CHRONICLES FROM THE NINETEENTH CENTURY

FAMILY LETTERS OF BLANCHE BUTLER AND ADELBERT AMES

Volume II

CHRONICLES FROM THE NINETEENTH CENTURY

FAMILY LETTERS OF BLANCHE BUTLER AND ADELBERT AMES

Married July 21st, 1870

IN TWO VOLUMES

VOLUME II

1874–1899

Compiled by BLANCHE BUTLER AMES, 1935

PRIVATELY ISSUED
1957

PRINTED IN THE UNITED STATES OF AMERICA
BY THE COLONIAL PRESS INC., CLINTON, MASS.

CONTENTS

Volume II

LETTERS between
BLANCHE BUTLER and ADELBERT AMES
and Others
1870 — 1899

(*Continued from Volume I*)

JACKSON, MISS., *August* 13, 1874

DEAR BLANCHE: I am glad to write you that the trouble in Tunica Co. which has caused me some anxiety and the reports of which are, I have no doubt, greatly exaggerated, has ended without bloodshed. The Democracy have magnified everything, believing it would tend to their advantage. How little the country knows of their falsehoods and duplicity. They have not changed since the days of the rebellion and nights of Ku Kluxism. Why should they? Their disappointments have aggravated their weakness, if not their wickedness, and now they pursue their old ways.

But I see the North is beginning to put faith in them for the first time for thirteen years. A most inopportune time, in my opinion. The cloud which hung over Tunica Co. portending a storm has passed. I hope we will not have any more. These events do not hurt me personally. On the other hand, they drive all Republicans to me as their chief and only harbor of refuge. To me they must look for deliverance and to me they do look for the aid and support which is to give them victory, if they are to have victory.

We all look for squally weather, and are awake and on watch for the heavy gusts of wind. We shall be free from danger till a year from next fall, when our election will take place, but we shall keep sharp eyes out on our neighboring states this fall—hopeful that another year will work changes for the better. So much for politics.

I receive your letters regularly, and receiving them before I get up in the morning I read them in bed. I ask George for my knife, that I may carefully cut the envelope, and then in a moment I am at Bay View with my dear ones.

I am sorry Butler has no better appetite. But is not thirty-five and a half pounds pretty good weight for a little boy not quite three? I do not think it wise to attempt to doctor him for the improvement of his stomach, to the end that his tongue may not be coated. The open, cool air he is now getting, and the very liberal diet he gets at your Mother's table must work his cure. It is possible his diet is too rich, and it would be better for him to come down to bread and molasses.

Poor Edith! How she must dread a spanking. If it develops in her, love, as you say, I shall unhesitatingly pound her well!

How very glad I am that my loved ones are not suffering from the heat we are having here. Hot, hotter, hottest is the cry here. We can have no more than two or three weeks of such weather, for then September will be at hand, when the heat of the summer passes away.

Then too, I shall be migrating to a Northern clime. When, I will ask now, do you expect to see me? I understood you to say about the middle of Sept., while in one of your recent letters you speak of my being back in about four weeks, which would make it about the first of Sept.

Yesterday I dined with Col. Breck. Rather, I invited him to dine with me. He is well, as is Mrs. B. They have been together on his circuit. He wishes to be remembered to you. They may not get North till the middle of Sept.

Kiss the babies for me. Love, ADELBERT

BAY VIEW, *August* 13, 1874

DEAR DEL: This morning Mother, Butler and I rode over to Gloucester. Mother was on her way to Lowell. Butler and I went for the ride and the morning papers. When Horace stopped the carriage in front of the book store I told Butler to go in and ask for the Boston papers and gave him ten cents to pay for them. He walked in as brave as a lion, and important as Cuff. When the clerk asked him what he wanted, he handed him the money and made known his wants, for the clerk came to the door and asked me if I wanted the "Globe or Advertiser." Butler waited patiently until he received the papers, then came out and climbed into the carriage apparently well pleased with himself.

Father came downstairs about dinner time with Edith in his arms. He was talking to her and she was coquetting in the most engaging way. As he passed the door he heard her voice, and looked in. She had just awakened, and put out her arms to be taken up. Of course he could not resist such an invitation. It is quite amusing. She will go to, and kiss, any strange man, but does not like strange women.

Mr. Moulton is here again. He came about five this afternoon, and says he is going away tomorrow. Perhaps he will change his mind. He had some business in Gloucester, and came to bring some documents to Father. Clancy and Father were in the billiard room when he arrived, and as they did not come down to the house for an hour or so, I had quite a long chat with Mr. M. He evidently feels that he is before the public, and quite a hero. He does not think matters can be compromised, and as Mr. Beecher's friends attack him personally, he regrets that he did not make a full statement and ventilate the whole subject.

I am a little out of spirits, because I want a letter from someone to whom I send unnumbered kisses. BLANCHE

BAY VIEW, *August* 15, 1874

DEAR DEL: I received a letter from you yesterday, and one this morning, and everything is bright in consequence.

I am sorry that you are obliged to endure such frightfully warm weather. It will take all your life and energy. The only satisfaction I can find is in the thought that three or four weeks will find you in the North, your time occupied with law reading and apple, pear, peach, and grape eating, and frolicing with the children.

Mother returned last night, and we shall all go up to Lowell for good a week from Monday. Uncle Webster will return with Aunt Sue's remains in the course of three weeks, and the funeral will be from our house. Florence and Aunt Lauretta sail today. The northeast storm is just over, so they will be likely to have a smooth passage.

Mr. Moulton went away last night. Mr. Beecher concluded to make his own statement, which was published yesterday. He did not accept Father's defence. Perhaps he thought it too kindly towards Mr. Tilton, whom of course he hates, as one man must always hate another whom he has wronged. Knowing the facts as I do, his statement is most wonderful. His brother Edward spoke truly when he pronounced him a "hypocrite, liar and libertine."

This coming winter will, I think, be an important one for you. In some way you must get control of the state and make *yourself* master of the situation. I do not care about the political triumphs or defeats you may have in consequence, but I do want you to show that you can *rule*, and neither Grant nor anyone else can ride roughshod over you. As you are quite indifferent to what the state can do for you, so you have nothing to lose, and are free to work out a course of action and follow it. You see, Sweetheart, I am ready for a fight. The idea that these reorganized Ku-Klux are likely to control the state for Grant is too much for *passive* endurance.

The children are in fine health and spirits. Your daughter Edith is becoming a great fighter. In six months she will be fully able to hold her own against Butler's aggressions. When he is looking at pictures on the floor, she delights to go and stand on the newspaper to dare him. Of course, she is "Papa's Own Girl."

Love from BLANCHE

JACKSON, MISS., *August* 15, 1874

DEAR BLANCHE: When I got up this morning to unlock the door to let George in and to get my law book to take back to bed with me I took my knife out of my pocket to carefully cut the envelope of your letter—but there was *no* letter. I did not use the knife.

Last evening Col. Cooley called on me. He says he is on his way North to find a new home. His wife is tired of Natchez as is himself, and they are in search of a home where they can have neighbors—which they do not have in N. Mrs. Cooley has another baby, now two weeks old. Their family now numbers *eight* children. He says it has been exceedingly hot in N. The thermometer has ranged up to 100° occasionally and at 94–5 and 6 degrees with effort. How would you like to be there? He also said that Col. Preston had left for good and gone to Iowa.

Mr. Brown and wife came in a day or two since. I did not see Mrs. B. She has gone to her plantation near Natchez, he is soon to follow. He seems as indifferent about his displacement as anyone well can. How contented Mrs. B. must be now that she has only a county to look after instead of a state. It was thought that they would not return. I fear they have not the good sense we attributed to them when we made up our minds we should never see them again.

Last night was the first night that I have not had croquet. Raymond was away taking care of Mr. Kimball, his partner, and it was so dusty and warm Mrs. R. did not get over.

There is a good breeze today, and the dust flies in clouds. I am doing the same things every day. I am diligent in reading law, and when tired go to the daily papers for relaxation.

My health is excellent—I am in good spirits—but I am in my thoughts often with you and Butler and Edith, so many miles away. Love from ADELBERT

BAY VIEW, *August* 16, 1874

DEAR DEL: All are well and in good spirits except Butler. He has been like a little bear all day. Anxious to get up into my lap, and when there fighting, kicking and slapping without the least provocation. This evening his mood is a little gentler, and he seems to feel better. I am relieved about him now, and think the crossness was caused by a slight cold.

Mr. Moulton came down again late last evening. He is deeply injured at the tone in which Beecher has spoken of him in his statement, and is determined now to expose the whole business.

We expect the Spoffords and Mr. Parton over from Newburyport tomorrow. As soon as they have made their visit we shall pack up for home. Mother would like to go the last of this week, but we shall not be likely to get off before a week from tomorrow.

I was mistaken about the yacht being in Boston Harbor during that storm. On the contrary, it went around to New London in the midst of the gale. They must have had a pretty rough time, especially the ladies. They will not return before Wednesday or Thursday. I suppose they will want to take part in the Isles of Shoals race on the 20th.

I think of you so often, and wish you were here. Not only on my own account, but to breathe this invigorating air, and get back the bright color of boyhood to your cheeks. In a few weeks more you will be North. I wish that instead of being sick I could be well, able to be a companion for you. However, we cannot have all the good things at once, and I am happy in the thought that you are to be near me.

I send you love, as do the children. BLANCHE

JACKSON, MISS., *August* 16, 1874

DEAR BLANCHE: Your letter of a week ago today reached me this morning. Enclosed find my note for five thousand dollars. I am sorry you are in that state of mind which causes you to think of such a matter. But it is doubtless due to your present condition of health. Before Butler was born I felt great anxiety, but now as this is our third child, and as you are so strong and perfect I, though anxious, have none of the biting anxiety I felt just three years ago.

By the way, this is the 16th of Aug. and six days from today—next Saturday—say the day after you get this, Butler will be three years old. What a long time it seems since he was born, and what events have been crowded into our lives since then. I hope the present ordeal you are to pass through will end as happily, and that this will be an event from which we will date time and count up the happy years which follow.

So be of good cheer, my Love, and hope and trust in the Kind Power above which has given us so much to be thankful for. I know you do, yet your letter shows you think of a change, which I cannot endure, and which I do not wish to consider.

In looking over a Washington paper I saw the enclosed announcement of the death of Mr. Ingalls, the artist. It was he who had the instrument by which a photograph was reflected on a canvass.

I send you a number of reports from Northfield and Fort A. Some of them you may have had. You can tell which mill they belong to by the amount of wheat, etc.

I am ready any day to start for Mass. you may feel like having me, though I think it will be better to carry out our arrangement of delaying till the time approaches. I send you a world of love. Kisses for the babies. ADELBERT

BAY VIEW, *August* 17, 1874

DEAR DEL: In a month from this time you will be with me. In less than a month, for you are to come before the 15th of September. I should suggest an earlier return, were it not that I think the later you remain into the fall after your return from the South, the better. I don't want you to go back in time to run the risk of chills and fever.

The Spoffords and Mr. Parton came as expected. I wish you knew Mr. Parton. He is a very delightful companion. Quite different from Mr. Spofford as a talker, for he does not monopolize the whole conversation, as does Mr. S., and his manner is more quiet. All seem delighted with the children. Mrs. Spofford thinks Butler must be half a head taller than her little niece, who is only two months younger. The young man has been having hot house grapes and Bartlett pears. Two or three baskets have been sent to Mother, and she keeps them almost exclusively for Butler. Edith has a few, but they do not seem to agree with her as well as with Butler.

I am rejoiced to hear, Love, that the disturbances are over in Mississippi. I watch the papers closely that no item of Mississippi news shall escape observation. Of course, we have only meagre telegraphic accounts, and those contain only a grain of truth.

I send you a slip from the Boston *Commonwealth*, which shows that the *whole* North is not deceived about the condition of things in the South. The New York *World* has been very unjust and coarse in its remarks about you. But it is not worthwhile to win the approval of such a low, contemptible sheet as that has shown itself to be.

I am quite well, Sweetheart, but very stiff and sore, more so than before,—and should prove but a heavy companion for you if you were here now. I send you love from the children and from BLANCHE

JACKSON, MISS., *August* 17, 1874

DEAR BLANCHE: You speak of returning to Lowell in two weeks from the day you wrote—that will be in nine days from now, and as it takes our letters five days to reach each other, I shall after next Thursday, write you at L. Your returning, as a mark of the flight of time, shows the summer is passing away, and that the new season is fast approaching with its events. I shall be with you in less than a month. My visit at Bay View this season was more pleasant than on the last summer I was there, and it is pleasant for me to think of you and the children being there in such a cool, invigorating locality. But Lowell at this season of the year will be everything heart can wish. How fortunate you and our babies are in having such pleasant homes—say summer homes.

H. W. Beecher seems to assail your friend Moulton most unmercifully. M. will retaliate of course. Tilton will sue for divorce—and all to result in getting your Father into a scandal and divorce case, to the great resentment and indignation of the Plymouth Church and all other pious people! So wags the world.

I do not know as I tell you daily that my health is good—as it is—and that I am pursuing so far as I can a quiet student's life—reading more than studying.

Love for you. Kisses for the babies. ADELBERT

JACKSON, MISS., *August* 18, 1874

DEAR BLANCHE: This is another cool day. I was glad this morning to cover myself with two thicknesses of woolen blanket. We do not expect to suffer much from the heat after this.

Judge Holland, the State Treasurer, has returned, and Raymond at least will be ready to start for the "coast" in a day or two. Mrs. Raymond will leave tomorrow night for the North. She has been intending to go for some time.

Last evening Mrs. R. and I played croquet as partners against her husband and Mr. Clover. We, our side, was successful both games. I find I have lost a little of my skill at croquet. I am glad to play, as it is my only exercise.

I have been carefully watching the papers to see if the "America" entered the races at Newport, and what her action was. As yet her name has not appeared in the list of yachts. It would be a pity if she fails to get into a race this season. She is a costly plaything and she should render some equivalent.

When I read in your letter this morning that "Mrs. Webster was dead" I could but think of the selfishness of Mrs. Hildreth who delayed going abroad to avoid giving a little time and attention to her sick sister-in-law. How rejoiced she must now feel, as she sails across the Atlantic, to know she will find an empty space—a void—instead of a sick, suffering woman, whose heart would be gladdened by faces and voices from home. I wonder what she expects when time draws to an end for her. I hope she will receive better than she has given.

What an amusing account you give of the meeting between Ben and his cousin George. Unfortunately for George, he failed to make the thrilling impression he intended, and only because his subject was not well selected. What a shallow life a fellow must lead, who wanders over the earth with one thought uppermost and that to impress people!

I will go to the coast probably next day after tomorrow, the 20th, and will stay there till about the thirtieth or later—but at any and all times I shall be ready to obey the summons of my beloved. ADELBERT

JACKSON, MISS., *August* 19, 1874

DEAR BLANCHE: I shall go to the coast tonight and remain there a week or ten days. Raymond will go down with me.

Everything is quiet here. I keep my correspondence well up and feel free to give much of my time to my reading. I have taken to dictating my letters, and I find it a great relief. It is much less laborious, and I write better letters.

We are having another cool, windy day, and a little while ago it was sprinkling as though we might have a heavy rain. So you need not think we are suffering from the heat. I am enjoying the weather of the last few days amazingly.

Our cow is well cared for, and she will be of service to us next year. Our rabbit is here running about, making friends with everybody. He is tamer now than he used to be. We will have to buy a mate for him next year.

I thought Mrs. R. went North on the 4:30 train, but she will not go till the 3 o'clock train tonight. Although the grass was wet she came over and had a game of croquet. As has been the case heretofore, we, she and I being partners, beat. Her boy, Warren, will go North with her. Her husband goes down with me at 10:30. Our Treasurer, Judge Holland, will go to the coast with us.

I find real pleasure in reading your letters, and never get enough of your details relative to yourself and the children. Health is all we need ask for—having that we should be happy, as I think we are.

It is true I sadly miss you, but the separation is but temporary. To you and our babies I send love. ADELBERT

Custom House, NEW ORLEANS, LA.
Surveyor's Office, August 20, 1874

DEAR BLANCHE: We arrived here at eight o'clock, brought our satchels to Mr. Parker's office, went out to a restaurant for breakfast and I have returned here to write a letter to you, while Mr. Raymond and Judge Holland have gone to attend to some business and do some shopping. At 3:15 this afternoon we will take the train for Bay St. Louis—rather, Shieldsborough is the proper name. I have ordered my letters sent there. You will, of course continue to write me at Jackson.

The contrast between this weather and that we had when I was last here is very marked. Then it was hot—now it is quite cool and pleasant—not at all uncomfortable. I am traveling in light marching order. I have the hand satchel and a law book strapped to it—also my gray coat on my arm, to be worn in bad weather. Could anyone have less baggage for a ten day's trip? I started with an umbrella, but left it in the car, but have sent one of Mr. Parker's many hangers-on for it.

We expected Major Gibbs to go over to the "coast" with us. It is said he is making love or engaged to a young lady there. Certain it is that he has been very attentive to her—but we think he does not want to go now, either because he does not care to have witnesses about, or else because Matt Sullivan, a former beau of hers, is there. Perhaps his loss has been so recent he prefers to make his new demonstrations less prominent than they would be, were we all there to see.

Last evening Mrs. Raymond before going off gave me a little gossip about the Powers family. They (even his own friends)

say that the Ex. Gov. has bought a place in St. Louis, and that he is expending a great deal of money—more than he could have come by honestly. His unmarried sister is there in charge of a sister, Mrs. McKee, who has sent her own children to her Mother, and is devoting her time and talents in getting her maiden sister into society. Judge Hill called on them a few days since, and was taken by the family to a German beer garden. The point of the story is that a beer garden is now the summit of the social struggle. What a strange story of a strange family. I have no doubt Gov. P. has made dishonestly much money. Yet he was upheld by the "oldest and best" while an honest political opponent is denounced. It only shows what a class of people they are.

I am getting on quietly and pleasantly, disturbed by nothing. I shall go over to the "Coast" and forget the Governorship, or at least do the next thing to it. I shall also eat fish, oysters, and shrimp, not to speak of crabs, and get fat. I shall not forget, however, to dream constantly of my wife and our babies. To them I send kisses without number. ADELBERT

BAY VIEW, *August* 20, 1874

DEAR DEL: Mother and I have been alone today. Kinsman, Percy, Paul, and Father went over to the Isles of Shoals race starting at five in the morning. It has been stormy and blowing quite heavily all day, so that the "America" will have an excellent chance to win the race, although she did not enter for the prize. A silver cup (two hundred and fifty) is to be awarded. Paul was quite provoked that they did not enter the yacht properly.

Butler and Edith have great contests. Edith will not give way, but fights and scolds with all her little might. She has a fearful temper, and is not inclined to control it in the least. Something did not quite suit her today, and she threw herself down on the gravel walk in front of the house, rolling over and over, screaming, at the top of her voice. She is in such perfect health and spirits, I suppose it is necessary for her to work off the extra vitality in some such way. I chastised Butler today for continued disobedience. The fish-man had just brought some unboiled lobsters. Butler rushed to the door, flung it open, and called "Oh, lobsters, lobsters, come in and bite Mother's ears off." When I explained to him that I could whip the lobsters, he was most anxious to have me try it, evidently in some doubt as to my prowess. I satisfied him by saying that I would whip the lobsters if they were bad, but while they were good I did not care to hurt them. I write all this, which I suppose seems very simple, that you may more clearly picture to yourself the children with their little troubles and repentances, and the quiet life I am leading in which such foolish incidents as these I narrate form the excitement.

We are all preparing to go up to Lowell on Monday. I am still so stiff that I rather dread the long ride, on the cars.

The days are passing, Love, and each one brings you nearer to us. The girls have letters from Jackson reporting that typhoid fever is prevalent there, and you speak of Mr. Raymond's absence to attend upon Mr. Kimball. Be most careful, Dearie. What should I do if you were to fall sick. I send you love and a thousand blessings which I wish were powerful to guard you from all harm.

BLANCHE

BAY VIEW, *August* 21, 1874

DEAR DEL: Your letter enclosing note came this morning. Do not think me morbid or unhappy, Love, because I made such a request of you. No doubt all women, without really fearing death, think of the possibility at such times and govern themselves accordingly. Perhaps it is something of the same feeling you may have had in going into battle. Full of hope, yet counting the chances.

Tomorrow Butler, as you remind me in your letter, will be three years. I cannot realize it. Four happy years I have been married. Each succeeding one more full of love and content than the last. I have to thank you, Del, for all your gentleness and loving kindness to me during these four years, which has made them the happiest of my life. You have humored my whims, been forbearing with my faults, and seemed so content with your wife, that you have left me nothing to wish for. I have, and do appreciate this, Dearie, and my only desire is that you should feel the same. If you do not, tell me wherein I can add to your content, and I am sure I shall not fail you.

Butler says "Father is in Mississippi, he will be home in a momph." At dinner he informed me that "Butler's tapetite is very well" which meant that he could eat some more corn. How strange it will seem to have another little one calling upon us for care and love. Three small steps.

The yacht came back about ten o'clock this morning. All were exultant. It seems she was entered for the race, but owing to her size the judges decided she must beat the others by twenty-eight minutes and four seconds. This, as the wind died away when the race was half over, she failed to do by four minutes, yet had passed the stake *nearly* half an hour before the other yachts. Paul was in great glee. The Captain told Father Paul was the best sailor he had—that he could go up to the mast's head quicker than any man on board.

This afternoon we have all been employed in putting together a venetian glass chandelier Father bought in New York. It is very pretty, and it seems a pity that it is to be seen only two months in the year.

I am delighted to hear that the weather is a little cooler. I do not like to think of your strength being sapped by the great heat. I will not ask you to change your time of coming North, although I should be so happy to have you with me sooner. I think all things will happen as we expect, and it will not be needful for you to come earlier. Love for my Sweetheart.

BLANCHE

BAY VIEW, *August* 23, 1874

DEAR DEL: We are all packed and ready for a start tomorrow noon. Paul and Percy drive up the gray horse. Horace the carriage. Mother, the children, Kinsman and I go by the way of Boston. It is so cold here that all are inclined to dress warmly and crowd about the fire at evening. I think it well that we are going to Lowell. It is possible that I shall not feel quite so rheumatic and awkward. Besides Mother must be there when Mr. Webster arrives.

I amused myself last night reckoning up the work and receipts of the Fort A. mill. It has made about 8500 bbls. of flour—but the price per barrel has been so low that latterly there has been quite a loss per bbl. so that after expenses of milling, transportation, etc. are paid you will not be more than two thousand dollars ahead. This is rather poor work, is it not, Del? Still you cannot blame the old mill. It has capacity enough, and if the 8500 bbl. had sold at the price of Northfield, you would have made at least twelve thousand this year. Bear this matter in mind, and think of some remedy. It would be impossible to make a change for the worse. I suggest that you do as you proposed in the spring, change the name of the brand, change your agent in New York, and make better flour if possible.

By the way, I saw a Mississippi *Pilot* yesterday, which gave an account of an assault on Geo. McKee in Vicksburg. Is that kind of warfare likely to prove common? Certainly the South, as viewed through the medium of the newspapers, is not a very inviting section of the country just now. Even the Attorney General views the situation with fear and trembling, while expressing his opinion of the inability of the General Government to interfere, although all parties are calling for aid to keep the peace. It is evident that you will have to "paddle your light canoe," without assistance.

I send you the *Graphic* which you may not happen to see. It gives Moulton's statement in full. I am very tired of the whole thing. Everybody connected with the matter seems more or less tainted. I have yet to hear of a perfectly honest, upright nature on either side of the controversy. No doubt Moulton prides himself upon his conduct, but I fear he has been a little inclined to the free love doctrines. I believe in being free to express my love for my husband and babies. To the former I send kisses and caresses from the latter and

BLANCHE

SHIELDSBOROUGH, MISS., *August* 24, 1874

DEAR BLANCHE: We got up at six o'clock this morning and took a bath. Returning I took up my law for a short time, but we are too many in this contracted space for study. Shortly after eight we went to breakfast—back to my room I am immediately engaged in writing to my far-away home.

A day or two since I gave you the remarks of a French lady (?) to her child on eating with her knife. I have since found out why she made the lady-like remark. Directly opposite to her sits one of our party, Judge Holland, who as you know is a simple, good-natured and honest man, and one we all highly respect. But unfortunately for the eating question he was brought up in the wooded Choctaw country, and is not as polished as he might be. The French lady saw him eating with his knife, hence her remarks. They were made aloud and for the benefit of us all.

Yesterday we did almost literally nothing. After the six o'clock train passed we took a trip across the bridge in the sail car. We had a good breeze going over, but our captain had to push us back. With a fair wind, it is a very agreeable way of travelling.

You can imagine I am having a quiet time here, one entirely free from annoyances of any kind, when I tell you that the only news of the outside world we get is from the N.O. papers, and that we read only the telegraphic dispatches. No business comes to us. However, I feel and know my time is being wasted. It goes into talk, talk by the hour. I wish you were here, or rather I was with you. I shall, without fail, receive a letter from you today. It is a long time since I have had a letter—almost a week, and I am hungry for some word from you. I send love to you, Dear, and kisses to our children.

ADELBERT

SHIELDSBOROUGH, MISS., *August 25, 1874*

DEAR BLANCHE: Yesterday we did little or nothing except to accept an invitation from Judge Chandler to eat some cake and drink some wine at six o'clock, in celebration of his birthday. Mrs. Chandler asked for you. I did not forget to thank her for the japonicas she sent you last winter.

By the morning's papers I see that Mr. Cordoza has been arrested for frauds charged to have been committed a year or so ago when he was circuit clerk of Warren Co. He was required to give $5,000.00 bail, but could not and was sent to jail. I am mortified and chagrined at the event, but can do nothing. I hope he is innocent. His former clerk and present deputy has been arrested and is now in jail because he could not give bail. I removed him and appointed another person. I am here out of the atmosphere of the transaction, and wherever I may be shall try to avoid thinking of the matter. But it is an illustration of the character of the material we have to work with, and gives me new cause to wish to be absolutely separated from it.

This morning's papers also give an account of the hanging of three Negroes for committing a rape on a white woman. Such lawlessness is common in other states, but has rarely occurred here—again I find cause for wishing myself in different community. But all in good time, my dear.

I see also that Penn. through its Rep. Convention has pronounced against a third term. So the world moves.

I do not know how long I will remain here. Judge Chandler has invited us to take a sail out to the islands. Should we go you will not get your tomorrow letter. I am inclined to go to N.O. to Mr. P's house, and there rest and study for a week.

You are now in Lowell, and there I must picture you rather than at Bay View where I left you and the children. Kisses for them, love for my beloved wife.

ADELBERT

LOWELL, *August 25, 1874*

DEAR DEL: How well you timed your letters. I received two from you this morning, both directed to Lowell, and two yesterday at Bay View. I am happy in the thought that you are well, and in good spirits. The days are passing, and you will soon be with me. The journey up was made quite comfortably, but I was very tired and sore by the time we arrived. So much so that I was glad to lie down and rest, and did not get up this morning in time for breakfast. I am entirely recovered now, however, and find the air pleasanter here than at Bay View. It is remarkably cool for August, and the children are obliged to wear their outside wraps.

Speaking of the children reminds me that they fight nearly all the time. Butler is very selfish and unkind to Edith. He takes from her everything, and is more inclined that way because she is beginning to resent his treatment, and screams and holds on with all her little might. I cannot keep punishing Butler for it. His life would be a burden to him.—All I can do is to watch development, and see if time will not work a cure. Edith is brighter and more knowing daily. This evening we were all much amused to see her attempts at dancing. Her nightgown was tied up behind, and she kept turning around to the music until her little brain was dizzy. As an instance of her brightness I will tell you that when asked what the cow says she will reply "*moo*" but when interrogated as to the dog's remarks she gives the same answer. Perhaps you will not think this as remarkable and cute as we do.

Father and Mr. Moulton are here. I suppose Mr. M. will remain a day or so longer.

Love, Dearie. I shall not return your compliments, although I could with truth say something to counterbalance your pet name for me of "Beautiful." Good night.

BLANCHE

LOWELL, *August* 26, 1874

DEAR DEL: In one of your letters of a day or two ago you speak of Aunt Lauretta's selfishness in not going to Europe sooner. What will you think when I tell you that no one is coming over with Aunt Sue's remains. The consignment is made to Wells Fargo & Co. New York, and Mr. Read is requested by letter to go on and bring the remains to Lowell. Mother and Mrs. Read are desired to attend to the arrangements for the funeral—an account to be kept of the expenses which will be paid upon presentation of bills. Uncle Webster wrote to Aunt Sue when she was here last summer that he should never allow her "to cross the ocean again alone." He has forgotten that and has left to others to perform those last attentions and duties which were his right and privilege. I do not think this neglect is owing to any lack of feeling, for he was proud and fond of Aunt Sue—but in his grief, as in all other things of life, he is selfish. I do not speak of the boys, because even if they desired they could not come without his counsel and permission. The funeral will take place upon the arrival of the remains. Probably next Tuesday or Wednesday.

Have you written to Northfield lately, Del? Your Mother will be anxious to hear from you, fearing the effect of the warm weather upon you. The Northfield Mills have made 37,800 barrels of flour up to Aug. 8th. This is not exact, for several reports are missing, but it is near enough.

By the way, Del, you are either a poor lawyer in spite of your late studies, or else you thought it well to humor your wife even to allowing her to remain in ignorance. I asked Father today if a note between married people was good. He replied no—unless the note is made out to a third party and by that party endorsed in favor of the husband or wife, as the case may be. I said "It seems to me this marriage relation in its legal aspect is very difficult to understand." "Not at all, if you will only bear in mind that two people are regarded as one person." My opinion of your legal knowledge, Sweetheart, is small. I prefer to think you ignorant rather than to suppose you could trifle with your wife and smile while humoring her foolish attempts. In which light do you prefer to be regarded?

I must say good night, Love—for having been rubbed in oil I feel a little cold. Love, BLANCHE

SHIELDSBOROUGH, MISS., *August* 26, 1874

DEAR BLANCHE: Another day and no letter from you. But you and the babies are well settled in Lowell by this time, in your commodious, comfortable home there. How fortunate you are, and also the children, in having such a resting place to go to, even though I am a wanderer with all my comforts in a hand satchel. I surely am content, for a limited period of time, with the contrast.

Yesterday there were gathered here some three or four hundred colored people, men, women, and children, from New Orleans, Mobile, and intermediate points, to enjoy themselves at a basket picnic. They had a band of music, and of course dancing, and evidently an excellent time. They were as peaceable and orderly as a Sunday School picnic in New England. When I saw them so quiet and well behaved, I could but wonder at the barbarity of their white brothers, late their masters, who seek every opportunity to kill them—and who do kill them, for political reasons only. Mrs. Cass and Mr. Raymond were walking out to the grounds, and I joined them. They were assembled together under the wide, spreading, moss-grown oaks —the band and dancers surrounded by friends, who seemed to enjoy the scene highly.

I was visited yesterday by some of the judges and chancellors along the coast here, and did not have an opportunity to take my usual bath. This morning has been quite warm, but the sea breeze is springing up—it is now about ten (the mail has not yet come) and will, if the day is like its predecessors, continue to blow all day.

Our arrangements are definitely made to sail out to the islands tomorrow. Ship Island will be one of those we propose to visit. That I shall view with interest, as one whereon your Father and Mother flourished a dozen years ago.

The train has stopped at the head of the bridge, and in a half hour I shall know whether I shall receive today a letter from my sweetheart. Whether I do or not, I love her all the same. Kisses to our children Butler and Edith. ADELBERT

LOWELL, *August 27*, 1874

DEAR DEL: There was no letter for me this evening, but no doubt tomorrow's mail will bring one. Perhaps I was a little harsh in my comments upon Mr. Webster in my letter of last night. Mother had one from him today, in which he speaks of being under the doctor's care, and it is written with so much feeling, and such a sense of his loss, that his failing to return with the remains was owing perhaps to the very magnitude of his grief, rather than from selfishness or want of consideration. Still, if well enough I think he should have come.

The children are well, but I feel that they are rather unruly. Miss Edith is exhibiting a good deal of temper, and it is sufficient to ask Butler to do a thing to have him conclude that he would rather not. Still, I ought not to complain, for they are quite as good as children average. Butler has grown much older in his ways, and talks more distinctly. He is frequently much amused at Edith's pranks, and I am in hopes he will soon learn to treat her decently.

I intend to send for Leslie Grant to come up and make him a visit tomorrow. He met her on the street yesterday and told me he would like to see her. You like to hear of Butler's remarks. Perhaps you will not think it very delicate when I tell you that whenever the young man falls down he picks himself up with a laugh and says "Oh! Butler fell down and bust his drawers." As he talks much plainer than he did, no one can mistake his meaning.

You will think my letter very foolish but I have no news for you tonight—and will close by telling you the old story that I love you, and am counting the days till your return.

Love, from the babies and BLANCHE

SHIELDSBOROUGH, MISS., *August* 29, 1874

DEAR BLANCHE: I did not write you day before yesterday because I was out sailing, nor did I write yesterday as we slept late in the morning and I failed to find the opportunity before the mail train passed. Mr. Holland and Raymond left for Jackson on that train, and they kept up such a furore that to write was impossible.

We had a very pleasant sail. We started at four o'clock in the morning, and returned at two o'clock the next morning. The wind was light almost the entire day, and we did not arrive at Ship Island until after sunset. The wind was ahead, and when a mile to the leeward of the lighthouse beating up to it the full moon rose behind the island, and made the scene quite beautiful, as well as unique. As we moved along, the moon would be at one time behind the lighthouse, at another behind the fort, and again behind the buildings between the fort and lighthouse, which were built for, and once occupied by our troops. We landed, and lighted by the moon and a lantern carried by the keeper of the lighthouse, we walked through the deserted street formed by the officer's quarters, and soldiers' barracks on either hand, to the fort, which we inspected. It is in perfect condition, and last winter some guns were mounted on its parapet. The buildings used by the troops as quarters are fast falling to decay. The wind has drifted sand about like snow. Some of the houses have thus been undermined, while others have been banked up. There is one house they said was your Father's Hd.Qrs; though my impression is that he lived in tents or some temporary wooden house he could and did transport from place to place.

I recalled much I had heard of the sojourn there of your parents, and also some of Kinsman's narrations, and withal enjoyed the moonlight visit much—though there was a feeling of sadness—a lonesomeness always incident to visits to scenes where those we know have been, especially when every step indicates decay. I found an old artillery sergeant who is in charge of the fort, acting as light-housekeeper. He has a family there—five children—and aside from his assistant there is no one else on the island. We had a drink of excellent milk and started at nine o'clock on the way back.

Of course you are now at Lowell, and the children are rolling in the grass on the hill sides. I shall see you all in a couple of weeks.

I have had a most excellent night's sleep last night, fully making up the time lost the night before last, a large part of which was passed in lying on the hard irregular hatches of our fishing craft. This morning I was up early and took a good bath. Since then I have had my breakfast and been chatting with you, except when interrupted by the crowd in which I find myself.

Love for yourself, Butler and Edith, from ADELBERT

LOWELL, *August* 31, 1874

DEAR DEL: Two letters came for me this morning, and I have felt the day to be bright and joyous mentally, as well as physically in consequence.

This afternoon I went out to make a call on poor Mrs. Greenhalge, but she is away on a trip to the White Mts. Her health has been very much broken by her loss and grief. I next proceeded to call on Maria Nesmith. She has been home from Europe about two weeks. I cannot say that the call was particularly agreeable, owing to the fact that both Maria and her sister Lucy did not express the least delight at being home again. On the contrary, Maria said she wished to stay abroad longer, and was very sorry to return. I believe it hard to feel an interest in people who are and who only desire to be mere wanderers on the earth. They seem to lack strength and stability, and we are obliged to regard them as the moths or butterflies of humanity.

On my way to the house across the lawn—our house, I mean—I saw a strange lady with Mother near the piazza. Miss Palfrey had been calling and was evidently awaiting my return. Butler was picking and adorning himself with scarlet geraniums, much to her delight. Edith, on account of her poisoned mouth, was not presented for inspection. I said I would send her down in a day or so, or call with her myself. This I fear will prove to be a society fib, for it was a great effort for me to make myself presentable for the calls of today, and I am not disposed to try it again soon.

Mr. Moulton is coming again tomorrow for a day or so. Mr. Read has gone to New York to take charge of Aunt Sue's remains, which are expected Wednesday, or Thursday. Paul has been planning a trip to the Adirondacks but will wait until after the funeral.

Aunt Maria is better. We have hopes that she has found a cure.

Your immediate family, Love, are in excellent condition. Mother rubs me every night with sweet oil and I feel most beneficial effects from it. How glad the children will be to see you. No doubt they will have plenty for you to do for their amusement and will repay you with love and kisses.

BLANCHE

LOWELL, *September 2*, 1874

DEAR DEL: I did not write you last night. Mr. Farrington has just returned and made such a long, late call I was too tired before going to bed, and this morning I was so disappointed at not having a letter from you that I could not set myself about it. I suppose you were away at Ship Island, out of reach of the mail.

Mr. Read telegraphed today that he should be in Lowell Friday with Aunt Sue's remains. The funeral will be on Friday. Aunt Maria and I are not going over to the graveyard. I am a little afraid to go, and Aunt Maria is so nervous about it that I doubt if she will even come over here. Mr. Moulton is still here, also Mr. Redpath. Mother is in hopes that they will go tomorrow. It is very distracting to have so many people to attend to just at this time, when of course her attention is wanted in another direction.

Your family is well, and in good spirits, looking forward to the time when we shall see you. Edith's face is better. She is growing taller and thinner, so much so I am surprised when I look at her. She seems to have changed since we came up from Squam. The photographs are not very satisfactory. I was most anxious to get a good one of the baby as I should like to paint her picture this winter. Perhaps it will be well to try again when you come *home*.

Love, Dearie, from your children and BLANCHE

SHIELDSBOROUGH, MISS., *September 2*, 1874

DEAR BLANCHE: This is to be my last day here. I will leave tomorrow morning at seven o'clock and will write you next from N.O. Since yesterday I have done literally nothing. Senator Little came on the morning's train and went away this morning, and as he came to see me I felt constrained to give him my whole time. I took him to ride along the shell road, and showed off the village as if I owned it.

I shall leave word with Judge Chandler to buy the Boulange place if he can get it for its encumbrances—some three thousand dollars. It will be very cheap property at such a figure.

It has been blowing a brisk breeze for the past two days, and though warm where there is no air stirring, one has only to get in the wind to feel comfortable. The day breeze is generally a sea breeze, and coming from salt water it brings no malaria with it. Hence chills and fevers are not indigenous at this point, though back on the fresh water bottoms such diseases prevail, as in all other parts of the state.

Soon to see you—I send my love to my Beautiful. Kisses for the babies. ADELBERT

LOWELL, *September* 3, 1874

DEAR DEL: This has been quite a busy and a very warm day. By far the warmest I have felt since we came North. This evening, however, the storm clouds are blowing over and there is every indication of a rain, which has not yet fallen. I wish there might be a short rain, just enough to lay the dust, which is very disagreeable, and will be especially so tomorrow at the time of the funeral.

Mother is expecting the Spoffords up. Mr. Moulton has not gone yet. The house is likely to be more than full unless someone makes a move.

Your letter describing the trip to Ship Island came this morning. It seems to me it could not have been over pleasant, though I suppose anything is acceptable for a change.

Thinking of this seems to bring you much nearer, also another nameless one. Mother has been talking lately of raising the roof of this house, for the reason that the family is growing so large we cannot be accommodated pleasantly enough. When Paul, Ben, and Hattie come home for good and I come visiting with my family of five or six, there will not be many spare rooms for guests. What do you think about it, Sweetheart? Good night. BLANCHE

LOWELL, *September* 4, 1874

DEAR DEL: This day is almost over, and like yesterday it has been a busy one for us all.

This morning we were all anxiety lest Aunt Sue's remains should not get here in time for the funeral and were much relieved when a telegram removed all doubts. The coffin had to be covered with black cloth, as it was marred and jammed by the long voyage, so that it was not brought up to the house until nearly three o'clock, the time of the funeral. There were great quantities of beautiful flowers from relatives and friends, and a most beautiful day to welcome her back to her old home. Poor Aunt Sue. I wish her husband and boys could have gone with her to the last resting place.

I have been thinking, as the time of your return draws near, what arrangement we can make as regards sleeping. Miss Edith will have to give up her crib, and Butler cannot sleep with me. Will you take them, Del? Butler can sleep on the floor beside your bed on the mattress, while Edith would be only too happy to creep up close to you, sucking her thumb and pinching you if anything should wake her. The girls can sleep in the nursery, Mrs. Faunce in the room next to mine, and you and the children occupy the lower room. In this way you can have someone ready to take charge of them in the morning. Our family occupies considerable space in the world, does it not? If this arrangement does not suit you, the girls and children can sleep in the nursery and you can occupy a room by yourself. All this, of course, is to be after your nose is put out of joint by the new-comer. We are all well, Dearie, and I think you will find an improvement when you make an inspection of your army corps.

By the way, the morning papers give the message (if it can be so called) about affairs in the South. The Government, it seems, has decided to interfere and try to put a stop to the terrible outrages which have been going on all over the South. High time, I should think. Even the Democratic papers applaud the action, although as they say "it will tend to give the vile carpet-baggers a new lease of power." I want Mississippi in such a condition that she can take care of herself and control all disturbances, without aid, and this while my Love is Governor. But perhaps I am desiring something unattainable.

I shall expect you the last of next, or the first of the following week. As you may not hear from me again until you see me, I send an extra allowance of kisses to last until you meet your babies and loving wife, BLANCHE

NEW ORLEANS, LA., *September* 4, 1874

DEAR BLANCHE: After writing you yesterday I saw Dr. Barrett on his way from Jackson to his family on the Gulf and was surprised to hear him say no, when I asked him if there were any letters from Mass. awaiting my arrival at Jackson. Were you sick I am sure you would have telegraphed me. I am not a little anxious about you. I shall go up on tonight's train and in a day or two will start North. I shall reach L. about the tenth or eleventh.

I see by a letter of Mr. Parker's that his wife is quite sick and that he even seems much concerned about her. How unfortunate especially for your Mother, as she will feel the loss of her sister more than any other one person.

This morning's telegrams bring the word that the President will send troops to the South. I am heartily glad of it. This act of his will do infinite good and no harm whatever. The White Leaguers who have been preaching a third term for Grant will now recoil from him as would a coward from danger. Of course the Republicans here are jubilant. As the dispatches appear for the first time in the morning's papers there has been no echo therefrom, but it will be, we can imagine, a shriek of wrath and hatred against the President and his advisers. The necessity for troops was no less great when I called for troops than now. Time has brought forth its developments, and an indignant North has forced action today where a month ago everything was passive.

I was much interested in the Isles of Shoals Regatta and it was yesterday only that I learned the results of the race. So the "America" was beaten. I am sorry. I believe a better captain and a different trim for the yacht (though I am absolutely ignorant of the details of the race) would have resulted, if not in victory, at least the next thing to it.

In a week from today I expect to be with you. This may be my last letter before I start, for I can, judging by the time it takes your letters to come to me, overtake one giving it one or two days' start.

Love, for you, Dearie, and for our babies, ADELBERT

Governor Ames was in Lowell, September 11th, 1874. He went back to Jackson, Miss. on October 6th. A daughter was born on October 1st, 1874, and was named Sarah Hildreth.

LOWELL, *October* 8, 1874

DEAR DEL: I write to tell you that we are doing nicely and getting on as fast as possible. The children seem to miss you very much. I need not tell you that your wife does.

I enclose two letters from Northfield—and have informed

Father of their contents. John must be wild to sell the goose which lays the golden eggs.

Chancellor Dennis wrote you that a movement was on foot to declare the Executive Office vacant and to install Davis in your place. How full of mischief and insubordination your subjects are, Del. You will have to get them into a condition of subjection. You have quite a contest before you, Sweetheart. Don't be discouraged.

The baby is a week old tonight. Of course I am not strong yet, which will account for this queer-looking epistle. Mrs. Faunce is cautioning me against exerting myself too much, so I must not write longer.

I send you love and kisses from your babies and

BLANCHE

The Mansion, JACKSON, MISS., *October* 9, 1874

DEAR BLANCHE: I arrived here safe and well last night, after a journey of three days and nights, and a few hours.

When in Boston I had a few hours to spare, and in my walk on the Common I found a set of scales, and curiosity prompted me to get weighed. With the light shawl on my arm I weighed one hundred and sixty-one pounds—somewhat heavier than I thought myself. My whole journey was pleasant and as I was much preoccupied in reading, it seemed very brief.

I find things here in a better condition than I expected. That is, the railroads have not got the school money yet, and the time has passed when Davis can do harm. Otherwise the situation is about the same as when I left. The quietude which of late has been upon me is now with me, and will no doubt continue to be as the cause therefor still exists.

Two of your letters awaited me here. I have not read them as I have not had time. The news therein will be old, but the love new and warm. I find no letters from Northfield, except reports. I have no letter relative to the Bay St. Louis purchase and so am uninformed on that subject.

The temperature is very pleasant—a Southern fall day which is unsurpassed anywhere. Since I left there has been but one rain, which long since dried up. It is now very dry and everything is covered with dust.

As I came in the gate last night, I observed that the plants in the vases looked strong and vigorous. I will have them put into pots and brought into the house.

I have already ordered down some law books, and shall go to work with them at once. I have a large amount of work on hand which I shall despatch as quick as possible and then take a trip to the "Bay."

I have been interrupted quite a number of times as a matter of course, and now comes another visitor. It is now late. I have been talking a great deal and now write hurriedly to get a visitor to take my letter to the hotel.

Love, to you, Dear, and our babies. ADELBERT

The Mansion, JACKSON, MISS., *October* 10, 1874

DEAR BLANCHE: The heading above was written last evening, but I could go no further because of the press of callers. Today is the 11th, Sunday, which has been a very busy day with me. I did not get up very early. But as soon as I did and ate my breakfast I went up to the penitentiary and since then have been talking or listening to somebody else till a few moments ago—it is now ten o'clock.

Howe is now here. He came today. Senator Pease is here but has failed to call, fearing, I understand, I may snub him. "The wicked flee when no man pursueth."

Everybody is to start tonight for Chattanooga to attend a convention of Southern Republicans. I shall not go. I find none of our friends who favor the third term idea. I was surprised to see the colored people so unanimous on the subject.

About a ton of hay was cut, which will be converted into milk for the children. Our cow will not be available for such work. She will not have her calf till next February, and I am at a loss to know what to do for milk till then. I gave the calf to the man who has been keeping the cow, and with his, ours will be sent to the cane break this winter. He will look up a cow for us if he can. I am sadly ignorant of the ways of cows, but half suspect the element of time has not received the consideration in this business it should have. Notwithstanding all obstacles, I expect to have a cow here when you arrive.

I feel I am writing this letter in a very jerky way—I feel it in my fingers, and all over. Howe who left me when I began this has now returned to take this to mail.

I send love to my dear wife and our babies.

ADELBERT

LOWELL, *October* 11, 1874

DEAR DEL: This is Sunday, and I have been up in the large rocking chair for the first time. Only for a few minutes, however, just while Mrs. Faunce was making the bed. Long enough, however, for me to appreciate the comfort of bed—it was delightfully fresh and cool and restful. Tomorrow I shall remain up a little longer, and so on day after day until I am perfectly well. The baby improves hourly in grace and strength, but not in beauty—for she is fatter, and the pretty outline of her face is marred by the heaviness of her cheeks, which have begun to hang down as Edith's did. Edith is as fat and rosy as it is possible for a child to be. I feel she will not be likely to receive her share of petting and attention. She was lying in my arms last night—Butler was beside the bed—Edith soon began to squirm and cry out. Investigation showed that Butler was slyly pinching her. Does he take after his Father?

Col. Kinsman is here. He has given me a diamond ring. I have not seen him, of course. Mr. Moulton came up from Boston by the milk train this afternoon. So you see the house is very full.

Father is hearing good news from his district. The opposition have only nineteen delegates out of the one hundred and twelve already chosen. He says they have worked unsparingly and used a large amount of money in their efforts to defeat him.

I shall expect some word from you, by tomorrow or next day. The troubles in Miss. will at least enable you to spot your enemies, and that is an advantage worth having.

I close my letter with love. BLANCHE

JACKSON, MISS., *October* 13, 1874

DEAR BLANCHE: I did not write you yesterday for the want of an opportunity. Major Howe was here and after attending to business I accepted a challenge to play a game of billiards. Dinner followed—then croquet. In the evening I had company till it was too late to write. We sat by a good fire in my room last evening and I had one this morning to dress by. It is unusually cold for this season of the year.

Judge Holland, our State Treasurer, was with me till late. He is to bring his family here. He lives about half way between here and the north end of the state. He will move by the "dirt road" and it will take him six days to come. I requested him to buy me a good cow on the way, and also a span of horses. The horses will be only ordinary ones, nothing extra. When we get them we will have to buy a carriage of some kind. As times are dull in N.O. I may be able to buy one reasonably there. I shall not be particular as to the quality.

This morning's mail brought me a letter from Mr. Maguire whereby I learn that he was not present at Bay St. Louis at the sale of the Boulange place. The sickness of Parker's Chief Clerk kept him away. Consequently I do not know what was done. I know no bid was made in my name. I felt a little disappointed. I have written down to know what has been done.

Father's and John's letters came today. I was mortified and disappointed that they did not send the $5000 owed by me. I feel confident they will when they get my letter and learn the real state of the case. I ordered them to hire the money if they could not get it otherwise.

Today's telegrams inform us of your Father's renomination for Congress. I am glad of this, for his new house can be occupied by him for at least two years. Your Mother will have time to fix it up—and she wants something to do.

I send you, my dear Beloved, love—the same to our babies.

ADELBERT

JACKSON, MISS., *October* 14, 1874

DEAR BLANCHE: Tomorrow will be the 15th—two weeks since the stranger came. It will be the time fixed upon for you to begin your journeyings from your bed. I hope—I certainly think of you as strong and well, only waiting for permission to move about.

The time passes very rapidly with me here. My habits are very regular. I do not intend to get to the office before eleven o'clock. The morning I devote to study. Between three and four dinner—then home again. Croquet comes on early these short days. I hope the evenings will be my own soon, but they have not been yet. In this quiet way, while I am trying to get something out of the days, I realize how rapidly they pass away.

I think we had a frost last night. I fear our plants in the vases may be touched a little. I have ordered tubs at the penitentiary to be painted and made so as to be moved, also stands for them. The frost is very early, and if they are killed it will be not that I have not been diligent, but because the frost has been more so.

I think you misunderstood John's letter. I think he referred to my mill rather than that at Northfield. He said "our" mill, yet I believe he meant mine.

I feel more and more the uncongeniality of this latitude, as do many of my friends. The present troubles in La. and the rampant spirit of rebellion here somewhat disgusts us with this section. The will to protect loyal people, and a feeling against aggression is what makes not a few stay here. Of this more anon.

I send as ever love to my loved ones so far away.

ADELBERT

JACKSON, MISS., *October* 15, 1874

DEAR BLANCHE: We had another frost last night and your plants are not yet in. I asked George about the geraniums and learned that he had put them in the house. The cold here seems very penetrating. Although I had blankets enough for a regiment, I slept cold. I suggest you bring the eiderdown quilt.

I will give you a word of politics, showing lost opportunities for the Democracy. They sought to induce Davis to assume the Governorship on the plea that I had abdicated! Their second scheme was still more startling. Had the rebels succeeded in Louisiana, their programme in this state was to have Ex. Gov. Powers (and it is said he consented) declare by proclamation that he had returned after a temporary absence; and that the election last fall was null and void, and order a new one this fall! I have no doubts that it was thought of and discussed, and that Powers is weak enough and corrupt enough to lend himself to such a purpose. It all amuses me very much. Personally I am quite indifferent. I incline more and more to a quiet life with my beloved wife and babies. All this will come, I hope, in due time.

Election returns from Ohio and Indiana have come to us today, and indicate Democratic successes. This crazy Democracy here are made wild by the news and on them build up the loftiest hopes. Our Republican friends feel the defeat of our friends there very sensibly.

Judge Hill dined with me today. He and his family are well. Mrs. Cass is on the seacoast. So we have no neighbors. In fact I have seen no lady: and as usual keep to my old track to the Capitol and back. I enjoy getting up here in my room by myself and in my way delving in my books and the papers.

This is the day you were to get up. I hope you were able to do so. You will not begin to think of coming here for a month. I will not begin to clean up till next month sometime. I send love to my dear wife and our babies. ADELBERT

LOWELL, *October* 15, 1874

DEAR DEL: I received a letter from you night before last, and it was very welcome because I had not been feeling as well as usual, and it was enlivening to know that you were safely in Jackson.

Yesterday I was better, and today feel still brighter. I am making haste very slowly, so as to be on the safe side and have nothing happen which can prevent my joining you in November.

Lizzie had a letter from her Uncle, in which he said everything was quiet. As soon as it was known that you were returning all disturbance ceased. Be careful of yourself, Sweetheart, and do not go out much after dark. You are in a community which harbors cutthroats, and encourages them.

The children are well. Butler said to me the other morning, "I saw Father last night." "Did you, what did he say"? "He laughed and said hulloa Butler." His dream must have been very vivid, for two or three times I heard him speak out in his sleep and say "Papa, Papa." Mother thinks it quite remarkable that he should tell his dreams.—It is quite unusual with children. Today he has gone out to ride with Mother, and Edith has gone to have her photograph taken in a state of nature. The baby has a cold, which she probably caught from my having the room so cold to avoid night sweats. All the relatives pronounce her the prettiest baby there has been in the family. All the aunts want her named Sarah Hildreth. Aunt Nina is quite determined about it. Mother says nothing, but I know she would like it very much, and was quite disappointed that we did not name Edith for her. So was Father for that matter—you remember he tried to bribe us with a silver cup. If it were not that you do not like the name I should yield to their wishes.

Time is passing, Del. In a month I shall be packing up and your family will join you and put an end to your bachelor existence. Love from BLANCHE

JACKSON, MISS., *October* 16, 1874

DEAR BLANCHE: I have just come in from the croquet ground where Cass and I beat our opponents two games, and as one of them, Capt. Clover, is the champion, we won a great victory. I do not think, however, that the Republican Convention at Chattanooga won a victory. Our delegates have just returned and are loud in denouncing the cowardice of the convention. It failed to endorse the civil rights bill! Instead of building up respect for Southern Republicanism they have drawn down upon it (so I should say) the contempt people ever bestow on a pusillanimity. I will not speak further on this matter as it disturbs my equanimity.

This has been a busy day with me—my way of being busy. In the morning shortly after daylight I got out of bed for my law book (as is my habit just now) and studied in bed till between eight and nine. Then I am up and dressed when George brings my breakfast at about nine. With my breakfast he brings the mail. This morning came your second letter. My letters are few now-a-days, and soon read. After breakfast I go back to my study, which I keep up to half past eleven, when I go to the office. Today I had little else to do than sign letters. Upon finishing the little I had to do, I went with Mr. Noonan to see a kiln of brick he has just burned.

I read till three, when I went to dinner. I am still at the restaurant. Returning I attended to callers and then went to croquet.

Such has been my day. Inside of my house and myself all is well; but Republican disasters in Ohio and Indiana and the gradual and seemingly certain falling away of Republican states in the South makes us all a little gloomy and full of forebodings of a like fate.

My heart was made glad by your letter today, as it shows me that you are well and happy. I suppose you will be going downstairs when this reaches you.

Love for my beautiful wife and sweet, pretty babies. How very proud I am of you all. ADELBERT

LOWELL, *October* 17, 1874

DEAR DEL: I am troubled about you, for in your second letter from Jackson you speak of your letter as looking "jerky" and that you "feel jerky all over." I am afraid that you are having chills. It is a very unpleasant thing to picture you in that old Mansion all alone, sick and a prey to the gloomy feelings which always accompany ill health. I hope and trust that I am mistaken, and that you are well.

All here are doing nicely. I am partially dressed and sit up the greater portion of the day, lying down occasionally as I feel weary. I have not been out of the room yet, and shall not go until next week some time. Since the furnace fire was started we have all suffered from the heat and I have not felt as strong and fresh as before. The baby has had a very heavy cold, but is now better. I have a slight one, but it is of no account. When the rooms are so warm we are all in profuse perspiration all of the time, and the least change or draught of air causes a cold. After this month I am determined to have the window open at night.

Butler and Edith are perfectly well. Edith has had her photograph taken. I have not seen the proofs yet, but Mary says she had two which must be splendid. How pleased I should be to get a fine picture of her. I believe I told you that the photographer said he had never seen a child so beautifully formed, so straight, and plump.

I told you wrong about the diamond ring. Col. Kinsman did not give it to me. He brought the stone from California and left it in Boston to be set and cut. He said Mrs. Dodge gave it to him in the rough. The jeweller took it to Father while Kinsman was at Panama and Father paid for the cutting. Now Kinsman for some reason desires to leave it here and have it worn. I made the mistake of supposing he desired to give it to me because Mother brought it into my chamber one day and said "Col. K wants you to wear this until he asks for it." Of course I could not say "no"—but it troubled me a little, for I knew it would compel me to paint a picture for him. He has often asked me, but I have excused myself upon the plea of not having time. This would hardly answer while I consented to take his ring. So I am quite relieved to be free from obligation. The ring was left for Mother's use as much as for me and I shall never wear it. Don't say "much ado about nothing," Del. My life just at present is quite monotonous, and I must write you about trifles.

You write of the beautiful weather of the Southern fall. It cannot surpass that which we have been enjoying for a week past. The air is bracing, without being cold, and the landscape is glorious with the varying tints of autumn.

I send you love and begrudge every beautiful day which I cannot share with you. BLANCHE

The Mansion, JACKSON, MISS., *October* 17, 1874

DEAR BLANCHE: This morning's mail brought me a letter from Bay St. Louis whereby I learned that the Boulange property was not sold. The lady who owns it was able to raise money to meet the mortgage and the sale was indefinitely postponed. That is, the suit was withdrawn. I will watch the papers to see if any new places are ordered by the courts for sale.

In looking after your geraniums today I found but a sorry remnant of the grand array you left. Two plants, one barely more than a stump—the other fast traveling, evidently, the downward path. I have not seen George to learn the cause of such ruin.

I am getting in wood and coal for winter. How would you like to have a new kitchen stove? Would it not be economy to get a smaller one than the one we now have? I think so, and shall make a change as soon as I go to N.O., which will not be till after the Nov. elections which take place two weeks hence.

This is very pleasant weather. I wish you and the babies were here. It is not pleasant in the streets because of the clouds of dust which are constantly flying. But nothing can be more agreeable to the senses than such fall weather as this.

Do you not mistake when you say I would rejoice in Butler's precocity as indicated by his slyly pinching his sister Edith!? I thought I was constantly striving to induce him to treat his sister with kindness? It must be my wife who finds cause for congratulations in such feats of her eldest. He gives evidence of cuteness in other ways enough to satisfy his Father. Kiss him, his suffering sister Edith, and the little one for me and take many with love for yourself. ADELBERT

JACKSON, MISS., *October* 18, 1874

DEAR BLANCHE: This is Sunday and it has been a very quiet day with me. I have hardly been out of the house. I sent for my dinner as well as my breakfast and with the exception of the time given to a few callers have been diligently reading all day long. And now, as the shades of night are falling, I take a seat by the window for a chat with you.

This house seems bleak and barren. As I wander through the rooms and see a thick layer of dust on everything I am reminded of a barn in the spring when the hay is all gone and only dust and chaff are to be seen on the timbers and in the crevices. It will brighten up by the time you get here, I have no doubt. Before then, however, I shall try my hand at the work of housecleaning, an undertaking so fatal to the equanimity (so said) of housekeepers.

I hope it will rain before you get here, as I have no doubt it will. I also expect to be able to bring you up from the depot in your own carriage.

By the quiet life I lead here you may know that I find little I care for outside of the house and my own thoughts. I am more and more inclined to abandon these surroundings and all they proffer and seek a new life in a different atmosphere. But we will have time to talk of this before the day of action shall come.

I expect the tubs for your plants tomorrow. I asked George about the geraniums and he said all had died but three last summer and that one of the three remaining had been stolen. So you will not have much of a flower garden next spring.

I was disappointed in not getting a letter from you this morning. You must be quite well by this time. Surely we should be thankful that you are doing so well, and that the baby is strong and growing fat, even if it loses its beauty thereby. If it gets a good start, as did Edith, it will be all the better able to withstand the ills young folks are subject to.

I shall expect to see a month hence a bouncing baby—almost a brunette—a good-natured child—to be a joy to its parents and the neutral ground at least on which her belligerent brother and sister can meet in peace.

To you all, dear ones, I send love—especially to my beloved wife.
ADELBERT

The Mansion, JACKSON, MISS., *October* 19, 1874

DEAR BLANCHE: Another day has gone. Time brings us nearer together. The day has been rather a busy one, yet I miss you much.

This morning as I was looking over my morning's mail, in which I found no letter from you, Mr. Raymond came walking in my room. He returned with his family last night. This evening while we were playing croquet I saw them riding by in their own carriage. He has bought a horse and buggy. They presented a grand appearance, but I am sure that they, inordinate lovers of croquet as they are, wished their turnout somewhere else and that they were with us footpads with mallet and ball.

Major Gibbs went away early last week. He has just returned. He has been spending the time at the "Bay."

There has been quite an influx of carpet-baggers within the last twenty-four hours, Col. Warner and Mr. Sullivan being of the number. Mrs. Warner is in Connecticut. The Brecks are well, and sent me word to come up there. I shall not go however at this time.

This is a very healthy season. There is so little sickness that the doctors are complaining—a poor crop for them. But this continued dry spell is exceedingly favorable for cotton. It has been a bad season as a whole, but this is such good picking weather the yield will be materially improved.

I suppose you are moving about the house a little now. And I have no doubt Butler and Edith are glad of it, while the youngest young lady is quite indifferent so long as she has her meals regularly.

Let me know how Ben I. is doing. I shall be glad of any news of you and ours—yours.

Love for my beautiful wife and our sweet babies.

ADELBERT

LOWELL, *October* 20, 1874

DEAR DEL: All are getting on bravely here. I have Edith to take breakfast, dinner, and tea with me—and Butler quite frequently although he is such a disturbing element that he is coaxed away as often as possible.

Edith is getting to be Mother's baby very fast, and fights and cries for her place in my lap. Mrs. Faunce insists that I must not lift her yet, so she climbs upon the stool and then sits on my knee, or someone gives her a helping hand. The little one has also learned to know me, and prefers to have me hold and rock her even when she does not care to nurse. You will have to make much of Butler, for he is evidently likely to be pushed out of his place.

The Avery baby is very bright and pretty looking—but has an awful name. There will be too many Blanches in the world by the time our youngest is grown up. We must think of some other name for her.

I am very sorry that you were troubled about the $5000 from Northfield. It was, and is a matter of no consequence. If you had not spoken of paying it Father would not have thought about your doing so at present, and if it will be any better for you or for the firm to leave it longer you ought to do so. By the way—is it not time to ask them to send you some flour for this winter's use, in order that it may arrive by the time we begin housekeeping again?

For the plants, if they are a little frost bitten it will not hurt them—but for a short time. They will put out fresh leaves very soon when in the house.

I was quite astonished to hear that you had ordered a span of horses and mean to have a carriage. Are you not growing extravagant, Love? I have a suggestion to make when you choose a carriage, that the wheels shall be so arranged that they can turn clear under. Otherwise I shall never feel perfectly at ease. I hope the horses will not be *too* frisky.

Mother starts for West Point this afternoon. Father will go on to New York with her tonight. He is to speak to the

Army of the James tomorrow evening—so I am to have no one but Mrs. Faunce and the children for company.

I do not write you every day—Love, so you need not fear that some of my letters are missing.

Love as ever—from BLANCHE

JACKSON, MISS., *October* 20, 1874

DEAR BLANCHE: I was glad to know that my boy still remembers his father, and that he enjoys seeing him in his dreams if not in his waking hours. It seems a long time since I left you, and I should not be surprised to hear any day that Edith was talking like a lady and telling her thoughts and dreams. I am free to say I do not expect that much at present of our second daughter.

This afternoon the Raymonds came over for a game of croquet. Neither played very well. When R. warms up to the game we will have the old exhibitions of temper and thereby a token of interest. Mrs. Dedrick was over also. I went to supper with them, the first supper I have had since my return.

Capt. French came to town today. He says he is doing well at his present business, which is working as a contractor grading a railroad over in the east part of the state. He has contracted for the hire of two hundred convicts and is going over on the river to work on the levees. He is a peculiar fellow, and all say very unreliable, but I must confess I was glad to see him.

Yesterday George brought up your geraniums, and this morning I had the pots washed clean and with a stick loosened the earth which was quite hard and watered them. I also cut off dead leaves and stalk. This is my first attempt at farming! I will also attend to your plants in the vases as soon as the tubs shall be ready.

Kisses for you, dear One, and for the babies, one, two, three.

ADELBERT

JACKSON, MISS., *October* 21, 1874

DEAR BLANCHE: I have just come up to my room from the croquet ground. I gave my mallet to Raymond and took his place in a two-handed game with Mrs. R. I won the first game but lost the second and third. She was better satisfied with herself than if she had lost. She charged me with letting her win. Though the suspicion was in her mind she was none the less content.

I wrote down to N.O. to a friend to buy me a second-hand carriage. Today he replies that he can get a phaeton which has been used but twenty or thirty times—a four-seated one and I presume with a top—the price being about $250.00. I do not know that you would be content with such a carriage. For one, I care little for any excursions outside of our own fence. If we had two horses we could ride horseback. Should we have such a season as was the last, we could go out but little.

I have been thinking I would delay any purchase till later in the fall. It costs at the boarding stables for keeping one horse one month twenty-five dollars. Poor folks will be obliged to sell by and by, and there is no haste for us. I begin to think an occasional horseback ride and croquet would be more conducive to health than carriage exercise. We can hire saddle horses.

I am becoming disgusted with the political atmosphere about me. It annoys me a little in spite of myself. It is almost impossible to shut my senses to it. I shall run down to N.O. in a couple of weeks for this purpose of purification.

Everything is quiet here. Nothing new. My days are all much alike, and I am never so well content as when left alone with my books.

Tell Butler he must be a good boy, and take care of his Mother, Edith and little sister. Tell him he should not strike them nor pinch them, but be kind to them and love them like a good boy as he is. I send love to you, Dear, and to them.

ADELBERT

JACKSON, MISS., *October 22*, 1874

DEAR BLANCHE: Another day has gone and its similitude to all its fellow days so strong that it is hardly distinguishable from them. The same routine of meals, office work and croquet.

The only new thing I have to record is this. I shall not wait till next month before going down to the Bay. I shall go in a day or two, exactly how soon I cannot say, as I must wait for the coming of some of my friends who wish to see me. I have no particular reasons for going except that I think a change will be beneficial to me. However, my health is excellent and today the restaurant at which I am boarding congratulates itself on having a French steward from New Orleans. I am glad to say I see a change for the better so soon in the food.

It is now seven o'clock here and about eight o'clock with you. Just three weeks ago at this time we were congratulating ourselves on the happy termination of an event we had waited so long and anxiously for. But it is human nature to forget such fortunate events soon after their occurrence and to worry ourselves with all kinds of indifferent things day by day. It certainly is very foolish to be building up windmills to fight. Even where we fight a real foe we might as well be cheerful about it and not permit ourselves to be unhappy till the time comes. You see I am permitting myself to be annoyed by things which I have no possible control of—things which could not have been forseen nor averted. Of course it is very unwise in me. It is, however, only temporary—soon dispelled.

Nothing brings sunshine like thoughts of my wife and our babies. To you I send love. ADELBERT

LOWELL, *October* 21, 1874

DEAR DEL: Another letter came for me in last evenings' mail, and it seems to me you are leading rather a lonely life. One more month and you will be ready for a change.

I have not been downstairs yet, and shall not go until Sunday. I am getting on nicely, however. The only trouble is that a very little exertion tires me, and brings on such an unpleasant headache. For this reason Mrs. Faunce is inclined to keep me in good subjection.

I wish you could see Edith. I cut her hair day before yesterday—after the fashion of Butler's. It is very becoming to her, but I am sure anyone would take her for a boy. Yesterday while they were playing about the room Butler as usual gave her a push, which she resented, and she went at him with both little fists clenched and so much determination in her face that Butler was amused, and made no resistance. She gave him one or two taps on the head (he was stooping down) and so the fight ended.

Mrs. Faunce never ceases praising the baby. She thinks her the brightest baby for her age she has ever seen, as well as one of the very prettiest. Certainly the child is as good natured as anyone could desire. We are fortunate in our babies, Dearie, and it is of very little consequence how matters go in Miss. politically, our contentment and well being does not depend upon anything there. But while you are head, you must direct and control as far as possible.

Love, BLANCHE

JACKSON, MISS., *October* 23, 1874

DEAR BLANCHE: This morning I had another letter from you. I am glad to know you are improving.

When I spoke of being and writing "jerky," not an elegant term perhaps, I only referred to the state of my nerves. As I wrote you yesterday, I am perfectly well—never better. So, you need not be anxious about me on that score.

Your plants of the vases are now in the hall of this (second) floor in tubs, painted white within (where the earth is) and blue without, black hoops, the tubs resting on little low stands which are also painted blue. Thus much have I been able to accomplish in the gardening line!

This morning a package came to me from Louisville, so said the express man, but it was marked as starting, or as having stopped at, Newport, Ky. Upon unrolling it I found a very large seal-skin rug with blue and red edge like those you have, the red constituting the back. It is larger than the polar bear skin in your library, at least it seems so to me. Its shape is oblong. The color of the fur is that of the mouse. The long hairs of the seal skin are left in in all parts or pieces except one, where the soft fur shows to excellent advantage. It is very heavy. I assume it is for a rug—say a chamber rug—for I cannot conceive of any other use to which it can be put. I have no notice from anyone of such a present. Unless General Swift, U.S.A. sent it, I am at a loss to know who did.

I write this by daylight before my usual exercise. Some friends have come in for croquet.

As ever, I send you love. I would not repeat this so constantly did I not know how pleasant such repetition of such words from my Love is to ADELBERT

LOWELL, *October* 23, 1874

DEAR DEL: Today the baby is three weeks old, and we all celebrated by going out to ride.

The fresh air was delightful, and the day remarkably fine. We rode over to Aunt Lottie's. Mrs. Faunce, in displaying the baby to Aunt Lottie, said she was the prettiest baby she had ever nursed. I think Aunt Lottie took a little exception to this statement in favor of her first baby, which was also a little girl. But Mrs. Faunce stood her ground and said "Yours were nice-looking babies, Mrs. Pearson, but not equal to this baby. Don't you think her the prettiest child of her age you ever saw?" Aunt Lottie answered "Yes, and that is Mrs. Read's opinion." I write you all this Del, in order that you may feel that although the stranger is of the weaker sex—she may do you as much credit as a boy.

I notice you make no reply to my remarks about her name.

Mother's silence in regard to the subject shows me that she felt our rejection of her name for Edith after it was urged, so strongly, by herself and Father; and I feel some pangs of self-reproach especially when I think how very kind, solicitous, and painstaking she has been during the annoying times of my confinements, and in fact at all times. I also remember how gentle and thoughtful you have been to me, Sweetheart, and I do not wish to insist upon anything to which you are opposed. But I cannot decide against the name myself. I really have not the heart to.

This morning another letter came from you. Perhaps the Boulange place is still for sale at a small advance over what you were willing to pay for it at auction. Of course that poor woman cannot desire to hold on to it if she can get anything for it. She did not ask but $4000 in the first place, did she?

You speak of buying a stove. It certainly would be desirable to have it smaller than the old one, and I would suggest that a Stewart stove is the best and that a large tin boiler on the back part of the top for holding water is a great improvement. While there is any fire in the stove there is plenty of hot water for washing and other purposes.

Never mind about the geraniums. We can start some more slips this winter. I think the trouble is in the soil in which they were potted. I stood by the men while they were putting the plants in the vases, but went in to dinner and left them to do the geraniums. They probably did not take pains, but thrust them into that poor, clayey soil.

I grieve when I think of the miserable meals you are having from that old restaurant. I am sure that we must have done better last winter, and we all know how poor that was.

I asked Butler today to tell me who loved him.—He was cross at me and answered "No one, but Father." "No one, Butler!" "No, not one." I knew his pique would not last long, and did not feel much grieved.

Love for my Dearie, from BLANCHE

JACKSON, MISS., *October* 24, 1874

DEAR BLANCHE: Enclosed is a letter which speaks for itself. I imagine the writer thereof did not expect me to read it first of all; consequently I am forced into this position—that I should not have opened it at all. If I have injured him by reading the letter, I can but say there was no malice in the act. The next one from the Executive Chamber of the State of New York will be forwarded unopened. I also enclose a second letter which shows something else. This is the letter to me. You may recall a letter I received from the same writer when in L. I did not reply to it. Kindness met my neglect, and the "carriage robe" (not a "seal skin rug") was but the forerunner of this suggestive letter. The key of the letter is in the last paragraph. He wishes my cooperation to secure a reappointment for his son. Though I failed to attend his call before, how can I do so now? Is it now a piece of bribery and corruption, as delicate and flattering in its way as your letter in its? Evidently we both are "wictims." I am not certain that I should feel mortified for not knowing a beaver skin from a seal skin. Surely I am not qualified for a fur merchant. I showed it to some friends from a county nearby, who pronounced it beaver, and said the beavers are very numerous on the Big Black, and that skins can be bought at a dollar apiece—and that otters were quite plenty. I requested him to buy me thirty or forty dollars worth. My robe is six feet long and five and a half wide. There are eleven pelts in it.

I had made my arrangements to go to N.O. tonight, but the State Fair begins on Monday, and all agree I had better stay. This I shall do till the middle of the week, if not the whole week.

Please ask your Father if he has received the additional $5000.00 from Northfield. I have not had any word from N. and begin to doubt if my letter there has been received.

Love for beautiful ones so far away. ADELBERT

LOWELL, *October* 25, 1874

DEAR DEL: I went downstairs yesterday, and took Mother's place at the head of the table. I found waiting on the people, cutting bread, pouring coffee, and those little duties, quite onerous, so that I know I must not overtax myself.

I rode out in the morning with Butler, the baby, and Mrs. Faunce. Edith had just gone to sleep when the carriage came around and I thought it best not to disturb her.

We called at Mrs. Lawson's for Leslie Grant, took her to ride and here for dinner. At first Butler was a little shy, but that soon wore off and before the afternoon was over he had told her the steamboat story—turned somersaults in which they mutually assisted each other by taking hold of the heels and pushing over. They took hold of hands and jumped up and down in the middle of Mrs. Faunce's bed and ended up by trying to see which could jump the farthest, making such a noise that Father sent upstairs and requested us to make less disturbance.

But the poor boy was too much excited. His little face was flushed bright red and he was so crazy that he did not take the least care of himself but threw himself about in the most reckless manner, receiving every few moments such severe knocks (for which he did not cry however) that I was obliged to put a stop to such rough sport.

Edith ran after the others, and laughed with her little mouth stretched wide open, now and then doubling herself up like some old woman with her fat hands laid upon her stomach, as you might imagine Harriet would do.

Butler has outstripped the Grant child in many ways, but she understands frolic and play far better than he does.

Kinsman had some candy the other day, and gave some to Butler saying "Where is Edith? I want to give her some candy." Butler answered "Little Sister has gone to Boston." "Has she?" said K., pretending to believe him. "Yes, her has gone to Boston." By this time all the visible candy was eaten, and *your son* looking into K's face with a smile and roguish eye, said "Man was only fooling, Sister is in the kitchen." What are you going to do with the boy, Del? You see he is equal to anything.

Mother will be home tonight with news of Ben.—I am happy when you feel satisfied to speak of "mine" as "ours" as you did in your last letter in reference to Ben's affairs.

Father has started off for a week of stump-speaking through his district. I don't know why he is taking so much pains. His election I suppose is sure. Perhaps he wishes to show the world how strongly he is seated in the hearts of his district men.

I send you as ever love, BLANCHE

JACKSON, MISS., *October* 26, 1874

DEAR BLANCHE: Would it not be well for you to bring down your riding habit? I am of the opinion that horseback riding will be better for us than the more luxurious exercise of carriage transportation. You see, I am hesitating about buying a carriage and horses.

I find that I have no winter underclothing—at least not in the quantity I expected. Please buy me three undershirts and one pair of drawers and bring them with you.

Why has your Mother gone to West Point? Not because Ben is retrograding in his studies, I hope. As she did not intend to go when I was in L. I fear some such cause impels her now.

The State Fair begins today. Unlike Northern fairs, this,

the first day, amounts to nothing. Tomorrow there is to be a horse race. Then we shall be interested. I rode to the Fair grounds this evening with Raymond in his turn-out. We then rode about town till dark. I supped with Mr. and Mrs. R. Mrs. R. and Mrs. Dedrick were over here, playing croquet. Such has been the day with me.

A gentleman from N.O. yesterday told me he saw Mr. Parker the day before, and in talking of politics Mr. P. said he (P) was a "Jeffersonian Democrat"!! What an old humbug he is. I wonder if he knows he is a swindler; or is he ignorant of that fact. I suppose he does not realize that by so proclaiming himself and so acting, that he prostrates himself in the dust before the Ku Klux there who would rejoice to see him a corpse.

Your account of Edith's demonstration against Butler with her clenched fists was very amusing. I am glad to know that Butler had the wit to see the ludicrous phase of the affair and was generous enough to submit to the chastisement. How like her Mother Edith is. Poor Butler.

I send to them love and kisses, also the same to their little sister. To their Mother I send love. I am glad to learn that you are doing so well, though it seems to me that you are not gathering your strength as rapidly as heretofore.

ADELBERT

LOWELL, *October* 28, 1874

DEAR DEL: This has been rather a bad day for me. I was quite sick last night, Mrs. Faunce says owing to over-exertion on Sunday, causing loss of appetite and poor digestion. I am feeling better this evening however, and expect another night's rest will cure all trouble.

Beef tea has driven off the night sweats, which is a great step in advance. How strange it will seem to you by and by to have a wife perfectly strong and well and uncomplaining. Can you imagine it?

Two letters came from you last night, in which you speak of games of croquet, your attempts at farming, and among other things a carriage for $250.00 and your uncertain frame of mind as to carriage and horseback exercise.

I agree with you that if the coming winter at all resembles the past, and there is no reason why it should not—the weather will prevent all daily carriage exercise. Then again, your time is very much occupied during the session of the Legislature, and you will have but little to spare to ride with me, and I am sure I do not know of anyone I should care to ask to go with me constantly, and certainly it would be quite lonely to go by myself.

Suppose we compromise, and instead of horses and a carriage you purchase a billiard table—which will be little or no care, cannot get sick or break its legs, does not require an extra person to take care of it, and costs nothing for board.

Then, if you wish, whenever I feel disposed to ride I will have you hire a vehicle, or if you will go with me and we can get a good horse for a lady to ride, we will try a little horseback exercise.

You can inquire if the stables afford such a creature. If so, and you think it worth while, I will bring my riding habit, etc.

I believe, Del, that the billiard table is a good suggestion. What could you do next summer with a carriage? It would not give you half the pleasure and exercise you could get from a table, and would be far more care. Perhaps you think I am very anxious to keep care at a distance. I confess I am, unless I can get a fair equivalent for the annoyance of its company. Get a table, Del, and please your wife.

This letter will reach you before the last day of Oct. and you can order it and call it a birthday gift. With it take love untold from your absent wife. If my suggestion is not sufficient, I order you *to obey*.

Mother returned this morning from West Point. Ben is well, and doing nicely. He expects to be made corporal. He has had more recommendations for it than any member of his class, and the only thing against him is his size. He likes his teacher in mathematics very much, and is doing better than last year.

I am very sorry to see by the tone of your letters that political matters are annoying you. It is useless for me to say "How foolish, Del" for you know that it is so, as well, if not better than I. But I will remind you that all these things would sink into absolute insignificance if sickness should come to any of us, and you would be the first to turn from them and exclaim what petty troubles in comparison to what may come. Then again, Love, the very things which seem most untoward now may be productive of great good in the end. Do not be downcast. There is nothing in Mississippi worthy of it.

With perfect confidence that all will be well, I commend my Sweetheart to the care of all those good spirits present on All Hallow E'en at the time of his birth. They will fight his battles and bring him out victorious. BLANCHE

JACKSON, MISS., *October* 27, 1874

DEAR BLANCHE: We went to the fair today. As we were gazing about at next to nothing, for next to nothing is on show, I met Capt. Raymond and his wife and spent the remainder of the afternoon with them. There was a good sprinkling of the beauty and chivalry of the town. As I passed them, or gazed on the crowd as they were grouped to see the race, I felt as much a stranger as when in your fair grounds at Lowell. The whole attention of the visitors centered in the races. The trotting was looked upon with apparent indifference, but when the running race began there was a clapping of hands which was kept up during the whole heat, a display I never saw before. I interpreted it as indicating intense preference of running over trotting—a people who never ride in carriages declaring in favor of their own saddles. Everyone seemed to bet on the issue.

After it was over I was invited, and I accepted the invitation, to drive Mrs. R. up here to the croquet grounds. Mrs. Dedrick came over when we drove up—soon R. appeared, when we had a four-handed game. Mrs. R. and I, being partners, beat. Mrs. D. is a peculiar woman, and moans most ludicrously when beaten. As a specimen she will amuse you, as a neighbor she will bore you.

I expect soon to begin to clean house. One of the first things I shall do is to have the chimneys cleaned out. Then have our slamming blinds provided with proper fastenings, then the glazier, then soap, water and elbow grease. I will commence next week if I can get some men. It will be so well done you will think you superintended it yourself.

Shortly after my return I saw Mr. Howard, Lizzie's uncle. He says L. writes home that she likes you very much indeed, also that she never saw such good children as are ours. Kiss the babies for me. Love for yourself, my Dear,

ADELBERT

LOWELL, *October* 28, 1874

DEAR DEL: I write you a hasty little note, in order that you may not miss your daily letter, and begin to have doubts as to the well-being of your family. We are all doing nicely, Mrs. Faunce leaves next Saturday, and we are all hurrying to get things ready for my start South. Mrs. F. does not think I shall be well enough to go by the middle of the month. I think I shall, however, unless something unforseen happens. I am anxious to be with you, Dearie.

Your letter of yesterday, or I should say that received yesterday, speaks of a seal skin rug—which from your description I should judge to be very handsome and most costly. I suppose it to be a carriage rug or robe. I should advise that you fold it up with camphor to protect it from moths, which in that warm climate must still be on the wing.

Our upper hall must present quite an appearance with the flower tubs, and the addition of a billiard table will make us quite flourishing. There is only one drawback, and that is the plants will not flourish where they cannot have the sun and if I remember rightly there is never any in that part of the house. Still, they may do well enough.

I notice on Father's table a letter in an envelope with the Northfield heading. Of course I do not know what it is about and Father will probably not be home until after the election, which is next Tuesday. I am very sorry Sweetheart that you felt annoyed about the $5,000 more especially because I do not think you had any cause.

Love, BLANCHE

JACKSON, MISS., *October* 28, 1874

DEAR BLANCHE: Things here are much as usual. The Fair has brought quite a number of people and a strolling theatrical troupe. The city is full of politicians of all stripes, and many and startling are the schemes on foot for future glory.

It is the "outs" or those who soon will be, who seek to make the tumult. Just now a determined effort is being made to induce me to stop fighting railroads, those which seek to get the subsidies granted them by an over-liberal legislature a couple of years since.

The roads seek to plunder the state, and I alone stand in their road to about a million of dollars. They are now "wire pulling" with my friends, but they will "pull" in vain. I shall stand by my trust, if the last friend (?) leaves me.

As my contingent fund is exhausted, and as I do not know exactly what kind of a stove would suit you best I will delay the purchase till after the first of January, when you can make your own selection.

Raymond is making arrangements to put his horse in our stable. One of the men stopping in the house with me, Gibb's clerk and bosom friend and bedfellow, has had a horse in the yard for a number of months. He will take him away when you come, and as a matter of course I expect R's horse will be brought over here. I do not remember when I asked him to bring it. The only objection will be the danger to the children, but as it is a quiet horse, I think there need be no cause for anxiety.

I had fixed on no particular name for the baby. Having the feeling you express, you had better name her in accordance with your own preferences.

I am glad to hear you have began to ride out and take the fresh air. I have no doubt it will do you much good. The baby may be very pretty and beat the Pearson children,—but it is only "pretty." It may be well for *her* but "a *him*" can manage to thrive without beauty—since it is a girl let us hope her beauty may hold with her.

Love, ADELBERT

JACKSON, MISS., *October* 29, 1874

DEAR BLANCHE: Enclosed is a letter from John. You will see that the $5,000.00 due your Father has been paid. I am glad it is off my hands. Will you attend to this business so far as to receive the mortgage I gave him, and have it cancelled if it can be done in Lowell? I do not think it necessary to send it to Iowa for that purpose. Your Father or his agent can so endorse the deed as to render it a harmless instrument, as it is not now. I have replied to John's letter and suggested that my share of this year's work of the mill should amount to just $5,000.00. Whether my suggestion will avail aught remains to be seen.

The new steward at the restaurant has revolutionized the kitchen and we now have most excellent meals for this latitude. I have no cause of complaint. So my Love need not feel concerned about my food. It is not equal to your Mother's which, in my opinion, is often wasteful, but it is good enough for one like me.

I was surprised to hear that you had cropped Edith's hair. How you could do so is hard to imagine. It is a long step towards bringing her up as you do Butler. Fashion has such a hold on even infants that a one-year old must have different styles of dress, if of different sex, and to depart far from the path it points out is too much for any Mother. But so far as the "cropping" goes, we have done well, and gathering courage therefrom we may do better. Perhaps you cut it off because of the mop-like appearance it presented in the photographs you sent me.

The Fair is doing finely. The city is crowded. I failed to get down to the grounds today. I did not care to go particularly, though the carpet-baggers are running the only attractive part of it—the races. What an audacious, pushing crowd carpet-baggers are. From the day Columbus imposed upon the simple Indians of this continent to this act of capturing a State Fair they have not permitted quiet folk, or any other as for that matter, to have a moment's peace.

Mr. Clover and Mr. Raymond beat Sullivan and myself this evening, about my first defeat at croquet. Mrs. R. and Mrs. Dedrick were over.

Love for the babies and yourself. ADELBERT

LOWELL, *October* 30, 1874

DEAR DEL: I did not write you last night, so you will miss one letter. I received yours enclosing DeKay's and correcting your mistake about a "seal skin rug." I am delighted that you have such an elegant present, and renew my remarks about camphor and moths.

Gen'l. Palfrey's wedding cards have been received. I trust he will have a happy life, although he has begun this new part of it rather late for perfect contentment. I think he may find it difficult to change his old bachelor habits.

For the last week Edith has had her chair at the table during breakfast and dinner. She behaves like a little lady and can feed herself nicely with a spoon. The weather has been glorious for the last three weeks, and the children have had the full benefit of it. Edith was out hunting chestnuts this morning and found eight—which shows her quite an expert.

Father has received word from Northfield that the $5000 is at his disposal. Clancey came up for the mail, and I had Mother ask him about the Northfield letter. I think the money is subject to his draft in New York.

You speak of otter skins being plenty on the Big Black. Is the fur nice? I should not think it would be as good in a warm climate as in a cold one. But any kind of fur is worth far more than a dollar a skin.

Love, from your *undemonstrative* wife (except on paper).

BLANCHE

JACKSON, MISS., *October* 30, 1874

DEAR BLANCHE: Another day has passed and it has been—nothing but a horse race. The renown of carpet-bagger management of racing at a fair must have spread like wild fire over the state for this day has been the most successful that Mississippi's State Fair has ever known. It is probable that five thousand people were present. I was lost in the crowd. I tried to find Mrs. R. but failed, and as a consequence spent the time with horse-men. I felt it my duty to go, but I was glad to get away and come up here in my own room by myself.

I have been annoyed a little today in this wise. Six months since I endorsed a note for Dr. Barrett to the amount of $330. He has permitted it to go to protest, and I am now called upon to pay it! The Doctor is a fair specimen of some of the boys! I can hardly believe he will persist in making me pay it. Should he, I shall lose all confidence in his integrity and so doing shall not want him in my office, nor near me. I imagine I have treated him with great kindness and consideration. Why he seeks to treat me so is what (as Lord Dundreary says) no fellow can find out. It seems to me that a man with money would buy the whole crowd. This is rather reckless writing when my letter goes through hands which, in my opinion, would not hesitate to open it. Please let me know (a la Irish) if you get this.

You should be glad you are not here. It has not rained enough to lay the dust for months. Today has been quite windy and clouds of dust have filled the air. A good, thick layer of it is over every part of our house. This morning I spoke to Mr. Noonan about sending me some men which he will do next week. I shall put them at work at first on the walks and out buildings, and leave the indoor work for the last.

Closing of letter missing.

JACKSON, MISS., *November* 1, 1874

DEAR BLANCHE: We had a very heavy frost last night. Although I had a good supply of bed clothes, I awoke once or twice from cold. George said the frost was so heavy that the grass looked as if snow had fallen on it. Within the past week the leaves have fallen, and now the trees, with few exceptions, are bare. All this forenoon I have been toasting my shins, over the fire. I am using wood rather than coal, and find it quite sufficient for the weather.

Yesterday when at the Fair Grounds, I was introduced and shook hands with Jefferson Davis, traitor. I did not wish to meet him, but could not well avoid it. He looks old, and by the glance I had of him, I should say his vigor and strength were fast departing. His coming (and he is visiting the state) I have no doubt is for political reasons. The October elections have had the same effect on rebel and "copper head" that sunlight and warmth have on the viper half torpid from cold. I do not think the few who saw Mr. D., I refer to *his* kind, manifested any particular interest in him. I did not detect a ripple. Yet I have no doubt that one and all will do him homage should the opportune moment occur.

Yesterday a colored man and his wife and child came to my office for *justice*. He first shrewdly committed me to admit that this "is a State Fair,"—referring to the Fair near the capitol. He then asserted that he had lost four dollars there by his own mistake and that of the ticket seller, who treated a five dollar bill as a two dollar bill. He then deliberately demanded restitution from the *state*:—the errors of a State Fair should be corrected by the *state*. Evidently good reasoning. We differed. He then wanted to borrow some money to buy meat for his family. Upon questioning him, I learned he had, with the four dollars claimed to have been lost, devoted eight to the Fair in buying tickets, etc. for family and friends! We differed again.

The "getting even" or "paying up" his innocent sister "when we go down stairs" sounds very much like Mary. He must have been repeating her very words. Surely, there was a cold-blooded, cut-throat twang about his utterance that should cause us to watch and switch.

To him and his sisters, and to you, I send love,

ADELBERT

LOWELL, *November* 1, 1874

DEAR DEL: Last night, or rather yesterday was your birthday. I thought of you many times, Sweetheart, and felt sorry to be so far away from you. In about three weeks I shall be starting with my little family to join you.

You will be surprised to hear that your youngest daughter is to have milk and water as part of her diet. She is very hearty—and for some reason does not always seem satisfied with nursing. It may be that she does not have sufficient. I am not yet well enough to digest easily and cannot eat as heartily as I ought to give her a full supply. She has been fed about three times, and not only likes it, but seems to feel the better for it, and falls off to sleep perfectly contented. I trust, however, that in a few weeks I shall be in such good condition there will be a surplus rather than a lack of food for her.

Your decision in regard to the horses and carriage is good. I want you to have the billiard table—however. You see I have forgotten, or rather ignore, my old jealousy of that one in Washington, and am willing to subject myself to the possibility of like causes and sensations. It would seem very strange to go riding with you, Del. I should forget, perhaps, that I am an *old* married woman and imagine myself a girl again. In such a case, do you think I should be satisfied with my escort? Who can tell.

I saw Mr. Carney this morning. He was here to see Father, and I took occasion to ask him about the Convers mortgage. He says that it will all be right as far as I am concerned eventually, but that I shall not have the interest to spend this winter.

Have you heard from Northfield lately? Perhaps they do not care to be written to in the way I am sure you did from the nature of your letter to me saying you had done so.

I can imagine your house-cleaning, Del. Do not lose your temper over it. Remember that you have no family to look after and annoy you. You have only to pretend that you have sent us all off to the restaurant for our meals—as most housekeepers would willingly do at such times. I am sure everything will be in fine order for our arrival.

I do not feel sure that I shall send you any love and kisses. That would be too demonstrative for your Wife.

BLANCHE

LOWELL, *November 2*, 1874

DEAR DEL: This is Monday evening, and I have been busily employed all day about things which would seem to be but of little importance, but which consume considerable time. I have nothing new to write you.

Tomorrow will decide the election. Father does not express himself very decidedly as to the result. Perhaps he fears that the Democrats will win. Mr. Gonch asked him to make a speech in his favor in Lynn. Father replied that he would do so if Gonch would get Dawes to speak for him in Salem. This Dawes most unwillingly consented to do, and he has been unmercifully abused for it by all the papers opposed to Father in the state. I think Father felt considerable satisfaction in compelling Dawes to endorse him.

You will be pleased to see Butler's cheeks. They are growing very rosy, and improve his appearance vastly, as they take away that rather sallow, delicate look he had. This afternoon he rode over to Mrs. Atwood's with us. There was a carpenter at work on the front steps. Butler watched him quietly for a few moments while we were waiting for Mother to do her errand. Finally he stepped up to the carpenter and gave him a piece of candy out of paper his Gran has bought him. This done, he helped himself to the hammer and nails, evidently considering that he had paved a way to an understanding with the carpenter. Of course the carpenter did not interfere with him and he was happy. Don't you think that he will be capable of making his way in the world, if he develops according to the promise he gives at present?

The babies are well, and some time will amuse us quite as much as their elder brother, no doubt.

Good night. If anybody would like a few kisses, I do not know that I should seriously object to having some *taken*.

BLANCHE

LOWELL, *November* 3, 1874

DEAR DEL: You will have learned through the papers before this letter reaches you that Father has been defeated in his district. The disaffected Republicans joined with the Democrats and elected the candidate of the latter. Father I think is a good deal disappointed, although he has had doubts about receiving votes enough to give him much of a majority. All the evening we have been quite excited, waiting for and reading the telegraphic returns. Enough towns have been heard from to settle the question, and Tompson has been elected by a majority of fifteen hundred or thereabouts.

I saw Carney today in reference to cancelling your mortgage. He looked through all of his papers but could not find it. He showed me, however, *two notes* of $5,000 each which you had given Father. They are exactly alike except as to date, one having been given in April, the other in May, I think. Mr. Carney last winter endorsed on the back of one the receipt of $2,840 last winter. He says that one of them probably belongs to the mortgage, and should have been worded "this note is secured by such and such a mortgage." Of course I could do nothing with him in regard to it. I asked Father if he knew where the mortgage was. At first he said "yes" but when I told him that Mr. Carney knew nothing about it, but had only two notes, he said—"Then I do not know where it is. I supposed that he had it. Has it ever been returned from being registered? I don't believe it has, however I can give the Gen'l. a deed of cancellation which will be all that he wants." I said "Very well, he wishes me to attend to it before I go away." Now, Dearie, it seems to me it might so have happened that you would be in a nice position. Carney has two of your notes and somewhere there is a mortgage, making in all $15,000. I must get the deed of cancellation and have Father destroy one of the notes, that on which there has been no payment. So much for business.

I took Butler over to Mrs. Pearson's with me this afternoon. Gardiner was there and we had the two stand up together to measure them. Gardiner, although two years older than Butler, is not two inches taller. I was astonished, for Gardiner has always been considered quite a large boy for his age.

I have ordered Edith's photographs. He will make them any size I wish for three dollars apiece. Of course they will not be finished up with india ink or anything of that sort. If longer than eighteen by twenty-four inches he will be obliged to use two sheets of paper, or greatly increase the expense.

We are all well. Butler has begun to go out of doors by himself, and rakes leaves with Richard and Lynch. His cheeks are like roses. The children send love and kisses. Good night, Love,
BLANCHE

Custom House, NEW ORLEANS, LA.
Surveyor's Office, November 4, 1874

DEAR BLANCHE: The telegraphic dispatches this morning proclaim the defeat of your Father for Congress. They also assert that the Democracy have triumphed in every quarter. Surely it is startling news. I have just come in from the streets. While walking along, three young men passed me, one of whom said, "They have beaten Ben Butler, that is glory enough for one year." What sorry times have befallen us! The old rebel spirit will not only revive, but it will make itself felt. It will roam over our land, thirsty for revenge, and revenge it will have, all to end in a re-action at the North (but never at the South) which will again hurl them from power unless perchance their rotten boroughs of the South wherein men will be terrorized over, will enable the Democracy to remain in power till rebel debts and rebel slaves shall be paid for. The great reaction at the North is an enigma to me. I cannot understand it. Your Father's house in Washington will hardly know him as a Congressman. How futile the plans we make. The best course for us to take is to do what we believe is right and smile at fate. What a revolution. In fact, I hardly realize it. A Democratic congress! And the war not yet over.

I am pretty well today. The doctor gave me some pills of quinine, which my stomach finds difficulty in disposing of.

I have a slight headache, but am better than yesterday. I will be well in a day or two.

I went to Parker's for breakfast. He is well, but somewhat crestfallen. I attempted to tease him about being a "Jacksonian Democrat," but he pleads ignorance.

Love, ADELBERT

LOWELL, *November* 4, 1874

DEAR DEL: We were amazed this morning to hear of the election of a Democratic Governor for Massachusetts. No one had dreamed of such a thing. Even Gaston himself says that he can hardly believe it is true. The Lieut. Governor is a Republican, so is the majority of the house and senate.

I trust our Southern friends will not derive any consolation or countenance from the state of politics here. The rum sellers and drinkers were determined not to have Talbot, and all voted a pink ticket without caring much what names were upon it so long as Gaston was at the head for Governor. Why would it not be a good idea to have a pink or yellow or blue ticket for the Republicans of Mississippi next fall. Of course, it would have to be kept secret until election day or the Democrats would have a similar color. It seems to me it would be an excellent thing for some of those poor colored men who cannot read. Father is a good deal disappointed, as is natural. It may however, turn out to be the best thing for him.

Mr. Blaine is filled with consternation at the prospect of a Democratic Congress, which will of course dethrone him as speaker, and put Banks or Fernando Wood in his place, thus taking away from him all chance for the Presidency and leaving him to fight all his battles on the floor of the house unaided by any prominent member from this section of the country. It is all very strange, is it not?

This seems to be a letter of politics, but from it you can judge that we are all well here. Mrs. Faunce has gone, and we are preparing to make a start Southward. I believe I will send you love and kisses this evening, if you care for them.

BLANCHE

Custom House, NEW ORLEANS, LA.
Surveyor's Office, November 5, 1874

DEAR BLANCHE: The news of yesterday morning is more than confirmed by the telegrams this morning. The only consolation we can find just at this time is this—it is very much better that our defeat should come this year rather than two years hence. It is possible we may lose there, but a couple of years of Democracy will awaken the people to the mistake made this year. Of course, that which comes nearer to us now is the defeat of your Father. It is a personal defeat which we feel very sensibly, the more that enemies, personal and political, exult so openly. You can well understand that personally I am in nowise disturbed by the disaster of Tuesday. On the other hand, I think it will make my labors much lighter this winter, and the beneficial effect will extend over to next year. What will your Father do?

I have been to look at a billiard table this morning, but it did not suit. I shall look further. My headache still holds on. But as my tongue is somewhat coated I ascribe it solely to the disturbed condition of my stomach. Except being a little unpleasant, I suffer no inconvenience.

I shall go over to the "Bay" at four this p.m. and remain but a couple of days at most. I send you love for you Dear, and for our babies.

ADELBERT

LOWELL, *November* 6, 1874

DEAR DEL: I did not write you last night because of an attack of biliousness which made me dizzy and ill. I am much better this evening, although not entirely well.

I saw Mr. Carney again, or I should not say that I have seen him, for he sent some papers to me by Paul, one of which was the missing mortgage, the other a letter from Father, written in Washington a year or so ago, enclosing the mortgage to him. The mortgage is for $10,000 instead of $5,000, and states that it is to secure two promissory notes of $5,000 each of previous date. So you see the notes are all right and Father says he will cancel the mortgage, it is so nearly paid. I am very glad you were able to pay that $5000 this fall, although I have thought it of little moment. Father said last night that he felt a good deal pressed for money, and I have learned through Mother that he intends to borrow $30,000 if possible. He is not receiving any income from the mill at present, and a great deal is required for the house in Washington, as well as for the Cartridge Mills to which they are making additions. Your mortgage is for seven percent, payable semi-annually. I believe I heard you say you thought it was for ten.

You would be surprised to see Butler's rosy cheeks. He is looking finely. The day that Mrs. Faunce went away he seemed to realize that I had a new charge and that he must depend more upon himself, for he was content to stay out playing with Lynch and Richard, and since then he has been out every day by himself. Lizzie puts on his outside garments and he goes where he pleases and comes in when he is ready. Of course, we look out, or send out from time to time to see that he is not in trouble or mischief. The men have been gathering leaves lately, and it has proved a great delight to him. He has helped to load the cart and ridden back and forth to his heart's content.

Yesterday morning I went down to the nut trees with Butler and Edith and we gathered nuts for a while, then sat on the wall to crack them. They could eat faster than I could crack. I should think a bird would be about distracted to see four mouths open at once. I suppose I remained out too long and exerted myself too much, which caused my illness in the evening. I feel that I ought to be well and act as if I were, but soon find myself at a standstill. However, the baby is only five weeks old, and I must not expect too much.

I am a little anxious because I have not had a letter from you. So much so, Dearie, that I cannot put on airs, but send you love, kisses and caresses without number.

BLANCHE

Custom House, SHIELDSBOROUGH, MISS.
Collector's Office, November 7, 1874

DEAR BLANCHE: I came over here day before yesterday and today I have been out of my room for the first time. I had a touch of, or the continuance of, the diarrhoea which came upon me a week ago; and believing discretion the better part of valor, I carefully kept to my room. Today I am much better, and hope I will be annoyed no longer by the complaint. Yesterday I ate nothing, and for medicine took pulverized charcoal and before going to bed a good dose of French brandy. I shall return to N.O. tonight probably.

I have offered $3500.00 for the Boulange place. The mortgages on it amount to $3,165.00, so I shall at this time be compelled to advance but $335. on the place. The mortgages can run on, and I will only have to pay interest. I do not know that I can get it at these figures, but believe so. I have engaged a cook for you, and shall have her on hand when you arrive. I write hurriedly, as I am in the midst of a crowd. Love to you and the babies.

ADELBERT

LOWELL, *November* 7, 1874

DEAR DEL: Your letter received yesterday has made me quite uneasy about you. It is plain you are not well, and I have so little faith in Dr. Mitchell's pills. It is some relief to know that you were to start at once for New Orleans. There at least you can have better medical advice. Now is the time of all others when I should be with you, and I am not. We shall certainly start the latter part of next week. That is about the 20th, unless something should happen to detain Father a day or so later. I am most anxious to start to be with you, also because I am fearful that as the cold increases the children may feel sick and detain me still longer. At present we are looking and feeling remarkably well. You have not telegraphed me, Del, and it is now five days since your letter was written, so that I am trying to believe that you are well again. If you are not well and want me, I will start at once without waiting for anyone to go on to New York with us.

You ask me about Lizzie, or another nurse for the children. I hardly know what to say. Lizzie has not proved trustworthy. That is, she has taken a number of small articles, of no great value to be sure, but quite sufficient to show that at any moment she may do more. When I told her I had found such and such things among her clothing she declared by all the powers above that she had never taken them and had a dozen different excuses to make, not one of which covered the case. Now, if I keep her this winter, will she not think that she can steal with perfect impunity, the only penalty being that if I miss the things and can find them she has lost nothing, while if I fail to find them or miss them she has gained just so much. With another girl it will be just the same, for I am convinced that stealing is universal, and I am at a loss what to decide.

I hope you will be able to get a cook. She should also be willing to assist about the housework. But on this point I fear you will fail, and we must be satisfied if she can cook. I think I can promise you good bread, at least this winter, and that is a long step towards good living.

I send you love. BLANCHE

LOWELL, *November* 8, 1874

DEAR DEL: I have not had a letter from you yet, and am still in an uneasy state of mind about your health. I am very busy these days, getting all ready to start. Certainly there are a thousand things to remember, all of which are of course of great importance.

You speak very doubtfully about a billiard table. I think I gave a good many reasons why it would be preferable to a carriage, and I still hold to them. I have no doubt you have been playing croquet too late in the evening, staying out after the dampness had begun to rise. With a billiard table you would be more willing to give up the other game.

Next week I shall think of you as busy house-cleaning. Make the men do it thoroughly, dusting the walls and washing the windows. Of course, the carpets will have to be taken up.

It is provoking about that protested note. But after all it will be a good lesson. I think one should never endorse a note unless they are prepared to give away that amount of money. If a man's note is not good enough to be taken without endorsement is it good enough to endorse?

I send you love, BLANCHE

NEW ORLEANS, LA., *November* 9, 1874

DEAR BLANCHE: I did not write you yesterday as I had no opportunity. I left the Bay at twelve and was more than over-run every moment of my time. I offered, as I told you in my letter of Saturday, $3,500. for the Boulange place, but the old lady wants $4500.00, which I fear she will never get. I withdrew my offer. I am still seeking, and hope to find a place by and by. I was charmed with the climate of the Bay, as I always have been. Mr. Cowan is looking, and will negotiate if the opportunity occurs.

I hired a cook, rather an old woman. Ann is her name. She has a good character, and I believe will suit. She will go up to Jackson next Thursday—this is Monday. When she gets there we will keep house at once. I have Cowan looking for a table, or rather a dining-room, servant which we can send for if you wish. The cook is to receive $12.00 per month. She has no family. I think I have been eminently successful in my search for a cook.

In obedience to your orders I have been looking for a billiard table, but as yet have found nothing which suits me. I have bought a carriage for which I have paid $250.00. It has been used some thirty times, and for actual service is, barring such service, as good as new. One man calls it a phaeton, another a baroche. It will answer well for a family carriage. The front wheels will not turn wholly under the body of the carriage, but nearly so. They turn till they strike the iron bar which couples the hind and fore wheels together. I think by turning so far it will be perfectly safe. The pressure being on the coupling, there is no leverage on the body to upset it. In thinking of the table and a carriage, I find no difficulty in discarding the former and purchasing the latter. The carriage means horses and harness. But you and the babies will enjoy a ride more than I the billiards.

I am going up to J. at 5 this afternoon. I have quite recovered from my ill turn. I am feeling lonesome. I need my wife and babies—to whom I send love, ADELBERT

LOWELL, *November* 10, 1874

DEAR DEL: I did not write you last night. We had been out all the afternoon making calls, and I was quite weary. Everyone is astonished to see me about so soon, and looking so well. Poor Sweetheart, while your family is being made healthful and rosy by this beautiful fall weather, you are ill and are not gaining strength for your work next summer.

We shall start the last of next week, and expect to meet you at Louisville. Butler talks of nothing else. It is "Oh, Mum, Mum, want to go home so bad. When are we going to Sip?" Certainly no one can accuse him of being a carpet-bagger.

You ask me what Father is going to do. He will finish the house next spring and expect to have it furnished and ready for living by the following fall. He will spend the winter in Washington and practice his profession. All the people about here express themselves as heartily sorry about the election, say that the state has lost her only smart man in Congress. What the future will bring in the way of political life for Father no one can tell, but he has his profession, and I think will prove sufficient.

I am very happy to hear that you think the elections will prove favorable for you. Mother says if "Gen'l. Ames can only be returned I shall feel that the great barn of a house is of some account."

Love, Dearie, from the babies and BLANCHE

JACKSON, MISS., *November* 11, 1874

DEAR BLANCHE: I was glad to get back again to my steady, even-going life here. I found everything much as I had left. Our party here is a little shocked at the elections North—and many of them, especially the ambitious ones, are shocked into good behaviour. Surely long continued success is very demoralizing to individuals as well as to parties. The *politicians* of this state were born and bred in victory and look upon it as a natural inheritance. Consequently they are shocked, if not alarmed, at the order of things as brought about by the silent falling ballots of the third of this month. The benefits of defeat come to us. We have no lost candidates to mourn, and hope we may escape such a sorrow.

This morning a letter came from John T. He says he is going East and that he will visit you. He writes that business is dull. He also sends me my settlement with the firm. The $5000 paid your father by me is assumed or paid by the firm. Charged with that sum, I stand, on a settlement, indebted to the firm to the amount of $3,655.00. Thus you see I am reducing my indebtedness rapidly. I can easily *carry* that sum inasmuch as I let my part of the dividends pay it. Should we do but one quarter as well this year as last, this sum will be cancelled at the end of the year as my share of the profits will equal it at least. My efforts now will be to meet my indebtedness in Lowell. I am glad to know they are being reduced so I can see a hope of an early escape from debt. Debt may be highly advantageous to some young men just entering into business, but it is not at all necessary for me. We will carefully avoid the embarrassment in the future, as I think we can do.

I shall sell my house in Natchez if I can for anything near the price which I paid for it.

You must let me know when to meet you in Louisville. I am busy at work cleaning, but it is so dusty we can do but little. I have had the chimneys cleaned out and glass put in, etc. but it will be of no permanent good to wash or shake the carpets. The cook will arrive tomorrow when we will go to keeping house. Unless it rains, expect nothing but dust, for I cannot clean up when everything is dust, dust.

Mother, writing to me, sends her love to you and the babies. Love to you and the little ones. ADELBERT

LOWELL, *November* 11, 1874

DEAR DEL: Another day has passed and the time of our separation is rapidly shortening. It is possible that Father will not start for Washington until a week from Monday, in which case of course we shall wait for him, as it will be far pleasanter to have his assistance, in New York. If we do not leave until Monday we shall not probably reach Jackson before Saturday, as I think we had better spend one night in Louisville. We are all well, and if this fine weather continues until after we start I shall feel that we are highly favored.

Edith and Butler have not had any colds to speak of this fall.

You will be pleased with the underclothes I have purchased for Edith. She is perfectly protected, as much so as even you can desire.

By the way—how is the water? You write that it has been very dry for a long time. Do you still use from the same cistern? Perhaps it would be well to have the cistern cleaned before the rainy season.

We have just heard from Florence. She has been to Berlin and gives a lively description of an encounter with and invitation from Prince Frederick Charles to a grand hunt. Mrs. Hildreth, Rowena, Hattie, and Florence were on their way in a landau with a guide to visit the Prince's Palace. He passed them on the way to the hunt, and sent his adjutant to invite them to join the party, which they did. There were five carriages, including theirs, containing Princess F. Charles and her ladies of honor. After the hunt was over the Prince rode up to the carriage, chatted a little about the hunt and America, and ordered the band to play again for their benefit. Florence thinks that they must have been very prepossessing in appearance to have received so much attention, inasmuch as of course they were perfect strangers. All are enjoying themselves very much.

I send you, Sweetheart, love and kisses. BLANCHE

LOWELL, *November* 12, 1874

DEAR DEL: Your letter from New Orleans saying that you are well came this morning. I feel relieved, for I was fearful that each day might bring me news that you were quite ill. I shall be very, very glad, Dearie, to be with you, not only for the sake of your companionship, but because although perhaps a poor nurse, I should prove far better than none, in case of sickness, and a consoler in case of trouble.

I saw the moon this evening, far over my left shoulder. Trouble in store for me during this month, if signs can bring it. I am very glad if you have been successful in getting a cook. I have spoken to Lizzie, and she desires to stay with me until we return North next summer. I told her that I had one very serious fault to find with her, which she well understood, and I could not be subject to that kind of annoyance. She replied "I will never do it again, Mrs. Ames." "That is right, Lizzie, for your own sake, as well as mine." We shall probably be troubled in the same way—whoever we may get—and I doubt if we can do better than with Lizzie.

So you have purchased the carriage, and ignored my commands about a billiard table. Well, I believe there was nothing in the wedding service about your "loving, honoring, and *obeying*," but for all that you owe me some obedience. If you will take time to ride with me I shall enjoy the carriage, otherwise I shall feel that you have been too extravagant for my sake. Who is to drive?

You will be amazed to see the change that has taken place in Butler since you left Lowell. He is getting to be quite a man. He can imitate a train of cars in quite a remarkable manner. Edith is amusing, and dances like a young elephant. Our youngest still promises to be a beauty.

I am tired and will say "good night" with love,

BLANCHE

JACKSON, MISS., *November* 12, 1874

DEAR BLANCHE: This afternoon our cook came. I have given her bedding, etc. and will try to make her comfortable. I shall send her out to market tomorrow morning and will let her go to work cooking. By the time you arrive she will be at home and ready for any call. In the meantime, I will lay in a stock of provisions.

It rained heavily last night. In fact, we have had a rainstorm. The bad humor I was in last evening and yesterday foretold the storm. The dust is laid, and I am hopefully at work cleaning. The dining room was torn to pieces and put together again today. The windows were washed and the woodwork scrubbed. The sitting room is now in a transition state. In looking into our store room I find all the cooking utensils, though no stores. I presume you left none. I will take all the carpets up and have the floors washed, and you will not have so heavy a task when you come.

Col. Breck was here today. In my anxiety for a cow I asked him if he knew where I can get one. He says he does, so I feel easier on that score.

I do not think it advisable for your Father to cancel my mortgage till he is fully paid. He should hold fast to his security while it is no disadvantage to us to have the mortgage hanging over us. Let him look well to his own interest and leave us to take care of ourselves. I only wish I had the money to pay the remainder of the debt. The Northfield mill cannot conveniently aid more. The first thing I shall do with my salary when my warrants shall be cashed will be to pay him what I owe him. You had better tell him I only await to cash my warrants to aid him.

I am glad to hear the babies are so well. I regret you are not so strong as usual, but perhaps we are in too much haste. You must let me know when you are to be in Louisville. On your way, telegraph me at the Galt House so I shall know the train you are to come on. Love, ADELBERT

JACKSON, MISS., *November* 13, 1874

DEAR BLANCHE: The event of this day has been the first step in our housekeeping. Our new cook prepared our breakfast and dinner and soon I shall go down to supper. I can hardly tell how good a cook she is as this day's trial is not a fair one. She is better than any we had here last spring and summer. With a little advice from you on the bread question, I have no doubt she will be quite satisfactory.

I have received a letter from Parker relative to a billiard table. He was to look up a second-hand one, but has failed to find one at any reasonable price. A second-hand one will cost $250.00, while a new one costs $350.00. There are no second-hand ones of the last and newest size and style to be had. A new one will be a too expensive luxury—and the second-hand one a very poor investment. I probably will buy at the "Bay." Principal and interest swell into frightful proportions at a time of stagnation like this. You see, I am clearly justified in being solicitous. Do not suppose I fret about my finances. It is only occasionally I think of them, and even then I have an abiding faith that something will turn up to rescue us from the poor-house. So situated, a billiard table is an unjustifiable extravagance, though a carriage for my wife and babies is not—though it is true a horse eats while a table does not.

I take much pleasure in picturing my family as you describe it. It will soon be seen by the real eye instead of the mind's eye, as now. Permit me to say by the way of a parenthesis, the sooner the better. In ten more days I shall expect to be with you. Love, ADELBERT

JACKSON, MISS., *November* 14, 1874

DEAR BLANCHE: Aside from a little office work and a little reading nothing has transpired today. There was no Northern mail, and of course no letter from you. Nor did I receive a letter from you yesterday. My sphere seems to narrow down day by day, and I must confess that I prefer my quiet life to any noisy one this latitude affords.

You will be better satisfied with our cook than either we have had. This morning she made some most excellent corn cakes. Her cranberry pie was far above the average. I give no orders to her—one excepted, which was to clean up the china closet.

I do not read local papers, but my attention has been called to the fact that some one has, in a letter to a paper, proposed my name as a candidate for Vice President, and that some of the Northern papers are noticing it. If I know myself, I never possessed so little political ambition as today. Events are constantly transpiring which cause me to look with disgust on many things which I am forced of necessity to meet. My purpose is to give a good government, and let the future look to itself. So I am not subject to annoyances I might be, were I trying continually to build. Judging by the late elections, political investments are not safe. A word to the wise is sufficient.

Come down and see us—bringing the babies. To them and to you, I send love,

ADELBERT

LOWELL, *November* 16, 1874

DEAR DEL: Two letters came from you yesterday, in one of which you bewail the dust, in the other rejoice over the rain. It is most fortunate for your reputation as a housekeeper that there has been a storm, and equally fortunate for us who are so soon to be travellers. Last night brought the first rain to us that there has been for at least two months.

Katie is quite disappointed that I do not remain to attend her wedding, which takes place on the 2nd of Dec. This I cannot do, and would rather not have delayed thus long if I could have avoided it. Next Monday evening we are to start, and shall make no delay in New York, if the trains connect. I will telegraph you en route, as you suggest. How glad I shall be to see your dear face again. You can understand that my life at Jackson last winter must have been pleasant when I can say that I think of returning there without a regret, and without the slightest desire to go anywhere else. This shows either great adaptability of character or that I was content last winter.

I believe I told you that Mr. Carney found the mortgage and it has been cancelled, which is quite as well for your note on which the endorsement for $2,800 received is sufficient security, if any is needed for the rest of the payment. I am amused that you seem so much relieved to be out of debt.

I send love.

BLANCHE

LOWELL, *November* 17, 1874

DEAR DEL: Yours enclosing the cook's recommendation came this evening. I am sure if any capacity can be inherited from long training in the family, we ought to have a treasure in the culinary line. I trust for your sake that we are to live well this winter. As for me, I am so fat that if it were not for the baby it would be well if I had next to nothing to tempt the appetite. Your wife has lost her girlish figure, and looks as weighty as an old woman.

Mr. Tom Nesmith brought up an invitation to a series of parties, six in number, to be given in Lowell this winter. This recalls the days of my youth, when I was greatly interested in such affairs. Were it not for Aunt Sue's death I should probably go to the first party given tomorrow evening.

You speak of your debts, and include your note to me. Of course you are in fun, Del. You know why I requested it. Your debts are mine. I cannot be in debt to myself—consequently you cannot be in debt to me. But if I cease to be, you could be to my heirs, your children. Is not that good logic?

I am sorry about the billiard table on your account, but glad upon my own, as I shall be likely to have you more exclusively to myself without such a rival.

Tomorrow I shall put our things into the trunks, some of them at least. Paul has purchased for me some nice mackerel and cod fish in Gloucester, which has been neatly packed in a box, and I intend to take it as baggage. Mississippi will think that all Yankeedom is coming, and "will snuff the battle from afar." Love and kisses, Del, from BLANCHE

LOWELL, *November* 20, 1874

DEAR DEL: The Spoffords came up Saturday to spend the Sunday—so as you can imagine the house has been quite lively. Mr. Spofford and Father talked over the political prospect and both agree that the Democratic and Republican parties will make each split on the money question, but with what result to individuals in which we are personally interested it would be impossible at present to predict. Father's defeat in the district may prove a great blessing in disguise. Let us hope so. I have not had a letter from you for two days, and suppose that you have left New Orleans for Jackson.

Butler can talk and think of nothing but his journey "to Mississip." Mrs. S. says that he seems much older, and is brighter than her little niece. She agrees with all the rest of the world in saying that the baby is the prettiest child of her age she has ever seen. I am beginning to look upon her with some misgivings. She is so very fair, with dark lines under her eyes, and all the little veins showing so distinctly over her head. The expression of her eyes is always so gentle and at the same time languid and rather weary. She excites great sympathy, and although so round and plump I cannot feel that she is very strong. I suppose I am foolish about it—still she is certainly different from the other children.

Edith is delighted with the new moon (which by the way I saw over my left shoulder). She thinks it is someone looking at her, for she hides her face a little shyly and peeps out at it.

How glad we shall all be to see you, Dearie. I was happy to hear that you were homesick for your wife and babies. They send you love and kisses. BLANCHE

Mrs. Ames, children, and nurse Mary journeyed to Jackson, Mississippi, November 25th.

JACKSON, *November* 30, 1874

DEAR MOTHER: We arrived yesterday morning, all well and in good spirits. The journey was long and rather tiresome, and we seemed to have a little streak of ill luck from the time we left Lowell. In the first place, you remember we started in a snow storm. When in the hack at Boston, both of our horses fell down, not doing any injury, but frightening us a little.

We passed Point Judith without trouble. Mary was the only seasick one. But all at once the wind changed, blew down the sound, making such a sea that our old boat simply tossed and tumbled about, making no headway, and instead of reaching New York at five o'clock in the morning, it was five in the afternoon. Of course we were all sick. Lizzie and Mary could not hold up their heads. Edith, Butler and the baby were in bed with me. First Edith threw up, then Butler, then came my turn, while all the time the baby tugged at the breast as nothing less would keep her quiet. You can imagine I was happy when we reached New York. The drawing room engaged for the previous morning was lost, and we were all too sick to go on by the night train, so remained over until the following night at the Fifth Avenue.

Everything went on smoothly enough after this until we reached Pittsburg. Just as we were eating breakfast the porter came into the car with the information that the wheel of our car was broken and we must transfer into another. So all our breakfast, bags and baggage had to be collected together and we were moved into our car, then out again into another. After this we had no other disturbances. Gen'l. Ames met us at the first depot in Louisville, so that he was in readiness to help us at the other. We took the night train for Jackson, stopping in Louisville only through the day, and completed our journey in two nights and one day, reaching Jackson about five in the morning instead of ten o'clock the previous morning as we should have done. Gen'l. Ames had telegraphed for a carriage and truck to be in waiting for us, but owing to the lateness of the hour there was nothing of the kind—so with babies and bundles we were obliged to trudge home. Here, however, the aspect changed. Everything was in nice order, fires burning brightly and a good breakfast to refresh us. The lunch basket you prepared stood us in good stead, and we ate up almost everything. The tea was spoiled however, before we left New York.

Your letter came yesterday morning by the same train which brought us. I was glad to hear so soon from you, it made the distance seem much shorter.

The weather is delightful, cool, but not too much so. The children will enjoy being out in it immensely. I have been down in the kitchen this morning about bread, and my fingers are rather stiff with cold, so that I have written you a miserable looking letter.

Butler and Gen'l. Ames join me in love for "Gran." With many kisses,

BLANCHE

LOWELL, *December* 4, 1874

DEAR BLANCHE: As the beginning of your journey was disastrous, we have a right to hope the close was favorable. All I have heard is that you were tossing all night and all day on the Sound, that you got in only in time to take the night train. That much from your Father. It is a long journey. You are safe through it now. I suppose you were all sick, children included. Poor things, they would rather have stayed with Gran.

The wedding is over. They left on the same evening at half past nine train, while the house was still crammed with company. Milton invited many more after he came, so that there was a jam. He certainly had credit for all he did, for when it was over there was not a thing left to eat. Yet I believe all were fairly served. There are some you know who gormandize all evening. He had a large average of that sort.

I wore the black satin and with some changes I made in it, it was very handsome. Katie's dress suited her style, and she looked as pretty as she could look. The day was mild and fair. Altogether it was enjoyable and very successful. I am thankful it is over. Maria was very tired, though Milton took the charge and looked after things well. She cannot endure much. Yesterday she was in bed. She had taken her large dose of oil. I have not been over today, but I think she will be up in a day or two as well as before. Milton is secretly determined that she shall go to New Orleans. He has begged me not to say anything against it, and offers to pay all expenses if Nina will go with her. It is an inducement to Nina for the reason that Phil is there. Katie declares she will not take charge of the house. But that might be easier than the care of the house and her Mother too, if she should be sick. I think Maria would be better off at home, and shall say so if I say anything, though now the wedding is over she may grow dull and restless when he has gone.

Your Father writes we had better open the middle house. I have decided not to go on till after the first of January. Ben wishes to know where we are to be at Christmas. I think he has a vague hope of coming home for a week. I wish he might, poor boy.

My days glide on, enough to do, no time to spare. Yours are the same now. How is Nub? His picture startles me forty times a day. Poor snipe, is he having a good time? And Edith too! Do you find yourself well, and the baby too? Gen. Ames was telegraphed here to hurry back, that mischief was brewing. My love to him, to you and the babies.

Your most affectionate MOTHER

JACKSON, *December 5*, 1874

DEAR MOTHER: This has been quite a busy week, for although Gen'l. Ames had attended to the house and put it in nice order, there were quite a number of little things to be done, in directing which all of my time has been occupied. I say all of my time; this is not exactly the fact, for every afternoon from half past three till six we have played croquet.

The weather has been delightful. The days sunny and bright, and so warm that at noonday I open the doors and windows to let in the soft warm air, and drive out the damp chill of night and morning. The children are out from twelve till half past two, the rest of the time is spent in my chamber and the nursery, where the fires are kept burning constantly, in order that there may be no dampness. We have been troubled with colds in the head, but are now somewhat better. Edith is the worst sufferer.

The cook is good, and besides understanding her business she is kindly and obliging, so that there is no trouble in having things to suit. Above all she is very neat and saving. We are extremely fortunate.

Last Thursday I purchased some poultry. Sixty chickens and five geese. The chickens were twenty-five, thirty, and thirty-five cents apiece, according to size. The geese one dollar. I intend to have some turkeys next week, and shall then feel that I have a pretty good supply. Tomorrow we are to have a cow, which with the horse will make considerable live stock. The cats have disappeared, much to my delight, so you need not feel uneasy about the little baby. She is very quiet and good—too much so perhaps, if the goodness is any indication of want of strength and vigor.

Gen'l. Ames is quite troubled about affairs in the State. Perhaps you have seen by the papers that the white men in Vicksburg have intimidated and driven away some of the colored office holders in that county. Of course, this is perplexing and annoying, but will soon be settled I hope.

If Butler were awake he would join me in love and kisses for his "Gan" and Uncle Paul. Good night, Mother.

BLANCHE

LOWELL, *December* 11, 1874

DEAR BLANCHE: What a miserable time you had the beginning of your journey. That is over now, and I trust you are all well, and living and breathing in a lovely atmosphere, where the children can still be out daily. There is nothing to complain of here. It is still temperate, but sparkling. Kate has returned from the bridal trip. They went to New York. They seem very happy. Kate, according to her Mother, thinks she has just the right one. If he thinks the same, as no doubt he does, why all is well.

Milton, Maria and Nina start for New Orleans next Thursday. It is laughable, I never dreamed Maria would go again, but so it is and perhaps just as well. Mrs. Read will be with Phil and escape all care unless Maria should be sick.

Hattie Heard has written a long letter to the Lowell Courier. In it she describes the Hunt that Florence wrote about. It is very well written. She may take up that kind of writing. She is ambitious, and evidently wants to be at something.

How does Gen. Ames get on with the political work? I am very desirous of that Senatorship. I suppose it is too much luck to expect. If you do the best you can, you can do no more than that.

There is a Shakespeare Club here. I was invited down to Mr. Talbot's for one of the meetings. I took my big book, supposing it might be possible I should be asked to read the part of "Lear," as that was the Play. But the parts had been given out by lot a fortnight before. Mr. Coffin, filled with the importance of the occasion, labored through the words of "Lear." They offered me the part of Gloster as Mr. George Richardson was not there to read it, but I declined, and gladly listened while they called all the words of the Play. They pretended a dread of me. But I think every one there felt as nearly perfect as it falls to mortals to be.

I expect Paul every minute, and it is tea time. Love to Gen. Ames. A kiss for you, that snipe of a boy, and the little females from *Your affectionate* MOTHER

JACKSON, *December* 14, 1874

DEAR MOTHER: I received your letter of last week describing the wedding and was glad to hear that Aunt Maria may possibly spend the winter in New Orleans. Of course it is pleasanter for me to have some of the family at least within a day's journey.

Gen'l. Ames and I, with some of our friends and neighbors, play croquet every afternoon. This is for exercise as well as amusement. We have not taken any rides yet, for just at this time Gen'l. Ames is quite busy, owing to the troubles at Vicksburg, and has people calling on him constantly about one thing or another.

I wrote you last week about my chickens and geese. I am sure you will smile when I tell you that six of my chickens committed suicide by drowning themselves in a slop barrel, two lay down and died. We have eaten three, and I shall feel that every one we have cooked is just so much gain. However, lately they have been doing well, and perhaps there will be no more fatalities amongst them.

If you have not seen the papers lately, no doubt Uncle Parker has told you that there has been serious trouble in Vicksburg. The city has been, and is, controlled by a mob, known as the "white leaguers." There was a contest the other day with some colored men who, in response to the call of the Sheriff of the County, attempted to enter the town. They were shot down like dogs, and those that fell wounded were murdered. Gen'l. Ames has called an extra session of the Legislature, which will assemble here next Thursday. Preparations are being made in anticipation of disturbances here, but I think we shall escape it. It is to be hoped so, at least. Two judges were obliged to fly from Vicksburg to avoid being imprisoned, if not hung. One of them, Judge Hill, is at the Mansion a good deal, and though anxious to return to his wife, who is expecting to be confined every day, he does not dare to show his face in his home.

My household is in good order, and runs quite smoothly. At almost every meal we have some visitor, so that the table has to be well supplied. I am glad to say that with this new cook I am able to do better than last year. The bread now is very good, and that is half the battle. Last week I made some mincemeat, taking my receipt from the cook book. It is very nice, and just the right quantity. A large soup tureen full.

I am feeling so much better this winter than last, that all my surroundings seem far pleasanter, and nothing is wearisome or burdensome. How much our happiness is influenced by our physical condition.

If you think of housekeeping this winter, Mother, I am surprised that you remain in Lowell until after Christmas. You will have a great deal of trouble for a very short season, unless you remain in Washington after Congress adjourns. I hope Ben will have a chance to spend the holidays with you. Poor fellow, he has been disappointed so many times.

Tell Paul that I have heard of a place in Mississippi where twenty-five deer were seen in a space of a few miles, quail in abundance, with now and then a wild turkey, splendid fishing. He will want to emigrate.

Say to Father that we are in the midst of warlike times, and no one can tell what a day may bring forth. We pull down the shades and close the blinds at night, lest some foolish person might think it well to fire in. Perhaps we are unnecessarily cautious, but this is a strange community.

If Butler were awake I know he would send kisses to his "Gan." Love for you Mother, Father and the boys, from

Your affectionate daughter, BLANCHE

LOWELL, *December* 15, 1874

DEAR BLANCHE: I see by the papers that Gen. Ames is in trouble. All the papers have been teeming with the Vicksburg statement that throws all blame upon Gen. Ames. His side is quite silent, except to call a meeting of the Legislature. I shall send an article from the Boston *Journal.* I thought, owing to their hatred of your Father, that the Republican papers of Boston intended only to publish the report of the Vicksburg murders. The *Journal* seems at last to have thought the better of it, and approves the call for the assembling of the Legislature. Gen. Ames has heavy work before him to govern that state. Let him gird himself firmly for the work. I think he is able for it. He is not rash, but he is firm and courageous, and those are qualities likely to be needed. Political life is but a game of chance, hardly worth the struggle, but coolness and decision are great requisites for winning. I see that Congress has ordered a Committee to be sent down to inquire into it.

The weather here is so cold yesterday and today that I could not look out of doors. The windows are thick with frost, the thermometer down below zero. Now I wish myself in Washington. I am glad the children are not here. They are better in that mild climate. You play croquet too late. Four o'clock is late enough for that damp atmosphere.

I am very glad you have a good, reliable cook. Look carefully after the baby. I think she is very gentle, perhaps delicate. Do not let Mary sing loud to her, or right in her ears, or breathe in her face. Only observe and speak of it quietly every time she does it. Poor little rats, the three take up a great deal of time, but there is nothing better to do that I know of. Be careful of yourself and them.

Love to you all, from *Your affectionate* MOTHER

Message of Gov. Adelbert Ames to the Extraordinary Session of the Mississippi Legislature

Executive Office
JACKSON, MISS., *December* 17, 1874

GENTLEMEN—It is with deep regret and sorrow, but with an overpowering sense of my official duty, that I have called you together at this time; regret that the high hopes entertained for the continuance of peace and contentment among the people, seem about to be dispelled in a manner which must shake our society to its very foundations, arousing prejudices, discord and distrust, to be followed inevitably by heavy burdens, and possibly the utter prostration of every interest of the State;

sorrow that any number of our citizens could find it in their hearts to deprive, by violence, their neighbors and fellow-citizens of their political rights; with an overpowering sense of official duty, because a portion of our territory is under the control of insurgents, and because I have not the power, under existing laws, to suppress such insurrection.

To-day, in Warren county, the laws and authority of the State are set at defiance. Although there is not in that county a single militia officer, they have organized companies and regiments, officered by men who pretend to act by authority of the State, exercising all the functions of an independent sovereignty, even so far as to search the homes of citizens of different political faith—to take from them their arms, incarcerate them in jail, compelling legally elected officials to resign their offices, and above all, putting citizens to death without even the formalities of law.

Officials and prominent men, holding political views different from the insurgents, have been compelled to flee, and even the Judges of the State Courts, though one of those Courts was in session, were forced to escape under cover of night, that they might not fall a sacrifice to the mob.

It is pretended that their acts of bloodshed were a necessity; that men were fighting for their homes, their families and their firesides. But how inadequate the plea, when we know that those who went to the City of Vicksburg, from Warren county, as many did, left their homes, their families, and their firesides, absolutely unprotected, in the midst of a large population of the very class they were engaged in shooting down. Had they believed there was danger, they would not, they could not, have abandoned them; for had those they pretended to fear the purpose to destroy, they could have done so without opposition.

By armed men riding through the county, this persecuted class have been maltreated and intimidated, till a perfect reign of terror prevails. Such has been, and is the condition of affairs in Warren county.

What is the real or pretended cause therefor? A recent Grand Jury indicted one county official, two ex-officials (clerks of the Courts), and the Sheriff's bonds are claimed to be insufficient and invalid. It is also asserted that another cause of action was a fear, real or imaginary, that the Petit Jury, for the trial of these indicted persons, might be organized to acquit.

These are proclaimed as the causes for the attempted expulsion of those officials from office; the interruption of the State

Courts; the violation of the laws, and defiance of the authority of the State.

No single legal remedy had been exhausted. The Petit Jury had not been organized. The Sheriff could have been restrained from continuing to act as Sheriff and Tax Collector until he should comply with the requirements of the law with regard to his bonds, by injunction, upon application to any one of the thirty-three Chancellors and Circuit Judges of the State, or any one of the Supreme Court Judges; and, upon proper showing to the Chancellor, could have been required to give new bonds, either as Sheriff or Tax Collector, or both. Yet not the first step was taken to remedy any grievance by such injunction, nor by such application to the Chancellor.

We have been taught by the action of our fathers that a people laboring under grievances were in duty bound to petition for their removal, before revolution or insurrection, with war and its attendant evils, could be justifiable.

The causes of complaint in Warren county, if any there be, would, I have no doubt, have received full and favorable consideration by the Legislature; but we are forced by the facts to the conclusion that a legal or legislative remedy has not been desired. The action of the insurgents bears a strong resemblance to that which so frequently occurs in Mexican or South American States, where legally constituted governments are overthrown by restless spirits who may assemble around them the means of so doing.

Is Mississippi to sink to a level of such communities? Are we to believe any considerable portion of our citizens can lend aid or countenance to such lawlessness? What is more likely than such action to destroy the peace, prosperity and safety of every community within our borders?

Mississippi is peculiarly situated, with a problem to solve quite unlike any presented to the world previous to these recent years. Our population comprises two races, who by revolution have been thrown on the same civil and political level. We cannot ignore the fact that issues have been made which have placed them, it is to be deplored, in political antagonism. With one race it has been a struggle for personal liberty and personal security. All else has been made subordinate thereto, and men with high appreciation of the magnitude and importance of that struggle, have generously and zealously labored therein. There can be no higher political issue in our land than that which is to give to the individual freedom, equality and security. That the masses of the people of this

State are prepared to give that to both races, we fondly believe. To do so will destroy every antagonism which now exists, harmonize all classes, obliterate all animosities, and purify all future political contests of class or race distinctions. What nobler aspiration can we have? What higher destiny can we anticipate for the State?

We find in Warren county, that violent white men have been for months appealing to the prejudices of their class, and urging on a war of races, for political purposes. At this very moment, when the State and county authorities are successfully resisted, when free action on the part of the officials is impossible, the armed insurgents procure orders for a local election, with the intention that ballots shall be cast in the midst of such a reign of terror, that the will of the great majority may be undone by a minority. It is well for us to face the facts as they exist. To evade them or ignore them, would be cowardice and crime. The insurrection has its sympathizers and supporters in other parts of the State. They have deliberately and knowingly entered upon this work of revolution, with a purpose co-extensive with the limits of the State. It is insurrection in its fullest sense. If successful, it must necessarily reduce a majority to the will of a minority, and that minority which shall thus have gained power by force of arms, will be bound logically to maintain and retain that power by legislation as harsh and cruel as their first acts of violence. In which case one race of our people will be deprived of their rights and remanded back to as unfortunate a condition as they have ever known, or else be compelled to wander forth seeking freedom rather than homes, as is now the case with many of their race in other States. Are the people prepared for such a contingency, even though they may be ready to sacrifice material interests for political success? Is there not a higher motive by which we should be actuated? Is it not our duty, the duty of every lover of liberty and justice to secure for whatever race or color those privileges and blessings which we hold for ourselves as dearer than life? If the people of the State insist on making a race issue or have the disposition so to do, then is our condition deplorable indeed. If successful it would be a success founded entirely upon the degradation and serfdom of a class.

At a former time a Governor of this State felt called upon, in his message to the Legislature, to announce the fact that twenty-six (26) Tax Collectors, when there were fifty-six (56) counties, were defaulters in one year, and that large sums of money were collected that were never accounted for in any manner.

The State, to-day, has no such grievance. Of the defaulting office-holders during the past year, which we are glad to say, bear no proportion to those referred to, the greater number are to be found in those counties where the colored man and his party are so far in the minority as to have no influence in their selection.

The indebtedness of the counties and cities is not to be attributed to the complexion of the voters. Many such localities are free from debt, and but few heavily burdened.

Of the State debt a large part is due its own school fund, a portion of which has been outstanding many years. The remainder of the State indebtedness, when this year's taxes are paid to meet this year's expenditures, will amount to but some six or seven hundred thousand dollars. Herein Mississippi stands equaled but by few of her sister States.

The expense of the State government is but the average of the expenses of other States. That there may be advantageous changes made in our revenue laws, there can be no doubt.

These facts I give to dispel all impressions that the colored men of the State, as a class, or the party to which they incline, have forgotten the great work of human freedom and equality in which they are engaged, or have stooped to plunder the State of its wealth.

The history of every State in the Union, shows that dishonest and unprincipled men have been elevated to official positions, but even at a time like the present, when parties are revolutionized by charges of corruption against officials, happily for this State she is exceptionally free from just complaint of that character.

With the State in such a fortunate financial condition, the insurgents have pretended to act in the interest of the taxpayers. Though the legal remedies for wrongs of which they complained were ample, they were hardly entered upon when a body of violent men combined together, overthrew constitutional authorities, assumed the functions of government, and have organized as a military despotism, recognizing no law but that which suits their humor or convenience.

The Executive of the State is without means to meet such an emergency. He has no well organized or disciplined militia, not a single policeman or detective at his command, and even were the men and material in abundance, he has not a dollar to expend for such a purpose.

Under such circumstances I have called you together. I invite your attention to this matter, than which none more vital to the State or more intimately connected with the welfare of the individual can come before you for your consideration, and I recommend that you take, in your wisdom, such steps as will overthrow the insurrection in Warren County, and prevent in future similar occurences there and elsewhere; and I venture to express the hope that there are but few of our fellow-citizens who will not cheerfully respond to any demand you may make upon them.

ADELBERT AMES

December 19, 1874

To His Excellency, U. S. GRANT, President, U.S.A., Washington, D.C.

Whereas, It is provided in the Constitution of the United States, Article 4, Section 4, that the United States shall guarantee to every State in the Union, protection to each state against domestic violence, on application of the Legislature of such State; and

Whereas, In the county of Warren, in the State of Mississippi, several of the legally elected and acting officers of said county, including the sheriff thereof, by force and violence on the part of lawless persons, have been compelled to abandon and have been prevented from exercising the duties of their respective offices; and the public property, including the court house, the jail, together with the prisoners lawfully confined therein, and the public records of said county, have been taken possession of by like force and violence, and all still held by such lawless and unauthorized persons, contrary to and in defiance of the laws of said State; and

Whereas, In consequence of such illegal and violent acts, as aforesaid, many of the peaceable citizens of said county have been killed, and a large number, through fear of violence, have been compelled to abandon their homes and families, and forced to seek protection by flight and concealment, and are still unable peaceably to return to and occupy their respective abodes; and

Whereas, Certain lawless, armed and riotous persons, in flagrant violation of the Constitution and laws of the United States, and of the State of Mississippi, have made illegal searches of the private houses and persons of citizens of said county of Warren, and such lawless, armed and riotous persons have, also, imprisoned and held for a number of days many of the citizens of said county, including public officers, without any legal authority or process of law whatever; and

Whereas, A large number of armed men from adjacent States have invaded the State of Mississippi in aid of such lawless and riotous persons and acts therein, and others have signified their willingness to assist such lawless and riotous persons whenever called upon; and

Whereas, The courts of the county have been paralyzed to such extent that they cannot be held, and thus rendered incapable to suppress such violence and to enforce the laws; and

Whereas, The Chief Executive of the State has no sufficient force at his command, by calling out the militia, nor other adequate power, to suppress such domestic violence, to execute the laws, and guarantee full protection to all citizens, irrespective of race, color, or condition, without causing a conflict of races, and thereby endangering life and property to an alarming extent; therefore

Resolved by the Senate of the State of Mississippi, (the House of Representatives concurring), That the President of the United States be and is hereby called upon and urgently requested, by use of the military power at his command, to suppress such domestic violence, to restore peace and order in this State, and to guarantee to all citizens the equal and impartial enjoyment of their constitutional and legal rights.

Be it further resolved, That His Excellency, the Governor of this State, be and is hereby authorized and requested to transmit, forthwith, the foregoing resolutions, properly attested, to His Excellency, the President of the United States.

WASHINGTON, D..C, *Dec.* 19

Governor Adelbert Ames—Jackson, Miss.:

Your dispatch of this date is received, and the proclamation called for by the law in such cases, will be forthwith promulgated.
U. S. GRANT

LOWELL, *December* 21, 1874

DEAR BLANCHE: I have waited till past seven o'clock for your Father and Paul. Neither has come. Paul went down this morning for two or three recitations, then to return this evening, or rather at four o'clock. But no Paul. I do not believe Congress has adjourned. Your Father wrote he should be at home Monday. But he has not arrived.

You see I am staying in Lowell over Christmas. The time

will be short in Washington, but no doubt we shall stay after Congress is over. Besides I go more to have things put in order, cleaned and made over than for ought else. What we have shall be put in good repair, and then we shall be ready for the new house. Your Father had the mattresses made over, those had enough in the pillow and bed to make three mattresses. Those will be enough for this winter. He bought a set of furniture in New York like that in my chamber, chairs and all. He writes that he bought it very cheap.

December 26, 1874

Your Father came home Thursday night. While we were listening to his news a youthful voice saluted us, and there stood Ben. He had dodged in through the kitchen and stood before us a complete surprise. You may be sure we were delighted. All of the children at home but you. But you and the babies leave a wide gap. Ben was allowed but one day. By good luck he arrived at night instead of morning, so that he was here two nights and Christmas day. He left early this morning, will be at West Point tonight. He had a good time. He took a stout bag of provisions, the day is fine, and he and his brother Cadet, who will join him at Worcester, will have a jolly day in the cars. Ben has grown tall, he looks well, and is doing well. I think he enjoyed every moment of the time, and goes back satisfied to begin again, and to wait till next summer for a longer holiday. I am very glad he got this little run home. It will do him good, and me too.

We start for Washington a week from tomorrow, Sunday. Your Father talked with the President something more than two hours on political matters, and Gen'l. Ames and his affairs. The President says he believes in Gen'l. Ames, in his honor and integrity and his ability, and is glad there is one Governor who means to carry out his work and govern his state. He believes every word that the officer telegraphed for, has stated that he, the President, will sustain Gen'l. Ames. Your Father talked with a man from the South about organizing a Militia. He said it would be a great thing. The danger would be that it would give Gen. Ames such prominence that his white friends might wish to pull him down. So you see, it requires circumspection as well as courage to govern. I think he possesses both and will manage affairs as well as any man living. I have read his Message. He states the full case, but leaves it for the Legislature to act. That I suppose is his policy. No doubt he has a settled conviction of the best way to govern the state, and will find means to do it.

I think it is well that you keep, at dusk, in the house. It is always better to avoid the dangers of climate and other things. Be as kindly and courteous to the residents as they desire. You must conciliate, however sternly Gen'l. Ames may be obliged to act. I have run into the old habit of counselling, you see. I think you both know very well what belongs to you to do.

Do your chickens have food enough? What is the matter that they die? Perhaps diseased before you bought them. Take care that those you eat are healthy and fat.

Dearest love to you all from your

Affectionate MOTHER

The Mansion, JACKSON, *December* 24, 1874

DEAR MOTHER: I have allowed the first of the week to slip by without writing you, not because I have been so very busy, but on account of many little interruptions. This is the day before Christmas, and Mary and Butler have just returned from a shopping expedition. I thought that Butler would enjoy seeing the toy stores more than the surprise of finding presents in his stocking in the morning. He is perfectly delighted with what he has seen, and a cart, a wheelbarrow, a bucket and tea-set will occupy his attention for some time to come. Edith is happy playing with a red wagon. She is inclined to be boyish in her tastes.

I received this morning a Christmas turkey from a Mrs. Carter, whose husband is under some obligation to Gen'l. Ames. I intend to celebrate with chickens for breakfast, turkey and goose for dinner, mince pies, cake, etc. You would be amused to see my poultry yard. I have now about fifty chickens, nine turkeys, five geese, six ducks, and three dozen quail. The country people bring in all that they have to sell about this time, in order to get money for Christmas. After the holidays I suppose it will be as it was last year, quite difficult to get anything in the line of provisions.

You speak in your last letter of the weather being very cold. It has been very delightful here. Since we came down it has not been cold enough to form ice, and some of the days are as soft and warm as in summer.

Gen'l. Ames has been anxious about matters in Vicksburg. But he has been so strongly supported by the Legislature that he hopes to be able to get them to pass some constabulary or militia laws, which will give him the power to stop such disturbances in the future. As far as his personal standing in the state is concerned, I think these troubles are to his advantage rather than otherwise.

The days are passing quietly but very pleasantly. We have a good deal of company. One or two at every meal.

I have asked Butler, who just now entered, what he wished to send to "Gan." He replied "A kiss to Butler and a kiss to Sister." The baby is very well, and everyone thinks her very pretty. She is very quiet and very little trouble. Butler makes the most noise, and disturbance.

Kisses for you, Mother, Love for Father and Paul.

BLANCHE

JACKSON, *December* 30, 1874

DEAR MOTHER: For several days past we have been anxious to learn the whereabouts of the Congressional Committee, in order to treat them with some hospitality. Yesterday morning I gave them up in despair. We could not hear anything of them, or their plans. You can imagine that I was a little concerned when about half past four in the afternoon word came that they had arrived and wished to call at the Mansion. Of course I had to give orders at once about supper and prepare to meet them. As is usual at such times, I was not really ready for them.

Last Sunday, the quail of which I wrote you came to an untimely end. I had them in a large enclosure, roofed in, but on one side there was a fence breast high. Their wings were cut so that they could not fly, and they had grown very fat and tender. Two great dogs came into the yard and evidently thought there was a feast prepared for them. They jumped over the fence and ate up nearly all of the quail, swallowing them feathers and all, so that there was nothing left to tell the tale except two or three dozen little heads here and there. Only nine escaped. They were so frightened that in spite of clipped wings they flew out of the pen and we caught them. Butler came into the house with eyes as big as saucers to tell the news. The little creatures were very pretty, and he delighted to look at them through the cracks of the pen. I was very sorry to lose my birds, and still more so when the Committee came upon me with so little warning. I tried to get more, but could not. However, the supper was very good.

We urged them to stay all night, but they were in a hurry

to get back to Washington and wished to leave Jackson for Vicksburg between six and seven in the morning, so wisely determined to spend the night at the hotel which is close to the depot. I am very glad that they could stay to supper. It gave an opportunity for a long talk and discussion of affairs. I said what I could to the Democratic members of the committee. One of them, Mr. O'Brien of Maryland, expressed his surprise that Gen'l. Ames was so young a man. He said that in some way he "gained the impression that Gov. Ames was about sixty." They came about five, and went away about half past eight or nine. It is quite possible they will stop in Jackson again on their return to Washington. This will depend upon the amount of time they have.

We are all well and have been having most delightful weather. Very unseasonable even here, for the peach trees are in bloom and should not be until the last of February. The fires were all out, windows and doors open, yet the perspiration flowed as freely as in mid-summer at home. Yesterday there was quite a change, and today we are having a cold rainstorm. We have to be a little careful of the children with such sudden changes. Butler is the most troublesome one, for we cannot keep him in one place. However the rain serves to keep him within doors, and the house is not yet damp or chilly.

Gen'l. Ames had a letter from Father this morning. He was glad to get it. His enemies are quite disgusted because this trouble in Vicksburg has united the party, ended all discussion for the time being, and made him the head and leader. As the wife of one of our enemies remarked "What a glorious thing this is for Gen. Ames. It has made a great man of him." He will do all that he can to get militia or a constabulary force well armed and drilled. But of course, he is dependent upon the action of the Legislature. The House will do anything he desires. It is not as certain about the Senate. Still I think something can be accomplished.

My love and a happy New Year for Father and Paul. The same with a kiss for yourself, from BLANCHE

Message of Gov. Adelbert Ames to the Legislature of Mississippi, Session of 1875

Executive Office, State of Mississippi
JACKSON, *January* 5, 1875

To the Senate and House of Representatives:

GENTLEMEN— As representatives of the people, you have assembled in conformity with the Constitution, to discharge the duties imposed upon you as the Legislative branch of the government. The questions for your consideration are of the highest importance, not only affecting the personal security of many of our fellow-citizens, but even their personal liberty.

Coming directly from the people, you are fully informed as to their necessities and aspirations; and the State looks to you in confident belief that you will give, by judicious legislation, peace and good order; promote its interests, and enhance its prosperity, so that the people may rejoice in the greatest advantages and the least disadvantages incident to human government.

It is my duty to give you such information relative to the condition and interest of the government and State, and to recommend, for your consideration, such measures as may be deemed expedient.

Detailed reports of the condition of the several departments will be furnished you by their heads, to which I respectfully refer you for full accounts of their workings.

Aid by Congress to Sufferers by Floods.

Long continued rains in the spring caused our rivers to overflow their banks and threatened a general inundation of the low lands. Happily, our worst fears were not realized, yet so imminent was the danger that an appeal was made to Congress to furnish provisions to those whose stock and supplies were washed away or destroyed by the rising waters. This appeal met with a most generous response, and large quantities of provisions were placed at my disposal for distribution. The demand for help came from one end of the State to the other on and near the Mississippi river. I designated gentlemen of experience and position to distribute the supplies thus furnished, selecting, so far as practicable, sheriffs of counties and mayors of cities, and others most likely to know the real condition of the people. The total cost of supplies given to the State by the General Government amounted to $6,985.72.

Great care was demanded in their distribution, that none should go to those not needing assistance, and that they should be devoted to the purpose for which they were donated. It may be possible that small quantities fell into the hands of those not actually in need of them, but as the area over which they were distributed extended hundreds of miles, and in places difficult of access, because of the floods, it is a source of congratulation that small quantities, if any, were misapplied.

The sudden subsidence of the waters restored to the planters their credit, and further distribution of supplies was suspended. I recommended an appropriation be made to return the money so generously given for our suffering citizens, at a time when help could be looked for in no other direction. Justice to ourselves, as well as to the United States, demands that we refund this amount. We can the more easily do this as it is comparatively so small. Had our Legislature been in session at the time, it could not well have avoided doing what was done by the Congress of the United States.

Public Institutions.

The reports of the officers in charge of the various public institutions have been made. I most earnestly commend the skill and economy with which they have been managed.

The Penitentiary, alone, has received and expended an appropriation for purposes other than that needed simply for its maintenance. At your last regular session, acting on the principle that the proper place for the convicts was within the prison walls, an appropriation was made for the construction of a building for a factory. That appropriation has been most judiciously and economically expended. Machinery is now needed, and, if upon a thorough examination, you should be satisfied with the efforts made in the past, and have confidence in the future management of the Penitentiary, I would recommend that a suitable appropriation be made for the purchase of the necessary machinery.

By the report of the Superintendent, we find that the Penitentiary is over-crowded. Cells which were built for one have in every instance two, and in some three prisoners. This, with the additional fact that the number of prisoners is increasing year by year, presents a subject of grave importance for your consideration. Even now, the treatment usually accorded such prisoners would necessitate the extension of the prison walls, and the construction of additional cells. At this time of financial depression, which is felt by the State as well as by the individual, it seems almost unavoidable that the convicts should be employed beyond the prison walls, as there is nothing for them to do within. It will be seen by the report of the Superintendent, that the expense of conveying prisoners to the Penitentiary is very great. In some instances prisoners are sent there for so short a period as six months. While it might not be advisable to materially modify the laws which fill the Penitentiary with persons guilty of grand larceny, yet they might be so amended as to consign offenders with so short terms as six, nine or twelve months to the county jails, from which they could be taken to work on county roads, and so forth, so far as to earn their own support, and thus relieve the State and county of a burden. I commend this subject to your careful consideration.

State Equalization Board

The work accomplished by the State Board of Equalization has been highly important. Attention is invited to its report. It will be seen that personal property (no action was taken as to realty), of substantially the same value in different counties, varied greatly, its assessed valuation not being the same in any two counties, and differing as widely as fifty-seven per cent. With such inequality goes a corresponding injustice. The law, as it now stands, permits the equalization of personalty but once in four years. It should be done yearly; our law is defective and imperfect. I recommend that it be modeled after those of other States where the system has been brought to a high state of perfection.

We have no law relative to the assessment and taxation of railroads. By an agreement between some of the railroad corporations of the State and the State Board of Equalization, they were assessed at five thousand dollars per mile, and agreed to pay accordingly. Legislation relative to this question is imperative.

Payment of Taxes in Currency

The law passed last year, requiring taxes to be paid in United States currency, has proved eminently beneficial. It is believed that sufficient money will be paid into the treasury, upon a settlement of Collectors with the State, to pay every warrant outstanding for the last fiscal year, and had the season been in any degree a favorable one, there would have been a surplusage to meet, in part, the expenses of this year. A repeal of this law, and a return to the system recently in existence, I would deem a great misfortune to the State and an injury to the tax-payer.

Railroads

I renew the recommendation made last year, that the law granting a subsidy to the Vicksburg and Nashville Railroad, be repealed, or that it be required to give additional and satisfactory security; and that the charter and the law granting a subsidy to the Vicksburg and Ship Island Railroad, be repealed. The latter road, which was brought into existence at about the same time as the Vicksburg and Nashville road, received, over a year ago, upon the construction of eleven miles, a State subsidy of $110,000. Although the law required interest on this money, and it was taken with the understanding that it would be paid, none has been paid, and I can see no indication that it will be. Little, if any, progress was made on the road for months after receiving that large sum. Since then, for violation of, or deviation from its charter, it has been enjoined and forbidden to perform any act. The liberal assistance granted these roads by State, county and city has failed to infuse into them the necessary vigor. They evidently want the confidence of capitalists. The paper representing the subsidies has been sacrificed, in some instances, for less than half the value written on its face. Yet the tax-payers are compelled to pay it in full. Counties and cities are much embarrassed and groaning under the taxation which has resulted therefrom. The subsidy granted these two roads will amount to about one million of dollars. Is the State in a condition, at this time, to have its indebtedness increased by that amount? Every one is striving to reduce expenses, and is gratified at any success. Here is an opportunity to relieve the people of the burden of a million of dollars. It is as direct a debt as the appropriations made to support any branch of the government, and must be as inevitably met. I cannot see how one holding the interests of the people at heart can let pass such an opportunity to serve them. An additional reason for action relative to the Vicksburg and Nashville Railroad is, that it has been granted franchises and exemptions which, sooner or later, must prove greatly oppressive to the State. I call attention to my special message of last year on this subject.

Compulsory Education

I renew my recommendation made last year, in favor of compulsory education. It is the surest and safest avenue of escape from embarrassment of every kind which may surround us. Such laws have been in operation in other States, with great advantage, and can be copied by us with like results.

Temperance

The laws relative to temperance, passed at your last regular session, have failed to give those beneficial results so much desired. Appeals come from every quarter of the State that the work so bravely entered upon a year ago may be pressed forward and perfected. I commend this subject to your careful consideration.

Dueling

During the past year the State has been put to some expense in arresting and attempting to arrest and bringing to trial citizens of neighboring States who have come within our borders and taken human life in duels. It has been found that our laws regarding dueling are inadequate to meet the purpose for which they were framed. The duelist fights either to prove the absence of cowardice or to kill his opponent. The years are but few since every one had the opportunity to perfect his record for bravery. No law can be too severe upon those who seek the medium of a duel to take the life of a fellow-being. I recommend that the law against dueling be revised, so that no violator thereof can escape its penalties.

Centennial Commission

Last year an Act was passed authorizing the appointment of local Commissioners to act in conjunction with the State Commissioners to the Centennial Celebration, which is to be held in Philadelphia in 1876. It would be not only well but seemly that Mississippi should participate in that celebration. That this may be done and the interests and products of the State properly represented and displayed, an appropriation will be needed.

Immigration

I recommend such action as will best make known to the world the great advantages of climate and soil of the State, that immigrants may be led to turn their steps in this direction. Inducements may be held out in the way of exemptions from taxation for a limited period of such property as may be brought here. Capital and labor are necessary to develop our resources, and any action which attracts them must be beneficial.

The Bar at the Mouth of the Pascagoula River

Heretofore an appropriation was made for improvements of the bar at the mouth of the Pascagoula river, but before expended it was covered back into the treasury. The lumber interests of that section of the State are important. The freshet of last spring seriously impeded the navigation of that river. I recommend that the State extend to the lumber interests there direct aid, as it has done heretofore, or authorize a tax for the improvement of the navigable waters of the counties most interested, as is done in those counties on the Mississippi river, where a tax is authorized for the construction of levees.

Grand Juries

Grand Juries are now selected by the Boards of Supervisors of counties. These Boards of Supervisors control and direct the finances of the counties. It is asserted that they select their juries to save themselves and their friends from the consequences of corrupt or illegal acts, which they may be base enough to commit. That all such criminal deeds may be followed by the severest penalties, it will be necessary for the law regulating the selection of jurors, to be modified. No man, who is to be tried or whose official conduct is to be inquired into, should select the jury to do it. I recommend that the selection of such juries be given to Jury Commissioners, to be designated by the Circuit Judge. Such Commissioners should be above reproach, respected by all, and known to be free from any connection with the monied affairs of county officials.

Constitutional Amendment

The inconvenience and expense of yearly elections are apparent to all. I renew the recommendation made in my inaugural address, that there be submitted to the people, at the next general election, such an amendment of the Constitution as will make our elections biennial instead of annual. To accomplish this, it will be necessary that the terms of all elective officers, State, Legislative and county, be reduced one year, or extended one year.

I also recommend that there be again submitted to the people an amendment to the Constitution for the reduction of the number of Chancellors. The minimum number now possible is nineteen, the actual number twenty. The labor required can be performed by ten or twelve, especially if the terms of court held in each county yearly, be reduced in number. An amendment to this effect was submitted to the people at the last general election, but by reason of a want of interest in the subject, or the absence of information relative to its purport, it failed to receive general consideration.

Finance

During the past year we have experienced the effects of one of those financial revulsions which periodically occur, and which human wisdom seems incapable of preventing, causing great embarrassment and distress, not only in our State, but throughout the whole country. Its disastrous effects in our State have been very seriously augmented by the heavy rains and consequent freshets of last spring, and the long months of drought which followed, whereby the crops, if not wholly cut off, were more or less injured; consequently we find, at this time, no little suffering among the people, and great complaint on the part of the tax-payer. I recommend the most stringent economy in appropriations for the support of the government during the ensuing year, and that every possible step be taken in the direction of retrenchment and reform. With this in view, I have recommended a change in the Constitution of the State by which our elections shall be biennial instead of annual, an amendment by which the number of Chancellors may be reduced; and, in the same spirit, I make the following suggestions and recommendations:

Ours is an agricultural State. The products of the soil are the one source of income to the people. Either because of the defects of our revenue laws, or the refusal of the people to make full returns of their personal property, or the failure of the assessor in detecting it, the personal property of the State escapes its proportion of taxation, and the realty is unduly burdened. To reform our laws, that the people at large may be the more generally benefited, it will be absolutely necessary to reduce taxation on lands. As all property by our Constitution must be taxed ad valorem, and as personal property is not easily discovered, at least not generally returned, land can be relieved of its burden only by partial return to a system of taxation which formerly prevailed—that of taxes on privileges and so forth. The lands in our levee districts are especially burdened. There the taxes for the ordinary purposes are increased by a tax for building and keeping in repair an extensive system of levees. It is possible that the planter there attempts to hold large areas of land, part of which only can be cultivated, though all is taxed. Whatever the cause, it is a remarkable fact that one-third or one-half of the land in some of those counties are now, and have been for years forfeited to the State or levee boards, and on the remainder the burden of taxation falls.

The money received in the State Treasury, under the operations of section six, article eight, of the Constitution, which consists of the proceeds of swamp lands, of lands vested in the State by escheat or purchase, of forfeiture of taxes, of the clear proceeds of all fines collected in the several counties for any breach of the penal laws, or moneys received for licenses for the sale of intoxicating liquors, etc., shall be securely invested in United States bonds, and held as a perpetual fund, which may be increased, but not diminshed, the interest of which only can be appropriated for the support of free schools. Here is appropriated to a perpetual fund a revenue which, by various modifications of the laws, may be made to amount to hundreds of thousands of dollars. That is, the State, though poor, with ignorance wide spread and general, is taxing such poverty and ignorance to educate future generations. The schools have not heretofore, and do not now receive any interest from this principal; nor can they in the future, to any considerable extent, under existing laws.

Efforts have been made in years gone by to accumulate a perpetual fund for schools, but it has been diverted from its true purpose, either being misappropriated, or has fallen a prey to those who have given to railroads an importance greater than to schools. It is a question, whether it is at any time advisable to have a large sum of money beyond that necessary for current expenses in the State Treasury. If the Treasury be not plundered, as is often the case, the funds serve little or no practical good. Money can never be better expended for education that at this moment. This generation needs schools as no other generation can. By making education general now, taxation for future schools will be but lightly felt and gladly borne. Consequently, I recommend that there be submitted to the people, at the next general election, an amendment to the Constitution, by which all the revenues derived under the provisions of the section of the Constitution above referred to, with the exception of the proceeds of such lands as may have been given by the United States exclusively for school purposes, be devoted to the general purpose of meeting the expenses of the State government. That the public schools may receive no injury thereby, I recommend that specific appropriations be made to them as a substitute for the interest that otherwise might be received. In this way, public education will not be retarded, and the State will receive the full benefit of the principal. A change of laws, especially as relates to the licensing of the sale of intoxicating liquors, may be so made as to put large sums into the Treasury, which would materially reduce taxation on property.

I recommend such additional legislation as will prevent counties, cities or towns incurring oppressive debts or liabilities.

That the number of Tax Collectors in a county be reduced to one, if possible. There can be no necessity for County Clerks or Treasurers to handle money intended for the State Treasury, much less that it should pass through the county treasury on its way there. All who handle it must be paid commissions, and a multiplicity of tax-gatherers divide and dissipate responsibility, and it is believed divert moneys from their proper destination.

That a law be enacted which shall authorize the inspection of the books and accounts of all officials who collect or hold public funds, and empower the State Board of Equalization, or some other authority, to suspend such officials, on proof of embezzlement, fraud, neglect or incompetency.

That Sheriffs, County Treasurers, and all other officials collecting or holding public funds be required to keep daily record thereof, subject to inspection.

That the costs of juries in civil cases be paid by litigants, either when the juries are summoned or before entry of judgment.

That a tax be collected, for the support of the judiciary, of all persons bringing suit in courts of record.

The expense of the judiciary is far greater than that of any other branch of the State government, and it seems but just that those who appeal to it should be thus taxed for its support. No one would be likely to go to law with its proverbial expenses and delays, who would hesitate at paying such a tax.

That grand juries, State witnesses, and other court expenses, be paid by the counties rather than the State. It is not just that the peaceable, law-abiding citizens of one county, where criminal cases are few, should be taxed to support courts in other counties where disorders and lawlessness prevail.

Then, again, county officials will be the more likely to scrutinize expenses if they are to be paid by their own county rather than by the State.

That the appropriations for the two State Universities be reduced, possibly, to fifty thousand dollars. Both now receive from the State, by direct appropriation and interest, about one hundred and twenty thousand dollars. This is a renewal of my recommendation of last year.

That Boards of Supervisors be prohibited from making allowances to any one claiming to be a pauper, unless the beneficiary be an inmate of a legally established poor-house.

That inquests be paid by counties.

That the expense of public printing be reduced.

That all laws exempting any property from taxation, be repealed. The Constitution demands that all property be taxed ad valorem. All property is not taxed. It should be, and when done, the lands will be greatly relieved.

That all lands forfeited to the State for taxes, be restored upon the payment of the taxes for the past two years. Should former owners refuse to redeem them on such terms, then so enact that they be forfeited forever, and the purchaser from the State be insured and secured in his title.

That some relief be extended to the land-owners of the Levee Districts. Now, the tax for the construction and maintenance of the levees is on land and cotton. If the land only is benefited by the levees, then the taxes are wisely laid, but if other property is also benefited, it should be correspondingly taxed.

I make these specific recommendations with the conviction that they can be practically carried out, and that if carried out, great relief will be experienced. A reform bill should contain many important features which I abstain from alluding to, not only reducing expenses, equalizing the burden of taxation, but simplifying and perfecting that part of governmental machinery which relates to the revenue.

The condition of affairs in Warren county was brought to your attention at your extra session. The lawlessness and violence there began in August last, at the city election. As you have appointed a committee to proceed to that county to investigate its condition, you will have the facts more in detail than I can give. The whole question now rests with you. But I feel it incumbent upon me to renew the recommendation made in my message at your extra session.

A free people should resort to every legitimate means to maintain, for their government, peace and order; and for themselves, personal security and liberty. It is now for you to decide how that can best be done. The nation cannot regard with favor the appeal for help which is sent forth by those who supinely refuse to help themselves. It cannot be possible that the people of the State will permit a few lawless, violent men to inflame the mind of a community appealing to class or race prejudices, and then by force overthrow regularly constituted authorities. To prevent such acts, and punish those who have participated in them, the whole power of the State should be invoked. The freedom of a race is at stake. No act should be left undone to assert the authority and majesty of the law. I recommend specifically that a State police or constabulary be organized, and that provisions be made that the power of the State can be appealed to. I cannot believe that only one class of citizens will respond to a call to enforce the laws and protect its officers. If such be the case, we cannot know it too soon.

ADELBERT AMES

JACKSON, *January* 5, 1875

DEAR MOTHER: By this time you are in Washington, trying to get the house in living condition. I do not envy you your task. I am very sorry that I am not there to assist you in labors. Here we are all very quiet. The weather has grown colder, and has been very rainy for the last week. The children are a little uneasy under the long confinement to the house, and are somewhat trying to the temper.

The baby is a wonderfully good child. Day after day passes without the least complaint from her. She sleeps a good deal, and when awake is full of dimples, cooings and silent laughter. She has an enchanting little dimple in her cheek, and is fond of showing it. She will be quiet for an hour at times on the bed, with her eyes wide open, looking at her hands or sucking her fingers. Time and time again we take her up when she is apparently perfectly content, simply because it does not seem right to leave her in one position. I do not exaggerate when I say that she is a remarkable baby and not nearly as much trouble as either Butler or Edith. I have written to Aunt Nina to get me a canvas in New Orleans, and intend to begin on Edith's picture at once. My household runs smoothly, and I shall never have a better opportunity.

We were delighted that Ben had a chance to spend the Christmas at home. Two nights and a day was very little time, still I suppose it was enough to please poor Ben. How much he will have changed by next summer. Two years next April since I have seen him.

Politics seems to be the absorbing topic here. Everything seems to be working satisfactorily. I trust the Congressional Committee will give a fair account of Vicksburg affairs.

Gen'l. Ames has just written a letter to Father in regard to a fire ladder he wishes to have patented, if it proves to be an original invention. I am experimenting a little, in a small way, and threaten Gen'l. Ames that I shall achieve a fortune in that direction long before he will.

This evening I send to the Inter Ocean a poetical effusion. I suppose it is the last I shall ever see of it. However, that is no matter, as nobody will know who wrote it.

This is not a very interesting letter, but from it you can judge how the days are passing, and how my time is employed.

Gen'l. Ames sends regards to you and Father, I join him in love for you both. BLANCHE

The Governor's Mansion, JACKSON, *January* 9, 1875

DEAR MOTHER: I have just completed some experiments I have been making with great success, and want to have my invention patented. You remember I wrote you that there was a rivalry between Gen'l. Ames and myself as to which should first invent something which would make a fortune. I have been trying to compound a starch which would not stick and wrinkle up the cloth, and which would give without trouble a fine polish, such as we see on new shirts. I have succeeded, and want to have a patent. I expect my invention to prove as great a blessing to washer-women as the sewing machine to the sewing community. I have been making starch and ironing all week, and so speak from experience when I say that by the addition of white soap (colored would not do) to starch, all sticking will be prevented, the clothes can be wrung out of the stiffest starch and ironed at once without the least difficulty. Collars, cuffs, and shirts can be done up with as much ease as napkins, handkerchiefs, etc. If the starch clings to the iron, pass it once over a damp rag and it will be perfectly clean. The articles ironed will have a fine gloss, and by placing them on a board without an ironing blanket, and using a polishing iron—they will have the appearance of new. Now if I can get a patent, it will only be necessary to put a certain quantity of soap into each package of starch to produce an article which will out-sell all others. Flour and soap work just as well, and as far as gloss and finish go, it is impossible to tell it from starch, but the color of the clothes might not be as good. Of this I am not sufficiently experienced to judge. Ask Harriet to try both, and give me your judgement upon them. A tablespoonful of scraped Castile soap to three of starch or flour, making it as you always do, only boiling it well. Ring the collar and cuffs or shirt out of the starch and iron at once, without drying and sprinkling, although you can do so if you wish. I know that by this time you are very much amused, and inclined to think me joking. Alas! I am patent mad, and was never more serious in my life. The only thing which will restore me to sanity will be an application for a patent. Will you ask Father to interest himself in this, and out of compassion for my state of mind attend to it for me? I will have the patent taken out in Mary's name, as I do not think it will be seemly for Mrs. Adelbert Ames née Blanche Butler to make such an application. All my experiments have been made in secret, and it will be well to keep my discovery so. Perhaps this process has been known for years, but if it is so, I want to know it.

Love and a kiss for you and Father from BLANCHE

The Governor's Mansion, JACKSON, *January* 11, 1875

DEAR MOTHER: I sent off by the last mail a letter to you with an application for Letters Patent. The application is not worded quite right, and I wish Father would interline and say "starch, flour, and other such substances for stiffening goods." This will make the patent a little more comprehensive. You see I am very much in earnest about this matter, and if Harriet does not say that she can do up her starched clothes far easier, I shall be much surprised.

We expect the committee[1] here Wednesday night. They will stay a day or so and examine some witnesses. I must put my wits to work and have something for them to eat. Fortunately I am better prepared than I was last season. Gen'l. Ames will ask them to spend what time they are here with us.

I am glad to see that the people at the North are getting aroused to the condition of things South. But it is perfectly disgusting to see the newspaper comments upon Sheridan's course— "The rights of Louisiana taken away. . . . The State throttled by United States soldiers, etc." As if a community of murderers could have any rights to be respected, and to complain of throttling when most of her citizens ought to be

[1] The Congressional Investigation Committee.

hung. (Nota bene—the colored man is not considered a citizen.) It is useless, however, to talk politics. We have nothing else from morn till night.

Love and kisses from BLANCHE

WASHINGTON, *January 12*, 1875

DEAR BLANCHE: You judged rightly. I have been full of care, and covered with the dust of humiliation. Healthful as that is for the soul, the body after a time rebels, and at the end of the week I was tired to death and my spirits at zero. I found I must break away from it, so last night Mrs. Spofford, Capt. Pearson and I went to the theater to see Olive Logan in her play of "Surf" and to look at her new French dresses. She played two parts in the same play. Therefore, several changes in dress. She has been abroad, and the dresses are beautiful. The play is not much, but it was a change of scene for me, so that I felt pleased and cheered. I was very tired again before it finished, but it was another kind of fatigue.

I shall go into the House today about one o'clock. There will be a debate on Louisiana affairs. The country is more stirred about Southern politics now than anything else. Finance has now less interest than the troubles at the South. I hope you see most of the leading papers that you may know the conflicting opinions. If you like I will forward the New York papers day to day, but maybe you see enough to know the different states of feeling here. If Gen. Ames can get a militia, or constabulary force, so as to really hold the power, and can steer the ship of state in safety, he will do an able work. Sheridan was a little rash in the word "Banditti," however truthful it might be. To be guarded, prompt and courageous are rare qualities combined. A man may possess all these and still fail. But I have good hope that Gen. Ames will govern that state, difficult as the task is.

I am very glad you have started your various avocations. Send me a copy of the verses.

The baby lies contented on her back precisely as Mother told me I used to lie by the hours together. I never gave her any trouble, the only one of a large family who did not. You cannot tell the reason of such quietude. It may be some harmony of spirit that keeps her quiet, some gentle grace of soul—or a little want of physical force that leaves her just content to lie at ease and rest. Mary must handle her gently, but do not let her lie too long, lest she become rickety and feeble for want of exercise. Remember this, and take her up. No wild tossings, but a gentle trot, and even exercise every day. She really needs your careful attention more than the others ever did. I should be glad to shake, tease and kiss Butler and Edith, but for the baby to take her up tenderly seems to be the thought, to watch and see if she is all right. When she is undressing, pass your hand under her clothes and rub her back and body all over, the friction is good for her.

You will like the house. It is said to be the grandest looking house in Washington. This we did not expect. But when it is complete I do not know but it will be so. It is certainly very handsome, and it looks like one house. If you come back to the Senate, you cannot fail to be charmed with your residence. The house we are in is very pleasant, and more than commonly grand looking, even among the best houses.

You really got on just as well with the Committee as though you had known it days beforehand. It is more the cordiality than the food.

I shall now begin again on the house. Put up curtains, wax the floors, etc., but I shall not tire myself again. I am too old for that. It tells upon me. Dearest love to you all from

Your affectionate MOTHER

The Mansion, JACKSON, *January 25,* 1875

DEAR MOTHER: It is more than a week since I have heard from you, and Gen'l. Ames has as yet received no reply to his letter to Father in regard to politics, and more especially, his patent. He is anxious to find out if anything like his application of the ladders has been patented. Of course there are hundreds of fire escapes, but he thinks none that work on his principle. As for my patent, I am still sanguine, and want to hear from it. It seems to me you have very little consideration for the impatience which afflicts poor patent-struck mortals. I wish you would get the inventive mania, and could know how to sympathize.

I saw a perverted account of affairs in Vicksburg in the New York *Times,* which we receive daily. Gen'l. Ames requested Captain Head to eject Flannagan, who claimed to be de facto sheriff, so that the office might be vacant, to allow the peaceable occupancy of McGee, who was appointed by Chancellor Hill. This appointment is temporary, continuing only during the present term of court, and he can perform only such duties as the court may require. The Legislature had repealed the law providing for special elections—consequently that held in Vicksburg during the reign of terror was illegal, and Chancellor Hill ruled that a de facto officer was a trespasser, and as such could not be recognized by the Court, lest it should be claimed that it had counter-ruled such trespass.

McGee was appointed as it was the duty of the court to make the appointment "in case the vacancy shall not have been filled by election or appointment in the manner prescribed by law, on or before the commencement of the term of any court which such sheriff is required to attend." Crosby is under indictment, and this McGee is one of his deputies. Now the citizens of Vicksburg are inclined to sing small, and will probably arrange Crosby's bond, declare it sufficient and pretending that the insufficiency of the bond was the only objection to him, be ready to have him reinstated. They do not enjoy the presence of U.S. troops.

The legislature will pass a bill giving Gen'l. Ames some power to control the State. I doubt if it will be sufficient or satisfactory. Everybody seems to think it so much better to rely upon the protection of the United States. Instead of Mississippi being in condition to assist the general government if necessary, she is like a puling infant hanging on to the skirts of its Mother, crying for aid. She has been a Sovereign State for fifty years, and is rather old for that kind of demonstration. *We* are sick of it. I write this for Father, that he may know a little of what is being done here. It is all very mixed, and quite discouraging.

My mind is full of projects for Bay St. Louis. I want to have a fine orange orchard there—and all the tropical fruits. It will give me some little trouble to furnish it, but all that will be in the simplest manner possible. Just what will make it comfortable and pleasant, nothing more.

Last night we were awakened by the barking of dogs and yanging of a goose, and investigated to find that the man had neglected to house the geese and the dogs were killing them. Gen'l. Ames took his pistol and went down into the yard. The dogs ran when they saw him coming, and he could only fire one shot at them. Two geese died before morning from their wounds, and one we have been obliged to kill. I do not know whether the other will recover or not. Poultry raising in this country is attended with some drawbacks. Twenty-four quail, twenty chickens, and four geese is the mortality, within six weeks.—It is temper-trying, and more so because I cannot easily replace them.

The children are well, but the weather has been stormy and they have chafed at the confinement. Today they have been out enjoying the bright sunshine.

Write as often as you can, Mother. It is very pleasant to get news from home.

Love and a kiss for Father. The same for *my Mother*.

BLANCHE

WASHINGTON, *March* 3, 1875

HON. A. AMES, *Governor*
Jackson, Miss.
Confidential.

MY DEAR AMES: I had a conversation with the President yesterday, in which he said that on Sunday he sat down to write a private letter to you; that he thought as Congress had not interfered and would not interfere in the Arkansas matter, it was quite probable that you might have trouble and he intended to say to you in the letter which he will write in a day or two, that he wished you to check in the very beginning anything that looked like revolution after the manner of Arkansas, such as calling a constitutional convention, otherwise than as provided by law, or any movement of conspiracy or fraud, to overturn the government, and to assure you that he will stand by you in every emergency to the full extent of his power. Of course all this will be, when you get it from him, confidential. But I thought you would like to know it as soon as you could.

Meanwhile, why don't I receive back the papers about Blanche's starch patent which I sent you. I had them all properly drawn out, but have not heard a word from you since, and that must be nearly a month ago.

All well here. Florence is to be married on the 17th—St. Patrick's day.

I am, *Yours truly*, BENJAMIN F. BUTLER

The Mansion, JACKSON, *March* 14, 1875

DEAR MOTHER: Spring has fairly come. It is eight in the evening and it is quite warm, with windows and doors all open. Of course the weather will change in a day or so, and we shall have fires again. Still the warm atmosphere causes the grass and flowers to grow visibly.

Next Wednesday we all go to New Orleans. We shall remain in the city about a week—by that time the house at the Bay will, I trust, be ready to receive us. I shall have considerable shopping to do, which will give Aunt Nina an opportunity in which she delights. I am almost sorry to leave Jackson. We may not be as comfortable at the Bay as here, although we shall have the advantage of the bathing, and no doubt it will be well for the children. They have been remarkably well all winter, scarcely troubled with colds—but in Jackson there has been a great deal of pneumonia and typhoid fever. We have been most fortunate.

I notice the *National Republican*, which we get regularly, had a little squint in regard to Father, and suggested that he might return to Washington from Buffington's district. Is there any such programme? We also see startling rumors of his going to Europe this summer. These, of course, are without foundation.

We were pleased, and also amused to hear of Kinsman's nomination as Judge of Western Arkansas. This will make him rather a neighbor of ours.

You will be surprised to see the children, they have grown so much, not in beauty, grace or goodness, but in stature. I shall never suffer from conceit of their good looks. Butler talks a great deal about Lowell and "Gran" and never fails to recognize a caricature of his Grandfather. Gen'l. Ames sends regards. He has written about the bear skins. With love and a kiss for you and Father, BLANCHE

WASHINGTON, *March* 15, 1875

DEAR BLANCHE: I have read Gen'l. Ames' letter to your Father and I am delighted that he feels even more secure in the good will of the people than ever. I trust all good things may continue, and that next winter may put them on a firmer basis still. The Howes arrived here the Sunday before they left for the South. He goes, no doubt, to secure his re-election. She goes with him.

(middle part of letter missing)

. . . he (Butler) will suit his *Gann* exactly, there will be good reason why his little, lithe figure shall be made to skip. And his comical face will not disarm his *Gann*. Strong little Edith, too, will pummel him well this summer. The little one of all Gann will handle tenderly— There will be a nice gathering this summer, if nothing happens.

Your Father and I go to West Point in June. He is leader of the examining Board. I do not know but I wrote it before.

The weather has been so bad they have not yet plastered

the house. I have finished cleaning the furniture, and it is covered. We think of going to New York some time this week, if your Father can get away. I want to look at various things, and this will be the best time.

Do not overwork in settling your house. That is sure to bring on sickness. Be careful, and get safe home.

Dearest love to you all. *Your affectionate* MOTHER

NEW ORLEANS, *March* 25, 1875

DEAR MOTHER: As you have already heard through Gen'l. Ames' letter, we are all in New Orleans, and I for one am as busy as a bee. I don't know that I should have taken time to write, were it not that I think I have something of importance to tell you.

Everything in this market is very cheap. Aunt Nina and I purchased this morning some pink and some blue cretonne, or India sateen, of the best quality that is made, for sixty cents a yard. You will remember it was a dollar and twenty-five in Boston. I enclose some patterns of dress satin, which is sold at ninety cents a yard by the piece. Aunt Nina thinks of buying a piece for window curtains. It is very glossy, and when lined would be just as handsome as a heavier quality. Don't you want some for your parlor chamber?

Furniture is being sold at auction for a song. This morning a beautiful rosewood set, with two extra pieces sold for *one hundred* and thirty dollars, and Mr. Parker purchased two *very large* mirrors—one for sixty, and one for forty dollars. I shall attend the next sale, and buy anything that is cheap and attractive. It does not seem right to allow such opportunities to pass. The people here are so poor they cannot buy anything that is at all extravagant. Write me if there is anything that you would like.

All send love—I join with kisses for Father and my Mother.

BLANCHE

WASHINGTON, *March* 27, 1875

DEAR BLANCHE: By this time you are at Bay St. Louis, fitting up the house. However easy you may strive to make it, you will still find it full of care. Make it as light as possible. You fit up this house, I conclude, that Gen. Ames may have a healthy spot to flee to during the summer. I know the difficulty there was last year to his leaving the state.

I shall engage my chambermaid to do the washing for the children. I think we saw enough of Jerry's laziness last summer not to try that method again. If you keep two girls let them be exclusively for taking care of the children and your rooms. If you do not want the expense of bringing two so far, I can get you one here. But you must let me know at once, because I expect to go home in about a fortnight. I write about this because you may feel a little uncertain what to do, and to show you what aid I can give in hiring servants. If you have such ones as suit you, you will be likely to keep them, if it is a little more expensive.

I have written to Paul to get the water works in order to be ready for us. The house is going on slowly. It has been cold until now, too cold to plaster. The house does not lose by daily examination, the satisfaction increases. You will be a fortunate woman if you come into it all furnished next year for six years, in prospect. I do not suppose such good fortune can be relied upon. But we will look to the bright side, and hope for it. There will be a change for me next winter in some things. Paul will be at home, I shall be likely to see more people, and maybe Hattie Heard will be with us.

You would be amused at the way I have passed my evenings reading the Beecher-Tilton trial till about eleven o'clock in the fine print of the *Tribune.* I thought I would send it to you, but consider on the whole that you had better not muddle your mind with it. Dearest love to you all, from your most loving MOTHER

BAY ST. LOUIS, *April* 6, 1875

DEAR MOTHER: We came over yesterday from New Orleans. The house is not yet quite ready for us, but will be so in a day or so. I thought we could hasten the work by being here and have it done more satisfactorily. Our visit in New Orleans was very pleasant, and everything was done to make our stay agreeable, but I was all the time uneasy about the children, for there was a great deal of smallpox throughout the city, and some cases in the neighborhood.

Here it is very delightful. The house looks directly over the water to Ship Island, and the glare of the sunlight on the waves is softened by the trees, which grow to the edge of the shore. The rooms in the house are high studded, large, and will look quite tasteful when furnished.

You advise me not to overtask.—I shall not. While in New Orleans I had all the sheets, pillow cases and tablecloths made up. Uncle Parker purchased for us a Wheeler & Wilson sewing machine for twelve dollars—or to speak more correctly, he paid eleven and we bought it of him for twelve. It is a fine machine in a mahogany cabinet case, so that when not in use it looks like a commode. Lizzie turned the hems and Mary used the machine. At present we are stopping in the Hotel of the place— Our chambers are large, airy and pleasant. The floors are without carpets, the beds furnished with mosquito bars, and everything is very simple.

The roses are all in full bloom, and the orange trees filled with fragrant blossoms. A gentleman from Jackson who came to the place for the first time a few days ago, and intends to remain here, says that "it is a place where one ought to be content to wait the coming of the Lord." At this season it is certainly charming.

I do not intend to take but one girl North with me. The children can easily be cared for by Mary—and if you engage a girl to wash for them I should have nothing for a second girl to do.

Say to Father that Gen'l. Ames received his letter, but has been moving about so much that he has not had time to answer it.

We shall be in Lowell the middle of June. What a fine reunion it will be, when we are all assembled. I am fearful that you will find yourself full of care. The children are well, and growing very fast. Butler is tall and thin, and full of quirks and smart sayings. Edith is prettier, and the baby will speak for herself when you see her.

Tell Paul that there is the finest kind of duck shooting about here, and we offer him the use of a shooting box on the Gulf of Mexico.

Love for Father—a kiss for you, Mother, from the babies and

BLANCHE

WASHINGTON, *April* 6, 1875

DEAR BLANCHE: By your arrangements I think you are intending to stay late at Bay St. Louis. There I think you are wrong. You risk too much, both for yourself and the children. That journey across the country, after the heat fairly sets in, is too formidable. The few weeks extra time there is not a good reason for the great discomfort and even danger too, of staying there late in the spring. There is much said in the papers of smallpox in New Orleans, and yellow fever along the coast. I do not pay any great heed to this, nevertheless it is not well to remain in the vicinity of such diseases. You and the children, Nina and Maria had better be moving along up toward the North.

I am a good deal disappointed that none of you come before I leave. I wanted you to see the houses, while I am in this one. We shall leave the latter part of next week. Your Father must be home before the nineteenth. Just now the weather here is lovely. With you it must be summer heat already.

It would be very difficult, as you know, to bring articles of furniture from such a distance, and then, nothing matches. I am afraid you have undertaken a heavy load to fit up a house in summer weather, as it must be there. Be careful what you do. To be sick there, with those children to look after, would be a hard matter. Whatever you do, take it easy. The baby is, I think, toward nine months old, but you will not be likely to wean her this summer.

This will be to you a most uninteresting letter, because it is all about what you are doing, when you know better, you will believe, than I possibly can, what are the best things for you to do there. And what you really want to know is what we are doing here. Well, the workmen are now plastering the house. Men and horses are all over the capitol grounds at work, so that by another year we may look out on our domain and find it perfect, with trees, shrubs, and fountains. The rooms you will have look out as though you were high up in the heavens, the horizon far below you, and bewildering scenes as though you were moving through the air or water above the rest of the world.

Come home as soon as possible. I will endeavor to have everything ready. Dearest love for you all, from

Your most affectionate MOTHER

WASHINGTON, *April* 13, 1875

DEAR BLANCHE: Your last letter, in a very cheerful spirit, and you evidently like Bay St. Louis at the present time. That is not strange, with roses and orange blossoms in full flower and the weather not too sultry. I approve of it now, but not up to the middle of June. I have tried it, so have you, and in my case and in yours, the risk was great. You remember how you looked when you came home, and what a condition Butler was in. The middle of June is too late to travel across the country with three children. It is the hottest month in the South. Come away the last week in May. I want you at home while we are at West Point.

I shall make such arrangements that I can send to Washington for another girl, if you want two to take care of the children. You seem to think I shall be burdened with care. I have no fear of it. "Never came trouble to my house in the likeness of your Grace." This empty house echoes departed joys. It is better to fill it so full that there is room for the present only.

Ben will be so full of excitement he will have no room for content. I thought we should leave here this week, but your Father has several suits in the courts, and we shall be here for a fortnight longer.

Paul, I think, will be elated with the vision of shooting duck on the Gulf of Mexico. I think he has a roving nature, like others of his race.

I wander through the new house almost daily. There is a staging from the window where we live to the windows of our house that is to be, so I have easy access.

I went all over Gov. Shepperd's house. It is furnished like a palace, but the rooms are too narrow. Ours will be plainer, but I like the proportions better. They have no inlaid floors. Their heavy carpets can never be cleaned. The carpets are woven for the rooms, and the frescoes match in coloring. Very rich. More than we can afford. But the views from our windows surpass them all.

Tell Gen. Ames to bring you away the last of May. The other fortnight will be but a drag to live with the heat and the restlessness of the children. Love and kisses for them all. My best regards for Gen. Ames.

Your most loving Mother

Lowell, *May* 12, 1875

Dear Blanche: I am alone in the house, and have been for nearly a fortnight. Only Paul comes on Sunday. Your Father is in Maine, trying a case. It holds on well.

Yesterday I went to Boston to buy some things for Bennie, but mainly to see Dr. Cabot. He is not willing to touch my face. As he says, he is not sure he could improve it. I know he could if he would do it as I desire. But it does not look much different from the other wrinkles now, so that it is not worth while to worry over it.

A terrible calamity has fallen on the Crosby family. Mrs. Caverly and her daughter are lost at sea in the shipwreck that has just occurred. Between two and three hundred drowned. A German steamer. It is a fearful thing.

I have (with the gardener) three men and three women, and

no one here but me. To keep them all at work taxes my skill. But I am doing it.

Perhaps you and Gen. Ames would like to go to West Point. If you would, I will take care of the children and I should like it just as well, or better, than to go.

I shall be all in order, outside and in, when you come, and it is a pity these three women should have nothing to do for all the time that somebody is away to West Point. You had better come home!

The robins are more numerous and fatter than ever. The children will find it jolly. Kiss them all for me, and tell them Gann is ready for them. Best regards to Gen. Ames. You can work now to better advantage here than there. The weather is just right.

Your most affectionate MOTHER

BAY ST. LOUIS, *May* 20, 1875

DEAR MOTHER: Your letter came yesterday and although you urge our departure North most eloquently, still we must adhere to our first determination to remain until the 11th or 12th of June. Indeed, it would be very difficult to leave just now. The carpenters are still at work, as well as the painters, and altogether we are full of business. As far as the weather is concerned, we have no need to hurry; for nothing could be more delightful than these days and nights. It is a little too cool to enjoy the bathing constantly. The temperature of the water is agreeable, but the wind is too fresh except at mid-day, and then I do not care to bathe on account of my complexion. I have been in several times, with the children. They are perfectly wild with delight, and Butler teases to go daily. The only drawback to this place is in the shape of gnats, flies and mosquitoes. Still there are many days when we have few, if any of these, as the Gulf winds drive them all inland.

You must not expect to see Sarah such a bouncing baby as was Edith. On the contrary, she is very slight and small. She does not sleep quite enough, which I think may account for her spirituelle appearance.

I doubt if Mary can go North with me. She has made a fool of herself and is married. She is quite unhappy, as she is most anxious to go to Lowell, and cannot bear to leave. I dread a new girl on that long journey North, with the children all unused to her—but we shall manage in some way no doubt, and it is barely possible Mary can go.

I am all alone. Gen'l. Ames has gone up to Jackson for a

day or two, and I take advantage of his absence to have the floors rewaxed. You would be surprised to see how fine they look. When we came they were fearful to contemplate, but are now quite elegant, and the whole house is satisfactory. Capt. A. pays for half of this Bay St. Louis property. It will cost, when completed, about four thousand dollars.

What is Father thinking of? Is he going on steadily with the law, or will he make some political move this summer? I am very glad he had nothing to do with that old Beecher trial. He has given up all thought of a trip to Europe in that yacht this summer, of course. I wish he could have some of the nice, soft-shell crabs we have here—thirty-five cents a dozen, and very delicious.

A gentleman by the name of Claibourne wished to be remembered to him—as the first Union man who met him at Ship Island.

Three weeks from today we shall leave here and go directly through to Lowell. I have a great deal to do in the meantime.—My projects always seems to be too numerous for the time allowed for their completion.

Love and kisses for you and Father.

Your affectionate daughter, BLANCHE

LOWELL, *May 22*, 1875

DEAR BLANCHE: Your Father has gone to New York and Washington. Started yesterday. He will return here before we go to West Point. We shall go there the last of next week, or the beginning of the following. What I write for especially is to know when you will leave, and if you could not return by the way of Washington. I could join you there, as I wish to look after the house, and I wish you and Gen. Ames to see it. Senator Jones, the millionaire of the West, wants it. Your Father is inclined to sell it to him. This worries me. It is like taking the eye teeth to part with it. Yet the stake is so great, and the chances of selling so expensive a house so few, that for all your prospects in the future, I dread to stand in the way. And yet, if Gen. Ames should come to the Senate, I want you in that house. I have telegraphed to your Father to defer the sale if possible till you come to Washington, where I will meet you. I should like you to see it, whether it is sold or not. If it is not sold, you can help me give directions, and if it is, we shall have to finish it. I want you to see it. You might be content with the middle one. It is a beautiful house. But I want your judgement and Gen. Ames'. You are as much interested as I am, more, indeed—you are young. We can sleep in the middle house. The beds are all in order. And we can take our meals at the hotel opposite. That your Father is doing now. You could telegraph us at West Point when you start. If the weather is hot, and you have concluded to start earlier, telegraph here or at West Point as the case may be, and I will join you. MOTHER

BAY ST. LOUIS, *May* 31, 1875

DEAR MOTHER: I have your letter, in which you speak of the possibility of a sale of the corner house in Washington. If Father can get a good price I should think that he would take advantage of his opportunities. As far as I am concerned, the center house would be more than satisfactory, even if Gen'l. Ames were to be elected to the Senate, which is by no means certain.

We shall start next Monday—that is a week from today. This will take us into Washington Thursday night or Friday morning. I will telegraph you when we start, and I hope you will meet us in Washington.

I write in haste, for I have many things to do, and I have had the house full of company. They have not all gone yet, and will not for a day or two. This, with the change of servants, makes it quite laborious, especially in the warm weather.

The children are all well, and Butler is highly pleased at the thought of seeing "Gan." Mary will take charge of the house here, and cook for Gen'l. Ames when he returns.

Love and kisses for Father and Ben. The same for yourself.

Your affectionate BLANCHE

Governor Ames returned to Mississippi after a month's absence in Massachusetts. Mrs. Ames and children spent the summer at Bay View.

The Mansion, JACKSON, MISS., *July* 22, 1875

DEAR BLANCHE: Again do I begin a series of letters to you—written only when time and space separates us—which may serve as an imperfect record of our lives. As we look back, we find the years running the one into the others so as to be hardly distinguishable, and were it not for these letters all record of the years would be lost,—except of course the happy memories kept by you and me alone. By and by, when we shall have "settled" in life, and when we may wish to penetrate the mists of our past, we will look up these love letters of ours and read, reflect, and recall.

I did all my business in Boston in short order. I saw the head of the Fire Dept. there and though I did not receive the encouragement I wished, I did not lose faith in my ladder. Simplicity is a requisite, so that ordinary men could use the ladder even on dark stormy nights, or when the snow falls and ice is rapidly made. I fear I must expect nothing for or from my ladder till I shall have made one for actual use which shall meet the various requirements demanded. This I think can be easily done. I shall try to experiment on it.

Your Father told me that the Convers mortgage would soon be paid and asked me about the reinvestment of the amount. He said you, he and I consenting (although I do not exactly see what I have to do with it) the trust could be revoked, etc. I told him that his judgement was better than mine, and I am free to say to you that I do not think I ought to be consulted. He said that he thought it best to buy U.S. bonds bearing .365 percent interest—that is an interest of a little more than three and a half percent. The bonds, he said, could be bought for about 70 or 75 cents on the dollar. If bought at seventy-three cents on the dollar, they would bear an interest of just five percent. If the interest be paid in gold, you would get the .3–65/100 of a cent in gold instead of greenbacks. Thus the interest would not vary much from five percent. Your Father said it would be seven, but his calculation must be wrong. I have said I ought not to be consulted; yet I venture to say that such an interest is not very large. It may be in the East, but it is small for the West and South. Certainty of interest and principal is an item. Yet nothing is more sure than real estate. Your Father sees, or says he sees, trouble in the future for U.S. Bond holders. Whether he does or not, bonds dependent on the will of a political party in times of great excitement are not the best security. Are we, as a nation, approaching such a period, may be a pertinent question.

Often mortgaged property is obtained quite below its real value by the mortgagee. Of course, with good security you want the best interest. We may do the best in the West. I would not advise you to put a single cent in the South. It strikes me that much money could be made by hiring it cheap in the East and loaning it in the West. I have occupied so much space with business that I will defer the recital of the incidents of my trip till tomorrow.

Everything is quiet here. Nothing of especial note is transpiring. I am a long way off from you and our babies, and realize it. Three months will soon speed by and bring us together again.

Love to you, Dear, and the babies—with regards to all members of the family.
ADELBERT

BAY VIEW, *July* 24, 1875

DEAR DEL: Directly after breakfast I went down to Bennett's office to carry my letter, and draw a check for fifty dollars. He told me that the storm of yesterday smashed up a sail boat in Lanesville. There was a party on board, but all escaped. He did not know the particulars. But from this you can judge somewhat of the violence of the storm.

I enclose a letter from Bruce which came in the morning's mail. I answered it by telegraph saying "Gov. Ames left for Jackson last Monday via Long Branch."

I have been occupied in two ways today. Painting and watching the race through the telescope. The sun rose this morning bright and clear, and there has been a passable breeze all day from the north. We could see the yachts quite plainly at the Shoals, and throughout most of the course, but my inexperienced eyes could not detect which was which, and I amused myself by deciding first on one, then on another. We have not yet heard which was victorious. The wind was not strong enough for the "America" to do her best.

After tea we took a long walk towards the lighthouse. I am anxious to reduce my flesh and improve in color.

Sunday Evening

The "America" has returned, bringing Mr. and Mrs. Hastings, Florence and Tom—Maria, McDaniels, Hattie, Pearson, Farrington, Ludlam, Father and the boys. Quite a house full.

The race was a failure. It seems the stake boat got out of position in some way, probably dragged its anchor during the storm of Friday. None of the yachts could find it, nor could the revenue cutter. But the "Rambler" claimed to have found it and sailed around it, so although she was the hindmost yacht in the race, she received the prize. There is a great deal of hard feeling, and all of the yachts except the "America" and one or two others left the Shoals this morning early, refusing to remain for the race on Monday, saying there was "no use racing with so little fair play." The "America" and one other yacht have challenged the "Rambler" for a twenty-mile race to the windward and back. The punch bowl to the winner. The challenge has not yet been accepted.

I must say good night. The crowd will think it strange that I am away so long. I came upstairs to put Butler to bed. Hattie is to sleep with me tonight, and I shall have no chance to write before going to bed.

I send you love and am thinking with pleasure of our settling in St. Paul or somewhere in the course of *years*.

BLANCHE

JACKSON, MISS., *July 24, 1875*

DEAR BLANCHE: Seated in our room upstairs I renew the story of my trip.

We had a pleasant run from Fall River to New York. I was up early enough to watch the varied scenery as we sailed through the East River; and when the boat got to the wharf I walked up Broadway to get my breakfast. Having an hour or two of time on my hands, I viewed the city afoot—my baggage in my hand. In fact, the comfort of baggage in a compact form was never more apparent to me. From this time out I discard large valises.

At half past nine I left the city for Long Branch. I first went to Gen'l. Babcock's but as he was bathing I did not see him, and so went to the President's alone. I was shown into the parlor to wait the departure of a visitor who was occupying the President's time. Mrs. Grant was there and we had quite a chat. She asked for you and the babies—also, for the fine-looking—she might have said the handsome or pretty cousin of yours she had met in Washington—Miss Hildreth. I married Miss Florence off at once, and she ceased to be of further interest.

We talked a little of the Ames side of the case when I went to the Grant side. I spoke of the promotion of the President, of his having become a grandfather. This remark of mine touched a responsive chord in a grandmother's heart, but still more strongly that of the mother's. She talked some of the child, but more of Nellie. She showed me some photographs of her home in England, and explained them in such a way that I could see she would have me, as all the world believe and know, that she had a good, happy home there. Mrs. G. showed she did not regard England as America for a home for her daughter. I asked if Mr. Sartoris (accent on first syllable as she pronounced it) would not make this country his home. She said no, with evident sorrow. On this point I said, in a kind and tenderly tone, as I felt, that it was too bad for the President's grandchild to be a foreigner. She spoke of the constant care Nellie would find in her boy. I replied that mothers only become young again after their children grow up, when they become more the mistresses of their time. I believe I dragged my wife and babies into the conversation at every opportunity, and the last remark was made with the restraints your babies put upon you full in mind. She said her son, Col. Fred, would not leave the army although she said he had formed a company with young Sherman for banking business in Wn. By the way, in speaking of Nellie and Sartoris, she said that at first they had no idea that there was any particular interest between them, but said Nellie was quite content to live in England and was very happy. My talk with the President was lengthy, though no particular conclusions were reached—none however asked. He showed his old interest in me, I judged.

I met Senator Spencer at the hotel, who told me that the President was much out of conceit with Postmaster General Jewell. Spencer said that the President told him (S) that "Jewell was a fool" that he "was much deceived in him," etc. Jewell, by the way is a candidate for the Presidency. Your Father will be amused at this item of Long Branch gossip.

At two o'clock in the afternoon I left L.B. for New York and at five I took the train for the west and south.

I send you love and love for the babies. ADELBERT

JACKSON, MISS., *July 25*, 1875

DEAR BLANCHE: We are enduring a hot Sunday. On my way here I met Major Gibbs at Milan, on his way home. His bride was with him and his child, a girl three months younger than Butler. Both Gibbs and his wife were looking well and seemed very happy.

Upon arriving here I found Gen'l. Packer up, and by his assistance got into my room. Mary and Battles had left for Bay St. Louis a week before I arrived. Up to that time they had made our room their home, and our bed theirs! I found some clean bed linen, and went to bed, to become a prey to mosquitoes.

Osborne says a gang of Negroes played croquet every evening until he took the balls and mallets and hid them. He also said that our neighbor Mrs. Deason said that Mary received crowds of her friends in the parlors. I can well understand why she should, when she takes such freedom in our own chamber.

The flowers in the vases are doing very well, but I noticed the number of plants had diminished. George informs me that Mary came one day, and with a trowel dug up and took away some of them. He said Mary asserted those she took up were dead, but he denies it. I see the remnants of a vine, which must have been alive ten days ago. I have no doubt she divided with us. I wonder if she is occupying our room at the Bay and using our best things. I presume she is. I will go and see when the Legislature adjourns. Her husband was indicted as you know—Mary got friends to bail him out. His case was continued till the next term of court, and he is now rusticating at the best sea-side residence on the Gulf. So much for friends.

The second crop of grass is about ready to cut, and the weeds in the vegetable garden—there are no vegetables—grow rank towering high above the fence. Our croquet ground looks neglected. Some of the arches are missing, and others look battered and bruised. The grass too, is getting a good start on us there.

It has not been dusty this season, and the house is quite presentable. I found the old, familiar, dusty odor augmented by escaping gas.

Although the objects in and about the house are quite familiar, I have known them for years, this does not possess the charm of home. It is seven years since I came into this house—and five years last Wednesday since we were wed. Five years is quite a period of time. I wonder if you remembered our wedding day on Wednesday last, and did you celebrate it? I must confess it never entered my head that day when I breakfasted in Pittsburg, Pa. and supped in Cincinnati, Ohio. While I did not think of the day, I nevertheless thought of you and our little ones. This place is very dull. Hardly any of our friends are here. So I have an abundance of time on my hands, and consequently think a great deal. I send you love, and kisses for the babies. ADELBERT

JACKSON, MISS., *July 27*, 1875

DEAR BLANCHE: I did not write you yesterday only because I was so much occupied I did not have time to do it. I can write but briefly today.

The legislature met today, a quorum in both houses, and have gone to work apparently with the best of feeling. I judge they will complete their labors and adjourn by the end of this week.

Major Howe, Col. Warner, and everybody else are here. Col. Warner and Mr. Warren quietly told me that they never found Mass. so delightful and attractive as this year, and that they never left her with more reluctance. The contrast between here and there was never greater, and their capacity to see it increases year by year.

Love for you, Dear, and the babies. ADELBERT

BAY VIEW, *July* 28, 1875

DEAR DEL: The household is now reduced to Florence, Hattie, Mother, Father, and *yours*. The boys are in Boston, waiting to return on the yacht. Your Father has been in Boston. He called at the office to see Father, who invited him down here, but he declined for the present, saying that he wished to visit Rockland first, and would come to see us on his return.

I have had a letter from Mary. It seems that she and Battles are at Bay St. Louis. We can try her, but I fear she is overloaded and will cause us more trouble than comfort. Still, poor thing, I am sorry for her. I agreed to give her ten dollars a month for looking after the place. If you take your meals at the hotel, and I think it would be well, she can make your bed, keep the house clean, and do your washing. The ten dollars is sufficient wages for this. Battles is working as waiter at the hotel, so they will get on very well.

I understand that the Convers matter is soon to be adjusted, and agree with you that U.S. bonds are not the most enticing security. The only trouble about the West is that we do not know any place sufficiently well to enable us to invest with safety. Neither do I know of anything here.

It would be an advantage now if we knew what our future abiding place is to be. With a cheerful, beautiful home I should be content at St. Paul, in spite of the cold weather. I feel sure that the close communion engendered by the long evenings and chats around the fireside would be most excellent for the children, and although it's not necessary or right for us to give up everything in life for their good and advancement, still our future happiness will depend largely upon them, and we shall feel better satisfied to be where it is well for them. More than this, I really think we might like it better than any place in the country. There are many reasons why it would be best for you there. I mean to speak to your Father when I see him—if for no other purpose—to have it reach Nellie's ears that we think of residing West. If I do not mistake her nature, it will do a great deal towards rendering her contented.

The papers say that the legislature of Mississippi proposes to impeach the Lieut. Gov. What does this mean? Have you called the Legislature together, and find assembled only a quorum of Democrats? I am not aware that Davis has done anything especially bad.

As you say, Del, three months will fly swiftly—but I am a little anxious about you, and beg you to take the greatest care of yourself.—I wish I could get you into my happy state of mind.—No matter how politics turn in Mississippi, I shall feel content and be perfectly satisfied that nothing so fortunate could have happened.

Good night, with love. BLANCHE

BAY VIEW, *July* 29, 1875

DEAR DEL: Butler is quite well today, entirely free from fever. I feel greatly relieved. No doubt I am suffering from a Mother's partiality—but Butler seems so uncommonly bright and precocious that I am always alarmed lest his brain may be affected. His smartness can be accounted for, however, by the fact that he is, and always has been, a companion for old people. Except at Bay St. Louis, he has never played with children.

I have been busy all day, painting and mending. Last week Father put five hundred dollars into his white vest pocket, and hung it up in the closet. Lizzie Carr, seeing that it was dirty, put it into the wash (so she says) without examining the pockets. When she found the bills they were all in a mash, and she threw them down the water-closet. Part of her story was true—but the indications are that she threw away two hundred and kept three. On being confronted with Father, she was very much frightened, and said she would look under the barn for the pieces. She did so, and with Horace's aid has produced four dilapidated fifty dollar bills and four (which Horace found) simply torn in three pieces. There are no traces of the hundred which she no doubt still has. I have assisted Florence in pasting the bits together, and the banks will redeem those that we have. If she had torn up the other fifties, we should at least have found some extra pieces. Of course there are missing bits to the bills we have tried to make out, but no extra pieces to indicate others. I am sorry for Lizzie. It was too great a temptation.

Col. French has met with a bad accident. In driving over from the depot this evening, he undertook to race with a man. This man locked wheels with another carriage, which caused his horse to shy, striking Col. F.'s team with such force that the sudden stop threw him out. Col. French is bruised on the back, and badly cut on the arm. I do not think he will be able to go on the race Saturday.

Butler is constantly asking "When is fall?" He understands that you are to return at that time.

I am startled to see by the papers that the yellow fever is so violent at Pensacola. I hope and pray it will not reach Mississippi. Be very careful of yourself, Del, and do not play croquet too late in the evening.

I had no letter yesterday, and hope the fates will be good to me this morning. I feel lonesome when I do not hear from you daily. Love, enough to last until tomorrow. BLANCHE

JACKSON, MISS., *July* 29, 1875

DEAR BLANCHE: Your second letter came today. Why do you ask me how I would like to go to St. Paul and live? What has put that into your head? I think a city would be more acceptable to both of us than a village—and St. Paul to Northfield. Now pray, why do you ask?

Things here are moving rapidly. Political excitement is on the increase. The animosity in our own ranks among the various candidates for office is very great. They are trying to destroy each other, and appear to prefer that our opponents should succeed rather than their party friends though personal enemies. The legislature is showing a good spirit, and will no doubt complete their labors tomorrow. It is saddening, yet with ludicrous phases, to see the strifes, envies, jealousies, animosities existing in our own ranks. Little of this exists in parties, as they usually grow up. The ignorance of the people is sadly worked upon and every man is induced to run for office. Hence, inextricable confusion. Could anything be more ludicrously grim than this? A colored man by the name of Jones sent the following telegram to Capt. Pease: "Circumstances over which I have no control compel me to be absent from the State Central Committee. I authorize you to act as my proxy." He was at the time in charge of the U.S. Marshal, and on his way to prison, having been convicted of robbing the mails. The opposition are commenting on the character of some of our leaders.

It is now nearly 3 p.m. Friday, and I find I cannot add anything for want of time and opportunity—I am being talked to now. Love, ADELBERT

BAY VIEW, *July* 30, 1875

DEAR DEL: The carriage has been used only to take Father to and from the train. The rest of Horace's time has been employed in searching for the missing bits of bills. One hundred dollars is probably gone beyond recovery.

The yacht sailed for the Shoals this afternoon—Father, Ludlam, Harry French and the boys on board. Col. French was kept at home by his injuries.

I have been painting all day. You will be surprised to see how much the original picture is improved. The copy is nearly completed, and will be a pretty portrait. How would you like me to paint and sell pictures, Del? It might cause me to work harder, improve faster, and in the course of time become a source of income. It would be a great *source* of *pleasure* to me, if in some way I could be instrumental in building up a fortune for ourselves and children, no matter how small the part I might take in so doing.

It is very annoying about Mary, Del. If she behaved so in Jackson, she will be utterly untrustworthy at Bay St. Louis, and you will have to send her away, and look after things yourself.

When you go to Northfield, Del, could you not inquire about property mortgages, etc. there and in St. Paul, with a view to the investment of the Convers money? Also about the law of the State. I understand that many of the richest families of Boston have been awfully nipped in western investments, the laws of the states being such that they could not get any satisfaction. Many cottages at Nahant and vicinity are for sale, their owners being compelled to spend the summer in the city. We do not wish to follow in their footsteps, and *lose one of our little nest eggs.*

I must acknowledge, Sweetheart, that I did not recollect the anniversary of our marriage. But I thought of my husband many times, and as each day passes I feel thankful for my happy fate. Perhaps that is sufficient. Good night, with kisses from the babies and BLANCHE

BAY VIEW, *July* 30, 1875

DEAR DEL: There is very little of interest to relate.—The first part of the day I spent with the children. The afternoon in painting and riding. In the evening Mrs. French and Mrs. Kensel called. While they were here young Thompson came over to bring news of the race. The "America" won—although the breeze was not very strong, and the course was not weatherly (if you know what that means). At first Father refused to sail, as the breeze was not eight knots, and the course was not what was expected. Finally he consented, and Capt. Reid said "Gen'l., we are beaten." "Well, never mind, Reid. I felt morally bound to try the race, and we will do the best we can." As they passed the judges coming in, Reid, to gain time, ran very close to a ledge, so much so that a pilot who was on the stand started from his seat, struck his hands together and exclaimed "In an instant you will hear a crash, Butler's yacht is on the rocks." But Reid luffed her off just in time, and saved a few moments. The "Resolute" gave the "America" eight minutes time allowance. The "America" beat by two minutes, forty-five seconds. So that the difference in sailing time was five minutes, fifteen seconds. Close, was it not? Tomorrow they sail for the punch bowl sweepstakes, no allowance. I fear the "America" will not come off victorious. Still it looks quite stormy, and that would be advantageous.

Just after we had finished supper, the "America" came in to take Col. French over to the Shoals. All hands came up to the house for supper—notwithstanding the fact that there is a fine cook and steward on board the yacht. By all hands I mean Mr. Ludlam, Harry French, Col. F's brother, Father, and the boys. They will sail back to the Shoals again in a few moments.

Carney wrote me yesterday. He wishes to know what is to be done with the stray three thousand—the mortgage being fifteen thousand and Carney's trust for me only twelve. It was understood that the three thousand was to go to the children, but I think Father wants it, and if you do not object I will return it to him. Mr. Convers agreed with Gen'l. Butler to pay eight percent in consideration of Gen'l. B's forbearing to collect the debt and interest at this rate. Now, the persons to whom the mortgage is to be assigned propose to pay only six percent from the time of the last payment, Nov. 18, 1873, nearly two years, a difference in interest of about $300. Carney writes "I must do as you direct." I do not see why I should accept any such proposition. If the Convers creditors who wish to settle up this mortgage have been two years about it—it is their fault not mine, and they must pay for it. If they had settled two years ago I might have been able to reinvest the money at eight percent. At least, so it seems to me, if I understand the question rightly. Carney also writes "I intend to invest the proceeds in bonds of the District of Columbia, guaranteed by the U.S., unless you desire otherwise." I do not believe in District bonds, and shall direct nothing of the kind unless you write me that you think best.

I have filled this letter up with business, and have only room to say goodnight, Dearie. Love from BLANCHE

JACKSON, MISS., *July* 31, 1875

DEAR BLANCHE: The legislature adjourned today at twelve, and now nearly all have called on me and departed. With bills to sign and favors to grant, and talks, I have not had time to breathe—yes, I have breathed to be sure, but I have done so under difficulties. The action of the legislature has been quite satisfactory to our party. The work laid out to be done has been done and all legal embarrassments for an election and the collection of revenue for this year have been removed. Some of our party have attempted to injure me, but the blows intended for me recoiled on their own heads. The strife in our own party will come to an end next month, for the simple reason that all the nominations will be made and our guns necessarily turned upon the common foe. I never was more placid than now. I will not be too explicit here as my letters pass through doubtful hands.

Major Gibbs gave a reception at the hotel last night. It was not a brilliant event, and probably he did not expect it to be. Not because he and his bride did not have the kindest regard and good wishes of those who were present, but because it all seemed an attempt at display by people who knew the amenities of civilized life in a community where they were regarded as pariahs, lepers, and a refuse to be sedulously shunned. He had a fine entertainment of cakes, candy, lemonade and champagne—music and dancing. All the carpet-bag male world was there; and aside from Mrs. Fisher and Mrs. Musgrave only ladies whose husbands or brothers are in the Auditor's office—yes, Mrs. Clover and Mrs. List. I have named four—Mrs. Gibbs was five, and the others three in number (eight ladies in all) belonged to the Auditor's office. The reception took place in the hotel parlor. The doors and windows were open and the hotel gallery crowded with strangers, white and black. A *home*-like feeling, or a *home* appearance, was not visible.

I must close hastily for the mail. Love for my loved ones.
ADELBERT

JACKSON, MISS., *August* 1, 1875

DEAR BLANCHE: You know I have always been adverse to bathing in the cold sea water at Bay View. I do not think *one* plunge would do harm, but more than one, with a sun bath which necessarily follows, results in harm. I have suffered by salt water bathing in New England. It has already had its enervating influence on Butler. If persisted in, it will surely injure him. So don't do it.

Hattie had better be content with her Isles of Shoals triumph. If she is so constituted that peace of mind and contentment are to come only when she belles it over you, then indeed is she unfortunate. That time will never come. She has never appeared so pretty as when she stood on the steps the afternoon I first saw her. Since that moment she has been losing ground. Yet, she is pretty and has but few equals. She is well enough —yes, of the superlative degree—till she comes into comparison with my wife. The contrast results in her confusion. I write upon deliberate reflection—unbiased and unprejudiced—at least so far as human nature is capable of so doing under the circumstances.

I am unable to understand why you say nothing of Father. I understood your letter to say he was to be in Boston a week ago last Thursday—a day or two previous to your last letter. I hope you will give me some information on the subject. Since my arrival here I wrote him at Northfield to send me a pass on the Chicago and St. Paul road. I should get a reply tomorrow or next day. I had not received your letter speaking of his going East when I wrote. I told him I would go to Minn. but I now doubt if I can get away. We are likely to have trouble at Vicksburg and all want me here. Davis is in trouble. The legislature has a committee to inquire into his action in pardoning one Barratine. Barratine and a young friend went to cowhide a woman for speaking unkindly of Barratine's sisters. This woman said that white girls, among them B's. sisters, came to her house to meet men. The facts evidently sustained her in making the statement. B's. friend was to hold her, perhaps whip her at the same time, but as she was strong, he could do no more than hold her, and while doing so Barratine shot her dead in her own house, in presence of her children. All this Lt. Gov. Davis told me yesterday. He said his chief reason for issuing the pardon was to suppress the scandal! The woman killed belonged to the class known as poor whites. The Barratines are "first families." Davis is charged with selling the pardon, but I can hardly believe it. His action is creating, has created, much talk and is condemned by all.

My room is full of the hungriest, blood thirstiest crew of

mosquitoes that ever presented a bill to me. And I am compelled at every period to slash and cut around with my handkerchief to drive them from my ankles and neck. There is no peace except under the mosquito bar. I have never before seen so many fleas in our room, nor such lively ones. I wonder if they were bequeathed us by Mary.

We have not had a drop of rain since I came till this morning, and then barely enough to lay the dust. The rain cooled the air, and for the first time I drew the sheet up over me. You can judge of the warmth of the nights. On two or three occasions I have, after getting ready for bed, put on my slippers and traveled up to the top of the house where it has been perceptibly cooler.

This is Sunday. I have been in the house all day. Breakfast was brought to me. I ate it, and sat down to the papers. I had my bath ready, but before I had finished my papers Mr. Raymond came in and I had to dress and as the bath tub was leaking I sent it away. I had dinner alone, here in my room. Since then I have been sitting here by our window, writing to and thinking of her I love. I send you love. Kiss the babies for me.

ADELBERT

BAY VIEW, *August 2*, 1875

DEAR DEL: My last letter was mostly about business—but I have still more to say. I think Father was at the bottom of Carney's proposition to buy D.C. bonds. I know that he has a good many, that at the present time they are very low, and he hates to sell and make a sacrifice to outsiders. Perhaps he would not mind so much if I had them, and in addition he will be paid in ready money, which he greatly needs, for his house. As I said in my last letter, I do not think these bonds the best kind of property. So I make this proposition as a compromise. The three thousand dollars I withdraw claim to, with the suggestion that at some future time he can give it to the children as he proposed. Then Del, I want your note and interest, which I suppose is about five thousand dollars paid. This will give Father eight, and leave us seven, which I think could be better invested than in D.C. bonds, more especially as you did not seem to like them. Then for the payment of your note I shall want settled upon me an equal amount, either by note to Paul, as before, or by a mortgage on your mill. All this is not for a division of interests as you know, but as additional security for ourselves, and the children.

I suppose the only person who could give you trouble is

Uncle Parker, and I do not feel afraid of him. Still for all concerned, I think it would be better as I suggest. Then we shall be out of debt—except to Northfield. Perhaps when you see Sam you may think the seven thousand would do more good at Fort Atkinson than elsewhere. If so, it would be best to use it there.

We are all well. The baby has learned to creep, and seems stronger. We send you love, Dearie. BLANCHE

JACKSON, MISS., *August 2*, 1875

DEAR BLANCHE: This is the sixth year of our married life—we have not traveled far into the sixth year—still it is the sixth. How we should make the most of the fleeting years. Since we are so much happier together, it is unfortunate that we should lose even one day, much less these long months of absence.

The mosquitoes are untiring. Having shoes on I have been compelled to wrap my ankles in newspapers. In defending my hands and face I have strewn my table with mosquito corpses.

We have about forty cords of good hard wood piled up in the yard, ready to be cut and put into the cellar. I have had the old hen house pulled down and put away for fire wood. Tomorrow or next day I will have the second crop of grass cut.

I am sorry to hear of the sickness of Butler. Suppose you dose him with a little quinine if he shows any of the symptoms of chills and fever. It was rather rude in him to laugh at his sister on her first attempt to say her prayers. She surely shows a laudable ambition.

I intended to go to the Bay tonight, but have deferred my visit for a day or two. The Democratic convention will meet here tomorrow.

I send love. Kiss the little ones for ADELBERT

BAY VIEW, *August* 3, 1875

DEAR DEL: Before you receive this you will have learned through the papers that the "America" won the Sweepstakes. Yesterday there was so little wind that all here gave up any thought of the prize, and felt sorry that the "America" should have entered for the race. Last night it blew up a heavy east storm, and this morning it was so cold and damp that when the children got up I ordered a fire in the parlor. The order was timely, for before the rest of the family were up, Father, Mr. Ludlam and the boys made their appearance. Not one word was said about the punch bowl, but it was put upon the piano so that each member of the family might be taken by surprise as they came into the room with faces made up to condole with friends in disappointment. Of course the sailing party felt triumphant. Poor Mr. Ludlam was sick—from a bilious headache he said, but I think from the heavy gale which rocked the boat on its homeward trip. I send you the papers which will give you a better idea of the race than I can. The "Resolute" left a challenge for the "America" at the Shoals to sail over the New York course six days for six consecutive weeks, for a thousand dollars a day. Either boat refusing to sail on account of stress of weather to forfeit a thousand dollars to the other. Father laughs and says he thinks he sees himself sailing over the same course thirty-six times. The successful issue of this race has increased the value of the yacht.

Your letters do not come very regularly Del. Do you want me to scold a little? Do not write when it is burdensome Love. But I think the fault is with the mail, not the male.

The children are all well and join with me in sending kisses to our best beloved. BLANCHE

JACKSON, MISS., *August* 3, 1875

DEAR BLANCHE: Your letter of the 28th ult. was received this morning. In it you say Father had called on your father in Boston and after a visit to Rockland was to pay you a visit at the Bay. I am glad he has appeared. I have no doubt he will have a pleasant visit. I know you will try to make it so.

I see by a telegram today that the "America" beat the "Resolute" on time allowance. This, then, is one of the victories you have been looking for, for the yacht. It must have been an exciting race. I wonder if they have trimmed her by the head as I hold they should?

The Democrats are holding a convention here today. Lamar is their orator. I have not heard what the character of his speech was—only that it was very bitter. They have had a band of music, have been firing cannon and been noisy generally. Whether the convention will adopt the "white-line" or not I do not know. They all affect great confidence in success this fall. The only thing which will do us harm will be the intimidation and murdering of the poor negroes. If they extend their savage policy in Vicksburg we cannot predict the results. There they have acted as only savages act. They have been barbarous in the extreme. However, we shall see.

It is very healthy here, and the indications are that we shall have a healthy fall.

I send you as ever, love, ADELBERT

BAY VIEW, *August* 4, 1875

DEAR DEL: Two letters came for me this morning, so that I feel a thousand miles nearer you. You ask if I have seen your Father and why I talk "of living in St. Paul." I have not seen your Father, and I first thought of living in St. Paul as I rode home from Gloucester after seeing you go out of sight on the cars.—It occurred to me that we might be very happy there. That it would be for our interests to be nearer Northfield and Fort A., that your Father would not be likely to sell the mills if we were there, that as you are a young man you would have a chance to grow (in fortune) with the country, and if political ambition should again overtake you, you might have a chance to gratify it. That the climate, though cold, is healthful and invigorating for the children, and that all things considered it might prove the very best place for us. There are two things to be urged against it. We should lose a little of the refinement and culture of the East, and might find the winters long and severe. These long winters have advantages, however. They cause home and its advantages to be more studiously cultivated, and the long evenings serve to unite a family more closely in thought, studies, and amusements. I have thought it all over, Del, and know that I should be content if you could be.

I spoke to Father tonight, and told him I wished to pay your note, that you would give me one through Paul. I took this much for granted. He suggested that your note would not secure me against your creditors. I asked if a mortgage would. He said yes, that it would be better to have the note secured by a mortgage. Again I took it for granted, and told him that you would do this—that you did not know I was going to pay the note, but I judged it could not fail to be agreeable to you and convenient to him at this time. I also spoke of the three thousand, and said that this was the time to make a different arrangement in regard to it if he so wished. He did not reply directly, but I think he will leave it as it is. I was mistaken in what I wrote about the D.C. bonds. Father has none to sell, on the contrary he prefers to borrow money and leave his bonds as collateral security—as he expects them to rise and give him a large advance. I will wait your judgement as to what I had best do about them. If any money is needed for Fort A. you had best use some of this. I am glad that we can pay your note to Father and feel out of debt. Except for this failure of Convers we should hardly have been able just now. I will write to Carney and tell him to wait awhile before purchasing bonds. In the meantime you write me what you think I had best do. And Del, do not think that I am too self-sufficient or inclined to take too much for granted in regard to your affairs. It is necessary for me to come to some decision at once in the three thousand dollar matter, in the reduction of three hundred in the interest, and in regard to the disposal of the twelve thousand. I have tried to think it out and do the best I could.

Poor deKay has lost his baby. How fortunate we are that ours continue so well. The mortality among children in New York is frightful.

You must take great care of yourself, Del. Eat all you can so that excitement and worry may have something to feed upon rather than your not too well covered frame. If things do not go to suit you this fall, remember my proposal for a grand settlement and do not allow yourself to feel annoyed.

Good night. Love and kisses from the babies and

BLANCHE

JACKSON, MISS., *August* 4, 1875

DEAR BLANCHE: I am glad to hear of Butler's recovery. I hope you will not put him into the water again. A sponge bath is, in my opinion, the only one for children. Butler *should* be smart. Is he not four years old this season, and do not four-year-olds have books and go to school? He should be reading soon. I hope you will have Edith's portrait ready for Father to take it West with him. He will do well to buy a frame for it in Boston. You have not spoken of the baby lately. How is her cold?

It is pleasant to picture you all at Bay View—a place where real care or sorrow has never made its appearance—but so smooth is life there that a poor dinner or disagreeable weather is magnified into an almost insurmountable obstacle. Well, that is human nature.

Ben has but about three weeks more before his revelry will cease and he is again incarcerated in the highlands of the Hudson. How fast the days pass.

Our town is quiet again. The crew of yesterday has departed. The true sentiment of the assembly was "color line" though the platform says nothing about it. The understanding evidently is that each locality can act as it chooses, but the state convention shall put forth a platform for Northern consumption. Lamar was very bitter on me as well as on everything Republican. I am, perhaps justly, made the head and front of all Republican offending, and assaulted accordingly.

Raymond tells a good story on me, illustrating my present situation in the party. While the Democracy are firing into me in front, the soreheads of our own party are assaulting me from all directions.

I am blamed for everything and more too. Raymond says that sore-head Republicans when they have girl babies blame me because they are not boy babies. It may not be literally true, but it is not more absurd than many things said; although I care very little what is said for my convictions and conclusions are deep and clear. I think I know what to do.

Give my kind regards to all the members of the family. Kisses for the babies and love for my Beautiful.

ADELBERT

BAY VIEW, *August* 5, 1875

DEAR DEL: All here are well. I will heed your warnings and commands, and will not allow Butler to go in again. I should not have done so anyway.

The "Resolute," the rival of the "America," has had bad luck this season. Seeing the "America" leave harbor at the Shoals and go home, she started for Boston in the storm, and when off Thatchers Island, although only sailing with mainsail and jib, she was blown all to pieces—and they were driven into Portsmouth. There the party left her, and went by rail to New York, stopping in Boston, where Father saw them. A fine vessel to sail thirty-six days in all kinds of weather.

Father does not want the three thousand dollars—that is to say, he leaves it as it is. I have written Carney to pay the note, and am now waiting to hear from you about the bonds.

I am sorry you cannot go to Northfield, because if at Fort Atkinson you could tell better what is needed. Ah, well! we can't have everything. Good night, Love. BLANCHE

JACKSON, MISS., *August* 5, 1875

DEAR BLANCHE: I am somewhat disgusted today. Last evening I had a telegram from Warren, who is in Holmes Co. (the second county above us on the railroad), asking me to receive a person bringing me a letter at one o'clock this morning. I went to bed at twelve and between one and two was awakened to receive a messenger. The message was that Col. Lee and his friends in Holmes Co. had made an attack on their own party friends, and killed one and mortally wounded another. There has been a feud in our own party there and has resulted as above stated. The persons killed (the second has since died) were both colored—the cause was "you lie" and "you are another."

Lee is here—he came on the last train. I have not seen him, but I have had a talk with Packer who went up there yesterday, and from him I judge it was a clear case of Ku Kluxism. I understand Lee was backed by the Democrats. I know not what the end will be, but it is easily forseen that such deadly feuds in our own ranks can but result injuriously.

The poor, dead Negroes are to be buried today. Those who killed are at liberty, but are to be examined before a magistrate's court next Monday. Never before has the strife among our own friends been so bitter. What I have described above is being enacted in all directions only with not such violence—such deadly results. Do you wonder that I am disgusted?

French left last evening and asked to be remembered. His family is in Ohio. He has bid adieu to politics in this state and engaged in planting on the Miss. river.

Since I began this letter a heavy shower has come up and cooled and purified the air. It is the first real shower we have had since my return. It has been very dusty. The heavy wind which preceded the rain filled the air with dust. The dust and low hanging clouds which were closing in upon us with the thunder and lightening forcibly reminded me of a battle.

I am beginning to be much alone. I must think, of course, and I find no subject so attractive as my own family. I miss you more than I can tell.

Love for my Beautiful and our sweet babies.

ADELBERT

BAY VIEW, *August* 6, 1875

DEAR DEL: I have not been doing much of interest today—sewed some in the morning, then went in bathing with Mother, Hattie and Fannie French. Fannie and I tried racing to see which could swim the best. She can beat me, so now I must practice, and excel her. I taught Hattie to float. She learned at once, and had no difficulty in lying on the water for quite a long time. I exercised so much that I was glad to rest on the bed and read in the afternoon.

Butler was out of sorts this evening, and tried to strike and bite me. I allowed him to bite me once, he did not hurt, but I pretended to feel greatly troubled. When he went to bed I asked him if he thought I could care for a boy who bit me. Like his Father, he became the injured party at once, and replied "You don't care, nobody cares, not nobody." Of course I was obliged to abandon the ground, and said "What will your Father say? He writes that you must be a good boy to your Mother, and take care of your sisters." "He won't know it, he won't know it." "Oh, yes he will. I write him about Butler every night. Shall I tell him Butler is sorry and wants to be a good boy?" So we kissed and settled all difficulties—and he went to sleep happily.

Edith talks more and more every day. She is much happier and a better girl. She enjoys picking berries, and is content to see me safely in the parlor while she plays on the gallery. She is devoted to her baby sister, who always crows and jumps to see her coming. Butler was in great trouble the other day because Edith told him she was going to look at the steamboat. He was afraid she was going down to the wharf, and came running to me crying and saying "Stop sister, Mother, she is going away." I brought her back, and with great indignation in his tone he said, "Her thinks her can take care of herself." Yesterday he went down with me to see us go into the water. I was a little in advance of him, going over the stones on to the beach, and he called out "Wait, Mother, wait, don't leave your child." His intonation was most amusing. So much for anecdotes of the babies.

When you go down to the Bay, Del, don't forget your promise to me about billiards, poker, pin-pool. Ask me now to do something, so that we may stand on equal footing—then you can keep your promise, as I keep mine.

I want *my* "Chevalier Bayard" to be sans peur et sans reproche *amongst his enemies,* and I am fearful they might find a pin-pool hole in his armor, through which to thrust an arrow poisoned with malice.

Good night. Love and kisses for our dear one, from the babies and

BLANCHE

JACKSON, MISS., *August* 6, 1875

DEAR BLANCHE: It will not be possible for me to go North to Minn. unless I do so to keep Gov. Davis here. We propose to have a delegation of our leading men go to Washington to see the President and the National Republican committee. No one wants Davis to go, as it is believed he will do more harm than good. It would not be well and seemly for me to go, and to keep my Lieutenant from going it may be necessary for me to go to Chicago to meet our folks. Such is our talk just now.

I shall go to Bay St. Louis tonight. Raymond will go with me. I shall remain there Sunday and Monday, returning Tuesday morning.

Why should you not sell pictures? You know I hold that necessity is the best whip to urge us on to great deeds. The necessity of making a saleable picture will do more for you and your genius than years of trifling with your brush. So I say *sell* a picture. Not a family portrait, but anything else. Paint Wendell Phillips or some other prominent personage and you will find purchasers if you do your work as you are capable of doing it. Portraits are of the highest order and you should travel in that path, but if you hesitate on portraits have photographs taken of Prince and Teedle and put them, at least their heads, on canvass—take a horse's head—take a fish—anything. You will do better on things like these than on landscapes, for they are more of detail than the latter where an effect is sought to be produced by omitting details.

I have had hands come from the penitentiary to cut the grass —a second crop. They have cleaned up our croquet ground well. I have had heretofore the wickets put up and played on two occasions. The red bugs abound in the grass, and now about half a dozen are on my legs working assiduously towards the bones. I avoid scratching as I regard sores which must follow a sorrow which would more than counter-balance the fun—of scratching.

Give kisses to the babies and take, Darling, much love for yourself from ADELBERT

BAY VIEW, *August* 8, 1875

DEAR DEL: This is Sunday evening. Everyone is preparing for bed, as I shall be when I have finished my evening chat with you.

Mr. Farrington and Col. Kinsman came down last night. All but Kinsman, Mother and myself went around to Gloucester for a sail. The yacht was on her way to Boston for supplies to go to Martha's Vineyard next Tuesday. There are to be some races there, I believe.

Father has made a miserable speech. The occasion the O'Connell centennial. A thousand dollar dinner was given in Boston to one hundred guests, and he not to use too strong a phrase, made a goose of himself. He has left himself a loophole to squeeze out of, for he can say that he prefers the Catholic religion to none at all. Still I consider the speech as ill-advised, and smacking too much of the demagogue.

I had a letter from Carney yesterday, which I enclose. In my letter to him I only said that I wanted him to pay the note and interest to Father. I did not say that you would give me a note secured by mortgage on your mill—for you had not told me you would, and in a business letter I could not arrogate so much authority to myself as to say you would. If you will give me the note, the money paid will be invested, not "expended," and Carney's trouble as trustee will be over.

Write me what you will do, and think best, Del. I know that Father was pleased with my proposition to pay the five thousand, and surely it is better for us to be out of debt when we can as well as not. Of course, Carney is satisfied when the money is secured, and you surely do not object to doing this, at least until I am *thirty years old*.

We are all well, Sweetheart, and miss you very much. Edith asks every day "Whars Bapa." She will be able to talk to you when you see her again.

You ask about the trim of the "America." I do not think she was down by the head any more than when you saw her. But in the Sweepstakes race everything was taken out of her above the water-line—guns, boats, davits, chairs, water out of the cistern and ice out of the chest. Except when trimming the sails everyone on board laid down flat to the deck. It was a very exciting race, and the "Resolute" was so sure of winning. When they started the Capt. of the "Resolute" flung up his cap and exclaimed "We've got 'em." I wish you could have been here to have sailed in the race, you would have had great satisfaction in the victory.

Good night, Dearie. I think of you constantly, with a lonely longing to see your dear face. BLANCHE

BAY VIEW, *August* 9, 1875

DEAR DEL: This evening I had a great contest with Butler. He exhibited such complete depravity that I was forced to take him in hand.—It was laborious, but at last he was subdued and we parted with a kiss and his prayers. I expect to have some furious times this week—for Aunt Lottie and her boys are coming tomorrow. Mother asked Butler just how he was going to treat them. He said "I can fight them." "Oh, no, you must treat them like a little gentleman." "Oh, yes, I only fights bad boys." Not very encouraging, was it?

I had two letters from you today "as welcome as the flowers in May." You speak of the abuse they are heaping upon you from all sides.—After all, hard words do not hurt much, especially if you are conscious, as you must be, that you are right. When the history of this country is written some fifty or a hundred years hence, the only interesting events of this present time will be the events which have been and are taking place in the South, and the motives which prompted all the actors in them. Your record will be a pure and prominent one. You cannot tell how large a part you are to play in bringing those poor people out of "*darkness* and the shadow of death." A thankless task, I think I hear you say. Not so, Del, you surely ought to feel that as a body the colored people have been and are ready to express their gratitude. But I have preached enough, Sweetheart. The upshot of it all is to keep up a brave heart.

I have acted upon your advice, and have been painting again, on your Mother's picture of Edith. It is now a pretty picture, and a better likeness than the larger one. I hope to have it ready for your Father to take to Northfield. All are well and send kisses and love. BLANCHE

BAY VIEW, *August* 10, 1875

DEAR DEL: Aunt Nina, Lottie and the boys came down about four o'clock. We expected to have a week of quietude, by which I mean that Father would be away. A trip to Martha's Vineyard had been planned. Father, Paul, and Ben and some friends were to set sail this evening. Well, about five the ladies of this family went into the water. The water was quite warm, and delightful. I am learning to swim pretty well.

After tea, when the children had all been safely put to bed, Mr. French's coachman drove up to the house to tell Horace to hitch up and drive down the road to meet Father and seven gentlemen who were on foot, also to tell Harriet to get supper ready. This news, of course, threw everything into confusion, and it was decided that we had all better go to bed. There was a little feeling that such a party at such an hour of the night was an imposition, especially as we had every reason to suppose that they were on their way to Martha's Vineyard. At length the party arrived. I had not yet undressed. Lo and behold, your Father was one of the number. They met him at Salem. Harry French was another of the gentlemen, and with Mr. Hill, the architect, made up the seven. A good supper was ready for them, and after a little chatting, as it was late, we all came to bed. The reason of this sudden appearance was that they had a collision. In going out of the harbor they ran into a ferry boat, or the ferry boat ran into them, staved in some of the planks at the water line, smashed up the rigging, and did so much damage that it will take three or four days to repair her. The ferry boat lost her railing.

Your Father is in fine health and spirits and quite happy over the advance in wheat and flour. They had about sixty thousand bushels in wheat and flour when the rise came, and of course they will make a good year's work. *Fort Atkinson he says is doing finely.* "I told you so" is my reply.

Love and good night. BLANCHE

JACKSON, MISS., *August* 10, 1875

DEAR BLANCHE: I am back again to J. as you see. The weather at Bay St. Louis was more oppressive than here. I felt it more because I was on the street nearly all the time, going to and returning from meals. The "Bay" is eminently a French town. I met all the people at the hotel and found them a French-speaking people. The private boarding houses and their occupants are French also. I like the place all the better for it. They are far superior to the whiskey drinking, pistol carrying Anglo-Saxons of this latitude. The Bay is the best place in the state to live—yet, it was a lonesome place to your husband, who could not forget his wife and babies who were with him there but a short time previous.

I paid Pierre, our neighbor, $20.00 for repairing the banquette in front of our place. He raised or made a walk next to our fence, which will keep the water from running from the road into our yard.

Mary seemed to be getting along pretty well. She is sewing and ironing she says, and is making money enough to live by. I offered her ten dollars due her for the month, but she said as she did not need it she would not take it. She took $1.75 in change. I saw no particular cause to send her away. I imagine the evil influences there are far less than here for one like her. She and Battles were occupying the children's room, and when I suggested that they had better go to the cottage she said you told her to take the room she occupies. So the matter ended.

We left the Bay at one o'clock—arrived in N.O. in time for a leisurely dinner at the city hotel—to reach the train by street cars.

Upon entering the sleeping car my eyes fell upon Gen'l. Comstock. He had been at the mouth of the Mississippi River to examine Ead's work—an undertaking to get more water at the passes—it is known as the jetty system. Comstock was returning to Detroit, his regular station.

I found one letter from you this morning. I am glad it is so cool with you. I do not like this hot weather here. Though my health is excellent I can but believe a marked difference in one's vigor and energy must exist between this latitude and that of New England. This difference may not attract attention while we are feeling well, but I have no doubt the difference appears in all our efforts and works.

A Negro by the name of Hill, brother of the man killed in Holmes County by Lee and his friend Mills, threatened to kill Lee, and Saturday morning at nine o'clock was the hour fixed upon when they were to meet in the streets of Jackson and fight it out. They were arrested, and have agreed to suspend action till after the examination of Mills and Lee in Holmes Co. before a proper magistrate. The examination was to take place yesterday. I have not heard of the results. If Lee was thought or found guilty, Hill was to shoot him at sight.—Such is the white man's code, and to such a code must the poor Negro resort if he is to be anybody in this civilized and enlightened community. I have just been interrupted by a messenger from Holmes Co. who reports everything quiet there, and that the examination was put off till today.

It is near sunset—the shadows of the trees are lying on the green grass of our lawn. I hear Mrs. McKee who lives opposite singing a Scotch song and playing on the piano. An occasional cart rattles by.—So passes the day away.

Love for my Beautiful, and for our babies. ADELBERT

JACKSON, MISS., *August* 11, 1875

DEAR BLANCHE: I received two letters from you this morning dated the 4th and 5th.

I have unintentionally neglected to write on the business points you have heretofore presented. I would by all means claim eight percent interest on the Convers mortgage. You should not suffer by their neglect. You are clearly entitled to eight percent. Claim it. You can lose nothing by so doing. I do not think I would have advised you to pay my note to your father; but now you have done so I think it a wise act. If I ever have any money you shall be paid and I will feel easier to be owing you rather than your father. Thanks for your thoughtfulness.

I do not feel that I can advise you as to the disposition of the Convers money. It is true, dear one, that what is yours is mine and what is mine is yours; and that I ought to advise you in this as well as in all other matters. But the question with me is, am I competent to advise you wisely? Surely I can do so disinterestedly. Disinterestedly in this, that I will not consent for you to put it into the Ft. Atkinson business or in anything I am engaged in (not at this time surely). I do not propose that you shall lose a cent by me. A disinterested person is the best judge. Where a person needs money for his own business he cannot weigh accurately the chances—especially when it is used to help him from bad luck to good. As to myself—I have not handled money enough to have unqualified confidence in my own judgement. Those who make money and keep it know the best. This money your father has made, and you would not be likely to lose it by following his advice.

By and by, when we know more of business matters, we can act ourselves. If the money be put into bonds, they can be converted any day. A good mortgage is good—as real estate is low, an investment in it when it reaches its lowest ebb might be a good speculation. A chance to speculate on others' necessities usually proves the most lucrative.

You and I may be right, theoretically, in our views, but would not your father be more competent to *act?* You see, I doubt my judgement—I do not want to be a party to the loss of your money. Your father's judgement is good—the money in bonds will be readily convertible—and we need not have any pride of opinion in this matter *now*, whatever we may have one of these days, when we shall have made a fortune.

It has just occurred to me that I write that you might, as your father suggests, buy bonds which will pay six or seven (he estimates seven) percent, and if the opportunity presents itself do as he is now doing; that is, raise money equal to or in excess of the amount in bonds for which but a small interest need be paid, and invest it in the West or elsewhere where a much larger interest can be obtained.

You may think I have taken much ink, paper, and time to say little. I have been trying to reason both with you and myself. Please ask your father if ten thousand dollars of U.S. bonds as security will enable one to borrow more than that sum. This is the first time I was ever called upon to invest money—actual hard cash—and I hesitate as to the *how*.

Ask my father about Western investments, if he has not already left you and gone West. Of course, you shall be secured by a mortgage on the mill.

Love, for you and for the babies. ADELBERT

BAY VIEW ON CAPE ANN, *August* 12, 1875

DEAR DEL: I did not write you last night—for when night came I was so tired I could hardly see. In the first place, fearing that your Father would get up early and feel lonesome, I tumbled out with the children about six o'clock.

By the time I was dressed it was half past six, and I went down stairs to find your Father and mine drinking seltzer and rum. Father was up early to go to Boston. We sat down and continued our little conversation of the night before, which ceased about half past eleven. Your Father is very sorry that he wrote you such a *harsh* letter about adorning the soil of Mississippi. I asked him how he would like to have us live in St. Paul. He seemed to think that Northfield was the place. I then suggested New York. He thought that would be as well, in a business point of view, as someone was needed East all of the time. I showed him your ladder, as printed by the Patent Office. He seemed much taken with the idea, and wanted me to give him the drawings so that he could have one made for trial at Northfield. I told him I would, when I had shown it to Father, as you also wanted his opinion. It was lying on the table in the parlor in the large envelope. I find the envelope, but the inclosure is gone, and I think he must have taken it with him. I will write today and ask. Your letters patent also came today. I showed them to Father. He would not express an opinion, but I think he was pleased with it.

Yesterday morning Paul, Ben and your Father went out fishing. They caught about twenty small mackerel and a string of cunners. In the afternoon, your Father, Butler, Ben and I went over to the mouth of the Ipswich River to fish.

Your Father managed the sailing of the little lap streak boat we had, and as there was a fine breeze, we had a fine sail of six miles, three there and three back. Our luck in fishing was not great, only a few mackerel.

I thought he would be better pleased and contented if I went too, and though as you know not a great sailor, I risked it and enjoyed the sail.

I told your Father that you might meet him in Chicago, and let him read your letter. I did all that I could to keep him, so did Mother and Father, who promised if he would stay over, to go out to Halibut Point cod-fishing. Mother got clams for a chowder for dinner. All to no purpose. He would go because he had some business in New York and he must get on to Chicago or to Northfield by the fifteenth. He thought that perhaps you could spare a day or so more and run up to see your Mother, who it appears was quite ill last spring, although perfectly well now. So determined was he to go that we were forced to let him have his own way, and Horace drove him over to Gloucester at nine this morning. I am to write, or telegraph, if I have any more news from you, to the Stevens House.

Butler behaved his prettiest while his grandfather was here. I had given him a bad reputation, and your Father seemed to think I had slandered him. Edith pleased him much. He thinks her more like you than the others. The baby he pronounces a Southern baby, she is so frail-looking, but says she resembles me, whom he is delighted to see in such fine condition. I showed him Edith's portrait. He liked it much, but when I showed him the full figure he thought that the prettiest picture, although not such a pretty face or good likeness as the head. I proposed he should take the head with him and suggested that he could have it varnished in about six months or a year. He finally thought I had better send it by John, who will be on soon. I think he wants it all varnished and finished before he takes it. The thought of selecting the frame was, perhaps, burdensome. I will try to do it myself before John comes. He thought it the most life-like face he had ever seen, and was puzzled that the eyes moved when he did.

Love from BLANCHE

BAY VIEW ON CAPE ANN, *August* 14, 1875

DEAR DEL: This is Sunday night, and as usual I am writing for both Saturday and Sunday. I wrote a letter to Mary yesterday in which I told her how much she had annoyed me, and directed her to move the children's bed into one of the back rooms in the cottage, to put the paints in the store room and the pieces of wood to be saved into the hen house, and use that little room for her clothes. To clean up the house, and lock it up. She did not tell you the truth when she said I had told her to occupy the children's room. On the contrary, I had distinctly forbidden it, and told her she was to take Lizzie's room. Of course I had no idea Battles was to be with her, and made no provision for him. She seems to me a little crazy. Perhaps my letter will bring her to her senses.

I am glad that you found things looking so well. As the yellow fever is at Pascagoula, I doubt if you go to the Bay again this summer. Do not run any risks. It makes me shudder to think of it. If your letters do not come regularly I shall feel sure you are sick. I am convinced that the fault is in the mail, not in you Del, at present, for when a day passes without bringing me a letter, the next day usually brings me two, unless you say that you have not written.

Here we are very quiet. Mrs. Read, Mrs. Pearson and the boys are still here. They get on nicely with Butler, or he with them, and there has not been a single contest. Aunt Lottie's boys behave very well, much better than I should have thought they could, under her method of training. The baby can crawl all about the floor, and has another tooth. Edith cries less and is more and more attractive. Your Father admired her very much, and quite aroused the indignation of the servants by pronouncing her, in his judgement, the prettiest of the family.

Butler came to me this morning before I was out of bed and asked me if he might have "two apples." "No," I said, "one is enough for you, you can have one, and get one for your sister also." "I wants two, Mama." "Why do you want two? One at a time is enough." "Can I have another?" "Oh, hoh, so you have had one already." He looked a little sheepish and said "Yes." I laughed and told him he might have two if that meant he was only to get one more. Don't you think he was rather cute about it? He evidently thought that if I knew he had already eaten one I might not allow him another, besides he had taken the first without permission. So he was trying to cover the ground by asking for two.

Father, Ben and the Frenchs have gone over to Rye Beach in the yacht. There has been a *fine* breeze and they must have had a *fine* sail. I continue the daily bathing, and I think, feel better for it. After the first plunge I do not feel cold, and it is really very refreshing. We have been having some rather warm days, but the nights are cool enough for us to pull up the blankets and I rise two or three times in the night to see that the children are covered. As the windows are left open, I fear that they may take cold. Edith is tossing restlessly, and seems to want my attention. She no doubt thinks it is time for me to go to bed. So I will say good night, with love.

BLANCHE

JACKSON, MISS., *August* 15, 1875

DEAR BLANCHE: This has been a very quiet Sunday with me. I have had but two or three callers. All the rest of the time has been devoted to reading.

I am feeling better today.

Lee and Packer returned last night. They have not yet

called on me. They probably feel ashamed to do so, although George says Lee is in excellent spirits. He certainly has lost all political influence there.

The contest in this city between aspiring congressmen is spirited. Delegates to the nominating convention have been chosen and McKee's friends are trying to have them instructed for him, but thus far have signally failed. A meeting was held in the courthouse yesterday to instruct. It met in the afternoon and when I went to bed at eleven o'clock the silence of the night was disturbed by shouts and noise. But who will win it is hard to tell.

I had seen an abstract of your father's speech at O'Connell's Centennial, and quite agree with you in your criticism. Why does he do such foolish things? He loses far more than he gains. There is no wisdom or sense in taking the unpopular side because it is unpopular. Your father evidently is always for the under dog in the fight—and yet the "under dog" may often be wholly in the wrong. Right and principle for which we all fight ought generally, as they are, to be "on top."

I am sorry to hear that our son is so pugnacious or as you say, depraved. I hope with the aid of the birch he will outgrow it.

Love to all my beloved ones. ADELBERT

BAY VIEW ON CAPE ANN, *August* 16, 1875

DEAR DEL: Last night Edith seemed restless and feverish when I went to bed. Towards morning she woke up with the nightmare and I took her into my bed. Of course the baby thought it would be a good time for her to make a fuss. As a consequence I did not enjoy the morning hours, and began the day rather drowsily. Edith did not feel sprightly, but slept on the bed in Paul's room. I took off her shoes and stockings and tried to perfect the foot in her picture. It was slow work, but I made an advance.

After dinner (I painted on Edith's picture until that time) Mother induced me to mount a step ladder on an ironing table in the dining room and color the bunches of grapes which are frescoed on the ceiling in the four corners of the room. I painted two of the corners, and she is highly delighted with them. I suppose I shall have to complete the others as well as the center piece, which is a wreath of grapes and leaves. Perhaps you will remember to what I refer—the ceiling is simply painted in brownish tints, and lacks color. What do you think of having your wife turn frescoe painter? It is certainly neck-breaking work.

I will write Mr. Carney that you will give me a mortgage on the mill at Fort Atkinson. By the way, what was done with the old mortgage? As this will be an investment, there can be no objection under the terms of the trust, but unless the money is secured in some such way I doubt if Carney will be willing to let me use it until I am thirty, or a year and a half longer.

Love from the babies (your youngest promises to be a scold). Good night, BLANCHE

BAY VIEW ON CAPE ANN, *August* 17, 1875

DEAR DEL: I received your letter saying that you were bilious and that Col. Warner acted as your medical attendant. I have no doubt his advice will be quite as beneficial if not more so than that of the *resident* physicians of Mississippi. Notwithstanding the attempted joke, Love, I shall not feel at ease until I hear that you are entirely well. You speak of dieting. My impression is that that is all you have done since you went South. I am sure that you have not overeaten of that restaurant fare—and you, yourself, write that your appetite has not been good. So do not continue the dieting system too long—you will need vigor for your work this fall.

Sam speaks of another mill. The property may some day be valuable, but I do not think, sanguine, as I am, that it would be well to have any more invested in *flour mills*. I should rather vary the enterprise.

You do not write that you are going to Chicago or Northfield. Your Father will be a good deal disappointed, as he fully expected to see you. He said they would keep on with the mills until you got through with that political business and then he should expect you to attend to your share of the work—that you could attend to business East, and make far more than you can get in Mississippi.

Butler is at my side while I write, grumbling because I will not let him go in wading. He has not improved much since you left, except about going to bed. Now he allows Anna to undress him—then I go up to hear him say his prayers—sing "Twinkle little star" once, and leave him. He is perfectly content with the arrangement. Edith still stays close by me. The baby also cries when I leave her, and is showing a great deal of temper. *Your* children, Sweetheart, are hard to manage. Love, BLANCHE

JACKSON, MISS., *August* 17, 1875

DEAR BLANCHE: I feel better today than I have since Friday last. I do not eat much, and consequently feel a little weak. My tongue is somewhat coated. I take six grains of quinine a day. I will be quite well tomorrow, I have no doubt.

Yesterday afternoon, shortly after I had sent your letter to the P.O. I heard three or four pistol shots about a square off, and immediately the hum of excited voices; and saw the people running. It was the shooting of one colored man by another because improper conversation or remarks were made to his (the assailant's) wife by the person shot. It is believed the wounds will prove fatal. The act is the natural outgrowth of the morality of this section, and especially due to the acquittal of Taz Jones, who killed Williams here last spring. I cannot express my disgust at such depravity and my regrets that with such my daily life is mixed. This will be a great country when its order of civilization shall be improved, but that will not occur in my day and generation.

You have seen the yellow fever news. I see it is reported that there is one case in New Orleans. If so, it may spread. There is plenty of time for it to do so. I shall keep a sharp watch out, and will studiously avoid it.

I am just now reading a little law, and a little of anything I can get hold of. If you get the novel I have just finished, *The Way We Live Now* by Trollope, tell me if Melmotte, he around whom the story swings, reminds you of anyone you know in any particular. I will not make any suggestion.

During all the time I have been writing this letter I have been compelled to stop every half minute to slash with my towel the swarms of mosquitoes which are pestering me—they distract.

Love for my dear wife and babies from ADELBERT

JACKSON, MISS., *August* 18, 1875

DEAR BLANCHE: I am quite well today. I went to the office and attended to my business and took my dinner at the restaurant for the first time since Friday. I had tea, toast, and half a broiled chicken. I am the better for my dinner. From the restaurant I went to the book-store to buy a novel, and while there ordered Gen'l. Sherman's reminiscences of the rebellion. My order was taken, but the shop man, not knowing me, asked for my name! A fair illustration of our intimacy with our political opponents.

Col. or Gen'l. Warner's chances for Congress are excellent. The indications now are that he will be nominated. In this district they had a contest for this county yesterday and Secretary Hill was victorious. Mr. McKee was signally defeated. The chances here are now in Hill's favor. I shall be much pleased to see McKee beaten.

Wells, of Holly Springs, has been lying about me and bringing French into the case. It is expected, so I am informed today, that certain friends of mine will make him swallow his lies or fight. I protest against pistols. I give the item to show how strong the friendly feeling towards me is on the part of some of those near me.

I am glad you made Father's visit a pleasant one to him, and, also, that in trying to please him you, yourself, found pleasure. I wish he had stayed longer, for I know he enjoys his visits at your father's, and likes you as much as one can like one not of their own flesh and blood. I wonder he did not stay and go around to Newport in the yacht to participate in the races.

The examination of Lee is still in progress. Packer has just brought me a telegram bearing the news of Howe's renomination. Wells, his opposing candidate, bolted the convention but with every bogus delegate he could get he failed to have enough for a quorum. Howe was nominated by a vote of thirty-five (35) to one (1).

I send love for my Beautiful and our babies.

ADELBERT

JACKSON, MISS., *August* 19, 1875

DEAR BLANCHE: I was much amused at your account of your effort to get into water "over your head." The age of boys when they find themselves in your frame of mind is from six to eight years. I am very proud of your success, only when once firmly ahold of the ledge, I fail to see the necessity of cutting your fingers and toes by hasty scrambling. But then you were there and knew best. Edith must be educated with Butler on this water question and not live nearly half a century (?) as her mother did before she *dare* plunge in over her head. Woman's rights must and shall be preserved.

Warner's convention will meet tomorrow, and everybody is going up to Canton on the evening's train to see it out. The chances are now in his favor. He says his wife does not know he is running.

Wells played a very scurvy trick. Being beaten, he would

not let his delegates go to the court house where the convention was to be held, but kept them in a private boarding house he had hired, and then held his convention and telegraphed to the world that he had been unanimously elected! Stearns, one of his men, and the chairman of the congressional committee, and the proper one to call the convention to order would not do so, but deserted and went to Wells. The soreheads sustain W. Their motto is anything to beat me. And they would prefer defeat to our party rather than to see me succeed. If they only knew my own indifference—even my determination not to take another office, they would be ashamed of their own extravagances.

The leak in our house at the Bay was in the roof through the shingles. You may remember that standing on the stairs you could see the light of the heavens through chinks in the roof. There was a high wind from the east, and the rain was driven through the shingles. That is the trouble. I do not think we need do anything about it now. We had better wait till next fall before we put on any more repairs.

I infer from your letters that Father no longer wishes to sell the mill, for you say he thinks New York would be a good place for us to settle. He certainly would not think so if it were not in connection with his business.

Love for you and our babies, ADELBERT

BAY VIEW ON CAPE ANN, *August* 20, 1875

DEAR DEL: I had two letters from you this morning, which relieved my mind very much, for I was fearful you were quite ill. As I write, the children are playing about—Butler as usual has just imposed upon Edith, she eases her mind by repeated loud yells—I come to the rescue and threaten to make a disturbance if they do not stop making such a row. Butler says in a low tone to Edith, "Go away, you hateful thing, you are nothing but a booby." "You're a booby," retorts Miss Edith. "No, I am not a booby, you are a booby." Now their attention is diverted. Butler is singing, Edith joins in with her little voice. "Stop your singing," roars Butler. "You don't know how to sing, you make too much noise." Poor Edith evidently thinks his judgment good and ceases. So they go, from morning till night. Can you not seem to see and hear them?

My frescoing proceeds finely. Tomorrow I shall finish it, I hope. You will pronounce it very well done, and think it improves the looks of the room greatly. When I began the grapes, of which there are thirteen bunches, I did not know how to do them very well, but I have improved, so that I can now do them nicely and quickly. In this, it is no waste of time.

Good night, Dearie. Your bad children join me with love.

BLANCHE

JACKSON, MISS., *August* 21, 1875

DEAR BLANCHE: This being the 21st of the month reminds me that the 21st day of the month (July) was our wedding day and the 22nd day of August, tomorrow, will be Butler's birthday. Tomorrow he will be four years old. He enters upon boyhood's estate. When I think how brief the time since we were wed, and how fast it flees by us, I realize that youth for us is passing, and our children are beginning to present their claims as representatives of another generation. Yet I can hardly realize we shall ever be old folks. Not at least for many and many a year.

Yesterday Warner was nominated for Congress. There is great dissatisfaction at the way his friends managed the convention. This dissatisfaction is felt of course by his opponents. The complaint is he was not just in his treatment of delegates —ruling out his enemies and ruling in his friends. I do not think there will be any split in that district.

This day has been like all my days. I find myself better than I have been of late. I ate, for me, an enormous dinner. I think I could relish a bowl-full of clam chowder. By the way, they can clams. I have seen them at Father's in Minn. It would be well to get a few cans for our use here. Also some of the Newburyport herrings.

Love and kisses for those I love. ADELBERT

JACKSON, MISS., *August* 22, 1875

DEAR BLANCHE: I have done literally nothing this Sunday. As usual my breakfast was brought me at eight and I got out of bed to let George in. I was a little sleepy this morning as Secretary Hill continued his call till one o'clock this morning.

Before I had finished my papers this morning Warner walked in and we had a long chat. Before he went "Bob" Alcorn came in and a little later Capt. Shaughnessy. The last one did not go till three o'clock. My dinner was brought at half past two—My guest refused to share it with me.

Since writing you last night I have not been out of my room but for a few minutes, and have only seen the persons whose names I give. So you see I am living a very quiet life here, by and with myself.

Need I tell you I miss you and the babies a great deal? And yet, while I would like to have you with me now I know it is best you should be where you are—and I would be the more content to be with you away from here than to have you here with me.

Our state convention will meet here on Tuesday next. I shall advocate a short canvass. If we have one only during the month of October I may be able to visit Father during Sept. I send love to you and the babies. ADELBERT

BAY VIEW ON CAPE ANN, *August* 23, 1875

DEAR DEL: Two letters came for me today, but not three as I had hoped. I am troubled that you cannot say that you are perfectly well. Remember my advice, not too fast, too much or too long.

All here are well, as usual. Edith is happy in the doll which you bought her. I found it was so strong that it was likely to last a long time, so concluded it was worthy of a dress. Edith keeps it constantly by her, and prefers to go to sleep with the doll beside her. I am satisfied that you should take advantage of one of your few opportunities, and say "I told you so."

Father and Hattie returned this evening. The "America" did not sail in the race, for the course was over too shallow waters. Only small boats took part. The "America" went on to Newport from Oak Bluffs and there Father, Hattie and the Frenches left her, as the gentlemen had to return to their business. Paul and Ben will be home tomorrow or next day.

Young Blair—son of Frank—came this morning. He is to be Ben's roommate this year. He has been stopping for some time over at Eastern Point with his brother's wife. I should say that he seems to be a nice boy. He stands very high in his class, and we hope as he is very studious, that he will be of some advantage to Ben. They will have to be at the Point next Saturday.—Poor Ben has not much more time for amusement.

I was rejoiced to hear that your friends are likely to be successful. How pleased Mrs. Warner will be to go to Washington. Was it not a great disappointment to Wells to lose the nomination? May all your enemies be similarly confounded.

What are your prospects, Del? Is it too soon to judge? Love for my Sweetheart. BLANCHE

JACKSON, MISS., *August 23*, 1875

DEAR BLANCHE: Last evening I had a call from Judge Hill of Vicksburg, and later one from Judge Warren. The former is very bitter towards Warren. He seems to indicate that his county will not vote for Warner. It is an indication of the strength of the feeling among the candidates, and while the masses of our party are united and are content to work and vote for the candidates whoever they may be, our party is more susceptible to harm from ambitious men than parties usually are.

Gibbs has returned with his family. He says he had no fear of the yellow fever at the Bay. He also says it has about disappeared from Pascagoula. I had a telegram from there this morning to the same effect. All danger seems to have passed away. I was fearful we might have a general epidemic this fall, but now I think otherwise. The season has been exceedingly healthy everywhere in the state up to the present time, and I doubt if an epidemic could get a foot hold before frost.

The delegates are assembling for the convention day after tomorrow. I doubt if many will come. Raymond is fighting hard for young Holland, who will probably be defeated.

You see I have nothing new today. I am well, and gladly see the days pass so rapidly. I send love for all.

ADELBERT

JACKSON, MISS., *August 24*, 1875

DEAR BLANCHE: Another day has gone, much as they do of late except that I have talked a little more and listened a great deal more. Tomorrow the convention will assemble, and the delegates are coming in. Our party is to be here through its delegates to select a candidate for State Treasurer. There does not seem to be much feeling, except as between the two candidates. I think I have told you before that Holland, Raymond's friend, will probably be beaten. Howe, though a friend of R., is against him in this.

Then, as a matter of much interest, perhaps of chief interest with some, my opponents will make an attempt to open war on me. Those who are fighting me are men who by their acts have shown a disposition to destroy the party. I do not think they will make any progress. In fact, I am indifferent as to what they do. Not exactly that—I can say I am not so concerned as I might once have been.

I suppose you will soon be preparing to return to Lowell. If

I mistake not, you do not remain at the Bay (Cape) much after the first of Sept. I see they have had a heavy frost in the Northwest already.

I see a crowd of visitors coming—so I must stop.

Love, ADELBERT

BAY VIEW ON CAPE ANN, *August* 26, 1875

DEAR DEL: I think, Del, if possible you should go to Northfield in September. In the first place the trip will be of benefit to you, and it would be well for your business arrangements. Then again, your Father and Mother are most anxious to see you. Your Father told me to tell you that he would pay your expenses if you would come—if it was only for a day. He would like more, but would be content with that. I am more especially interested in your going from the fact that I think the change would be of benefit and would tone up your system. You cannot get on well with tea and toast, Del, and must insist upon the people at the restaurant putting on the beef to broil, not stew or fry—or a chicken. If they will not do it, George can. He was cook for his mistress, and if you told him to broil a chicken or a piece of beefsteak or bake a potato, he could do it for you. I know you are very careless about what you have to eat, but that will not do. In order to work you must have proper nourishment and in that debilitating climate it is especially needed. Mind what I say, Sweetheart, or there will be trouble in store for you in the future.

The babies are not in perfect condition, but are doing pretty well for all that. Butler has a cold, and the baby is getting another tooth. Edith is perfectly well and happy. I bought a baby carriage for her doll in Gloucester on my way home from Boston, and a trombone for Butler. They were very much delighted. Butler had asked me to buy him "a band," and he seems to think that he has one. I have made a hat for Bessie, and she sits up in state while Edith pushes her about from place to place all day long.

Love, Dearie. BLANCHE

JACKSON, MISS., *August* 26, 1875

DEAR BLANCHE: I did not write you yesterday as the convention occupied all my thoughts. Although my few enemies have made much noise of late, the opposition to me in the convention dwindled to contemptible proportions. Its organization and management was wholly in my interest. In fact, the chairman of the convention, Col. Morgan, and Howe, who was a member, came to me to ask my permission to let my name be put by an endorsement of the convention before the people as the Republican candidate for the U.S. Senate. I refused to consent to it. They intimated they would do so if any opposition was offered to my endorsement as Governor. Holland was beaten as candidate for State Treasurer. Buchanan was successful. Raymond feels badly over his defeat, as he regards it as a personal matter. I could have turned the tide either way, but it was due the party that I should remain a neutral. The vote stood Holland 110, Buchanan 121. The office belonged to a Southern Republican, and though I am wholly a friend of Raymond's I could not in my position use my influence for his candidate.

I was unanimously endorsed in the resolutions. Pease and company were in the convention, but they did not have the moral courage to utter one word against the resolution. There was one exception, Mr. Lake—but they jeered him into silence. He was so much under the influence of liquor that he was not able to read the resolution, endorsing me, yet he tried to speak against it. They say his effort put the whole convention in good humor by the ludicrousness of his effort, and the response he received. They would cheer me, thus interrupting his remarks. Then he would say the mob would not let him speak—then many voices would say "go on" "go on"—"read the section" etc. Then he would try again, only being able to read the number of the section—No. 10— Then cries of "read," "read," "speak," "three cheers for Ames" etc. etc. till finally he subsided, being even himself in good humor and forgetting to vote in the negative when the question was put. The convention did not adjourn till about half past three this morning. The long session was due to the delay in deciding questions between contesting delegations from some half dozen counties. It was a tiresome day to me. In addition to seeing everybody I had on my mind the thought that I must make a speech to the convention. I expected to be called upon any moment after they assembled, but they did not organize till midnight. When I heard of the delay—that it would be into the small hours of the morning before I could get an opportunity to *begin* I gave up my purpose and at midnight I went to bed. Thinking, knowing I can speak better on an empty stomach, I would not eat my supper, and as I say midnight found me supperless —my supper being on my table, cold. A cup of tea (so called) and a piece of bread sufficed. I tossed on my bed for an hour or so, hearing the echoes from the convention as they floated over the night air. This morning I have seen many who could not get out of town. They all seemed pleased with the work of last night—especially are my friends jubilant.

Judge Hill is lying on my sofa fighting mosquitoes, as I am here, while writing.

Love to my loved ones. ADELBERT

BAY VIEW ON CAPE ANN, *August 27*, 1875

DEAR DEL: One of our household has gone. Ben started for West Point at noon. He felt badly to go, as we all did to have him, but I think he looks forward cheerfully to the work which lies before him. Paul returned in time to see Ben. The yacht had head winds all the way from Newport so that they did not make very good time. Paul says the expense of running the yacht is enormous. While at Martha's Vineyard there were twenty people dining there every day. Father asked everybody on board and then tried to feed them.

We shall remain here another week, and then go to Lowell. There is a great deal to do for the children, something for myself, and painting without end, if I undertake what I desire to accomplish. I want to get that debt to Mr. Chadwick paid, although it seems a most conceited thing, both as a woman and an attempted artist, for me to give my portrait painted by myself. However, Father and Mother seem to think it right. Perhaps they can judge better than I.

Your youngest daughter is quite a character. She is far more pugnacious than Edith, perhaps because she has not had Butler to keep her in subjection. If they attempt to take anything away from her, she strikes and fights for it with real venom. Last night, after nursing her for nearly an hour and finding that she would not go to sleep, I laid her down on the mattress, and put my face beside of her, trying to soothe her off to sleep. She tried to slap it, and then getting on her hands and knees, set her little wedges into my cheek. They were too small to bite much, but tickled, and I laughed. She joined with great glee, and I allowed her to play about the floor until I was undressed. She can appreciate her situation when she thinks she has the best of it. Love, BLANCHE

JACKSON, MISS., *August 27*, 1875

DEAR BLANCHE: I have been quite busy today. I went to bed early last night, so early that I failed to see a number of callers who came to the gate and turned back because all was dark in the Mansion. This morning I got up early and fully completed my toilet before breakfast. I not only took a bath and shaved, but in the industry of the hour washed my watch chain which was so black and dirty as to quickly soil my white vests. Of course, while washing the chain I could but think that a man's wife should do that for him. But we know all wives are not alike.

Let me say here, by way of a parenthesis that the mosquitoes are "awful"—hungry and numerous—and nowhere do they abound as in my chamber. If you and the children were here, they would bite you and let me alone. What a lot of drawbacks there are in life.

While reading my mail this morning the Board of Trustees for Alcorn University came in and we had a meeting which continued till twelve o'clock. Then I went to the office—at three I had dinner—have just returned again to my room.

The convention to nominate a congressman for this Dist. is now in session here. The chances have been in favor of Hill, but I believe his men bungled in the organization of the convention and he may miss it, through the committee on credentials. Judge Brown is the most sanguine—and just now Shaughnessey next. I still think Hill will get it. All of our prominent men are here. I shall succeed in having a committee sent on to Washington. Some of them are insisting that I go with them. I do not think I should go—furthermore I feel too poor to go. But if they persist I will go. I doubt if they do persist, especially now when Lieut. Gov. Davis is under charges of receiving money for a pardon granted while Acting Governor. He was before a committing court for examination the other day, but waived it and was put under bonds to appear at the next session of the Circuit Court. His case *looks* very bad. I think our party is afraid of him, and would regret to see me absent myself for even the shortest possible time. Should I go to W. I shall keep on a day or two longer and pay a visit to my world—my Beautiful wife and babies so far away.

Ben Israel is to be at West Point tomorrow, I have no doubt, as the 28th is the day the furlough class returns. Well, he will have the satisfaction of knowing he has had the best opportunity of having a "good time" of any boy in the country. Human nature is such that those boys without his opportunities have been no less happy in their way, many being really happier. Boys ought to be poor. What a jolly chance we will give ours.

I send you, Beloved, love, ADELBERT

JACKSON, MISS., *August* 28, 1875

DEAR BLANCHE: About three o'clock this morning I was awakened by loud shouts, and heard the name of "Hill" called by what was evidently the Congressional Convention at the State House. It was evidence of his nomination. Shortly after Mr. Osborne came home and stated that Hill had been nominated. He had a hard fight, but was at last victorious. McKee was not put in nomination. He received three votes, however, which, I have no doubt, indicated his whole strength. Shaughnessey was Hill's chief opponent. McKee is most thoroughly beaten, and he shows it in his bearing. He must have spent a great deal of money. He has been going night and day. Raymond told me a few days since that he had suggested to Mrs. McKee that last winter I offered peace to her husband if he would join me in keeping down troubles in Vicksburg. She replied that then Gov. A. was in trouble, and had more on hand than he could attend to. Which evidently was sufficient cause why her husband would not aid me, thinking I would fail and my failure would redound to his advantage. Result—he has been ignominiously defeated. In fact, the conventions thus far, state and congressional, have all been in my favor, and my friends have come forth triumphant and my enemies laid in the dust.

We are sending a committee on to Washington. Howe is of the number. He left this afternoon at 5 o'clock for Mass. So did Warren. I felt much like going with them.

I send love, to you, Darling and to our babies.

ADELBERT

BAY VIEW ON CAPE ANN, *August* 29, 1875

DEAR DEL: This is Sunday evening, and I believe for once I am correct about the date.

I have not much news to tell you, as nothing of importance has happened here. Katie Parker has a little girl, born last Tuesday.

The yacht starts Wednesday for New York. It is Col. French's party. Father will probably join it in New York.

The last of this week or the middle of next we shall go to Lowell. I am in no haste, for the children are quite well, and they might not be there, certainly not unless the weather grows cool. Here it is delightful.

Did I tell you that my frescoing is considered a great success by everybody except Father. He has not as yet expressed an opinion. I am not sure that he does not resent having the change made without his sanction. Still I cannot help that, and he will no doubt feel reconciled as it is a great improvement.

Every day after bathing we have some hot lemonade brought up stairs. There is no stick in it, and your son has a fancy, although he does not go into the water, that he is entitled to a share of the entertainment. So he is always on hand at such times. He usually provides himself with a small glass from the dining room. This is the result of experience, as he has been sent down for one several times. Today he was unfortunate, or, as he expressed it those "nasty stairs made me slip." The glass fell and broke in pieces. Poor Butler was quite overpowered, and like his Father made himself the aggrieved individual. So much so that his grandmother had to comfort him instead of scolding for his carelessness. Like Father, like son, in this connection. I will say I love my boy with all my heart.

BLANCHE

JACKSON, MISS., *August* 29, 1875

DEAR BLANCHE: This has been one of the hottest days of the month. It is now, as the day departs, more sultry than it has been at any earlier hour. This Sunday I have had a succession of visitors. First came Raymond and then Bruce and Hill. The two latter stayed for three hours or more. Then came Warner, and before he went Raymond came. Lee and Packer were on the look out for their departure, and I had but time to write the few lines at the beginning of this letter when they entered.

I have been indicating that I might go on to Washington but I will not be able to do so. I must remain here the whole time till the election. You say that your Mother would like to see us occupying her house in Washington. This she cannot see, for I am fully determined not to accept the Senatorship if I can get it. I do not like anything in the life I lead here, and I know we will be happier elsewhere, and elsewhere we will go.

I will not commit to paper my many reasons, but that I can convince you of the correctness of my position I firmly believe.

George has just brought in my supper, and if this is to go out in tonight's mail I must close now; though I had intended a long chat with you today.

I send as ever, much love to my Beautiful wife and our babies.

ADELBERT

BAY VIEW ON CAPE ANN, *August* 30, 1875

DEAR DEL: I am very glad to hear that the Convention was so satisfactory. You must have felt quite elated. Why did you object to having your name used, or rather endorsed for U.S. Senator? Was it because you do not intend to take the position, or because you thought it more politic? Decide nothing rashly Del. Although your Father would like so much to have you join business with them, still he would not counsel such a move, for he said when he was here that you had made a mistake in not taking it the last time when you could get it, that the Ameses were all too honest. I speak of this in order that you may not allow your present unpleasant life to so far influence your decision that there may be danger that in the future when you have forgotten the discomforts you may regret it.

Oh! I have another little bit of news for you. Phil's wife has signed an engagement to sing for the next four years in all the principal cities of Europe, and can spend two months of each year in the United States. The offer was liberal, so much so that she did not hesitate to accept. I suppose now there is no doubt but that she will be a success. Phil writes to his mother, "Good God, can I stand this sort of thing for four years longer." It is worse for him than if he were a woman, and wife of a sea Captain. Isn't it?

Enough gossip for today. Love Sweetheart. We are not so badly off as some people. Don't be downhearted.

BLANCHE

JACKSON, MISS., *August* 30, 1875

DEAR BLANCHE: My positive determination not to accept another office in this state, as presented in my letter of yesterday, must have startled you, coming as it did so quickly after the action of favorable conventions of the people. I am constantly thinking of my life and surroundings here, and have calmly and deliberately arrived at this conclusion. After writing you as I did last night I felt relieved of a great burden. I know I would be happier elsewhere, and I question not that it will be better for you and our children for me to abandon politics here at the earliest possible date. I was glad to get out of the army into civil life, and I know I shall be far more gratified to leave politics, such as I know it, and attend to any honorable business. I am growing day by day more and more dissatisfied, and I am sure when you hear all I have to say you will agree with me. We can visit your Mother at her house in Washington, if she will be content with such a compromise, and our business (?) permits, but beyond that we are not prepared to go. So please do not set your heart on our being a Senator.

This has been a very quiet day—everybody has gone away. It is warm, with slight showers. The ground was well soaked by the shower of last night.

I am glad to learn that Father does not feel that my action hurt his financial condition, and that he is in good humor.

John T. will be in Mass. soon and I suppose you will get his side of the case.

I send love to my loved ones—whom I miss a great deal.

ADELBERT

BAY VIEW AT CAPE ANN, *August* 31, 1875

DEAR DEL: I have been painting all day on the foot in Edith's picture. It is very difficult. Edith took her nap on the table placed under the window for a good light, and her little bare foot laid up for a model. Ah, well! I suppose I have advanced some, and must be content with small favors.

I received a letter from Mary this morning which I enclose. You can judge from the tone of it that my letter to her produced rather a disturbing effect. Poor Mary. She finds life pretty hard, and it is entirely in consequence of her own misdeeds.

You will be amused to hear that I am collecting peach stones for our *plantation* at the Bay. Father brought some very large and delicious ones from Boston, and I thought of our mile and determined to try some of the stones there. Of course peaches like other fruit have to be grafted to insure successful fruit. Still if you run your risk the seeds may produce some delicious varieties. At any rate, we will try. There is no harm in that. Your Father and Mother will spend part of the winter at the Bay. If they are there in February they can plant for us.

I have Edith's small portrait all ready for Paul to take to Boston tomorrow for a frame. He thinks some of going West to try some shooting with your Father. But whether he goes or not it is better to have the picture framed. It will then be ready for John when he comes on.

Butler seems to have that same kind of a cold which you will remember by his sneezing five or six times in succession. His eyes are a good deal inflamed and he cannot breathe through his nose. This makes him quite restless at night, and although he has no fever he kicks the clothes off frequently and calls me up to put them on again. Ordinarily I should advise him to pull the blankets up himself—but now fearing that he will not do so, and fall asleep uncovered, catching more cold, I jump up four and five times in answer to his calls. It seems to me something like a hay fever. The others are well. The baby crawling all about the floor, and Edith playing with her inseparable dolly and carriage, from morning 'till night.

Love Sweetheart. Remember my advice to have George cook your meat for you. BLANCHE

JACKSON, MISS., *August* 31, 1875

DEAR BLANCHE: Your letter describing your trip to Boston was quite entertaining, possessing as it did just a spice of romance. Was it not rather humiliating to get lost, after such a successful day? I think you must have enjoyed the trip, both because of the change—what you saw, and the release from the care of our three babies for one whole day. You doubtless felt young again—young in the sense of being without care and responsibility.

Another day just like yesterday and the day before is passing away. I have been to the office—have had long talks about nothing but politics—have had my dinner at the restaurant—and home again to chat with you, the pleasantest part of the twenty-four hours with me. I have just been interrupted by Treasurer Holland, who brings a report of the situation from Capiah Co.—the county next south of this. The Democracy are trying every means to defraud us as well as to intimidate our voters. They seem utterly devoid of honor or principle. I have never read of such depravity among enlightened people. Fraud is attended by murder in all political struggles here; and what seems the saddest is, that no class of Democrats, it matters not what may be their intelligence or position, frown upon these crimes, but on the other hand the higher orders are the leaders in that which is the most wicked.

I have come into the N.W. chamber to escape the mosquitoes—shutting the doors behind me. My effort has proved quite successful. The setting sun shines into the window and falls upon the bureau and its glass vividly, lighting up a broad spider's web which extends from the glass and its frame to the marble slab which forms the top of the bureau. Dust covers everything. I shall not go on to describe further. Before you come we shall have everything put to rights and every nook and corner made as clean as the hands from the Penitentiary can make them.

My health is excellent—never better, though I suppose I am not very weighty. I have not tried the scales.

I send love. ADELBERT

BAY VIEW ON CAPE ANN, *September* 1, 1875

DEAR DEL: Mother has just said "Blanche, are your trunks partially packed?" I answer "Yes, it will not take me long to get them ready." This is plainly a signal for departure, and the first of next week we shall start for Lowell. Father leaves for New York tomorrow, then to Washington, then to Dayton. Paul will go West. Father is willing that he should. So only the women of the family will be at home. Perhaps you will be in Washington at the same time Father is, that is, if you go on at all. I trust you will be able to, so that we can have the happiness of seeing your dear face again, without waiting two months and a half longer.

Butler has a new companion. A girl called Janie.—She can swear, and is not over nice in her selection of words. I told Butler to go up stairs and wash his hands and face and clean his teeth, that if he wished he could use some of my soap. "You is good to me ain't you, Mama, you isn't stingy is you?" "Why, Butler, what do you mean by stingy"? "Mrs. Quinn is stingy. She would not let Janie get me some cherries." I explained to him that Mrs. Quinn was not stingy, for she was always giving him good things, and had made him a nice little mince pie. That she did not want Janie to take her cherries because she did not like her, as she was a bad girl, said bad words, and swore. He seemed to comprehend the situation. He is sharp enough to keep one busy all of the time. I wish that he might rid himself of his cold, for it makes him look badly and feel worse. Edith grows prettier daily. Annie did her hair up in curl papers yesterday, on the front—so that she seemed like a young lady. You see when I have no news to tell I go into the details about the children.

I am entirely opposed to this feeling of yours about being poor. Do you know that it is likely you have saved fifty thousand dollars counting this year since we were married, that is five years. For young married people I think this is pretty well, don't you?

I am sorry that I do not please you about dates. I will try to do better, and I will not arrange the matter with my own conscience, but with your lady friend, of whom I have nothing spiteful to say. Love and kisses for you Dearie, from your affectionate but much abused wife. BLANCHE

JACKSON, MISS., *September* 1, 1875

DEAR BLANCHE: A letter from you, one from Butler, and two boxes of "boneless herrings" came to me by this morning's mail. Butler's letter was entertaining, but I suggest he be more explicit in the future. The wrapping on the herring boxes was torn and the boxes broken enough to display their contents and to permit an escape of an odor which in its way was emphatic enough. I was glad to get the herrings, and shall proceed to eat them for lunches. Though I dislike ale and beer, I have taken to beer, and drink a glass every day at dinner with the hope that it may prove fattening. If I should grow thinner year by year, and you fatter and fatter, what a contrast we will make in course of time! I shall protest when you raise more than two hundred pounds. Perhaps I may consent to two hundred and twenty-five—your health may demand that—but not another pound will I countenance. So be careful if you care for peace in the household.

This day has brought nothing new. I have read all the novels I could get hold of or buy, and now have taken up a history of England (Shield's) which I find interesting. I have a map of England and am trying to revive and correct my knowledge of that country.

Father has sent me another check of $1200, which, with three hundred dollars I have, paid for our house at Bay St. Louis. Please send father the $1200 check you have, scratching or marking it so it will be valueless should anyone get hold of it.

This is the first day of fall. I am glad to see it come. Ben of course has returned to West Point. What is Paul going to do?—And how much longer are you to remain at Bay View? I am quite willing to see time making history, as time ever does.

I send you of what I have in abundance, love for you.

ADELBERT

BAY VIEW ON CAPE ANN, *September* 2, 1875

DEAR DEL: I have come to the conclusion that Butler is really troubled with the hay fever. Perhaps the change to Lowell will be beneficial. It is a terrible pity if he has to be afflicted with this disease all of his life. Everybody who sees him pronounces it hay-fever. It is useless to consult a doctor, for it is well understood that up to this time nothing is known that will cure it except a change of air. This is Mr. Beecher's trouble, and drives him to the White Mountains yearly. Mr. Tucke, Katie's father-in-law, so Uncle Parker told me, "was congratulating himself that so far he had escaped his yearly affliction, the first season for twenty years." Paul came down from Lowell last night, and his first words were, "Mr. Tucke is miserable with his hay fever, his eyes all swollen, sneezing and blowing from morning till night." So much for this subject. Of course, this trouble is not serious, only annoying.

Mr. Moulton came down with Paul, to whom he said in Boston that he was on his way to visit the Frenches—but when he reached Gloucester, our carriage not being there, he rode over with Col. and Mrs. French and they brought him to our door and left him. We are of the impression here that Mrs. French and her friend Miss Sweasy had intimated to him that his presence would be agreeable, but as Col. F. did not second it—he found himself in an unpleasant position.

Paul is going West. His gun has been pronounced by Meigs dangerous—liable at any time to let the charge through the side of the barrel. So he is going with Father to get a new one. The expense of the gun and trip was considered, but finally Father thought he had better go if he wished. Paul would not urge it. So Mother and I did the talking. Not that Father required it at all—but it was difficult to get Paul's wishes about it.

I made a mistake in my last letter. Father does not go to Washington until next Friday instead of this. Poor Ben writes that he is dreadfully down in the mouth. His studies will occupy him, however, and he will soon be content. Percy is getting on well, and is liked.

Father went up stairs with Butler the other night to take him up to bed. Butler wanted someone to go with him. Father offered, and his offer was accepted.

Love. BLANCHE

JACKSON, MISS., *September 2*, 1875

DEAR BLANCHE: This is a very hot day. The thermometer ranges well up towards 90° in my room. Walking up to the office and back suggests a moderately heated furnace. As I have so little to do now-a-days I do not go office-wards till about midday. At half past two I aim to be at the restaurant. This morning in starting out I met a man with a pail full of thick skinned native grapes for which he asked forty cents. I made the purchase. I hold they are most excellent to regulate one's interior.

The only business just now is to listen to reports of outrages by the Democracy. Today a telegram came that a Republican meeting at Yazoo City where Col. Morgan was speaking was attacked and one or two Negroes killed, and quite a number wounded. Of arming and intimidation by these white liners reports come from all sides. They will do anything to carry the state. I hope our committee which is to go to Washington will bring some succor. So far has this intimidation gone that I cannot organize a single company of Militia. In fact, months ago when I was laboring to do so, leading Republicans came to me and besought me not to. Today everybody is against it, and I can get no one to take a commission. The old rebel armies are too much for our party, and the colored men dare not organize even though they know their liberty is at stake. You see how unsatisfactory my position is. Our only hope is through the U.S. enforcement laws.

I did not go to bed last night till twelve o'clock. I was interested in my history of England, which I read till eleven when my thoughts went to a patent boat.—I use "patent" for fun, as there is no patent in the case. I was thinking of having a pleasure boat made in this manner. Have two hollow cylinders fastened together, though some three or five feet apart. These boats or runners, water tight, could be made with bottoms like regular boats. Cross pieces would hold the hulls together and on these the deck could be fastened—deck and cabin. Such a boat would need no ballast, and could not be upset. I think much speed could be obtained. Of course it would be "wet" in a sea. When I shall have some money to waste I will try an experiment. In such a raft our family could cruise with comfort, speed and safety! I do not blame you for thinking my time could be better employed than working out the details of such a plan.

I agree with you in failing to see the propriety of painting your own portrait for Mr. Chadwick. Charity begins at home —better paint one for my folks. Then again, perhaps we would prefer you were not making such presents.—Suppose you compromise and return to him his wedding present.

Love, kisses for the babies and yourself from

ADELBERT

BAY VIEW ON CAPE ANN, *September* 3, 1875

DEAR DEL: There is one thing of which I feel sure, and that is that you are not strong and well. If you think it safe to go through New Orleans, fill your pockets with camphor, now and then put a grain into your mouth (not more than a grain, for too much would give you colic), and go to Bay St. Louis for a while. Get something good to eat and have some nice baths. I am sure you will feel more capable and in better spirits for the coming campaign. My impression is that you have been in the physical condition which precedes a change of weather for some time. Not on account, however, of the atmospherical effect, but from lack of perfect health and strength. So once *more* I insist by some means or other you must get something to tempt your appetite and fit you for the work which lies before you. If you go to the Bay, besides your regular meals you should have Mary fix you something nice and tempting to eat, between times.

I can picture you so clearly, with your face still thinner than when here, great hollows all around your eyes, and know that your soul is filled with disgust for your present life and its surroundings, not only on account of its many disagreeable features, but because you are in that state of mind and body which will not allow you to pass them gaily, and lightly aside. You remember I once told you that shortly after Butler was born, although surrounded by all the comfort, luxuries and good things which are attainable in life, I still felt that existence was going to prove a great burden and not worth the effort. If this was the case with me, when so pleasantly surrounded, how natural that you should have the same feeling with so many annoyances to contend, political and physical. Of course you hate it all, and long to get out of it. I have only one thing to say in regard to it. Be sure that you *make no mistake.* Fate has fixed us for two years more in Mississippi, and we must do the best we can with the time, perhaps the time will come when we shall look back to these days with pleasure, not only you and I, but the children, on account of the name you have won, and the position. But be that as it may, we have two years to stay, and in view of that I will tell you what would please me, and what *I* think would be the best course to take. You do not desire to be a Senator, and tied to the State for the next six years. Well, I should like to escape one of the two remaining years as Governor. If you can, by all means get the Senatorship. Do not resign in Mississippi, but serve one session or half a session in the Senate. Then resign—so that at least the world will know that you had the capacity to obtain the place you resign. If you decline to accept the nomination in Mississippi the world will say, he declines a place which he only dreams he can attain. Beat your enemies, take the place, and then give it up when in all respects you will be better able to judge accurately what will be the most conducive to your contentment and happiness. What I desire is, that by no acts of yours at the present time you should debar yourself of a thing which men will say he could never have had, and which you, yourself, might regret at some future day. I hold that when a man is in a position he can judge best whether it suits him or not. Do not say to anyone that you have no desire for the place, let that be your secret and mine for the present. This is good advice, Del, which at least it can do no harm to follow.

The main thing just now is to get well and strong for the campaign—that lies before you and is inevitable. Do this, and hold firm to all the points in the game. We always have this in our favor, that if the position does not come to us, we are not so ambitious for it that our hearts will be broken. I am sure you will smile at this long letter on one subject, but I have a feeling that I should prefer to have the game in my own hands to checkmate or not as I saw fit, rather than to let it slip gradually from the beginning.

Butler's cold is better, I think. Mother has been having the floors waxed. Butler assisted in the operation, as I thought the smell of the turpentine might prove beneficial. I think it has, for he has not sneezed nearly as much. He will wax some more tomorrow.

Good night, Love. Keep up good heart and spirits. I would give a great deal to be with you now.

It is not best to tell Mother positively about the house, inasmuch as I don't think it will make any difference in the retention or sale of it. You know she would feel that it was a terrible thing to give up a Senatorship. So would everybody in the world except you and one who must always stand by and approve your action, whether worldly wise or not. Kisses and caresses. BLANCHE

JACKSON, MISS., *September* 3, 1875

DEAR BLANCHE: I had a call from a lady this morning before daylight. Col. Morgan was addressing a 'club' of Republicans in Yazoo City, a few evenings since, when some white liners interrupted, broke up the meeting and killed two men. Col. M. escaped. Immediately the city was filled with armed men. Companies were marching to and fro and pickets and sentinels established as in active warfare. The only way our friends there could communicate with us was to send a lady, a sister-in-law of Col. M., his brother's wife, to us. She came in on the night train and at once came here to the Mansion with Mr. Cardoza, and related the facts. The Democracy are organized into military companies and have assumed control—taken military possession of the county. I shall issue a proclamation ordering them to disperse and retire to their homes. Of course I can do nothing by physical force, but my proclamation will, I hope, pave the way for national interference. The canvass here is waxing warm, and I shall have to remain constantly to my post.

Just before I sat down to write you I received a telegram from Capt. Avery at Bay St. Louis, informing me that the yellow fever still existed at Pascagoula and that it was said there were cases at the Bay. He advises me not to go there. Of course I will not do so.

I send you, Sweetheart, love in abundance.

ADELBERT

JACKSON, MISS., *September* 4, 1875

DEAR BLANCHE: I am glad to know the babies are well and I suggest that you remain at the Bay as long as you deem it well for them so far as your wishes may be consulted. However, as this letter goes to Lowell I do not suppose you will get it till your arrival there. But surely it must be cool and healthy in L. at this season of the year.

Everything is reported as being quiet in Yazoo. Mrs. Morgan is to return tonight.

Yesterday evening Mrs. Dedrick and Mrs. Gibbs were among those playing croquet here. Mrs. D. and I played against and beat Capt. Raymond and Mrs. G. Mrs. G. is looking very well and seems bright and happy. Major Gibbs little girl was along and played with her father, knocking the balls about as Butler used to do.

I am afraid you are spoiling our eldest by undue petting. Why did you not show him that it was his fault and not the stairs' which broke the goblet? He has been up and down stairs often enough to become acquainted with their slippery character and should have been prepared. Instead of that you seemed to have put the blame entirely on the stairs and me.

I send you love, ADELBERT

BAY VIEW ON CAPE ANN, *September* 5, 1875

DEAR DEL: This is Sunday night again, and I believe I am right about the date of my letter.

The house seems quite deserted, for Paul left yesterday morning and Mr. Moulton last night. To be sure, Mr. Stetson of New York and Mr. Devlin rode over from Swampscott, a distance of twenty-five miles, starting at half past six, and were here to dinner. They came unexpectedly, but as the larder was easily supplied Mother did not care, and I think they had a pleasant visit. We are all talking of and planning our expected homeward march next Wednesday. Dog days are over, and the weather is cool and bracing. So much so that I think it will be safe for the children.

Mrs. Bennett's boy has been quite ill. She took him up to Lowell a week ago for change of air, and left the little girl with Mr. Bennett. He, of course, feels lonely and miserable, in anxiety about his boy, and troubled for fear the girl may get sick. I do not know why Mrs. B. did not take the little girl to her Mother's except that she went away in great haste. I write this thinking that it may possibly afford you some consolation to know that you are not the only man separated from your family.

This brings me around to my discussion in Friday's letter, or perhaps it would be better to call it a dissertation. Please bear my remarks in mind and gratify my ambition if possible. I care so little for the opinion of the people of Mississippi that it would not give me half the pleasure to flaunt my plumes, and then throw them aside before them as it would before home folk. By home folk I mean those among whom we have heretofore flourished. Keep up your spirits, Sweetheart. The days will fly more quickly when you leave Jackson to go about the country, and we shall soon be together again and can snap our fingers (a very elegant expression) at the whole world.

You do not say how Raymond felt about your action, or non-action, in regard to Holland. You should not be surprised if he shows resentment. There are few men who are willing to have what is best and right for all concerned considered before their own individual interests. Their good and bad feelings should be nothing to us, Del. We shall have that kind of thing to contend with wherever we are.

Also remember my instructions about getting something to eat and building yourself up strong and well. I am uneasy about you, Del, and would give much to be with you. I do not mean that I think you are sick enough to be in bed, but I do not believe you feel well and strong enough to ward off annoyances which sometimes would appear mole-hills, but at present are mountainous. As I cannot go to you I beg you to take great care of yourself, pet, and consider yourself for me.

Butler is, I think, a little better—he does not sneeze quite so much and breathes easier. The baby still looks pale and big-eyed—but is bright and saucy as possible. Edith is my little woman. You will be surprised to hear that for the last week I have turned over a new leaf and have been getting up with the children, thus lengthening the days for painting, etc. Oh! by the way, Father does like the fresco, and takes visitors out to see such evidences of his daughter's skill.

I do not think I have sufficient force of character to get out of bed so early if I could turn towards you and with your dear head on my shoulder nestle down for another nap. So you need not flatter yourself that because of my present well doing I am likely to do as well or better in the future.

You will also be amused to hear as a little church gossip that there has been held in Lowell a retreat of three days by the *Anglo-Catholic* clergy of the United States, and that the orphan asylum of St. Ann's church is to be under the direction of the Sisters of St. Margaret in London. Our beloved pastor, Dr. Edson, is becoming rather wild with his high church notions. A retreat is a Catholic arrangement, and means that those who take part in it retire from the world for a certain time, and give themselves up wholly to fasting and prayer. Does it not also strike you as absurd that an orphan asylum, dependent upon the subscription of Lowell people, should be managed by a set of English recluses? I spoke to Father the other day about Dr. Edson's antics, and his reply was— "The Doctor has given up his whole life to the study of these matters, and is more likely to know what is best and right for all concerned than I am." Such affected humility from one who does not hesitate usually to express most determined opinions on all subjects aroused my ire—and I retorted more flippantly than filially, "I *think* that Dr. Edson has probably given as much, too much time to the study and consideration of spiritual affairs, to the exclusion of temporal, as you have to temporal matters to the exclusion of spiritual." Father laughed and said "It may be so." He and Mother had just made up a quarrel, and he felt good-natured.

Well, Del, I have written you a long letter. Hattie and Mother wonder what I can find to write every day, but there is always something.

Love from your family, but the sweetest and best from

BLANCHE

JACKSON, MISS., *September* 5, 1875

DEAR BLANCHE: I had finished my letter to you yesterday and was looking for George to mail it when Capt. Fisher came to me out of breath and out of heart to tell me of a riot which had just taken place at Clinton (a village ten miles west of here) and from which he had just escaped, with his wife. He was speaking when the riot began. It was a premeditated riot on the part of the Democracy which resulted in the death of some four white men and about the same number of Negroes and quite a large number of Negroes wounded. There were present at a Republican barbecue about fifteen hundred colored people, men, women and children. Seeking the opportunity white men, fully prepared, fired into this crowd. Two women were reported killed, also two children. As the firing continued, the women ran away with the men in many instances, leaving their children on the ground. Today there are some forty carriages, wagons and carts which were abandoned by the colored people in their flight. Last night, this morning and today squads of white men are scouring the county killing Negroes. Three were killed at Clinton this morning—one of whom was an old man, nearly one hundred years old—defenseless and helpless. Yesterday the Negroes, though unarmed and unprepared, fought bravely and killed four of the ringleaders, but had to flee before the muskets which were at once brought onto the field of battle. This is but in keeping with the programme of the Democracy at this time. They know we have a majority of some thirty thousand and to overcome it they are resorting to intimidation and murder. It is cold-blooded murder on the part of the "white liners"—but there are other cases exactly like this in other parts of the state. You ask what are we to do. That is a question I find it difficult to answer. I told you a day or two ago that the whole party has been opposed to organizing the militia and furthermore I have been unable to find anyone who was willing to take militia appointments.

The Mansion has been crowded all day long with Republican friends and Negroes from the field of battle. I have run off to the northwest chamber for my daily chat with you, leaving a crowd in the other rooms. There has also been a crowd at the front gate all day long. The town is full of Negroes from the country who come to escape harm. The whites here are afraid of the Negroes who have come in. A committee of white men have just waited on me and offer to keep the peace so far as may be in their power. The Sheriff has selected a number of them to act as a posse to go out into the country and arrest those who are murdering Negroes. This last step has caused a subsidence of the excitement felt by the whites as well as blacks.

I anticipate no further trouble here at this time. The "white liners" have gained their point—they have, by killing and wounding, so intimidated the poor Negroes that they can in all human probability prevail over them at the election. I shall at once try to get troops from the general government. Of course it will be a difficult thing to do.

I send a world of love. ADELBERT

BAY VIEW ON CAPE ANN, *September* 6, 1875

DEAR DEL: I shall write you only a short letter, just to remind you that there is someone here for you to love.

The papers report troubles in Vicksburg, or at Clinton. I am fearful that you are having a trying time this fall. Do not allow these things to wear upon you. I can understand that you will not feel like being away from your post, although there is very little that you can do.

We go to Lowell tomorrow. The weather is cool here. A fire in the parlor every day keeps us comfortable. The baby will be likely to do quite as well in Lowell now. Her little pale face looks quite blue in this keen air. The weather changed instantly with the end of dog days.

This reminds me that Father and I have been having a discussion about the North Star and the Dipper. I maintain that the Dipper changes its position, revolves around the North Star. He says "No" and has threatened to get up and look at it in the morning early, to see if it has moved.

Butler is getting to be a great runaway. There is a family named Powers living behind us. They all seem fond of Butler. I asked him why they liked him, if it was because he was good or because he was smart. He answered at once "Because I am smart." Well, the men take him sometimes to the store, sometimes to the quarries, sometimes to the ledge—and yesterday he went to see *a sheep killed.* I would not have consented if I has known, but he goes to play with Janie, and then marches without permission. The change will be good for him in this respect—Lynch and Lewis will have to be his companions in Lowell. He seems to like older people better than children, if they will notice him.

Love, BLANCHE

JACKSON, MISS., *September* 6, 1875

DEAR BLANCHE: This has been a very busy day for me and an excited one for the county and city. I understand that squads of armed "white liners" have been scouring the county today killing Negroes. A large number of poor black men are in the city. I think the excitement has somewhat subsided in the city. Tomorrow I shall issue a proclamation ordering all armed bodies to disperse, which of course will have no practical effect, beyond making a record of the facts and situation which may be used as the canvass goes on as a basis of requisition for U.S. troops.

I was interrupted here by callers, white men, who represent a deplorable state of affairs in the western part of this county and in Warren County. Vicksburg is the county seat of Warren County. I may find it necessary to call on the President tomorrow. It is not particularly pleasant to write you so much about these troubles, for I get tired of hearing of them long before the day closes, but I know you wish to know how my hours are spent.

I had a letter from Avery at Bay St. Louis this morning and he tells me that there have been two or three deaths there of yellow fever, and that others are sick. So I shall beware of the coast.

I send you—Beloved—love. Kisses for the babies.

ADELBERT

BAY VIEW ON CAPE ANN, *September* 7, 1875

DEAR DEL: I go to Lowell tomorrow with the children and part of the servants. It is not yet decided whether Hattie will go with me or wait for Mother, who may not get away before Friday, as she is compelled to await the arrival of Lewis who is to drive up the white horse. He should have been down this evening, but as he has not come, he may have failed to get the letter of instructions, and of course will not move until I get home and send him.

Butler is, I believe, better, and I believe the turpentine must have had something to do with it. If he only continues well it will be a great thing.

I intend to write your Father this evening and enclose the draft on Northfield as you desire. You may feel sure that he is well pleased with the year's work, and is satisfied with your action about selling, at present. Of course you know he would not be if fortune's wheel were to turn in the opposite direction. I considered that we had done a great thing when he said—"That is good property at Fort Atkinson. Sam is doing finely." I wanted to say "I told you so."

Did I write you Del that since we were married you have saved about fifty thousand dollars? This is on the supposition that Northfield will pay you seven thousand and Fort Atkinson five—which they have not yet done, but I hope may do this year—thus completing five years of our married life.

There is no news to tell you. All is quiet here. Father brought home word this evening that Mr. Beecher had quarreled with the proprietor of the Twin Mountain House, White Mts. It seems, according to the newspapers, that Mr. Beecher was to have according to agreement his board and fifty dollars per week, and was to stay until the first of October. Now Mr. Beecher asks for two hundred a week and wants to go the first of September.

Funny, if true, isn't it? Rather a pleasant and economical way of spending the summer. Nast ought to caricature Mr. B. into a huge hand bill or poster, and have flowing from his ministerial lips a notice beginning "Delightful Summer Resort, etc., etc." The ways of the world are past finding out.

Good night. I may not be able to write you tomorrow evening, so do not feel neglected if the letters fail to come regularly.

Love, BLANCHE

JACKSON, MISS., *September* 7, 1875

DEAR BLANCHE: Today I issued a proclamation commanding the illegal military companies to disband: and I also telegraphed the President to make an inquiry before formally making a requisition for troops. I asked him if his proclamation of last December was still in force, and state that if he does not so regard it I will at once make a requisition as required by the Constitution of the U.S. The excitement in this vicinity is abating, but there is enough and more throughout the state. As I have already stated, the Democracy seek by violence to defeat the purpose of the Constitutional amendments and deprive the colored men of their political rights, to do which they do not hesitate to murder. Lamar and Gordon of Georgia are in the state making, it is reported, most incendiary speeches. The language they use is not of itself violent, but the conclusions they reach are that this election must be carried, even if violence be resorted to.

So much for politics. You may read to your Father such

portions of my letters as touch on the political situation. Tell him that in '60 and '61 there were not such unity and such preparation against the government of the U.S. as now exist against the colored men and the government their votes have established. Gibbs and Raymond report that Gen. Augur is ready to act but that he requires authority from the President. He holds, as I have told you our party generally does, that the organizing of the militia of colored men precipitates a war of races and one to be felt over the entire South. He says thousands in Louisiana are ready to come here to fight the Negro. As it is, the power of the U.S. alone can give the security our citizens are entitled to. If it is not given, then no effort will be made by Republicans to carry the election.

I send you love. ADELBERT

JACKSON, MISS., *September* 8, 1875

DEAR BLANCHE: Today I made an application to the President of the U.S. for troops to keep the peace and preserve life. We must have them, or the colored voters of the state will be deprived of their rights and liberties, which the amendments of the Constitution expressly stipulate to maintain. My telegram[1] went this afternoon, and I await confidently a favorable reply. I see my telegram of yesterday has been given to the press. Of course that of today will appear in tomorrow's papers. By them you will know what I am doing long before you get this. Of course I am working hard, and am anxious that the results may be favorable.

We have been having another scorching day. Just a few minutes since a wind and rain cloud rose up out of the east and it is now quite comfortable. The wind fans me through the window, and the dust is being laid by the few drops of rain as they slowly fall. It is time for cool weather, and I hope it will follow this shower.

I had a letter from Mary this morning. She still seems sick. I express myself as in doubt whether she be sick or well, as I was unable to read her writing. She says the yellow fever is there and seems ready to fly from it. She also says many

[1] *President* U. S. GRANT, WASHINGTON, D.C. (*No date*)

The majority of the legislative committee sent to investigate affairs at Vicksburg report to me a great feeling of insecurity prevails there and that certain officials can not safely discharge their duties.

The Sheriff of the county reports to me that "armed defiance of all law and lawful authority hold sway at the Court House."

Consequently I am compelled to ask you to send troops there to uphold and protect the lawful authorities. ADELBERT AMES

people are leaving, and not a few are camping in the woods. The epidemic may become general, but I doubt it. I am at a loss whether to advise Mary to come here or go to New Orleans or some other point, or to remain where she is for a time longer and judge for herself what to do. The objection to her coming here would be that she might bring the fever with her, which would be a great misfortune.

Capt. Avery of Tallahatchie Co. is here, and has a bed in the children's room. Raymond will leave tonight for the north. He will meet his wife in Chicago.—She is now in Kansas.

I am sorry Butler has the hay fever. While physicians may not be able to cure adults, they may advise as to a child. We must spare nothing to cure him. Kiss him for me and Edith and Baby— How long it seems since I last saw them! To you, Beautiful, I send a world of love. ADELBERT

LOWELL, *September* 9, 1875

DEAR DEL: We have changed our location, as you see by the heading of this letter.

We started yesterday at one o'clock from Bay View and arrived here at half past six. The children were very good on the trip. I suppose they seemed more so than usual, because Butler slept in my lap from Salem to Lowell. Edith was in Hattie's charge, and looked as pretty as a pink. The baby was full of coquetries and airs, ready to go to anyone, and very many asked to take her. Mother came up by carriage today, reaching here at seven. The weather has been warm, and they drove slowly. The place is looking very beautiful. Flowers, flowers everywhere.

There are a number of things I want to do this fall, and I feel as if every moment is to be crowded. Perhaps it is well that I should be kept closely at work, for I am too *fleshy*. You notice I say fleshy, Sweetheart, instead of fat. This shows that I am sensitive on the subject.

Mr. Carney came up this evening to see Father, and we had a few words on business matters. It seems that there was another clause to that trust, to the effect that the principal should only be invested in U.S. bonds. Mr. Carney said, "I would rather break the trust than not do what you wish, but I think I can arrange it without doing so. The trust does not extend to the three thousand, and the interest, etc. due from the Convers mortgage will be some three or four thousand." "Well," I said, "this would be perfectly satisfactory to me.

I partly wished to pay it now because I thought it would be agreeable to Father, as so much ready money is required for the houses, and because I thought it better to make a family affair of it, more especially as Gen'l. Ames has to pay large rates of interest for money in the West." "You are perfectly right about it, and it is better without taking your Father's needs into consideration that you should save the interest, and I can arrange it for you, and would have done so, so that Gen'l. Ames need not have known anything about it until it was finished, as you wished to surprise him." "Well," I said, "I could hardly have told you that he would give me a mortgage, when he did not even know that one was desired, consequently when it was thought best that I should have one, I had to write him what was on foot." Then Father came into the room and our conversation ended.

The day's papers record your call for troops and the President's favorable response. I regret more and more that I am not with you, Sweetheart. What a nice old age we will have together, Del. The children will have grown beyond our immediate care, and we will keep together. The only thing to be desired will be good health, which brings me round to my old stand point. Take great care of yourself *now*.

Love and good night. BLANCHE

JACKSON, MISS., *September* 9, 1875

DEAR BLANCHE: Yesterday I wrote you I applied to the national government for aid to maintain order, etc. but have not as yet received any reply. I presume, however, the President will act at once even if he does not notify me of his action. I am fully alive to the fact that my action will be like an exploding shell in the political canvass at the North. It may injure Republicanism there, but I had but one course open for me to take—and that I have taken. I anxiously await the action of the President. There is no special news. The Democracy are beginning to deny my statements and will by their lies attempt to deceive the North as they did last winter relative to the murders in Warren Co.

I saw Capt. Cass today. He says no one at Bay St. Louis is concerned about the yellow fever. Two children of a Northern man there have died, but he seemed to regard it due to their exposure in the water bathing, and on the bridge fishing, etc. admitting, however, the presence there of a malignant type of fever. He also reports the death of a colored man.

Your letter of advice came this morning. I do not think

we need borrow trouble on account of our immediate future. Circumstances will entirely control us. Our feelings may change a dozen times before the time for a decision will come. So as you suggest I may as well do nothing at present—in fact there is so little I could do at present.

I am always glad to hear of the babies—none of your letters are more interesting than those which tell of yourself and them —for is not a man's heart where his treasures are? To you all I send a world of love. ADELBERT

LOWELL, *September* 10, 1875

DEAR DEL: Last night after getting ready for bed, and finishing all my little arrangements I went to the window to put out the gas and open the shutters. The moonlight was glorious, and the scene such as you will remember it. My first thought was—if Del were only here to enjoy this with me, my next, he does see this same moon, and it is quite possible he may even now be looking at it.—So I threw some kisses to the moon for my sweetheart, which I hope he received, none the worse for having been carried to him by the man in the moon. Although we have been married so long, and have three babies, still it is very evident that one of us at least has not outlived all romance, otherwise such a performance as mine last night would not be possible.

Mr. and Mrs. Farrington, Capt. Pearson, and Florence were here last night. Florence stayed all night. Tom, you know, is away with Paul. Father left last night for his trip to Washington, Dayton, etc. None of the protectors of this portion of the community are at home, and we must ward off tramps all alone.

This— Oh, dear me! Butler has just asked me to do something for him, and while attending to him he has thrown my pen on to the paper and made that great blot. He had just said "Marmma, am I not a good boy," and I had answered "Yes, a very good boy," but had ample occasion to scold twice at him in as many seconds. If I were not so well and fat I should tell you that "this sort of thing is enough to break anyone down." As it is, I fear if you were to see me you would lose all compassion, so I make no complaints.

We are all going to the Bank. The others have some business to attend to, but I want some money, as I have the children's winter outfit to attempt next Monday in Boston. You remember that I have quite a number of your papers, among others, young Holland's bond. I did not know but it might have passed from your mind that you had given them into my charge.

I wish Del, you would write to your Aunt Marietta in Rockland, and ask her if she will please put one third white soap in her starch, and see if it makes her shirts polish any easier. Your Father had one on which she had laundered and it was finely polished, but was done by repeated ironing and strength.

Love, BLANCHE

LOWELL, *September* 10, 1875

DEAR DEL: This is for Saturday and Sunday, two days which have passed like dreams. I have been so full of thoughts and plans for the future. The papers Saturday brought me the news of Grant's dilatory shilly-shally conduct, and my indignation was without bounds. It is shameful. If the Govt. absolutely refuses aid, what can you do, Del? What a pity it is that you cannot catch an aristocratic leader or two just after one of these murderous riots—take them to Jackson and have a court martial instanter, and let the noose grace their necks. To be sure, it would make things pretty lively, and you might bid adieu to the Senatorship. What of that? If the State could be kept in good order, it would be worth more than forty Senatorships. You see I am talking at random, Dearie, but I am troubled on your account, as well as filled with wrath against these miscreants, which causes me to run on without much rhyme or reason.

You have not a strong, able connection in the whole State. Those who surround you are as a rule weak, timorous men on whom you can have no reliance. There is only one consolation I can derive from the state of affairs, and that is if the people of the South behave too outrageously, it may prevent our having a Democratic President next time. I am sorry however, that you will have to be so much annoyed in order that such a result may be achieved.

Well, to let such subjects alone and come to home matters. The children are all well. Butler's cold, or hay fever, is much better, and they seem in very fine condition. Poor Mrs. Bennett is in great trouble about her baby. He is nine months old, and was much larger for his age than our baby. They do not expect him to live, he is so ill with cholera infantum. Bessie is here. I called to see her, and although she has a little hope, the doctors and her family have none. How fortunate we have been, Del. Heaven grant that our good fortune continues.

Florence had a letter from Tom Saturday. He writes that your Mother gave them a most cordial reception. That she was delighted with Edith's picture and that they were going out to be gone three days—some eighteen miles from Northfield. The boys were evidently in fine spirits.

Del, I want you to have the men take up the carpets and have all the plastering in the Mansion repaired. It is dangerous for you to be in that room of ours, and going up and down stairs with the ceiling in its present condition. You can occupy one of the other chambers while it is being fixed—and it would be better to have it done as early as this in order that it may be fully dried before the children are to occupy the rooms. Our experience of last spring should warn us to beware of fresh plastering. When you move into the other room, take all your things, for it will not be dry enough for you to go back to it before we join you. I think this should be attended to at once.

With this long direction, I send you love, BLANCHE

JACKSON, MISS., *September* 10, 1875

DEAR BLANCHE: I have been very indignant nearly all day long at the treatment of my telegram asking for aid. But this afternoon when I heard that the sheriff of this county had reported to Attorney General Pierrepont that all was quiet —why—I subsided, thoroughly disgusted. Tonight Sheriff Harney has returned to town, and reports that he sent his telegram under compulsion. He will send another to that effect. Thus you see we are amidst exciting times. I had begun a long telegram in reply to that of the Attorney General, but desisted when I heard of Sheriff Harney's action. I will not send it tonight; perhaps not at all. My action will depend on the development of events.

Tolman writes me that they have word that Paul was on his way to Northfield. I hope he will have good shooting. I know he will enjoy knocking over prairie chickens. It is just the season for a good time. I have no doubt he and Father will become great cronies. I should like to be up there with them for a day or two. Paul will be amused, I have no doubt, to see such a demonstrative set as the Ameses are—in this, they are outspoken towards each other and keep nothing back, as his folks are inclined. I do not think your family confide with each other enough. I will not dwell longer on this idea. You and I have discussed it often. Paul may not be there long enough to see our traits. I wonder if he will think Fanny pretty. I have not thought of her before for a long time—how long I can hardly remember.

I send to you love and kisses—which you may share with our babies.

ADELBERT

LOWELL, *September* 11, 1875

DEAR DEL: Another letter to write, which shows that one more day has passed, and the time of our separation is shortening.

One day with me passes very like another. My chief anxiety is to see the papers, and read the latest from Mississippi. If I am unfortunate enough only to be able to get the Boston *Herald* I take it under protest, but still take it, for I would rather have the news, even though falsely presented, than not to have it at all. I can sift, and find some grains of truth.

I was reading over some of your letters to your parents during the war, and find that you were not contented, even with all the honors which were falling thick upon you. At the same time, in one of your letters, you gave your Father some very good advice on this same point.

I can see, or think I can see, that it is a family characteristic to fret and chafe against any restraint. It is a fine quality for success, but for happiness and contentment I doubt, and I have some misgivings when I look forward and try to picture our future condition. I do not mean, Dearie, that you would ever growl or grumble, but I always feel when you are not content, which is quite as bad, if not worse, than having a good grumbling. All of this talk tends to this point. Try, Love, to catch a little enjoyment as the days fly. I know how hard it is now, in the midst of such turmoil, and separated from those you love, and those who love you. Still the separation is not to last for life—God willing—and yet many of our acquaintances have suffered such a separation this summer, with some member or members of the family. Ah—Sweetheart, we have many things to make us happy in spite of present small annoyances, if we only compare our lot with that of those *less* fortunate and not more. In fact, the latter are hard to find. I wish I could be with you, Del, that you could feel that one at least, even though a woman, was with you, heart and soul, in all your troubles, all your hopes and plans.

Your Mother wished to know of Tom if Edith's portrait was not flattered. Florence has written Tom to tell her that it is

not as good looking, and that Edith is growing prettier daily.
Love, BLANCHE

LOWELL, *September* 11, 1875

DEAR DEL: I am glad to see, or rather to be able to draw the conclusion, from the tone of your letters that you are not despondent. Gen'l. Michie was here this morning to bring us news of Ben, and while speaking of you and Mississippi affairs he said "I hope Gen'l. Ames will not become gloomy and embittered. Everything has to be done for political effect. This may account for the President's apparent hesitation in sending troops, that he wishes to act with great care and to ask for thorough information in order that it may appear to the country that he was *compelled* to send troops to Mississippi, notwithstanding his hesitation and desire not to interfere if it could be avoided. Of course the Democrats will make a great handle of this federal interference in the coming elections. I hope the Gen'l. will not become entirely disgusted, and I do not think he will, he is not that kind of a man, when most closely pushed he is the most determined." He then related an anecdote about you and Gen'l. Rosseau in the mess hall, and another about the manner in which you overcame the insubordination of your Maine regiment, by leading them into battle, etc. etc.

I think he was led to the thought that you might possibly be disgusted from the fact that the morning papers reported that the Attorney Gen'l. telegraphed Saturday to Gov. Ames for more particulars and received no reply except from the Postmaster at Jackson who said that the disturbance was only such as a few determined men citizens of Jackson could easily quell if they were so ordered to do. Then the Attorney General telegraphed to Gov. Ames again and at length received an answer. Gen'l. Michie probably thought, although he did not say so, that you did not answer at once because you felt too disappointed and disgusted.

I have not given the exact words in any of the above reports, and conversation, but as nearly as I could remember. Gen'l. Michie's judgement I could see was that you should allow nothing to anger you, but continue to send telegrams and continue to give the conditions of affairs, until by constant persistence you forced the Gov't. to accede to your demands. That the affected hesitation of the Govt. is only for political effect, and that it desires to be forced into action.

Keep up your spirits, Dearie, and allow your natural and most powerful characteristics rather than your pride to govern you. Persistency will most always insure success. I should want to succeed if for no other purpose than to punish the meddling Postmaster of Jackson.

You will be glad to hear that Ben, although very homesick, is doing finely. He maxed this past week and Gen'l. Michie says that if he keeps on there is no telling what he may not accomplish. He had him up in the section room and examined him for fifteen minutes the other day, and found that he thoroughly understood his subjects. Gen'l. M. does not give the marks, but the instructor was so much pleased that he marked Ben away up.

The children are in fine condition. Butler's cold is cured. Love and kisses from us all. BLANCHE

JACKSON, MISS., *September* 11, 1875

DEAR BLANCHE: I have just sent off a dispatch to Atty. Genl. Pierrepont in reply to his asking me if I have exhausted all my power to protect. When you write, tell me what you think of it. You will probably see it in the papers tomorrow or next day. Nothing has transpired of interest today.

Col. Lee, who has been on trial before a committing court for murder up in Holmes Co., has been bound over to appear before the next circuit court in the sum of $2,000. He confidently hoped to escape without further action. He has no fears, but will be somewhat annoyed by being compelled to dance attendance on the courts.

I do not think there are any more cases of yellow fever at Bay St. Louis. Had the epidemic increased I think I would have heard of it, as Cass is in and out of my office daily.

As I made the last period I began to strike out fiercely at the mosquitoes which assail me, which reminded me of a patent mosquito exterminator some one was speaking of the other day. It is a candle, which burning, puts forth a gas or odor which causes the pests to abscond. The idea is excellent— Do you recall our smudge?

We had rain last night, and it is quite comfortable today. The days pass quickly and I am glad of it. My amusement is found in the history of England which I take up as we do novels. Then it diverts from my labors.

I close with love and kisses for my babes and their beautiful mother. ADELBERT

LOWELL, *September 12*, 1875

DEAR DEL: In your letter which I received yesterday you write of having received mine containing "good advice" and at the end of the same letter that nothing "pleases me so much as to hear about the children." This is very natural, Dearie, and I will indulge you as far as possible, still you must have a lecture once in a while. I should not feel that I was fulfilling my wifely duties else.

Butler is getting to be a much better boy. He does not make so much noise about the house, and is far more kindly to his sister. They play together quite good humoredly now. Once in a while he tries to domineer over her, she then sets up such an unearthly squeal—throwing back her head and opening her mouth to its widest extent—that the noise and annoyance of seeing such a spectacle causes him to desist. When she is cross, if he interferes she bites him. In short, she is learning to hold her own in divers ways, and they are both the happier for it.

Yesterday Mother was talking to Butler. He said "Butler, Edith, and little sister is all Mamma has got, a'int it?" "Yes" Mother replied "enough for the present. Don't you think so?" "Yes, them's enough for the present" he answered, with such an intonation on the present that we all laughed. The baby is growing fat. Every day I imagine I feel her limbs are larger and firmer. As she increases in size and strength, her temper increases in undue proportion. She is now the most touchy of the children, and yet she is a good baby. You will be delighted with Edith. She merits the name of "Sonsie" which Mother has given her, for she is always ready for a laugh and a frolic. She is a little shy of strangers.

Today while I was writing a letter, Butler and Edith were on the billiard table playing together. Finally Butler took out of his pocket an old penknife with only one blade left, and that was broken *nearly* short off, and said to Edith "Come here, Sister. Sit down and see me make a boat." Edith obeyed, and when she had seated herself he also drew from his pocket a small chip of wood, which he tried to whittle and pound into shape with the handle of his knife, in the most approved style. From this you may judge that your boy is progressing.

Love from your family. BLANCHE

JACKSON, MISS., *September* 12, 1875

DEAR BLANCHE: I have just put on my boots to protect my feet and ankles from the mosquitoes, and thus protected, seat myself for a chat. As this is Sunday, nothing of a political nature has transpired in my sphere of action. I have no news.

Additional news from the Gulf indicates that the yellow fever has really assumed an epidemic form there. It is also reported as prevailing in New Orleans. While I have no particular fear of the cholera, I do dread the yellow fever, and if it makes its appearance here I shall visit the north part of the state.

Mr. Rhodes had it two years ago. In speaking of his treatment, mustard plasters came under discussion. He said mustard mixed with the white of an egg was the only proper way to make a plaster, and when applied a thin piece of muslin should be put between the skin and the plaster. Do you remember the scorching plaster you once made for me? I took it off, knowing that something about it was wrong, but not until today did I fully appreciate the enormity of your offense in sandwiching me as you did. Remember in the future, mix with the white of egg and separate plaster from body by piece of linen or muslin.

Capt. Avery of Northern Mississippi came in last night, and is stopping with me—he was here a few days ago—he has returned.

It strikes me you are sending Butler out to "sheep killing" at an early age. He will be "smart" by and by with such tuition. Did you teach him the word "smart"? I fear he is already too "smart." Kiss the dear boy for me and repeat my message to him that he shall be a good boy and take good care of his mother and sisters. I send greetings and love.

ADELBERT

JACKSON, MISS., *September* 13, 1875

DEAR BLANCHE: I have no news today. Atty. Genl. Pierrepont telegraphs me that my telegram of Saturday has been submitted to the President and that I may expect action today.

Cass has had a letter from his wife today and she says there is not a case of yellow fever at Bay St. Louis. I am very glad of this for various reasons, one of which is I will not be compelled to wander about the north end of the state till frost comes.

Avery (of Tallahatchie) reports to me the following. Last Saturday morning just before day his house was set on fire by someone believed to be a Democrat, and had it not been for a timely discovery his wife and three babies would have been sacrificed. The house is a frame one, and is supported on wooden blocks—the floor being about three feet from the ground. The fire was built under one end, over the fire was the bedroom in which his family was sleeping. One of the children woke his wife up. The fire was extinguished, but was on the eve of bursting into the room at the head of a little bed in which his oldest girl was sleeping. This deed followed a Democratic political meeting where the people were advised to drive out of the state and county every carpet-bagger.—Avery himself was named as one who should be expelled. He was not at home when his house was fired. So much for the chivalry of this section of our great and enlightened country.

Mr. Rhodes, my private secretary, will soon have to leave his boarding place and has asked me if he can bring his family into the rooms of our attached building. I have consented. I could not well refuse him. If need be, I will ask him to go, when we shall prefer his space to his company.

I send you that of which I possess without limit—love for you and for our babes. ADELBERT

JACKSON, MISS., *September* 14, 1875

DEAR BLANCHE: I have but little news to write you today. I was interrupted here two hours ago, and it is now almost mail time. So I will have to write a brief note.

Today I had a telegram that the President would send me a messenger with dispatches. He will not arrive before next Friday morning.

Col. Morgan came in from Yazoo City where he has been secreted since the riot on the 1st inst.

I send you this, that you may have your regular letter. My supper is on the table, cold, but this shall catch the mail.

Love, ADELBERT

JACKSON, MISS., *September* 15, 1875

DEAR BLANCHE: Your letter from Lowell—the first one you have written—was received today. I hardly realize you have changed your quarters. My thoughts go more readily to you as I left you in July last than as you now are.

I saw in a paper today that an aerial-fire-ladder was on exhibition in New York a day or two since and that it broke, seriously injuring a number of men. If you get a description of the ladder, send it to me. I have no doubt my own is far superior to it. My ladder ought to be experimented with. I wonder if your father has done anything with it. I hope he will, for it will save me expense.

Politically, I have nothing new today. Nothing new has transpired. My spare moments are devoted to English history. When I awake in the morning I get up and take my book back to bed under the mosquito bar with me, where I read till George comes with my breakfast and the mail.

If you want something to do I can suggest you have the children's photographs taken and send them to me. Saving, always, copies for them when they grow up—and they are growing up and we are growing old very fast—more's the pity. If this sort of life continues for the rest of my term I shall be willing to settle down anywhere for a quiet life. I feel that these days are more than half wasted which are passed away from you and the children. With such a feeling it is wrong that we should be separated. Yet I know we cannot now be together—but the moral I am drawing is let us so manage that such another necessity shall not be upon us. So much for moralizing.

I send you, my Beautiful, love, the same to the babies.

ADELBERT

LOWELL, *September* 16, 1875

DEAR DEL: I have looked up my dates again and am right once more. I believe my letters have been as usual dated several days behind the time when they were written. However, this is not one of my worst faults.

Your wife is really a "jack of all trades" in addition to my many other employments. I was called upon this morning to mix paint to match the tints on the library ceiling. This I accomplished to the satisfaction of everyone, and the man is now painting the plastered heads of twenty-four dozen screws which have been put into the ceiling to keep it from falling.

Edith talks quite well now. When asked as to the whereabouts of her Father she answers clearly "gone to 'Sippi." She is very fond of naming over all of the members of the family who are going on the cars with her soon. It is really quite wonderful how fast the children are progressing. Two of them are quite capable of taking good care of themselves when playing about the yard. Of course Annie keeps a general supervision.

I am going to see Mr. Carney tomorrow and settle that note. He writes me that he has now in his hands $16,550—of this three thousand was not in the original trust, and the interest of that amount for five years, added to it will make nearly five thousand, probably enough to settle the note. There is one thing about it, however, Del.—When you come North in November I shall have to ask you to bring money enough to pay clothing debts, etc. for I shall have exhausted all credit. You will know in plenty of time how much will be needed. Won't it be fine for *us* to be out of debt, Sweetheart. You know I do not mind being indebted to you for any amount, as long as you are not backward and dilatory about granting my demands. Of course, I should not like it very well if you were to refuse to pay my bills—but as long as you do not, I do not, and shall not hesitate to call upon you to the extent of your ability to grant.

Remember the "*golden rule:*" "Feel towards others as they do towards you." With love, BLANCHE

JACKSON, MISS., *September* 16, 1875

DEAR BLANCHE: The only news I have today is a telegram from Warner, Raymond, etc. in Washington, saying that everything is all right there. Exactly what they mean by it I do not know, but I presume it is "all right." There have been no new developments in the state. The messenger the President sent to me I expect tonight—or tomorrow morning.

I have not had a game of croquet for a long time till tonight. Clover and I have been playing. Out of ten or a dozen games, he only won two. My science was wonderful.

George has just come in to light the gas and shut the blinds, and left me again with my thoughts.

I am glad you are not here in this tumult and excitement, but that you are so comfortably established in your old home in a civilized country. Yet, in a month and a half we will have our election and then we shall again have peace. This time will pass very quickly.

I wish you would send me the bond of the State Treasurer you speak of in your letter received by me today. I have looked high and low for that bond, of course, unsuccessfully. It is of no importance really. A new bond has been given, and the men on this one wish to withdraw it.

I should much like to see you all. I have been thinking that I have at times been too severe with Butler, and have tried to make up my mind not to whip his little hand for its naughtiness as I have formerly done. Yet, reason tells me that love alone will not control such little likenesses of Adam. When we shall be together again I shall try, be the result what it may.

I will look to the moon tonight for the kisses you sent me by her. You see I claim it is *her*, the moon—chaste goddess—and quite ignore the *man* who is there. Should a fellow kiss a girl he would not consider that he was kissing that other fellow she might have in her eye. We will look to the moon for your kisses. I will send them back again—no, not the same ones nor others near as *nice* but mine own—such as I have they are yours—many of them. With them find much love that grows with a strong, steady growth—more engulfing and consuming each day and year. ADELBERT

LOWELL, *September* 17, 1875

DEAR DEL: I am homesick and want to be with you, partly on my own account, partly on yours. I read Pierrepont's letter in the evening paper, and it aroused me so that I felt I must fly to you, and had quite made up my mind to start next Monday. Now second sober thought has prevailed, as well as Mother's opposition, and I will not go until I hear from you. This letter will reach you in four days, and I want you to telegraph me to come or not to come as you wish and think best. The children, of course, will remain here with Mother. I should not dare to change the climate for them before the frosts in the South. The baby is nearly a year old, and it is time to wean her. The weather here is very cool, and they are all in fine condition. I think I could leave them without risk. If your political campaign does not begin until the middle of October, I could have three weeks or a month with you, and then return here to get ready for our winter sojourn. Not knowing what your plans are to be, I fear to start without consulting you, lest on my arrival you might be on the point of leaving Jackson for some place where I could not follow. If you can have me with you, do not hesitate to say so, Del. I feel that I have deserted my post, and so much of my heart is in Mississippi that I am too uneasy to be happy when I know that things are not going to please you. I shall await your answer anxiously.

In one of your letters you say "If the President does not aid us there will be no fall campaign in the state." As an outsider, Del, I should say that such a decision was wrong. The President will come to the rescue, Del, if these murders continue, and if possible I think Republicans should steadfastly pursue the same course they would if there were no disturbances—only with this difference, that women and children should not attend the meetings and so far as possible the men should be armed for defense. If disturbed they should not only defend themselves but it should be understood that there would not be a single house belonging to a white-liner left standing above the ground. The Govt. has told the Republicans of Miss. to band together and protect themselves. Arson is less reprehensible than murder and likely to prove far more efficacious—for men after one or two lessons would stay at home to protect their firesides instead of stampeding over the country committing wholesale murder. The colored people of the state are indebted to you for much, but you will not have fulfilled your whole duty until you have set them an example for self-protection. Let the white-liners once learn to fear the Negro, as the Negro does the white-liner, and each will keep the other in check, and so keep reacting until at last all may stand a chance of becoming good citizens.

Indeed, Del, the North will sustain you better in anything, rather than apparent inaction. I understand how you are situated, Del, but the country does not, and will not. But a decided, bold attempt, no matter if it is a wrong one, will challenge admiration and do more for the state abroad than fifty Grants assisting could do. Of the home effects you must judge. But anything is better than nothing, and I would not allow myself and adherents to be bullied into silence. Bullies are always cowards when opposed with courage and determination.

Remember Gen'l. Rosseau.—I would not be too careful about always having right on my side. A little homeopathic dose would do those outlaws good—"similia similibus curantur" may prove correct in this case as in many others. How would it do to issue a proclamation instructing the people what course to take—for self protection—saying inasmuch as the Gov't. advises us to take measures to protect ourselves and refuses aid, this is the only course left us to pursue, and be the result what it may, let the praise or blame fall upon those who compel us to action.

You see, Del, I am excited and must write my mind on the subject or sleep will fly my pillow tonight. Let the row come, the sooner the better, and compel the President to action. A few white men killed and some burned cotton gins and houses, and the whole South (reb. I mean) would be a unit for federal interference.

Ah, well! I must say good night. You will be tired of this letter and yet I am sure I give expression to a feeling which is very general at the North.

Take care of yourselves, even if the consequences are somewhat startling. I shall be ready to start the moment I get word *come*. Kisses, Dearie. BLANCHE

JACKSON, MISS., *September* 17, 1875

DEAR BLANCHE: I have been nearly all the afternoon engaged in replying to a telegram from Atty. Genl. Pierrepont, relative to affairs. His telegram is rather severe on us and our party, simply because we have taken no action to protect ourselves. The fact is, however, that I have endeavored time and again to organize militia and have utterly failed. You will see my letter by and by, when you can judge of its merits. I have been heretofore disgusted at the condition of affairs, but Pierrepont's telegram has quite exasperated me. Perhaps, however, my own helplessness to protect has had its effect of laying the foundation of both my disgust and exasperation.

I shall turn to something else now. I never give you more than a page or a page and a half of politics in my daily letters.

I had a letter from Tolman today, containing his weekly report. He says that Paul and Nesmith both appear to be enjoying themselves. I suppose they are staying at Father's. What is the trip they have on hand?

Last evening after closing my letter to you, Mr. Osborne, who has a room up stairs now, occupying Mrs. Breck's (Packer takes his), came in with his chess board. The first game he beat me, but the second and third, which we played while I was eating my supper, were disastrous to him. Now, George has gone for my supper—it is getting on toward eight in the evening, and Mr. O. has come in with his chess board for another struggle.

I am a great deal preoccupied now-a-days, and find much difficulty in driving my more serious affairs out of my head, even when writing to you, my Love. I am such a serious fellow—when I am serious—and take my duties so seriously that it is uncomfortable to myself—however, I believe I hide it from all the rest of the world—at least I try to.

Love, ADELBERT

LOWELL, *September* 19, 1875

DEAR DEL: This afternoon Uncle Parker and Aunt Maria were over here. Uncle P. is going South next Thursday or

Saturday and asked me if I did not want to go with him, that he was sure I "ought to go, for Ames must be feeling like the devil and needs the comfort of having some of his family with him." I said at once that I would go, and then told him that I had written you Friday night to ask if you were to be in Jackson and if you wanted me to come. So if you say come, I shall have Mr. P. for an escort. This of course would be pleasanter, but I should not mind the journey alone. What a frightful shock that attempt to fire Avery's house must have given them all. They must be living in constant terror.

I am rather sorry that you have given Rhodes leave to live at the Mansion—for the reason that it will be likely to make hard feeling when we desire to make a change, and because in these times the more men you can have in and about the mansion the better. Mrs. Rhodes and her daughter only take up room without being able to render any service in case it is necessary. You remember how thankful we were that Barrett did not accept our offer. They will have quite as much difficulty in finding a boarding place in two months as at the present time, and will not be half so easily suited. If you have not gone too far I am sure it will be better to put them off. I know women well enough to appreciate the fact that they are not so easily disposed of at will, and will hold fast to a good place when they find one. Mrs. Rhodes is pleasant and all that, but I feel that our winter will be pleasanter if we are by ourselves. Our attempt to make it pleasant for Lee and Packer did not, I fear, make them any more kindly disposed or more inclined to do what they knew would be agreeable to you. Any way, Del, have it fully understood that the Mansion shall have no lady occupant when I arrive.—All this is much ado about nothing, is it not Del, and you must be heartily sick of the subject?

Butler said to me today "Are you going to write to Papa, Mamma? He will be lonely if he do not get a letter from you." You would have laughed to have seen him take up his Gran's eye-glasses, hold them in one hand up to his eyes with the fingers all spread out exactly as she fixes hers, the newspaper in the other held off at arm's length, as if he were very far sighted. All this with perfect gravity of countenance, and evidently satisfied that he was doing the thing exactly right. He is a droll boy. Yesterday I told him all about the picture of the Madonna with the little cherubs, and about the death of Priam.—Both these pictures hung in Mother's dressing room. Mother gave him the history of Columbus. You can judge that he is growing learned fast.

I am writing in the nursery, and even now I hear a cry "wants my hat." It comes from Edith who has been aroused from her sleep by Annie, who always takes her out of my bed and puts her with Butler for the night. She was greatly pleased with an old hat I found and insisted upon taking it to bed with her. Now, though scarcely awake, it is her first thought. So much for vanity.

I send you two copies of the *National Republican*. You may have seen them, but if not, it is well you should.

Father will be home in a few days. I shall be glad to hear his opinion on the state of affairs. Do not allow anything to make you lose your temper. Now is the time for nerve.

McGuire, writing Mr. Parker from New Orleans, says there is a good deal of division among the Republicans of Miss. Some in favor of, and some against, Gen'l. Ames' course, but with his coolness and courage he will bring matters out all right.

I close this long letter with love from your babies and

BLANCHE

JACKSON, MISS., *September* 19, 1875

DEAR BLANCHE: I did not write you yesterday for the simple reason that I was over-run with visitors till long after the mail closed. I do not deem it safe to leave my letters at the hotel for five hours, to be inspected by strangers and possibly stolen.

This day has been clear and cool, and for comfort's sake I have had a fire, though I have one window open. I greet with pleasure this cold weather. To meet it I now have in the basement forty cords of dry, hard wood. I have also sent for two carloads (20 tons) of coal. With such a stock well housed we will be able to be quite comfortable next winter. The Rhodes came yesterday through the rain, and are occupying the two western rooms of the detached house.

It is two months ago today that I left you at the depot on my way here. What with the legislature, the party strifes, party nominations, and with a murdering white league, I have had a very lively time. A month and a half more and we will take a rest.

I spoke in my last letter of a communication I was writing to Atty. Genl. Pierrepont. I have not sent it. I do not know as I will. I fear I was in too belligerent a state of mind when writing it. We will decide definitely after seeing the delegation which have been to Washington. What I regret more than anything else is that the North cannot and will not understand the rebellious and barbarous spirit which prevails among the whites here. I do not know that there is any use in fretting about it. Yet their ignorance places us in a false position. The postmaster you speak of is Pease of Vicksburg. Thus he buys his peace from the Democracy who despise him beyond any and all of us.

I send you with this the accumulated reports from Iowa and Minnesota. You will find Sam's estimate of the past year's work by the Fort Atkinson mill. I suspect your calculation is somewhat too large. Tolman writes me that it takes five (5) bushels of wheat to make a barrel of flour. I anticipate a far better season during the next twelve months than the last has been, especially for our Iowa property. It now has a reputation, which it had not then. The Northfield mill succeeds fairly at all times and seasons. We may have made a good many thousands this year, but I feel a little stinted when no dividends are declared.

As you say, Beloved, we are remarkably blessed—more so than we appreciate or comprehend. Our woes thus far have been one and all imaginary, and it would be wicked for us to murmur—but I don't murmur—but I do get wonderfully "mad" at times! We have agreed that "man never *is*—but *to be* blessed." So it is all right now.

I can only say about your picture for Mr. Chadwick that I want you to paint my picture *soon*. I am growing old, and who cares for an *old* picture. If you won't paint my *face* I shall declare you haven't the capacity to do so.

Kiss the babies for me and tell them that I am often thinking of them—yet not so often as I do of their beautiful Mother. I sent some kisses to you by the moon last night—did they reach you? If not, the moon must have given them to young lovers who make her their messenger, never for a moment supposing any kisses would be sent in such a way to an old married lady with three babies. Love. ADELBERT

LOWELL, *September 20, 1875*

DEAR DEL: I write you only a few words tonight, because I am quite tired, having been in Boston all day with Florence, shopping. It seems to me that there is no end of the things to buy, but there is an end of money to pay for them.—Some little suits for Butler, well made, but perfectly plain, they ask twenty-five dollars for. Do you think that you can afford eight winter suits at such a price? Ah, well, we shall manage after some fashion.—In the meantime, all are well and send love, kisses, and caresses to our dear one.

Two letters came from you this evening, in one of which you say that you are in expectation of a special messenger from the President. I only hope that they may contain something more consoling than Pierrepont's letter.

I shall expect a telegram from you in a day or so about going to Jackson. I cannot determine in my own mind what you will say.

Good night, Sweetheart. BLANCHE

JACKSON, MISS., *September* 20, 1875

DEAR BLANCHE: I was quite amused at Butler's way of agreeing with your mother on your possessions "at present." I am glad he is putting aside his tyranny towards his sister Edith. I have looked upon his disposition to command with a little apprehension—especially as he showed so little heart in his treatment of his sister.

I saw Cass today, and was informed by him that Mrs. Gallagher of Bay St. Louis who lost two of her children by yellow fever has since died, also their third and last child is dead, and that her husband Mr. G. was dangerously ill of the same disease. Cass said that there all agree that it is the yellow fever, but that it was carried into that family by a friend who had had it in New Orleans, but who visited them in his days of convalescence. No other cases have been reported.

Warner came home yesterday and brings good news from Washington. The situation here remains unchanged.

We are having delightful weather. It does not look like fall, yet. The rains have kept the grass in our yard green, and the trees have not yet begun to turn their leaves except here and there a tree. I do not go out much. In fact, I keep as close as ever to my own vine and fig tree.

Noonan says someone has written him to see me to buy my house in Natchez. I have offered to sell it for $5000. That is $1100 less than I paid for it. I am willing to lose that much to get rid of it. Perhaps the writer will not give so much.

I greet you with love, ADELBERT

JACKSON, MISS., *September* 21, 1875

DEAR BLANCHE: Another day has gone and we the same except another sun is to be numbered among the past.

I have begun to organize the militia and have sent on North

for some muskets. They will be here in ample time for use. Even now Genl. Warner is opposed to the organization of the militia. He wants me to call again on the President for troops before we do anything. This of course I cannot do. We will organize and do all we can.

The weather keeps cool and pleasant. I see that there has been quite a heavy snow storm in Canada. If so you must be suffering from the cold in Lowell.

I got out of bed by sunrise this morning and taking my history back to bed with me read till your letter was brought in. I read the papers till ten o'clock when some gentlemen came in for consultation which lasted till midday. At half past two I went to dinner, taking Warner with me. After dinner I came home and have been reading till now.

Mr. Rhodes came into my room last evening and found me in the large rocking chair reading. He said "I should think you would feel lonesome here by yourself." I think myself it would be more cheering to have somebody here I know.

I called on Mrs. R. last evening, or in the afternoon just before dark. I thought it was due our neighborly relations. I found her with disheveled hair and in an old gown. She was in dress and ornament quite devoid of those frivolities known under the head of fashions. I thought I had met her before, but she said we had not met. She talked of herself—California —religion, and finally came to spiritualism. She claims to be a Swedenborgian, if anything. They, you know, have different heavens, or grades of heaven. I suggested the inconvenience of being in one and having the best beloved in another heaven. I told her of an old army officer who in discoursing of the future said—there is Major —— —he is a good man. He will go to Heaven where he will never see any of his old army friends, while the rest of us will all go together happy in each other's company. She was eager to discuss spiritualism, but I offered unappreciative remarks. Soon her husband came in. Mrs. R. was uncomfortable all the time, for she was not dressed *up*.

I believe I have given you all my news.

Will my lady accept a kiss from ADELBERT

LOWELL, *September 22, 1875*

DEAR DEL: I am heart-sick every time I take up the papers. You well know that usually I do not mind them, or their comments, and I suppose I should not now if we were together. But as it is, when I see anything disagreeable I think Ah! that will be annoying to Del, and I am not with him to lighten the gloom. I do hope you will telegraph to me to "come," for I am sure I should be far happier to be with you for the next month, although it will separate me from my pretty babies.

Butler said to me this evening, "Mother, where did you get so many babies, me and Edith and sister? Who did give them to you?" I was a little taken aback, but finally answered "Your Father gave them to me." He thought it over a few moments and then asked "Who gave them to Papa?" Again I was nonplussed, but told him "God gave them to your Father." This seemed to satisfy him entirely and he changed the subject by telling me how much he liked to climb trees. I quite innocently said "What makes you like to climb trees so much?" He turned slightly on his heel in a kind of half pirouette, and answered "God makes me like to." You can judge he is rather a queer fellow.

Poor Edith has been disfigured for the last day or so by a boil on the end of her nose. Fortunately it has come to a head on the inside, so that she will not have an ugly scar to disfigure her face. She is quite tall, and is so restless at night that she must be troubled with growing pains. I used to be greatly troubled in that way, and can have full sympathy for her.

Tomorrow the young men of Lowell are to have an amateur horse trot at the Fair Grounds. Five hundred invitations have been issued. We, of course, are among the number and are to don our prettiest robes to grace the occasion.

You will be glad to hear that Ben has gone up a section. This is good news, is it not? I wonder if it is because he really deserves it, or if it is because Gen'l. M. is determined that he shall go up. Young Blair said if Ben had been fairly treated he would never have been put down last year.

Father has not yet returned, but we are expecting him daily. Also Paul.

I have not seen any mention of the fire ladder you speak of—but from your account draw favorable auguries for (ours) yours. I want your Aunt Marietta to try soap with starch before I make any more experiments.

(*Closing of letter missing.*)

LOWELL, *September 22*, 1875

DEAR DEL: Your telegram came this evening. I found it on the library table when we returned from the horse-trot. The tone of your letter which came this morning had somewhat prepared me for such an answer—for in it you said that you were glad that I was enjoying such a good home in a "civilized country." I think you have decided this question from the standpoint of what you deem best for me, not what you think best for yourself. You have made a mistake, Del, for I could have spent the next month with you as well as not, and we should both have been the happier for it. As you have said "No" I have no support to fall back upon when Mother is opposed, and it is quite clear that Mr. Parker will go South without me unless you change your mind and telegraph "Come."

Father came back this evening. He says that he had a long talk with Pierrepont and urged that he should order the troops now in Mississippi to report to you, saying that you would use them only when it was really necessary. This he agreed to do. How he has kept his word you can best judge, for you know all the circumstances and we have so far only newspaper reports.

Father met in the West a Mr. Bowles of Springfield, Ill. This gentleman had just returned from Long Branch, having seen the President, who he says has given up all expectation of renomination for a third term, also all hope of a Republican victory in the next presidential contest. So little hope has he that he is quite content to let things take their course, and has given himself up to the enjoyment of the remainder of his term.

If when you have seen his messenger, you write that you are not satisfied, Father will go to Long Branch and try to stir him out of his apathy. So much for politics. Now we come to home matters.

John T. is in the East. Father met him on the New York boat last night. They had a chat about Paul, Northfield, etc. Then someone came up to speak to Father, and they separated not to meet again, for when the man had gone Father searched the boat to find John, and could not. He had probably gone to bed. In the morning I will telegraph to the American House for him to come up. Paul and Tom have gone up to the Northern Pacific, and expected to have joined Father at Milwaukee on the 22nd, but will fail in that, as Father is here.

We had a fine race today. Willis Farrington was the victor. McDaniels next. The Bunting Co. was triumphant. Ned Tucke won the race for the slowest walking horse. A pair of reins made of leather. The other prizes were whips.

When in Boston I bought for Edith a little bag such as you sometimes see the ladies wear. She is perfectly delighted with it. Night and day it does not leave her, for she insists upon sleeping with it tucked under her cheek.

I gave all your messages to Butler. They did not seem to take great effect. But he asked "What will Papa say when he knows I can climb way up in a tree?" Good night,

BLANCHE

JACKSON, MISS., *September 22*, 1875

DEAR BLANCHE: I telegraphed you today "No." By which you of course understood that you were not to come here at this time. You can do me no good here. I will not say you would embarrass me, but fear of sickness for you and the probable necessity of leaving you here alone would have their influences. Really, you could do nothing beyond the pleasure your presence would give. I am alive to the unpleasantness of my position. I think I have told you already that I have most zealously sought to organize the militia, but owing to the universal protestations of all Republicans I have failed. I have not been able to find even *one* man to co-operate with me. Although we had troubles like those of Vicksburg before, the legislature last year would give me but $60,000 for militia purposes which is a trifle compared to what is needed. Of course all the blame comes on me. All you express and far more has been felt by me, yet I must possess my soul in patience.

I have taken steps to put all the arms I have or can possess (get) into the hands of colored people and shall demand that they fight. The white liners are intimidated by the attitude of the national government. What is to be the result I cannot say. I shall, for one, insist on severe measures. Some of our friends want me to call the legislature together—others think the insurgents will prevent Republican members coming. Then again, there are such men as Price and Campbell who feel and will probably act as has Pease. I shall arm.

It is very loving in you to wish to come so far to me. I would have sent you a longer telegram only I did not care that all the world should know what we were telegraphing about. Every telegram can be and doubtless is taken from the wires at each station, at least in this state where I am the central figure.

We can have but five weeks more of this at most. After

the election I think I will go to Mass. to get you and not be so sparing of my time as I was last year.

I love you all the more, Beloved, for your letter of today.

ADELBERT

JACKSON, MISS., *September* 23, 1875

DEAR BLANCHE: This has been a busy day for me. I had appointments for friends to meet me here in the Mansion this forenoon at 10 o'clock, and from then till now I have been listening to the excited talk that times like these call forth. I am really tired of the clatter.

The Democracy have played a game on us today. I have an appropriation of $55,000 for militia purposes made by the last legislature, but shortly after going to my office I received notice that the Auditor of Public Accounts had been enjoined and forbidden to pay out that money. The unpleasant part of it is that they can enjoin any appropriation the legislature could make. We could appeal, but the supreme court is against us, and can delay till after the election. I cannot call the legislature together because we cannot maintain a quorum should the Democrats in the senate absent themselves, which they will do as they have done heretofore. So I must fight it out as I have been doing alone. In our consultation today I found they all wanted me to again call for troops, which I could get using a formula the Atty. Genl. gave me. But I would not consent to ask again before an effort on our part. Act we will. I have begun to organize colored militia and shall continue till the last man of our side is in the ranks.

I had no letter from you today. Tomorrow I will receive your Sunday letter. We are having delightful weather. It is so cold at night I have to tie myself up into a knot to keep warm and even then fail. I will have some more blankets for tonight.

I send you of what I have in great abundance—love,—for you, Beautiful, and our babies.

ADELBERT

LOWELL, *September* 24, 1875

DEAR DEL: John came up today and reports all well at Northfield. But he is uneasy, and acknowledges that he is a victim of nervousness and indigestion, that he cannot sleep nights, and is impelled to constant action. He has consulted a doctor in Boston in regard to a burning spot on the spine, which has troubled him. The doctor told him it was the result of indigestion, that he could do nothing for him, that he was at the change of life, which is the same for men as for women although not so dangerous, and he would probably settle into a hale, strong man. That he must not confine himself too closely to business, but should sit on a rock in the sun, and keep all troublesome thoughts out of his mind.

I said to him, "John, you would sit on that rock the doctor speaks of about ten minutes and then you would feel your inherent restlessness creeping over you, impelling you to throw that rock with all your force from you and driving you on to seek rest somewhere else. I think your Father has something of the same temperament, and Del the same, though not to the same degree as your Father even. I do not believe that any change in your business will lighten your cares one particle, on the contrary it would tend to increase them, for I know of no business which will allow a man to absent himself for three and four months at a time except that at Northfield. Then again, you have a large family, chiefly girls, and if in making new ventures they should prove disastrous, what a fearful thing it would be." "I have not the least fear about it Blanche, and of course should keep the farm, anyone could make a living out of that. There are some men in New York who want to buy one half of our property and I am ready to sell one half of mine, and have written to Adelbert about it and told him I should speak to you."

We talked the matter all over. He admitted that it was good property and in the worst times would pay a reasonable percentage. Still he wants to sell partly owing to his health and partly from some wild idea that he can do better. You and I know, Del, that there is no business which he could undertake requiring so little attention, and so well adapted to them now as is the Northfield. The only thing that will be left for us to do is to go and take part in it, and keep the firm in good order. I am sure that there is nothing else for which your services are required, although it is possible if you were there that John and your Father would go travelling and leave you at the helm.

John says the firm paid eleven thousand dollars for commissions last year. This did not include storage. I suggest that this would be a good place for some one. There is one thing, however, of which we may rest assured. Poor John will never be content. In addition to his own restlessness, he has an uneasy wife, constantly urging him to this or that. In this your Father has greatly the advantage, for your Mother is calm and content, and adapts herself to her surroundings.

John has gone to Rockland. He had directed his letters to be sent there, and wanted to get them, so in spite of all our endeavors and persuasion (Mother urged him very strongly, and so did I), he would go, but promised to return in a week and make us a visit.

After saying so much about your brother, I have something to tell you of Paul. It seems that John sent them out shooting in the river near his farm, the first day or so they arrived, and they killed some ducks and shot at many more. At last, just as they were giving up for the night, Paul saw a goose fly up and fired a couple shots at it, making feathers fly in all directions. As they had floated down near the mill when he fired, John inclines to the belief that it was old Mother Jackson's goose which was so unfortunate as to fall in the way of our enthusiastic sportsman. They could not find the goose, so it escaped, or went over the dam, and old Mrs. J. has not made any complaints. John was hoping that she would, so that he might fix the joke firmly upon Paul. They have had fine sport, and having exhausted the fun of killing prairie chickens, partridges, snipe, etc. have gone with your Father, a cook, tents, blankets, etc. two hundred miles north, for geese and ducks.

This evening I read in a Boston paper that colored troops were trying to organize in Mississippi, and the movement was meeting with great opposition. Also that the sheriff of Amite Co. officially reported to you the presence of one hundred armed men from Louisiana stopped by pickets. All this put me on thorns, and I again insisted that I would go with Uncle Parker next Sunday. Mother said it would do no good for me to go. Of course I understand that, but if there is to be trouble I want to be with you, even if I am in the way. Father decided that it was entirely out of the question, but I was none the less decided until your letter came saying that Warner had returned from Washington with good news. I suppose you will not write me what it was, owing to the uncertainty of the mails. I am content if you call it "good news" and will remain satisfied until I have gotten another scare. Do not be careless about yourself Del, and have the bolts fixed on our doors. You are not dealing with a noble foe, but a murderous one.

John thinks the baby the handsomest of the children, and says that she resembles her Mother more than the others. Don't you resent this?

I will paint your portrait this winter, Sweetheart, if all goes well with us, and as for your growing old, every gray hair and every wrinkle belongs to me. There are many things which you had before I knew you, but all which have come since are more truly mine—and I prize them a little more highly. Love,

BLANCHE

JACKSON, MISS., *September 24*, 1875

DEAR BLANCHE: I have no news for you today, except that I am organizing my militia and preparing for an emergency by and by. The programme of the Democracy now is to remain passive till two or three days of the election, when it will be too brief a time for Grant to issue his proclamation—he needs five days—at least that seems to be the minimum time to make his proclamation generally known—and on the day of election or two or three days preceding—bring forth their guns, rifles and pistols for slaughter. I will try to meet such demonstrations, but even now there are no Republicans in the eastern part of the state who will consent to the organization of the militia there. Such is the report I get from there today.

Carrying the election by violence and murder, the Democracy intend, so they say among themselves, to impeach me and turn the state over to the president of the Senate, one of their own men.

You ask what is to be done with Lt. Gov. Davis. This,—The charge against him of receiving a bribe for the pardon of young Barratine will be sustained (information received by me convinces me beyond a doubt of this fact). The charge sustained disqualified him and at the same time displaces him. A jury might disagree, to be sure,—but such a legislature as the Democracy expect would impeach him. In fact, the Democracy at the last extra session in July introduced resolutions of condemnation of his act, and would have tried to present articles had there been any hope.

You may feel astonished at what I say and ask what under the sun they can impeach me on. To which I reply I cannot conceive of anything done by me that a single charge against me can attach to. But a party that will take innocent blood for success will not hesitate at anything else. While they will have the will to do anything to advance their own interests I do not imagine they will have the power to impeach anyone. They may however, get control of the lower house. Time flies, and will solve these problems.

I had no letter from you yesterday nor any today. It is unusual that two days in succession should pass without word from you. I hope you have not started on a journey to me. No, I cannot believe it. The mails are somewhat irregular here anyhow, and your letters could well have been delayed.

We are having delightful weather—cold enough for a fire if you want—and warm enough without one if you be so minded.

I send you, Beloved, much love. ADELBERT

JACKSON, MISS., *September 25, 1875*

DEAR BLANCHE: We are having a cold, rainy day to meet which I have a good coal fire.

Capt. Raymond has returned. He was in the office just for a moment today, and in reply to a query relative to Mrs. R. I understood him to say she was here. As I wrote the above Capt. R. appeared. He says Mrs. R. and their boy are here. He is in fine spirits. He saw Paul for a moment in Milwaukee.

John T. has found someone in New York who will buy half of the N. mill for $50,000 and he wants to sell. The buyers to have the sale of the flour in the N.Y. market! Why, the commissions will pay them a good interest on their money aside from the profits of the mill. And the Ameses would be left as they are now, to do the work and drudgery of the business. I cannot see wherein we would be benefitted by such a step. When you see John talk him out of his fancy to do something else or to come East, which latter is, I have no doubt, at the bottom of his desired change. If he desires to go into some new business he can raise money on his part of the mill. Only he should know positively what he is to do.

Mr. Warren has returned. Warner withdrew as a candidate for congress and his county has nominated someone in his place for the state senate. Consequently he is left out in the cold.

Love, ADELBERT

LOWELL, *September 26, 1875*

DEAR DEL: Yesterday Florence and I went to Boston. I ordered three suits and an overcoat for Butler. The other suits I will try and get made at home. This reminds me, Del, that I would suggest if I were you that they should declare dividends at Northfield. If by any chance they should sell out, all that you get out of it will be twenty-five thousand, and what you have drawn to invest in other places. Do you not think it well to make demands, even if they are not acceded to?

John complains bitterly of having all the eggs in one basket. Now my remedy would be not to sell the basket, not to withdraw the eggs already in, but to carefully abstain from putting any more eggs into a receptacle which from all reports seems to be too heavily laden.

After the campaign, Del, you must try to go to Northfield, if only for a day or two. One thing which makes them so unsettled is the want of your presence and steadying power. John says that he was at Fort Atkinson and went over all the figures, and that you have made about three thousand dollars. He is not satisfied with Hicks & Co. and contemplates making another change.

Partridge and Wells[1] have broken down. John seems to still believe in Wells, and wants to get him in with Hicks & Co. as selling agent. I don't know how Mr. Wells will come out of the breakdown of Partridge, but I should doubt the policy of putting great reliance in a partner of an insolvent firm.

Paul came home last night. He enjoyed his trip very much although they were rather unsuccessful in their trip to the North, as it was too early for great duck and goose shooting. He says that Fannie is nearly as tall as I am, and is very pretty —that the sisters are very unlike, so much so that they do not look as if they belonged to the same family. Fannie will go South with your Father and Mother this winter.

Del, we have one satisfaction in this Mississippi business. After you have done your duty the whole thing may go to the dogs, and it will probably be just as well for you in many respects. I mean that you are entirely independent of any honors the state can confer. Your own affairs are in such a condition, that to accept a position were one offered you, you would be likely to interfere with your success financially. We are fortunate to be so situated, that success or defeat will still keep our chariot wheels turning in the right direction.—As for me, I am still ready to face towards Minnesota when it is deemed for the best. But all that is in the future. Love,

BLANCHE

JACKSON, MISS., *September* 26, 1875

DEAR BLANCHE: This is Sunday—a very quiet, peaceful day. Mr. Musgrove has just left me. He came to tell me that the Democracy propose to hold off their dogs till the day of election. I have no doubt he was sent, and his purpose was to dissuade me from organizing the militia. I talked peace as loud as he, but could not forbear to take steps necessary to

[1] Commission Merchants for sale of Northfield and Fort Atkinson Flour.

protect the people. I shall go on with the only work left for me to do.

Gen'l. Augur is here and called on me today. He can do nothing unless ordered from W——n but when the orders come will act promptly.

Gen'l. Augur said that there have been some twenty or thirty cases of yellow fever in New Orleans, but that the season is so late the fear of an epidemic no longer exists. I am glad of that, for our troubles here would keep me here, epidemic or no epidemic.

I have not been out of the house but for a moment during the entire day. The history of England occupies most of my time.

I send you greeting in love, ADELBERT

LOWELL, *September 27, 1875*

DEAR DEL: Your letter dated the day you sent the telegram "No" came today. I knew, Sweetheart, when I wanted to go that I could do no good except in the way you suggest, as a pleasing presence. But even this, with the knowledge that there was one heart devoted to you, might have been good for you, as it would have given some restful, contented moments in which to recuperate for others of struggle and inconvenience.

You say "It is very loving in you to wish to come so far to me." Why, Del, do you not know that but for the babies, we should never have been separated, and that a trip around the world, if for the purpose of joining you, would be pleasant to me? The truth is, I wished, and still wish to be with you, more on my own account than on yours (love is always more or less selfish) for I am uneasy about you, and if I were near you I should be rid of the feeling to a certain extent.

The Northern papers report that you have two colored militia companies. How unfortunate that the Northern men around you have not more determination. Ah, well! I am convinced that this trouble will all turn out for the best—in the end.

This reminds me that Tom and Florence were here this evening and Tom says, pardon the term, that "the Capt. is a brick. Everybody likes him in all the country around, but nothing goes quite to please him, for instance, he does not want the trouble of going down to that Bank. It takes a great deal of time and it is fuss, fuss, about something or other. It is good property, though, it pays fifteen percent." Of course it amused Tom that anybody should complain of a little trouble a bank might give which paid fifteen percent. Tom wrote your Father last night to thank him again for the pleasant time he had had, and for the great attention shown him. He says everybody did all in their power for them. He thinks that Fanny is very pretty, bright and chatty. I think that both he and Paul appreciate the great kindness shown them.

The house in Washington is rented to Jones for three years and a half, at thirteen thousand dollars a year. Mother is well satisfied with the arrangement, as it still leaves the middle house handsome and comfortable to live in, relieves her of a great care in furnishing the corner house, and the two rented buildings give an income of nineteen thousand.

Father wants Paul to go on to Washington this winter and study law for six months. Paul has not yet said whether he would prefer to do this, or go into the Cartridge Mills at once.

Butler is the man of the house, and except for a bad habit of calling his Mother names when she displeases him, fighting Edith and tormenting poor Teedle, would be a model boy. He is the brightest child of his age I have seen. This is not spoken out of a Mother's conceit, but from a careful comparison with other children of his age.

I send you kisses, Dearie, and am glad to hear of your determination to make a little stay North when you come. Not that I reluct in the least at the thought of going South, but because I want you to have a little freedom.

Take great care of yourself for my sake and for the children. Good night. BLANCHE

JACKSON, MISS., *September 27*, 1875

DEAR BLANCHE: I received from you by today's mail two letters and the Treasurer's bond. I was glad to see that the style of paper is changed, for now I shall be almost sure of having a reasonably long letter. Why do the young ladies, who as a class are not renowned for much learning (slander of course), submit to a fashion which demands much ink or a glaring blank of fancy paper? I hope you will buy so large a stock that it will last long after the next new fashion which may revert to the pigmy sheets which have been so familiar to the world of late.

It is not because I would not like to have you near me that I telegraphed the "no"; but because you had better be with the babies and out of this tumult which envelops us. Like all who have to *endure* I get disgusted, but believe it is all making me a better man and preparing me for a quiet happy life (D.V.) with my Beloved Ones so far away.

What hurts me most is that the cowardice of our party since its organization is now visited on my head, and there seems no escape from it. Also all the sins and iniquities of Republican rule in South Carolina, Louisiana, and other Southern states are weighed against me in judgment of the country. Also—this—I am fighting for the Negro; and to the whole country a white man is better than a "Nigger."

Gen'l. Warner, Gibbs, Raymond and others have been playing croquet this evening. Judge E. Hill has just come in. He has interrupted me for some time and is now talking. He wishes to be remembered to you. Love, ADELBERT

JACKSON, MISS., *September* 28, 1875

DEAR BLANCHE: I have nothing new today. I had a thousand muskets arrive today and soon will equip as many men. Please ask your Father to look up the laws (U.S.) which authorize the use of U.S. soldiers to protect citizens at elections. There are a number of Statutes bearing on the subject—the "enforcement" acts—the civil rights acts—the elective franchise—and perhaps a general law under which the U.S. marshal called in U.S. troops in the case of Burns (?) in Boston, years ago. If we can get troops to protect us at the election we will be all right. If your Father finds the law and gets Pierrepont to instruct his marshals to call and the troops to obey, he will render us a great favor. May I ask that you will not overlook this?

Love. ADELBERT

JACKSON, MISS., *September* 29, 1875

DEAR BLANCHE: I have just come from the office, and being at leisure take advantage of the opportunity to write you a note. I send you today newspaper slips containing three letters from "Civic" on the situation here. The body of the letters I first dictated to be sent to the Attorney General U.S. as a reply to his and Grant's letters to me, but when our committee returned and reported them in sympathy with me I withheld what I had written and neglected to finish what I had intended to put on paper. Mr. Rhodes took what I had dictated and published it as letters.

I see by the *Sea Coast Republican* that Mr. Gallagher is recovering from his sickness of yellow fever. You may remember him as the Michigan man I pointed out to you, who lived near the new houses Mr. Ullman was building. He has lost his wife and children. I believe I told you that because of the lateness of the season no one anticipates an epidemic.

I congratulate you on Ben's advancement and hope he will not stop till he reaches the first section.

I do not think you distinguished yourself in your dialogue with Butler. Judging from that dialogue one would say he did not inherit his "smartness" from his mother. What say *you*? *I* think he did—because—I love you. ADELBERT

JACKSON, MISS., *September* 30, 1875

DEAR BLANCHE: In your discourse with John T. you show a very accurate estimate of his peculiarities and surroundings. He never could pursue the same object six months in succession. He tried a number of things as a boy before he could decide what business to follow, when he finally selected what in the East they call "store keeping" and here "merchandising." To buy and sell after his style required little effort of mind and less restraint. It was some like politics where one need not think of any one subject longer than is convenient and also like politics in this, one met all the world in daily gossip. John's predisposition to dyspepsia could be met in no better way than by traveling and change of scene and diet. Our present business permits of any amount of traveling which he could make exceedingly profitable to the firm if he would studiously attend to it.

In a letter the other day I stated that John can hire at a low rate of interest what his part of the mill will bring, and invest it as he may wish. The mill will pay the interest and give him a surplus. He will have principle and interest too. If you are so inclined you can read him what I have already written.—This you had better keep to yourself—to wit: I think his wife is the chief cause of his present desire to change. She has made him make many changes since their marriage—and will not let him alone till he finds himself in Boston or some other eastern city. I but reflect your own views. I will not say I blame him much, for I have no doubt I would do as he has done did you, Dear, make the appeals I believe Nellie has.

You refer to my letter wherein I spoke of good news from Washington. That good news was only the report of Grant's sympathy with me and his purpose to support us when we had done something for ourselves. Nothing more—and yet all we can ask. I have no news today. All is quiet at present simply because the Democratic generals have so ordered.

Tell John T. that I will not write him in N.Y. but ask him to regard this as my answer to his letter. Tell him I will buy his part of the mill as soon as I get out of politics. Tell him also that he should not have any plans which prevent his staying one whole day at Lowell. If he is to traverse the East at such high pressure he will never get an advantage over his dyspepsia.

Love, for you, and our babies, from ADELBERT

JACKSON, MISS., *October* 1, 1875

DEAR BLANCHE: Our baby is one year old today. But a few years ago you and I cared little for any birthday but oneself's; now there are five which equally command our attention. I suppose the baby can walk whenever she is inclined to take exercise. I shall be glad to see her, who is more of a stranger to me than her brother or sister ever were. We, all, will meet in November, in a happy, loving union which shall continue till late next summer at least. Heretofore I have been over-diligent in watching the interests of our party here. I am not convinced it has resulted in good. Hereafter we will not seek to carry so much of the world on our shoulders.

Today I wrote Father that I would try to visit him next month, when I will fully discuss our business matters. When our political career shall terminate, we shall be at liberty to attend to business and then, things holding as they are now, we could go to Minnesota to try one or two years residence there. We could carpet-bag there as we did here, to remain or not as we should subsequently decide.

I am surprised to hear that Fanny has grown so tall. I believe you were about her age when you attained your height. I am suprised you did not get your information from John T. rather than from Paul.

I received a letter from Father today. He pleads for a sale of the mill. I wrote him as I have stated herein.

The unsafe plastering has been taken down in the nursery and they are now at work in the hall. As the rooms are plastered I will have them cleaned up and made ready for occupation. I have a man at work digging the grass out of the brick walk, wheeling away ashes, etc. that our "house" may be in perfect order when my loved ones shall return.

Love to you from ADELBERT

LOWELL, *October* 2, 1875

DEAR DEL: Miss Richardson is here sewing, and I have been running the machine. I shall be very glad when the furnace fires are started, for it is quite difficult to keep our little family in good order. Butler is somewhat under the weather. He has a little, croupy cough, and requires some attention. Altogether I feel that my hands are full, as usual.

Edith is happy with a stove and tea-set. Butler aids in drinking quantities of water and setting the table. When I brought the things home to Edith, Butler said "What did you bring me Marma." "I did not bring you anything this time, Butler, you are not sick—Edith is." "My Papa would brought me a tea-set and stove, I know he would." "I will get you something when you are sick, Butler, but Edith wants the pretty things now, and you can play with her." Not long after, when I was tucking Edith into bed, and saying kind words to her, Butler sneezed, and immediately fell down crying out at the top of his voice. I thought he had strained himself, and flew to his rescue, but the sly fox put his arms around my neck and said "I am sick now, what will you get me?" I laughed at him until he hid his head on my shoulder a little shamed-face, and out of conceit with himself. "He is more like his father than any child I have ever seen." Love,

BLANCHE

JACKSON, MISS., *October 2*, 1875

DEAR BLANCHE: Gen'l. Warner came to tell me he is going up to Breckville to see the Brecks who returned last Thursday. Yesterday I learned Warner is exceedingly anxious to run for the state senate in his county, but the party there will not have him. Did I tell you that Raymond has gone to find President Grant somewhere in Colorado on our party business? The one purpose being to effect a change in some of the federal officials.

I was not expecting to hear that your Father would ask Paul to study law. If P. begins it I suppose he will be your Father's office lawyer. If P. is so inclined it will be a good training, both in study and close business relations, to get the run of the whole business of your Father.

It occurs to me as I approach the bottom of the page, to express regret that my letter is so stupid. I have been wearied today and am dwelling too much on our struggle here. Nevertheless—I love you.

ADELBERT

LOWELL, *October 3*, 1875

DEAR DEL: This has been a quiet day, spent chiefly with the children. In the morning after Horace returned from taking Hattie to church, I took the children over to see Katie, who is not yet well enough to go out. Mrs. Faunce has been quite urgent to have me do so, and this delightful day afforded a good opportunity. Mr. Tucke, Katie and Faunce were at home. All were astonished at the beauty of the children, and their large, dark eyes. Faunce put Katie's baby into Edith's arms.—Edith was sitting in my lap, so that while my arm was really supporting the baby, Edith thought she was holding it. She thought it a doll, and was delighted with it—and said to me "my baby, Mamma, my baby." When the baby cried loudly, she was much concerned, but a little too bashful to sing to it.

Butler went into the garden with me when we returned, and we picked pears and apples, and broke off some ears of sweet corn which had escaped the gardener's notice. Butler called my attention to the corn, saying "Look, Mamma, I am going to take this up and have Harriet cook it for my dinner." Corn is his favorite vegetable.

I was much amused today at a little conversation of his in Mother's room. He had followed me in there, and while I was putting away some things he was looking fixedly at the sea-gulls wings and eggs which are hung over the mantle piece. Presently he spoke— "Mamma, if that old hen should hatch those eggs, what would you do? All the chickens would tumble down all over the floor and break their heads off." This little speech will give you some idea of the speculations which are constantly passing through that young brain, and of which he allows every now and then a glimpse, much to our astonishment. He is very bright, and never forgets anything.

Hattie thinks she would be very fond of him if he were not so malicious. But when, for instance, he has been sent out of the room for making a disturbance, and happening to meet Hattie on the stairs, says to her "You are making too much noise, Hattie, you will wake the baby," she feels inclined to slap him for his impudence. Mother thinks our youngest is "a perfect beauty," which is enough to say about her in this letter, except that taking advantage of her sickness, she is as far away from weaning as ever.

I am more contented now that I hear you do not anticipate any more disturbance in Mississippi. It is harassing to be on the watch for the latest telegraphic reports of outrages. You are wise in your determination to have all done that can be, in expectation of more trouble. Father is going on to Washington in a week or so, and he will see Pierrepont. I wish

Grant were to be there. He will urge them to give such orders that you can command at once. The days are slipping away, Del, and the exciting times will soon be over. Although we have many things to complain of, we have more to be gratified for, and are far better off than the majority of our neighbors.

I have good words about my starch from Aunt Lottie, who recommends it highly. Aunt Nina has been asked for an unbiased opinion. All is not lost yet. Write to your Aunt Marietta.

Love, Sweetheart. Have you made George get you anything to eat? You have much to encounter in the next six weeks, and should be well sustained. BLANCHE

JACKSON, MISS., *October* 3, 1875

DEAR BLANCHE: I am getting cross I am sure. I have been trying to teach people to call on me at the office rather than at the Mansion, and have been flattering myself that I had met with some success, but in these exciting days all barriers are broken down and I am a victim. My grievance just this moment is that I am angry with myself for permitting myself to be imposed upon. Major Howe spent the forenoon with me with others, and will call again this evening, as he will return to his county on tomorrow morning's train.

We all discuss the situation, and all hold very similar views—which are that force, violence, intimidation and murder are the means to be used, and which are now in use, by the democracy, to carry the election. With such weapons in such hands, the chances are against a fair election, and of course likely to prove fatal to a Republican victory. Well, in a month we will know all about it.

It is overcast without, and gloomy, and judging by my nerves (temper) I am inclined to believe that a storm is imminent, or at least we will have the wind from the East.

Mr. Rhodes sent me this morning with my breakfast an oyster stew—a luxury to him, but a dish I care nothing for. My natural diet is clams. This reminds me of that wonderful chowder I made at Bay View last July.

I greet you Beautiful, with a world of love. Kiss the babies for me. ADELBERT

JACKSON, MISS., *October* 4, 1875

DEAR BLANCHE: This day's labors are summed up in this—I begin to be convinced that my Negro militia has not the courage or nerve—whatever it may be called—to act the part of soldiers. That is today. Excuse me if I discuss political matters with so brief a statement.

Major Howe sat late with me last evening. During the course of our conversation he stated his family were indirectly connected with the two events most talked of during the last twelve months—the events referred to being the Beecher scandal and the abduction of Charlie Ross. His wife's brother married Mrs. Ross' sister; and his wife's sister is the Mrs. Bradshaw who was a witness in the Beecher case. As Mrs. Howe accepted your hospitality, and failed to invite you to her own home, I watched sharp for a history of her family. Her father went to Boston as a poor boy, walking, with a bundle on his back. He grew into the firm of "Crocker and Brewster" publishers, Washington St. Boston.—His name being Brewster. I give this item to you as I had an impression that they pretended to aristocratic exclusiveness. Howe says his father-in-law asserts that Beecher is innocent and will not permit anyone in his family to utter a word to the contrary. This shows he is an old granny and one likely to be proud of his ancestry. All of which spite is put forth because you were not treated as you should be.

While writing the above one of the Judges of our Supreme Court came in and solicited from me a promise that I would reappoint him. I could not make the promise.

I send as ever, everything to you, except my presence, that you can desire, yet I would prefer to present myself.

ADELBERT

LOWELL, *October* 5, 1875

DEAR DEL: I will have Father look up the laws you desire, and he will see Pierrepont when he goes on to Washington in the course of a week, or so. We had already planned that he should make a determined appeal to Pierrepont, using all the arguments and documents at command. There are certain passages in your letters, which Father and Mother thought might be effective, as showing the condition of affairs and the difficulties under which you have been and are laboring. These I have arranged, ready for Father to take, and he will do all in his power to have orders so given that you can call for instant aid. Del, I read your letter to Father this evening, and he has looked up the laws in regard to U.S. troops at times of elections, and says they are all to be found in the 24 Article Revised Statutes, that he will see both Pierrepont and Grant when he goes to Washington, and will call their attention to all the points which he thinks are amply sufficient to cover the case. Also, that the troops were called in the case of Burns in Boston to aid in the *execution* of a *warrant* under the fugitive slave laws, which of course are now repealed.

This has been a lovely day.—Miss Richardson is still here, consequently I have been busy running the machine, and about four o'clock I felt a slight headache and fearing it might increase, and unfit me for Florence's party tomorrow night, I put on my hat and went up on the hill to join the children, who were hunting for a few enterprising chestnuts which were very rare, and the more precious when found. Then we went to the grove and cracked green walnuts, picked bright leaves, ate apples, and until sunset enjoyed the bright, warm weather.

Edith, I am sorry to say, has formed a very bad habit of whining. I have thought it owing to her health, but she is so persistent that I am inclined to think she has allowed herself to do it so much that she is now unaware of the noise she is making. Butler and I have had one or two contests, because when crossed he thought it elegant to call his Mother "a nasty, stinking old fool." One more spanking will, I think, cure him.

The baby has come to the conclusion, owing to having her own way, when ill, that the proper place for her at night is on my arm, with her head on my breast. This she will have to change her mind about before many nights are over. Thus, you see, I have my hands full to bring up your family in the way they should go. Still, they are good children and I have not much fault to find with them.

Ben writes "by the way, I went up another section last night." This makes an advance of one in chemistry, two in philosophy, since he returned to the Point. Of course, Ben feels very proud. When Michie was here he said "If Ben keeps on studying as he has begun, there is no telling where he will stop." I am very glad he is doing so well, because it will make him happier.

I send you love, without limit. BLANCHE

JACKSON, MISS., *October 5*, 1875

DEAR BLANCHE: We are having a rainy day. I am glad we have, as it justifies the inclination to "temper" I have felt during the past few days.

A couple of weeks since some one wrote to Mr. Noonan asking him what I would sell my house in Natchez for. He consulted me and replied that I would sell for $5000. He has received a reply saying that it was too high, and the negotiation terminates. This is a very favorable season for crops and the impression prevails that the people will be better off this fall than ever before. The railroad will be completed in a month from Natchez to Fayette, and it is believed it will enhance property in N. I will hold on for the present, at any rate.

The plasterer has finished the nursery and hall. I do not know whether he has found additional places of defective plastering or not. I shall proceed to clean up.

Your descriptions of Butler are quite amusing. He always had an old head, and his youth causes it to appear more so. I hope the babies will not forget me during this lengthened separation. Kiss them for me. Kisses for yourself.

ADELBERT

JACKSON, MISS., *October* 7, 1875

DEAR BLANCHE: I received a telegram today from your Father, signed by Major. I suppose it was sent in view of the troubles reported yesterday in Coahoma County. It is difficult for me to get any reliable information from so remote a point. I am investigating and shall do all I can.

Mrs. Raymond, Mrs. Gibbs and Mrs. Fisher were over playing croquet with us this evening. Mrs. F. was calling on Mrs. Rhodes when we began. Mrs. F. plays just as she talks—gushingly and ludicrously. When she finds herself in the way of a moving ball she jumps over it.

Everything is quiet in this vicinity. The news you get by telegraph about the same time as I do. I believe I told you that Col. and Mrs. Breck have returned. Warner is ill now of the fever. The condition of health of this community is better than it has been of late. A visitor comes. Love.

ADELBERT

LOWELL, *October* 8, 1875

DEAR DEL: I promised you a long letter last night, but have disappointed you. Florence and Tom were here to tea, and remained until our youngest woke, which always puts an end to any attention to anything or anybody except herself. We had a struggle during the night, for Miss was determined to sleep in my arms. Of course, I was victorious.

The Boston *Herald* is abusive, and heads an article on Mississippi troubles "Our Son-in-Law in Mississippi." This is pretty good, is it not, as an exhibition of personal and political malice. The other papers have nothing of this kind, but publish Alcorn's exculpatory article on the riots at Friars Point. I am glad that our worthy Senator has at last reached his old stamping ground, having thrown over his sable friends for his ancient allies.—The colored people may consider themselves well rid of him.

But you, Sweetheart, with all these troubles, must not allow yourself to get despondent. Having done all that is in your power, the rest must be left to the guidance of fate. I am glad that people call at the Mansion and occupy your time, as I am not there to share it, for if you spend too many hours by yourself you will surely grow morbid and gloomy. So I cannot give you any sympathy in this imposition of which you complain.

As for me, for the first time in my life I have cause to envy Mrs. Raymond, for she has a chance to chat with you now and then. Does Mrs. Rhodes use the library and parlors? I think she should not. Resist any encroachment, for my sake, if there should be any, for you know I shrink from intruders on what I hope will be a very happy household this winter.

You will smile when you hear that Paul and I went with Nina Hildreth to take a dancing lesson this afternoon. Mrs. Darracut said that I need nothing but practice, but as Paul will not care to go without me, unless Hattie will take my place, I must take the remaining lessons. It is a private instruction. We three are the only pupils.

Florence's party was a great success, and Tom was well pleased. Mr. McDaniels said to me "what a remarkable, capable, energetic woman your cousin Mrs. Nesmith is. She not only knows exactly what she wants, but how she wants it, and how to do it." John Kimball has returned for the winter, and was at the party. He expressed himself as "totally unprepared for so much splendor and elegance as he found in Lowell." He has been living in Scotland, and looking so long at the dowdy Scotch girls, he had forgotten those he left behind him. As for your wife, I am not called upon to express any opinion of her, but others said she "never looked so beautiful in her life, and not a day over sixteen." Of course you are at liberty to make all the allowances you please. The things were not said to her. She told me in confidence that at one time in the evening she really felt ashamed of herself—for when towards the last of the evening she was sitting down chatting to Wendell Goodwin, a young man about twenty-three or four, nephew of Wendell Philips, he had the presumption to draw off his glove and twirl his mustache, in order to display a unique ring in the form of a coiled serpent which adorned his finger. She felt that she must have appeared very young and foolish, when a coxcomb of that age had the temerity to put on such airs. She could not bring herself to speak of the ring, and after a few moments of vain attempts to attract attention he *resumed* his glove. He was introduced the first of the evening, and although your wife did her best to put him off on the girls and talked of you a great deal, and her children, still he seemed to like her company and her conversation. She would have thought very well of him if he had not maneuvered with that ring. Perhaps you had better write to her, to stay at home and look after the children.

Father saw John T. in Boston today. He is going to New York, and when he returns is coming up to Lowell. Father urged him strongly to come up.

This is enough for tonight, is it not? Love, from the babies and BLANCHE

JACKSON, MISS., *October* 8, 1875

DEAR BLANCHE: Neither yesterday nor today have I received a letter from you. The mails must be sadly out of joint when two consecutive days pass without a single word from you.

This day has been like all of late—much excitement—much talk, and towards sunset, a game of croquet. Mrs. Dedrick was here today with Mrs. Raymond and Mrs. Gibbs. Of course, I was repeatedly interrupted by callers, much to my annoyance. These days are so momentous that I cannot well refuse to see callers, though I am drawing my lines closer and demanding that my official business shall be done at the office.

October 9, 1875

Interruptions prevented my completion of the above in time for the mail. The general excitement was increased by my orders to a colored company to march out to Edward's depot—a town thirty miles west on the railroad—as an escort of arms and ammunition for colored companies. Quite a number feared a battle would result from this movement of the company. I did not fear it. The day is passing away, and I believe no trouble or battle will ensue.

But this is the cause of the non-action of the white liners. They know that if they bring on a war I will call for troops from the U.S. Consequently they have given orders to their well-disciplined army to avoid battle for the present, but with the intention to open fire along the whole line about election time, when the time will be too short for the President to issue his proclamation for them to disperse—a proclamation which gives at least five days grace.

Not a few of our Republicans are now demanding that I should at once call on the U.S. for troops, even before we attempt anything. The trepidation in which they find themselves causes them to appeal to me even before my troops move out this morning. But all the world agrees I should help myself before calling on the President for troops. The fact that my company has not been molested today shows two things—first; that the "white-liners" are not willing to bring on hostilities at this time for the reasons I have stated—and second; that, as my militia has not been interfered with, I cannot consistently call on the U.S. for troops.

I believe I have already written you that our party is sadly demoralized. None of the white Republicans seem disposed to enter the militia, being intimidated by the white liners, and the Negroes are no less intimidated. Election day may find our voters fleeing before rebel bullets rather than balloting for their rights. The troubles in Coahoma result simply and solely from the action of the white-liners, led on by Alcorn, who openly proclaimed that they would take possession of the county by force, although the whites number at most but four hundred while the blacks number two thousand. All this is a race war. Alcorn shows his true colors when he deliberately kills Negroes to gain the ascendency in his county where such a disparity of numbers exist. The assault on the Negroes was most uncalled for and unjustifiable.

The difficulties in the way are apparent. I have neither arms nor men nor money to send up there on the river. I can send a few arms there, had I the money, which I have not. Again, without a guard, it would be impossible to get any munitions of war safely to that point. I see that the U.S. Supreme Court will deliver its opinion on the "Enforcement Act" on Monday next (Oct. 11). Should it decide favorably, we may do something under it. We must wait and see what turns up—yet, feeling and knowing that my own army though the most numerous is without arms, without discipline, and without the morale which is indispensible even where other things abound. Should we fail, all the blame will be put upon me. I see that more clearly day by day. Call on the President, call on the President, is the constant cry—and the more delinquent the individuals in efforts in their own behalf—the louder and more persistent is this appeal to me. How I can retain my own manhood and guard the dignity of the state and yield to this cry under existing circumstances I cannot well understand. It is so safe and easy for Uncle Sam to do our work that that sentiment has numerous advocates. It is true, too, that the white-liners mean to win if they have to shed blood. This is their policy everywhere.

I believe I have given you politics enough for one day. Love, ADELBERT

JACKSON, MISS., *October* 10, 1875

DEAR BLANCHE: I have nothing new to tell you today—except perhaps that our friends are very much dispirited and seem almost ready to abandon the contest. In fact, many have lost all hope of success unless aided by the national government. Consequently they are very persistent in urging me to make a call. Even in counties where there is no actual killing, the Republicans are paralyzed through fear, and will not act. They refuse to accept arms, and organize militia. As this feeling is general, you can well understand what little hope we have of success. The company I sent out to Edwards Depot has not been disturbed as I understand. The result will be that the colored man ceases to be a free man—serfdom awaits him as certain as fate.

Your letter telling of your Father's visit to Washington was received today. I do not know that he can accomplish much when the administration will not even make a change in the U.S. Marshal here, which is a necessity, and which was asked by our committee which went to W——n and also by myself. By what I have written, you will perceive I see nothing very flattering ahead.

This is Sunday—hardly a day of rest. Yet, I have read a good deal of my history of England. Love and kisses.

ADELBERT

LOWELL, *October* 11, 1875

DEAR DEL: This day has been well occupied, although I cannot say that much has been accomplished. Hattie and I went to church in the morning. Poor Dr. Edson forgot part of the service, and dismissed the congregation while on his knees before the altar. He seemed to recollect that he was wrong, just as the people were passing out of church, and rising, stood with his head a little bent, his hands clasped together, and his eyes fixed on his daughter Lizzie, with such a mournful gaze that I shall never forget the picture. It was as I should imagine one who felt himself dying, a painless death, would look upon those around him, powerless to save. You know I do not altogether admire Dr. Edson, but my heart was filled with compassion for him today.

After church, Mother and I took a drive and returned in time for dinner, after which Butler, Edith, Annie, the baby and I took a walk through the woods, gathering nuts, eating apples, pears, etc. Butler saw some strange boys in the hill gathering his nuts, so he took up a stick and ran up on the hill straight to the boys. What he said we could not hear, but could see that he was talking. He afterwards called out to us that he had told "the boys they might have some chestnuts," so I conclude that they asked permission and it was granted. He informed me a day or two ago that "a coward was some one who was afraid of everybody and everything." You can judge that he is picking up a great deal of information.

Father said to me at dinner today "What a very large head that boy has, *very large*. There is nothing the matter with him, is there?" I answered "Oh, no, nothing that I know of." "He will have to be put on the right track or he will run away and bust the machine," Father added. He notices Butler a great deal, and is, I think, quite proud of his grandson.

Father will go on to Washington the last of this week for the purpose of seeing Pierrepont and urging Mississippi affairs. He is to make a speech Thursday night to the New York Board of Trade on finance. He expects that it will set the pot to boiling with renewed vigor. I should judge from the exertions and abuse which your enemies are using in Washington, that they must feel their cause is a desperate one, and growing more so. What have you been doing that has so frightened them? Or is it that they are endeavoring to screen Alcorn by berating you?

Edith is better than she was. A slight cold is the only trouble. The baby is growing fat and can walk about by pushing the chair before her. She is very fond of being held, and likes to play with the other children. When Butler speaks unkindly to her, she is quite heartbroken at times, at other times she looks very impudent and shakes herself slightly.

I have not thought about a cook, Del. Mary of course will want to try. How well she will do is another question. I suppose we shall have to board Battles, which will about affect Aunt Annie's fondness for giving away what does not belong to her. If you write to Mary do not make any agreement about the price. She should receive reduced wages on account of Battle's board. Perhaps Lizzie is as well as we can do for table girl, in spite of her faults. It is pleasanter to have the same servants as far as possible. If you think best you can speak to Merriman Howard about her. She will be glad to return to Jackson.

Good night. I must be up early in the morning for my trip to Boston. You would be more than content if you knew how much and how often my thoughts turn to Mississippi, and it would not be needful for me to tell you that I send love.

BLANCHE

LOWELL, *October* 12, 1875

DEAR DEL: I have made my trip to Boston and have returned a little weary. Paul went down with me, and when I had finished the few errands which I went for, we wandered about into all the picture stores in the city. Paul had never seen the Montpensier pictures, so we visited the Atheneum. You will remember I wrote you that I went the first time by myself. I find company more agreeable.

Father leaves for New York tonight. When we parted at the depot this morning he invited us to join him at the office and go with him for lunch at half past one. This we did, and had a fine repast of broiled oysters, compote of pigeon, stewed chicken and dumplings, apple fritters, etc. Our lunchroom was the Bellevue Cafe on Beacon Street. After lunch we went into one or two more picture places and Paul's favorite book store, returning to Lowell on the four o'clock train.

It was not at all discouraging to look at the paintings in Boston, so few of them have much merit. In looking through two or three rooms full there would not be more than that number which one would really care to possess. You will, no doubt, think me lazy when I tell you that I have not painted any since we came from Squam. The fact is, Del, every moment is filled, either with the children or plans for them or myself, and I try in vain to break away and let matters take care of themselves. In another week I may have more time. Do you "suggest" getting up earlier?

Sarah is getting quite ambitious. She can walk all about, holding onto things, but wishes to do more, and occasionally tries to stand by herself, not very successfully however. Edith is quite well—looking as plump as ever. I am sorry to say that she is now the most quarrelsome and noisy one in the family. But a little time and she will be good again.

Paul is going to finish his boat, because he says he does not like to begin things and leave them incomplete.

I believe I have given you all the news of our household. I have already told you that Father goes on to Washington especially to see Grant and Pierrepont, and urge that they do something to defeat the plans of the "white-liners," but I did not tell you that he has taken all of your letters to me containing any politics which it would be advisable for the departments to see. They are all arranged in book form, and the portions to be read clearly marked, and I have charged Father to read them himself, or have them read before him, as I did not wish the world to see all of my letters—although there is nothing in them of which we should feel ashamed, on the contrary everything of which to be proud. I suppose you do not know how clearly your letters have told the whole story. Father thought that such a statement made to me, so evidently without expectation of its being used, might have more influence upon Grant than all the men of Miss. in Washington, whom he might suspect of changing the truth for their own personal motives.

Love, BLANCHE

JACKSON, MISS., *October* 12, 1875

DEAR BLANCHE: I had thought I would not be at liberty long enough to write you today, but just at this moment I have dismissed visitors till a later hour, and write you just one word while George is arranging my supper on the table in the center of the room.

Caldwell's company (colored) has returned from Edward's Depot, not having been interfered with. But the excitement occasioned by his march is very great. The Democracy say they see in it an effort to intimidate the white people. It is strange that they should assume the position they do while at the same time they assert the superiority of the whites over the blacks, and that the former should rule. Asserting substantially that the Negro shall be disfranchised, notwithstanding the constitutional amendments, they pretend they will secure him in his rights if I will call off my militia. They began this campaign with the assertion that they would win if they had to wade in blood—they now are on the eve of other outbreaks. Each of these days is important. Tomorrow the election will be held in Ohio. I hope it will go Republican, and yet I fear it will go Democratic. Today I understand the Supreme Court of the U.S. delivers an opinion on the

Enforcement Act— We look for a favorable decision—yet, it may be against us.

While I have been scrawling the above, my supper has been getting cold. I think I will stop a moment to make (pour out) my cup of tea and when my first visitor comes I will take a moment of his time to close—I have had half of my supper.

I enjoy your accounts of yourself and the babies. Kiss Butler and Edith and the baby for me, and keep many kisses from me for yourself. ADELBERT

JACKSON, MISS., *October* 12, 1875

DEAR BLANCHE: This has been another busy day for me. The militia question is agitating the "white-liners" very much. They are prepared for another New Orleans affair if need be, so they say. The leaders have asked me for an interview, which will take place tomorrow. I think, among other things, they really fear the militia will disturb their families in case of a disturbance. We began too late to organize and have too little means to accomplish much with the militia. Inasmuch as peace exists—or rather as there is no open violence—the militia cannot be called out. I understand they are willing to promise almost anything if I will cease with my militia movements.

Through the terror caused by murders and threats, the colored people are thoroughly intimidated. They cannot be rallied unless we have U.S. troops and it is now too late for that. It is too late for this reason. My demand must be made in writing—not by telegraph— Four days will be thus consumed. A number of days will be taken by the President for consideration, and when he decides to act, five days must be given. I do not believe a call at this time would be heeded. Ten days at most would be all the time allowed in which the troops could act. Of course they would have to be moved from where they now are to points of action. The result would be that hardly a day would be left for them to act in.

Yes, a *revolution* has taken place—by force of arms—and a race are disfranchised—they are to be returned to a condition of serfdom—an era of second slavery. It is their fault (not mine, personally) that this fate is before them. They refused to prepare for war when in time of peace, when they could have done so. Now it is too late. The nation should have acted but *it* was "*tired* of the annual autumnal outbreaks in the South"—see Grant's and Pierrepont's letter to me. The political death of the Negro will forever release the nation from the weariness from such "political outbreaks." You may think I exaggerate. Time will show you how accurate my statements are. In fact, look at other Southern states.

Last night I made up my mind to resign after the election when this revolution shall have been completed. Why should I fight on a hopeless battle for two years more, when no possible good to the Negro or anybody else would result? Why?

After all this I turn from myself to you, Beautiful—the bright, happy dwelling place of my thoughts, and send forth to you a world of love without end. ADELBERT

JACKSON, MISS., *October* 14, 1875

DEAR BLANCHE: This is the first opportunity I have had during the past forty-eight hours to have a chat with you. I doubt if I, even now, have an opportunity to say what I have to communicate to you. The telegraphic dispatches have doubtless informed you of a "compromise" here. They have said perhaps—I have not seen them—that I have disbanded and disarmed my militia and that the opposition was to cease its lawlessness. The facts are, in brief, these. Yesterday a committee of the leading citizens of the state—at least this part of it—waited on me, and proposed that they would do all in their power to preserve the peace and secure a fair election if I would disband my militia. I refused to disband or disarm the militia or in any way impair its efficiency.

But I did agree to do just what I had intended to do, even before the interview; which was to order the companies (two) on active service, to their homes to await orders. I had brought here two companies to aid in re-instating Sheriff Morgan of Yazoo County. Morgan, fearing assassination, would not go. I had nothing to do but dismiss my militia, to be called upon whenever new troubles occur. I also agreed that the arms should be kept in armories instead of in the hands of the members of the companies. This also I had previously intended. The reasons of the opposition for asking this was to keep them (the arms) from the Negroes and by me and also by the Negroes that the "white-liners" should not take them. Thus far I have agreed to do nothing I had not intended to do. That the arms should be safe I agreed that guards of U.S. soldiers should guard them if they could be had—always subject to my orders. The militia is to be ordered out at any and all times when necessity may demand. Thus my power through the militia is not curtailed in the least. I also agreed to stop organizing more militia. Here I yielded little as I had organized about all the militia I could organize.

Since I began I have been able to organize only in this one county and all the rest of the state is militia-less, because in other counties they would not organize—one or two counties excepted.

The opposition were content that I should do what I have told you—in fact it constitutes all they asked except that they wanted me to disband and disarm, which I could not and would not do. They were moved by at least two reasons—first they and their families *feared harm* from the Negroes.—Second the planters wanted this movement stopped on account of their cotton still unpicked in the fields. They began to carry the election by violence but the consequences of the attempt grew to be more portentous than anticipated and they, at least the leaders, have not withdrawn. I believe them honest in their promises, and believe much good will result. Some doubt their sincerity, but be that as it may, all of my means to protect had been exhausted.—The U.S. had substantially refused to aid us.

While I have not departed from principle or yielded a single right or duty, I believe the compromise has saved many lives. The facts which prove it I will give you at some other time.

This has been written hurriedly.—George has come with my supper. Love, ADELBERT

LOWELL, *October* 15, 1875

DEAR DEL: Your letters show me that you are growing more and more dispirited. The sky is always darkest just before day, Love, and you have done all for the best, according to your judgment, and no man can do more. Do not allow affairs to prey upon you. When we have done all in our power for some object there is a force beyond our control which perfects or defeats our wishes, according to some plan of which we have no conception. What the world says of us is of little moment, for it is apt to praise when we least deserve it, and blame where praise is due. Keep up your spirits, Dearie. If all goes wrong in Mississippi we will all go to Northfield, or wherever you make money, and establish a happy, luxurious home for ourselves and the children. I am quite confident you would be content. It would only be necessary to turn your ambitions into another channel. Perhaps the Ohio and Iowa elections will change the aspect of things a little in the South. Perhaps Pierrepont will not be ready to bid so high for the Southern vote. In fact, there are many perhapses, and if they all fail it will probably be quite as conducive to our happiness as that they should all succeed. "Then let the wide world wag as it will, I'll be gay and happy still."

This reminds me of Maria's German which we all attended last night. Paul did not dance, not having acquired quite confidence enough. Hattie was somewhat disappointed because Nina and I had full as much and more attention than she did. The two gentlemen from Boston of whom I wrote you in describing Florence's party, came up and stopped at Aunt Lauretta's. Tompson came up, and is staying with us. He did not care to go down on the first train this morning. Then there is Mr. Smith, staying at the Parkers. Had it not been for these young gentlemen, there would have been a great lack of that necessary constituent for a German. Mr. Hedges, one of the Boston youths, politely asked to be my partner. But I had some compassion on him and refused, saying that he would surely enjoy himself more dancing with one of the younger ladies, and, ignoring his protestations, I insisted upon introducing him to any lady he might point out. Finally he suggested Miss Read, and I went on to take my place with the wall flowers and older ladies, like Mother and Mrs. Farrington. But Mr. Smith came, a tall, good-looking fellow about twenty-two. Both Hattie and Nina had, I knew, refused him because they were going to dance with the Boston men, so I accepted him and had a merry dance all the evening, being called out by all the gentlemen in the room, but three. Hattie has just passed through the room and said "Are you telling Gen'l. Ames what a dancer you have become? Say to him that I am perfectly disgusted, that you have come home with two flags and two trinkets, while I have only one of each. Not because it is you, but because anybody should have more than I." So much for your wife's frivolity. How I should enjoy dancing with you, Dearie. I think I could do so now, for I have improved very much since I tried with you at Squam.

Butler has his new clothes, and looks like a pink. His little figure shows to great advantage. If it is fair tomorrow I will have their photographs taken.—I mean I will have the children's photographs taken. They are all well now.

Poor Bessie has lost her boy. How unfortunate she has been. Poor baby! he has been in great suffering for weeks. How can we complain, when we are and have been so favored. There are many things much worse than having a riotous state.

Have you noticed what a great, lovely moon we have for a messenger? I send many kisses by *her*. BLANCHE

JACKSON, MISS., *October* 15, 1875

DEAR BLANCHE: What busy days these are for me. So absorbed my time and thoughts that your name looks strange to me as I write it; and you seem far off both by space and time.

The arrangements made on Wednesday (the 13th) are being faithfully observed by me. Because one of my militia companies refused to obey orders and put their arms in an armory and deserted, taking their arms with them, I have disbanded the company and revoked the appointments of the officers. It was absolutely necessary I should take decisive action. My word was given that these companies should do certain things. Many of the opposition distrust me as many of our friends distrust them. That they should have perfect faith, I resorted to the harsh measure of disbanding this particular company. By this act I deprive those of the opposition who might be disposed to cavil, of any excuse to do so. Of course some of our party are indignant at me because of my action. By and by they will thank me for it. It was the only way that they could be secure.

You may wonder to read this letter, and that of yesterday. I cannot give you all the facts as I know them. But you must know all were on the eve of a revolution—some crash was inevitable. A revolution has occurred, but instead of one of blood, it was one of fraternity, which all seem thankful for. My dread is that I fear somebody will think I have "sold out"—but I have not, in any sense.

Please note my letters of the last few days, and see if they are tampered with. I have no reason to suppose they have been—but as I am making important history and everybody knows it, it is possible that somebody may want to see what I say to you on the various subjects. See also if you receive all my letters. Your letters are coming very irregularly.

I send you love—kiss the babies. ADELBERT

LOWELL, *October* 16, 1875

DEAR DEL: The newspapers this evening report trouble in Mississippi at Friars Pt. I happened to say to Father that all Memphis would fly to the rescue. "That would be a case of invasion, and Ames should demand troops," he replied. I at once wrote a telegraph which he corrected, and it was sent in Major's name, in order that it might not appear to come from Father. He seemed to think that the point would suggest itself to you, without your attention being called to it, but I feared that your mind would be crowded with so many things that it might escape you, and that at least it would do no harm to suggest it.

Florence's party takes place tonight. The rain is pouring down furiously. All the horses are sick, still they will have to come out for this occasion.

The children have been as noisy as possible, owing to the rain, which has made it necessary for them to expend all their surplus energy in that way instead of exercising in the garden.

I believe I did not tell you that Mr. and Mrs. Coffin called the other night to ask Hattie and myself to attend some Germans given by a club composed chiefly of married people. There will not be more than one given before we go South. Maria Nesmith is soon to give another. So society seems to expend itself in this form of entertainment. Hattie is very earnest that I should have one, really on her own account, but she says in order that I may show people that I am not to be left out in the cold. What do you think of my tripping the light fantastic toe? I think I hear you say "Are you not satisfied with the good things I have given you, that you desire a new departure?"

Good night, Love. BLANCHE

LOWELL, *October* 17, 1875

DEAR DEL: Another Sunday evening has come, and we are another week nearer each other.

The papers give no news from Mississippi, so I take it for granted everything remains quiet. There is but little time now before the elections, but plenty for mischief. I am looking anxiously for Father's return to hear the news from Washington.—Now the Ohio elections have gone in our favor, something may be done for Mississippi.

Butler looks very tall and boyish in his new suits. His pants have pockets, and button up in front "like my Papa's." There are pockets also in the jackets, and he comes in every day with chestnuts, sometimes more, sometimes less, but no matter what the quantity, there is an equal distribution in each of the pockets. He says he "can cut down trees, bring in wood, dress himself, and drive the horse." Mother suggested to him that we need not keep any servants. "No, I can do all the work, Gran, every bit." I suppose you would have felt quite grand, if you could have seen him yesterday driving Phil up the Avenue in the cart. Louis was sitting in the back part. Butler in front stood up and handled the reins. He is a capable, bright boy.

Edith also is keen enough in her way.—For instance, about a week or so ago Paul brought home a paper of candy which he hid away in the lower drawer of his bureau. The next day Edith brought the candy to me. I supposed Paul had given it to her, so we divided it around and ate it all up. It was not very good, so I asked Paul where he "found such miserable stuff." "I should like to know where you found it," he said. "I hid it away." "Edith brought it to me. I thought you had given it to her." "No, indeed, she has been pillaging in my room." Every day now she makes a pilgrimage to that same spot. The other day Paul caught her, and asked what she was looking for. She would not answer, but pointed to a picture of some children and said "pretty babies." Paul still questioned her, but she pretended not to understand until he asked "Are you looking for candy?" "All gone," said she pointing to the drawer, "all gone." She frequently visits Hattie's room and puts hair pin box, tooth powder box, soap box, comb and brush bag, everything of that nature into the middle of the floor and changes the contents of the boxes to suit her taste. Whenever she is out of sight and quiet, be sure there is mischief afloat.

The baby also is not without her tricks. She takes advantage of every open door to start for the front or back stairs. —Under the sink would be her favorite playground, if allowed there. When you ask for a kiss she puts up her little face with open mouth, and can apply a handkerchief to her nose when told to do so, with a flourish. *There* I have told you all the little details I can think of likely to amuse you about the children.

As for the remaining member of your family I do not think she has changed much since you last saw her, although at a little family party given by Aunt Lauretta last night, the lady of the house told her that she looked "Eighteen, not a day older." How do you like that, Sweetheart?

I send you, as ever, love. It is the same with which you have been kept supplied for nearly six years. I trust you are satisfied with your purveyor. Good night.

BLANCHE

JACKSON, MISS., *October* 17, 1875

DEAR BLANCHE: I had a telegram from Whitney (at Washington) asking if peace reigned here. I reply that I expect it will. With this I will dismiss politics for today.

This is Sunday. I have done nothing but read—read till my eyes ache. A gentleman from New York is here by the name of Chase. I have invited him to take a room in the Mansion, which I expect he will occupy till election. He has acquaintances in Maine, well known to me, and this has caused us to appreciate each other a little. Do not get jealous. I will explain at some other time.

Senator Pinchback spoke here yesterday. A supper was given him last evening, which I attended and made a very poor speech. And speaking of speeches reminds me that the condition of affairs has been such that I have not been able to go out into the canvass; and the time is now so brief I will not attempt to.

Did I not leave my winter clothing at the Bay (St. Louis)? I shall write Mary for it. I will not make any arrangements with her about staying with us. I will wait till I hear from you again before writing to Howard for Lizzie. That is, I do not interpret your letter as final in your decision relative to employing her. I concur in what you say—that she will doubtless do as well as anyone. There is plenty of time yet.

In about two weeks this contest will be over, and I shall then start for Father's, where I will stay for a day or two and then—for Lowell. Were the battle over today I would feel tired, but I cannot afford to be tired for a fortnight longer.

Love, ADELBERT

LOWELL, *October* 18, 1875

DEAR DEL: I write but a short letter tonight, for we have company and I steal a few moments for a letter to my Love. You are growing more and more despondent. This is not well, Dearie, and although I am willing to remember your prophetic words so that if you are right I can acknowledge that you told me so, I am not yet ready to accept all you say as a fixed fact. But even if I were, I should still say "Where is your philosophy, Love?" As far as we are personally concerned, the worst results in Mississippi may prove the best for us.

As for the colored man, our experience of the race would surely lead us to the conclusion that only through trouble and contest will a spirit of self-reliance, assertion be developed by which they will be enabled to maintain their manhood and rights. This struggle must have come sooner or later, and it does not follow at all that because they are to be overcome at this time they will remain so for all time. As each man is fitted for freedom, he will grasp it. The race will suffer for a time, but I do not think with you that it will be forever. Don't despair, my Love.

Butler had a visitor today. He took her all about the place. Miss Hastings. He had a stick of candy, and after taking it out of his pocket, he broke it in two, and like all children, picked out the biggest piece, but unlike most children he walked up and gave it to Miss Ethel.

Edith picked some asparagus branches with berries upon them. Butler said "Don't eat the berries, sister, they are poisonous." Florence and Etta, who came up with Ethel, were amazed at such care and attention. A stray horse came into the grounds today, and Butler and Teedle started in full pursuit, and drove the creature out. He is not afraid of anything, and feels equal to any man.

Are you sick of hearing so much about the children? I do not believe you are. BLANCHE

JACKSON, MISS., *October* 18, 1875

DEAR BLANCHE: The indications now are that we will have a fair election. I am of the opinion that the schemes of the opposition were monstrous and their detection caused a halt. I can but feel sore at the treatment I have received at the hands of the general government. When the liberties of the people were in jeopardy the nation abandoned us for political reasons. Were it not for the merest accident we would have had a bloody massacre on the thirteenth of this month, which would have finally disposed of every prominent Republican here, your husband among the rest.

The whole programme is now known. The U. S. Government would not even move troops as I have asked, to have a force near at hand for an emergency. The national administration has acted in a selfish, cold-blooded spirit in this whole trouble. I am disgusted with the whole affair. I have let it be known that I will not be a candidate again for any place. When my term as Gov. shall end we will bid good-bye to politics here—if I do not resign before. You see, I feel *ugly* towards the whole world, and, as President Taylor said, the rest of mankind. I say this in fun, though I am in earnest.

I have done little today but chat, and as evening advanced play a few games of croquet. Mrs. Raymond and Mrs. Gibbs were here. My boarder, Mr. Chase, is still with me. He occupies a bed in the nursery. His breakfast and mine are sent in together—so is our supper—thus I live.

Love, ADELBERT

LOWELL, *October* 19, 1875

DEAR DEL: At supper this evening a telegram came for me. I opened it with fear and trembling, but it proved to be from John T., saying that he would leave Boston for Lowell at six o'clock. Paul went down to the train for him, but missed him, and a few moments after he had returned, John drove up. He seems in good health and spirits. Says that all the flour the Northfield and Fort Atkinson mills can make is selling at good prices, and as fast as it arrives. I told him that you were entirely opposed to selling at Northfield, and read him your letters. "Well" he said, "he must have his way, and we will talk it over when he comes to Northfield. These same men are going West with me, though, to look at the property." Then he explained that he wanted to sell, not because he thought it would be well for himself personally, but because your father is an old man and worries so much over the business that he would rather sacrifice himself than to have his father fretting so much.

I laughed and answered, "Why John, you know as well as I do that your father is bound to grumble, no matter what he is doing.—It is constitutional, and does not wear upon him a bit. His cheek is as rosy and his form as full and strong as ever. If he were really troubled as much as he would make the world believe, he would be a mere shadow. Then again, you say that he would be perfectly content with one hundred and twenty-five thousand dollars safely invested at a fair rate of interest. Now, if you will think about it you will acknowledge that when he is fretting the most it is not because he does not expect to make a fair percentage, but because he wants to realize a great one. Neither you nor he pretend that at the worst the mills will ever fail to pay a good percent." "No," said John. "It will always pay something, and if Adelbert will only join us, we can do a splendid business."

By so much of our conversation, you will readily see that is entirely useless to argue the matter. John's idea is, and I am sure I judge correctly, that you should bear your part of the burden. That your lines have fallen in too pleasant places. That he has the laboring oar. If when you go to Northfield you will insist upon it in answer to everything, that you will buy John out if he wishes to go, you will hear no more about the sale of the mills than you have about the sale of the farm, after you proposed to take it. John now says that "when Nellie complains and he talks of selling and building a nice house in town, she says 'we can't part with the farm—it is our home, and a home for our children.' " It will be the same with John's share of the mill, when it is supposed you want it.

Now Del, I come to my proposition, which I am sure will make you smile. John has talked so long about selling that I have desires in that direction, and intend to suggest to him tomorrow that inasmuch as these men are going West and will be entirely disappointed about the Northfield Mills—as you will never consent to sell—that he had better take them to Fort Atkinson, show them the property there, and then offer to sell for sixty thousand dollars. Fifty for the property and ten for name and business. That they can take it or leave it, just as they choose, that he does not even know as his brother will take that, but thinks he might, as the fifty thousand will fairly cover his expenditures, and the ten will in some part repay him for the trouble and time it has cost to establish the business. That he would not sell for seventy-five thousand if it were possible for him to give it constant personal supervision, but he is so situated that this is impossible and a good offer might be accepted. What do you think of this Del? I write you of it, so that if you hear anything of this nature you may understand the state of the case.

Love from your babies and your BLANCHE

LOWELL, *October* 20, 1875

DEAR DEL: I have made my proposition to John about offering the mill at Fort Atkinson for sale, and it did not meet his approval at all. He says it is a very fine property, that they have started in splendidly this fall, and that all the other mills on the river have busted up, and he acknowledges that to us it is equal to fifty thousand well invested. These men will probably be West when you are, and you can make your own proposal if you wish to sell. I do not think John will do anything about it. Although one of his arguments in favor of selling at Northfield was that milling property was so poor that there was danger of losing everything.

I do not wish to seem harsh in my judgment, or to speak unkindly of John—quite the contrary—but I do think that in his heart he feels that it would be more satisfactory if you two brothers were a little more evenly blessed with worldly goods. He will never think of leaving Northfield if we go there.

A kiss and good-bye until this evening. BLANCHE

LOWELL, *October* 20, 1875

DEAR FATHER: Your note has just come. Paul is away, and will not be back in time to take your shirts, so we send them by express.

Mother is still very hoarse, too much so to go from home. We are sorry that you are to go back at once, without coming home for a night at least.

I enclose another letter from Gen'l. Ames of later date than those you had. By it you will see that all your efforts have been useless, unless the President will *at once order the troops* to report to Gen'l. Ames so that he can order them into action the moment there is any outbreak. If he has to wait and make a formal call, the President's aid will be worse than useless. Urge this point above all others.

Your affectionate daughter, BLANCHE

LOWELL, *October* 20, 1875

DEAR CAPT. AMES. John came last night, and went away at noon. He is going to New York, then to Philadelphia, then West. He talked over Northfield matters, and said that those New York parties who propose to buy half of the mill for fifty thousand dollars are going on with him to look at the property and talk it over. I write to suggest that it is a most unfortunate time to urge this selling upon Gen. Ames. I hear from him almost daily, and he is greatly annoyed by political matters in Mississippi, and is quite despondent. Also, just at this time it is impossible for him to decide definitely what he is to do in the future. He is strongly opposed to selling the mills (as I read to John from several letters), and to urge it upon his attention now is simply adding additional annoyance and trouble, and he has quite as much as is good for him already. He writes me that he is going to Northfield before coming East—so you will see him soon.

The election which takes place early in November will settle all political questions, and he will know upon what to depend. What I desire is that you should do nothing, and urge nothing upon his attention, until after the election. I suggested to John that he should take the gentlemen to Fort Atkinson and offer them the property there for sixty thousand dollars, nothing less. I do not know, however, that Gen'l. Ames would sell, and am very doubtful if it would be good policy for him to do so. If he asked my advice however I should say that, "If your Father is determined to get rid of the Northfield Mills, sell at Fort Atkinson for all you can get, then mortgage your part of the Northfield property and borrow money enough to buy out your Father and John, settle in Northfield, and conduct the business yourself." Don't you think this is sound advice? This is surely a business letter.

Give my best love to Mrs. Ames and accept the same for yourself. *Yours affectionately*, BLANCHE

LOWELL, *October* 20, 1875

DEAR DEL: You ask me if your letters come regularly, and if they bear traces of being tampered with. Each envelope looks as if it had been smeared with the mucilage brush. Aside from this I can discover nothing, and I receive them all, although they come irregularly—that is, a day will pass without any, and the next I may get two, sometimes three.

John went away at noon. We urged him to stay longer, but he said he was getting homesick and had promised to meet some men in New York. He now wishes to have your Father sell his half and leave you and himself owners still. In fact, Del, it is hard to tell what he does want. After he had gone I wrote a little note to your Father, the original of which I enclose to you. I was a little fearful that your Father might be urged to sell and would trouble you with it at a time when you had other things to attend to. Perhaps you will regard it as *an interference*. If so, I cannot help it. I have done as my judgment directed.

Mr. Farrington went down to Boston today and saw Father, who had made so much progress on his way home, when he was called back to Washington again. By the time this reaches you, the news will already be old to you. Father told Mr. Farrington to say to Mother and to me that he saw Grant and he had half written the telegram ordering the troops to report to you, when your telegram arrived saying that you had effected a temporary compromise, but could not tell how long it would last. Then Father went to Pierrepont and they looked up all the laws in the case and decided that as Governor you were the senior officer in command in the state, and Grant again agreed to send the troops to you. Father has gone back to Washington on other business, and says that if he finds they have not done as was promised he will see that they do. I sent your letter by him, in which you speak of the impossibility of the government aiding, even if you were to make a formal call for troops—the time being consumed by what it would take for your letter to reach Washington, the President's delay, five days to disperse, etc. etc. I have taken a good deal upon myself lately, Del. More perhaps than you will think I am warranted in. I hope all will so turn out that at least my action will not be productive of harm, even if it does not lead to good. As I am in disgrace in your estimation I do not feel at all sure of my position on any point.

The children are well. Kisses, BLANCHE

NEW ORLEANS, LA., *October* 20, 1875

DEAR BLANCHE: As peace had been declared, and as I believed a change would be beneficial to me, I ran off here with Gen'l. Warner and Mr. Chase. We were due here last evening at nine, but an accident to a freight train blocked the road, so we could not get here till this morning. I shall return this evening on the six o'clock train. I am now in the Post Office, writing at Parker's desk. Everybody says I am thin, and I *feel* it.

I see it is thought here I sacrificed something substantial in the treaty up there. But the fact is, we understood that the Democracy was not to do any deeds of violence till about the day of election, when it would have been too late for the U.S. to interfere. What I did do, I had intended to do, inasmuch as I could do nothing else. I had no money—no arms—and was powerless to invoke anything beyond myself. The companies I had called out were to go home till disturbances occurred. I could not feed them elsewhere. In fact, I had ordered them home to await orders. This I may have already stated to you. I repeat the points perhaps, but I do not want you to mistake the facts.

I did not get a letter from you yesterday morning. That you may not be a victim of neglect I write this note to you in the midst of much talk, noise and confusion.

I greet my Beautiful with many caresses. ADELBERT

LOWELL, *October* 21, 1875

DEAR DEL: There was no letter for me today. Perhaps you have heard the news from Washington and are indignant about something—I do not know what it could be unless you resent a wife's meddling. You can hardly do that, however, inasmuch as you requested me to have Father call Pierrepont's attention to the laws. You see, I do not feel quite easy about having shown your letters. Yet were it all to do over again I should take the same course, and I await your rebuke with bowed head.

Last night Mrs. Farrington, Mr. and Mrs. Willis F., Florence and Tom, Etta Hastings, Nina and young Smith came up to practice waltzing. Mrs. Farrington started the party. All were very lively. Paul has learned to dance very well. Not being in the frame of mind I did not take part, but was a looker on, and musical performer. Mrs. Farrington has invited the same party and more to dance again tomorrow night.

I think I have given you all our little news. There does not seem to be much of interest. The children are not as "cute" and bright as usual, so that I have no anecdotes to relate of them.

I am anxiously awaiting news from Washington and Mississippi. Oh! Del, how grand it would be if you could bring it all out right, in spite of "white-liners" and recreant Republicans.

Love, Sweetheart. BLANCHE

JACKSON, MISS., *October 21*, 1875

DEAR BLANCHE: I am back again, as you will see by the heading of this note.

We had a very pleasant trip. We called on Parker and as usual left him disgusted. Mr. Chase had never been to N.O. and Parker proposed to show him something, but when the time came Parker suggested to me (Mr. C. and Warner being in a carriage at the door) that *we* could do what he had promised—rather offered to do. We did it.

We are having nothing new. Mr. Chase is here representing the Attorney General's department. He is evidently inclined to appreciate me. He had a letter today from Atty. Gen'l. Pierrepont in which he, the Atty. Gen'l., warns Chase not to be misled by me, as he had heard hard stories about me. Pease and Wells are the story tellers. How gratifying to me to know that the world is believing all their lies.

I am sorry you have taken to round dances—perhaps I should say I am sorry you have told me you had done so. However, the sentiment entertained by me on this matter is only—a sentiment.

I judged by my face that I had fallen off in weight quite a

number of pounds, but I was weighed in N.O. and found I had lost but three or four pounds.

Love, ADELBERT

LOWELL, *October* 22, 1875

DEAR DEL: Your letter bringing word that you expected a "fair election" came this morning. I am very glad you can say so, but I am not glad that as you say you "have let it be known that you are not a candidate for any office." I wrote you some time ago about this, and asked you for many reasons not to resign a position before you had it. It was good advice. Those do best who keep their own counsel and do not allow the world to meddle with their private affairs. I say "private" because I think no one has a right at this time to force you into an expression of your intentions. I asked you before for your own sake, Dearie—now I *demand it* as *my* right that you should take the Senator's position and then resign. I have a great pride in this, Del, and surely if you can gratify it as well as not, it is your duty to do so.

In many ways, Del, our going to live West is not altogether agreeable to me, and I should like this satisfaction before I go. However, I will not discuss this further at present. All I ask is that you do not commit yourself to anything. I think that at least you might have given yourself time to talk the matter over with your wife before taking any decided step. It was a little exercise of your manly right to decide for yourself *and your family*, which I have not observed in you before. I cannot say that I approve or admire the development. So much for this, Del. I have written partly in fun, but more in earnest.

By this time you know that Chandler has the Office of the Interior. I should be glad to show Mrs. Hale that our family has not been left in the lurch, even that we valued some positions too little to keep them. "A petty ambition" you will say.—Be it so, the world is made up of such.

Father has not yet returned. It would seem that his efforts have been useless, as you now feel independent of governmental aid.

I cannot send you the proof of the children's pictures, as I could not get them. Tomorrow you shall have them. You will be very proud of your boy. He is a little man. I allow him to take his sister out to play alone, and he takes very good care of her. He is somewhat domineering, but that is to be expected, but he does not allow her to go where she should not.

He is "hail fellow" with all the men. Whenever the gardener goes down town he takes Butler and allows him to drive Phil all by himself whenever they come to a straight road and no carriages. I hope and pray that he will keep well and strong.

Why—Del—you ought to accept the senatorship (if you can have it) were it only to say to your boy—"Your Father was *twice* elected Senator and once Governor." You are sick of the whole thing, but other men would barter all the best years of their lives for your chances. Again I say, do not throw them away until you have reaped a little benefit from them.

I am not very happy these days—because as I wrote you I do not feel quite sure what position I hold in your good graces. I cannot come to any conclusion, whether you are annoyed with me for what I have done, or whether you think it well advised. Of course I know that in the end you will excuse it—for if I made a mistake it was through my desire to save you.

Edith is playing at my feet with her tea-set and stove, trying to get supper. She has recovered her health and spirits, and is again a merry little girl. The baby is now the fretful one, she is cutting teeth. She sleeps with me and will no doubt make some disturbance when called upon to give up her place.

Love from the babies and kisses in addition from

BLANCHE

JACKSON, MISS., *October 22*, 1875

DEAR BLANCHE: I have just come in from a game of croquet with Mrs. Raymond, Mrs. Rhodes and a half a dozen gentlemen. The weather is delightful and we are as happy as weather can make one. I will condense all I have to say on political matters in this—I am inclined to resign the very first day I can do so honorably. It is folly to expect anything but murder and violence till the state becomes Democratic. Why I should endure what I do endure till '78, with the inevitable result indicated, I do not know.

Raymond was at Denver, Colorado, and speaks in glowing terms of that country, dwelling especially on the cordiality with which all strangers are received there. We are having nothing new here except that it is exceedingly difficult for the Democracy to keep their part of the peace arrangements.

As I am entertaining some now, I ordered when in N.O. a barrel of scotch ale—bottled. Mrs. Raymond learned the fact, and has asked me to divide. I would not if I thought the barrel would make me as fat as she is. She is dressing well—not richly, but rather tastefully—but she is looking far older than I have ever known her. Her face is flabby, and dark, heavy lines are under her eyes. No one would say she is but eighteen, as some people are kind enough to estimate your age.

We have been separated three months.—I hope we will be together again in less than three weeks. Till then, love, for my Beautiful and babies, Butler, Edith, and Sarah.

ADELBERT

JACKSON, MISS., *October* 23, 1875

DEAR BLANCHE: You may think by my recent letters that I am getting soured. I half think I am. I am, as you see by the papers, made responsible for the cowardice of our party and the desertion of the South by the general government. The white-liners inaugurated war here, and I alone am to blame. Everything comes upon me. There is no end to this. Next year will be worse than this, if next year finds us a Republican state. A year or two will end it all. Thus we see nothing but a fruitless contest—an humiliating failure.

I must stop this strain, as it is nearly time for the mail and as Warner and Raymond are in my room talking loud and violently on the "situation."

This evening (afternoon) Mr. Chase and I called on Mrs. Dedrick, but she did not appear and our call was devoted to Gen'l. D. I returned home and played croquet with Mrs. Raymond and Mrs. Rhodes till they went out to ride. These two calls (one the other day on a Mrs. Fisher) are the only departure from my regular walk between here and the State House, during the past three months. All this will end in ten days.

No letter from you today— What is the matter?

Love. ADELBERT

LOWELL, *October* 24, 1875

DEAR DEL: I send you the proofs of the children's photographs. How do you like them? The baby's are fearful. I shall have to try with her again. We could not make her keep still, and the motion has given a wavering, uncertain look to her face which is very funny. Still, they look like her. Perhaps you think Edith's beautiful enough to make up for the plainness of the baby's? We think it a very lovely picture. Paul pronounces it stagey, and that were it not for the hands, which are imperfect, one would say it was a made up fancy picture. Butler's, although not very handsome, are just like him, with perhaps a little extra touch of sobriety or crossness.

He looks ready for school, does he not? It will not be well to send him young. His brain is already too active.

Edith is now the mischief maker of the family. Butler stands aghast, as do we all, at her performances. This morning she disappeared from my side while I was painting. Butler came in to show me "how many chestnuts he had in his pockets." As he had to count them out in my lap—it took a few moments. Directly however, I started in search of Edith. I went first to my room, instinct or reason told me she would go there, for I had put some grapes in a paper bag in one of the corners out of sight, but the odor was so strong that the moment Edith entered the room after breakfast she said "Give me some gapes Mamma, give me some gapes." I took the precaution to send her out while I selected a bunch for her. Well, on entering the room in search for her I beheld in the middle of the floor a pile of grapes. The bag had been emptied. Some teapots, sugar bowls and dishes belonging to her tea-set were standing about filled with grapes. A number of stems showed the havoc which had been made—very few skins, for she usually swallows them, more especially on this occasion, for she must have eaten in great haste. Of course, I stopped to pick up the remaining battered grapes. While so employed Miss came in. A glance was quite sufficient to show that more mischief was afloat. Her little hands were clasped behind her and she looked out of the corners of her eyes over cheeks powdered as white as snow.

"Where have you been?" I asked. "In Hattie's room," was the answer. I went to the scene of disaster, and found Hattie, who had just returned to her room, on her knees in the center of the floor, striving to scrape up her Lubins powder off of the carpet where it had been emptied in three or four little piles. I told her the next time she caught Edith with her things it would be advisable to slap her hands. Hearing a scolding voice, and guessing who might be the culprit, I hastened to the encounter, and was in season to hear Mother say—"Let me catch you at my venetian glass again, you scamp. It is you who have pulled off these glass leaves after we had so much pains to get them stuck on, and it is you, I have no doubt, who has spilled ink all over the silver inkstand in the library." She might have added, and it was you who emptied the vase of flowers into the punch bowl and mixed the playing cards into the mess, and it was you who threw all the clean clothes in the parlor chamber over the ballusters into the front entry, etc. etc.

You can understand why Butler looks about, astonished, when he sees such deeds.

You ask me in your letter about the servants. We cannot do better than to employ Lizzie and Mary. If the latter does not prove steady enough, we can send for Aunt Annie.

Do not forget my advice of Friday, Sweetheart. I am sure I am correct about it. If, fearing your own indecision in the matter, you are thus endeavoring to close the doors against yourself, you are surely making a great mistake. Take my advice this time, Love.

In less than three weeks you will be with us, and this long separation will be like an ugly dream. I shall never consent to your leaving me for more than a month at a time again. This I am determined upon.

Good night, Love. BLANCHE

JACKSON, MISS., *October 24*, 1875

DEAR BLANCHE: This morning I received two letters from you. I was amused to read your conversation with John T. He is only acting consistently with his whole life in this, that he is always anxious for a change. He never had any persistency. His determinations have always been short lived. I believe he would blindly break up his present business without a moment's consideration of what he was to do, in the immediate future. As you suggest, I think he only wants to have me in active cooperation with him. Yet, were that accomplished he would not be content. You put my mill too high. I will gladly sell it for a much less sum than you propose and be glad of the chance.

I received two checks from you the other day, one of three and the other of two hundred. I do not expect to use them. I will be able to have my pay cashed this fall.

Yesterday I wrote to my tailor in Boston for a suit of winter clothing. I am in doubts as to the style of coat. Some one suggests an English walking coat (suit). Perhaps you may be able, after ascertaining what kind of a "suit" that is, to express an opinion.

Mr. Chase is still with me, and will remain till election. He is something of a talker on certain subjects. He is a friend of Pierrepont, Atty. Gen'l., and has come here as a favor to him. He is a partner in a flour house in N.Y. and recommends his firm in case we change. He is acquainted with Moulton, and by his own account often acts the part of a "friend" in money transactions or in work of which his present is an unusual example. I have said he is a "talker"—but his chief talk is of "life" in N.Y. and a more immoral picture thereof I never heard presented. What he parades is *his* life, if not the life of the average New Yorker. He is a good liver, and in his company I find I am eating more than usual. As I take two of my three daily meals in my room, company of any kind would probably prove beneficial.

We went over to Mr. Raymond's last evening. Warner was there. We played euchre, and had half a bottle of poor champagne. We returned home at about half past ten.

It seems to me we have never been so long separated as since I left you last July. Surely I have never missed you as I do now. I am resolved that we shall not again—never—if I can help it—be so long apart. My happiest moments are those devoted to thoughts of you and our beautiful babes. I am glad you are so happily surrounded—and yet, I fear I have at moments resented in my mind the happy life you lead, so free from disturbing care. Of course, this comes only when I fancy I am a kind of a martyr.

It is pleasant to hear of Butler's manliness. I have great hopes of him. I sometimes dream of him as a young man stepping into life's arena for battle. Edith, poor girl, as presented most vividly by you of late is a candy-thief! But as her mother shared the stolen plunder, two-years-and-a-half old could not well have learned better. I cannot well conceive of Sarah's tramps around the room. She was unable to make any headway on hands and knees when I left her at Bay View more than three months ago.

I send you a world of love, with kisses and caresses thrown in, in quantities sufficient to make continents and oceans. Tell the babies I send love to them. ADELBERT

LOWELL, *October* 25, 1875

DEAR DEL: Your letter dated at New Orleans has just been received. I hope by the time you get back to Jackson you will find the "order" about which I enclose a copy[1] of your letter

[1] (Enclosure in letter of Oct. 25, 1875 from Mrs. Ames to her husband.)

October 16, 1875

Hon. Ed Pierrepont, Atty. General

SIR: Through the timely and skillful intervention of Mr. G. K. Chase, a bloody revolution has been averted. The condition of affairs which preceded the Clinton riot grew worse from day to day, and soon attained gigantic proportions under the feeling of hostility to the Militia I was organizing. The danger became apparent to all, and in the interest of peace and a fair election, an understanding was had to this

to Pierrepont and Father's endorsement. I trust troops will not be needed at the next election, but if they should be it is something to have them at your command.

We will see what can be done to cure the thinness of which you speak. If this colder climate does not develop chills—your weight will increase at the rate of five pounds a week.

Butler went through a grand performance today. You must know that the "Artillery" [2] visited us last night, no, Saturday night, and deposited the fruits of their labors in a deep hole arranged for the purpose in the cow yard near the wall. Of course it was very well filled with earth and leaves and the same spread over the top, to cover up everything obnoxious to sight or smell. Some strange freak led our son in that direction. The pile evidently looked inviting. Perhaps he thought it a fine pile of leaves and just the place for a boy of his size. At any rate, he took a flying leap from the cow-yard wall and landed in the middle of the heap, up to his middle. Although quite a man, the situation overcame him, and he raised his voice in lamentation while he pulled himself through and out, and made his way into the house. A careful scrubbing and a little cologne improved his condition, but oh! those boots and that pair of trousers, those stockings and under-drawers. He does not like to have the subject mentioned, and in the future, I am sure he will give wide berth to all strange piles of leaves, be they ever so tempting.

Good night, Sweetheart. There seems some limit to our separation now, and one even dares to count the days.

BLANCHE

JACKSON, MISS., *October* 25, 1875

DEAR BLANCHE: By your description of the appearance of the envelopes of my letters, I judge they all have been tampered

---

effect. The opposition was to do all in their power to preserve the peace. I have faith in their honor and implicit confidence that they can accomplish all they undertake. Consequently I believe we will have peace, order, and a fair election.

I write this letter chiefly to thank you for sending here a gentleman who has succeeded in inspiring us all with confidence, and who by his wisdom and tact has saved the state from a catastrophe of blood. Personally I feel under the greatest obligations to him. *Very truly yours,* A. AMES

MY DEAR BLANCHE: The within (above) is a pencil copy of letter from the General to Pierrepont. The President has ordered the troops to take orders from the Governor. Pierrepont told me the order had been sent by the Sec. of War. I am all well, but when I shall get home depends upon the Superior Court. Love to you. Tell Mother that I am much annoyed because she is not here. I am so lonely at night in a great house, all alone, nobody to comfort me. FATHER

[2] "Tewksbury Artillery," so-called—vault cleaners.

with. I use no brush and no mucilage. I will enclose a part of an envelope that you may judge between it and those you have already received; though if this letter should be tampered with a specimen envelope within would also be.

I have just come in from a game of croquet. Mrs. Fisher, Mrs. Gibbs, and Mrs. Raymond. Mrs. Gibbs and I were opposed to Mrs. Fisher and Capt. Raymond. Our side was beaten, much to the delight of Mrs. Fisher and Capt. R. While playing I received a note from Mrs. Dedrick, inviting us over to her house for a game of cards—and in case we cannot come in the evening to come in the afternoon for a game of croquet. Thus you see, we are no longer a recluse, but again are entering society.

Politically, things look ominous. Our friends look only for violence and intimidation. As you suggest, it makes little difference to me personally—and what I now fight against may prove in the end the greatest boon that could happen to me.

I send you love, ADELBERT

LOWELL, *October* 26, 1875

DEAR DEL: I have not had a letter today, which is owing doubtless to your having been occupied by your trip to New Orleans.

I am pleased that you have such an agreeable companion in Mr. Chase. Is he as thin as you are? In your last letter you say that the people in New Orleans think that you "gave up something substantial when you made your compromise." Of course, I know to the contrary, and I wish to say just here that you must not care in the least what the world says of your action. You have done the very best you could under the circumstances, and the clatter of the world's idle tongues is of no account. Success is the only thing the world appreciates or respects. If unsuccessful your wisest reason will be pronounced as wanting in judgment. If successful, the results of accident or folly will be regarded as evidences of great penetration. Therefore, I say, Del, be a philosopher and do not give too much weight to such an unstable opinion.

Here there is nothing new. Edith amused herself this morning by spilling a book full of gold leaf about the entry. I do not know where she found it. Butler told me in confidence that "Horace was setting traps for him all about. That place in the cow-yard was a trap for bad men and bad boys. Horace put him into a trap." "Oh! no," I said, "Horace did not try to put you in, you jumped in yourself." I then explained how the pile came there, and satisfied him that it was not a trap set by Horace.

We had some partridge for dinner. Butler was helped to a piece of the breast, under the impression that it was chicken. But the instant the young epicure tasted it he looked up and said, "Did you shoot this Uncle Paul?" There is nothing that escapes his observation, and very few things his comments.

Hattie has just returned from a musical party, where she was one of the performers. About one hundred people were present. She hopes to have such an assemblage here two weeks from Thursday. She wished me to go with her tonight, but I declined, thinking she had asked me only for politeness' sake. It seems, however, that she really desired me to go, and keep her in countenance, and I ought to have gone. Instead of that I remained at home and planned children's garments.

Tomorrow night the crowd comes again for dancing. So you see we are all given over to frivolity. You will be surprised to see how finely Paul gets on. He owes that much to his sister. Day before yesterday, Paul, Hattie, Mother and I drove down to the dancing school. I was rather tired of the business, not having had much satisfaction in it since the lecture I received on "youthful pretentions," and when we reached the place I declined to go in. Paul's countenance fell, he urged, but I was obstinate, and I really think that if he could have found any excuse he would have backed out of going himself, although he had hurried home from Boston in order to be in time. Therefore I say he owes what he has learned in the dancing line to his sister Blanche.

Mother is still very hoarse. She has not been able to speak clearly this summer. I trust she will improve now, as she has ceased taking the medicine for the throat, which I believe has produced all the hoarseness.

Ben is second or third in his section, and thinks he has the best average marks. He says nothing would induce him to go over the last two months.

I have told you everything I can think of tonight, and being very sleepy, will say good-bye until tomorrow. Love,

BLANCHE

JACKSON, MISS., *October 26, 1875*

DEAR BLANCHE: About nine o'clock last evening, after having wearied my eyes reading—and it was the first evening for a long time I have had to myself—I went down to call on Mrs. Rhodes where Mr. Chase had gone to consult about the "spirits." Mrs. R. does not like to be known as a medium. Sometime since she sent me a warning to be careful and not expose myself to "white-line" bullets—a message from A. Lincoln through her to me. An evening or two ago she gave Mr. Chase a specimen of her powers charging him with secrecy. He told me. When I knocked at the door, I heard sounds indicating the spiriting away of something. Entering, Mr. and Mrs. R. and Mr. C. were in as many corners of the room, but on the table was some paper—a chair was by the table unoccupied. As soon as I well could, I called attention to what I knew had been the subject of conversation, and seating myself at the table, wrote a message from Napoleon. Mrs. R. finally went to some tea grounds, and told our fortunes. I tried it afterwards, with a better-spoken fortune. My skepticism was fatal to a serious consideration of the absorbing subject, and we departed.

Warner and Raymond came in just then, and Warner did not leave till about one o'clock this morning. He was telling Mr. C. of the situation. As Mr. C. represents the U.S. we lose no opportunity to inform him. Politically, things are looking worse.

I send love, ADELBERT

JACKSON, MISS., *October 27*, 1875

DEAR BLANCHE: It is midday and I have just come up to the office. It is my usual time for appearing here. My friends (?) have long since learned my habits, and now seek interviews with me at the Mansion, instead of waiting till I get here. The preceding was written at the office, but interruptions prevented further progress. I have just returned from dinner. The Republicans of Madison County—the next above this—have been so far intimidated that they are about to give half of their offices to the white-liners. They were sent for, and a committee came here this morning at half past two to see me. Warner was to be present, and so spent the night here, sleeping in the only spare room. He and Mr. Chase kept up a most distracting conversation over hot rum punches till half past one. I went to bed when my other visitors left, but was awakened from time to time till they had drank their last punch. I sent out and got a breakfast for Warner—mine, which was last, came in about ten.

A letter from Pierrepont, U.S. Atty. Gen'l., indicates that he may send troops, provided the opposition break their words of honor. However, I can say nothing more to him. It is now too late for success. The state will go Democratic, and forever remain so, at least so far as Republicanism is concerned. Next year the Republican Party of the nation will look in vain in this direction for an electoral vote. Exactly what I shall do must be left for consideration till after election day, Nov. 2nd.

I was surprised that you should imagine for a moment that I could be displeased with your action in asking your Father to aid us here in this our day of trial. On the other hand, I have been looking with anxious eyes to see good results from his labors.

I believe I have not written you more than one letter wherein I have vented my spleen upon my wife rather than on myself—or the rest of the world, either of which deserved it rather than said wife. When we meet I will try to make amends for anything you may have taken amiss. Of course, I add a present apology.

I am annoyed *now*. People will loaf about town, attending to their own business first, and then come to the Mansion to see me. I have just declined to see a number of persons and while they were writing me a note, another individual deliberately walks upstairs to my room. They have all gone, but my nerves have hardly tuned down—so little is needed to disturb our equilibrium.

I see Mr. Chase returning—so this must as it should close.

Love, ADELBERT

LOWELL, *October* 28, 1875

DEAR DEL: Two letters came from you yesterday, in which you speak of the Attorney General's advice to Mr. Chase. It does not make me so indignant as it seems to have made you, Love. Pierrepont's difficulty, in my mind, is that it is impossible in his estimation for a man situated as you are to do a right thing if it conflicts with his interest, and he is therefore prepared to hear and believe any and all hard stories. As for resigning, Del, I cannot counsel that while it would have the least appearance of your having been beaten and driven out of the State. However, this question is not to be decided just at present, and at this time no one can tell what a day may bring forth.

The weather here is now delightful, although I fear you may find it cold. The children have been on the hill gathering leaves and chestnuts. Butler has quite a little hoard, which he has locked up in the drawer of my dressing-glass. He and

Edith have just stepped into the room. Seeing me writing Butler steps up to the table to inquire what I am "going to tell Father?" I say that "Butler is a good boy." "How will he like that? What will he say when I show him my chestnuts?" "Father will be here in about two weeks, and you can show him what a lot you have." Edith follows suit as usual, and in her imperfect language endeavors to repeat Butler's questions, about Father, and holds up a tin pail in triumph, with about a dozen nuts in the bottom. The baby has been out in the wind. The moment she came into the warm house her little eyes closed, and she is now enjoying a glorious nap.

You did not seem to relish the remarks about my age, Del. They were not made to me, but of me. I will give you another, made on the same occasion, which will perhaps prove more acceptable. This remark was made by a gentleman to Aunt Lottie, by her repeated to Mother, thence to me, and now I give it to you for your *gratification*. "God is love, love is adoration, and we adore the beautiful," a wave of the hand towards *Mrs. Ames* completed the sentiment. I would not have told you this, Del, if you had not made so much ado about a simple *truthful* little compliment in regard to age. Next time, "do not try to sit on your wife," to use Paul's favorite expression. If Mrs. Farrington tells Mother that I am the best dancer in the room, I am prepared to believe it—more especially as she tries with all her might to imitate. If other ladies tell my relatives that I do not look more than eighteen I am prepared to believe it, more especially as my glass tells me so. Now if you choose to consider this conceit and vanity, why swallow it with your glass of ale, and reason thus— My wife and I are one. She is the better half. I had better be a little careful how I detract from her, on account of the position in which it may leave me.

In a few days more I shall have to write to Northfield, as you will have left Jackson. I want the days to fly now. I must hunt up the eiderdown spread, as I am sure you will be frozen in this Northern climate. We have a new steam boiler which heats the house finely, which is one comfort for you.

Love, Sweetheart. BLANCHE

LOWELL, *October* 28, 1875

DEAR DEL: This will probably reach you the day of election. I do not understand why you have made no reference to Father's attempts in Washington, or why you say nothing of the troops having reported to you. At the departments they assured Father the order had been sent. Does Mr. Chase hold it, or why have you not received it? I do not put full faith in the promises of the "white-liners" and in case of an outbreak I long to have you in a position to say "check-mate." I shall with the greatest interest watch every word from Mississippi.

When you go to Northfield, Sweetheart, make no definite promises. Only offer to buy out John T., your father, and everybody and run the mill for yourself. If I do not mistake the characteristics, they will not care to sell to you. In my opinion your Uncle David could run the mills for you as well as not, at least for a while. Speak to him about it. If worst comes to worst, and they are determined to sell, I think you can raise money enough to buy them out—and surely it will be better to do that and mortgage the mill. If you cannot run it and find you have to sell, you will be no worse off than you will be if they sell out now, and you have a chance that it may work finely.

I must say, Del, that since my last talk with John, I am very little inclined to go into a concern where he is chief partner—where I shall be near enough to be influenced by his discontent and desire for change. Perhaps you smile and say "Yes, Blanche, but *you* are not to be a partner." Indeed I am, sir, and where your interests are, there are mine, and whatever can affect them affects me. However we cannot settle this matter by letter. Only on this point I am determined. I can never go to Northfield to have you the third wheel of that slow coach. To have you give up a salary of five or six thousand or more, which you can easily get in many positions if you desire, for the purpose of assisting to run a concern which has too many heads already and attempting to live and save money on the proceeds of your quarter share of the mill. So you may tell your Father and John. If the latter is ready to sell out—buy; if not, have nothing to do with it, or if both want to sell—say we will talk the matter over and buy if possible.

I have not any news for you, as everything is running in the same ruts.

Butler and Edith have a good deal to say of Father and "Sippi." My painting of Edith I mean to take down to Boston and ask Mr. Brackett's opinion. I want him to criticize it so that I may know what to change in the next one.

I send you love, enough to last until tomorrow. You shall judge of the quantity requisite. BLANCHE

JACKSON, MISS., *October* 28, 1875

DEAR BLANCHE: Today the Attorney General of the U. S. has telegraphed me that U. S. troops will interfere if the Democracy fail to keep faith in their pledges to me to preserve peace and give a fair election. This shows that my former call was a legal one, and at this, the eleventh hour, they are willing to honor it. Many Republicans have abused me for not calling on the national government a second time. It would have been folly, as the sequel proves. Mr. Chase is the representative of Pierrepont, and is now holding conferences with the Democratic leaders, to ascertain if they will pledge peace. An answer will be given tonight. Tomorrow we may telegraph the President that our peace arrangements are at an end. Then he will have to act, and afterwards troops will have to be moved. Thus you see we will have but a day or two at most during which they can act. We look for little good from this late support of the national government. Our side is so thoroughly demoralized that I doubt if they can be rallied. The election will have taken place before this will reach you. The sequel you will know when you read these lines.

Mrs. Hale heads you now, but—my Beloved, Mrs. Hale has not the loving husband you have. She does not know what it is to be worshipped by her husband— Tears, doubts, fears, have been her portion, bitter drops in her cup—while yours has been as free therefrom as my love for you is pure—my devotion deep. It is a cruel world, my dear, full of sorrow, and yet you have no just cause to envy Mrs. H. because of office which hers may have and yours may not have.

Love, and kisses for the babies and yourself.

ADELBERT

LOWELL, *October* 29, 1875

DEAR DEL: I write you a short letter tonight, for it is quite late, and if tomorrow is fair I must rise early to go to Boston. Father came home this evening, and says that he saw both Grant and Babcock, that they understand the situation in Miss. to be exactly what your letters show. The troops were ordered to report to you. He also saw Pierrepont, who said to him "If you, General, had heard as much about Mississippi affairs as I have in the last three months, you would begin to think that there was not a man in the state fit to be out of the penitentiary." "Pardon me, if I were in your place I should think that every man in Washington, out of Mississippi ought to be in a penitentiary."

Some colored men called on Father and asked him to subscribe for arms. "Not one dollar" was the answer. "I will give you twenty-five cents for a package of lucifer matches, and if you cannot take care of yourselves with that you are not worthy to be freemen. If you and your friends are molested, why do you not burn the dwellings and cotton fields of your persecutors. Take it when there is a high wind, and you will not have to burn more than four or five before they will be glad to let you alone." Oh! Pierrepont told Father that a colored man by the name of Williams had told him that you had sold out the colored men, in order to get the Democratic vote for Senator. Never mind about this, Del. We are independent of them all, and of their opinion. They will understand all in good time, who worked to serve them. We can afford to let them take time to find it out much better than they can afford to take it.

I send you love and kisses, Sweetheart. Whatever betides, keep up a brave contented spirit. Fate took you to Mississippi for some purpose which will be worked out in spite of all our small efforts, and the only thing to guard against is lest we leave some opening for conscience to prick us for not having striven to do our duty.

Good night, Dearie. Sarah has just crawled out of bed and is coming to my knee for a second supper. BLANCHE

JACKSON, MISS., *October* 30, 1875

DEAR BLANCHE: Tomorrow will be a birthday for me. I do not care to say which one. It is not very gratifying to me to have you write that you look as young as when eighteen. I first saw you some eleven or twelve years ago, and would be content on the score of age, if you did not look (?) better now than then. But when people make you but eighteen, I feel that I have not done my duty, that I should impose upon you some of the drudgery and worry and sufferings which I have to bear, and which I have heretofore assumed, that folks might say how young she, how old he. We will turn over a new leaf.

Everybody was playing croquet tonight but me. I began, but visitors and committees absorbed all my time. Mrs. Warner arrives tonight.

Politically, all goes wrong. Major Howe's brother is a refugee from white-liners' bullets and halters. The same is true of Warren and many others, and yet all is peace and we are having a quiet election. The election ceases to have any interest for us. It is lost. Gone forever. The Republican candidate for the presidency next year may want this state, but he as well might want the moon for a toy. In this sad plight, I can but think that I have conscientiously done my duty, and also predicted consequences.

I only said "kisses" but I meant enough to last till the next day.

ADELBERT

JACKSON, MISS., *October* 31, 1875

DEAR BLANCHE: As I wrote the date above, it occurred to me that it marked a year-stone in my life. The regret, if any, that the number is so large arises chiefly in connection with thoughts of you and our children, wherein lies the most precious part of myself and my life.

This day has not been a happy one. In fact, these days, one and all, are quite the reverse. I lay awake not a few hours last night as miserable as one cares to be, thinking over defeat which will befall us next day after tomorrow—Tuesday, the 2nd. As I thought—pondered—I fell into bad humor with all the world, and with a will to avenge my many wrongs, finally, in my helplessness, went to sleep with an aching head. I have been irritable all day long; and now only in good humor so far as to admit my savageness. Let us leave this subject. I saw the new moon over my *right* shoulder just a few moments ago. It portends good luck only so far as defeat by intimidation, violence and murder is good luck.

I read your description of Butler's flying "artillery" leap to Capt. Raymond. He was much amused. Why did he think Horace did it to "trap" him? What put that into his head? I hope someone did, otherwise the thought would indicate a suspicious mind, and an inclination to attribute to others the cause of all his woes.

I send you love—the same to the children. I am in hopes to leave here for Northfield by the end of this week.

ADELBERT

LOWELL, *November* 1, 1875

DEAR DEL: It is with quite an effort I write you, for I feel that by the time this reaches Jackson you will be on your way *home*, via Northfield. So strong was this feeling yesterday that I did not write you at all last evening, firmly believing that your letters of today would give me instructions to direct to Northfield or discontinue. Three letters came this afternoon, and in one of them you say that you can have no definite plans until after election. I conclude that you do not leave for the North so soon as you expected.

You mistake, Sweetheart, if you think I envy, or could envy, Mrs. Hale under any circumstances. I appreciate my great good fortune, and am so well content that I do not really think I am anxious enough about affairs in Mississippi.—Except the desire that you should check-mate your enemies, and succeed in all you undertake. I care but very little about the result. While you are content and happy with me, you will find me the same. *Except* that I do not care to go to Northfield unless you have a much larger interest in the concern, for reasons I have already given you. But I should be happy there, or at Fort Atkinson. You would only need to show me that you were doing what was best for your interest.

Tomorrow will settle the election. We shall hardly get news from Mississippi before Wednesday.

> "Then let the old State
> Wag as it will
> I'll be gay and happy still, etc."

In case the Democrats drive you out, Love, you will not come home to find a family of mourners.

This morning I went down to Boston, partly for shopping and to see Bracket about Edith's portrait. He puzzles me, and I have about come to the conclusion that he is puzzled himself and doesn't know exactly what to say. He considers the "drawing very fine," "the flesh tints admirable," "the coloring and surroundings appropriate and pleasing." He objects to covering the further hand with flowers, as it is "against the rules of art to cover the extremities." He suggests that it might be well to change the outline of the shoulder and thigh, but warns me against it unless I can get the child into the proper position, and feel sure I am right. Also a little change in the direction of the cloud is suggested. Here he stops, only repeating that it is a very difficult subject, and that I have managed it wonderfully. I have concluded that he really knows little or nothing about it. I will try to have Hunt, who is another good artist, see it. Perhaps he will be more positive.

You must not stay too long in Northfield, Del. We have two large chests of pears which are waiting some attention from you, and Butler has a horde of chestnuts for his Father.—Now it is so near time for you to be here we are getting impatient. I send you love, and am happy tonight in the thought that you are not displeased with me. How easy it would be for you to take all the sunshine and sweetness out of life. You *are* good to me, and I love you for it. BLANCHE

JACKSON, MISS., *November* 1, 1875

DEAR BLANCHE: The canvass is at an end, and tomorrow the voting will take place. The reports which come to me almost hourly are truly sickening. Violence, threats of murder, and consequent intimidation are co-extensive with the limits of the state. Republican leaders in many localities are hiding in the swamps or have sought refuge beyond the borders of their own counties. The government of the U.S. does not interfere, and will not, unless to prevent actual bloodshed. But no preparations have been made by a proper disposition of troops to meet the murderous designs of the white-liners. I have copies of the orders to the troops. They are to be used to "prevent bloodshed in case of disorders." Observe, they cannot be used to prevent *disorders* nor to prevent intimidation nor to secure to all men their political rights—only where disorders may occur are they to stop the flow of blood. What a mockery are such orders, when as the troops are now disposed, there are but three points where they can act and at those points no disturbances are anticipated.

Warner has gone up to his county to vote. His wife is almost distracted, as she fears he will be assassinated, and the government detective reports to us that the probabilities are that he will be. Mr. Chase has gone to see the chairman of the Democratic state committee to get protection papers for Warner! You can thus surmise what my power, or the power of the civil authorities, is. I am glad this state of affairs is drawing to an end. I begin to speak of the situation in a fair frame of mind, but before I close I lose all patience. Today—now—I have held out longer than usual.

I send you love—for yourself, Beautiful, and for the babies.

ADELBERT

LOWELL, *November* 2, 1875

DEAR DEL: I write again to Jackson as you have not intimated that you have any thought of leaving for the North at present. Tomorrow we shall get the election returns, and see if they verify your predictions. For us, personally, Love, I shall never give one sigh of regret for any of the lost honors the State of Mississippi might have conferred upon us. I only wish that you might feel as independent of its praise or censure as I do for you. After completing your duties in the state, we will seek our home elsewhere. Your babies are expecting you, and Butler looks at the nuts he has been saving for you every day. As he always takes away a few in his pocket, your share is not likely to prove large.

Father has gone to Washington again, to try some cases in the Supreme Court. He is looking remarkably well, and happy. I think it agrees with him to be out of politics.

I have not much that is new to write you. This morning I was out for two or three hours, doing errands. It is very cold here now, and you will need all the warm clothing you can get on to be comfortable. Look in the linen closet and see if I left the eiderdown quilt there done up in a sheet. I am sure I did not, yet I cannot find it here. You will need it, you are so thin-blooded.

Butler stands beside me and says "What will you tell Papa through his letter?" "I don't know, what do you want me to tell him?" "That Butler is a good boy." He has watched these lines with great interest to see that I write his message.

How much you have to make you proud and happy, Love. I know you will be delighted with the children. With Butler, especially, because he is a man. We send you love and kisses.

BLANCHE

JACKSON, MISS., *November* 4, 1875

DEAR BLANCHE: I did not write you last night, not being in a writing humor. The reports of disasters which came to us then were mild as compared to those of today. So complete and thorough was the intimidation of Republican voters that we have yet to hear of the first county which has gone Republican. There may be a few counties on the river which have been neglected by the murderous white leaguers that have maintained their virtue, but of such we have no word. The legislature will be nearly unanimous in both branches and will be able to do anything it may incline to do. The election has been a farce—worse than a farce.

To this point I had written at the office, when Mr. Huntington, a friend of Gen. Warner, came in and took me down to the hotel to dinner with Gen. W. Capt. and Mrs. Raymond were present. The dinner was good. Fish, crabs, chicken, beef. Mrs. R. and I drank each about a bottle and a half of ale. I told her what you said about an extra car to take her West. After dinner we came up to the Mansion, and had a game of croquet. Mrs. W. and I against Mrs. R. and Gen'l. W. We were beaten. Madames have gone off to ride the gentlemen to the hotel, and I have come upstairs to finish this, my letter to you.

Today I have had some hands at work cleaning the chamber opposite ours. When that is done they will go to the parlors below. Osborne will leave in a few days. His and my rooms will be the last. I have given Mr. Rhodes directions to have the gas fixtures attended to, the bells and wires renewed. I have no doubt we will find the house very comfortable when we return.

My visitors are increasing, and I must stop. Mr. Chase starts for the North tonight. I expect to leave for Minn. next Saturday.

Love, ADELBERT

JACKSON, MISS., *November* 4, 1875

DEAR BLANCHE: You again refer to your loving labors in seconding my efforts to induce the national government to put forth its hand to secure the poor colored people of this state their rights. I most heartily approve of everything you did, but I have long since known that I would not receive the much desired aid. I have already told you what the President did do for us. He tells your Father that he ordered troops to report to me He simply orders Gen'l. Augur—or Gen'l. Augur orders—that troops shall be used to "prevent bloodshed in case of disorders!" Threats, intimidation, violence, anything and everything, provided no blood is shed, and troops will not act. As a result the state has gone about fifty thousand (50,000) Democratic. Two years ago, the state went twenty thousand (20,000) for me. A change of some 70,000 is wrought, notwithstanding Grant's professed order that troops should be at my disposal. His order was a sham, and the election a fraud.

Need I tell you I hold the state has gone beyond redemption. The Republicans know it, the Democrats know it—and while the former are inclined to blame me for their defeat, the latter are making an effort to cultivate us—me. The Democracy has been denouncing me for years—the Republicans say I have "sold them out." Grant will probably say "It was Ames' fault, I gave him all the troops he would use!" With the Democracy I never had a character—with the Republicans it is lost!

While Grant may thus try to shield himself—if he does—and Pierrepont repeat what he knows to be false, and newspapers howl, I am convinced upon a careful examination of my heart that I am a better man than any in the whole crowd, and that my head work has not been defective in any important point. This I can prove.

I think I shall leave for Minn. next day after tomorrow morning, Saturday morning. I shall not be able to reach Lowell in less than a week from that time.

Love for my Beautiful and our babies. ADELBERT

LOWELL, *November 5*, 1875

DEAR DEL: I am grieved, Sweetheart, to find that you are so depressed and unhappy, although I know that you have had quite enough to endure to make you so. The state has gone Democratic to be sure. But Maryland and Mississippi are the only Democratic victories, and their success in these states only makes their defeat in the others more exasperating. They ought to have carried nearly all, and lo and behold, they have only two, and all the world understands that these were carried by violence and fraud. The Northern papers do not hesitate to comment loudly on the facts. "Those who laugh last, laugh best" and although things have gone so sadly for our state I do not by any means think they are past all redemption. As for the Senatorship, Love, I do not and have not given it a thought. I have been troubled and annoyed at your helpless position, and angry that you could not have a chance to get the better of your enemies. But for any personal interest we might have in a republican success, it has not entered into my calculations.

I have one great regret, that I could not have been with you during these hard times. I know you could have taken things with more placidity if I had been with you. You should have said "yes" instead of "no" to my proposal. You did not leave Jackson, and I could have been with you as well as not. That was a mistake. The next time I shall not ask you.—No, better still, there shall be no occasion for asking, for I do not intend to have any more such long separations.

I want to write you my opinion of Mr. Chase. You have always spoken of him most kindly. But I believe him to be like his chief, an unreliable trickster, with no conception of propriety or the dignity of the Government, he has tried to represent.—If a Catholic, a good Jesuit. Thank kind Fate for one thing at least—that our Attorney Gen'l. is to be disappointed next year. In fact, is so this. The election did not go as he expected, and there will be no chance for him as Democratic candidate, or failing that, no nice fat place in a

Democratic administration. I wonder if our worthy President has received backbone enough to attend to his affairs, and has yet found nerve enough to do what is right, instead of what is politic. I am glad I am not a *man* of that stamp, forever sacrificing what is right to what is expedient. No doubt you will say "Oh, no Blanche, you misjudge Mr. Chase." I only want to put myself on record against him and his director, that is all. I am always suspicious of middlemen, and I take it that Mr. Chase has been acting in that capacity lately.

Enough on politics.—You wrote me that you should probably start the last of the week for Minnesota, so I will direct my letter to Northfield. Do not commit yourself, Love. We have many things to talk over and plan for the future, and it is better not to be too hasty about it. You notice that I claim without hesitation my right to a share in your plans and deliberations. No doubt you have been learning to do without me lately. All things of this kind you will have to unlearn.

Butler and Edith are well. The baby has lost her appetite and does not seem so bright and lively. It is only temporary, however. I want her perfectly well by the time you see her.

Father is still in Washington. Tomorrow Paul, Mother and I go to Boston. I want Paul to take Edith's picture to Hunt. I am quite determined to get somewhere an opinion which shall at least convince me the picture is worthy of criticism or the reverse. I send you, Love, kisses. In a few days more you will be with us. Good night, Dearie. BLANCHE

JACKSON, MISS., *November 5*, 1875

DEAR BLANCHE: I had made preparations to leave tomorrow morning for Minnesota. I came home after dinner, and have been steadily at work to get ready. I packed the few things I am to take in my satchel, and also put everything in the room away, that there should be the least possible confusion, when the men get to work here cleaning up. The room looks quite bare now, after my stowing away process. The barrel of apples which I had in my room is gone, and a small basket of apples in the middle of the mantle piece, is all that remains of its grandeur as it stood by the wardrobe. A corkscrew, box of matches and four books are the mantle companions of the apples. On the bureau is a piece of sealing wax and a few letters I have yet to attend to. *One* pair of boots—I usually have *three*—and two trunks are the only other adornments.

A little while before I sat down to write, I received a telegram from Mr. Chase, who is in Vicksburg, saying he will not be out till tomorrow afternoon, and asking me to wait for him. As he waited a day or two for me, I could not do less than to wait for him. Sunday morning at three we will start. I have today issued a proclamation setting a day for Thanksgiving—the same as that fixed by the President.

The indications now are that our Democratic friends (?) are disposed to cultivate us. It is mooted in the aristocratic circles of this city. I have given you something to think of.

Love, ADELBERT

JACKSON, MISS., *November* 6, 1875

DEAR BLANCHE: It is now nine o'clock in the evening. I am packed, ready for a start.

This letter will go as far as Milan, Tenn. on the same train with me. I will reach Chicago Monday evening, and will be compelled to stay there till Tuesday morning. At ten a.m. I will leave, and arrive at Northfield at about the same hour Wednesday. I suppose twenty-four hours will be the extent of my stay there. I cannot now tell whether I shall be able to reach Lowell Saturday, Sunday, or Monday next. I will probably telegraph you of my coming.

George is strapping my trunks, and will put them in the closet. The key of the closet I will leave with Mr. Rhodes. I have commissioned Mrs. R. to get curtains for our chamber. I have told Mr. R. to finish cleaning up and repairing.

The carriage will soon be here to take us to the hotel where we have taken a room so we will have a little sleep before the train arrives at 3:45 tomorrow morning. I will not seal this now, but carry it with me on the train to add a P.S. as we progress on our journey, and before we reach Milan. Politically I have nothing.

I send you, my Beautiful, much love. A few days after you shall receive this I hope to be with you. I rejoice that these long months are drawing to a close. I hope we will never again be apart for so long a time.

Kiss the babies. ADELBERT

TENNESSEE, *November* 7, 1875

We have passed Grand Junction, and are plunging onward towards Milan, where Mr. Chase who is along will turn to the right, towards Louisville, while I go on to Cairo. We spent the evening with the Warners, only leaving them at 12:30. They sang, talked, and drank hot rum punches. After leaving their room, we went to Mat. Sullivan's and continued our sitting up process. We had but about one hour's sleep before the arrival of the train. Wells got on the train at Holly Springs, and is bound probably to Washington to take his seat as a M.C. How successful is roguery! Senator Price and others attended him, to bid him who deals exclusively with the d---l *God* speed. I do not speak to W.

By the irregularity of my writing, you can tell the exact condition of the road we travel on, as I have been writing while the train is in motion.

A Memphis paper of today says in its Washington dispatches that Pease has been removed as P.M. of Vicksburg, and that Raymond has been appointed. This and *more* we have been expecting.

Love to my Beloved. ADELBERT

LOWELL, *November* 7, 1875

DEAR DEL: I write again to Northfield, nothing doubting but that you will be there by the time this is.

Father is still in Washington, and writes home to Mother as follows. "So Ames has lost his state. Poor fellow, I sympathize with him. He will feel very much chagrined about it. Tell Blanche not to let him resign till next year. Tell him hold his place till Grant's chance for nomination comes off, and then he may have a chance for something in the future, but of all that we will talk when I come home." My only request of you, Sweetheart, is to keep up a stout, cheerful heart. As I wrote you before "those laugh best who laugh last." We may have our chance next, at any rate, we can afford to smile a little now. What a dreadful disappointment it must have been to the Mississippi "rebs" to read the returns from the Northern states and find that after all their efforts, they were not on the winning side. For my part, I care but little for the whole matter if you will only be happy.

If you go to Fort Atkinson, Del, will you bring on with you a mortgage on the mill? The notes have all been paid and do not require any more interest, but Carney has not endorsed them paid and does not wish to do so until he has something to show for it. Do not forget what I said about going to Northfield with you as *third* director of the concern. I cannot agree to such an arrangement. It is too great a waste of raw material. Perhaps I should say *good* material. At any rate, I think too highly of the Ames's to suppose that three of that name are required to run a little one-horse affair like that at Northfield.

Saturday I went down to Boston with Aunt Nina and Paul. We remained to go to the Opera. Kellogg was the Prima Donna. She has grown very stout, and is losing all her beauty. Johnnie Kimball came to talk to us during the intermission. He is just the same as of old.

Every morning Edith asks to have on her new shoes, to go and see her Father. Every time Butler eats a chestnut, he asks "What will Papa say if I save this nut for him?" Every act of mine is with reference to your coming. Mother is pondering over what she can get that you will like to eat, and wonders if the pears will keep till you can eat them. Thus you see there is quite a little circle thinking of, planning for, and loving our absent one.

Try and be happy, Love, for we are so much better off than the rest of the world. I would not change places with anyone in the world, and I am very grateful that fate has been so kind to me. The bloom will be somewhat taken off of my rose, if my Love is not contented too.

Good night. BLANCHE

Governor Ames left Mississippi for Northfield, Minn., November 7th. Visited Lowell, Massachusetts, and returned with wife and children to The Mansion, Jackson, December 8th.

The Mansion, JACKSON, *December* 8, 1875

DEAR MOTHER: We are here, all well, and were fortunate in having one of the pleasantest trips I have made South. We missed connection, as it was surmised we might, in taking the morning instead of the evening train, and stopped in Pittsburgh four or five hours, also twelve hours in Cincinnati. Perhaps these pauses were better—for the trip seemed shorter, and all were less wearied than usual.

We reached Jackson about half past three in the morning. Most of our journey had been made in the rain, which laid the dust, and kept the cars quite clean. Fortunately, however, we had just passed from the rain clouds when we arrived here. The air was soft and warm, and the stars shining brightly as we rode from the depot to the Mansion, through mud half way to the hubs of the wheels. The house was in nice order, fires in the chambers and everything ready to receive us. The children flew at once to their old box of playthings. Our breakfast was brought in from the restaurant and proved quite good. We are having all our meals served in this way at present. Perhaps will continue to do so. Mary is not here, and I cannot tell how soon she will be. The expense is about the same and the variety, but home cooking is a little better. I have also some doubts about establishing the household with large supplies from New Orleans, as the clamor for impeachment is great among the Democrats, so great that those who are really friendly do not dare to stand against it. This may change during the next three weeks, but is not likely to, as it is entirely a party move, and as the party has sufficient majority to impeach. I do not see that there are any favorable signs for our remaining here long. It is folly to say that they cannot find grounds for impeachment. Of course we know that there are none. But it is easy enough to concoct any number sufficient for their purpose. This is what we are looking forward to now, but changes are liable to occur in all things.

The weather has been and is quite spring-like. The thermometer has been as high as seventy for three days or more. This morning it is cloudy and threatens rain and the air is a little more raw.

Mrs. Judge Tarbell sent me this morning a large bunch of roses and other flowers grown in the open air. The blue violets are in blossom, but in a day or so it may be cold enough to blight the buds and retard more blossoms until the last of February.

Butler said this morning, "I do not like Mississippi." I think he misses his "Gran, Grandfather, and Uncle Paul." Last night Edith was troubled with a little touch of croup. The syrup you gave me was brought into requisition, and this morning she is much better. I keep her up stairs close by the fire, as the air is damp, though not cold. I had hoped she was not going to be subject to that difficulty.

I purchased today four turkeys, not having quite decided about my housekeeping arrangements. It wouldn't look well, would it, to be obliged to sell out a lot of ducks, geese, turkeys, chickens, etc.?

Write as often as you can. Tell Hattie she must consider it a duty to keep us informed of events. If you can make her understand that it is her *duty*, I am sure she will attend to it. Paul also promised to write. Remind him of it.

Kisses for you and Father. Love to the others.

Your affectionate daughter, BLANCHE

JACKSON, *December* 8, 1875

DEAR MOTHER: Your letter came a few days ago, and I delayed answering it, in order to know the effect of Gen'l. Ames' message and be able to tell you prospects here. The message was, I think, a surprise to the Democrats, and troubled them a great deal. They no doubt thought the threats of impeachment would intimidate him to such a degree that he would ignore election matters entirely. They are full of wrath at his position. In the house a joint resolution referring that part of the message relating to intimidation and fraud to a committee of five (all Democratic) with power to send for persons and papers, was adopted. While the message has had the effect of arousing many, it has frightened some, but the timid ones will be whipped into the traces.

Gen'l. Ames wrote to Father this morning. He had to enclose the letter to his old clerk, for the mails are tampered with. A letter directed to Father would not be likely to reach him. The Democrats are determined to get rid of Gen'l. Ames and if they should not succeed in impeaching him, they would not hesitate to assassinate. Last summer they fired, and left bullet holes in the Mansion. A prominent Democrat said that Gen'l. Ames' life was not worth the snap of a finger. Nobody in the North can realize the condition of affairs.

I suppose you saw an account of the murder of Caldwell, a colored man, at Clinton. The only truthful part of that account was the statement that the man was shot. I will tell you the story, for it has made my blood boil many times within the last fortnight. Caldwell was State Senator last year, and he was one of the leaders in organizing the militia last fall (this was the reason of his murder). His nephew, a young fellow under twenty years of age, went over to Clinton and soon after his arrival was accosted by a white man, a member of the vigilance committee, who asked him if he was in the Clinton riot, and if he killed anyone. "No," he said, "I did not kill anyone that I know of." "Did you shoot at any one?" "I shot around, as the others did, when we were fired into." The young fellow then went up to his Uncle's house, but found that he had gone out fox-hunting. When Caldwell returned from the hunt and his nephew told him of the conversation, he said he would go down in the town and tell the man that the boy had done nothing at the riot. So far I have given you the boy's story as near as I can remember as he told it to Gen'l. Ames. The rest is the recital of a Judge Cabinis of Clinton, who had pretended to be a friend of Caldwell. Caldwell recommended him to Gen'l. Ames for a judgeship, and was very strenuous about his appointment. There were some forty men around Caldwell when he fell back wounded into the cellar, and he called out "Oh Judge, Oh Judge, don't leave me here to die like a dog." At the same time the Judge was standing in the door of a store across the street with a gun in his hand ready to fire, with the other men, the moment Caldwell should show his head above the cellar door. Then Caldwell asked to be taken home. They went into the cellar and brought him out into the middle of the street. Someone cried "clear the road." They dropped him, and like a flash, fifteen shots were fired into his body. This is the Judge's story to Gen'l. Ames and his excuse for his conduct was that it was done to protect the life of a man by the name of Rice. A mere subterfuge. The Judge said that fifteen shots were fired into the body, but those who have seen Caldwell's corpse report that the body had to be tied together, while on his head and neck there was not a space where one could lay a hand. After he was wounded, Caldwell said, "You may fire as many shots as you please, but you shall not say I did not die like a brave man." His brother, hearing the shooting, rode into town to find out the cause of the fray, and was shot from his horse.

That night a few colored men, hearing that Caldwell had been shot, assembled at a place called Wilburns, near Clinton, to see if they could learn the particulars, and if Caldwell were only wounded and able to get out of Clinton, to help him on his way. The town was picketed on all the roads so that no colored man could enter it. One of the women went in, however, and brought out the word that Caldwell was "dead." The men agreed to remain there that night, but about dawn, hearing the dogs bark, they got up and looked out, to find the yard full of armed men. They escaped through the windows, but not before the white-liners had discovered them, and firing at them, gave chase. The house was near a swamp or cane brake, and as the colored men ran in all directions they managed to escape and hide and make their way to Jackson.

Walker, who gave us the narration, did not dare to go back—in fact, Gen'l. Ames did not advise him to, but told him he had better get away from Jackson as soon as possible. Walker said he thought he would walk to Florida, he had a brother there, and after he got away from the country no one would know him. (He also took part in the militia). He did not feel safe in Jackson, for he said he saw Judge Johnson (a man who expected to be President of the Senate and Governor in case of Gen'l. Ames' impeachment) point him out to one of the murderers. Poor fellow. I felt sorry for him, a poor suit of working clothes on his back, no money in his pocket, and that journey in prospect. He had done no wrong, and intended none, only desired to help a wounded friend. The papers reported that Caldwell was drunk. On the contrary, he had just returned from hunting and went into the saloon to take a drink of settlement with the man who had questioned his nephew. He was fired upon when he attempted to come out. Enough of this story, but it shows you the condition of society, when the judges and principal men of the community bear a hand in such atrocities.

At night in the town here, the crack of the pistol or gun is as frequent as the barking of the dogs. Night before last they gave us a few shots as they passed the Mansion yard, by way of a reminder. I do not think they fired at the windows, only discharged the guns to disturb our slumbers.

I will send you Gen'l. Ames' message and want you to read it and give us your opinion of it. Of course he was very careful to make no statement he could not prove. The only thing we can do now is to await developments. I sent Father a Southern newspaper containing some extracts from his impeachment speech, with comments and application to Gen'l. Ames' case. I am sure if he gets it he will be amused, while at the same time he will see how very weak their charges and to what straits they are pushed. The Democrats think that Gen'l. Ames is in constant communication with Morton and Gen'l. Butler, and that they have put him up to writing the message and thus he is to be martyrized through impeachment.

The weather is charming. Every afternoon we play croquet. Every day the windows stand open. I will send you a couple of oranges by mail, which grew on the place at Bay St. Louis. Not a large crop (only nine)—still for size and quality, quite unsurpassed.

Butler is well, but full of old sayings and theories. The family who are living in the back building have told him about heaven and the angels, and he speculates constantly upon the manner in which angels take people up to heaven when they die. His last idea is that they put a chain around the neck and pull them up. He asked me yesterday if I should not "feel sorry for poor Butler if God should take him up to be an angel." He is very old. The baby does not seem to grow any larger, but is more and more pert. Edith is about the same but more interesting, as she talks plainer.

Suppose you and Father come down and see us in our difficulties for a while. You would not mind the trip. Charlotte could stay with Hattie, and I think it would be a fine plan.

The great change would be well for your throat. When you gave me the report of the Boston doctor, I felt there was a weight off of mind. This summer air might be of benefit.

How is it you always keep thinking of nice things for other people? I shall consider the cross a Christmas gift.

Love for you and Father. With kisses, BLANCHE

LOWELL, *December* 15, 1875

MY DEAR BLANCHE: Your letter came this morning. I forwarded it at once to your Father in Washington, together with one from me, urging him to give it his quick and complete attention, asking him in my letter if it would be better to have a lawyer from the North and fight it to the last, or to see Grant and see what presentation he will make of it in his message, which is yet to be given, as the papers say, on Mississippi affairs, among other things, etc. etc. Do not feel uneasy, for whichever way the thing goes, it is not worth your being troubled. The articles of impeachment as given in the newspaper you sent seem to me to have no weight whatever. I don't believe if Gen'l. Ames is well defended that they could make a case that they would themselves not be ashamed of. They may overleap the mark too far, and do Gen. Ames a great benefit.

This is your time of political effort. Do the work bravely and well, and have no fears of the result. For my own part, I should be thankful to get you back to Washington. But for all that, a Governor is a power, and it must not be lightly yielded. My idea is not to give up an inch of power while you possess it, unless compelled.

I think my throat is improving. The rest of the household are well. I miss the children very much and I know well enough that Butler misses his "Gran."

Dearest love to the children, Gen. Ames and yourself.

Your most affectionate MOTHER

The Mansion, JACKSON, *December* 23, 1875

DEAR MOTHER: I had two letters from you the first of the week. They were most acceptable, I can assure you. When away, one longs for news from home. Gen'l. Ames said (and he is not supposed to be as anxious for some word from you as I am), "It seems very pleasant to get your Mother's letters, she writes well."

We are still having our meals from the restaurant. We are abundantly served, and with great variety. The style of cooking might be improved. When we have company, we send for an extra plate, I suppose you would call it—that is, a meal for one more. In the course of a month or so, we shall go to keeping house. The impeachment supporters are growing fainthearted. Perhaps Morton's bill for a committee to investigate the election in Mississippi may have had something to do with it. Gen'l. Ames will not mince matters in his message, and the effect will be to arouse them once more.

Mr. Chase, from the Attorney General's department, is here now. He was sent for as a witness in the court-martial of the officer commanding the post here. He says with great emphasis, and continues to repeat it "Oh! no! it will never do, the Governor must not be impeached. He must not. What! with all these little children to have such a thing as that happen. Oh! no! It must not be. Not if the Attorney General's department can help it, not if I have to come down here myself, and it shall never cost the Governor a cent." All of which, in my opinion, means that Pierrepont is working for the presidency. It would not do for him, if he expects to win the delegation from Mississippi, to allow Gen. Ames to be impeached, for then the Democrats would have full power, and all the delegates to the nominating convention would be Democratic. Gen'l. Ames says I am wrong. It makes no difference with the nominating convention whether he is in or not.

We have not heard from Father yet. I have occupied my time painting, and have nearly completed that portrait of myself which I had begun. Gen'l. Ames thinks it the best thing I have ever done. I thought so yesterday, but today I am not so well satisfied. Perhaps this is owing to the weather, which is most oppressive. The fires are all out, the windows open, and a soft April shower is falling, but the perspiration stands in great beads on our faces, and the hair of the children is quite wet. The thermometer marks seventy-seven degrees. A man had up an umbrella to keep off the sun yesterday. This great warmth is unusual at this season. We shall have to take great care when the cold snap comes.

I wish when you go to Washington, you would look, or ask Hattie to look, for photographs of Charles Sumner. That photographer by the side of Thorpe who used to be in the Capitol would probably have the best.

The children are very well. Butler is growing still fatter. But while they are well enough in health, they are poorly off as regards discipline. In fact, I am inclined to despair. Butler is simply outrageous.

The clouds are breaking away, and the sun shines. It is going to be more sultry than ever. Just think of it, when in accordance with the season I must say "Merry Christmas to all, and to all a Happy New Year." I suppose the ice is a foot thick in Lowell.

Kisses and love for you, Mother. Father I suppose is still in Washington.

Love for Hattie and the boys.

Your affectionate Daughter, BLANCHE

WASHINGTON, *December* 23, 1875

Gen. ADELBERT AMES, *Governor*
Jackson, Mississippi

MY DEAR AMES: I have read your note of the 10th of December with some care, and also its enclosure. Of course, I agree fully and thoroughly with you that if the Democracy desire to impeach you, they have the physical and political power to do it. Upon the charges in the article in the newspaper, or upon any other they can bring against you, there is no possibility of just cause of impeachment being found. But that I need not stop to discuss. The question is how to meet the impending danger, if it is a danger to you to be made the victim of political injustice. It has always worked in the past, in the end, in aid of the man who suffered the temporary wrong. Now then, as to your message: I would advise that you put calmly in the most dignified way, a statement of all occurrences of the election in your forthcoming message. The facts should be stated with some boldness. I would then dwell particularly upon the financial character of your administration, showing what was the indebtment of the state, what it consisted of and what was the value of its warrants when your administration began. I would then show exactly the same items now and make the comparison between the two dates. This I would do as distinctly and tersely as possible. As soon as you get these items prepared, please send to me a full synopsis of them, so far in advance that I can get them into the hands of the printers of two or three leading papers to come out as telegraphic messages on the day your message is read. That I will endeavor to do. Assuming, as I have no doubt will be done, that the articles of impeachment, if found at all, will be found in accordance with the provisions of the constitution, by the House of Representatives of your state, and be duly presented to the Senate sitting as a high court of impeachment,

I think you are bound to answer them. I should therefore not advise your treating them with contempt or neglect. In that answer you can put forward your justification, and that should be a carefully drawn document. I should make that answer my manifesto and appeal to the people. For the purpose of preparing that answer you will require at your elbow a good lawyer and an eloquent writer. I have such a one in my mind, Mr. Thomas J. Durant of this City, formerly Attorney General of Louisiana, and I should say you had better have him employed, and I shall endeavor to have him take the retainer. Of course the articles of impeachment will hardly be got prepared and got through the House until after the election of the Senator. It certainly cannot get through the Senate, because time must be given you to prepare your answer. I think after the election of the Senator, whoever he may be, he will be somewhat adverse to having the impeachment go on lest the Republican Senate should visit upon him the outrages which he would promote upon you. Meanwhile, a pretty strong sentiment will arise against your impeachment; the timid and conservative men in both House and Senate will begin to pause. Morton's Committee under his resolutions will be down in your state about that time, and I think the general sense of the Democratic Party will see to it that they will gain nothing in the presidential election by this performance. I think also that the President will take a pretty decided stand in your favor; at least, he is now so inclined so that I do not quite look upon the contest as hopeless, and after a fair, stand-up and aggressive defence, which can appear in your answer to the articles, is made, I think the common sense of the country will go with you. If it ever comes to the answer, let a synopsis of it, giving its salient points, be also forwarded to me that I may get it in the leading newspapers of the country. It will never get there through the Associated Press of the South. I do not know that I can say anything more upon this subject that will be of advantage to you at present, but I think that this plan of campaign will be as likely to be successful as any other, and certainly it will be in accordance with the eternal propriety of things in view of the situation. Of course, I have not written many things that I would say to all the world if all the world should read it. Be not cast down or worried. That you will be annoyed I know. I think we can offset here all the personal or political harm they can do you there, and be like the honest Dutchman who, when he had the rheumatism, congratulated himself that it was not the gout. Do you congratulate yourself that the Democrats of Mississippi propose to remove their Governor by impeachment and not assassination. The same spirit that makes them do the one would prompt and justify the other, save that the last would have to be accomplished by the bravery and recklessness of some single man, while the first can be done by the cowardice of a mob calling themselves the Legislature.

With love to you and all yours, whom I do love very much, and none the less because I am not demonstrative in its expression, I am, as ever, *Yours*, BENJ. F. BUTLER

LOWELL, *December 27*, 1875

DEAR BLANCHE: "A Merry Christmas" to you all! Ben came home Saturday morning and stayed till Sunday night. This little diversion will clear his head for the examination. He is getting on very well, as you will see by Gen. Michie's letter, which I will this time enclose. Your Father arrived from Washington Saturday noon, in time for Christmas dinner. Poor Ben was a happy boy when he arrived, just in time for breakfast, chicken fricasee, and nice coffee. We admiringly watched his eating. As before, he came up the back avenue and took us by surprise.

I think we may go on to Washington the last of this week. Your Father will return here again to try some cases, but that makes it too late for us to put the house in order for the season. Florence and Nina both want to go. I want the house all equipped against your arrival. What do you think of the billiard room as a nursery for the children? The billiard table, if we buy one, shall be put in the room next to the front door.

There is a chance that Morton's resolution in the Senate may stop further action against Gen. Ames, if Lamar has any fears about getting into the Senate. Your Father seems to think if they push things to extremes that Durant will be the best lawyer to go down. I told him if that were so, he ought to engage and pay him. Gen. Ames' opportunity of making his record clear and known abroad is in his message, and in his defense if they attempt to impeach him. Do not worry over it, but meet it as people must the annoyances that are not to be avoided.

Your Father saw Grant, who professed great interest. He was to see him again; but Grant was away, at Philadelphia. He could change those officers. That would be the best proof of his sincerity. He will see him again as soon as we go on. I do not believe he is to be relied on. Your Father will test him with all the skill he has. Keep your Father or me well informed, and whatever can be, shall be done.

My throat continues better; the difficulty was partly owing to the medicine, though it is likely enough there may be something beside.

I expect to stop in New York to buy some furniture, and I wish you were here to aid me.

My best love to the children and Gen. Ames, and yourself.

Your affectionate MOTHER

LOWELL, *January* 3, 1876

DEAR BLANCHE: We leave Lowell tomorrow morning. Just started off twelve trunks to the depot. Horace takes with him six more. I write you a short letter now, because I may not find time for a week or more after I get on to Washington. I shall stop in New York one day to purchase some things that we must have.

Cut a little article from the Boston *Herald*, that paper you know is always in enmity to your Father. If the agent alluded to is Mr. Chase, you have need to be careful how far you confide in him.

If Grant is not for you, he is probably against you. But that will be seen by the men he puts in office.

Your Father read us a speech last night which he has written for Bruce to deliver in the Senate. I think it very good, and to the point.

It seems to be hard to tell just yet what they will do with regard to impeachment. Do not let it disturb you or Gen. Ames, as you are in no wise responsible and cannot avert it if they are determined to vote it. As Gen. Ames says, if they will kill the Negroes to prevent their voting, so they will vote him out without any scruples, if they are not afraid of the consequences.

Florence has just left. She and her mother and Nina are preparing their dresses for a Centennial Tea-Party Thursday night; old-styled dresses. Florence, Tom, Nina and Mr. & Mrs. Farrington all expect to go on to Washington this winter. I do not mind if I am able to take care of them. But I should naturally feel better pleased to see you and the children along.

Best love to the children, Gen. Ames, and yourself from

Your most affectionate MOTHER

P.S. Your Father says there is not a word of truth in the article, only the spite of the *Herald* against him, that Chase has written in favor of Gen. Ames and that I had better not send the article, as there is no truth in it, nothing but spite.

Annual Message of Gov. Adelbert Ames
to the Legislature of Mississippi
Session of 1876.

State of Mississippi
Executive Office, JACKSON, *January* 4, 1876

To the Senate and House of Representatives:

In the discharge of a duty, incumbent upon me, of giving you information concerning the condition and interests of the government and state, and the condition of the people, I call your attention to the late state election, and the events incident thereto, as a subject whose magnitude and importance demands the wisest and calmest consideration.

On the fourth day of September last a political meeting, at Clinton, Hinds County, was interfered with and dispersed by violence, which resulted in the death of a number of persons, and which was followed, subsequently, by the pursuit and shooting of others, by armed men riding through the county. Impelled through fear of violence, men abandoned their homes and fled by hundreds to this city for safety. The fifth and following days of September found this city crowded with panic-stricken fugitives, unconscious of offense, imploring such assistance as would enable them to return to their homes, and shield them in the peaceful pursuit of their labors.

While a city full of refugees was one illustration of the violence and the success of lawlessness, another was to be found in the fact that a Sheriff's posse, which was sent to Clinton from this point, was headed by a flag of truce.

At this juncture business was suspended, and disquiet or terror existed in the minds of all. The authority of the county was paralyzed. The Sheriff reported his utter helplessness to give the needed protection. It then became the duty of the state government to furnish him the means to overcome and suppress the lawless bands, which, for some purpose other than the punishment of crime or the pursuit of criminals, had established so lamentable a condition of affairs.

The spirit which precipitated the Clinton outrage by no means had its origin then and there. Previous to that day, the Sheriffs of two adjacent counties had been compelled by force—or what is substantially the same, after encountering much lawless violence, which no power at their command could control—to make their escape beyond the borders of their counties, leaving them without the chief peace-officer which the law has made so indispensable. Nor was violence, or the fear of it, confined to two or three counties. Appeals for protection and aid came from all directions.

The state was without a militia or constabulary force. Although previous political disturbances had occurred, of a magnitude too great for local or state authorities to cope with, the sentiment against a militia, or other armed force, was so powerful and so general as to prevent its successful organization. This hostile sentiment to maintaining peace and affording protection by force was chiefly due to a dread of a conflict of races. While one part of the people were thus discountenancing the militia in the interest of peace, another part was converting the state into a broad military encampment, which called forth a proclamation, bearing date of the 7th September, 1875, commanding, though ineffectually, their disbandment. The evil day anticipated, when the state should need force and be without it, had arrived.

Under such a combination of circumstances, which could exist only in a state where the inhabitants are of two distinct races, with strong race prejudices and antagonisms, I was constrained to call upon the national government for assistance to protect against domestic violence. This call was unsuccessful. It was followed by a succession of demonstrations by the armed part of the people towards the unarmed, causing a feeling of insecurity and danger, which continued until and after the day of the election.

A renewed effort to organize a military force developed the deep-seated bitterness of the race issue, and the extent of the intimidation which prevailed. While appeals for aid and protection came from all sides, and often from Sheriffs, it was held by them that such forces as might be organized under state laws, could not be serviceable. On the contrary, the conviction prevailed that they would only precipitate the conflict it was sought to avoid.

The seizure of state arms on their way to the Capitol, the liability of seizure in sending them away from the Capitol, and the necessity of storing the few arms on hand at the United States camp for safe keeping, were additional causes which embarrassed and prevented the organization of the militia. Consequently, only a few companies could be organized, and those (with one exception) but in one county—this, the seat of government. Many who took arms did so to obtain the means of self-defense; few were accustomed to their use, and instruction and discipline were quite impracticable.

The fund for militia purposes, appropriated by the late Legislature, was sixty thousand ($60,000) dollars, but with the condition that fifty-five thousand ($55,000) dollars should be used only in case the militia should be called into active service. An early injunction from the courts prevented the expenditure of any part of the latter sum. The remaining five thousand ($5,000) dollars were soon expended, and there were no means to transport beyond the borders of this county, the recruiting ground and depot, the few undisciplined companies formed within it.

Preparations had been made to protect the Sheriff of Yazoo County, in his return to his county, he having previously been driven away. Deeming the means inadequate, he declined to make the attempt. He has not been able to return to this day.

Because of the attempt to organize and use a militia to protect citizens in the exercise of their rights and privileges, as bestowed upon them by the Constitution and the laws, a class of people rebelled against it. To avoid threatened deeds of resistance and violence to state authority, as well as toward county officials and individuals, and the possible consequences, a committee of prominent citizens, powerful in controlling one of the political organizations of the state, gave their pledges that they would "do all in their power to preserve peace and good order, and secure a fair election." As to their power "to preserve peace and good order, and secure a fair election," I did not entertain a doubt.

This novel and humiliating spectacle, in the government of a free people, was presented: Regularly organized legal authority unable to preserve peace and good order, and secure a fair election, the leaders of a political organization assume to do it, with the accredited power, to accomplish all they might attempt.

The deeds of violence already alluded to, and many similar ones of greater or less magnitude, in various parts of the state, had the effect to intimidate many voters. The extent of such intimidation may be judged by the following facts:

In various counties the meeting together and consulting of voters before election, an important proceeding in a government like ours, had to be wholly or partially abandoned.

In one county not only was there no preliminary canvass, but the danger was regarded so great that no convention was held to nominate candidates for offices.

In certain counties, tickets could not be freely and safely distributed, and in one county not at all.

From one county prominent candidates for office fled before election, fearing violence, if not assassination.

In another county one party, through fear of the evil consequences if they refused, struck from their tickets names of candidates formally and regularly nominated, and substituted those of their opponents, with whom there existed no political affinity.

In certain counties, on the day of election, voters were driven from the polls by armed men, or so intimidated by them that they feared to vote.

In one county the principal county officials were driven away from their posts on the day following the election, and have been refugees since. This county, Amite, was the one remote from the seat of government where the effort to organize the militia succeeded.

These are effects, not detailed statements of causes which produced them.

The courts of the state have been unable to dispense justice in such cases. The conviction that frauds were perpetrated at the late election gathers strength by comparison of the returns with those of preceding elections.

That the great evil which has befallen the state may be remedied, it first becomes necessary to inquire into its causes. The happy financial condition of the state, and the comparatively small amount needed for its support, preclude the possibility of a financial cause. Intimidation was not proportioned to counties in accordance with their indebtedness. Thorough intimidation was effected in some counties whose finances were in the most flourishing condition.

The character of the events which have transpired compel the conclusion that the evil is to be attributed to a race question. It did not have its origin at this time.

The inhabitants of the state are somewhat equally divided between two races. They have, until recent years, borne the relation of master and slave. By a power external to the state, the slave has been made the civil and political equal of the master. The withdrawal of this restraining force leaves the formerly dominant race to re-assert its supremacy. Though the complete supremacy of former days may not be possible, still the tendency is toward supremacy. The effort in this direction has heretofore and elsewhere resulted, as in this election, in violence, loss of life and intimidation. How far this effort has resulted in the virtual disfranchisement of the one race, and revolutionized the state government, is a question worthy the most patient and careful inquiry.

Unless every class of citizens be thoroughly protected in the exercise of all their rights and privileges, our government proves unequal to its pretensions. The nation recognizing the race antagonisms has anticipated them in the interest of liberty and equality by modifications of the fundamental law of the land, and I recommend, as both right and expedient, action in harmony with such modifications.

The State Finances

The condition of the state's finances is unprecedently favorable.

The real debt of the state—that is, its outstanding obligations beyond its ability to pay at once with its current and available funds (the taxes received for 1875) amounts to	$500,000.00
The Common and Chickasaw School Funds—debts upon which the interest only is to be paid, the principal never becoming due (obligations incurred many years since), amount to	$1,530,620.00
The expenses of the state government during the past year amounted to	$618,259.18
The amount paid to the two universities of the state—to Normal Schools—and interest on Chickasaw School Fund was	$136,896.37
The Mississippi State bonds paid amounted to	$250,000.00
Interest on bonds	$37,664.00
Extra improvements—state buildings	$56,017.44

The progress made during the past three years in reducing the expenses of the state government is found in the comparison of such expenses, to wit:

The expenses in 1873 were	$953,030.13
The expenses in 1874 were	$908,330.72
The expenses in 1875 were	$618,259.18

The successful administration of state finances will be seen in the comparison of receipts and disbursements during the past five years.

Disbursements over receipts for 1871	$390,895.86
Disbursements over receipts for 1872	$347,552.36
Disbursements over receipts for 1873	$674,128.50

While on the other hand, the

Receipts over disbursements were, for 1874	$49,114.17
Receipts over disbursements were, for 1875, (based on moderate estimate of taxes, already received and due) over	$400,000.00

The amendment of the Constitution, adopted at the last election, authorizes the reduction of the expenses of the judiciary to an extent which heretofore has been impracticable.

The state indebtedness of half a million can easily be discharged in two or three years, when the comparatively light tax for the support of the state government of today, of about one dollar and thirty cents per inhabitant, can be reduced to less than one dollar.

I recommend a return to the financial system of 1874, when taxes were paid only in the currency of the United States. The receipts were in excess of expenditures, and had tax collectors been required to collect and pay into the treasury the taxes at an earlier day, the one defect of the system would have been remedied. Under existing laws state paper, by the manipulations of the speculator, fluctuates through a range two or three times greater than it ought. Should it be known that at the end of the year state warrants were to be cashed, they could not fall below a margin which would yield a liberal interest. The changes recommended will accomplish this end.

For a complete and detailed statement of receipts, disbursements and indebtedness your attention is called to the official reports of the State Treasurer and the Auditor of Public Accounts.

Amendments to the Constitution

The following amendments to the Constitution of the state were adopted at the general state election, which took place on the second of November last. That in relation to the Union and Planters' Bank Bonds, which adds to Section five of Article twelve of the Constitution the following words, to wit:

"Nor shall the state assume, redeem, secure, or pay any indebtedness, or pretended indebtedness, claimed to be due by the State of Mississippi to any person, association or corporation whatsoever, claiming the same as owners, holders, or assignees of any bond or bonds, now generally known as Union Bank Bonds, or Planters' Bank Bonds."

That in relation to the School Fund, which amends Section six, Article eight of the Constitution as follows, viz.:

"All proceeds of lands now, or hereafter vested in this state by escheat, or purchase, for forfeiture, for taxes, and the clear proceeds of all fines collected in the several counties for any breach of the penal laws, and all moneys received for licenses granted under the laws of the state for the sale of intoxicating liquor, or keeping of dramshops, shall be collected in legal currency of the United States, and to be paid into the treasury, to be distributed, pro rata, among the educable children of the state, in the manner to be provided for by law."

That authorizing a reduction in the number of Chancellors, substituting for the seventeenth Section of the Sixth Article of the Constitution, the following, viz.:

"The Legislature shall divide the state into a convenient number of Chancery Districts. Chancellors shall be appointed in the same manner as the Judges of the Circuit Courts. Their qualifications shall be regulated by law, and they shall hold their office for the term of four years. They shall hold a Court in each county, at least twice in each year, and shall receive such compensation as may be provided by law."

Economy demands that the number of Chancellors should be reduced to the minimum compatible with the efficient discharge of the duties of the office.

Railroads

The educational funds of the state, which a former Legislature granted to railroads, has been under litigation during the past year. Time but confirms the views entertained by me a year ago, and which I now reiterate.

I recommend the repeal of so much of an Act entitled "an Act to aid in the construction of the Vicksburg and Nashville Railroad," approved April 18, 1873, as surrenders to the Vicksburg and Nashville Railroad Company, under certain conditions, trust funds known as the three per cent. and the agricultural land scrip, which amount to some $320,000.

I also recommend the repeal of so much of an Act entitled "an Act to amend the several Acts now in force concerning the Grenada, Houston and Eastern Railroad Company, and for other purposes," approved January 17, 1872, as exempts said railroad company and its acquisitions from taxation.

The agricultural land scrip fund was recently bestowed by the United States, to constitute a perpetual fund—the capital of which shall remain forever undiminished—and the interest of which shall be inviolably appropriated by each state, which may take and claim the benefit of this Act, to the endowment, support and maintenance of at least one agricultural college. The state was authorized, at the same time, to invest this fund in "stock of the United States, or of the States, or some other stocks." Has the state done so?

The railroad company, to which this fund is proposed to be surrendered, has not completed a single mile of road. As projected, it will, when completed, extend some 250 miles in this State, and about 150 miles in the State of Tennessee, making a total length of some 400 miles. The section now being worked on is between Okolona, on the Mobile and Ohio Railroad, and Grenada, on the Mississippi Central (now the New Orleans, St. Louis and Chicago) Railroad, a distance of some 65 miles. It is asserted that some twenty miles are now ready for the iron.

Judging by its progress to the present time, a number of years must elapse before these sixty-five miles can be completed, and the road in a condition to pay interest on its bonds. Were it in working order today, between Okolona and Grenada, it would run through but one county untraversed by railroads, and would be but a feeder to two great railroads. Its Southern terminus is some two hundred miles from the Gulf of Mexico, and at almost equi-distant intervals the road is intersected by three rich and powerful lines, well established and in successful operation.

The history of railroads has taught that only through roads, which carry the products of a county to market, are successful, and especially is this the case in sparsely settled sections; and it has also taught that new roads are rarely, if ever, able to meet the lawful demands of stock and bond-holder.

Is a paper railroad, like this one but little more than projected, a safe investment? Is it one that can, in any reasonable period of time, from its legitimate business, pay an interest of eight per cent. to its bond-holders? Is it an investment from which the principal can be withdrawn at will? If not, it certainly is not the best investment that could be made, nor even a safe one.

In the consideration of this subject, it must not be forgotten that the Vicksburg and Nashville Railroad is not a railroad in reality—it is but a projected one.

Observe the security extended by that company to the state. Four hundred (400) miles of road at $30,000 per mile, supposed to be a fair estimate, when completed and in good running order, will cost some twelve millions of dollars ($12,000,000). The state is expected to advance to the road $320,000, and receive in return the note of the company, secured by first mortgage bonds, to the same amount. Can this note be regarded as "safe stocks"? Could the United States, in bestowing this fund for the education of our youth, have contemplated such an investment?

The first-mortgage bonds, proposed as collateral security, cannot be deemed of much value; for other first-mortgage bonds, to the amount of some ten millions ($10,000,000), may be issued. In fact, the law places no restriction upon the amount of such bonds.

The experience of the state, in aiding railroads with its trust funds, has not been of such a character as to cause its tax payers to contemplate effects of this law with any very lively satisfaction.

In our reasoning as to safety of this investment, we should not neglect to consider, should the law remain unrepealed, the possible action of some future Legislature, when this company, in days of adversity, appears before it and pleads poverty or misfortune.

The success of this road can in nowise depend on the sum of $320,000 expected from the state, which, though insignificant as compared to the cost of the road, is highly important to the state. To withhold it, cannot embarrass the road or impede its progress. However, if it should, then the "stocks" of the Vicksburg and Nashville Railroad cannot be regarded as safe, and the sooner the fact is known by the people who are paying taxes in the interest of the road, the better. We should be, if possible, more cautious and circumspect in the disposition of the funds of the state than with our own. Are we prepared, as individuals, to invest our own funds in this enterprise?

By the original Charter, and by the Act of January 27, 1872, heretofore referred to, the road is authorized to buy without restriction or limitation, and all its property and acquisitions, of whatever character, shall be exempt from taxation for thirty years, or till the road shall pay a dividend of eight per cent. to its stockholders.

Under such provisions, all the roads in the state can be consolidated, and their entire wealth, amounting to a tenth or fifth of the property of the state, would be exempt from taxation. And this, too, though only a small section of the road, in whose interest this law was passed, should be built. Who cannot foresee that such a corporation would delay for many a year the announcement that the stockholders were to be paid a dividend of eight per cent., and with such announcement, expose their millions to taxation?

Railroads, when friendly to the people, are of inestimable advantage, but when used to oppress them, are quite the reverse. Let this law stand, and there will spring from it a corporation which, if ruled by the spirit of the legislation that gave it birth, will sooner or later blight, if not destroy, nearly every other interest in the state.

The state should protect itself now, when the task is so easy, and not leave it to the people at some future day, when outraged and indignant, to rise in their wrath and show that what they create shall not be superior to themselves, the creators.

The law, which exempts the property of this road from taxation, is, in my opinion, unconstitutional. The Constitution reads as follows: "The property of all corporations for pecuniary profits shall be subject to taxation, the same as that of individuals." It seeks to accomplish by indirection or evasion, what is so plainly forbidden. The people who adopted the Constitution, and bear the burden of supporting the government, will never consent to such a flagrant violation of it. If any are to be relieved from taxation, let it be the poor rather than the rich and powerful.

All doubtless are in favor of internal improvements, but no true friend of the state, or of progress, can ask that unwise and unconstitutional laws shall find place in our statute books for that or any other purpose. A commercial necessity must breathe life into all enterprises for pecuniary profits, and that road which depends solely on state and county subscriptions, and is undertaken with money borrowed thereon, enticing no other capital, must be of problematical success.

There is an attempt to make it appear that this investment is a contract; that the company receives it as a grant! Is it a grant? Are we giving this sacred fund away? On the contrary, the state accepted it with the understanding that it would not do so. She is in honor bound not to do so.

We can but invest it. And the investment in this road should not put the state under obligations to it, more than she would be to the United States, or other states, were the funds invested in their stocks.

The road can regard it but as a loan. It is required to give securities, and additional securities may be demanded at any time. And were the law, relative to this railroad, defective in no other particular, it would be incumbent on the state, as its least duty, to demand full and sufficient securities.

It is asserted that by repealing this law, the reputation of the state, not now too good, will be still further injured. The repeal of unwise and unconstitutional laws, in the interest of the whole people and in harmony with the previously plighted faith of the state, must be far more to her credit than it would be to let such laws stand, pregnant as they are with so many evil consequences.[1]

[1] The preceding paragraphs concerning educational funds and railroads repeat those in Governor Ames' message delivered in March 1874.

I also call your attention to the case of the Vicksburg and Ship Island Railroad. This road received, over two years ago, upon the construction of eleven miles, a state subsidy of $110,000. The road neglected to pay the interest due on this sum as required by the law. Little, if any, progress has been made on the road since the completion of the first eleven miles. Because of a violation of, or deviation from, its Charter, the payment of additional subsidies has been suspended, and the question practically, as to such payment, is before the courts. A compromise has been requested by the road, but as a larger amount of money is involved, I have deferred action, preferring to submit the case to the Legislature, which alone may be able, by legislation, to save the people from the additional taxation the further payment of the subsidy may impose, or to obtain security beyond question.

Education

Neither argument nor statistics are necessary to make known the great extent of illiteracy which exists in the state. It is as much the duty of the state as it would be to its advantage, to effect a speedy change in this particular. Much has been done already, but the state is more capable at this time, since the amendment of the Constitution, to extend its aid and fostering care. By that amendment, moneys which otherwise would have been locked up as a perpetual fund can now be applied to educational purposes, year by year, as they are received. This will permit of the building of additional schoolhouses, the employment of the best class of teachers, and the extension of the periods of instruction.

The prosperous condition of the finances of the state is such that, with the slightest effort, school facilities can be extended to every child. But, unfortunately, ignorance, with its lack of appreciation, too often refuses to take advantage of the educational opportunities which are presented. To overcome this obstacle, laws should be enacted and enforced requiring the attendance of every child for a limited period of time each year. Money and labor can never be more beneficially expended in the interest of education than now.

Penitentiary

The total number of convicts in the Penitentiary, as shown by the register, is	513
The average number within the walls during the year	200
The number leased out	373
The number received in 1874	236
The number received in 1875	373
Deaths in 1875	33
The number of serviceable cells	175

While it is admitted that the only proper place for convicts is within the prison walls, necessity has compelled the adoption of a policy which takes the larger portion without the walls. It will be observed that while the total number of convicts is 513, the number of serviceable cells is 175. The safe keeping of this number of prisoners, in such contracted quarters, could not be compatible with humane treatment. Furthermore, no sufficient means has been provided for the useful employment of so large a number within the walls. The cost of keeping so many idle prisoners would aggregate, during the year, to tens of thousands of dollars.

This want of accommodations and employment forced the leasing out of hundreds of the convicts, whereby the state has been relieved of the expense of their support, clothing and guarding, and received, in addition, a small compensation for their services.

The convict, however, who is working on levees, railroads, or cultivating cotton, received a much less severe punishment than the law intended he should receive when it consigned him to the narrow limits of the prison.

That the convicts may be retained within the walls in the future, the number of cells should be increased, and suitable machinery purchased, before the expiration of the present lease—four years hence. At the present time all the labor-saving machinery, in use in the prison or owned by the state, does not exceed in value $300.00. Last year a large and substantial building was erected, which is well adapted for a cotton factory. It should be filled with machinery.

To increase the accommodations for prisoners, the foundation of an addition to the Penitentiary has been laid. I recommend that appropriations be made for the purchase of machinery, and also for materials for the completion of the new building.

Insane, Blind, and Deaf and Dumb Asylums

The management of the Insane, Blind and Deaf and Dumb Asylums has been eminently successful during the past year.

To increase the capacity of the Insane Asylum, and meet the numerous demands for admission there by the unfortunate, an appropriation of $25,000 was made by the last Legislature, and expended during the year in the erection of an additional wing to the Asylum.

The appropriation was very judiciously and economically expended—the greater part of the labor being performed by convicts from the Penitentiary.

I recommend a liberal appropriation for the continuance of this work; and, also, appropriations to relieve both the Blind and Deaf and Dumb Asylums of debts which have embarrassed those institutions for years.

Centennial

At the last session of the Legislature an appropriation of five thousand ($5,000) dollars was made for the use of the Centennial Board in preparing for a proper representation of the products of the state at the International Exhibition, to be held in the city of Philadelphia this year.

The Act of the Legislature making the appropriation provides that the Board shall make reports, from time to time, of their action in the use and expenditure of the same. A portion of the appropriation was applied to the payment of Centennial premiums at the recent State Fair. Other expenses have been incurred, a detailed statement of which will be furnished in the report of the officers of the State Board.

I recommend a liberal appropriation, that there may be a creditable exhibition of the products and interests of the state.

Conclusion

The people can justly demand of those to whom they have delegated the power, that the strictest economy be practiced in every branch of the government, and that offices should be reduced in numbers, where practicable, by being consolidated or abolished. All such efforts will receive my hearty and zealous co-operation.

The prosperity and progress of the state must necessarily depend upon the feeling of security and contentment of the people. Distrust and suspicion should be dispelled by just and liberal legislation. This done, the solution of the many difficulties of the present time will have been substantially accomplished.

Adelbert Ames, *Governor*

Jackson, *January* 15, 1876

Dear Mother: I will write you a little letter, enclosing one from Gen'l. Ames to Father. Everything here is very much as when I wrote you last. Gen'l. Ames, Sarah and myself have been complaining a little. The weather is much colder (though not unpleasantly so) and developed a great deal of biliousness.

Mrs. Breck has been visiting us for nearly a week. She went

home day before yesterday. Now and then a couple drop in for the evening, and we have cards, cake and coffee, but altogether, as usual, we are living very quietly.

The Democrats seem to be troubled about the impeachment. They cannot find any "high crimes or misdemeanors" to charge Gen'l. Ames with. The committee are now investigating and they find difficulty in substantiating the charges they are trying to make, such as "interfering with the judiciary," "inciting the Vicksburg Riot," "*not being a resident*," "sending militia to Edwards Station with arms," "allowing two of his appointees to exchange their offices." The men in question resigned, and were reappointed, each in the place of the other. I believe these are all of the things they have been able to hunt up so far, and they are now engaged in examining the witnesses in regard to them. The excitement seems to have died out a good deal, but no doubt it could easily be revived.

I know you must be very busy at this time. No doubt the house is looking lovely. Capt. Raymond is going on to Washington in a day or so. He will probably call to see you.

Butler is delighted with a bow and arrow, which he has. He has been trying to shoot a bird all the morning. When he pulls the string he works his mouth as he does just before drinking his tea. His whole soul is in the operation.

Love and kisses for you and Father. Love to Hattie.

Your affectionate daughter, BLANCHE

WASHINGTON, *January* 30, 1876

DEAR BLANCHE: Sunday has come round; the duties of the week are over. The piecing out of carpeting, fringing of the curtains, clearing the wine cellar, polishing of floors, all this is finished. The yellow satin furniture has not yet come, but the house looks very attractive.

I wish you were here. Butler's company would be a great attraction to me, as I do not make calls or go to parties. Florence and Tom left Thursday morning. She would gladly have stayed, but he was determined on her return with him. She brought her Saratoga trunk, but did not display but three of her dresses. I was very sorry, and would gladly have had her stay. It did seem a pity that that lovely wardrobe should go back without being seen.

Nina and Paul are still here. Your father went with them to the Chandler's reception. They went the same evening to the German. Johnny Kimball is in town, and was one of the party. He is delighted with Washington.

The furniture has gone into the new house—and Senator Jones to New York for his new wife. I shall expect to see this quarter of the town rather lively for the rest of the season. He delayed so long in coming and furnishing that a misgiving troubled me. As we did not go in ourselves, of course it was a matter of moment that someone else should. Hattie is ambitious of Mrs. Jones' acquaintance, and will call at the earliest time.

Senator Morton has been obliged to postpone his speech from a trouble in his throat. The Pinchbeck question is brought up by Morton on Thursday, I think; how soon he will complete his speech I do not know.

Your Father's impression seems to be that the impeachment of Gen. Ames will die out. But I do not trust to that; until it is finally dismissed every precaution should be taken, as though it were in full progress.

You must be very careful about your own and the health of the children on account of this warm weather. I sent your letter to Morton. It has been like summer here, so that it must be too warm there.

Best love to Gen. Ames, the children and yourself from

Your most affectionate MOTHER

WASHINGTON, *February 2*, 1876

Gen. ADELBERT AMES, *Jackson, Miss.*

MY DEAR AMES: I have your letters, but have not answered them for I did not see anything that I could say which would be of use. I have seen Durant and he promises to go if he can get away from the Spanish Commission, of which he is counsel for the United States. I have seen Fish and he promises to let him go. Still, I am inclined to think you won't need him. That is, I don't believe they will be so mad as to impeach, but yet they may do so. The case as stated by you is so bald and without possible justification that while I admit the force of your remark that men who have won two branches of the Government by the murder of innocent men and women would not hesitate to resort to this measure to get the third, the murder can be committed in the dark, but the impeachment must come in the light of day, and I don't think the Democratic Party can afford to do it. You have two warm friends Warner(?) and Raymond(?), who will keep you posted in all the incidentals of Mississippi politics, so that it will be useless for me to write you about that. The President still professes, and I think meaningly, that he has faith in you and in your attempt to do the best you can, and in your good judgment in what you have done, but he is very much troubled what to do. With Alcorn here in the Senate, and Bruce, who doesn't stand up like a man anywhere, I don't think the delegation amounts to much. Wells (?) is your bitter opponent, and that only leaves Lynch. Lynch has not called upon me this winter, although I sent him my card. I am to be absent three or four days in Massachusetts, but I have left directions with Mrs. Butler to see Mr. Durant in case you telegraph that you want him, and I think he will make no difficulty about going, nor would he be very expensive either for a lawyer of his ability and standing. I would come to you myself but I am afraid that I should do you more harm than good, and I know Durant is just the man you want.

Tell Blanche I read her letters and expressions of love which I don't need, although they are very grateful to me. A better daughter a father never had, and I don't believe any man ever had a better wife. Nor do I know of anything that you have done in your trying situation that I would not have had you do. I am a little inclined to think, however, that if I had been in your place I would have had somebody hurt, probably myself; but then your course was more prudent than mine would have been. I think the third term has come to an end and I would not advise you to be at all outspoken on that subject. We have got Blaine, Conkling and Morton in the field. It rests substantially between them, although there is an attempt to run in Hayes who is the representative hard money man; and while I have no doubt the Republican Party will go for hard money, yet I think they will be under such pressure as not to go for it offensively, as they would do if they took the representative man of the fight in Ohio. The Democrats in the house are not making much headway—much less than I supposed. The only thing they have done politically is to cut down the West Point boys, which will do them more harm than good, as every father who will have a boy there and loses a $100.00 will take care not to vote for the Democracy. I think your friend Babcock is in very great danger. There is an atmosphere in St. Louis that is not fit to try anybody in, especially Babcock. I regret that because I do not think he is guilty, and I believe he will be found guilty even if innocent.

I am sorry to say that Mrs. Butler is exceedingly ill, although I think she is mending slowly, yet she has lost flesh and is being pulled down. I am exceedingly glad that she has not the burden upon her of furnishing our new house; it would kill her. Jones is just moving into it. He has furnished it very lavishly! Probably costing him $40,000 to do so. He proposes to keep some twenty horses and six or seven carriages, and so many servants that he has in fact turned it into a "nigger" boarding house.

We had a great gale here last night which blew off the roof of the Coast Survey Building next to mine, but it did not disturb us. Cape Ann granite isn't very easily moved by wind. I hope you will retain your good health, and Blanche and the children theirs, compared with which politics and impeachment are of very small consequence.

I must tell you a little incident: At Governor Shepherd's party, I met a lady, a Mrs. Gen. Stevens, who had met Blanche. Lady Thornton and Mrs. Fish and Mrs. Stevens kindly inquired after her, and how many children she had. I told them three. They were then anxious to know if they were as pretty as their mother, and I told them that they were much more so. They wanted to know how that could be. I astonished them by telling them that beauty in a family always skipped one generation, and that children took their characteristics not from their father or mother, but from their grandparents. I don't think they have got over their bewilderment yet. With love to all, I am, Yours truly, BENJ. F. BUTLER

JACKSON, *February* 6, 1876

DEAR MOTHER: Your letter, written last Sunday, came this morning. I was beginning to despair, for it is fully three weeks since I last heard from you. I had come to the conclusion that you were all so taken up with pleasure that you forgot all about the absent ones. Now that the house is finished, I trust you will have more time.

You speak of Paul and Nina as attending the reception at the Chandlers, but do not mention Hattie. Did she not go? Poor Florence! It was mean of Tom not to be willing to have her remain a while longer. Is Paul enjoying his visit?

You have already felt the cold weather, which came so suddenly. The newspapers report a violent gale in Washington. Here we have had cold weather and rain. Half an inch of ice in the gutters. In spite of precautions, the children all have colds, and I am quite stuffed with one. I trust it will moderate in a few days, and thaw us out again.

The baby has a great appetite and eats very heavily. I remember you did not think it well to give Edith so much as she desired. How is it with the baby? We rather think she has a tape worm.

As for impeachment, I really cannot tell you what will be done, reports are so contradictory—but the indications are that they will go on with it. A week or so now will probably decide the matter. Morton is very slow with his speech. It will not do much good anyway, even if a committee of investigation is appointed. Gen'l. Ames will be impeached—the Lieutenant Governor also, and the whole state will be in the hands of the revolutionists. I do not see what can be done to prevent it. It is too late.

It is possible Mrs. Ames and John will come down for a while this spring. If we leave Jackson we shall go to Bay St. Louis for a while, and perhaps to Northfield before going East.

Butler wishes to tell Gran that he has lost one of his front teeth. The other upper one will soon follow, as it is very loose.

Write as often as you can. Has Father received any letters from Gen'l. Ames? We are suspicious that the mails are tampered with.

Love and kisses. *Your affectionate daughter*, BLANCHE

JACKSON, *February*, 1876

DEAR MOTHER: Gen'l. Ames received a letter from Father this morning, in which he says that you have not been well. Why did you not tell me? What is the trouble? Is it the throat difficulty? Have you been taking more of the iodine? Please write me about this. Father seemed to think you were a little better—Is it really so?

All here are well except for colds.

This week they will probably come to some conclusion about impeachment. The charges they can bring are perfectly absurd. The Democracy hesitate upon impeachment, though it is probable their desires will overcome their fears.

Write as soon and as often as you can, for we are anxious and lonesome. Love to all the household.

Your most affectionate daughter, BLANCHE

JACKSON, *February* 23, 1876

DEAR MOTHER: I delayed answering your letter a day or two, in order to send you definite news of impeachment. Yesterday the majority of the committee reported thirteen articles and recommended impeachment.—The minority report[1] Gen'l.

[1] The majority and minority reports follow after this letter.

Ames has sent to Father, and you will see by that how senseless the charges are. Yesterday the house was in secret session—reading the evidence. It will probably occupy them for two or three days.

The trial of the Lieut. Governor begins the 2nd of March. Gen'l. Ames' case will probably be taken up after that is finished, so that we shall be here at least six weeks or two months longer.

It has been suggested that the legislature may suspend Gen'l. Ames until he is tried—but this would seem a difficult thing to do, as there is no law for it. The laws of this state are not like those of Louisiana, where they proposed to take this course with Kellog.

Gen'l. Ames desires me to ask you to suggest to Father that Morton might like to make some use of the minority report in his speech on Mississippi affairs. Of course, Gen. Ames would like it, as in that way a more permanent record would be made of the report, than could be in any other. Morton's objections to using it might be that, having been already published in the papers, there would be nothing new or interesting in it for his speech, and it will be necessary to give it to the papers at once, or they will refuse to publish it at all. Still, he might make the suggestion to Morton, and see what becomes of it.

Gen'l. Ames is quite placid under his misfortune. I think more so now that we know the worst.

We are glad to hear that you are so well pleased with the looks of the house. It must be quite resplendent. But I am not content about your health. Are you still improving? Has the hoarseness nearly gone? Knight must have told you something unpleasant for it to have rendered you sufficiently nervous to affect your health. Tell me truly, what did he say?

Paul has not written to tell me if he received the check I sent him, and you did not write me if you sent my letter to Florence about the dresses. Perhaps you think it folly to send abroad, still I do not know any better or easier way to get the things. I shall have little or nothing by summer.

Butler is very old, and asks innumerable questions. Inquiring as to the strength of an elephant, he wished to know if an "elephant could throw Sarah up so high as to bump her head against the sky."

Gen'l. Ames has just come in from the office and says that the indications now are that the Democrats are doubtful about impeaching. The minority report has so shaken them, and the evidence they have been reading is such that they are a little uncertain. Thus the prospect changes from day to day.

How are the *young people* enjoying the winter? I see that Father is made to attend some parties. I send him my love and kisses, notwithstanding he says it is not necessary and that he will take those things for granted. It is not well to leave everything to the imagination.

Be sure to answer my questions, Mother. I am anxious about you. *Your loving daughter,* BLANCHE

Majority Report

House of Representatives
February 22, 1876

Mr. Featherston, Chairman of the Committee appointed to investigate the official conduct of Adelbert Ames, Governor of this State, asked leave to make the following report; which was received:

Mr. Speaker: The undersigned, a majority of a special committee appointed under a resolution of this House, adopted on the 6th day of January, last, to investigate the official conduct of His Excellency, Adelbert Ames, Governor of the State of Mississippi, and to report the result of such investigation back to this House, beg leave to submit the following report:

For thirty-eight days, your Committee has been diligently and industriously engaged in the discharge of the duties devolved upon it by the adoption of the resolution aforesaid. It has sat from three to five hours every day, and has examined fifty-five witnesses—thirty-six of whom are classified as Republicans, and nineteen as Democrats.

At the beginning of the investigation, your Committee directed the Republican member thereof to inform His Excellency, Governor Ames, of the points on which witnesses were being examined, from day to day, touching his official conduct, and to request him to send in, to the Committee, the names of such witnesses as he might desire to have summoned and examined, in vindication of his official acts.

Your Committee states, with pleasure, that this request has been complied with, and quite a number of witnesses have been summoned and examined, at the instance of His Excellency, the Governor, and, in fact, all whose presence before, and examination by your Committee, was requested by him, have been summoned and examined fully, with the exception of one, whose illness, after he was summoned, prevented his attendance.

The testimony taken has not been ex parte, and with a view of developing but one side of the case; but your Committee has, in fairness and justice, endeavored to reach a conclusion fully justified by the proofs on both sides, and impartial as between the people of the State and His Excellency, the Governor.

Your Committee has considered it a question of too much importance to admit of a hasty or superficial examination. And in pursuing the inquiry, its members have endeavored to divest themselves of all partisan feeling and political and personal prejudice, and to keep steadily in view the one great object to be attained by this investigation, that is, to ascertain whether the official conduct of Governor Ames has furnished the people of the State with grounds which would justify and demand his impeachment.

How far your Committee has succeeded in excluding from their deliberations all improper influences, and in basing their report upon the impregnable foundation of truth, as furnished by the testimony, they submit to the judgment of this House, and to the arbitrament of an impartial public.

This conclusion reached by your Committee, has not been sought or desired, but has been forced on them by convictions of duty, and gladly would they have arrived at a different conclusion, for the honor of the State and its chief executive officer, if the testimony in the case had justified them in doing so.

Your Committee, therefore, submit that Adelbert Ames, Governor of the State of Mississippi, should be impeached and removed from office, for his official misconduct in the following instances:

1st. In refusing to execute the laws by failing to remove W. M. Conner, Sheriff of Noxubee County, from office, in August, 1875, at which time he was reported to him as a defaulter holding twenty-two thousand dollars ($22,000) of public money, and refusing to pay the same over to the county of Noxubee; and in violating the law by appointing, without legal authority, certain persons to office, in Washington County.

2nd. In refusing to execute the laws in the case of M. L. Holland, State Treasurer, who was reported to him, by the Attorney General of the State in the summer of 1875, to be in office and in charge of the State Treasury, without having given bond and security, as the law requires.

3d. In calling for United States troops, in January, 1875, and causing A. J. Flanagan, Sheriff of Warren County, to be ejected from his office by said troops, and another man installed in his stead, in violation of the constitution and laws of the State.

4th. In permitting H. Cassidy, Jr., Chancellor of the —— District, and J. B. Deason, District Attorney of the —— District, to exchange offices, in violation of the constitution and laws of the State.

5th. In permitting the convicts in the Penitentiary, by contracts approved by him, to be leased out to his partisan friends, Messrs. French & Jobes, in 1875, without pay or compensation, when the same convicts were leased to other parties, within a very short time, by French & Jobes, for a large sum of money.

6th. In the removal of W. B. Peyton, Chancellor of the 16th District.

7th. In the removal of W. A. Drennay, Chancellor of the 12th District.

8th. In the removal of Thomas Christian, Chancellor of the 4th District.

9th. In the appointment of C. Cullens, L. C. Abbott, J. D. Barton, and William Beck, Chancellors of their respective Districts.

10th. In his abuse of power and violation of the law, in directing Peter Crosby's return to Vicksburg, in December, 1874, and in sustaining said Crosby in his efforts to take possession of the office of Sheriff of Warren County, by force of arms, whereby a conflict between the races was brought on, and much blood was shed, and many lives were lost.

11th. For his official acts in arming the militia of Hinds County, in September and October, 1875, in time of peace, and especially for detailing Charles Caldwell's company composed of colored men, to escort arms to Edwards' Depot, said company being officered, in part by, and the rank and file composed of colored men known to have participated in the Clinton riot, and causing them, armed and defiant, to parade the streets of Clinton, going to and returning from Edwards' Depot, with the deliberate intent to create a disturbance, and plunge the country into a war of races, with all its attendant horrors.

In support of the foregoing specifications, your Committee is of opinion that the proof will show that the Judicial Department of the State Government has not only been tampered with, by His Excellency, but that he has sought to paralyze, to dwarf, to emasculate, and to render it entirely subservient to his will.

That His Excellency has failed and refused to execute the

laws by non-action in some instances, and by the removal of officers in others, whenever his personal or partisan interests would be promoted thereby.

That he is responsible for the conflict between the races at Vicksburg, in December, 1874, and for the loss of human life that then and there occurred, and that he would have been responsible for a greater loss of life in Hinds County in the fall of 1875, but for the timely interference of prudent and discreet persons to prevent the same.

Without attempting to analyze, to classify, to condense, or to recite any of the testimony in this report, your Committee herewith submit it to the House for its candid, conscientious and impartial judgment, in obedience to the terms of the resolution under which your Committee was appointed.

A majority of your Committee recommend the adoption of the resolution herewith submitted. Respectfully submitted,

W. S. Featherston, *Chairman*
W. F. Tucker,
W. A. Percy,
H. L. Muldrow.

Resolution

Resolved, That Adelbert Ames, Governor of the State of Mississippi, be impeached for high crimes and misdemeanors in office.

Mr. Featherston moved that the resolution offered by the majority of the Committee be adopted.

Minority Report

Mr. Parsons asked leave to make a report from minority of the Committee to investigate the official conduct of Governor Adelbert Ames, which was received:

Mr. Speaker: The undersigned, a minority of the Committee appointed to investigate the official conduct of Governor Adelbert Ames, begs leave to report that he dissents from what he is informed would be the recommendation of a majority of that Committee.

The undersigned will state that after closing the testimony in this investigation, the Committee had a formal meeting, at which a majority, without making any specific charges, agreed to recommend that the *Governor be impeached for high crimes and misdemeanors.* The minority (the undersigned) expressed his dissent from that conclusion, and gave notice that two reports would be inevitable.

At this point it was suggested that the majority and minority should prepare their reports separately. Under these circumstances, in the preparation of this report, I labor under the disadvantage of not knowing what charges or specifications will be made by the majority of the Committee, upon which they propose to recommend that Articles of Impeachment shall be based. This must be my excuse for entering more minutely into the details of matters which came before the Committee than would, ordinarily, be required.

The undersigned takes pleasure in bearing testimony to the patience, industry, and especially the spirit of manly fairness which has characterized the labors and deportment of the Committee. Whether this movement against the Governor has been incited by political considerations or not, I bear witness to the fact that no evidence of it has been permitted to enter the committee room, and as a co-laborer with that Committee, although a member of an opposing political party, I extend to them my thanks for uniform courtesy and indulgence.

The investigation, the result of which I now report, has extended over the conduct of Governor Ames, for a period of not less than seven years, although he has been Governor but *two;* we have been engaged in it three or four hours, nearly every day, for the last six weeks. Many subjects have been discussed, and five volumes of testimony taken. Much of this will be found to be irrelevant—nearly all of it hearsay—and none of it proof of guilt of any treason, bribery or high crimes or misdemeanors.

The first point which was taken up by the Committee was the general charge that the Governor had attempted to "tamper with the judiciary" in what is known as the "Peyton case." It appears that Governor Ames appointed Peyton Chancellor of the 16th District, on or about the ——— day of ———, 1875, during a recess of the Senate, before the next session of the Legislature, and before the Senate had an opportunity to give its consent to that appointment. About the 30th day of July, 1874, a case was brought before Chancellor Peyton by way of injunction to prevent the Treasurer of the State from paying to the Vicksburg and Nashville Railroad Company certain moneys belonging to the universities, amounting to nearly $350,000.00. It appears that *that* fund has been loaned to the said Railroad Company by an act of the Legislature, approved in 1873. It further appears that Governor Ames did not regard the securities provided for by the act, and offered by the Railroad Company, as sufficient guaranty for the safety of the fund, *and hence the injunction*. Prompted by a desire to save this fund to the Universities, and to protect the State against loss, Governor Ames became deeply interested in the case pending before Chancellor Peyton. It appears further that Chancellor Peyton decided that the injunction should be dissolved.

At the next meeting of the Legislature the name of Chancellor Peyton was withheld from the Senate for confirmation. Common rumor charged that Governor Ames had attempted to control the decision of the Chancellor through the influence of his (the Chancellor's) father, the venerable Chief Justice, and that failing in that, he refused to send his name to the Senate. In the course of the investigation of this matter, it is ascertained that the Attorney General, Hon. Geo. E. Harris, and Gen. W. W. Dedrick were employed as counsel for the State. It is in proof that these gentlemen made great complaint to the Governor of the conduct of the Chancellor during the trial. Before the decision was made, it appears that Messrs. Harris and Dedrick called upon the Governor at the Mansion, and made their complaint against the Chancellor, in the presence of several other gentlemen. Gen. Dedrick stated to the Committee that: "I think I told the Governor that we had not been fairly treated in the case, and that his appointment of a Chancellor in this District was a failure; that in a case involving $300,000 to the State, he had not shown that discretion, that knowledge of the law which the position demanded."

The Governor seemed to be very much interested in the case, and determined, as far as his executive power reached, to protect the interest of the State. My idea was that Chief Justice Peyton, being the father of the Chancellor, might have a talk with him, that might be beneficial to all parties, with a view to a rehearing in the case. Gen. Harris was very much aggrieved at what he considered to be the prejudiced attitude of the Court toward him, and represented to the Governor that Chancellor Peyton showed from his conduct in that case, that he was entirely unfit for the position of Chancellor. The only idea of seeing Chief Justice Peyton was that he might advise his son as to what was the law in the case, and with a view of explaining the grounds of complaint that had been brought to the attention of the Governor. I do not think the Governor's idea was to influence Chancellor Peyton's final judgment in the case, but to show the Chief Justice how the case had been conducted by his son.

The statement of Attorney General Harris will be found to correspond, substantially, with that of General Dedrick. Mr. John B. Raymond, who was present at the interview, stated that Harris and Dedrick said to the Governor that Chancellor Peyton had treated them most outrageously; that his conduct was outrageous; and said that the Chancellor's object seemed to be to place the case beyond the power of the Universities to appeal; that while Harris was talking to the Governor about the treatment he had received at the hands of the Chancellor, he was so much affected that he actually shed tears, and declared his intention to tender his resignation. Chancellor Hill, who was also present, says that he inferred from the statement of General Dedrick to the Governor, that the counsel for the State thought that the Chancellor was entirely under the control of the counsel for the Railroad Company; and further, that some one suggested that Chief Justice Peyton be informed of his conduct; and from what Dedrick said, the Chancellor's conduct was improper and unusual. The purport of Maj. Gibbs' testimony is confirmatory of what has been said by the others. Mr. Little, the President of the Railroad Company, testified that he was in the city of Jackson at the time of the trial, wished to get possession of the money, but that the Governor opposed it; had no conference with him then, but saw the Governor in the following winter, and endeavored to induce him to send Peyton's name to the Senate. The Governor refused to do so, alleging as a reason that it was the opinion of the Attorney General that he was unfit, and incompetent for the place. General Tucker, another party to the Railroad interest, and a member of this Committee, testified that, in a conversation with the Governor touching this matter, the Governor said "the Vicksburg and Nashville Railroad Company had cost one Chancellor his head," or words to that effect. (The undersigned may remark, by way of parenthesis, that it was evident from the opinions of Messrs Harris and Dedrick, that the case had demonstrated the Chancellor's incapacity). But General Tucker does the Governor the justice to add, that the Governor assured him that Peyton did not lose his position on account of the decision he had made, but because he had refused to permit the attorneys for the investigation to dismiss the bill. That he had understood from a number of judges and lawyers, that a lawyer was always permitted to dismiss his case, or words to that effect.

Chancellor Ware testified that he had a conversation with the Governor about the Peyton matter, and that the Governor said that great injustice had been done him in relation to it; that the whole cause of Peyton's failure to be continued in office was the very general opinion among lawyers of the district that he was incompetent for the position, and that *that* was the cause of his refusal to send Peyton's name to the Senate, and that his active participation in the Railroad case was prompted by a desire to protect the State in the funds that he thought were about to be squandered.

Chief Justice Peyton, the father of the Chancellor, informed your Committee that he went to the Governor, at his (the Governor's) request; that the Governor commenced the conversation by stating that complaints had been made against his son, the Chancellor, on account of his conduct in the Railroad case; that the Governor did not say that he desired him (the Chief Justice) to influence his son's decision in the matter, but that he informed him that *that* was the object of the interview; and he at once became indignant, and stated that his son was an honest man, and would make an honest decision. Soon after this the interview ended. That is the sum and substance of the somewhat notorious Peyton case. I do not know that the majority of the Committee find in this case any cause for the impeachment of the Governor. His conduct in endeavoring to save the money of the Universities was silently imitated and commended by this House, *in an Act passed only a few days ago*, requiring additional security in that very case. The undersigned is of the opinion that this House cannot possibly give expression to a more complete vindication than it has already done.

Another case in which it was charged that Governor Ames had tampered with the judiciary, is that known as the Drennan-Walton case. It appears that Drennan had been appointed Chancellor of the 12th District by the predecessor of Governor Ames, during a recess of the Senate, and had not been confirmed by that body. In January, 1874, one A. T. Morgan, the Sheriff-elect of Yazoo County, appeared before the said Drennan, charged with the killing of one Hilliard, a citizen of Yazoo County. The Chancellor remanded him to jail without bail, and for safe keeping he was afterwards transferred to the county jail of Hinds County, located in this city.

It afterwards transpired that the name of Chancellor Drennan was not sent to the Senate for confirmation, but that Chancellor Thomas Walton was appointed in his stead. It is charged that the Governor removed Drennan because he refused bail to Morgan, and that he appointed Walton because he would admit him to bail. This was the rumor. It appears from the testimony and the record, that although Governor Ames did write a formal order removing Chancellor Drennan, by virtue of the Constitution of the State, Drennan was really not a Chancellor, and, in fact, was not a Chancellor, by virtue of the Constitution and laws of the State, when he tried A. T. Morgan, his time having expired by reason of the fact that his name had not been sent to the Senate within ten days, as prescribed in Section 106 of the Code of 1871. The order of removal was, therefore, of no effect; Drennan was not a Chancellor at the time. There was a vacancy in the office of Chancellor of that District.

Chancellor Drennan stated to your Committee that he sought an interview with the Governor within ten days after the receiption of the order of removal, and that the Governor did not assign any distinct reason for his removal; but, in a conversation, he said that he (Drennan) had not done right in the Yazoo matter in not granting bail to Morgan, as he (the Governor) had been informed that it was the opinion of the lawyers that the case, at most, could only be regarded as manslaughter, and therefore the prisoner was entitled to bail; and that the Governor further found fault with him (Drennan) because he had not given the Coroner sufficient time to give his bond as the successor to the Sheriff's office, but appointed a Democrat instead. Messrs. Prewitt and Scott concurred substantially with Chancellor Drennan as to this conversation with the Governor.

Mr. Morgan testified that Drennan told him that no court could convict him, and that he had refused to admit him to bail because he thought his life would be endangered if allowed to go at large. Morgan recommended no one to the Governor for appointment, but urged that a good lawyer be appointed; that he did not see Walton, nor have any conversation with him, prior to his appointment and confirmation; that Walton admitted him to bail upon a second hearing. Morgan further stated that he had tried to appeal from Drennan's decision to the Supreme Court, but could not do so, for the reason that no record of the evidence had been taken by the Chancellor, as the law directs, and that the lawyers could not, or would not, agree as to what the evidence was. Morgan further testified that at the term of the Circuit Court following the proceedings before Walton, the Grand Jury made a full investigation of the case and failed to indict him.

Col. Nugent, a lawyer of this city, informed the Committee that he had had an interview with Morgan, while he was in the jail in this city; that Morgan handed him a copy of the *Yazoo Democrat*, which contained a newspaper reporter's (Democratic) account of the evidence taken before Drennan. After reading that report, Nugent says he told Morgan that he was astonished; that any one making any pretensions as a lawyer should refuse bail on that testimony. Col. Nugent said he took a lawyer's view of the case, and was of the opinion that the decision was a great outrage. That Morgan told him, that Drennan had assured him that he had remanded him to jail because he thought that his (Morgan's) life would not be safe on the streets of Yazoo City.

Chancellor Walton testified that he had not sought the position of Chancellor; that he had not desired it; that he had never been approached by Governor Ames, nor by anybody else, in relation to the Morgan case; that he had endeavored to deal justly with the case, and had published his opinion to the world, which opinion he submitted as a part of the testimony in the case.

The undersigned fails to find, in this case, a single particle of evidence sustaining a charge of corruption against Gov. Ames. On the contrary, the testimony of Col. Nugent alone is sufficient to prove that Gov. Ames did right, and was amply justified in withholding from the Senate the name of Chancellor Drennan. Indeed, what claim did Chancellor Drennan have upon the office, greater than that of Walton, or any other lawyer of the State? In this connection, we do not forget that it was, at all times, within the power of the Governor to pardon Morgan; and thus, directly with a scratch of the pen, secure to himself the credit of relieving him without exposing himself to the hazard of attempting to corrupt the Judiciary. It was also proven before your Committee, that Chancellor Drennan had promised Morgan that he (Drennan) would join in a petition to the Governor, for pardon.

It is supposed that the case next in importance, touching the official conduct of Governor Ames, in relation to the Judiciary, is what is termed the "swap" between Chancellor Cassidy and District Attorney Deason.

It appears that Chancellor Cassidy had been duly appointed and confirmed as Chancellor of the 19th District, and that

Deason had been duly elected District Attorney. It seems that each of these gentlemen had a preference for the office occupied by the other, and that they agreed each one to resign, and with the consent of the Governor, to exchange offices, by appointment. It is charged, in general terms, that Governor Ames was a party to this collusion. Now, the undersigned begs leave to report that no evidence has been brought before this Committee, proving that Governor Ames was a party to the transaction; but on the contrary, that the tender of the resignations to him was absolute and without conditions; and that he was not made acquainted with the wishes of the parties before the resignations were placed at his disposal. No reason or objection has been assigned why the appointments were not good ones.

Cassidy was a young man, and wished for the activity of practice at the bar. Deason was an elderly gentleman, and preferred the more sedate duties of the bench. No complaint has been made of the want of competency or fitness in either one of them in their changed positions; on the contrary, we have indisputable proof, in his triumphant re-election to his office, that the people approved the appointment of Cassidy to the office of District Attorney. On this subject, the Hon. J. M. Smiley, Circuit Court Judge of the District in which Chancellor Deason and District Attorney Cassidy reside, said to your Committee, that the exchange between them was most excellent—conducive to the public benefit. Indeed, all the witnesses concur in the testimony that the people were satisfied.

The undersigned scarcely supposes that this will be made a ground for impeachment, even if the Governor was cognizant of the wishes of these gentlemen, which the testimony shows that he was not. Where is the high crime or misdemeanor? In the whole of the transaction, the interests of the people were carefully subserved, and no violence done to the Constitution or the laws.

In the case of Chancellor Christian, the undersigned will state that if there is anything in the whole transaction implying a crime or misdemeanor in office on the part of the Governor, the undersigned has failed to discover it. The Governor did not appoint Chancellor Christian as Chancellor of his District, and the undersigned supposes that there are hundreds of lawyers in this State, equally competent, whom he did not appoint to office; and if Governor Ames is to be *impeached* for appointing his political friends to office, other things being equal, then every President that the United States ever had should have been impeached for the same reason. It is not alleged that Chancellor Dennis has not made a good and acceptable officer. In the various acts of appointment and removal connected with the Christian-Dennis case, the Governor acted in accordance with the opinion of his legal adviser, the Attorney General. In this State, we should bear in mind that the registration and election laws give to the office of Chancellor a political importance, and it is not regarded as a *crime* in political ethics of this nation, or State, for the appointing power to have an eye to future party success, provided the means employed do not endanger the public welfare.

Grouping the cases of Barton, Cullens, Abbott, Sullivan, Buck and Stone in one paragraph, the undersigned begs leave to state that in no case does the shadow of proof exist that the Governor was prompted in these appointments by a corrupt motive, nor that he was guilty of any high crime or misdemeanor. The undersigned will content himself by simply inviting the attention of the House to the testimony in each case as it shall be read.

However much may have been said about the incompetency and efficiency of the Chancellors appointed by Governor Ames, it is a matter of record, and a fact open to the public, that the ratio of reversal of judgments by the Supreme Court, upon appeals coming up to it, is absolutely smaller than has lately been known in this State, as shown by the following statements made by the Clerk of the Supreme Court:

The State of Mississippi, Hinds County:

I, A. W. Little, Clerk of the Supreme Court of said State, do hereby certify, that during the years 1859 and 1860, the High Court of Errors and Appeals of this State rendered (266) two hundred and sixty-six decisions in cases that were appealed from the Chancery and Probate Courts of said State, of which number (169) one hundred and sixty-nine were affirmed and (97) ninety-seven were reversed.

And do further certify, that during the years 1872 and 1873, the Supreme Court of said State rendered (328) three hundred and twenty-eight decisions in cases that were appealed from the Chancery and Probate Courts of said State, of which number (221) two hundred and twenty-one cases were affirmed, and (107) one hundred and seven reversed.

In witness whereof, I hereto set my hand and affix the seal

of said Court, at my office in the city of Jackson, this 17th day of February, 1876.

A. W. Little, Clerk
By W. E. Cage, D.C.

The State of Mississippi, Hinds County:

I, A. W. Little, Clerk of the Supreme Court of the State of Mississippi, do hereby certify that, after examination, I find that of the number of appeals taken from the decisions of the Chancellors appointed by Governor A. Ames (41) forty-one have been decided up to January 1, 1876, of which number (33) thirty-three were affirmed, and eight (8) reversed.

In witness whereof, I hereunto set my hand, and affix the seal of said Court, at my office in the city of Jackson, this the 4th day of February, 1876.

A. W. Little, Clerk
By W. E. Cage, D.C.

Of a total of forty-one cases decided in 1874, the following is a summary:

W. B. Peyton	5 affirmed.
O. A. Whitfield	3 affirmed — 2 reversed.
W. D. Frazee	3 affirmed — 2 reversed.
P. P. Baily	1 affirmed — 1 reversed.
E. H. Osgood	3 affirmed — 1 reversed.
G. L. McMillen	1 affirmed.
Thomas Walton	1 affirmed.
R. Boyd	1 affirmed.
E. G. Peyton	1 affirmed.
1875	
W. D. Frazee	2 affirmed.
L. C. Abbott	2 affirmed.
H. Cassidy	1 affirmed — 1 reversed.
E. G. Peyton	5 affirmed.
J. N. Campbell	1 affirmed.
R. Boyd	1 affirmed.
J. J. Dennis	1 affirmed — 1 reversed.
Thomas Walton	1 affirmed.
Total affirmed	33 cases.
Total reversed	8 cases.

It is thus shown, that of the appealed cases in 1859 and 1860, 36 percent of them were reversed. In 1872 and 1873, 33 percent were reversed, while in 1874 and 1875, only 20 percent were reversed. This, I am aware, may be only a coincidence, but the coincidence is rather damaging to the declaimers about the incompetency of the Judiciary appointed by Governor Ames.

It was complained that the Governor approved the State Treasurer's bond, in 1875, when it was not properly verified by the oath of the sureties, that they were worth the penalty of the bond, over their just debts, legal liabilities and exemptions *in freehold estate.*

It was said that the words "in freehold estate" were left out. This complaint was made by the Attorney General, in a letter to the Governor, but that *that* officer has not yet furnished the Committee, to the knowledge of the undersigned, with a copy of said bond, if the statement be true.

It is a matter of public record, that many other official bonds were written in the identical language employed in this one. It seems that, whether right or wrong, that form of bond had been very generally adopted, and its approval by the Governor could be, at best, only a technical oversight, and was not done with a view of rendering the bond less secure. The subsequent examination of the affairs of the Treasurer's office shows that everything was found correct, and that the State had suffered no loss on account of what was supposed to be an imperfect bond. The undersigned fails to discover any cause for impeachment in that.

It was alleged that Governor Ames had violated the constitution of the State, and his oath of office, in appointing certain members of the Legislature to office, which office had been created by the Legislature of which said appointees were members. The whole force of this allegation turns upon the question as to whether the position was an *office* or an *agency.* The law under which they were appointed, declared them to be *agents,* and the decisions of the Supreme Court, especially in the case of Shelby vs. Alcorn, 7th George, page 288, in which the distinction between an agent and an officer is clearly defined, proves conclusively that the appointees of Governor Ames were merely agents, and not officers. In this view of the case, the allegation falls to the ground.

Another case which received considerable attention at the hands of the Committee, is the Conner case. It appears that the Board of Supervisors of Noxubee County, in March, 1875, called upon Mr. Conner, the Sheriff, for a settlement of the taxes collected by him in 1874. It seems that the Board refused to allow certain claims which Conner held against the county, and Mr. Conner declined to settle unless his accounts were allowed. He expressed himself as ready and willing to settle upon these terms. Subsequently, the County Treasurer reported Conner to the Governor, as a defaulter, and asked his removal. The amount of the defalcation was not stated. The report of Mr. Stevens was referred to the Auditor, and was, afterwards, returned to Mr. Stevens with the assurance that if he still insisted upon his original report, that the Governor would take action.

In the meantime, the President of the Board of Supervisors, Dr. Allgood, who was a candidate for the office of Sheriff and recognized as the principal mover against Conner, visited the city of Jackson, and requested Lieut-Gov. Davis, who was then acting Governor, to suspend any proposed action in the matter, pending the excitement attending a personal antagonism during a heated canvass for nomination. Soon after this, proceedings were instituted against Conner, in the Circuit Court of Noxubee County, and the grand jury not only failed to indict Conner, but made a written report, that in their opinion, if Conner should have a fair and equitable settlement, the county would be indebted to him. It may not be improper to state that *that* grand jury was composed of nine Democrats and seven Republicans, (Conner being a Republican).

The undersigned was impressed, during the examination of this case, that it was, at best, only a personal struggle over the Sheriff's office. Under the circumstances, how could Governor Ames have been justified in removing Conner? How could he decide upon the merits or demerits of Conner's claims against the County of Noxubee? Had he removed Conner, under the circumstances, it is possible that he would have rendered himself liable to complaint.

The investigations of your Committee have also extended into the contract which was made on account of the labor of the convicts in the Penitentiary. Rumor had charged Governor Ames with corruption in approving a contract made between the contractors, Powers & Jobes, and the Board of Inspectors of the Penitentiary. The Hon. G. Wiley Wells states that French told him that he (French) had been induced to write a letter to Governor Ames, which letter was to be used with the Attorney General of the United States to the prejudice of the said Wells, in his aspirations for the appointment of District Attorney of the Northern District of Mississippi, by a proposition from the Governor, that if he (French), would write the letter, the Governor would approve the contract for the Penitentiary hands; that Governor Ames declared the letter damaging to Wells, was the price of his signature to the contract. That he (the Governor), would not approve the contract unless the letter should, at the same time, be written and signed. Mr. French denies this statement, in every particular. The undersigned will not attempt to decide a question of veracity between French and Wells, especially since other testimony is at hand which renders that decision entirely unimportant. As far as the charge of corruption against Governor Ames is concerned, the House may take either or neither of the statements of Mr. French or Mr. Wells. The documentary proof on file shows, by their respective dates, that a collusion between Governor Ames and French was physically impossible. It is in proof that a contract for Penitentiary hands was made with Powers and Jobes, and signed by the Inspectors, on the second day of March, 1874. French's letter derogatory to Wells was written and dated on the 13th day of the following May.

In Wells' testimony before the Committee, he entered minutely into the manner in which both papers were said to have been signed. That when French presented the contract to the Governor, His Excellency presented the letter already prepared, to French, and with a significant air, said, substantially, favors are reciprocal; you sign this and I will sign that—not otherwise. Whether French told that to Wells, or not, the truth remains that the contract was signed by the Inspectors of the Penitentiary on the second day of March, 1874, and it is in proof, by Mr. Noonan, that the first hands were transferred on the 27th day of the same month, and after the contract had been approved by the Governor. The date of the Governor's signature must have been between those two dates, which, as before stated, French's letter was dated on the 13th day of the following May, not less than forty-seven days afterward. Time and space frequently come to establish a physical fact which is incontrovertable.

The official conduct of Governor Ames, in connection with the Vicksburg riot, and the troubles in Warren county, in 1874, was investigated very thoroughly, by your Committee; but inasmuch as those unfortunate troubles have been investigated by a committee of Congress, and by a former committee of the Legislature of this State, I deem it unnecessary to enter into a detail of the matters which have come to the knowledge of the public.

In this investigation, I have thought proper to confine my attention to such facts as were calculated to throw light upon the conduct of Governor Ames in the matter. It appears that on or about the 2d day of December, 1874, Governor Ames received the following note from the Hon. George F. Brown, Judge of the Circuit Court of Warren and Hinds counties:

VICKSBURG, *December 2*, 1874

To His Excellency, Governor Ames:

It becomes my duty to inform you that an armed mob, composed of several hundred men, has, this evening, taken forcible possession of the court house and jail of this county, and forced most of the county officers to resign, or flee to the country for protection.

The mob is in possession of the records of the office, and threaten violence to any one who does not recognize their authority. My court is in session, but I am powerless, and cannot execute the laws.

Relief must be furnished from abroad, in the way of military, by the State or General Government, and that quickly, to prevent a general riot and loss of life.

Geo. F. Brown,
Judge of the 15th Judicial District

It is in proof that Peter Crosby, Sheriff of the county, was one of the officers who had been forced to resign; had come to Jackson, and was present at the Governor's Mansion when the note from Judge Brown was handed to the Governor.

It appears that the excitement pervading the city of Jackson had caused quite a number of political and personal friends of the Governor to assemble at the Executive Mansion, and among them, the Attorney General of the State. It appears that a consultation was held as to what should be done in the premises. It is in proof that the Attorney General was appealed to for his advice to Crosby; which was, substantially, to carry out the provisions of the law as prescribed in section 235 of the Code of 1871, which, among other things, declares that it shall be his (the Sheriff's) duty to quell and suppress all affrays, riots, routs, and unlawful assemblages, for which end he shall be and is hereby empowered to call to his aid the power of his county.

It is not in proof that Governor Ames gave any direct advice to Peter Crosby on the subject, and if he gave any indirect advice, it was in strict conformity with the advice of Attorney General Harris. It is in further proof that Peter Crosby left the Mansion with that advice, accompanied with the assurance that the Governor would use all the power of the Executive office to assist him and sustain him. For Peter Crosby's manner of regaining the possession of his office, Governor Ames cannot be held responsible any more than Attorney General Harris, or anybody else, could be held responsible.

It is in proof that Warren County was in a state of insurrection. The chief executive officer of the county had been expelled by force. A mob was in possession of the offices. Court had been suspended, and the Judge had declared that he could not execute the laws. The sheriff had come to the capital for advice. What else could the Governor do but just exactly what he did do? He called to his counsel his legal adviser, and the advice of that legal adviser was recommended to the expelled Sheriff. Be it remembered that the Governor was comparatively powerless to do anything, and if he would be *impeached* for concurring with the Attorney General in his views of the case, what security can there be for the perpetuity of civil government in this State? Under his oath, he could do no less than he did do.

The testimony in relation to Vicksburg matters would fill a volume. The points to which my attention has been called are simply three: First, what was the condition of affairs in Warren County, at the time alluded to? Second, what was the Governor's duty? And, thirdly, what did the Governor do? I respectfully submit *that the testimony will establish the fact that the Governor's action was strictly in the line of duty.*

Much has been said about a remark which has been attributed to Governor Ames, about the benefit which the Republican Party would be likely to receive from the killing of 25 or 30 Negroes. The only witness who has testified to anything of that kind is Major Allyn. It seems that Major Allyn was present at the consultation at the Mansion, and he says: "The Governor made a remark which I think was not intended to be heard by everybody in the room, that very likely fifteen or twenty Negroes may be killed, but that it would result to the benefit of the Republican Party. I give the substance of it, not the exact language. It was a casual remark, and I think, was addressed to Shadd." At another point in the testimony, Major Allyn said, in substance, "I think the remark was made to Shadd, Lewis and Crosby." Shadd swears positively that no such remark was made to him; and out of that whole assembly, consisting of twenty or thirty individuals, not one person, except Major Allyn, has been found who has testified that he heard the remark. Is it probable that Governor Ames would make such a remark to three colored men, all of them more or less influential as politicians?

It is in proof that soon after the Vicksburg riot, a special session of the Legislature was called, which Legislature not only endorsed the action of the Governor, but also passed a resolution calling upon the United States for troops to assist in restoring the County of Warren to a condition of law and order.

It is a notorious fact that the regular session of the Legislature of 1875 investigated, by its committee, the whole subject of the Warren county troubles, and necessarily passed in review the official conduct of the Governor. Since then another session of the Legislature has been held—in all, three sessions of the Legislature, and not one word of censure has been pronounced against Governor Ames until now. It will not do to say that it was because a majority of that Legislature were his political friends, for it might provoke the retort that a majority of the present Legislature are his political enemies. However this may be, we are bound to concede that the old Legislature was entitled to as much consideration as any Legislature.

Perhaps the most delicate matter which has been brought to the attention of your Committee has been the official conduct of Governor Ames during the late political canvass. For some reason or other, the investigation into this matter was not very extensive nor exhaustive, and I might say very unsatisfactory to the undersigned.

Serious complaint was made on account of the marching of a militia company from the city of Jackson to Edwards, a distance of about thirty miles. It was in proof that *that* company was sent there to transport and guard arms and ammunition to an organized but unarmed company. It was proved that, on one occasion prior to the marching of said company, arms belonging to the State of Mississippi had been seized at Vicksburg and destroyed, or kept from the proper authorities.

Is it an impeachable offense for the Governor of the State, who is ex-officio Commander-in-Chief of the militia, to march a company on such a mission—quietly and peaceably through the country?

It was in proof that it was regarded as unsafe by the military officers of the State to attempt to send the arms to a company of colored militia by railroad, or otherwise, without guard, and it was also in proof that, as it was, there were parties along the line of march who sent telegrams to Jackson, desiring to know whether they should resist the company that was sent or not, that they were ready to do either.

But the undersigned supposes that the Governor will rely upon the statements set forth in his message to this body for the vindication of his conduct. As in the case of the Vicksburg riot, my attention has been mainly directed to the three points:

1st. What was the condition of the country?

2d. What was the duty of the Governor?

3d. What did the Governor do?

In considering these questions, I am forced to the conclusion, with, I hope, an unbiased judgment, that the Governor did not do anything except what the Constitution and laws of the State, and his own oath of office required him to do.

I apologize, Mr. Speaker, for this long report. As stated at the outset, I was not informed of the nature of the charges upon which resolutions of impeachment were to be recommended. I have, therefore, been necessarily compelled to make perhaps an unprofitable discussion over a broad field of testimony in support of various rumors.

At this writing, I have no idea of the nature of the report to be made by the majority of the Committee. Whatever points they may seize upon, and whatever specifications they may rely upon for Articles of *Impeachment*, I feel assured that they will not be sustained by the dispassionate and unprejudiced judgment of this House.

Not knowing the premises, I can only oppose the unannounced conclusion of the majority of the Committee, and therefore respectfully recommend the adoption of the following resolution:

Resolved, That the further consideration of the reports made by the Committee appointed to investigate the official conduct of Governor Adelbert Ames, be indefinitely postponed. Respectfully submitted,

Fred. Parsons,
Minority of Committee

Washington, *February* 25, 1876

General Adelbert Ames, *Jackson*, *Miss.*

My dear Ames: Your letter, telegram and minority report all came today, somewhat of a surprise to us. We did not know that things had progressed so far. Clancy will hand you this; he starts with Durant tomorrow morning.

I have got into communication with Lamar through Judge Black and Beck, and Lamar has undertaken to stop the procedure as well as he can. I have seen Black and I may send him down as counsel when the trial comes on, which may not be for a week. Lamar thinks that Wathall will be good counsel, and is against impeachment, and has gone or is going from Lamar to try to stop it. Lamar is very much surprised to think it has gone on so fast. I know he wrote the first of the week against it. I need not stop to write you now how thoroughly frivolous the charges are. I have been over them with Durant, in whom we have every confidence. I must start this Saturday night for Massachusetts to deliver a Semi-Centennial address before the citizens of Lowell and argue one end of the Beecher case on Monday. I shall return next Monday. We will do all we can at this end of the route. I believe Beck, Black, and Lamar are in thorough earnest in the matter of the impeachment, and they believe it will be a bad political move for the Democracy. I am sorry to tell Blanche that her mother is a good deal troubled with her throat, and what is worse she is getting a little discouraged with it. She has thought a little of breaking up housekeeping and going back to Lowell and having an operation performed. I have discouraged her. She is considerably weakened in her general health and worries a great deal over your troubles besides her own. I leave her with great regret, but it is imperative that I go to Massachusetts. If you want to confer with me at Massachusetts, telegraph to T. E. Major, 12 Pemberton Square, Boston, who is the same man who will answer you.

My love to Blanche and the children, I am

Yours truly, BENJ. F. BUTLER

WASHINGTON, *February* 27, 1876

DEAR BLANCHE: Your letter came this morning, before you get this in reply you will receive one written two or three days ago. In that I gave you strong assurance that the impeachment would not go on. It was believed a messenger would arrive there soon enough to stop proceedings. That part of it is too late, as the impeachment is now publicly recommended by the House. But the Senate have yet to act, and the best will be done that can be to stay it there.

Lawyer Durant and Clancy[1] are to start tomorrow. Your father left for New York last night. He goes from there to Lowell, to be gone one week. He made all arrangements before leaving for sending these men down to Jackson. Also spoke to Judge Black, a Democrat, to go. That will be determined whether he goes or not, a little later. Now, from your letter, I am in doubt whether Durant and Clancy should go so soon. I shall send for Mr. and Mrs. Spofford to dinner, and consult

[1] Mr. Clancy was General Butler's private secretary.

with him.—Still, delays are dangerous. I think they will go, I'll not interfere. Until Spofford (who as you may judge from my other letter is deeply interested in the case) comes, I will write of other matters.

Dear Blanche, I have just reckoned over the time and see they must start tomorrow morning. Cassels says they have agreed to go tomorrow morning at eight o'clock. I have forwarded your letter to your father in New York. He will write back to Morton.

Once more about myself—I am much the same as when you left, better, if anything. The hoarseness still continues in a degree. It would perhaps have been better if I had remained in Lowell. That is, I should have had less care. It was a dull day when I saw Dr. Knight. He was sorry that the sun did not shine, so that he could see clearer. I meant to have seen him again, but did not. I shall do that on my return to Lowell.

I think you had better return home with the children, when you leave Mississippi, and leave them with me when you go West; the shaking and fatigue of such a journey is too much for them, besides I want to see them. Hattie and I are here alone. The party season is about over, and she has had a tolerably fair chance.

Clancy is to send us a synopsis of the proceedings from day to day. I still think you will get through with it all right. There is no act of yours to regret. By that I mean Gen. Ames, and that is the only thing worth considering.

I sent for the Spoffords, and he is down with a headache, and cannot come. You see how all my promises have faded away. Still I have hopes, and you are strong in the integrity of your cause. Be firm and cheerful, let the result be what it may. My strongest desire is to get you all back home. You see I have been living apart from all my children about long enough. I understand that Clancy's synopsis is to be published—and I have no doubt that Morton will be ready to incorporate what you suggest in his speech. Gen. Ames has the reputation, even with his enemies, of an honorable and brave man. He has shown himself strongest in action, and will do so now.

I cannot fully explain to you the meaning of my last letter, because the matter is yet in progress there is still some hope from it. But nothing to alter Gen. Ames' action.

Dearest love to all, from *Your affectionate* MOTHER

WASHINGTON, *February* 11, 1876

MY DEAR BLANCHE: Your letters came this morning while we were at breakfast. You are still uncertain about the impeachment. Whatever happens, do not let it disturb you. Whatever is done will be regarded simply as a political movement. I do not know why Senator Morton's speech is still left unfinished. He was at a party last night at Brown's. That, you know, is quite out of town. It would seem to show that he is able to make it at all events. So what policy he is pursuing I do not know.

Your father has been in Boston for over a week. It always seems to happen that he is away if anything special is wanted of him. I expect him home tomorrow morning, or certainly by Sunday. He told me he had spoken to Durant to go down in case General Ames telegraphed.

I see that this is a most unpleasant winter for you and General Ames, owing to the uncertainty of things. I should think you would want to go down to Bay St. Louis before coming North, as you speak of doing. You must, of course, look after your real estate, even if you quit the state. You might be glad to retain that little piece of property. It grows delicious oranges. I do not know about your going to Northfield with the three children; 'tis a great journey. Butler, if he loses his teeth and makes that great journey, will look like a little old gentleman before he gets round to me. In that case he and his poor old "Gan" will have to hob-nob together, all the time.

My voice is still hoarse, but I manage to get along with it. I have made no calls thus far, and attended no parties. My health, apart from my throat, is very fair.

Hattie has been incessant in her demands for my going out, but I have steadily refused. Nina doesn't seem to care much whether she goes or not, but they have been out with your Father, and by themselves, with Paul, quite as often as they ought to go, that is two or three evenings a week, and calls in the day.

Sen. Jones and his wife, his two sisters—their two children each—their husbands, and Mrs. Jones' baby occupy the house. A French maid, nurse, French cook, and two assistants, two laundresses, a butler, an engineer for the furnace, a man to build fires, two coachmen, a maid for one of the sisters, and an errand boy, Mr. Jones' secretary, and last but not least Gerry, who related this stuff to us yesterday, and who says that not one of the servants is willing to do a single thing, make up this conglomeration of an establishment. Gerry says that they are all in confusion, but you know she is very *tongue-y*. Therefore you must accept all this with a reservation. I was quite displeased with myself when I found how much we had listened to her tattle, and would not repeat it to anyone but you.

Yesterday *our* yellow damask furniture came. It is very handsome. The house looks very well, but I can't exactly understand what we are here for. The tiger-and-bear skin makes quite a superb addition.

Oh—you asked me if I had been taking iodine. No—according to the Doctor's orders I have let my throat entirely alone. The fatigue of the journey and the arranging of the house prostrates me somewhat, and I sent for old Dr. Johnson. He thought I was run down, and therefore *nervous*, recommended bitters and building up, which I have been sedulously doing with good effect, so you need give yourself no trouble about that. I should have said nothing about it if your Father had not written of it to General Ames. If there were anything very serious I should send for you to come home at once.

It puzzles me almost every other day to understand why I'm here keeping house by myself. The only good result that I can see is that I have picked up and turned to the best use every old thing and new thing within the premises, so that the stuff looks more valuable than it did boxed up, and everything is clean.—If anybody wants to come here next winter it will not be so laborious a task. If not 'tis in excellent condition for sale.

There is one thing I'm determined upon, not to disturb myself much more by moving about, unless there is some reason for it other than the pleasure of opening and shutting up.

We have laughed pretty heartily at all this. You may do the same, but it is full of truth, nevertheless.

You'd better let the children eat what they want while they are South—tapeworms and all. When they get to Lowell I'll begin to discipline. Kisses for them all. Dearest love to General Ames and yourself from *Your affectionate* MOTHER

P.S. There is but little of impeachment in this letter. I will write you again when your Father returns and I have better information. In the meantime there is but little worth worrying over. Life is tragedy or farce, according to the temper you view it with. Be sure and look at it on the humorous side, especially when you have every reason—as you now have—to be satisfied with your own acts.

WASHINGTON, *February* 23, 1876

DEAR BLANCHE: I had a letter from Bennie this morning. He is very well, but reports no further advance in his class. I think he did best when he first returned from home—that is, when he was strengthened in mind and body by good, wholesome food, and plenty of it.

Paul and Nina returned to Lowell about a week ago. Just now there are three of us in the family. If you and the children could come I should be delighted—but I suppose it is useless to speak of that just at present.

Now I am going to write a little of the present situation of your affairs. You must draw conclusions, as I do not think it wise to write clearly or explicitly.[1]

Mr. Morton is slow in his speech because he is obliged to wait for the Pinchbeck matter. I thought it wise to consult our Newburyport friend. He has moved with alacrity, and brought men of influence to consult with your father. The consultation is highly satisfactory, and a movement will be made at once to check further steps toward that which is annoying you. In fact, so sanguine is this friend that he says to me: "Tell Gen. Ames to be perfectly at ease, for all will go right, to bear himself with dignity (that he always does) and *calmness*." The last allays the irritable spirit of opposition, and makes it more tolerant. Keep in readiness for the worst, but we trust and believe it will subside without much further manifestation. Say nothing to any of your friends that you expect anything, in fact I don't see how you could from these rambling sentences.

As you know on which side our "Deer Island friend" [2] belongs, you may conclude from that where the help will be found. They think you may rely upon it with security. I think so too, but I never feel absolutely sure till a thing is past and finished. I feel all the annoyance, Blanche, that you and Gen'l. Ames feel, and I wish this letter could reach you in a moment. I feel relieved, and when you get this I hope you will feel so too. Relax none of your exertions, but speak temperately so as not to stir up bitter feeling.

I don't know as I can consent to have you and the children go West before coming home. Mr. Raymond was in the office yesterday. He thinks impeachment will go on. We do not

[1] She feared her letter would be opened and read in Mississippi.

[2] Mr. Spofford, a Democrat.

think so, but did not so tell him. The old adage says, "The least said, soonest mended."

Dearest love to the children, Gen. Ames and yourself, from

Your affectionate MOTHER

JACKSON, *March* 1, 1876

DEAR MOTHER: You have heard that the legislature has brought articles of impeachment against Gen'l. Ames. Your letter received a day or two ago intimating that we might expect other action, owing to promises made by members of the Democratic Party, caused a smile of derision. Will the people of the North never learn that truth, honor and virtue do not and can not belong to Democratic ci-devant slave holders, that while those at Washington speak soft cooing words, make kindly promises and prate of peace and good fellowship, their hearts are full of gall and bitterness, and they are the fitting representatives of constituents who, with none of the virtues of human nature, have all the vices, and have perpetrated every crime forbidden in the Decalogue. Hill, Toombs and Davis are entitled to some respect as compared with those who, while wearing cloaks of hypocrisy in Washington, go home and expose their hate and ferocity to such an extent that no reports are allowed of their utterances, lest Northern men may discover the wolves in sheeps' clothing.

Of the principal men in Jackson, there is hardly one who has not, by counsel or action, taken some part in the Negro murders. These murderers, and I use the term advisedly, thinking that Father ought to be or might be interested in Gen'l. Ames' case and come here to lend assistance, have arranged a plan to assassinate him. No doubt you will think I am carried away by indignation; on the contrary, although I deplore impeachment because I fear some good men of the North may be deceived into believing that it is merited, yet as far as my personal preference goes you know I have never been contented with this country, and I hail with pleasure anything which will shorten our sojurn here. Nature has made it the garden of the earth. But with that law of compensation by which the gorgeous perfumed flowers of the tropics live side by side with poisonous reptiles and deadly seeds of miasma, so this lovely climate and fertile country is inhabited by a race which seems to have lost all the heavenly fire of noble purpose. There is hardly a spark left for rejuvenation.

I think I hear you say "But Blanche many of these Southern men are from the North, they are our kinfolk, our brothers."

When I spoke of ci-devant slave holders, it was with meaning. There has been a leveling process in this country, by which in proportion as the Negro acquired under the lash docility, humility, and subservience to authority, the master gained ferocity, arrogance and resistance to all law, human and Divine. I believe it impossible for any nature, however perfect and refined, to have lived with slaves and not to have suffered deterioration.

I have written rather more freely than usual, and given you *my* opinion of the South, and I venture to say if Mr. Spofford would live here three years, and take part in politics, he would go home to Newburyport and feel ashamed to acknowledge himself a Democrat. Do not think that we are wanting in appreciation of the kindness which prompted the efforts in Gen'l. Ames behalf. We are not, but recognize their utter futility, owing to the class of men with whom we have to deal.

March 2nd

Mr. Durant and Clancey came last night. Clancey brought a letter from Father. Don't you on any condition have any operation performed upon your throat unless I am with you. I can go to you at any time you desire, and it is possible I shall not go to Northfield, but return home with the children. I want very much to be with you, my sweet Mother. I enclose a newspaper slip. You will see at once the part of interest to you, as it is an indication that you are suffering from what appears to be an epidemic.

Sarah is cutting her eye teeth, I think. She has not been perfectly well lately. Butler and Edith are great cronies. They immersed themselves in the bran barrel to my great disgust yesterday, and covered themselves with bran from head to heels. Butler can print all of the capital letters, and spells out words in the small ones. He asked me just now "What will Gran say when she hears how much I can do?"

I come back once more to your health. Why can you not leave Washington and come here? Just as soon as the trial is over we shall go to Bay St. Louis. You will find the climate delightful during these spring months, and the change might prove very beneficial, especially if the east and northeast winds are productive of increased hoarseness. *Do come*. You would not mind the journey when once started—and you ought not to fail to try everything before you let your thoughts wander towards operations.

Think of this seriously Mother, and don't put it off from day to day—but make up your mind and come. You would really enjoy it at the Bay—and we will have Aunts Nina and Maria for company. *Come.* Love and kisses,

Your affectionate daughter, BLANCHE

Articles of Impeachment

House of Representatives
March 2, 1876

Mr. Featherston, on behalf of the Managers of the Impeachment against Adelbert Ames, Governor of the State of Mississippi, reported the following:

Articles of Impeachment

Exhibited by the House of Representatives of the State of Mississippi, in the name of themselves and all the people of said State, against Adelbert Ames, Governor of the State of Mississippi, in maintenance and support of their impeachment against him for high crimes and misdemeanors in office.

Article I.

That the said Adelbert Ames, Governor of the State of Mississippi, and while acting as such, on the 3d day of August, 1875, at the city of Jackson, in the State of Mississippi, unmindful of the high duties of his office, of his oath of office, and of the requirement of the Constitution of the State of Mississippi, that he should take care that the laws of the State be faithfully executed, did willfully, corruptly, and in violation of the Constitution and laws of the State of Mississippi, fail and refuse to suspend one W. M. Conner, then being the Sheriff and Tax Collector of Noxubee county, in the State of Mississippi, and acting as such.

That prior to the said 3d day of August, 1875, for many months, the said W. M. Conner as such Sheriff and Tax Collector of Noxubee county aforesaid, has failed and refused to make monthly reports and payments, or either, of such public funds as camc into his hands from the collection of taxes, or otherwise, belonging to the said county of Noxubee, to the County Treasurer thereof, Joshua Stevens; and the said Joshua Stevens, as County Treasurer aforesaid, had notified said W. M. Conner of the fact, as by law he was required to do; and the said W. M. Conner still failing and refusing to make report of or to pay over to said Joshua Stevens, such sums of money or any sum of money in his hands belonging to the said county of Noxubee, the said Joshua Stevens, as Treasurer of the county of Noxubee aforesaid, did, on the 3d of August, 1875, as well as on divers other days before and after the said 3d day of August, 1875, report the said W. M. Conner to the said Adelbert Ames, Governor of the State of Mississippi, a defaulter to the said county of Noxubee, in the words and figures following, to-wit:

The State of Mississippi }
Noxubee County. } August 3, A.D. 1875.

To His Excellency, A. Ames, Governor of the State of Mississippi:

I, Joshua Stevens, County Treasurer of the county of Noxubee, in said State, by virtue of said office, and in performance of the duties required of me in section 4 of "An act to reduce taxes and enforce prompt settlements and payments by Tax Collectors," approved March 5, 1875, do hereby beg leave to report to your Excellency that W. M. Conner, Sheriff and Tax Collector of said county, has failed to report and pay over to me the amount of revenue collected by him now due said county, as required by him under section 4 of the above Act.

That I have notified the said Tax Collector, as required under the said section 4, of his default, and his duty under said section, but the said Collector still fails to pay over the same to me, as Treasurer of said county.

I, therefore, in the further compliance with my duty under said section, do hereby make known the said default to your Excellency for such action as to your Excellency may seem meet and right, and in accordance with law ought to be done.

(Signed) Joshua Stevens
Treasurer of Noxubee County

Which said refusal to suspend said Conner by said Adelbert Ames, Governor of the State of Mississippi, was in violation of his official oath, contrary to the provisions of the Constitution of the State of Mississippi, and made wilfully and corruptly, with the intent to violate the provisions of an Act entitled "An Act to reduce taxes and enforce prompt settlements and payments by Tax Collectors," approved on the 5th day of March, 1875.

Whereby the said Adelbert Ames, Governor of the State of Mississippi, did, then and there, commit, and was guilty of, a high misdemeanor in office.

Article II.

That Adelbert Ames, Governor of the State of Mississippi, unmindful of the high duties of his office, of his oath of office, and of the requirements of the Constitution, that he should take care that the laws be faithfully executed, did, unlawfully, and in violation of the Constitution and laws of the State of Mississippi, at the city of Jackson, in the State aforesaid, on the 28th day of January, 1876, and on the 8th day of February, 1876, willfully and corruptly appoint and commission, in writing, for partisan purposes, the following named persons, Justices of the Peace and Constables in and for the county of Washington, in the State aforesaid, to-wit:

On the 28th day of January, 1876, William Minor, a Justice of the peace, and Charles Schaphnor, a Constable; and on the 8th day of February, 1876, Gilbert Norton, a Justice of the Peace, and Dan. Hays, a Constable, which said acts of the said Adelbert Ames, Governor of the State of Mississippi, in making said appointments, were in violation of the Constitution and laws of said State, and were willfully and corruptly done and performed, with intent to degrade the sovereignty of the State, and to bring her Constitution and laws into contempt among her citizens.

Whereby said Adelbert Ames, Governor of the State of Mississippi, did, then and there, commit, and was guilty of, a high misdemeanor in office.

Article III.

That said Adelbert Ames, Governor of the State of Mississippi, and while acting as such, unmindful of the high duties of his office, and of his oath of office, in violation of the Constitution and laws of the State of Mississippi, did, at the city of Jackson, in the State aforesaid, on the 19th day of February, 1875, unlawfully, knowingly and corruptly approve the bond of M. L. Holland, who had been appointed Treasurer of the State of Mississippi by him, the said Adelbert Ames, Governor of the State of Mississippi, and he, said Holland, as such State Treasurer, being required by the laws of the State of Mississippi to execute a bond, payable to the State of Mississippi, in the sum of eighty thousand dollars, with three or more good freehold sureties, whose solvency and acceptability should be established by their oaths, showing that they were worth the penalty of such bond, over their just debts, legal liabilities and exemptions, in freehold estate, to be approved by the Governor, and conditioned according to law, before he could be inducted into said office.

And he, the said Adelbert Ames, Governor of the State of Mississippi, knowing the same to be defective in form, and well knowing that the sureties had not sworn that they were worth the penalty of said bond, over their just debts, legal liabilities, and exemptions, in freehold estate, did approve the same on the day and year aforesaid, by virtue of which said approval, unlawfully and corruptly made, for partisan purposes as aforesaid, the said M. L. Holland was enabled to assume the duties of the said office of State Treasurer, on the day aforesaid.

Whereby the said Adelbert Ames, Governor of the State of Mississippi, did, then and there, commit, and was guilty of, a high misdemeanor in office.

Article IV.

That the said Adelbert Ames, Governor of the State of Mississippi, and, while acting as such, on the 28th day of August, 1875, at the city of Jackson, in the State aforesaid, unmindful of the high duties of his office, of his oath of office, and of the requirement of the Constitution of the State of Mississippi, that he should take care the laws were faithfully executed, did unlawfully, knowingly, and corruptly permit M. L. Holland, the Treasurer of the State of Mississippi, to remain in said office, in the possession and control of all the moneys, bonds, papers, and other articles of value belonging to the State of Mississippi, and required by law to be kept in the Treasury of the State, without having executed, as Such State Treasurer, a bond, payable to the State, in the sum of eighty thousand dollars, with three or more good freehold sureties thereon, who had justified and sworn that they were worth the penalty of said bond over their just debts, legal liabilities and exemptions, in freehold estate, conditioned as the law required, and approved by him, the Governor of said State.

That he, the said Adelbert Ames, Governor of the State of Mississippi, was advised, on the day and year aforesaid, by the Attorney General of the State of Mississippi, that the bond of the said M. L. Holland, State Treasurer, as aforesaid, was, in law, insufficient to authorize him, the said M. L. Holland, to act as such State Treasurer, by a written communication in words and figures as follows, to-wit:

Attorney General's Office
Jackson, Miss., August 28, 1875

His Excellency, Adelbert Ames, Governor:

Sir: A sense of duty impels me to call your attention to a matter which I regard as quite important to the interests of the State of Mississippi. I have, at length, succeeded in procuring a certified copy of the official bond of the present State Treasurer, M. L. Holland, appointed by your Excellency.

Your Excellency approved his official bond, on February 19, 1875, and I find, upon examination that the bond is insufficient, and not in due form of law. Nor have the sureties justified as the law directs.

The Revised Code of 1871, page 114, provides that "All bonds to be approved by the Governor, shall be payable to the State of Mississippi, verified by the oath of the sureties, that they are worth the penalty of such bonds, over their just debts, legal liabilities and exemptions, in freehold estate: *Provided,* That such bond shall be adjudged sufficient, if the aggregate amount for which surety justifies, covers the full penalty of the bond."

No such oath or verification appears on the bond, nor does it appear that the sureties on the bond are worth anything in "freehold estate."

I am clearly of the opinion that the Treasurer has not such bond as the law requires, and that the said M. L. Holland has no right to exercise the functions, powers, or duties of the said office, until his bond is perfected, and that we have now no State Treasurer authorized to act as such; and for the protection of the funds of the State, permit me to suggest that your Excellency should close the Treasurer's office and take possession of the keys of the office, safes and vaults, until the State Treasurer shall have qualified himself, by executing the bond required by law. Very respectfully,

G. E. Harris, Attorney General

And he, the said Adelbert Ames, Governor of the State of Mississippi, as aforesaid, being thus advised and requested by the Attorney General of the State aforesaid, to take immediate steps for suspending the said M. L. Holland from the Treasury of the State, and taking possession thereof himself, in violation of his official oath and of the Constitution and laws of the State of Mississippi, knowingly, willfully, and corruptly permitted the said M. L. Holland, State Treasurer, as aforesaid, for partisan purposes, to remain in office, in possession of the Treasury of the State, from the day aforesaid, until the expiration of his term of office, on the first Monday of January, 1876, without suspending him from office, or taking any steps to compel him to give bond and security for the faithful discharge of his official duties, as by law he was required to do; whereby the said Adelbert Ames, Governor of the State of Mississippi, did, there and then, commit, and was guilty of, a high misdemeanor in office.

Article V.

That said Adelbert Ames, Governor of the State of Mississippi, and while acting as such, unmindful of the high duties of his office, of his oath of office, and of the Constitution and laws of the State of Mississippi, on or about the 20th day of January 1875, at the city of Jackson, in the State aforesaid, did willfully, corruptly, and intentionally, in violation of the Constitution and laws of the State of Mississippi, and of his official oath, instigate and cause one A. J. Flanagan, the acting Sheriff of Warren county, in the state aforesaid, to be ejected from his office as such Sheriff of the county aforesaid, by force of arms, in the hands of certain United States soldiers then stationed at Vicksburg, within the said county of Warren, and who were moved and instigated in their forcible removal of said Flanagan from office, by the direction of the said Adelbert Ames, as Governor of the State of Mississippi, whereby the said Adelbert Ames, Governor of the State of Mississippi, and in his official action, as such governor, did, then and there, commit, and was guilty of, a high crime in office.

Article VI.

That the said Adelbert Ames, Governor of the State of Mississippi, whilst in office as such Governor, unmindful of the high duties of his said office, and of his oath of office, did willfully, corruptly and knowingly, connive at, assent to and assist in a fraud practised upon the State of Mississippi, by which said State was defrauded of a large sum of money, to-wit: Of the sum of thirty-three thousand seven hundred and fifty dollars, as set forth in the several specifications hereinafter written, in substance and effect, that is to say:

Specification First.

In this, that at Jackson, in said State, under the color of the provisions of an Act of the Legislature of said State, entitled

"An Act to amend an Act for the regulation, control, and support of the Penitentiary, approved March 28th 1872," approved February 26th, 1875, one O. C. French, then and at that time a member of the Legislature by which said Act was passed, and as such chiefly instrumental in having the same passed, and a personal and partisan favorite and friend of said Adelbert Ames, Governor as aforesaid, did, with the connivance, consent and assistance of Adelbert Ames, Governor as aforesaid, secretly and without any fair and open competition or public bidding, as was the true intent and meaning of said law, obtain from and make with the Board of Inspectors of said Penitentiary, by and with the consent, assistance and approval of said Adelbert Ames, Governor as aforesaid, on the 27th day of February, 1875, a contract by which two hundred and fifty of the convicts in the Penitentiary of said State were leased and hired to said O. C. French and his partner, one S. C. Jobes, for their personal use and profit, for and during a term of years ending the first day of January, 1880, without compensation or remuneration to said State other than the obligation to maintain, clothe, guard and care for said convicts without expense to said State, imposed by the terms of said contract upon said French and Jobes, when, at the same time, said convicts, had other and responsible parties been allowed or given the opportunity to bid for or hire them, might and could have been hired and leased upon the same terms upon which they were hired to said French and Jobes, and in addition thereto, for a large sum of money, to-wit: for the sum of eighteen thousand seven hundred and fifty dollars, which said last mentioned fact was well known to said Adelbert Ames, Governor as aforesaid.

Specification Second.

In this, that at Jackson, in said State, on the 13th day of May, 1875, said O. C. French, a personal and partisan favorite of said Adelbert Ames, Governor as aforesaid, under the color of the provisions of said Act of the Legislature, did, with the connivance, consent and assistance of said Adelbert Ames, Governor as aforesaid, secretly and without any fair and open competition or public bidding, as was the true intent and meaning of said law, obtain from and make with the Board of Inspectors of the Penitentiary of said State, by and with the assent, assistance and approval of said Adelbert Ames, Governor as aforesaid, a contract by which two hundred of the convicts then confined in said Penitentiary were leased and hired to said O. C. French and his partner, one C. S. Jobes, for their personal use and profit, for and during a term of years ending on the 1st day of January, 1880, without compensation or remuneration to said State, other than to relieve said State of the expense of maintaining, clothing, guarding and caring for said convicts; when, at the same time, said convicts, had other and responsible parties been allowed or given the opportunity to bid for or hire them, might and could have hired and leased upon the same terms upon which they were hired to said French & Jobes, and in addition thereto, for a large sum of money, to-wit: for the sum of fifteen thousand dollars, which said last named fact was well known to said Adelbert Ames, Governor as aforesaid.

Specification Third.

In this, that on the 27th day of February, 1875, acting under color of the provisions of said Act of the Legislature, said O. C. French, a personal and partisan favorite of said Adelbert Ames, Governor as aforesaid, and by and with the assent, assistance and approval of said Adelbert Ames, Governor as aforesaid, clandestinely and secretly obtained from and made with the Board of Inspectors of said Penitentiary, without any fair and open competition or public bidding, as was the true intent and meaning of said Act, a contract by which two hundred and fifty of the convicts in said penitentiary were leased and hired to said O. C. French and one C. S. Jobes, his partner, for their personal use and advantage, for and during a term of years to end on the 1st day of January, 1880, without compensation or remuneration to said State other than to relieve the State of the expense of maintaining, clothing, guarding and caring for said convicts; and on the same day, to-wit; the 27th day of February, 1875 with the knowledge, consent and approval of said Adelbert Ames, Governor as aforesaid, the said French & Jobes leased, hired and transferred to one Edward Richardson, in consideration of a bonus paid to them in cash of seven thousand five hundred dollars ($7,500), one hundred of said convicts, he, the said Richardson assuming all of the responsibilities, contracts, agreements and conditions imposed upon said French & Jobes under their said contract with said Board of Inspectors, thus making for said French & Jobes, with the assistance, connivance, consent and approval of said Adelbert Ames, Governor as aforesaid, at the expense of said State, in one day, a net profit of seven thousand five hundred dollars ($7,500), simple transfer of two-fifths of the convicts received by their said contract with said Board of Inspectors.

Specification Fourth.

In this, that at Jackson, in said State on the 13th day of May, 1875, acting under color of the provisions of said Act of the Legislature, said O. C. French, a personal and partisan favorite of said Adelbert Ames, Governor as aforesaid, and by and with the assent, assistance and approval of said Adelbert Ames, Governor as aforesaid, clandestinely and secretly obtained from and made with the Board of Inspectors of said Penitentiary, without any fair competition or public bidding, as was the true intent and meaning of said law, a contract by which two hundred of the convicts in said Penitentiary were leased and hired to said O. C. French and his partner, S. C. Jobes, for their personal use and profit, for and during a term of years ending on the 1st day of January, 1880, without remuneration or compensation to said State other than the obligation imposed by said contract upon said French & Jobes, to maintain, clothe, guard and care for said convicts; and on the same day, to-wit; on the 13th day of May, 1875, with the knowledge, consent and approval of said Adelbert Ames, Governor as aforesaid, the said French & Jobes leased, hired and transferred to one Edward Richardson, in consideration of a bonus of seventy-two hundred dollars in cash paid to them, one hundred of said convicts, he, the said Richardson, assuming all the responsibilities, contracts, agreements and conditions imposed upon said French & Jobes in their said contract with said Board of Inspectors, thus making for said French & Jobes, with the assistance, connivance, consent and approval of said Adelbert Ames, Governor as aforesaid, at the expense of the said State, a net profit of seventy-two hundred dollars, by a simple transfer of one-half of the convicts received by their said last named contract with said Board of Inspectors, by means of which said several contracts had and obtained by and with the assent, assistance and connivance of said Adelbert Ames, Governor of the State of Mississippi, a gross fraud was practised upon said State, whereby the said Adelbert Ames, Governor of the State of Mississippi, did, then and and there, commit, and was guilty of, a high misdemeanor in office.

Article VII.

That the said Adelbert Ames, Governor of the State of Mississippi, whilst in office as such Governor, unmindful of the high duties of his said office, and of his oath of office, did, at Jackson, in said State, on the 13th day of May, 1874, and upon divers and sundry other days in said year, conspire with one O. C. French, to defame, slander and libel one G. Wiley Wells, a citizen of said State, and thereby and in that way to prevent the appointment of said G. Wiley Wells to the office of District Attorney for the United States for the Northern District of Mississippi, then about to be vacant, and for the purpose of securing the assistance and co-operation of said O. C. French in said conspiracy, the said Adelbert Ames, Governor as aforesaid, on said 13th day of May, 1874, and on divers and sundry days before and after that time, did willfully, unlawfully and corruptly pervert and abuse the power conferred upon him by law, as Governor of said State, over the convict labor of said State, and did corruptly require and receive from said O. C. French, as a condition precedent to, and a consideration for the approval by him, the said Adelbert Ames, of certain contracts, bonds and papers, under and by virtue of which the said O. C. French, one Homer C. Powers, and one C. S. Jobes, were to and did secure contracts for a large portion of the convict labor in said Penitentiary, for their own use, and as a condition precedent to and a consideration for the exercise by said Adelbert Ames, of his influence as Governor of said State, in so securing said convict labor, that the said O. C. French would write and deliver to said Adelbert Ames, Governor as aforesaid, for the use aforesaid, a letter calculated and intended to injure, destroy and defame the reputation and character of said G. Wiley Wells, a citizen of said State, and to prevent his appointment as aforesaid, which said letter was, in pursuance of such conspiracy, written and delivered by said O. C. French to said Adelbert Ames, Governor as aforesaid, on the 13th day of May, 1874, and is in the words and figures following, to-wit:

Jackson, Miss., May 13, 1874

Hon. A. Ames, Governor of Mississippi:

Dear Sir: In reply to your inquiry of this date, I have only to say, that on my arrival in Jackson at the commencement of the last session of the Legislature, I met the gentlemen named in your note, and they requested my support and the favor of any influence I might have in support of Col. Wells for the United States Senate.

In the course of the conversation, it was suggested by them that in the event of their receiving my support, they would relieve me of the financial embarrassment under which I was then resting, by paying off the judgment issued against me by the Federal Court at the December session of 1873, and surrendering the same to me. Very respectfully,

Your obedient servant, O. C. FRENCH

And the said Adelbert Ames, Governor of said State, did in pursuance of said corrupt bargain and conspiracy, on said 13th day of May, 1874, and on divers and sundry days thereafter, at Jackson, in said State, in consideration of having received said letters, approve said contracts, bonds and papers, and use his said influence as Governor as aforesaid, to secure to said O. C. French, Homer C. Powers, and C. S. Jobes said convict labor of said State, to the great loss and damage of said State, whereby the said Adelbert Ames, Governor of said State of Mississippi, did commit, and was guilty of, a high misdemeanor in office.

Article VIII.

That the said Adelbert Ames, Governor of the State of Mississippi, whilst in office as such Governor, unmindful of the high duties of his said office, and of his oath of office, on the 5th day of April, in the year of our Lord, 1875, at Bay St. Louis, in said State, did corruptly, without authority of law, and in violation of the constitution of the State of Mississippi, permit, consent to, connive at, and assist in an exchange and swap of their respective positions, as public officers of said State, by and between Hiram Cassidy, Jr., then and at that time, the lawful incumbent of the office of Chancellor of the 19th Chancery District of said State, and J. B. Deason, then and at that time the lawful incumbent of the office of District Attorney of the 2d Judicial District of said State, by means of which said exchange and swap of offices, made and had, by and with the permission, assent, connivance, and assistance of said Adelbert Ames, Governor of the State of Mississippi, and of the appointment made by said Adelbert Ames, Governor of the State of Mississippi, on the 12th day of April, 1875, in pursuance of said swap and exchange of the said J. B. Deason to the office of Chancellor of said 19th Chancery District of said State, and of the appointment, on the 12th day of April, 1875, of Hiram Cassidy, Jr., to the office of District Attorney of said 2d Judicial District of said State, the said J. B. Deason became the Chancellor of said 19th Chancery District of said State, and the said Hiram Cassidy, Jr., became the District Attorney of said 2d Judicial District of said State; and said swap and exchange of offices was consummated and made complete, whereby the said Adelbert Ames, Governor of the State of Mississippi, did, then and there, commit, and was guilty of, a high misdemeanor in office.

Article IX.

That Adelbert Ames, Governor of the State of Mississippi, unmindful of the high duties of his office, and of his oath of office, and of the constitution of said State, and the laws thereof, whereby it is provided that "Chancellors shall be appointed in the same manner as Judges of the Circuit Courts," Article 6, Section 17, and "Judges of the Circuit Courts shall be appointed by the Governor, with the advice and consent of the Senate," Article 6, Section 11, and of the law of the land whereby it is provided "that the Governor shall fill, by appointment, with the advice and consent of the Senate, all officers subject to such appointment, under the constitution and laws, when the term of the incumbent is about to expire," Code, 1871, Section 106, did, on divers days, in the county of Hinds in said State, in the year of our Lord eighteen hundred and seventy-four, wilfully, and with intent to violate and subvert, in this regard, the constitution and laws, and to deprive the Senate of its constitutional right of sharing with him the filling of the office of Chancellors in this State, fail, neglect, and refuse to send his nominations of Chancellors to the Senate, at the regular session of the Legislature of this State, in the year eighteen hundred and seventy-four, which was the session of said Senate just before or preceding the ending of the term of office of the then incumbent Chancellors of said State, and which session of the Legislature was duly had and held, according to the constitution. That the said neglect, failure, and refusal of the said Adelbert Ames, Governor as aforesaid, was with intent to destroy the independence of the Judiciary, in his behalf, and make them subservient to the Executive will and power, and for corrupt and partisan purposes.

And having so failed, neglected and refused to make nominations of Chancellors as aforesaid, to said Senate as aforesaid, during its session as aforesaid, with intend as aforesaid, the said Adelbert Ames, Governor as aforesaid, did, in violation of said constitution and law of the land, appoint Chancellors, in the vacation of the Senate, and after the adjournment of said Senate, thus aggrandizing his executive powers, usurping powers belonging, in part, to the Senate, and subverting the said constitution and laws, by defeating the selection of an enlightened, upright, and pure Judiciary.

Specification First.

That he failed, neglected, and refused to nominate to the Senate, in session, at the regular session of the Legislature, under the constitution, in the year A.D. 1874, a Chancellor to succeed J. Fred. Simmons, the then incumbent Chancellor of the 10th Chancery District of said State, whose term of office was then about to expire, and did expire on the 3rd day of June, A.D. 1874; and afterwards, in vacation of and after the adjournment of said Senate, to-wit: on the 12th day of October, A.D. 1874, appoint as Chancellor of said District, one J. N. Campbell.

Specification Second.

That he failed, neglected, and refused to nominate to the Senate, in session, at the regular session of the Legislature, under the constitution, in the year A.D. 1874, a Chancellor to succeed Thomas Christian, the then incumbent Chancellor of the 4th Chancery District of said State, whose term of office was then about to expire, and did expire on the 1st day of July A.D. 1874; and afterwards, in vacation of and after adjournment of said Senate, to-wit: on the 23rd day of May, A.D. 1874, and on the 29th day of July, 1874, appointed, as Chancellor of said District, one John J. Dennis.

Specification Third.

That he failed, neglected, and refused to nominate to the Senate, in session, at the regular session of the Legislature, under the constitution, in the year A.D. 1874, a Chancellor to succeed DeWitt Stearns, the then incumbent Chancellor of the 9th Chancery District of said State, whose term of office was then about to expire, and did expire on the 10th day of June, A.D. 1874; and afterwards, and in vacation of said Senate, and after its adjournment, to-wit: on the 10th day of June, A.D. 1874, appointed, as Chancellor of said District, one L. C. Abbott.

Specification Fourth.

That he failed, neglected, and refused to nominate to the Senate, in session, at the regular session of the Legislature, under the constitution, in the year A.D. 1874, a Chancellor to succeed Wesley Drane, the then incumbent Chancellor of the 3rd Chancery District of said State, whose term of office was then about to expire, and did expire on the 7th day of June,

A.D. 1874; and afterwards, in vacation of and after the adjournment of said Senate, to-wit: on the 2d day of June, A.D. 1874, appointed as Chancellor of said District, one R. Boyd.

Specification Fifth.

That he failed, neglected and refused to nominate to the Senate, in session, at the regular session of the Legislature, under the constitution, in the year A.D. 1874, a Chancellor to succeed A. E. Reynolds, the then incumbent Chancellor of the 8th Chancery District of said State, whose term of office was then about to expire, and did expire on the 28th day of July, A.D. 1874; and afterwards, in vacation of and after the adjournment of said Senate, to-wit: on the 29th day of July, A.D. 1874, appointed, as Chancellor of said District, one J. D. Barton.

Specification Sixth.

That he failed, neglected, and refused to nominate to the Senate, in session, at the regular session of the Legislature, under the constitution, in the year A.D. 1874, a Chancellor to succeed T. R. Gowan, the then incumbent Chancellor of the 17th Chancery District of said State, whose term of office was then about to expire, and did expire on the 10th day of June, A.D. 1874; and afterwards, in vacation of said Senate, and after its adjournment, to-wit: on the 4th day of June, A.D. 1874, appointed, as Chancellor of said District, one R. B. Stone.

Specification Seventh.

That he failed, neglected, and refused to nominate to the Senate, in session, at the regular session of the Legislature, under the constitution, in the year 1874, a Chancellor to succeed W. G. Henderson, the then incumbent Chancellor of the 1st Chancery District of said State, whose term of office was then about to expire, and did expire on the 2d day of June, A.D. 1874; and afterwards, in vacation of said Senate, and after its adjournment, to-wit; on the 19th day of May, A.D. 1874, appointed, as Chancellor of said District, the said W. G. Henderson, as his own successor.

Specification Eighth.

That he failed, neglected, and refused to nominate to the Senate, in session, at the regular session of the Legislature, under the constitution, in the year A.D. 1874, a Chancellor to succeed G. S. McMillan, the then incumbent Chancellor of the

2d Chancery District of said State, whose term of office was then about to expire, and did expire on the 6th day of June, A.D. 1874; and afterwards, in vacation of said Senate, and after its adjournment, to-wit; on the 12th day of April, 1874, appointed, as Chancellor of said District, one G. S. McMillan, to be his own successor.

Specification Ninth.

That he failed, neglected, and refused to nominate to the Senate, in session, at the regular session of the Legislature, under the constitution, in the year A.D. 1874, a Chancellor to succeed O. H. Whitfield, the then incumbent Chancellor of the 6th District of said State, whose term of office was then about to expire, and did expire on the 21st day of July, A.D. 1874; and afterwards, in vacation of said Senate, and after its adjournment, to-wit; on the 18th day of May, A.D. 1874, appointed, as Chancellor of said District, one O. H. Whitfield, to be his own successor.

Specification Tenth.

That he failed, neglected, and refused to nominate to the Senate, in session, at the regular session of the Legislature, under the constitution, in the year A.D. 1874, a Chancellor to succeed Austin Pollard, the then incumbent Chancellor of the 8th Chancery District of said State, whose term of office was then about to expire, and did expire on the 1st day of July, A.D. 1874; and afterwards, in vacation of said Senate, and after its adjournment, to wit: on the 25th day of May, A.D. 1874, appointed, as Chancellor of said District, one W. D. Frazee.

Specification Eleventh.

That he failed, neglected, and refused to nominate to the Senate, in session, at the regular session of the Legislature, under the constitution, in the year A.D. 1874, a Chancellor to succeed Dallas P. Coffey, the then incumbent Chancellor of the 11th Chancery District of said State, whose term of office was about to expire, and did expire on the 16th day of June, A.D. 1874; and afterwards, in vacation of said Senate, and after its adjournment, to-wit: on the 25th day of May, A.D. 1874, appointed, as Chancellor of said District, one Peter P. Bailey.

Specification Twelfth.

That he failed, neglected, and refused to nominate to the Senate, in session, at the regular session of the Legislature, under the constitution, in the year A.D. 1874, a Chancellor to succeed Samuel Young, the then incumbent Chancellor of the 13th Chancery District of said State, whose term of office was then about to expire, and did expire on the 6th day of June, A.D. 1874; and afterwards, in vacation of Senate, and after its adjournment, to wit: on the 6th day of June, A.D. 1874, appointed, as Chancellor of said District, one William Breck.

Specification Thirteenth.

That he failed, neglected, and refused to nominate to the Senate, in session at the regular session of the Legislature, under the Constitution, in the year A.D. 1874, a Chancellor to succeed E. W. Cabiness, the then incumbent Chancellor of the Sixteenth Chancery Court District, of said State, whose term of office was then about to expire, and did expire on the 20th day of June, A.D. 1874; and afterwards, in vacation of said Senate, and after its adjournment, to-wit: on the 23d day of May, A.D. 1874, appointed as Chancellor of said District, one W. B. Peyton, whereby the said Adelbert Ames, Governor as aforesaid, did willfully, and in disregard of the trust and confidence in him reposed, degrade and dishonor the public justice of said State, and did thereby commit and was guilty of a high misdemeanor in office against the peace, interests and dignity of said State.

Article X.

That the said Adelbert Ames, Governor of the State of Mississippi, whilst in office as such Governor, unmindful of the high duties of his said office, and in violation of the Constitution and laws of said State, and corruptly intending and seeking to destroy the independence of a portion of the judiciary of said State, and make the same subservient to his will, did on the 30th and 31st day of July, 1874, at the city of Jackson, in said State, endeavor to persuade and induce E. G. Peyton, then and at the time Chief Justice of the State of Mississippi, to interfere with, direct and control, in such manner as should meet the wishes of said Adelbert Ames, Governor of said State, the rulings, decision and decrees of W. B. Peyton, then and at that time Chancellor of the Sixteenth Chancery District of said State, and a son of said E. G. Peyton, about to be made and rendered in a certain cause then pending in the Chancery Court of Hinds County, in said State, before the said W. B. Peyton, styled "the University of Mississippi et al. vs. the Vicksburg and Nashville Railroad et al.," and numbered on the docket of said Court number 234, whereby the said Adelbert Ames, Governor of the State of Mississippi, did commit, and was guilty of, a high misdemeanor in office.

Article XI.

That the said Adelbert Ames, Governor of the State of Mississippi, whilst in office as such Governor, unmindful of the high duties of his said office, and of his oath of office, and in violation of the Constitution and laws of said State, moved thereto by a corrupt desire and intent to control the Judiciary of said State, and make the same subservient to his will; and because of certain rulings, decisions and decrees made and rendered on the 30th and 31st days of July, 1874, in a certain cause pending in the Chancery Court of Hinds county, in said State styled the "University of Mississippi et al. vs. the Vicksburg and Nashville Railroad Company, et al., and numbered on the docket of said Court, No. 234, by one Wm. B. Peyton, who had prior to that time, on the 25th day of May, 1874, been appointed to the office of Chancellor of the Sixteenth District of said State, by said Adelbert Ames, Governor, as aforesaid, and was on said 30th and 31st day of July, 1874, exercising and performing the functions of said office of Chancellor, which said rulings, decisions and decrees were especially and personally distasteful and disagreeable to said Adelbert Ames, Governor, as aforesaid, did, at Jackson, in said State, on the 1st day of February, 1875, and on divers and sundry days thereafter, willfully, arbitrarily, and corruptly fail and refuse to report to the Senate of said State, for its advice and consent, at the regular session thereof, held at Jackson, in said State in the year 1875, being the session of said Senate next succeeding said appointment of said W. B. Peyton, as Chancellor, as aforesaid, the said appointment of said W. B. Peyton as Chancellor of said District; whereby the said Adelbert Ames, Governor of the State of Mississippi, did, then and there, commit, and was guilty of, a high misdemeanor in office.

Article XII.

That the said Adelbert Ames, Governor of the State of Mississippi, on the 7th day of February, in the year of our Lord, one thousand eight hundred and seventy-four, at the city of Jackson, in the State of Mississippi, unmindful of the high duties of his office, of his oath of office, and of the requirement of the Constitution, that he should "see that the laws are faithfully executed," did unlawfully and in violation of the Constitution and the laws of the State of Mississippi, issue an order in writing for the removal of W. A. Drennan, from the office of Chancellor of the 12th Chancery District of the State of Mississippi, the said W. A. Drennan having been theretofore duly appointed and commissioned to said office of Chancellor of said District, by R. C. Powers, then Governor of the State of Mississippi, on the 30th day of September, A.D., one thousand eight hundred and seventy-three, and the said W. A. Drennan, by reason of the premises, on said 7th day of February, being in the possession, performing the functions and discharging the duties of the office of Chancellor, which said order for the removal of W. A. Drennan, is in substance as follows, that is to say:

State of Mississippi, Executive Department
Jackson, Mississippi, February 7, 1874

Hon. W. A. Drennan:

Sir: You are hereby notified that your appointment as Chancellor of the Twelfth Chancery District has been this day revoked.

Adelbert Ames

By the Governor:
James Hill, Secretary of State.

Which order was willfully, corruptly and unlawfully issued by the said Adelbert Ames, Governor of the State of Mississippi, and for the reason that sitting as Chancellor for the trial of a writ of *habeas corpus*, sued out by a personal friend and political partisan of Governor Ames, one A. T. Morgan, charged with the murder of F. P. Hilliard, Sheriff of Yazoo County, the said W. A. Drennan had refused to grant the said Morgan bail, and had remanded him to jail; which judgment and decree of the Chancellor, made under the sanction of his oath of office, and in the legitimate exercise of powers conferred upon him by law, displeased and offended the said Adelbert Ames, Governor as aforesaid, who immediately thereupon issued the said order for the removal of said W. A. Drennan from his office of Chancellor; which said order was issued by the said Adelbert Ames, Governor of Mississippi, with the intent then and there to violate the Constitution and the laws of the State of Mississippi, and to corrupt, control, degrade and render subservient to his will, the Judiciary of the State, and with the further intent contrary to the provisions of law, in violation thereof, and contrary to the provisions of the Constitution of the State of Mississippi, to remove, and by said order, he did so remove the said W. A. Drennan, from the office of Chancellor of the 12th District, the said W. A. Drennan being then and there in possession of the office of Chancellor of said District, and being then and there in the discharge of the duties of said office, whereby the said Adelbert Ames, Governor of the State of Mississippi, did, then and there, commit, and was guilty of, a high misdemeanor in office.

Article XIII.

That the said Adelbert Ames, Governor of the State of Mississippi, on the 29th day of July, in the year of our Lord one thousand, eight hundred and seventy-four, at the city of Jackson, in the State of Mississippi, unmindful of the high duties of his office, of his oath of office and of the requirement of the Constitution, that he should "see that the laws are faithfully executed," did, unlawfully, and in violation of the Constitution and the laws of the State of Mississippi, issue an order, in writing, for the removal of Thomas Christian from the office of Chancellor of the Fourth Chancery District of the State of Mississippi; the said Thomas Christian having been therefore duly appointed and commissioned to said office of Chancellor of said District by Alexander K. Davis, Lieutenant-Governor, at the time of making said appointment acting Governor of the State of Mississippi, on the first day of July, in the year of our Lord one thousand eight hundred and seventy-four, and the said Thomas Christian, by reason of the premises, on said 29th day of July, being in the quiet possession, performing the functions and discharging the duties of the said office of Chancellor, which said order for the removal of Thomas Christian, is in substance as follows—that is to say:

State of Mississippi, Executive Department
Jackson, Mississippi, July 29, 1874

Hon. Thomas Christian, Meridian, Miss.:

Sir: Your appointment to the office of Chancellor of the Fourth Chancery District, Mississippi, dated July 1st, 1874, is hereby revoked. Very respectfully yours,

Adelbert Ames, Governor

Which order was willfully, corruptly and unlawfully issued by the said Adelbert Ames, Governor of the State of Mississippi, and for the reason that the said Thomas Christian declined to be used as a party tool himself, or to permit his high office to be used by Adelbert Ames, Governor of Mississippi, or his party friends for the purpose of advancing the interests of the political party to which they belonged, which said order was issued with intent then and there to violate the Constitution and laws of the State of Mississippi, to corrupt, control, degrade and render subservient to his will the Judiciary of the State, and with the further intent, contrary to the provisions of law, in violation thereof, and contrary to the provisions of the Constitution of the State of Mississippi, to remove, and by said order he did so remove said Thomas Christian from the office of Chancellor of the Fourth District, the said Thomas Christian being then and there in possession of the office of Chancellor of said District, and being then and there in the discharge of the duties of said office, whereby the said Adelbert Ames, Governor of the State of Mississippi, did, then and there, commit, and was guilty of, a high misdemeanor in office.

Article XIV.

That the said Adelbert Ames, Governor of the State of Mississippi, on the 29th day of July, in the year of our Lord one thousand eight hundred and seventy-four, at the city of Jackson, in the State of Mississippi, unmindful of the high duties of his office, of his oath of office, and of the requirement of the Constitution that he should "see that the laws are faithfully executed," did unlawfully and in violation of the Constitution and the laws of the State of Mississippi, issue an order in writing for the removal of J. F. Simmons from the office of Chancellor of the Tenth Chancery District of the State of Mississippi, the said J. F. Simmons having been theretofore duly appointed and commissioned to said office of Chancellor of said District by Alexander K. Davis, on the 17th day of July, 1874, the said Alexander K. Davis being Lieutenant-Governor, and, at the time of making said appointment, acting Governor of the State of Mississippi, and the said J. F. Simmons, by reason of the premises, on the said 29th day of July, being in the quiet possession, performing the functions and discharging the duties of the said office of Chancellor, which said order for the removal of J. F. Simmons is in substance as follows, that is to say:

State of Mississippi, Executive Department
Jackson, Miss., July 29, 1874

Hon. J. F. Simmons, Miss.:

Sir: Your appointment to the office of Chancellor of the 10th Chancery District, Miss., dated July 17th, 1874, is hereby revoked. Very respectfully,

Adelbert Ames, Governor

Which order was unlawfully issued, with intent, then and there, to violate the constitution and laws of the State of Mississippi, and with the further intent, contrary to the provisions of law, in violation, and contrary to the provisions of the Constitution of the State of Mississippi, to remove the said J. F. Simmons, and by the order aforesaid, the said J. F. Simmons was removed from the office of Chancellor of the 10th District, the said J. F. Simmons being then and there in the possession and in the discharge of the duties of said office. Whereby the said Adelbert Ames, Governor of the State of Mississippi, did, then and there, commit, and was guilty of, a high crime and misdemeanor in office.

Article XV.

That the said Adelbert Ames, Governor of the State of Mississippi, while acting as such Governor, unmindful of the high duties of his office, and of his oath of office, and in violation of the constitution of said State, which constitution makes it the duty of the said Governor to see that the laws are faithfully executed, did, at Jackson, in the county of Hinds, in the State of Mississippi, on the twenty-third day of May, in the year of our Lord one thousand eight hundred and seventy-five, and at divers other times, as well before as afterward, willfully, corruptly, and for partisan purposes, and with a reckless, wicked, and criminal disregard of the wishes, rights, interest, and happiness of the citizens of said State, bring into disgrace, contempt, and ridicule, the Judiciary of the State, by appointing to Judicial positions men who were notoriously incompetent, immoral, and dishonest, as more fully set forth in the several specifications hereinafter written, in substance and effect, that is to say:

Specification First.

In this, that at Jackson, in the county of Hinds in the State of Mississippi, the said Adelbert Ames, Governor of the State of Mississippi, while acting as such Governor, heretofore, to-wit:

on the twenty-third day of May, in the year of our Lord one thousand eight hundred and seventy-five, did willfully, corruptly, and for partisan purposes, nominate and appoint to the office of Chancellor of the 8th Chancery District of the State of Mississippi, one J. D. Barton, who, at the time of said appointment, the said Adelbert Ames, Governor as aforesaid, well knew, was wholly unworthy and incompetent to discharge the high duties of the office of Chancellor, by reason of the fact that the said Barton was guilty, or publicly charged, of the crime of forgery.

Specification Second.

In this, that at Jackson, in the county of Hinds in the State of Mississippi, the said Adelbert Ames, Governor of the State of Mississippi, while acting as such Governor, heretofore, to-wit: on the twenty-third day of May, in the year of our Lord one thousand eight hundred and seventy-four, did willfully, corruptly, and for partisan purposes, nominate and appoint to the office of Chancellor of the 8th Chancery District of the State of Mississippi, one J. D. Barton, who, at the time of said appointment, the said Adelbert Ames, Governor as aforesaid, well knew was wholly incompetent to discharge the high duties of the office of Chancellor, by reason of the fact that the said Barton had little or no knowledge of the law, or experience in the practice of the same.

Specification Third.

In this, that at Jackson, in the county of Hinds, in the State of Mississippi, the said Adelbert Ames, Governor of the State of Mississippi, while acting as such Governor, heretofore, to-wit: on the first day of June in the year of our Lord one thousand eight hundred and seventy-four, did willfully, corruptly, and for partisan purposes, nominate and appoint to the office of Chancellor of the 9th Chancery District of the State of Mississippi, one L. C. Abbott, who, at the time of said appointment, the said Adelbert Ames, Governor as aforesaid, well knew was wholly incompetent to discharge the high duties of the office of Chancellor, by reason of the fact that said Abbott had never practiced law, but was admitted to the "Bar" only a few days prior to his appointment as such Chancellor, and with the distinct understanding that when admitted to the "Bar," as aforesaid, he should receive from the said Adelbert Ames, Governor as aforesaid, the said appointment of Chancellor.

Specification Fourth.

In this, that at Jackson, in the county of Hinds, in the State of Mississippi, the said Adelbert Ames, Governor of the State of Mississippi, while acting as such Governor, heretofore, to-wit: on the sixth day of June, in the year of our Lord one thousand eight hundred and seventy-four, did, willfully, corruptly, and for partisan purposes, nominate and appoint to the office of Chancellor of the 13th Chancery District of the State of Mississippi, one William Breck, who, at the time of said appointment, the said Adelbert Ames, Governor, as aforesaid, well knew was wholly unworthy and incompetent to discharge the high duties of the office of Chancellor, by reason of the fact that the said Breck had little or no knowledge of the law, or experience in the practice of the same.

Specification Fifth.

In this, that at Jackson, in the county of Hinds, in the State of Mississippi, the said Adelbert Ames, Governor of the State of Mississippi, while acting as such Governor, heretofore, to-wit: on the sixth day of June, in the year of our Lord one thousand eight hundred and seventy-four, did, willfully, corruptly, and for partisan purposes, nominate and appoint to the office of Chancellor of the 13th Chancery District of the State of Mississippi, one William Breck, who, at the time of said appointment, the said Adelbert Ames, Governor as aforesaid, well knew, was wholly unworthy and incompetent to discharge the high duties of the office of Chancellor, by reason of the fact that the said Breck was publicly charged and reported to said Governor, as having defrauded and swindled, as assignee of the estate of one Green, in Madison county, the creditors of said estate, and as having been a party to illegal and fraudulent contracts let out by the Board of Supervisors of Madison county, in the State, he, the said Breck, being President of the said Board of Supervisors.

Specification Sixth.

In this, that at Jackson, in the county of Hinds, in the State of Mississippi, the said Adelbert Ames, Governor of the State of Mississippi, while acting as such Governor, heretofore, to-wit: on the fifth day of February, in the year of our Lord one thousand eight hundred and seventy-five, did willfully, corruptly, and for partisan purposes, nominate and appoint to the office of Chancellor of the 8th Chancery District of the State of Mississippi, one C. Cullens, who, at the time of said appointment, the said Adelbert Ames, Governor as aforesaid, well knew, was wholly unworthy and incompetent to discharge the high duties of the office of Chancellor, by reason of the fact that the said Cullens was, at the time of his appointment, a practicing physician; that he had never practiced law, but was privately examined and admitted to the Bar only a few days prior to his appointment as such Chancellor, and with the distinct understanding that when admitted to the Bar, as aforesaid, he should receive from the said Adelbert Ames, Governor as aforesaid, the said appointment of Chancellor; whereby the said Adelbert Ames, Governor of the State of Mississippi, did, then and there, commit, and was guilty of, a high misdemeanor in office.

Article XVI.

That Adelbert Ames, Governor of the State of Mississippi, and being, by virtue thereof, commander-in-chief of the militia of said State, and having power to call forth the militia to execute the laws, repel invasion and to suppress insurrections, unmindful of the high duties of his office, and of his oath of office, and of the constitution of said State, whereby he is made a conservator of the peace, and charged with the duty of seeing that the laws are faithfully executed, did, on the 10th day of October, A.D. 1875, in the county of Hinds, in said State, with intent to excite a riot and produce a conflict of arms between the two races of citizens of the State, cause a certain company of the organized and armed militia, composed of men of the African race, colored citizens, whose Captain was one Charles Caldwell, a notoriously dangerous and turbulent and obnoxious man of that race, and one or more of whose lieutenants were of the same character and race, to march, with guns and accoutrements of war, as an escort to a wagon train of arms, from the city of Jackson, in said county of Hinds to the town of Edwards' Depot, in the county of Hinds, and did cause these men, thus armed, to traverse, march and countermarch over and through the region of said county of Hinds, between the city of Jackson and Edwards' Depot, and to parade the streets of the town of Clinton, in said county of Hinds, which was within their said route of march, he, the said Adelbert Ames, Governor as aforesaid, intending and contriving to provoke peaceful and law-abiding citizens of said county and State to wrath and violence, and a conflict and collision with arms with the said militia, armed, as aforesaid, and well knowing that in consequence of the inflamed and excited state of the people along said line of march, and in said county of Hinds, of the existence of which he, the said Adelbert Ames, Governor as aforesaid, was well aware, such conflict and collision, and consequent riot, bloodshed, and death of many of the citizens of said State was likely to result, whereby the said Adelbert Ames, Governor as aforesaid, did violate and betray the trust and confidence reposed in him, and did, thereby, commit, and was guilty of, a high misdemeanor in office, against the peace, interests, and dignity of said State.

Article XVII.

That Adelbert Ames, Governor of the State of Mississippi, unmindful of the high duties of his office, and the dignities and proprieties thereof, in the county of Hinds, in said State, on the 3d day of December, A.D. 1874, when and where there was a large number of men of the African race, colored citizens of said State assembled, to-wit: Peter Crosby, J. J. Spelman, Jas. Hill, I. D. Shadd, and divers others of said race, did, then and there with a corrupt design, purpose and intent of bringing on an armed conflict between the white and colored citizens of said State, in the presence and hearing of said colored citizens make and deliver certain intemperate and inflammatory speeches, which are set forth in the several specifications hereinafter written, in substance and effect, that is to say:

Specification First.

In this, that at the Governor's Mansion, in the city of Jackson, in the county of Hinds and State aforesaid, on the day and year aforesaid, when and where the right of said Peter Crosby to the office of Sheriff of the county of Warren, in said State, was under discussion, and when and where an objection, by some person present, to any attempt on the part of said Crosby to take possession of said office by force, was made, and when and where a suggestion was made that such attempt would cause bloodshed, he, the said Adelbert Ames, Governor as aforesaid, with the intent aforesaid, did declare, in substance and effect, among other things, that is to say: "I and other white men have faced the bullets to free the colored people, and now if they are not willing to fight to maintain that freedom, they are unworthy of it."

Specification Second.

In this, that on the third day of December, A.D. 1874, (one thousand eight hundred and seventy-four), at the Governor's

Mansion, in the city of Jackson, in the county of Hinds and State aforesaid, when and where the right of the said Peter Crosby to the office of Sheriff of the said county of Warren was being debated, and when and where the remark was made by some person then and there present, that if said Crosby, attempted by force to take possession of said office of Sheriff, there would be lives lost, he, the said Adelbert Ames, Governor as aforesaid, with intent as aforesaid, did, in substance and effect, declare, among other things, that is to say: "What if it does cost blood, *the blood of the martyr is the seed of the church.*"

Specification Third.

In this, that on the third day of December, A.D. 1874 (one thousand eight hundred and seventy-four), at the Governor's Mansion, in the city of Jackson, in the county of Hinds, in said State, when and where the right of the said Peter Crosby to possess himself of the office of sheriff of Warren county, in said State, was being discussed, and when and where the suggestion and opinion of some person then and there present, was made and given, that an attempt by said Crosby to possess himself of said office by a posse of Negroes, only would cause bloodshed in Vicksburg, he, the said Adelbert Ames, Governor as aforesaid, did, in substance and effect, then and there declare and say "That very likely fifteen or twenty Negroes may be killed, but that it would result to the benefit of the Republican party."

Which said utterances, declarations, and speeches are highly censurable, indecent and unbecoming in the Chief Magistrate of the State, and said declarations, utterances and speeches tended to produce and bring about a certain riot and armed conflict in the city of Vicksburg, in said county of Warren, a short time thereafter, to-wit: on the 17th day of December, 1874, (one thousand eight hundred and seventy-four), between many citizens of said State, and which riot and armed conflict then and there resulted in the wounding, killing and slaying of many of the citizens of said State, to the great scandal and disgrace of all lawful authority—to the scandal and disgrace of the high position then and there held by the said Adelbert Ames, Governor as aforesaid, whereby said Adelbert Ames, Governor as aforesaid, did commit, and was, then and there, guilty of, a high misdemeanor in office.

Article XVIII.

That Adelbert Ames, Governor of the State of Mississippi, unmindful of the high duties of his office, and the dignity and proprieties thereof, on the third day of December, A.D. 1874, (one thousand eight hundred and seventy-four), in the county of Hinds, in said State, when and where there was a large number of men of the African race, colored citizens of said State, assembled, to-wit: Peter Crosby, J. J. Spelman, James Hill and divers others of said race, he the said Peter Crosby being then and there for the purpose of receiving counsel and advice of and from him, the said Adelbert Ames, Governor as aforesaid, concerning the office of sheriff of the county of Warren, in said State, and then and there claiming that he, the said Peter Crosby, was entitled to the possession of the said office of sheriff, he, the said Adelbert Ames, Governor as aforesaid, unmindful as aforesaid, and with corrupt design and intent, did then and there, in the presence and hearing of said colored citizens, make and deliver a certain intemperate and inflammatory speech, which said intemperate and inflammatory speech, together with unlawful advice given to said Peter Crosby, by the said Adelbert Ames, Governor as aforesaid, provoked and caused a certain riot in said county of Warren, a short time thereafter, to-wit: on the 17th day of December, A.D. 1874 (one thousand eight hundred and seventy-four) between the colored and white citizens of said county of Warren, and in said riot many of the citizens of said county of Warren were wounded and slain; whereby the said Adelbert Ames, Governor as aforesaid, did, then and there, commit, and was guilty of, a high misdemeanor in office.

Article XIX.

That on the 3d day of December, A.D. 1874 (one thousand eight hundred and seventy-four), Adelbert Ames, Governor of the State of Mississippi, unmindful of the high duties of his office, the obligations of his oath of office, and the Constitution and laws of said State, and intending to stir up strife between the white and colored people of said State, and especially the white and colored people of the county of Warren, in said State, and to provoke them to wrath and violence, did, as Governor aforesaid, on the day and year aforesaid, in the county of Hinds, and State aforesaid, corruptly and unlawfully counsel and advise one Peter Crosby to organize, without authority of law, an armed body of men in said county of Warren, to forcibly take possession of the office of sheriff of said county, which said unlawful counsel and advice was acted on by said Peter Crosby, afterwards, to-wit: on the seventh day of December A.D. 1874 (one thousand eight hundred and seventy-four) in said county of Warren, in pursuance of said counsel and advice so unlawfully and corruptly given by said Adelbert Ames, Governor as aforesaid, did unlawfully organize a body of armed men in said county of Warren, and by said means did then and there attempt to take possession, by force and violence, of the office of sheriff of said county of Warren, which said unlawful and armed organization of men, organized as aforesaid, by the unlawful and corrupt advice of the said Adelbert Ames, Governor as aforesaid, invited and brought about riot, bloodshed and death among the people of said county of Warren; and, he, the said Adelbert Ames, Governor as aforesaid, at the time he gave such unlawful and corrupt counsel and advice, well knew that if said counsel and advice was acted on and carried out by the said Peter Crosby, that the same would result in riot, bloodshed and death to many of the people of said county of Warren; whereby the said Adelbert Ames, Governor as aforesaid, did, then and there, and in the way and manner, and by the means aforesaid, commit, and was guilty of, a high crime in office.

Article XX.

That Adelbert Ames, Governor of the State of Mississippi, unmindful of the high duties of his office, the obligations of his oath of office, and the Constitution and laws of said State, contriving and intending to stir up strife between the white and colored citizens of said State, and especially between the white and colored citizens of the county of Warren, in said State, and to procure the killing and shedding of blood of some of the colored citizens of said county, for corrupt and partisan purposes, did, on the 3d day of December, A.D. 1874 (one thousand eight hundred and seventy-four), in the county of Hinds, in said State, corruptly and unlawfully advise one Peter Crosby to forcibly take possession of the office of sheriff of said county of Warren.

And the said Peter Crosby afterwards, to-wit: on the 7th day of December 1874 (one thousand eight hundred and seventy-four), in said county of Warren, in pursuance of said advice, so unlawfully and corruptly given by said Adelbert Ames, Governor as aforesaid, did unlawfully organize a body of armed men in said county of Warren, and with said body of armed men, unlawfully did then and there attempt by force and violence to take possession of the office of sheriff of said county, and said attempt did then and there result in an armed conflict between the citizens of said county of Warren, and the bloodshed and death of many of the colored citizens of said county.

And the said Adelbert Ames, Governor as aforesaid, well knew at the time he gave said advice to said Peter Crosby, that if the said Peter Crosby acted thereon and in accordance therewith, that the same would probably result in bloodshed and death to many of the colored citizens of said county, as he, the said Adelbert Ames, designed and intended it should do, for corrupt and partisan purposes; whereby the said Adelbert Ames, Governor as aforesaid, did, then and there, and in the way and manner, and by the means aforesaid, commit, and was guilty of, a high crime in office.

Article XXI.

That Adelbert Ames, Governor of the State of Mississippi, unmindful of the duties of his office, the obligations of his oath of office and the constitution and laws of said State, on the 3d day of December, A.D. 1874 (one thousand eight hundred and seventy-four), in the county of Hinds, in said State, did unlawfully and corruptly incite, provoke, counsel, order and command one Peter Crosby, then and there seeking counsel of him, the said Adelbert Ames, Governor as aforesaid (the said Peter Crosby then and there claiming that he was the sheriff of the county of Warren, in said State), to return to the county of Warren and city of Vicksburg, and assuming to himself the authority and duties of said office, to summon an armed body of men to possess himself of the office, books, papers, charge and control of the court house and jail, and all the actual insignia of the said office, against any opposing authority, in the actual peaceable possession of said office, and its outward insignia, when the question of the right of said Peter Crosby to said office, and the duties incident to it was a question which it was the duty of the said Peter Crosby to submit to the decision of the courts, and which it was the duty of the said Adelbert Ames, Governor as aforesaid, to have advised the said Peter Crosby so to submit the same to the courts of the said county of Warren, which were then and there open to the said Peter Crosby for such redress as under the laws of the land he was entitled to; yet the said Adelbert Ames, Governor as aforesaid, unmindful as aforesaid of the high duties of his office, the obligation of his oath of office, and the Constitution and laws of said State, and intending to stir up strife between the white and colored citizens of said State, and especially between the white and colored citizens of said county of Warren, and to provoke them to violence, did then and there, as Governor as aforesaid, corruptly and unlawfully advise the said Peter

Crosby to forcibly take possession of the said office of sheriff of said county; and that he, the said Peter Crosby, afterwards, to-wit: on the 7th day of December, A.D. 1874 (one thousand eight hundred and seventy-four), in pursuance of said advice so corruptly and unlawfully given by the said Adelbert Ames, Governor as aforesaid, did unlawfully organize a body of armed men in said county of Warren, and with said body of armed men did then and there attempt, by force and violence, to take possession of said office of sheriff of said county of Warren, and which attempt resulted in riot, bloodshed and death among and to many of the citizens of said county of Warren.

And the said Adelbert Ames, Governor as aforesaid, well knew at the time he gave said unlawful advice to the said Peter Crosby, that if the said Peter Crosby acted thereon and in accordance therewith, that the same would probably result in riot, bloodshed and death to many of the citizens of said county of Warren; whereby the said Adelbert Ames, Governor as aforesaid, did, then and there, and in the way and manner, and by the means aforesaid, commit, and was guilty of, a high crime in office, in violation of his oath of office, and against the peace and dignity of the State of Mississippi.

And the House of Representatives, by protestation, saving to themselves the liberty of exhibiting at any time hereafter any further articles, or other accusation or impeachment against the said Adelbert Ames, Governor of the State of Mississippi, and also of replying to his answers which he shall make unto the articles herein preferred against him, and of offering proof to the same and every part thereof; and to all and every other article, accusation or impeachment which shall be exhibited by them, as the case shall require, do demand that the said Adelbert Ames may be put to answer the high crimes and misdemeanors in office herein charged against him; and that such proceedings, examinations, trials and judgments may be thereupon had and given as may be agreeable to law and justice.

Which were adopted, by the following vote:

Yeas—Messrs. Aldrich, Amacker, Bailey, Baker, Barksdale, Bassett, Bean, Bell, Blount, Bridges, Byrd of Franklin, Bird of Lawrence, Campbell, Carter of Holmes, Causey, Clay, Clifton, Dabney, Dyer, Ervin, Fairly, Featherston, Fortune, Garrett, Bayden, Gibson, Gillis, Guyton, Hall, Hebron, Hicks, Horton, Huddleston, Hudson, Jagers, Jayne, Johnston of Winston, Lester, Massingale, Meade, Muldrow, McCargo, McCormick, McInnis, McNair, McLaurin of Jasper, McLaurin of Smith, McWhorter, Neilson, Nichols, Parker, Pennington, Percy,

Pound, Powell, Reynolds, Rogers, Rowan, Saunders, Shands, Spight, Stebbins, Sykes, Tison, Troup, Tucker, Turley, Wilkinson, Vaiden, Vaughan, and Yellowley—71.

Nays—Messrs. Hussey, Jacobs, Jenkins, Mallory, Millsaps, Monroe, McNeese, Overton, and Parsons—8.

Absent and not voting—Messrs. Boyd, Brown, Carter of Warren, Cochran, Crossland, Cessor, Chiles, Crum, Dear, Denson, Drake, Edwards, Floyd, Gowan, Guthrie, Harper, Hogan, Jarnagin, Johns, Johnson of Itawamba, Jones of Hinds, Jones of Issaquena, Leigh, Miller, Riley, Sanderlin, Shattuck, Shelby, Shrock, Southworth, Trice, Watkins, Warren, White, Young, and Mr. Speaker—37.

Mr. Percy offered the following resolution, which was adopted:

Resolved, That the Clerk of this House inform the Senate that this House has adopted specific Articles of Impeachment against Adelbert Ames, Governor of the State of Mississippi, and that the Managers appointed by the House, W. S. Featherston, H. L. Muldrow, W. A. Percy, W. F. Tucker, W. R. Barksdale, and Thomas Spight are ready to lay the same before the Senate, at such time as may suit its convenience.

WASHINGTON, *March* 3, 1876

DEAR BLANCHE: Gen'l. Ames' letter came this morning. Your Father is in Boston. I have forwarded the letter to him. Before he left he said he would write to Gen. Ames. I suppose he did so, and that in his letter he gave a good deal of advice as to what course to pursue.

It was mentioned, among other things, that there should be a Democratic lawyer besides Mr. Durant. By this time Durant is already there. Is there no good Democratic lawyer that you know in Mississippi, and can trust in the case? I suppose a man on the Democratic side would have rather more weight with a Democratic Senate. No doubt you have thought of this? And Gen. Ames may have provided for it, or Mr. Durant may have carried instructions to that effect from your Father. I only make a note of this that nothing may be left undone. I do not know that your Father could do anything further if he were here. But it is rather vexatious that whenever a matter comes up that I am deeply interested in, he is almost sure to be away.

I wrote you of some movements to be made in two former letters. Now I have no further knowledge and no means to gain any. Therefore, as much in the dark as you will be with my two former letters, in which I could give you no clearer knowledge than what I sent, rely on your own ability. I think it will be equal to the occasion, and whatever the result, be satisfied that you have done your best. You are both able, and I think Gen. Ames understands the art of fighting as well as any other man. For my own part I shall be best satisfied when I see you all home.—I am tired of living alone and want company. So fight your battle thoroughly and leave triumphantly, whichever way it goes. Spofford has been sick for a week, so I hadn't even him to counsel with.

Dearest love to Gen. Ames, the children and yourself, from your *Most affectionate* MOTHER

LOWELL, *March* 7, 1876

DEAR MOTHER: Today I am fairly installed as treasurer of the Cartridge Company, and have signed my name as such for the first time.

I wish you could have been here yesterday and today to enjoy the fine weather we are having. It is so warm that it seems impossible that there should be another cold snap, but I suppose we must expect one.

Last night Nina and I went to a musical at Mrs. Kittredge's. The playing lasted so long that everybody was tired of it and at the *end* of the last piece the applause was loud and joyful. After that, dancing. I did not dance much, as I felt tired and the room was crowded. I think everybody had a good time, however.

I saw Mr. Buttrick this morning as I was driving down Central Street. He said he saw you a day or two ago and you did not seem very well. I know you must be worrying about two things, your throat and Gen. Ames' impeachment. I wish you were at home, as I think you are more cheerful here than in Washington. Anyway, don't worry any more than you can help, as it can do no good, and does do harm because if you are ill, Blanche will have to leave Gen. Ames to fight it out alone. I have just seen Mr. Farrington, who thinks you are feeling a little better than you were a short time ago. He said he tried to persuade you to come home with him. I wish you had, and I would have gone on and closed the house. How long do you intend to remain in Washington? Do you know what Father's plans are as to going West? He was here Sunday, stopped with Aunt Lauretta, but I did not think to ask him about that. I believe he intends to leave Boston Thursday night.

Don't you try to do any packing or putting the house in

order. Send for me and I will start immediately. Love for yourself and Hattie. PAUL

JACKSON, *March* 14, 1876

DEAR MOTHER: I have delayed writing you from day to day in order to give you some decisive information about impeachment. The house has at last presented the articles—twenty-one in number, which Gen'l. Ames will today send to Father. They are substantially the same as those reported by the Committee, and as Mr. Durant says, there is nothing in them that reflects in the least upon Gen. Ames' honor or integrity as a man. As they are the result of two months of most careful examination of all acts, not only of Gen'l. Ames' gubernatorial term, but extending back over the five years previous, we should most certainly regard them as the most complimentary report it would be possible to make. Perhaps it would be well, if any notice is made in the papers, to insert something of this idea.

Davis, the Lieut. Gov. has been found guilty, as you have heard by telegraph. The vote was 32 to 4. Some of the Republicans voted against him. Six, including one colored Senator.

Gen'l. Ames does not count upon more than ten or eleven favorable votes. This number comprises all the Republicans. The Democrats will, without doubt, throw a strict party vote, at least this is the impression.

Gen'l. Ames had a letter from our Deer Island friend, urging the retention of Gen. Walthall as counsel. He feels that it would be worse than useless. Of course Gen. Walthall is recommended by Lamar. The warmest friends of Lamar here are the most violent for impeachment—and Mr. Lamar is a double dealer on whom no dependence can be placed, as it is well known that in all matters political he does not hesitate to be false. When in Jackson he made a speech urging on impeachment. Is it likely that such a person will make any efforts to retard it? Of course he talks smoothly to Mr. S— and is full of promises and suggestions. It is likely that he wishes some friend of his engaged as counsel. Times are hard in Mississippi. If he really wishes to be of service, let him call off the dogs—which he can easily do, as they are trained to hound or retreat at the word of command.

It is quite possible that Black might be useful, not so much on account of his legal ability—reason and law will have but little attention in the coming trial—but if he were willing to use his influence politically and instruct these people that they are injuring themselves and producing a bad effect in the North, it might do some good, although a very slender straw to cling to.

The Democrats at Washington are well informed as to proceedings here. They may not care to appear so.—Gen'l. Ames will not engage Walthall unless further advised.

I did not answer your telegram, as each hour we were expecting the report of the House, but it was not made until last night. They will carry the articles to the Senate today and I will telegraph you as soon as we know when the trial is to begin. The impeachment of Cardoza, the Superintendent of Education, is being conducted at present. You can judge that there is to be a clean sweep and all Republicans must leave. When Gen. Ames is impeached, the last state officer will be removed, and all the branches of the government will be controlled by Democrats. Is it likely then that the ability or influence of Mr. Walthall will be sufficient to interfere with a so much to be desired result?

All here are well, and contentedly awaiting developments of which I will keep you informed. My mind is so much relieved about your throat, Mother, that other matters seem of very small account. I wish you would come South, however. Don't you think the summer warmth would agree with you?

Kisses for you and Father.

Your affectionate daughter, BLANCHE

WASHINGTON, *March* 17, 1876

DEAR BLANCHE: I send you this note simply to take away all care and anxiety on my account. I have called in Dr. Johnson once or twice since we came to Washington. The first time I was really run down from putting the house in order and having a large family while doing it, also some cares and troubles that belong to me. Since then I have been better, but I suppose nervous, for the two or three times the doctor has been here he has told me so, and that there was nothing serious the matter with me. He said he would bring a doctor to examine my throat, to put it beyond all doubt. He came with his doctor (who makes it a specialty) today. The doctor has examined thoroughly, and says there is nothing the matter but a slight inflammation, which will probably yield as the warm weather advances, that the fulness in my throat that disturbs me at times so much is but a nervous affection, and that I am in no danger of losing my breath. They caution me to be careful to take no cold, but further than that seem to think the trouble of no great moment. I write this at once, for I am afraid you have been worried, and you have enough of that at present. I do not think I can visit you—the effort is too great.

A letter came from you this morning. It is a splendid one. You write well and ably—you are a strong woman, and can meet the ills of life or the splendors with equanimity—that is well.

Your Father is still away. I forwarded Gen. Ames' letter, and will attend to anything you or he send. I am glad that you intend to come home before going to Northfield. I think my family is too far separated, it seems to leave me by myself.

I hope you will find Durant able in your case.

Dearest love to you all, from

Your most affectionate MOTHER

JACKSON, *March* 21, 1876

DEAR MOTHER: Mr. Durant replies to the impeachment charges tomorrow, and the trial begins a week from tomorrow. There is but little suspense, as we can anticipate but one result —conviction. I suppose Father will send Black, if he can come. There may be some satisfaction in feeling that nothing has been neglected. Gen'l. Ames telegraphed Father last week when the trial was to take place, in order that he might know what time to send Black—also asked Father what was done "about the witness as in Johnson's case." The legislature has been getting up a bill to compel Gen'l. Ames to pay the fees of all witnesses called on his side—and it was in reference to this that he desired information in the Johnson case. No answer has yet been received to the telegram.

The Lieutenant Governor resigned last week and Gen'l. Ames has been most urgently solicited to fill the vacancy. The Attorney General gave a written opinion that he had such a power of appointment. Mr. Durant said that such was not the intention of the constitution. But the legislature evidently held the same opinion as the Attorney General, for it passed a bill a few days ago depriving the Executive of the power to fill such vacancy. The bill has now become a law by limitation. Gen'l. Ames would not veto as it would be passed over his veto, and he refused to make the appointment on the ground that the Supreme Court would decide against his power to appoint and that the Legislature would pass an act providing for a special election. "But" it was urged "if you appoint a Lieutenant Governor the impeachment will be deferred until such an election can be held, and then you can resign, and thus allow your Lieutenant Governor to take your place."

That is to say, the end of the matter was to be that Gen'l. Ames should make a sacrifice of himself for the good of the party, and *resign under charges*. This he declined to do. The wing of the Republican Party urging it was composed almost exclusively of men who have not been on speaking terms with him, and who by doing all in their power to pull him down and destroy his influence, have ruined the Republican Party in Mississippi and made impeachment possible. It is proposed to hurry through the impeachment very fast. The Senate will hold evening sessions until eleven o'clock. I should think Mr. Durant would find it rather heavy work to conduct the case alone.

The weather has been very cold for the last few days. This morning the ice was half an inch thick. The children have escaped with the exception of slight colds in the head. I have not been so fortunate, for two days my throat had a large lump in it, and my voice was almost gone. Mr. Durant prescribed a gargle of wood soot, Mr. Clancey a wet towel. I tried both remedies, and am now quite well. If it had continued I would have believed that I had your trouble, owing to the sound of the voice and location of the cold.

Write as often as you can. It is very pleasant to hear from home. Love for Hattie and tell her Sarah is growing fat and coarse. Kisses for you and Father. I would like very much to have you see this place before we leave it for good.

Your affectionate daughter, BLANCHE

WASHINGTON, *March* 25, 1876

MY DEAR GEN. AMES: Pryor[1] started for Jackson, as you have been informed by telegraph, full of faith, hope, earnestness and zeal in your defense. You will like him immensely. He will do you good service and if any man can save you he will. I know of no two men who are more likely to come to the most full and thorough concord in managing a case than Durant and Pryor, because both will look more to the interests of their client than any little question of professional precedent and etiquette. I have been thinking about the management

[1] Roger Atkinson Pryor, Democrat from Virginia. At the outbreak of the Civil War, he was a Colonel in the Confederate Army, was made a Brigadier General in 1862. He resigned, entered the Army again as a private, and was captured and imprisoned at Petersburg until the end of the war. Afterwards he practiced law in New York.

of the case. Durant now has been with you nearly three weeks making preparations, and so far as he knows, to play a lone hand, to borrow a metaphor from another profession. Now, Pryor comes down there new to the matter. Unless Mr. Durant has some objections which I don't think he will have, I would suggest that Pryor make the closing argument because it will take him through the case to get ready, whereas Durant is more than ready if he has, as he always does, bestowed that careful thought that I know he has given to it. Now, Durant is a more methodical and unimpassioned speaker than Pryor, and will put down the propositions of law and fact more ably after his thorough preparation than Pryor could do without preparation, and I think than Pryor would be inclined to do. As you expect Pryor to try to move the Democrats, I think he had better have the last word, not by any means that I have more faith in him than I have in Durant, but because I believe that that is the best way for that team to pull in the harness. If you think best you may show Durant this letter, because I am certain that he will gather from it clearly my idea of the condition of things, and he will know that I do not mean to advise any interference in a matter of talking. If he is the older lawyer and I believe him to be, he has the right to close. In the Johnson impeachment case I chose the opening argument, and I do not believe anybody ever read the closing argument, while over one hundred thousand of the opening argument were called for, and I suppose were read, although I pity the readers.

Tell Blanche that her mother is a little better, and is gaining strength, and that her trouble is partly nervousness, for she has really fretted a great deal over you and yours, sometimes almost fretting me out of patience, and that you know is very difficult. Moulton is here while I am dictating this letter and interrupting me, so that if I do not write as connectedly as I can, you must lay it to him. He begs to be remembered to you all and especially to Butler, whose head he will bump against his own. I am,

Yours very truly, BENJ. F. BUTLER

Additional Articles

House of Representatives
March 25, 1876

Mr. Percy, on behalf of the Managers of the Impeachment of Governor Ames, offered the following resolution:

Resolved, That the additional Articles of Impeachment against Adelbert Ames, Governor of the State of Mississippi, charging said Adelbert Ames with corruption and an abuse of the pardoning power, in the matter of the pardon of Alexander Smith, convicted of the crime of rape, and numbered twenty-two and twenty-three, offered by the Managers, be and the same are hereby adopted, and said Managers are hereby directed to prefer the same at the bar of the Senate.

Resolved further, That the Clerk of this House be and he is hereby instructed to inform the Senate of the passage of this resolution, and Articles of Impeachment.

Article XXII.

That Adelbert Ames, Governor of the State of Mississippi, unmindful of the duties of his office, the obligations of his oath of office, and the constitution and laws of said State, in consideration of a large sum of money, to-wit: the sum of twenty-eight hundred dollars, to be paid by one Alexander Smith to one William Noonan, and of the further sum of two hundred dollars to be paid by said Alexander Smith to one Fred. Parsons, and which said several sums of money, were in consideration of the pardon hereinafter set forth, so paid by said Smith, and received by Noonan and Parsons respectively, did, at Jackson, in said State, on the 11th day of March, A.D. 1876, unlawfully, corruptly, and feloniously grant and cause to be issued and delivered to said Alexander Smith, then, and at that time, imprisoned in the Penitentiary of said State, under a judgement and sentence of the Circuit Court of Chickasaw county, in said State, rendered upon the 8th day of April, A.D. 1873, by which said Smith was sentenced to be imprisoned in said Penitentiary, upon an indictment charging him with having committed a crime of rape upon the person of one ———, a female child, under the age of ten years, an Executive pardon, under the Great Seal of said State, by means of which said pardon, the said Alexander Smith was enlarged and set at liberty; whereby the said Adelbert Ames, Governor of the State of Mississippi, did, then and there, commit, and was guilty of, a high crime in office.

Article XXIII.

That Adelbert Ames, Governor of the State of Mississippi, unmindful of the duties of his office, and of the obligations of his oath of office, and of the constitution and laws of said State, at Jackson, in said State, on the 11th day of March.

A.D. 1876, did grossly, willfully, and wickedly abuse and pervert the power and discretion of pardoning criminals, vested in him by the constitution of said State, in this, that the said Adelbert Ames, Governor aforesaid, did, on said 11th of March, A.D. 1876, grant, and cause to be issued and delivered to one Alexander Smith, then and at that time imprisoned for and during the term of his natural life in the Penitentiary of said State, under judgment and sentence of the Circuit Court of Chickasaw county, in said State, rendered on the 8th day of April, A.D. 1873, upon an indictment charging said Smith with having committed the crime of rape upon one ———, a female child under the age of ten years, an Executive pardon, under the Great Seal of said State, by virtue whereof said Smith was enlarged and set at liberty; which said pardon, so granted and caused to be issued and delivered by the said Adelbert Ames, Governor as aforesaid, upon the petition of a few of his, the said Adelbert Ames' personal friends, who did not pretend any personal knowledge of the facts surrounding the commission of said crime, and the conviction therefor, and were residents of a totally different and widely distant part of the State; and which said petition states only one substantial reason for such exercise of Executive clemency, and that statement was known by said Adelbert Ames to be absolutely false; and, at the time of granting such pardon, said Adelbert Ames had, within his knowledge and possession, communicated to him by the Judge of said Circuit Court, and the District Attorney who prosecuted said indictment, the evidence adduced upon the trial of said Smith, clearly and indisputably establishing his guilt of the revolting crime with which he was charged, of which he was convicted, and for which he had been imprisoned.

Whereby the said Adelbert Ames did, then and there, commit, and was guilty of, a high misdemeanor in office.

Which were adopted.

JACKSON, *March* 26, 1876

DEAR MOTHER: I have not had a letter from you this week, but Gen'l. Pryor arrived this morning and says that he spent last Wednesday with you, and that you seemed in fine health. I asked about the hoarseness and he said it was scarcely perceptible, a little huskiness perhaps but nothing which interfered with perfect enunciation.

Gen'l. Ames desires me to have you ask Father if some

arrangement cannot be made with the New York *Herald* or some other paper to publish telegrams. Mr. Clancy knows not what to do, as he has not heard what arrangements have been made. Gen'l. Pryor is of the opinion that if the trial could be delayed and the facts telegraphed to and commented upon by the New York and Northern papers, that such an expression of opinion would have its effect upon the Democrats of this state and would influence the result of the trial. Mr. Durant, I think, is not of his opinion, and I am sure it is foolish to expect the people of Mississippi to care more for the opinion of the North than the members of the House of Representatives, and that body has not been very politic or careful.

Two additional articles have been presented against Gen'l. Ames. Their purport is to charge him with taking a bribe for granting a pardon. The only fact in the case is that a pardon was granted to a man whom all who knew the merits of the case say was not deserving of confinement or punishment. The trial was to have commenced next Tuesday—but Mr. Durant will ask for postponement for a day or two in order to attend to these two new articles.

You must not have any hope of a favorable termination of this trial. We can expect but one result,—Mr. Durant says, "If it is to be a *trial*, I know the result, and if it is not to be a trial I know the result." The question therefore is whether it is to be a trial or not. That is to say, if the Senate will listen to the case and vote conscientiously there is no doubt but that Gen'l. Ames will be acquitted. But if they are determined to get rid of him, in spite of law and justice, of course they have the votes, and can do it.

We are having a delightful spring, and all are in good health except Gen'l. Ames. He has not been quite well. I think these matters weigh upon him. It is natural that they should.

Mr. Durant, Gen'l. Pryor and Mr. Clancy are stopping with us. Our meals still come from the restaurant, and we have better variety and nicer meals than I could get at the market. I should be greatly troubled to supply the table if the cooking were done at home. Mr. Durant is very fond of sponge cake. Every other day it is necessary to cook or bake new. This, with coffee, and tea, comprises all the cooking done at home.

Write as often as you can. News from home is pleasant.

Love for Father, and a kiss for yourself from

Your affectionate daughter, BLANCHE

WASHINGTON, *March* 27, 1876

DEAR BLANCHE: We have all your letters, yours, Gen. Ames', two of Mr. Durant's. The trial begins next Monday. Your Father has telegraphed to Mr. Pryor to start at once, and act as counsel for Gen. Ames. We were in some doubt, but have finally come to Gen. Ames' view of the case. Your Father went to see Judge Black, to see if he would go, and to get his *real* inside view of the situation down there. Mr. Butler thinks he has got it. Judge Black cannot go, but approves of Pryor's going. Mr. Pryor is a very keen, incisive lawyer. Your Father thinks him very able.—Mr. Spofford is sick, and unable to go out, or he would have seen Judge Black instead of your Father, which would have been a mistake. You have now two able lawyers, his cause will be fully heard, however the vote may go. That is a satisfaction. It will give you some care to take charge of these gentlemen, but you are at work in a good cause.

We shall watch this case with great interest. Gen. Pryor will be here tomorrow on his way to Mississippi. If the case goes against Gen. Ames, it will be in defiance of law and justice. You will have at least two good witnesses to that fact, Durant and Pryor. Take it calmly in any event, but I need not counsel that. You are both calm and equable. I mean yourself and Gen. Ames. You will feel, as we do, that all has been done that could be accomplished, and more than all that, that in all respects you have acted rightly.

Dearest love to Gen. Ames, the children, and yourself from

Your most affectionate MOTHER

Resignation

House of Representatives
March 29, 1876

Mr. Featherston presented the following communication and resolutions:

Executive Mansion, Jackson, March 28, 1876

Messrs. DURANT & PRYOR, *Jackson, Miss.*

Gentlemen: In reply to your suggestion, I beg to say that, in consequence of the election of last November, I found myself confronted with a hostile Legislature, and embarrassed and baffled in my endeavors to carry out my plans for the welfare of the State, and of my party.

I had resolved, therefore, to resign my office as Governor

of the State of Mississippi; but meanwhile proceedings of Impeachment were instituted against me, and of course, I could not, and would not retire from my position, under the imputation of any charge affecting my honor or integrity.

For the reasons indicated, I still desire to escape burdens which are compensated by no possibility of public usefulness; and if the Articles of Impeachment presented against me were not pending, and the proceedings were dismissed, I should feel at liberty to carry out my desire, and purpose of resignation.

I am very truly yours,

(signed) Adelbert Ames

Whereas, Assurance has been received by the House of Representatives of the State of Mississippi, that Adelbert Ames, Governor of said State, but for the pendency against him of Articles of Impeachment, exhibited by the House of Representatives, would have resigned his office of Governor, and will now do so, as the Managers are informed by a letter addressed by said Governor Ames, to his Counsel, Messrs. Durant and Pryor, read to said House, on a resolution adopted, directing its Managers to dismiss said proceeding; now, therefore

Be it resolved by the House of Representatives of the State of Mississippi, That the Managers on the part of this House, in matter of Impeachment of Adelbert Ames, Governor of said State, be and they hereby are directed to dismiss the said Articles against the said Adelbert Ames, Governor as aforesaid, heretofore exhibited by them against him at the bar of the Senate.

Which were adopted.

Extract from the *Proceedings in Senate*, sitting as a *Court of Impeachment.*

Wednesday, March 29, 1876

Mr. Reynolds offered the following order:

Ordered, That the Articles of Impeachment, heretofore preferred by the House of Representatives against His Excellency, Adelbert Ames, be and the same are hereby dismissed, in pursuance of the request of the House of Representatives, this day presented by the Managers in their behalf.

Which was adopted.

WASHINGTON, *April* 1, 1876

MY DEAR AMES: We have got telegraphic notice of what has happened in Mississippi. You will see also that we have just got through the Committee on Investigation by the same mode of information. I have been expecting Durant home. I forbear even attempting an opinion of the wisdom of what has been done, although I am bound to suppose it wise when engineered by gentlemen in whom I have so much confidence, aided by your own good judgment, as Messrs. Pryor and Durant. But I will not conceal from you that the matter strikes the public mind unfavorably. I will, however, keep my own mind open until I hear the circumstances. Tell Blanche that I start for home on Monday morning, April 3, breaking up housekeeping here, with her mother. She goes home but the house will be open a little while. My stay there with her will be determined by her state of health, although I have got very pressing matters to call me here, so that if she is able to have me come away I shall come. Meanwhile, she intends to have some operation upon her throat, if so advised by her physician, Dr. Cabot, whom we shall visit in Boston on our way home. Now, don't be unnecessarily alarmed at this, but yet I do not conceal from you that Mrs. Butler would be exceedingly gratified if Blanche could be with her and relieve her from the care of the household during this painful and perhaps dangerous operation. So that if Blanche can come home and bring the children, I would not wait for warmer weather. If the exigencies of your position, of which of course I know nothing, require you to stay in Mississippi for the purpose of adjusting your affairs there, perhaps Parker would have no objection to coming home with Blanche. Everything goes well with me except the one thing, and that is Sarah's health, and the thought of her suffering and possible danger makes everything bad. We got a letter from Ben yesterday. He is getting along very well. Gen. Michie was here and insists still, which I do not believe, that Ben will graduate in the first third of his class. Paul has taken to business very kindly and is in charge of the Cartridge factory. Hattie goes home with us. Much love to the children. Butler will be glad to come home and see Gran. For myself I send no love to either of you; you both know you have that now. Mr. Moulton who is here staying for a few days begs to be remembered in the kindest manner to all, and especially to be recalled to the mind of his pet Butler. *Yours truly*, FATHER

NEW ORLEANS, *April 2*, 1876

DEAR MOTHER: By the heading of my letter you will see that we are visiting Aunt Maria.

Long ere this you have heard the result of the impeachment. Mr. Durant has, of course, seen Father and given him all the particulars much more clearly than I can write them. Therefore I will not make any attempt to go over the whole matter again, but I will make a record of a fact of which Gen'l. Pryor did not see fit to inform Mr. Durant, i.e.—that I was the one to suggest a compromise with the Democrats, and induced Gen'l. Ames to consult Pryor and Durant. He spoke to Pryor first, as he was a Democrat, and would have to be the negotiator, and Pryor objected to consulting Durant until after he (Pryor) had sounded the Democratic leaders on the subject. Finding them most favorably disposed, he consulted with Durant, but claimed that the plan was entirely original with him, which of course rendered it impossible for us to undeceive Mr. Durant, who if he should know all the circumstances might possibly feel that he had not been openly dealt with. I do not know Pryor's object, and now it is of very little importance, except that as I feel a little self-congratulatory I want to give you the facts. Mr. Durant is a very pleasant gentleman, and I like him very much. So also Mr. Pryor, although we did not have so long a time in which to study his characteristics.

Tomorrow we are going over to Bay St. Louis to put some things in order, and the first of the week following start for Minnesota, and intend to be in Lowell the middle of June.

Aunt Lottie writes Aunt Maria that you are expected in Lowell. Now, Mother, it is not possible that you intend to go to that cold climate at this season. The temperature in Washington is much more favorable. Have you any idea of having your throat tampered with? I insist that you must not. Leave it alone until you have tried the effect of the summer upon it, and on no account think of such a thing unless I am with you. I cannot really think you have any intention of it, but if you have I want you to telegraph me *at once* upon receipt of this in order that I may receive it before starting North and shape my course to Massachusetts instead of Minnesota.

Now deal frankly with me in this Mother, for I must be with you, although I am opposed to all action of this kind. The children are well and quite excited with the prospect of travelling.

Love and kisses for Father and yourself.

Your affectionate daughter, BLANCHE

Mrs. Butler was admitted to the Massachusetts General Hospital at Boston on April 6th, 1876. Dr. Knight and Dr. Cabot de-

cided on examination that the hard lump on the front of her neck which had seriously interfered with her breathing, was a malignant growth of such a nature that they abandoned the attempt to remove it. Thyrotomy was decided on. This failed and an incision was made below the thyroid and the trachea opened. Mrs. Butler was more comfortable the next day but died quietly on April 8th, at the age of fifty eight.

General and Mrs. Ames were notified by telegram as they were on their way from Mississippi to Northfield, Minnesota. They arrived in Lowell in time for the funeral.

WASHINGTON, D.C., *April 12*, 1876

MY DEAR BLANCHE: I know how desolate the house will seem when you wake up on Friday, and I feel as if I must write you, if only to take up your attention a few moments. I wanted to write you many times in the winter, and tell you I feared your Mother was a great deal worse than she thought she was; but I didn't know but it might be merely my fancy, and I should be alarming you for nothing, and it seemed like an intrusion anyway.

She gave me many of your letters to read, and was so proud of them—especially of one that she brought down here for Dick to see in one of his illnesses, written, I believe, the first week in March. She was wrapped up in you,—you satisfied her ambitions and affection, you were all she wanted you to be. I often thought few mothers had such another self in a child as she seemed to have in you,—perfect gratification; and she seemed too, to live her youth over again in yours. The last time I saw her, she said she longed to have you at home again, to take all the housekeeping on your hands, and let her rest. It startled me, though I did not let her see it, for I felt as if her strength must be greatly less, for her to be willing to resign care, or to put it upon you.

She was much excited by the Mississippi matters, and came down here almost every morning to see Dick about them, in your father's absence, and talked of nothing else for hours. I think your father feared it would worry her, but it really seemed to do her good, by taking her mind off herself. She spoke frequently of the comfort she expected to have with you next summer, of the possibility of your and her taking the children to Bay View if the yacht went to the Centennial, of the happiness the little children gave her, and of how she meant that you should always have the opportunity to develop your genius for painting, irrespective of children or care.

Except for the pathetic hoarseness all winter, you would seldom have known that anything ailed her; her cheeks were rosy, and her movements strong and rapid; and when Dr. Johnson said nothing *did* ail her but nervousness, she said then she should think of it no more, for she was not one to give way to nervousness. She told me she never had one moment's pain with her trouble, and would not know anything was the matter till she spoke, except for the occasional attacks—and that is a great deal to be glad of. Of course, she thought of *possibilities* for she and Dick talked a great deal about the future, and she didn't seem to regard it unpleasantly; Dick thought he would go before her, and she appeared to think so too, often speaking with me of the critical state in which he has been all winter; but I doubt if she had a suspicion of the truth concerning herself; if she had I feel as though she would have *hinted* here, she really talked so freely with me about her thoughts and feelings, and so did I with her, and it closes up a great side in my life.

She was interested in all that went on this winter; sometimes in a serious and reflective mood, sometimes full of gayety, arch and laughing, and in happy spirits. She was in those happy spirits the last day I was with her, natural sweet spirits—she had dismissed anxiety till she should see Dr. Cabot. I wanted then to offer to go and be with her during any operation, but feared it might embarrass her to decline if she preferred not to have me, I also disliked to remind her of the *possibility* of an operation. I meant, though, to see her again, and venture it, but Dick was taken sick, and I was so anxious—for it was his ninth attack this winter, and he has not yet sat up all day—that I did not. It is a great loss to him—he was very fond of her; indeed everybody was that knew her, she was so many-sided, with something in her that responded to all; she spent her life trying to make others happy.

I can't think of what your father must suffer—for nobody ever lost such a wife before—such women are only made once in a while. She was so entirely on the scale of heroic times, so tender and womanly on one side, with such courage and power and will on the other, such large and acute perceptions, such quickness and such sagacity. How brilliant and receptive she was, and how sweet and stately her manners were, like those of some uncrowned queen. I used to think that Portia, the wife of Brutus, might have been like her.

It is impossible that this magnificence of nature can have closed on nothingness; the economy of the universe where nothing else is wasted, could not allow it here. I am *sure* that she lives still, in some larger freedom, some great flight,—you know she loved solitude sometimes, and had a sort of intimate delight in nature; and more than once, in speaking of death, she said that the sense of timid loneliness that others experience at the thought, was unknown to her, she felt strong enough to *go alone*, and if it were not for leaving those she loved there would be a wild enjoyment in the thought. But those she loved, she loved intensely,—her husband and her children.

I don't know why I write this way,—of course you know it all, and much more, for I doubt if any daughter ever had such an intimate personal friend and companion in a mother. I don't attempt to console you, for consolation is impossible. Time makes the cruel thing easier to bear, but the sore spot is always there. It never seems to me that the dead are to be pitied—they are through with trouble, they "rest from their labors,"—but those who remain, and I know how to pity you, for *my* loss helps me to see how *infinite* yours is.

You must not think of her as *dead*, death never came near so great and beautiful a being. She is a free spirit floating outside the narrow limits of our grosser sense,—unless the world is all a hollow mockery you will have her again. Nevertheless, that knowledge will not fill the vacant place, the daily want, and I can't tell you how sorry I am for you, and for you all, and poor little Hatty.

Dick sends you his warmest love and sympathy,—and I am always *Your loving friend*, HARRIET P. SPOFFORD

Excerpt from *Poems* by Harriet Prescott Spofford:

Sarah Hildreth Butler

Do you remember, O you wondrous woman,
In those dim regions where you wander now,—
You, who were always something more than human,
With the large light upon your lofty brow,—
Do you remember all the hours we spent,
All the gay mornings when the tremulous hazes
Swathed the two silver rivers, and the heights
Of pillared Arlington shone through their mazes?

I seem to tread on graves since your swift going
The trembling gates of loss wide open threw,
And age its frosty breath upon me blow,
And still, though life is dear, and dear shall be

Love, and the fresh delights that are not few
My heart cries to you, wandering far and free,
O great, sweet ghost, do you remember me?

WASHINGTON, *April 22*, 1876

Mrs. Gen'l. ADELBERT AMES
Lowell, Mass.

MY DEAR BLANCHE: I am well, but very lonely at the table, and when I am alone. I hope you are all well at home.

The Mississippi investigation has not yet started because the deficiency bill has not yet passed. I will see Boutwell Monday.

I enclose this kind note of the Fitchburg Sentinel, which I think you will like to see. Please keep it, and send it to Mrs. Spofford, who is going to make a memoir of your mother.

Yours affectionately, BENJ. F. BUTLER

WASHINGTON, *April 23*, 1876

Hon. FRANK W. BIRD,
East Walpole, Mass.

MY DEAR MR. BIRD: I do not know when I have been so deeply touched by a sympathetic and kind word as by the receipt of your note of sympathy and condolence.

You and I have differed politically in the last few years, after having been together so many years, and an estrangement without reason and without cause, but not of the heart I now find, on your part, and know on mine, has somehow come between us.

You will see, therefore, how your very sympathetic and touching note must have moved me, coming as it did, in the earliest hour of my affliction; but I have had hardly the heart to reply to it before, you believe me, not from neglect, but because it opened an unhealed wound afresh.

Yours were not the poor common words of courtesy which are such a bitter mockery; they were more thoughtful, more tender, more consoling, and for them you have thanks, which are but a poor and almost an unmeaning expression of my gratitude.

I trust I may soon meet you and say face to face with warmth what seems so cold to write, and in the future as in the past, believe me,

Very truly, Your friend, BENJ. F. BUTLER

WASHINGTON, *April 25*, 1876

Gen'l. ADELBERT AMES,
Lowell, Mass.

MY DEAR AMES: I have not been able to see Durant, for in fact I have been confined since Saturday to my house with a very bad cold, from which I am now, I trust, almost recovered, but shall not go out today, but hope to tomorrow. I saw Clancy, however, on Saturday, and asked him to see Mr. Durant.

In the meantime I think you had better send Pryor his two thousand two hundred dollars ($2200). Tell Carney that I will make any arrangement that he desires about the money.

Yours truly, BENJ. F. BUTLER

General Ames was called to Washington to testify before the Congressional Committee investigating conditions in Mississippi.

WASHINGTON, *April 27*, 1876

DEAR BLANCHE: I found Kinsman in Boston and sat with him till it was time to go to the depot. I arrived in N.Y. yesterday morning after a good night's rest on the cars. I at once took my valise to the ferry and turned my face towards the city—a foot pad. I wandered about, most of the time on Broadway, till nine, when I breakfasted and at ten sent up my card to Florence at the Fifth Avenue. I saw her, Tom, and Mrs. H. till about eleven, when Tom and I took to the streets. We went first to Sypher's or Snyder's on Broadway, where Tom had bought a side board the style of which much resembles yours in Lowell.

We then went to Hicks and Co. our flour merchants. They report much as I had expected, that the business was about as usual—they were neither at one extreme nor another, but on an average level. From H. & Co.'s we went to Hastings, ship merchants, and then to two of his ships. The Capt. of one said shipping interests were at the lowest ebb—that not a dollar could be made at it at this time. Yet Hastings is building a new ship! Business (?) thus attended to, we went over to the west end of Brooklyn to see the yachts "Mohawk" and "Rambler." They are half again as long as the "America" and will test her highest speed.

At half past five I dined with Tom and the ladies. After dinner we had three games of billiards, when I started for the ferry. I arrived here at half past six this morning and came up to the house. After a slight attempt at dust cleaning I made a tour of inspection of the house. Of the two lower floors, the hall of the second floor and the dining room adjacent only are in order. The parlor is prepared for the long vacation of summer. The book cases and furniture of the hall are rich and elegant—the dining room is very attractive. Great taste and cultivation is apparent in everything. The plan of the house strikes me more and more pleasantly every time I come into it.

Your Father has had quite a severe cold and is still hoarse from it. Mr. Farrington said he was really indisposed a few nights ago and that a fever was threatened. But now the only remains of his sickness is his hoarseness.

I went before the Committee this morning at ten and am to be present tomorrow at the same hour. I think I will have said all they expect of me by the time they finish with me tomorrow. Possibly they may keep me till Saturday evening.

I began this letter shortly after returning from the committee. About one o'clock I went to the patent office to see sailing rafts. I looked over all the models and then over the drawings. I found nothing indicating that patents had been taken out on sailing rafts. One, and one only, had uprights to keep goods out of the water—and this was a raft for crossing rivers. The nearest approach to the bows of the "Mary Ann and Eliza Jane" are found on an oblong raft where the corners are somewhat rounded with the same upward and outward slant as they have. Read this part of my letter to Paul. Tell him that the "Mohawk" has been lengthened seven feet aft—and the "Rambler" fourteen forward. The idea is to lengthen the yachts.—Others have been lengthened. He must keep an eye on "Mary Ann and Sally Mana" and if need be stretch 'em out a little.

My leaving you day before yesterday was quite a different affair from what our parting is when I used to start for Miss. Now it is only a trip to Boston stretched out a little.

Kiss the babies—and take a world of love for yourself,

ADELBERT

LOWELL, *April 27*, 1876

DEAR DEL: I am really puzzled to know where a letter is to reach you. Today I went to Boston. Kinsman met me at the depot at half past two when I was returning, and he said that he thought it likely you would be detained in Washington a week or so. This rather interferes with my calculations, for

I had made up my mind that in a day or two you would be on your way to Northfield. At a venture I will direct to Washington until I hear from you.

The night you left was very dull. I was tired, and went to bed early—Butler was my bed fellow. In the morning I worked with great zeal to get the nurseries cleaned and the closets cleared out. I also made a change in the arrangement of the beds—Ben's bed was brought into the room where the children sleep. There are now in the room two iron bedsteads. Butler occupies one, Edith the other. Annie has gone into the attic to sleep and the baby is with me. When you return Sarah will sleep in our room on the little mattress on the floor. The nurseries look much more inviting and cleanly than they did.

Yesterday afternoon Hattie and I in the phaeton drove over to the woods on Concord river in search of evergreen. We were not very successful, but took what we found over to Dracut for Mother's grave. It was cold and late when we reached home.

I called at the bank this morning for some money and went to Boston at half past nine. An hour and a half was spent at Hovey's. The rest of the time I passed in making purchases for the children.

I love you, BLANCHE

LOWELL, *April* 28, 1876

DEAR DEL: My trip to Boston had a bad effect—for I awoke this morning with a severe headache and have been out of sorts all day. Still I have been as busy as usual, for it is not well to stop work.

Mr. Parker came home yesterday, and I have never seen him so quiet and overcome. He was here today and said that nothing was of any importance, except to be allowed to live. Col. Kinsman came up this afternoon. He is going to Washington Monday. He brought a string of coral for the baby, and a ring, which you remember he took down to have mended. Paul says that the "Mary Ann" is progressing rapidly. The floats are finished and are receiving the first coat of paint.

Our babies are all well. Butler was quite disappointed yesterday when we told him that the beans he had planted in the shed could not come up. He has transferred his garden behind the greenhouse. I am having a wire door made in the little passage which leads to our room so that I can feel safer when the doors are open between the nurseries and our room. Do you not think it a good idea?

I am lonely, Del, and every now and then the sense of loss comes over me terribly. It seems as if Mother must come back. I had a letter from your Mother today. She is expecting you soon. I should have been better contented if there had been a letter from you for me today. Yet I know that it is hardly time. Good night, I send you love and kisses. I am if possible more dependent upon your love and gentleness than ever before—I want you to fill Mother's place as well as your own. We must not desert each other.

Your loving wife, BLANCHE

WASHINGTON, *April* 28, 1876

DEAR BLANCHE: It is now five o'clock and I am rather tired by reason of my hard day's work.

Your Father and I breakfasted together, and it was ten minutes of ten when we left the table. At ten I was in the Committee room and was examined till twelve when Mr. Redpath and I came over here to the house where we have been ever since, I giving facts about Mississippi and he writing them down. He is writing for the New York *Times*, which has recently changed its Editor. Redpath writes a long personal sketch of me. Both he and I were tired, and so we suspended our labors till tomorrow.

The table is set, I hear your Father coming, and so will dinner instanter. I shall send this to you today even though it may not be completed, for I know, at least I make myself believe I know, that a letter from me daily, as has always been the case when absent from you, will be gladly received.

April 29, 1876

DEAR BLANCHE: I did not have the opportunity to send this yesterday. It is now almost six o'clock and at that hour I am to dine with Mr. Durant.

Your Aunt, Mr. Butler and cousin Charlotte were just in to see your Father, but he is out. I will write you more fully tomorrow. I will have to remain till Monday next.

Love for you, my Beautiful, and for our babies.

ADELBERT

LOWELL, *May* 1, 1876

DEAR DEL: I received your letter written in Washington Saturday and was happy to know that you were apparently in fine spirits. I meant to have written you yesterday, but going to church and attending to visitors so filled up the day that I could not find time. Gen'l. Kinsman, young Lamson, Florence and Tom took tea with us. We had quite a table full.

The babies are well—Butler is very obstinate, and complains of a pain in his stomach so that I am inclined to indulge him more than is well.

I went over the place after returning from church with Kinsman and Paul to pick out the finest location for a house. All were decided that the most attractive spot is that open level space between the two groves, where the rose path turns up parallel with Wyman's road. The ground slopes off finely, and a house facing the Avenue would look grandly.—Such an arrangement would permit of an equal division of the land by a line direct from Ludlam's to Brady's, and so Paul suggested the expense of carrying on the place could be so divided as to permit, or rather make less burdensome for each the gardening and improvement of the place. Carney writes me that a painter named Heywood has the refusal of the Mecan property till the 1st of July, for $12,000. Just at present I am more favorably inclined to the last idea, and so we build air castles to have them overthrown.

I love you, and with the children send kisses to our absent one. BLANCHE

WASHINGTON, *May*, 1876

DEAR BLANCHE: I did not write you yesterday because I did not have an opportunity. I have but a moment to write you now. You may wonder at my statement and possibly question the veracity of it. But such is really the case. I have been badgered by everybody and everything.

Mr. Redpath has been with me writing up Mississippi affairs and he sits by the hour. The time selected to write is captured by someone. Yesterday we had breakfast at ten. I did not go to bed till midnight. Redpath was here till then. Soon after breakfast yesterday Chase, Morgan, Redpath and Judge Walton of Mississippi came in and they all did not get away till after five o'clock in the afternoon. I sit as long as possible with your Father, generally about two hours at dinner. I had other visitors—we, your Father and I, had a late supper and to bed at eleven. Thus does the time go. Today I have been no less busy. I have a hundred pages of manuscript to read.

I have much to tell you of what I have heard and seen. Now I will only say I love you dearly. Everybody I meet praises you to the skies. I will not tell you all now as you may be made too vain and I do not care to have you vain when I am absent.

Love and love for you, Beloved, ADELBERT

WASHINGTON, *May 2*, 1876

DEAR BLANCHE: Another busy day for me. Last evening I thought it possible I might get away to-night, but it is impossible. My evidence will not be printed till Thursday morning and then is to be read before the Committee. I understand my presence then will be necessary.

I was up early this morning reading the manuscript over. I came home and worked at my correspondence and received callers till about three, when I went to the Senate to see Senator Conkling, thence to the Ebbritt House to see Senator Morton. Conkling I had seen before. I found Morton in bed with a bad cold. His room and surroundings looked like a pig sty. It is possible that the neat rooms you keep and the elegance of your Father's houses may have demoralized me, but it is the fact that the hotel furnishings and dirty-looking bedding strongly appealed to my sense of sight. I am just back from Morton's and am taking advantage of the short time before dinner to write this.

The carriage has gone for the Spoffords to dine with us. They are expected every minute— Eight o'clock, the Spoffords have just gone. From five till now we have been sitting at the table. Our dinner was tomato soup, baked stuffed shad, roast chicken, vegetables, an excellent dinner. The Spoffords would not go to the theatre to hear and see Rose Eytynge in *Rose Michael*, because Dick was afraid of catching cold.

I repeat what you know so well, I love you,—kisses for the babies. ADELBERT

May 2, 1876

DEAR DEL: Your second and third letters in one sheet came yesterday. I am delighted to hear that you are hard at work in such a good cause, i.e. putting yourself in a proper light before the country. Your great fault is that you never talk of yourself enough, and when by chance you do mention your own affairs it is always with such an effort and unaccustomed air, as to make you appear unnatural. I trust that Redpath pumped you. If I mistake not, he not long ago wrote something not over complimentary of you, but as I take pains to drive from mind all that is disagreeable I cannot now remember the purport of the article to which I refer.

I direct this letter to Northfield, as you speak of leaving Washington. Give my love to them all, and thank your Mother for her kind letter.

Here we are still busy at our work of reconstruction and do not pause one moment. I have had a wire door put in the narrow passage which leads to my room so that I can leave that suite of rooms entirely open and still be protected from thieves.

I would give a great deal if I were only a great sculptor. I have an idea for Mother's monument which would be grand if I could only carry it out. I have half a mind to undertake a miniature model of it anyway—which will probably result as all my attempts do.

Our babies are well. Butler tries his Mother's angelic temper fearfully. He was enraged with her yesterday and said "I am glad Gran is dead and gone away from you—you treat me so." Love and kisses, BLANCHE

WASHINGTON, *May* 3, 1876

DEAR BLANCHE: As I have remained here longer than I expected—and as I think you are a little lonesome and would like to see me—and as I would like to see you—and as I love you I have decided to break my Western trip into two parts, the first to end when we meet. I think I will start for Lowell to-morrow evening. I intended to leave to-night, but your Father has invited Mr. Durant to dinner to-morrow evening and asked me to stay till then. I will spend Friday in New York City and Saturday morning will be with my Beloved. I wonder if all this is evidence of love of my Beautiful? What think you?

I have an engagement with a number of Mississippians at this hour, corner of 15th St & N.Y. Avenue—so I must hasten.

Should I say I love you and the children at the end of *this* letter—yes I do. ADELBERT

LOWELL, *May* 4, 1876

DEAR DEL: You complain, or rather explain, that every moment is occupied. I can well understand it, and am quite content if you find time to say "I am well and love you."

We are to have visitors next week. Florence is having her room at the Nesmith's put in fine order, and as the smell of paint is not beneficial in some cases she proposed coming here, saying that as her Mother had a "sewing woman it was not pleasant there, no one could care about seeing dresses made in which one had no interest." I was rather wonderstruck with the proposition, but am perfectly willing to have them come.—It will be quite pleasant.

The "Eliza Jane" or "Annie Maria" is nearly completed. Paul says it is a very queer-looking craft. He has been planning a center board and rudder. There is to be a rudder at the end of each cylinder and the center board will be on the outer side of each cylinder. He is inclined to launch it on Haggett's Pond, as there is much better chance for sailing.

That cistern under the barn has been attended to as you desired and it is now restored to its original condition so that the waste water runs off into the garden if desired. This feat was accomplished today. With the thought that possibly we may be here for some time comes the desire to have everything restored to the condition in which it was before this place was so much deserted. The house has been open just a month, and Paul and I have been making calculations and find that counting our family as six people—each person's yearly expenses would be seven hundred dollars. As our *immediate* family consists of three, I leave the sum for you to work out. This includes horses, carriages, care of the grounds, servants, and all except rent, with which we have nothing to do.

Butler has been driving Phil in the cart today, and planting a garden. I have cut Sarah's hair, and she looks much better. Edith is as fat and saucy as ever.

Love, Dearie. BLANCHE

LOWELL, *May* 11, 1876

DEAR DEL: Your postal card came yesterday. I shall take your experience in catching the train as an omen of your future business prospects. Although you will have to struggle with many troubles, such as starting late in life, have long distances to travel in limited time, and be weighed down with the cares of a family, still you will succeed, and when once on the way will get over the business road as smoothly and quickly as those who started long before you.

I, as you may suppose, have been modeling. Paul is assisting me, and as he has a great idea of muscle aids me greatly. I will not tell you what I think of my success so far. It is best to say nothing, as the result will speak for itself.

I send you quite a number of letters which have come in the last two mails. One from Sam saying that he is making a margin of sixty-seven and a half cents per barrel, I will keep.

I have not much that is pleasing to write you about, but will tell you what I always find most agreeable in your letters. I love you, and miss you very much. The children send kisses with mine. *Your affectionate wife,* BLANCHE

NORTHFIELD, MINN., *May* 11, 1876

DEAR BLANCHE: I arrived here this morning none the worse for my journey. I never before realized so fully the comfort and certainty of connection of the great through lines of the North. The contrast with Southern travel is very marked. The distinction being that of a civilized country as compared with a semi-civilized one.

The spring here is but a little behind yours of Mass. Everybody is planting or gardening. I saw quite a number of immigrants on our train. They look like excellent material to build a country up with, but I was a little shocked to see how devoid they seemed to be of the decencies of life. Perhaps it was more or less due to the condition they found themselves in. Your Father shows how Mass. will soon be a foreign state—that is, the inhabitants will be largely of foreign birth.—I was reminded of what he said by hearing Father say that we all would be foreigners in fifteen or twenty years. It seems so by the way the immigrants still come here. This state is quite prosperous. I see that Father expects me to buy and that all expect me to settle here. I have said neither yes nor no.

All are well except Father who has "stitches" in his side and back, due to a cold he believes he caught in changing his winter clothing. It may be rheumatism or it may be an affection of the kidneys. It comes on in a night. He goes out all the time and is now in the mill as I write. The mill is doing very good business now.

Need I tell you I am not a little homesick and that I miss you much. Love, kisses and courage, Beautiful— Kisses for the babies. ADELBERT

NORTHFIELD, MINN., *May* 13, 1876

DEAR BLANCHE: I enclose you reports from Ft. Atkinson which I found awaiting me here. I do not know as it will be necessary for you to keep the account any longer.

Yesterday was a busy day for me— Not that I did anything in particular—I was running to and fro all day and when night came I was quite tired and glad enough to go to bed. This morning we had breakfast at six, the usual hour—dinner will come about midday. Thus our life line begins. I hardly realize I am here to *make money.* I have not yet become impregnated with that thought. It is a necessity and I have no doubt I will adapt myself to the inevitable which I hope is to *make* money. Speaking more accurately, I should have said I have not grown to a business frame of mind—an occupation.

My folks are very kind and considerate—only as loving relatives can be. Mother has been building up great expectations on your coming and bringing the children with you. You need never have fear that she would ever tire of you so long as she holds you in the esteem she does now. I have given her, Father and Fanny a cordial invitation to visit you when they go East this summer. Mother has been undecided about going though. She wanted to see her sister Mary and also the Centennial and only decided to go yesterday when I insisted that you would like to see her. She wants to see you and the babies.

As yet I have not talked about buying although Father has no doubt I will. I do not know as he will be willing to take my paper which is about all I can now give him.

Love for my Beautiful wife. Kisses for the children.

ADELBERT

LOWELL, *May* 14, 1876

DEAR DEL: Of course I did not write you last night, knowing that the letter could not go until Monday morning. We have all been to church. By "all" I mean Hattie, Paul, and I. Aunt Nina was there, and I persuaded her to come up and take dinner with us, as we were to have a nice one.

Poor Aunt Nina—the house and all the familiar things without Mother made her feel very sad, and yet I think she was glad she came.

About the only time I find for modeling is in the evening. There are a great many things requiring attention during the day. Still the cares are not unpleasant, and I do not speak of them in order to complain.

You, my loved one, are now with your people, but I doubt after all if you find much more affection awaiting you, or more desire to aid and do for you than those you leave behind. Alas! I forgot for the moment that the one who planned most and cared most for us is gone. Well, I except your Mother, and allow my statement to remain, and when I say this it is with no desire to under-rate the love your family have for you, only I feel that there is unusual kind feeling and affection for you here.

Butler was naughty the other day, and I asked him how he would like to have me go to Northfield and leave him and his sisters with Uncle Paul and Hattie.—He answered "Papa would ask 'where are the children' and would leave you and come to take care of us and make us happy." I have given you his words almost exactly or as nearly as I can remember, and surely he not only speaks like a wise boy, but also shows unlimited confidence in his Father.

All are well, and comparatively happy. Give my love to *our* people Sweetheart, and take for yourself an unlimited amount from the children and BLANCHE

LOWELL, *May* 15, 1876

DEAR DEL: Father came home this evening and I received the first letter from you so that the house does not seem quite so lonely as it did. I am very glad the journey West did not seem very long and deary to you, as it will be another reason why you will not be opposed to remaining in Lowell.

Father asked me if you had said anything of Mr. Moulton's proposition to go into partnership.—I answered, "Yes, but it seems to me Gen'l. Ames would have to do all the business, Mr. Moulton is not very energetic." "Oh, you mistake, he is the most thorough and active of business men. Why he built up the business of Woodruf & Robinson." "They were very mean then to turn him out." "It was because one of the Robinsons is a deacon of Plymouth Church and it was one of the methods of oppression." I was silenced, but not at all convinced, and the proposition is one I shall oppose with all my might.

I think it better, Del, that your Father does wish you to buy the mill. There is nothing here in which you could invest your money so well, and I think that it might be possible to carry it without constant personal supervision. Father manages his interests in this proxy manner, and I should hope you could do the same.

Do not get too homesick, Sweetheart, but investigate the business thoroughly, so that by acquaintance you may cease to feel that you are to have an incubus on your hands. I say this, Del, for I know that if I were in your place and you and the babies in mine I could not stay long away from you unless compelled by some stern necessity, and that you have not. Then again, I want you to so arrange matters that you will not be obliged to go out there again until fall. You can occupy yourself here this summer in starting your commission business.

You see I am planning far ahead, but I love you Del, and want to keep you by my side. Our babies are well.

BLANCHE

NORTHFIELD, *May* 16, 1876

DEAR BLANCHE: Enclosed are the only photographs in my collection that I thought would be of any value to you— Some may be of very little assistance—if any. It has occurred to me that you would profit by a study of the Venus de Milo[1]—she without arms—and of Apollo. There is a statue of Minerva which may be of great service. I would be glad to be at your elbow to suggest.

I send you a couple of newspaper slips relative to your Mother. The first is from the N.Y. *Herald* which I cut out at your request on our way East. The second you may already have as I think I have already seen it. As I was not positive I send it.

I have been busy looking over my Mississippi papers preparatory to sending them to Washington for the benefit of the investigating Committee. I may have to copy them. Col. A. T. Morgan gave me some letters relative to the outrages in Yazoo County—which he had received from his wife and brother. Those letters I cannot find in the chest. Will you look into my trunk and see if they are there—if so send them to me. I have written to Rhodes to learn if he can tell me where they are. The chest of papers and of books and the box we packed at Bay St. Louis arrived here all safe. We opened the latter this forenoon and Mother will attend to the robe and other things. One of the table cloths was stained slightly with water, but with that exception they were in the same condition as when they were packed.

I have nothing new relative to the mill. I expect to buy Father's part and then sell one sixteenth to Jack—the miller. By selling to Jack we will secure him permanently and when absent will have his best, not only as miller but to oversee everything. It will also be advantageous in making me more free and independent of this place. My business will not be so confining and I can travel more and be absent longer. John T. and Father agree that it will be better to sell Jack a part of the mill. Butler's bear was taken out of the box and I hear Fannie and Alice frightening Johnny with it. Johnny was

[1] Bronze purchased by General Ames in Europe and left with his mother.

seven last February—some two and a half years older than Butler.

Kiss the babies and take for yourself a world of love,

ADELBERT

LOWELL, *May* 16, 1876

DEAR DEL: I enclose a little proof of Sarah's photograph which I am sure will delight you. Is it not very pretty, and sweet, and is it not just like her? Show it to your Mother and ask her if she ever had a more lovely grandchild.

You say in your letter that your Father may not be ready to take your note, which is all you can offer at present. If you want more, Sweetheart, you must not hesitate to write to Father and ask him to endorse it. If you do not wish to make the request I will. You can offer him such good security that there is no possible objection.

I am very glad if your Mother feels kindly towards me. We have not seen much of each other, and her visit will give me a great deal of pleasure. I told Father yesterday that if he did not get a good rent for the house at Bay View he had better not let anyone have it, as in case of a very warm season or sickness of the children it might be agreeable to go down. He said "I shall not let anyone go in unless they pay seven hundred and fifty dollars. We don't want anyone in the house for nothing." I spoke to him of this because he had said that Cassels would have gone in if he (that is Father) could have insured her a homeopathic physician in the neighborhood. This thought set my blood in a ferment, and I wished to prevent it if possible. I do not think Cassels would be likely to pay much.

Our babies join with me in kisses for our loved one.

BLANCHE

NORTHFIELD, *May* 17, 1876

DEAR BLANCHE: I received your first letter last evening and the second this morning. I was glad to get them. I have no doubt your labor on the statue will be successful, and we one and all will be very proud of it when it shall be completed.

This morning I went into the garden and aided in planting beans, melons, having in view first exercise and then to learn how to farm. My horseback riding has come to an untimely end. Father uses his ponies all the time and John has taken possession of his ridinghorse and I am left to go on foot. My mare Kentucky has another colt, but because of her exceeding fatness (so say horsemen) her colt is but a pindling affair. My two-year-old is hardly equal to the saddle.

I am looking about and accustoming myself to the surroundings. I will not take hold seriously till the transfer of property shall be made. The business is very good at this time. There is much money in this business if conducted properly. The question which will naturally occur, Can *I* conduct it properly? I have no doubt of it when so many experienced persons are about me. By letting it run on as of old it will do well. I have only to introduce reform from time to time, we shall see.

Love to my Beautiful wife. Kisses for the babies.

ADELBERT

LOWELL, *May* 19, 1876

DEAR DEL: In your letter which came last night you ask me if you have promised too much in telling your Father that I would endorse your note. Certainly not; as your wife I am only too happy to do anything which will assist us in making money. But Sweetheart, I have, as your business partner, several things to say and questions to ask. What rate of interest will your Father charge you? I am not ready to pay more than six percent., for I can raise the money here at that rate. Why is he to have your note endorsed by me, and in addition a mortgage on the mill? This is being doubly sure, and it seems to me the endorser of the note should be secured by the mortgage.

I committed a breach of confidence, Del, and showed your letter to Father, thinking it better to ask his advice. He said at once, "What interest does Captain Ames want?" I answered: "I do not know; the general rate is twelve or fifteen percent. If you would endorse Gen. Ames' note he can get fifty thousand at six percent." "Write on and tell Gen. Ames to hold on and not conclude this definitely until he writes to or sees me." Father will, I am sure, be perfectly willing to endorse your note, or if I were to endorse it, it is possible Carney could raise the money at six percent with my endorsement. Anyway, I repeat, hold on until you have informed us further. We cannot afford to pay more than six percent.

I am glad to hear that you are exercising and also making yourself useful. If you feel a little homesick, remember it is better than Mississippi.

Last night, Paul and I had an exhibition of our model. Father, Uncle Parker, and Low were spectators. They were very much pleased with the conception, and when we have completed our work Father will be more than willing to have it put in granite. Today we shall probably take a plaster cast of it, as Paul wishes to preserve it. This may not be successful, and I wish very much that you could see it before we make the attempt to cast it.

Butler has been putting the road in fine order out by the shed, and I have been with him to admire. He has just come into the room and wishes me to tell papa that he has a garden. We send you love and look forward one month to a reunion.

BLANCHE

NORTHFIELD, *May* 20, 1876

DEAR BLANCHE: Two of your letters reached me this morning via St. Paul. One came last evening via McGregor. So you see I am luxuriating just now.

I am not surprised your Father should ask what you were copying when he found you at work on your statue. I think, had I been there, I would have told him my purpose and shared with him the enjoyment Paul and I have—of pride, faith and great expectations. Perhaps you know him better than we do, and are convinced it will give him more pleasure to see the accomplished fact than follow you step by step on your way.

The river, which rose suddenly last night, has again subsided. The mill is not running today on account of a piece of broken machinery.

Brother, Father and Uncle David have spoken to me about some old Medford rum. Uncle David thinks it possible it might be good for his rheumatism. The suggestion of alcohol was mine. He is sorely afflicted with the rheumatism in his wrists, and I told him he should vary his diet as much as possible and see if he could not find something beneficial. He is exceedingly temperate and a fit subject for my kind of liquor. Father says he has been expecting some nice old Medford your Father promised to send him. If your Father has not any large supply on hand, I wish you would have five gallons of the genuine article bought, carefully packed in a box and sent to Father as a present from yours—as coming from Lowell—as he would be quite likely to appreciate such rum more than any he can buy. I will be responsible for all expenses. As this is a temperance town, you will have to enclose the rum in an innocent-looking package.

I am glad to know the children are well and happy. Perhaps it would be well to send Butler to the kindergarten school.

At least you might try it if you so feel inclined, and if you doubt the results you can take him out anytime.

We are having summer weather and I have worked out in the sun or walked about in it and the wind till I am the hue of an Indian—that deep mahogany color you know I am so capable of taking on with the aid of wind and sun.

Give my kindest to your household and kiss the babies for me. Love, Dearest, from ADELBERT

LOWELL, *May* 20, 1876

DEAR DEL: This is the most lovely day of the season. All the trees have soft tender leaves and blossoms. The grass is full of violets, innocents, and dandelions, the soft warm breeze brings to the ears a thousand love songs from the birds. We have been walking through the grounds and returning found near the piazza a little stiff bird, lying by the fern bed. The constant reminder that death is all around in the midst of this beauty and joyful sound. I told Butler to get his spade and dig a little grave in the fern bed. I brought him a little box. He put the bird into it, and adorning it with dandelion, buried it. He put up a little wooden headstone and planted all kinds of flowers about it until the little space looked like a garden. The babies are very happy in the sunshine.

I wrote you yesterday a business letter, in which I asked you not to make any definite arrangement with your Father as to the terms of payment until you let me and Father know the rate of interest, etc. I repeat this, fearing that something may miscarry the former letter.

A week from Tuesday Father will deliver an oration in Music Hall, Boston, to the reunion of the Grand Army. He then goes to Maine, trout fishing. From thence to Washington. The last of June to Philadelphia. So that we shall not see much of him here for some time to come. We expect you back by the middle of the month. Are you going to wait until fall before going to the Centennial? I do not think I can go before that time, but you could take two sights of it.

Keep up your spirits, Dearie. I have *an impression* that all will go well. We send you love, kisses and caresses in abundance. Your *forsaken* wife, BLANCHE

LOWELL, *May* 22, 1876

DEAR DEL: I am delighted to hear that the business in Northfield does not look so formidable, and hope if the business is doing well that you will have something from division of profits to use as running capital. I feel sure you had better hire the money here, as your Father will never be satisfied with six percent.

The horses and carriage came last Friday night. They are great luxuries, especially for me, as I do not enjoy driving behind a horse which is only separated from me by the dasher. You smile at my timidity. I intend to conquer it. Butler and Edith went over to the grave yard with me yesterday and then to Aunt Nina's. They had a delightful time and were very good.

You have spoken lately of "taking the liberty to invite, etc. etc." Now, Del, I do not like that form of expression. If we are to make our home here, you must lay aside all of that, and feel that it is your home, and that all your friends must feel as free to come, and as welcome as though there was no one in the house beside. Visitors incommode no one but the mistress of the house, and that I intend to be. There will be three masters, however, and the friends of each will be always expected and welcome. I want you to say, "Blanche, I wish to, or am going to, bring Mother and Fannie *home* with me." Or "Mother and Fannie will visit us." For you, love, Sweetheart, and regards for our friends. BLANCHE

LOWELL, *May* 23, 1876

DEAR DEL: Two letters from you came today. It is a fine thing that you have some work to do, or you could not content yourself. Why does not your Father settle the matter and give you the papers? I think if you wish the mill and he expects you to take it that there should be no more delay. You see I am anxious that you should be in a position to look into and comprehend the business. Perhaps your Father does not intend to give you possession until the first of September, the beginning of the working year. This, perhaps, will be just as well, as it will be easier to settle up the business and divide the profits.

There seems to be a working capital of over thirty thousand. This would give you and John as partners fifteen thousand, which with the addition of five thousand as your share of this year's profits and two thousand as John's would be twenty-two thousand. A sufficiently large capital, I think. John, however, would of course desire to have only a quarter of the capital, so I have estimated his share too high. We must take off a quarter, which will leave eighteen thousand for your capital and his. I have written all this because in this way I think over your matters and plan them over and over according to the various probabilities.

In six years the mill at Northfield has made you about twenty-two thousand dollars. I don't feel sure that it is quite as much as that. To be sure, you own the mill at Fort Atkinson and the house at Natchez, but you will remember that they are paid for by money which you have saved and borrowed elsewhere, and that the Northfield Mills have only done part. This has not been anything very wonderful, and I conclude that when everything is settled you will have a proper proportion of the working capital coming to you. Do I reason well?

Your Father and John, who do not notice accounts very carefully, may quite likely feel that Fort A. has all come out of Northfield. I would undeceive them in this matter. It is only right to do so.

Before you return, give some days to Fort Atkinson and look over the books carefully to see what the mill has done for the last few years in the way of paying debts, making improvements, and what the running capital is. It is possible if the result is not satisfactory that you may desire to sell. Besides, it will make Sam feel better.

This seems to be a business letter, and I have written a good deal in detail because I know that I am looking at the thing through a different medium from yours, and it presents itself in another light to me from what it can ever do to you. By comparing notes we may judge more clearly.

Our babies are all well except Butler, who seems to be having a return of his hay fever, or rose cold. If he does not get over it soon I shall try all sorts of simple remedies.

Love and kisses. BLANCHE

NORTHFIELD, *May* 24, 1876

DEAR BLANCHE: I did not feel very well yesterday morning. The forenoon was spent at the mill. In the afternoon I was to write you, but after dinner I had a headache, and was heavy and drowsy, and spent the rest of the day on the sofa. Mother insisted upon doctoring me. I went to bed before nine. Mother soon appeared, to put a jug of hot water at my feet and tuck me in. It is a long, long time since she did the like for me. This morning I was up by six, much better than I was yesterday.

John T. went to St. Paul yesterday as a delegate to the State convention with this county pledged to him for Cincinnati.

I shall go up to St. P. this morning to return this afternoon. I go as a looker-on. John thought it better that I should not go with him, as somebody might say I was using him to forward my own schemes. As the *work* will be done by the time I shall get there, I venture on the trip.

Your business letter was received yesterday. Father says he prefers the money to anybody's paper and prefers we should hire money in the East at six percent. I did not feel like asking your Father to endorse for me if I could make any other arrangement. First, because he does not care to—second because he wants me to go into business in the East at once, and may regard my buying here as putting off that step on my part.

I think this a good speculation. In twelve years on our original capital of $18,000.00 Father can retire with a home worth $15,000.00 and about $100,000. out at interest bringing in from eight to twelve thousand a year. Times are not so good as they have been but they are good here—I believe.

Love, ADELBERT

LOWELL, *May* 24, 1876

DEAR DEL: Your little family is well except Butler is sneezing a great deal. This morning he came into my room and took his morning nap. When he awoke he asked "Where is Edith?" On hearing she was in bed he exclaimed with great emphasis "By George I must hurry up stairs and get dressed before her." He also said, "Mother, that little boy who comes over to play with me says his Mother told him that 'the stars are bigger than the earth.' Are they?" You see he grows older and older, and his mind is at work upon rather heavy subjects.

Edith asks me daily when is Papa coming home, and now and then she gets an idea that you have come when she hears a stir in the entry, and she flies like a shot to meet you.

I am taking active measures to have the rear of the house arranged more acceptably. Paul is looking for men to dig the drain to the barn. It may be all complete by the time you return. Next Saturday Paul and I are going to Boston to look for head stones. We were not successful with the plaster cast. The plaster was air slacked and would not harden. We are to begin on the second sized figure directly.

Love—from the babies and BLANCHE

NORTHFIELD, *May* 25, 1876

DEAR BLANCHE: I find Father anxious to sell and John anxious for me to buy, but I find at the same time that I can have no influence here till I buy. I can not buy till I raise $40,000.00. I cannot raise that sum till I go East. The sooner I buy the sooner will I receive the benefits of the mill's profits. John and Father think I had better go East at once to procure the means to buy. I do not know what else to do. I shall try to raise the money somehow. You must not expect me to remain East till fall if I go into this business. I must learn to direct before I stay so long.

As I write I half conclude not to go East till after Cincinnati. I may induce Father to agree to a sale based on the books as they will appear on the first of June. If I wait till then Mother and Fannie will go with us part of the way.

John was elected yesterday by the Republican Convention at St. Paul as one of the delegates to Cincinnati. If I stay we will go together. I was at St. Paul yesterday, going up in the morning and returning at night. It is quite an attractive place.

Love, ADELBERT

LOWELL, *May* 26, 1876

DEAR DEL: I did not write you yesterday because as I did not sit down at once after breakfast so many things were crowded upon me that I had not one spare moment until nine o'clock at night. Your letter requesting me to send some rum to your Father came night before last, and I will attend to it without fail.

I am delighted to hear that your Father is going to let you have the mill for forty thousand. How does it happen? I asked Father if he would endorse your note, if you gave him a mortgage on the mill and he said "Certainly." Carney told me that he could get the money for you at five percent., so that it would seem as if everything were working satisfactorily.

I know, Sweetheart, that you are homesick by this time, and want to see the babies. They are well. Butler's rose cold is better. I shall try and have our house cleaning and improvements finished before you return, so that there will be nothing on hand but the modeling.

Remember me to all our relatives. Love for you, Del, from the children and BLANCHE

NORTHFIELD, *May* 26, 1876

DEAR BLANCHE: I have decided to remain here till after I leave for Cincinnati, which will be on the 12th of next month—two weeks from next Monday.

All my people are anxious that we should come here and live. For political reasons I still hold my residence in Miss. and so can frankly say I am not taking up my residence here at this time, but am here only on a visit. Nor do I think it wise for you to fix in your own mind to the rigid conclusion that Lowell is to be our permanent home at this time. If Father and John so thought and believed, they would take fright, hesitate to deal with me and lose half their interest in things which now give them the greatest satisfaction.

I have been studying over the fascinations of your Lowell home and I find them to be this—there you have the comforts, luxuries and pretensions of a home worth one hundred thousand dollars ($100,000)!. I never thought of it till just now—or at least a day or two since while I have been trying to find some place in St. Paul and elsewhere which could bear any relation to it in attractiveness to your loving husband. Such places cannot be made, they must grow with the country and cities in and near which they are found. We must have such a place of our own some day but it is not best that I should abandon my efforts at turning honest pennies for such elegance and ease till I shall have learned something of my own occupation. You tell of your Father's movements and call attention to the brief space of time he is with you. I fear his business and pleasure excursions will leave you so much alone that you can hardly be said to be keeping house for him. With Paul it is different, he is always at home. I think neither of us had better proclaim our home at this time but let this uncertainty of old continue a little longer.

I shall try when I get East to raise fifty thousand dollars. With it I think I can make money.

I am talking with John and gradually getting him to think my way and will try my innovations in the smaller details of management. My health is very good now.

(*Remainder of letter missing*)

NORTHFIELD, *May* 26, 1876

DEAR BLANCHE: This is Sunday. Yesterday John arrived from Milwaukee. I now expect to get to Milwaukee by the end of this week on my way home. Thus you see another week intervenes between us. In the first place the Tolman matter cannot be finally disposed of till John goes to Sioux Falls, which is in the southwest corner of the state and off of the R.R. In the second place comes something of more importance. John learned of the sale of a flouring mill in Milwaukee which he is inclined to buy. The mill was thrown onto the market by the death of its owner. I will not give you the details, but will say in brief that both Father and John hold it as very cheap property. It is a twelve-run mill—in good order and is offered for fifty thousand dollars. John's household is eager for him (or us) to buy. Nellie is very forward to argue with me. I decline to sell this mill or permit Jack or any of our crew here to go to M. in case of a purchase. In fact I make that a condition of participating in the purchase.

I will buy only if I can sell my Fort Atkinson mill for $20,000.00. This amount I am willing to put into that mill. It would be as you see a transfer of mill property from Ft. A. to M. Both J. T. and father hold that Milwaukee is a better milling point than Minneapolis. I agree to much said in favor of the former place. Certainly the figures show in its favor. The property is certainly quite cheap. Sam says Glass is again on the anxious seats. There is a possibility that this transfer of a part of our business to Milwaukee may be made. The contingency just now seems to be the sale of the Ft. A. mill. I shall regret much John's withdrawing from active service in this locality. It will diminish the value of this property somewhat. But his going sooner or later seems inevitable. His going will of course cause Father to sell out and go to Milwaukee with him. Thus you see how marked and startling are the possible changes on the board.

From the nature of the business on hand you can see how impossible it is for me to start for the East though I made the last necessary preparation yesterday.

I send you love, ADELBERT

NORTHFIELD, *May* 28, 1876

DEAR BLANCHE: I did not have an opportunity to write you yesterday and so write you today, Sunday.

We, that is Father, John and I, left the house at just six o'clock yesterday morning, in Father's carriage, behind John's horses, for Faribault and did not get back till five o'clock in the afternoon. We went to look over the papers transferring the mill. They were made out two or three months since, but I had detected errors in them and another week is given for their completion.

We went by John's old farm up near Faribault and though Father could not praise it enough and expressed regrets he had parted with it, it was very evident that down in their hearts both rejoiced that they were no longer burdened with it.

I have made one change at the mill of some advantage. I have been protesting at the cost of barrels. In fact, I have been protesting for years. At Fort Atkinson our barrels cost less by ten cents than they do here and I have insisted we should make our own barrels. Father and John have never been willing to act. But day before yesterday John spoke to the cooper who reduced his price pr. barrel so that the saving to us will amount to $1,800.00 a year! I want to take the making of the barrels into my own hands but I think John does not want to and it is possible he made it appear to the cooper that he must reduce or retire. As soon as possible I shall make my own barrels and not be at the mercy of any one. By this and similar changes I think I can save about as much as the interest on forty thousand would amount to. The arrangement with Father now is that I buy one half of the mill for $40,000.00 to be paid in cash and am to receive the mill as it may stand by the monthly settlement on the first day of June. The mill is doing well now and I of course will receive the profits from that date—also, I take my chances on the losses.

I send love to you and the babies, ADELBERT

NORTHFIELD, *May* 29, 1876

DEAR BLANCHE: Two weeks from today I expect to be on my way to Cincinnati. From C. I will go to Philadelphia for a day or two. John T. will go to Phil. with me and I doubt not will visit us at Lowell. It was not my purpose to stop at Phil. but we are making arrangements to exhibit our flour there. We are late, and we now act only at my solicitations. Tomorrow morning I shall go to Fort Atkinson. I shall take our head miller with me. I shall not return till towards the end of the week.

I was up at John's today to see our two-year-old colt from Kentucky broke to harness. She behaved as demurely as possible. She was mastered once about a year ago. I rather regretted she did not "get mad" and make a "row" but the man was skillful and gentle. It is better to have her gentle than ugly—vicious is the word. She is a very handsome colt and will be quite large. I am much pleased with her. I have seen but little of Nellie—and when I do only the usual salutations pass. Do not understand that anything unpleasant exists.

John's two youngest, Alice and John, go to school in town and dine every day at Father's. The boy is not smart, judging from his standing in school. I think his parents hold a very uneven hand over him. I wonder what his parents will say of our son?

The old mill has been doing but little of late. I have started the firm to put in some improvements over there and keep it running. I believe I shall be a better business man than I was sailor, soldier or politician—which is saying a great deal in my own behalf as a money maker, and yet I do not know but that my part will be in *keeping* rather than in *making*.

Mother often speaks of you as in fact all do. You are held in high esteem by all of my kith and kin. It appears from conversations with Mother as to where she will pass her time East that Fannie's chief pleasure is expected at her Aunt Blanche's.

Love, for you and for our babies. ADELBERT

LOWELL, *May* 30, 1876

DEAR DEL: Your letter desiring caution in regard to settling permanently that this is to be my home, came this morning. I agree with you that it is not necessary to say positively anything. When anyone asks me about it, I say "Mother desired it, but it will depend upon Gen'l. Ames' business. His interests are West and South." Still, Sweetheart, in my own mind, I desire very much that we may remain here for many reasons. I am sure I can make you happy here—but I will say nothing about the matter at present.

You have not, or had not when you wrote, received my letter saying that Father would endorse your note. I hope this will relieve your mind somewhat as to the matter of raising money. You can, no doubt, get fifty thousand at five percent. This will not be such a terrible burden to carry, and yet with your lawyers' fees and other debts, you are taking up a pretty heavy burden. I have hope, however, that all will come right, especially *if you try to please your wife.*

Paul and Father start today on a fishing excursion to Lake Umbagog. They will be gone a week or ten days, and Hattie and I are left to defend the citadel. I shall take advantage of their absence to finish up all the household arrangements and have nothing to do when you return. I shall be very glad to see your Mother and Fannie. Will not your Father come on with them?

Butler came in just now and said "Are you writing to my dear Father? Tell him that you bought me a rake, hoe and spade, and that I let Ethel Hastings take them and she has lost them somewhere." Father has a great fancy for Butler. A few days ago he and Butler were the first at breakfast. Butler said "I want some of that, Grandfaryer." "Do you know what it is?" "No, but I want some." Father took a small piece of liver on the fork and was about to put it on Butler's plate, when the young man said "That is not big enough. I want more." Father put another piece on the plate. "No, I wants more." So a third piece was added. Butler tasted of it and did not like it, and called for fish balls. Father gave him the fish balls, but at the same time pointed out to him the fact that he would have appeared better to have been more moderate in his demands for liver. I speak of this to show how patiently Father attended to his whims. Last night he brought him a paper of candy from Boston. Sarah and Edith usually pay Father a morning visit while he is dressing. The babies are in fine health. Butler sneezes a little, but otherwise does not seem troubled. Since weaning the baby I have grown fat, and if the warm weather does not take effect, expect to rival Nellie.

Butler has come in again, and brings four sticks of rhubarb which he shows in triumph as the product of his garden. He has staked his peas and beans in imitation of Lynch's and feels proud of the plants which have come up from the seeds he has planted.

Love from the babies and BLANCHE

FORT ATKINSON, IOWA, *May* 31, 1876

DEAR BLANCHE: Jack, our head miller, and I came here yesterday. Sam met us at Calmar and drove us over. I find the mill in excellent condition and very economically managed. The two freshets in the spring injured the apron to our dam to the amount of about five hundred dollars. New machinery has been put into the mill which will not have to be replaced for years. Though this mill has done better than any in this part of the country it has not done much. Never before has the wheat been so poor. This has been due to a wet harvesting season and a mild open winter. The inferior quality of the wheat requires more for a barrel of flour and even then the flour is of an inferior grade. This mill has done better than any here and it has paid but about six percent. on the capital invested, excluding money paid for dam and machinery. Including such expenses it has paid about nine percent on capital invested. The miller is very sanguine that he can do better when better wheat can be had. I think so too. Jack has made some suggestions to the miller which I have no doubt will be of value.

My impression of the business here is—that it is a little too far South for spring wheat of the best quality. One or two hundred miles further South they find it difficult to raise either spring or winter wheat and devote their lands to corn and fruit trees. Thus you see there is a limit to the spring wheat section and that we are not far from it. Unfortunately the market for wheat does not make the distinction between spring wheat of different latitudes, it should. The burden finally comes upon the flour manufacturer when the flours from the different wheats are put in competition with each other. I believe we will have a better year after the new wheat comes in.

Everybody here plays croquet. Even here at our house are two sets, and some of the folks real champions. I have not been beaten yet but I half expect to be by every one I see come at me with a mallet.

Love to you and the babies, ADELBERT

FORT ATKINSON, IOWA, *June* 1, 1876

DEAR BLANCHE: I labored all day yesterday. Sam brought forth all the papers which had been accumulating since the mill was built and we went to work to examine and systematize. The culling process consumed six hours. It is now midday nearly, and our briefing is hardly half done though we have been over the papers for nearly six hours. I am trying to teach Sam how to keep his papers. Should I succeed, he is quick enough, I will not have another such task on hand.

It is very dry here and the crops are said to be suffering. However the quality of the wheat is always excellent in dry seasons. The river is somewhat low and they stopped last night for the first time since midwinter. They started up again this morning.

The families are well pleased with each other. In the house are three small pianos—not exactly pianos, but organs—which answer all the purposes. Last evening Mrs. Davy, the wife of one of the assistant millers, played and sang for us. She was good-natured about it and sang a long time, furnishing to every one his favorite piece.

I sleep at Clara's—Clara is wife of Nathan[1] and sister of Sam and is the silent power which regulates—and eat first with Sam and then with Nathan just as they arrange to ask me.

I think one of the reasons why I feel lonesome here is because

[1] An employee at the Fort Atkinson mill.

I some way associate you with the place—recall your visit here —and of course miss you much. I love you— Kiss the babies for me.

ADELBERT

LOWELL, *June* 1, 1876

DEAR DEL: Again I am as busy today as yesterday, and go from place to place a great director. The weather is lovely and the out-of-door work goes on very well. My indoor corps are rather undisciplined and skittish. They require patience.

In two weeks you will be on your way home. For some unexplained reason your absence this time seems longer, I won't say than ever before, but very long. The two weeks will be two months, and yet the days pass quickly.

Butler has just come in. I asked him where he had been. He answered "Playing with Georgie and I told him, Mamma, that he must not do that no more, and he said he wouldn't." Poor little man. He is so earnest. His hands are full of rhubarb which he has brought in from his garden to have made into a pie for himself. I discovered *Ames* in pencil on the wall by the front stairs. I should prefer to have him print upon paper. Edith is in the library with me, looking at a picture. She is a good little girl.

The days are getting warmer. The house at Bay View is still unrented, so if you get tired of Lowell you can change your location. I send you love,

BLANCHE

LOWELL, *June* 1, 1876

DEAR DEL: We locked the house up carefully last night and slept without fear of molestation.

This morning my hands have been full. Paul had started several projects which I am left to carry out. A carpenter came at nine and an upholsterer at ten and some masons, whom I sent away, at eleven. They all came to begin jobs.

Lewis was trying to chop off the heads of dandelions with a sickle, and succeeded in felling one in ten minutes. I sent him for a scythe and the work was soon finished. I then set him to turfing and left for half an hour to direct one of the girls about clearing the sideboard. When I went back his job had to be done over again. Thus I move from pillar to post, and rather enjoy it, although sometimes the great carelessness exhibited makes me furious. In a few weeks now you will be home again, and I hope will feel contented with everything.

I have not yet begun on the second sized model, but will

have the carpenter set it up for me this week. I was anxious to have the house matters off of my hands first.

I send you a letter from Redpath. I trust the sketch he made of your career will prove satisfactory.

Love, Dearie. BLANCHE

FORT ATKINSON, IOWA, *June 2*, 1876

DEAR BLANCHE: We had a slight shower yesterday, but not enough to benefit the pond. With additional "lead" in consequence of higher slash boards less water is needed. They have been running since yesterday morning without any perceptible diminution of water above the dam. The last twenty-four hours they have made eighty barrels. This would give four hundred and eighty during the week. One week some time ago five hundred and six barrels were made in one week. Everything was favorable then, especially the wheat which is tough and soft and has been since the last crop came in. I am much pleased with the management of this mill and continue the present force for another year—unless I may have a favorable opportunity to sell.

Inasmuch as the last year has been very severe on millers I anticipate a change for the better this year. There is hardly a mill in this part of the state which has not lost money during the past season. As we stand high above our neighbors in repute, I am forced to the conclusion that we can do excellently when they can live.

One of the best illustrations of the depression of business in the last year was shown in Northfield a day or two before I came here. Every dry-goods merchant there put down calico prints of all qualities to six cents a yard. Mother bought quite a quantity and I noticed that some she bought was made at the Merrimack Mills, Lowell. Cotton factories must be at a discount.

I shall leave here at nine this morning—riding over to Calmar to take the train and if possible to search the mail for a letter from you.

I send you love. Kiss the babies for me, ADELBERT

LOWELL, *June 3*, 1876

DEAR DEL: I have several important letters to enclose to you, one about your witness fees, one about the price of the house at Bay St. Louis, and one from Raymond whom you will probably meet at Cincinnati. You will be glad to hear of a purchaser for your house. I would hold to my price, it is cheap enough, and you ought to be able to recover your expenditure.

I am delighted that things are working so well at Northfield and Fort Atkinson. I believe with a little experience you will be very fond of money-making. It is very pleasant to see anything grow under one's hands, whether the trees and flowers, horses, cattle and houses, or business. That sentence is constructed very poorly, but the meaning I trust is apparent.

Yesterday I went to Boston to make some small purchases and to buy a border for a carpet for Paul. His room I trust will be finished next week. I have been directing the carpenter today as to the quantity of material requisite to mend the barn door. He is a very dull old man and is slow to comprehend a situation. I have been standing over him, trying to have the framework of the second model made. He said to me "You never learned this trade did you? You seem to understand about it, and how things go together better than any lady I ever saw. Most ladies do not know how things are made." He evidently feels that I am an able director.

I can see you smile, Sweetheart, at such conceit. Well, you may smile. I shall love you all the same even if you do laugh at me, and I long to have you home again. In less than two weeks now you will be here. Tell your Mother she must expect to see the children's faces very much sunburned. Love from the babies and BLANCHE

LOWELL, *June* 4, 1876

DEAR DEL: The children are very restless, owing to the approaching storm (for as yet it only sprinkles at intervals). Butler has given me a great deal of trouble, to say nothing of Edith and the Baby.

Aunt Nina was here to dinner. She says she never "saw such a change as has taken place in Sarah since her return from the South. In New Orleans she was pale and delicate, with a winning smile which was almost pitiful, owing to her fragile appearance. Now she is as solid and robust as a child need to be." I was glad to hear such commendation.

I send you Mr. Parker's bond, which he desires you will sign as Mr. Tucke and Father have done. He says it is all right and gave me some explanation which I have partially forgotten. Still, as Father has signed it we may conclude that, as he says, all is right. He wishes you to have your signature witnessed just as the others have had theirs and to return the paper to him as soon as possible. He asked me to say all this to you, and *much more,* which I promised I would do without fail. It does not seem necessary, however, to write out a long explanation of why it was necessary to re-sign. You will be satisfied without, no doubt.

Nina and Aunt Lauretta have returned, and are delighted with their trip. I look forward with a great deal of pleasure to our visit to the Centennial together.

What a delightful thing it is to know that there is one person in the world above all others, or any combination of others, with whom one can enjoy a thousand fold more all the pleasant things of life, and whose presence is sufficient to render all that is unpleasant endurable.

This is the preface to—I love you, BLANCHE

NORTHFIELD, *June* 6, 1876

DEAR BLANCHE: I have been looking over salaries and will be able to make reductions amounting, with former reductions, to about $4,000.00 a year. Some of my reforms have already gone into effect, others will begin July 1st next.

They had decided not to send our flour to the Centennial but I have insisted on it and we are now at work on it. We can not enter our flour after the 15th inst. and so have to hurry. Had we taken leisure as others have, our chances for a prize would be better. Jack tells me that the Minneapolis millers have obtained California wheat to whiten their flour. The fact is this firm has been doing an honest plodding business and are far behind others in the details which often amount to so much in a year. Surely I have much work before me.

I believe all the papers are ready and all of my suggestions made—at least such as I feel competent to make at this time—and I will be ready to pack my valise and take the train on the 9th inst.

The indications now are that Blaine will go into the Cincinnati Convention with a strong force. I sympathize with him in the effort of the rebels to strike him down by their secret investigations and am glad to see him clear himself but I would regret to see him receive the nomination. Yet to be wholly frank about the subject I would confess that I care but little at best about the political contest we now are in.

I am rather anxious to be with you and our babies—my first wish. My second is—that our financial efforts may be reasonably successful so that we may not be constantly beridden by a nightmare. Money I want for the glorious privilege to be independent. I will not attempt to tell you what a revolution

I have seen and am going through. The change from the dreamy idleness of politics preceded by the army to the certain monotony of a money-getting existence cannot be wholly analyzed and realized much less intelligibly expressed. I make progress whenever I comprehend what is to be done and how to do it. As I become interested the difficulties of the change disappears.

I have been writing and attending to numerous things as they have come up—as to time a dawdling letter. Love,

ADELBERT

LOWELL, *June* 6, 1876

DEAR DEL: I had two letters from you yesterday, both written at Fort Atkinson. I am content that you should feel a little lonesome, and desire my presence, and am glad to hear that matters are carried on to your satisfaction at Fort A.

Paul and Father came home yesterday. They did not have great luck fishing, but enjoyed the trip. Father walked over a rough road through the woods three miles and a half, and it took him three hours and a half to go over it and four hours to return. The snow was on the ground in the hollows, although the flowers were in bloom and mosquitoes so thick that they were quite uncomfortable.

You will return here, Del, in the loveliest season of all the year. Paul, Father and Hattie will all go away about the last of June or first of July. Do you think of going to the Centennial with them? It will do no harm to go twice, and I shall expect your escort in the fall, of course.

I am as busy as a bee, and have no desire to stop for thought until you come home, and then my mind will be taken up with your affairs to the exclusion of all that is harrassing or sorrowful. Dear Mother, how she planned and worked for us all.

You will find a happy wife and babies, when you return. Sarah even will be able to make some demonstration. Love,

BLANCHE

NORTHFIELD, *June* 7, 1876

DEAR BLANCHE: It is about eight o'clock in the morning, I have had breakfast, helped Mother transfer some plants from pots to the beds by the walk, came to the mill, waited for the mail which had no letter for me, read the papers and after a thorough going over of the mill seat myself for a chat with you.

On Mother's account I have finally succeeded in arranging for the migration of our family East. Mother could not get ready to go East when John and I start and it was too early for her. She wanted Father to go with her which he was not inclined to do on account of crowding somebody. So I held out the yacht race to him and arranged about John's return. I think the sail was the chief motive power, consequently I am bound to beg an invitation for him in the "America." If I can get one for myself I will transfer it to him. I will trust this delicate diplomatic service to you if you will take it. I think Mother and Fannie will be in Lowell about the 20th inst. I do not think they will be there earlier, they may not arrive quite so soon. I am free to confess I impose them upon you with a little hesitation—I will not say on you, but into your household.

I have done an unpardonable thing I know—I may have written you about it before. I invited the Raymonds to visit you. Visions of the *face* your mother caused you to put aside when they were with you before rise up and I shudder. I know you do not want them but you see, I shield myself with a but, Johnnie is fighting my battles now and—I like him.

Everybody here is going to the Centennial. The town will be deserted by and by. You should thank your stars you do not live in Philadelphia. Few things are so bad they could not be worse.

Love to you and the babies, ADELBERT

NORTHFIELD, *June* 8, 1876

DEAR BLANCHE: I have just returned from John's farm where I went after dinner to see my ponies. I am inclined to believe that my mare is the identical one sent me by Gen'l. Swift, but that she was much injured by harsh treatment on the way here. Surely she is very handsome. My two-year-old will make a grand horse with but moderate speed. The young colt is so young no judgment can now be formed of her points. I shall endeavor when East to buy some breeding stock. I want something with a pedigree.

My business here is about all arranged for the present. John and I will start tomorrow morning. We will leave Cincinnati as soon as possible after the nominations shall be made —will stop two or three days in Phila., one day in New York City, and then to Lowell. I have invited John to go to Lowell with me. I wonder what you will say to see Father, Mother, John and Fannie all there at one and the same time! It is awful to contemplate. Your Father and Paul will then be away at the regatta.

John and I are closer than ever. Our business is now the same while, if I am not mistaken, Nellie and I are further apart than ever. I do not think John observes it at all. Whereat I am much pleased. Nothing has passed between us, Nellie and me, which differs in the least from what our relations have always been, except that she is in manner and conversation in the superlative degree of what has heretofore been the comparative degree.

As with you our present separation seems to me somewhat different from any previous one and disproportionally long. We, both, are taking upon ourselves new parts which, not being fully learned, fit less comfortably than our occupation of old. I think I shall be quite content with my business if the next turn of fortune's wheel shows I am making instead of losing. This feeling is due no doubt to my inexperience in business and not a little to necessity.

Kiss the babies for me and reserve a world full for yourself from ADELBERT

CHICAGO, ILL., *June* 11, 1876

DEAR BLANCHE: We, John and I, left Northfield as proposed day before yesterday morning. We reached Milwaukee at half past three yesterday morning. Intending to remain till noon only we amused ourselves as best we could till business hours. We walked to the Lake and saw the sun rise. It rose at about four o'clock and twenty minutes. I give you the exact time as I know it will be both instructive and amusing. I dare say you have never thought nor known that the sun is up about his day's work when you have more than a third of your night's sleep to enjoy. We went out to the "Soldier's House" but accomplished nothing as nobody was there.

We arrived at this town at four yesterday afternoon. Rose Etynge (Eytinge is the proper orthography) has been playing here during the past fortnight. I called to leave my card and met her and George just about to step into the elevator. I accepted their invitation and went to their room for a few minutes. George has been here but two days. He is going to Cincinnati to benefit Warmouth so far as it may be in his power. Warmouth intends to run for Governor of La. and I infer wants to be let alone by Grant. As John cares no more than I for the blood and thunder play Rose Eytinge is engaged in, we went to see the Negro minstrels.

We will leave this evening for the Convention. By the papers I see that everybody is already there and that the fight waxes warm. I do not imagine any thing will occur to deeply interest me in either one of the candidates.

John is now lying on the bed napping and I—why I am dreaming of you and my pen has been idle for the past quarter of an hour. I send love for the babies and yourself.

ADELBERT

CINCINNATI, OHIO, *June* 13, 1876

DEAR BLANCHE: I have been quite busy since my arrival yesterday morning though I have done nothing of course. I am sorry to say that Blaine's chances seem very brilliant and he may receive the nomination on the second ballot. Everybody from Mississippi is here. Warner, Chase, and I are at this House while the delegation is at another hotel.

I am feeling better than I have been for the past three weeks. It is very warm here. I am anxious for the days to pass so that I may be with you once again.

I can not now write conveniently as Chase and Warner are talking and laughing and commanding my attention in spite of myself. Love, kisses and caresses, ADELBERT

LOWELL, *June* 14, 1876

DEAR DEL: Your postal card directing me to write you at Philadelphia came at noon, and I hasten to reply at once to your questions as well as I can.

The yacht will be in New York by the twenty-fourth or fifth. The race comes off on the twenty-sixth. Paul will be on board of her and sail from Boston. Father intends to meet her in New York, and after the race to sail around to Philadelphia. There are no restrictions as at the Isle of Shoals in regard to the number on board during the race, so that your party of gentlemen will be cordially welcome. Paul is my authority, as Father is in Washington. You well know that all the plans of this family are liable to be changed at any moment. I will keep you advised, however, as far as I am able.

You are wrong to talk as you did about Raymond and my sour face. If his stay had only incommoded me I do not think you would have observed a change of countenance. I was not content, however, to make the move to Bay View any more laborious than was absolutely necessary on Mother's account, and their stay all night would have made it harder. Be just, Sweetheart. Everything will be in good order I hope for your return, and as far as the number of visitors at once, why it is all the pleasanter. If they will not find fault with my housekeeping, I shall be only too happy to entertain them. My sympathies are all with Nellie, who is left behind. Why does she not come too? Surely she will visit the Centennial. I can appreciate her feeling toward you, and while I cannot say it is a proper one—I am sorry for her.

You will be pleased with the babies. They have aged considerably since you went away. Butler just said "I will pick only the flowers, not the buds, that will be the *proper* thing to do."

This is rather a rambling letter. The only remark to the point I can make is to say I miss you, and shall be happy when you return. I am also glad that you are to visit the Centennial. Now you will be better prepared to act as my guide next fall.

Kisses, Sweetheart. BLANCHE

CINCINNATI, OHIO, *June* 14, 1876

DEAR BLANCHE: I have time to say but a word. Maj. Howe, Gen'l Warner, Capt. Raymond and Mr. Chase are in this room as I write. Howe and Warner are occupying two of the four beds in the room, Raymond and Chase are by each other at a window and one and all blaggarding each other.

John, who dined us (and we are just up from the dining room), has just come in and joins in the banter. John came to me in the Convention and came down to the hotel with us. We came away before an adjournment was had. We will not get to work seriously till tomorrow morning. We rather expect to leave tomorrow evening.

Love, ADELBERT

CINCINNATI, OHIO, *June* 16, 1876

DEAR BLANCHE: This is the third day of our Convention. It is now nine o'clock. I have just had my breakfast and came upstairs to drop you a note before going to the Convention which will meet at ten. On my way upstairs I met Gen'l. Negley of Pa. who told me that Blaine would get the nomination. John has just stepped in and is no less confident.

I have no doubt we will finish our work today—leave tonight and arrive at Phila. tomorrow, Saturday, evening at seven.

Love, ADELBERT

LOWELL, *June* 16, 1876

DEAR DEL: Paul went to Boston today and found that the "America" is in fine condition and will sail next Tuesday for New York to take part in the races. Thinking that your

Father might enjoy a sail around in her, as well as—or in addition to—the race and trip to Philadelphia, Paul will telegraph you care of Beattie, Hay and Co. so that you will have a chance to tell your Father about it and he can have time to come directly on. No one sails around in her but Paul, the Captain and crew.

I have had two letters from you dated Cincinnati. They were short, but very sweet, inasmuch as they proved that I was not forgotten in the midst of your friends and excitement.

The news of the nomination of Hayes and Wheeler was quite a surprise to us, as all had made up our minds in spite of the teaching of history that Blaine would get it. I trust matters in the Convention were agreeable as far as you personally were concerned. At least Alcorn's man was beaten.

This afternoon Hattie, Dr. Parker and I went out for Scotch heather and arethusas. The day was delightful and the ride very pleasant. The Doctor is quite entertaining, yet I felt out of place that you were not with me. A few days now and you will be home again. Remember the pretty sights at the Centennial so as to lead me aright when we go together.

Love, dearie. Kindest regards to our relatives.

BLANCHE

General and Mrs. Ames were together in Lowell and at Bay View, Cape Ann, through July and August.

WEST POINT, N.Y., *August* 1, 1876

DEAR BLANCHE: I have received a letter from neither you nor Father for about two weeks. I hope no one is sick at home.

I suppose Father is on the yacht. The last race did not turn out very well for the "America," though I think she did very well under the circumstances, and was just showing them what she could do, and stood a very good chance of winning the race when she carried away her bobstay and jibstay, especially as she was at that time on her best point of sailing and had begun to overhaul the other boats rapidly. Well, better luck next time.

By the way, yesterday I finished my last July at West Point and the time really seems to be going at last.

I think you said Father was going to run for Congress from the Lowell district. Of course I hope he will win if he runs, but I almost wish he would not run, he has to work so hard when he is in Washington, and it wears him out, although he does love dearly to stir them up and go in hot and heavy.

How are you all getting along at Bay View now? Is Paul staying there all the time? Does Prent enjoy himself as much as he ought? I hope he will come up here before he returns.

Write soon and let me know how you all are. Good-bye. Love to all from *Your affectionate brother*, BEN

WEST POINT, N.Y., *August* 5, 1876

DEAR BLANCHE: You were right in saying that I was disappointed in the "America's" not winning the race, and I do not believe the "Wanderer" could beat her. The "Idler" might have done so but still I have my doubts. Is the race to be with the "Wanderer" or the "Idler," as it is a very different affair.

Prent did not give me the impression when I saw him that Randolph was as unfortunate as you say, but that he was rather wild. Poor fellow. I am sorry for him, for he was very good-hearted but rather weak, although obstinate. I hope he will be able to control himself and that there will be no break between him and his father.

As you want me to promise I will not drink anything this year, I will do so without any hesitation, and promise not to drink anything until I return home again, and I hope you will feel at ease about it, especially as I am doing what I always said I would not do, that is, to promise not to smoke or drink.

Write soon and tell me everything that is going on, and how you are enjoying yourself.

Love to all from *Your affectionate brother*, BEN

LOWELL, *September* 3, 1876

DEAR DEL: I wrote you all the news up to Friday night. Saturday morning as soon as I had given directions about the daily work and mended a pair of pants for Butler, who is almost raimentless, I went down cellar and puttered about the statue with indifferent success until dinner time. After dinner Hattie went out in the phaeton and I returned to my work. At four I went into the dining room to assist about arranging the table, as I desired it in nice condition for Mr. Phillips.

I had barely finished dressing when Dr. Parker called to see about Butler, but he had gone down to the depot for Father. The doctor waited his return and upon inspection pronounced him greatly improved. The swelling and inflammation in his nose had decreased and he could breathe with his mouth shut. This was encouraging and I am now in hopes we can get the poor boy cured.

Hattie was most anxious to attend the ratification meeting and as I had never heard Mr. Phillips,[1] I consented to go, although slumber was heavy on my eyelids. The babies were very restless Friday night, Sarah especially. We rode to the hall with Father and Mr. Phillips and expected to get seats in the gallery, but the crowd was so great fifteen minutes before the meeting was called that the only place for us was the stand. Thither we went in the procession, to the tune of "Hail to the Chief," sandwiched between Father and his companion, Phillips and his. The crowd divided to make way for us, and Hattie was so overcome at the situation that she would have backed out if there had been any chance, and could only wonder at my self-possession and tranquility, which was only due to the fact that unlike her I was thinking more of other matters than myself. Phillips made a grand speech. Father did not as well as usual in my opinion, although Phillips congratulated him upon his happy effort. Father has eighty-three delegates so that he is sure of the nomination. Mr. Phillips went to Boston on the eight o'clock train so that I missed the Sunday morning snooze. Aunt Nina was here for dinner. The rest of the day has passed much as usual except that I did not go to church.

I trust you find all things well in Northfield. You are greatly missed here by your wife and little ones. Even little Sarah, when she saw a carriage called out "Papa coming," and fairly screamed with delight. Do not allow yourself to feel homesick. You must gain at least ten pounds, and how can you do so with a heavy heart? Our watchword must be "it is better than being in Mississippi."

Love, Sweetheart. BLANCHE

NORTHFIELD, *September* 4, 1876

DEAR BLANCHE: We arrived safely Saturday evening twelve hours later than we expected owing to a heavy train and a weak engine in Canada. The baggage car broke down in the Queen's dominions, and those of the travelers who had trunks, of whom I was not one, found themselves in awkward positions when they reached Chicago. As Mother's trunk was checked to St. Paul we came through via McGregor, the only route by which we could get home on Saturday. We have sent to St. P. for the trunks. We found everybody well and glad to see— I will not say *us* but Mother and Fanny back again. Father was delighted and showed it in his quiet way.

On our journey I had a good opportunity to observe Fanny.

[1] Wendell Phillips.

I found her defects were, in the main, due to her education. She is a little too selfish, which I suppose is owing to the high consideration with which the lass has been treated. She would calmly take the seat by the window and leave Mother next to the aisle. When I appeared with a morning's or illustrated paper it was her hand not Mother's which was first, and that quickly extended to seize it for her own use. Of course I did not yield to such peculiarities. She was benefited by at least my own deference to Mother.

The business is doing fairly. I have not had an opportunity to investigate much. The weather is remarkably fine. I wish you and the babies could be with me.

I am looking out for a saddle horse and when found, I shall take regular exercise. I do not resolve but I shall try to get into regular hours both for business and amusement.

John thinks he is now in the hands of a physician who will cure him—not of dyspepsia, for he is informed his trouble is not that but of nervous hunger—or hunger of the nerves. He is full of life and hope.

Father's package from French has been here since last June. There was no name on the box and of course no one knew its consignee. I found among Father's papers the shipping bill sent him by Paul. Father has gone to Faribault today and John and I have brought the box to the house and now have it on tap.

Love for you, Beloved, and for the babies. ADELBERT

LOWELL, *September* 4, 1876

DEAR DEL: An uneventful day this has been. The greater part of it I have devoted to modeling. This afternoon Hattie, Edith, and I took a little ride, attended to some shopping. Hattie walked home, Edith and I returned in the carriage, and I called at Mrs. Richmond's to inquire about the school. It does not begin until the middle of the month.

Paul has not returned yet. He will know the Centennial by heart. We miss you, Sweetheart. I have not been in a good, happy humor since you went away. Hattie has thought me as cross as a bear, and I have no doubt. I am recovering my equanimity now, however, in a degree.

We have a tramp at work here. Father gave him some money and told him to come here to work. He sleeps in the barn and eats at Lynch's. He is a good-looking fellow—a brushmaker by trade. Bennet sent back the pistol—but it is unloaded, and as yet I have not had energy enough to reload it.

Father has a plan for a circular grapery for the Avenue. Paul is to look about a green-house in Philadelphia. Kinsman is to go to Hartford tomorrow as stamp agent at a salary of twenty-five hundred.

Our babies are quite well. Butler's cold does not improve as fast as I wish. I send you love, Dearie. BLANCHE

NORTHFIELD, *September* 5, 1876

DEAR BLANCHE: This forenoon was spent by me at the mill looking over our accounts. The aspect of affairs is not so satisfactory as I wish it was. I have a long road to travel before I shall be able to take the position in our business I must of necessity take. Exactly what has been done during the past year is to be ascertained. But it is much less than any of us had believed—if our accounts as given by our bookkeeper are correct. I shall go over everything myself. During the past year times were hard. The crop in this year is very poor—small in quantity and inferior in quality. My shoulder must be applied to the wheel for more times than I have heretofore thought it to be necessary. As you may perceive by what I have written, I am much at sea as to my own movements because I am not conversant with my own business affairs. While I am ploughing, Father is laying out programmes for playing. He has given me a most excellent muzzle-loading shot gun which I shall have converted into a breech loader. Will you ask Paul to see a Mr. Adams of Boston and see if the change can be made? I am not certain that the man's name is Adams—but he is a friend of your Father who sent my Father and me to see him when we were last in B.

I have one more commission for you now. I contracted a habit of reading Boston papers during the past summer. I feel its weight upon me and so ask you to send me one of the papers your Father brings home with him every evening. But a package of one cent wrappers and your labor will not be heavy. I am not particular about dates—a day or two later or earlier will make no difference. I am chiefly desirous of following your Father's triumph.

I send you, love. Please kiss the babies and tell them Father sent the kiss. ADELBERT

LOWELL, *September* 5, 1876

DEAR DEL: It seems as if you had been gone a month, and I am foolish enough to wonder what has become of all the letters I should have had in that time. I shall really expect one tomorrow.

Mr. Read received a letter last night from a banker in Paris with whom money was deposited for Phil's wife which said "As Madam Philip Reade was in the habit of calling daily for letters, etc. and as two or three days passed without such a call, we made inquiries and have just learned of her sudden death. We therefore send you the letters which were uncalled for." This is all that anyone has heard of this sad affair. I think it very strange that the people who were boarding with her, or with whom she was boarding, have not written. Uncle Read telegraphed to Phil. He wishes to know all the particulars, but there are none to give. She had decided to remain two years longer, and the family were very much pleased with her letters in regard to staying. Poor girl—this is the end of her ambition and projects for future enjoyment and well being. It is very sad to think of her dying alone. No one sufficiently interested in her to write of her death to her friends. Let us be content, Sweetheart, that we are well and try to get some contentment out of the days as they fly—not looking forward to the morrow with such earnestness that we are oblivious to the present.

I must tell you a smart remark of Sarah's. She was playing with Edith's baby carriage. The latter took it away from her. Sarah cried a little at first, but consoled herself by saying "Ha, ha, my callidge is in the barn" with such a triumphant air that I am sure Edith thought her wagon of small account. Love for my Dearie. BLANCHE

LOWELL, *September* 5, 1876

DEAR DEL: I have been busy all day upon my statue. I believe I am making some progress.

Father has been going the rounds with the Water Board of Boston. He took them to dine at the Washington House and I thanked him from my heart for his consideration, inasmuch as sixteen men would be rather troublesome to take care of.

This afternoon I had a call from Gen'l. Palfrey. He was looking well, and inquired as to my future residence. I told him Lowell probably, if you could arrange your business so as to make it practicable, as Mother wished to keep the family together as much as possible. I do not think it causes much satisfaction, this meeting of old admirers. One feels that time has left its traces and it is not a particularly pleasant thought.

We are growing old very fast, Sweetheart, without being aware of it—until some guide post of a friend shows us the number of years, instead of miles, that we have passed.

Father is in fine spirits tonight, because of the action of the Republican Convention at Worcester. His name called forth more applause than any other, and he has been put on the State Committee, which gives him a hold of the party machinery.

The children's school does not begin until the middle of the month. Sarah is getting to be such a woman that she will feel she ought to go with the others. She has managed to get into the dining room for several meals lately. Rather than have a row, she has been allowed to remain, and has behaved like a little lady.

The weather has been very cool but no rain yet. The nights seem frosty and I watch Butler's fever to see if he is well. He is decidedly better, although he sneezes occasionally.

My letters do not seem very interesting lately, Del. They are written badly and in poor style on very bad paper. When I have time I will correct the latter fault—but I fear you will have to endure the former and make excuses on the ground that—well—you love me. Kisses. BLANCHE

NORTHFIELD, *September* 6, 1876

DEAR BLANCHE: I am plodding over our accounts but nothing has appeared to change the rather unsatisfactory phase they first presented. I feel called upon to labor all the more strenuously, which I feel inclined to do.

I do not know as my movements today would interest you—this morning I rode up to John's, horseback. Mother is sick with a cold and a fever threatened. Nellie is much the same. Fat and over forty. She seems to be a little lugubrious. The forenoon was spent in the mill at work adding and multiplying. I have just been to dinner and am writing you now to catch the four o'clock train North.

I see Father in his grapery showing it to some farmers, one of whom I recognize as one who was in the mill this forenoon to borrow money on his farms at 12% probably. Father's grapery is a grand success this year. He will have many hundred pounds of excellent grapes— Many times more than you will be able to put into or get out of your new grapery by the barn.

Kiss the babies again for me—and take for yourself a world of love. ADELBERT

NORTHFIELD, *September* 7, 1876

DEAR BLANCHE: Your letter of last Friday was received today. It bears a post mark of the 2nd. So it takes a letter five days to pass between us. How very busy you must have been.

Alas! poor Maria— Alas! poor McDaniels! I can well understand his feelings when he persisted in having his lost love buried in his own lot. No animosities or enmities with the Nesmiths can embarrass him or cause him to feel that he intrudes when he visits his wife's grave. The Nesmiths might have such feelings but the husband is infinitely nearer. I am glad that you did something for them at such a time. Now two of our bridal party have gone—first, Atwood; now Maria. When we think that their sun has set how bright and warm ours seems.

With your letter came two from Prentiss. His information has filled me with new ideas as to our business and I am now full of contemplation. It is this—our old mill is doing nothing, nor can it do anything in our present grades without great expense, more than we can afford at this time. The wheat this season is like that of last, poor. Poor wheat is cheap. I think we can profitably turn the old mill to making the very lowest grade of flour for the European market. The samples Prentiss sent us were far inferior to anything we ever made. I shall begin to cipher on this new work at once. I am also studying the process of flour making and need a magnifying glass. Will Paul lend me his microscope? It may be too strong, but if it can be sent safely, I would like to have him do it.

Our miller has been away on a wedding tour. He has just returned, but has not as yet settled down to business. If I do half I have in mind I will have to stay here till next spring. I may fail in every effort.

Love to my beautiful and the same to our babies.

ADELBERT

LOWELL, *September* 8, 1876

DEAR DEL: A letter came from you last night and I feel less lonesome than before. I am happy to hear of your safe journey and hopeful expectations for the future, although I am a little doubtful about the success of the horse-back riding. Do not forget that you must be home by the last week in October at the latest, to go with me to Philadelphia.

We have been putting up tomato and between times I have

worked on the statue. You see I am persevering, if nothing else. At half past four we rode over to Dracut to carry flowers, and on our return found Charlotte Stevens and Lizzie Batchelder. They spent the evening and went to Boston on the nine o'clock train. Charlotte is on her way to Washington. She cannot hear as well as formerly—but says the doctors "can cure her when she has two months to spare." Singular, is it not, that anyone afflicted as she is should be willing to wait an indefinite time before being cured?

Butler has become his Grandfather's companion. He goes to the depot for him and with him. Edith also went down so that Father is well received. It is an odd sight to see those two small mites riding in the barouche all alone. We are expecting Paul today, as the races are over. It is time for him to come home, as the greenhouse is not yet commenced, and many things require attention. I remail some flour samples sent by Prentiss. You can now compare your product with that in the English market. Perhaps you will become a shipper. We sent to Nichols yesterday for another barrel of flour. He will think we appreciate you.

I am glad to learn that the rum arrived all safe, and that it was not owing to any fault here that it was so long on the way.

Love, BLANCHE

NORTHFIELD, *September* 8, 1876

DEAR BLANCHE: Yesterday this town was the scene of a very remarkable tragedy.[1] Your letter of yesterday was written immediately after dinner and I took it at once to the mill to be mailed. I had been at the mill but a few minutes when some one rushed in and reported that the bank was being robbed. This was about two o'clock. Going to the door I heard rapid firing across the bridge. I walked over and made my way across the square to the corner of the stone building occupied by Mr. Schiver. As I went I saw quite a number of the citizens hiding behind houses and a few firing up the street towards or in the direction of our house. Going to the corner I found that it, the corner, was being raided on by some one and that those, as I went up, had run away excepting one man. I looked around the corner with that man, who had a rifle, and as we were warned by those on the other side of the street, we both left. I soon returned and saw half a dozen men riding away on horseback. The following facts soon became known: eight men had attempted to rob the bank. They had been

[1] The raid on the Northfield Bank by Jesse James and his outlaws.

about here during a part of the forenoon and some say two of them were seen here a week ago. Four rode across the bridge and joined the other four who came into town by the way of Dundas and at once began operations, which were first to fire off their pistols into stores and ordering everybody out of the streets. Three went into the bank, jumped over the counter and tried to make the cashier open the safe. A second assistant ran out of the back door but was pursued and shot near the arm pit—the ball passing between the arm and body. They knocked the assistant cashier down and threatened him with death unless he opened the safe.

In the meantime the citizens were making it so warm on the outside for those on guard that they called lustily for those in the bank to come out. This they proceeded to do and as one of them jumped onto the counter to go out he turned upon the cashier and shot him dead through the brain. They went out, joined their friends, and rode away. But they left two of their number dead in the street. They lost two horses, one being killed and the other captured—one, in fact two, of those who rode away were wounded. They have been pursued and the latest word is that another has been wounded and a horse killed.

You can little appreciate the excitement in this town. Every old musket, shot gun and pistol was drawn from its hiding place and put on duty. The two dead robbers were left lying in the street in pools of their own blood, to be looked at by the world. Men, women and children had their fill. Country folks came in or were in town and sat in their wagons by the dead bodies and chatted by the hour. I now refer to women and children. All the women and children in town nearby went to see them. Poor Mr. Heywood, the murdered cashier, was taken from the bank to his wife. They were married about a year ago.

Considering the fact that the town did not expect the raid it did well. Such robbers have of late captured quite a number of towns. An effort was made to get up a company and pursue them but both for want of arms and horses it was abandoned. A dozen or so went in pursuit, among them Frank Wyman with a little pistol of no earthly use.

John T. was the ruling spirit in town. He and Father—the people did about as they said—especially Father; he is just the coolest man at such a scene of excitement I ever saw.

What I did after the robbers rode away and why, I will let you know tomorrow. Of course I did no business yesterday afternoon. This forenoon I went to the bank and with others owning stock, counted the money there. The president is away and the cashier also. The person killed was acting cashier.

The time yesterday reminded me of an election in Mississippi.

I am called for by Father to ride down to the mill. I shall try to make a little progress in my business.

Love, ADELBERT

NORTHFIELD, *September* 9, 1876

DEAR BLANCHE: I believe I promised to tell you of my movements after the bank robbers left. I was with John and father for a time while they were urging the men to organize for pursuit—and looking about, talking a little.

Soon word came that the robbers had gone to John Ames' house. This word was on the street for a few minutes when I met John in great trouble. He said they had gone to his house and he must go up and look after his daughters. I told him they would not harm them at such a time and counseled calmness. No, he was going to look after his daughters. We were walking up the road to his house when some one coming back said they had gone and went as far as Dundas. John was put much at ease but still he was going on to attend to his girls and calm them with assurance of their safety. As the people were looking to him I made him turn back and went to his house myself. Arriving there I found they were not excited as they knew nothing of the facts.

I do not know for a certainty that Nellie was the cause of John's anxiety but I believe so. She was downtown and was on the streets when the robbers were about and had to run from them to get out of the way. I think she suggested to John to go and look after his daughters when the news came that they, the robbers, were stopping at his house. She got someone to drive her up to the house, arriving there almost as soon as I did. She bundled Mattie down here while Fanny and a dressmaker were quite content to stay where they were. This work done, she went to the village again and put a day's work in as good as any of us. It was all right, everything she did. I only account the facts. My criticism, quite uncalled for, to be sure, is that the seeming to be half frightened to death, was really enjoying herself right royally.

Frank Wyman came back from the pursuit last night. Up to this time they have not been captured. The whole state is on the lookout.

Is it not strange that Mississippi should come up here to

visit me. The killing of Republicans by a set of Mississippi K. K. produces a similar state of sensation as the murdering of a number of men by Missouri cut-throats who are after plunder. It is thought they are of the James and Younger brothers of Mo.

I wonder if your father beat Hoar in the contest for delegates in Concord.

Love for thee, Beautiful, and our babies. ADELBERT

LOWELL, *September* 9, 1876

DEAR DEL: Two letters from you this evening and I am grieved to hear that business matters are not quite satisfactory—for the reason that in order to be happy you must be successful. For this reason, more than any other, I pray for good luck. But, Dearie, the profits of last year do not so much concern you as those of the year to come. I understand that you do not undertake to be responsible for the mill's work only since June last. Have you been running behind since then?

I send you a letter from Hicks. He speaks more encouragingly of the future. Keep up your spirits, Sweetheart, and follow your advice to Paul. Learn the detail of the business so that you can feel at last a complete master of it. This is the first time you have ever been over books and accounts. Perhaps other years the showing would have been quite as unsatisfactory if as closely inquired into. I mean those years when the mill has paid but little in comparison to what it has done at other times.

I will ask Paul about the gun. He returned at noon. Has seen little or nothing of the Centennial, all of the time being occupied with the boat racing.

The newspapers I will also attend to. All of the towns have elected delegates and out of 104 or 5, Father has 93. Not much chance for bolting is there? You know that Father is not to take his seat until the 4th of March and there will be no session probably until a year from next December. Of course you have thought of this. I only was the ignorant one. Father is going on to Washington next Friday, to be gone a week or so. I am busy every moment about one thing or another.

Tell your Mother that I made yesterday about seventy quarts of crab jelly. We had the apples, and as the tree bears only once in two years, made enough to last two years. I was very successful—but alas!—my hands bear marks of my labors. I helped squeeze the juice and very black stained hands are the consequence. Peaches, pears, pickles and tomato still claim attention.

You speak of your Father's grapes. Of course he has more, but think of the quality of those we shall raise. I mean to have some native grapes planted along the wall by Brady's. He gets a great many and there is no reason why we should not do the same. There are so many trees on this place it is difficult to find a sunny exposure.

Butler is such a man that he is out with Jimmy or West the greater portion of the time. Edith has taken his place and stays with me. We get on finely until Butler comes in and then there is a fight, of course. *We* send you love and kisses. Be of good cheer—all will come right in time. BLANCHE

LOWELL, *September*, 1876

DEAR DEL: I am out of sorts this morning—partly for want of sleep and partly owing to the presence of Moulton. Last evening without any previous warning, Sherman of Lawrence, Mr. Stone, and Moulton made their appearance. As Miss Richardson is here, we have quite a houseful. Father is full of the nomination, and oblivious to all else. The library was full of delegates all the evening, and as Mr. Moulton had nothing in common with them, it was my lot to entertain him.

Dr. and Mrs. Kimball called just after tea. You know she is an enthusiastic admirer of dogs, and of course had to take Teedle on her lap. Shortly she put him down in haste and explained that "dogs always do so when they smell others, and I have been holding my pet in my lap coming up here." I said "Would you not like to see the baby?" and led the way to the dressing room, where water and a towel repaired the damages. Father and Dr. Kimball were in the room, but did not understand what had taken place.

I sat talking with Moulton until eleven—then said "good night." The baby awoke and would not go to sleep until the rest of the household had come up to bed and the clock had struck twelve. She was dozing off—when I heard Father talking to himself. "Poor Sallie, poor Sallie, I wish you would be here tomorrow to witness my triumph. But that is not to be, that is all we can say about it—it is not to be. In two or three years I shall follow." This of course disturbed me, and after all was quiet and I was drowsy, Teedle came yelping at the wire door to be let in. I could not endure her noise, so I got up, thus waking the baby who was lying on top of me. I took Teedle to the dining room and fastened her under the table.

Returning I found the baby walking about the entry. I tried once more to get her to sleep, but was so unsuccessful that I took her to Annie, who had the advantage of a two hours nap. Once more I got into bed, when from Butler came the cry "I can't find the cover Mamma, come find the cover." Out again, the cover was fixed, and I crawled into bed quite cold from my frequent wanderings, and was soon growing warm and comfortable. "What could that sound be—water is running somewhere. I must get up again." Father had left the water running full head in the basin. Again to bed, and this time to sleep until sunrise, when Edith wished to go up stairs and have her dolly carriage taken up. To avoid an outcry and get rid of her I did as requested, and also ran down to tell the cook, who was not up, that she must send for a beefsteak for breakfast, as we had so many men to entertain.

Small annoyances you will say, Love, and you are right. I tell you of them because it is these and such as these this morning that have made me out of sorts. All are as well as usual, and send you kisses.

I have looked at the skins. They are very fine. They will be handsomely mounted this fall.

Good-bye for a day, Dearie. BLANCHE

LOWELL, *September*, 1876

DEAR DEL: Father brought us word tonight of your trouble in Northfield with a band of roughs. You will begin to think that Mississippi manners have followed you North.

It was raining this evening and very dark. I had been out through the billiard room, which was unlighted, and noticed through the open window in the passage that the light was streaming brightly through the parlor window on to the fern bed. With the thought in my mind that I would go down and turn off the gas as the rain would be likely to keep away all visitors, I put my head out of the window. There at the dining room door, looking through the slats at the girls clearing off the table and putting away the silver, was a man. He had an umbrella under his arm, a dark coat and light pants on. I thought at first it must be Father or Major, and yet why should they be looking through the slats in that manner. I called "Is that you, Father?" The man did not answer, but drew back behind the pillar. He could not see me owing to the intense darkness. His figure would have been invisible but for the light from the windows. He could only judge of the direction of the voice. I called again "Can't you answer, what are you doing there, what do you want?" I was a little excited and spoke quick and sharp. While I was asking the questions he had jumped from the piazza and disappeared. I went down to the library and asked Uncle Parker, who was there with Father, if he had brought anyone up with him. He said "No" and started out to look for the man but returned after blowing his little whistle, saying that it was too dark to see anything. I then went into the kitchen and started up the three men, who were playing cards. They searched about but could find no one. The upshot was I concluded I should feel safer to have a loaded pistol ready for use. Bennett had extracted the balls from the one left at Bay View. Don't laugh, Dearie, you know the trigger goes very hard, that is, it is hard to stop when it gets going, and I was a little fearful about loading it. So I went up stairs and took the other revolver out of your trunk.

When bedtime had come Father asked where his pistol was. I answered, "I have not seen it lately—perhaps Paul has it. I have one you can have if you will load it."—"Get me the ammunition and I will attend to it." Hattie and I went up into the attic. Annie was there preparing for bed. I took out the stocking full of cartridges, (if you do many things up in that way it may account, Sir, for the disappearance of your hose) but seeing the little pistol said "Hattie, perhaps you would like this for your protection. Father will load it—if you dare to shoot it," and pointing the pistol towards the trunk cover I fired, and whew!—I thought my head was off. Hattie and Annie were dumb with astonishment and I could hear Father stumping heavily but swiftly up stairs to see if anybody was killed. I sent Hattie to tell him we were all right—and contemplated the hole in the trunk lid with rueful countenance. I had held the pistol not at arm's length, and my forehead smarted as though some of the powder had lodged there. I suppose such a thing could not be, however. But, Del, I did not dream that it was loaded. Of course, I was careful not to point it towards anyone on principle. But no one was ever more astonished at anything than I at the report.

We tied Teedle to the dining room table, and feel safe for the night.

All are well. Father brought some candy home to the children this evening. At breakfast he remarked "The children seem to bring back the old home feeling again."

Love—Dearie. BLANCHE

NORTHFIELD, *September* 11, 1876

DEAR BLANCHE: This is earlier than my usual time for writing you but as Father wants me to go for some game with him I think it necessary to write a word that the afternoon mail may be caught. It is about eleven now and we will be gone till toward night. We are going for pigeons at the same place we went together for them some six years ago when our married life was young.

Mother did not want me to go out gunning today because of the cold I caught yesterday and the day before. Last night I piled a mountain of clothes upon me and with the jug of hot water at my feet I perspired profusely. I should not forget the large glass of rum punch Father sent up to me. I am almost free of my cold today.

Yesterday funeral services—or a funeral sermon—was preached in the school house over Mr. Heywood, the murdered cashier. There were at least five hundred people present, a very large gathering. John T. was the ruling spirit till the preacher began his sermon—and even after that. In the first place he seated the people—in the next place he notified the congregation of what was going on out of doors. As for example—he said, "The robbers have been turned back this way from Le Lesur" (a town forty miles from here) "and any young men who feel inclined may aid in their capture." Further on he notified us that a special train was at the depot to take a company the Mayor was organizing to the nearest point to the robbers. The preacher urged young men to go to the front. You can thus judge of the excitement our town is laboring under. Father comes to tell me that John is coming with my gun and ammunition and that we must away. Rest assured I shall not tramp through the swamps and marshes as I did when you were along.

Love to my loved ones. ADELBERT

NORTHFIELD, *September* 12, 1876

DEAR BLANCHE: I went gunning yesterday against Mother's advice as she thought the cold I had would be made worse. During the past week it has been cold and rainy and disagreeable.

To the better care for myself, I put on a pair of Father's stockings over my own and plunged my feet into John's India rubber boots. I put on his buffalo-robe overcoat and seated myself in Father's carriage for a ride to the hunting ground.

We went to the same place you visited with me but met with no success. I trudged about till I became quite warm trying to scare up some game but with no success. It was about two o'clock we abandoned those grounds and rode towards town one mile and tried another. Here we were more successful. Between us we killed five pigeons. But at the latter place we had to force our way through marsh and underbrush till with my fur overcoat and heavily clad feet, I became perfectly wet with perspiration. Literally all my underclothing was wet through. To keep from a too-sudden stoppage of the perspiration, I turned up the fur collar about my neck—tied it close to my throat with my handkerchief, and covered my knees with my overcoat (cloth). I came home all safe. We had the fire brightened up and had supper. When I went to bed at half past eight—nine is my usual hour—Father gave me a good allowance of rum which I modified with hot water and sugar. I awoke this morning with the cold of yesterday annihilated. Should you get cold, go ahunting, clad as I was, work as I did and you will be cured. No charge for the recipe. No patent.

Love for you and kisses for our babies, ADELBERT

LOWELL, *September* 12, 1876

DEAR DEL: I did not have a chance to write you last night, so I make it my first duty this morning. I asked Paul about converting your gun into a breech loader. He thought it would not pay, but Father said it would if it was one of those nice old-fashioned double and twisted bores. I will have Paul inquire into the matter thoroughly and send particulars of price, etc.

Miss Richardson is here sewing for Hattie. I have been as busy as a bee preserving, pickling, etc. The children's winter garments come next, and thus the days fly by, all too swiftly. You speak a little discouragingly of the time you feel called upon to give the business. You feel that you have a great deal to do. If you persistently devote yourself day after day to one point or another, you wish to accomplish, you will be surprised to find that your work is done long before you expected. This is my experience with my small household matters. They loom up before me mountainous—but a mountain which crumbles swiftly when strongly attacked.

Butler told me yesterday morning that he had been dreaming you were at home. Keep in good spirits, Love. All are well and send kisses, BLANCHE

NORTHFIELD, *September* 13, 1876

DEAR BLANCHE: If you have not already sent Paul's microscope do not, as I have a glass that answers all purpose. But I wish you would buy me a cheap instrument for measuring the moisture in the atmosphere. I think I can make such an instrument quite valuable in our business. As to our business I can only tell you we have as yet learned nothing. The books and accounts are all being overhauled by our clerk to ascertain wherein arose the discrepancies between the reports made to me on the blanks I had prepared and what the books now show. I have been a little savage at times at the slipshod way in which the business is recorded but now I am mild again and awaiting patiently day by day for some denouement from their labors. Of course I begin to question the way the whole business is being and has been done. It looks now as if it would be necessary for me to stay here for the next six months. However, I do not think it will prevent our visiting the exhibition at Phila.

There is an interesting incident in the life of Mr. Heywood, the murdered cashier of our bank. By his first wife he had one child, a girl. When she, the wife, died they arranged for him to marry an old friend and schoolmate of hers as the one she preferred to succeed to his affections and the care of her child. This "friend" was made a widow last Thursday by an assassin's bullet. The first wife now has her husband, and her friend, her child.

Yesterday Father and I took our guns for a hunt about the ponds and river in this vicinity but came home empty-handed. Consequently I concluded that game is getting scarce in this vicinity. However it is a little early as we have as yet no frost.

With my magnifying glass I am inspecting a grain of wheat and closely observing the process by which it is converted into flour. As a result my head is full of notions as to how the thing should be done. In putting forth ideas to Father, I find I have been anticipated—and yet I am going on with some experiments. I am not saying that my ignorance and genius(!) in inventing will result in any very great good to anybody.

It has been raining today. The northeasterly storm which has been with us more than a week is drenching us again.

I send you unlimited love. ADELBERT

LOWELL, *September* 14, 1876

DEAR DEL: The convention was over by noon yesterday and you will have learned the result long before this reaches you.

Our company left by five o'clock, and I took a ride up to Park Parker. The family had gone up for the afternoon. It was so late that of course we could stop only for a few moments —but that was long enough to see that he (Uncle P.) has really quite a nice place there. He has cleared up the underbrush, put out stone seats and wooden benches, dug a well, and altogether has a good picnic ground. He is to have a clam bake there next Saturday, 200 men are expected.

We have the catalogue from West Point and are sorry that Ben's standing is not better. He is 60 out of a class of 78. I shall write to urge him to greater efforts, but his lack of concentration will not, I fear, allow of great improvement. We had a small procession and serenade here last night. It was the first appearance of the Cadets for this campaign. The white uniform and scarlet trimming was very fine in appearance, and the young fellows evidently felt becomingly dressed. I expected our flower-beds would suffer terribly, as the following crowd was great. Those on the right coming up the Avenue have been trampled upon, but not destroyed. We did not allow any light on the parlor side of the house. I promised Butler I would wake him when the band came, so he was at the open window well wrapped in a bed blanket.

Your description of Nellie's fright was amusing. I should think young Wheeler would be fearful that he might in the future be punished by some of the gang for doing such execution.[1]

When you come to Lowell, it is possible you will bring with you such an atmosphere of disturbance that we shall have mill riots, bread riots, etc. You must feel that you are doomed to that kind of annoyance.

The weather is now lovely, and I have made up my mind that a part of each day must be given to riding or walking. Soon the cold winter winds will keep us indoors and we can then make up by increased application for our remissness now.

We send you love, Sweetheart. Remember me to your Father, Mother and John.

Good day. BLANCHE

NORTHFIELD, *September* 14, 1876

DEAR BLANCHE: The morning's paper informs us that your Father was nominated by a large majority but that there were ten members of the convention who refused to make his nomi-

[1] Wheeler killed one of the Jesse James gang.

nation unanimous. His opponents, if the Hoar Stripe, have dwindled in numbers greatly when only ten can get into a convention. The papers concede his election, but papers so far away cannot well judge. I wish he could beat Rice for Gov. and his supporters.

I have just come up from dinner. Our family is larger at dinner than at any other time. John's children, Alice and John, are going to school and dine with us every day. They are very well behaved children. In fact all of his are. Fannie is in disgrace with Father and me. She has been cuddled and pitied by Mother since childhood—rather babyhood—and Mother evidently expected to make her a child of her old age. But Fannie won't. She will take favors but will give nothing in return. She has been here to the house but twice since we returned and stayed altogether not more than ten minutes. As Mother has been ailing since she returned and as attention such as she might give would be acceptable—and as she keeps away, why, Father and I occasionally give Mother sly digs. Mother says, which I have no doubt is mainly true, that Nellie has interposed to some extent and prevented Fannie's coming. Fannie is young, Mother is old, and close intimacy is not expected; yet, we did think a little attention would not have been misplaced.

I have nothing new. Rumors innumerable come about the bank robbers. This morning we heard that three of them had been captured. Later, it proved that three of their rubber blankets had been found! The pursuit indications are more favorable to their capture.

As to business—our books are being searched and a summing up is being attempted but nothing definite has been reached. We know the year has not been so profitable as we expected.

I had my horse, Kentucky, brought here yesterday. I have undertaken to take care of her—feeding, watering and cleaning her and of course saddling and unsaddling her when used. How long I shall continue in such well doing is a matter of speculation with me. I try to do a little work by the way of exercise but going to the mill at half past seven in the morning, coming home at noon only long enough for dinner and to write a letter to you—returning and staying till about five o'clock, so consume the day that I have but little opportunity for exercise.

I must put this letter into an envelope and direct it to her who is dearer to me than all the rest of the world.

ADELBERT

NORTHFIELD, *September* 15, 1876

DEAR BLANCHE: Father wishes me to make inquiry about his rifle that Col. Diamond ordered of the Whitney Manufacturing Co. I wish you would make an inquiry of Paul and learn its whereabouts. Father is anxious for it. He does not want it today but will next week.

I had a compliment from Jack, our miller, today. He said he was "real glad to see me take so much interest in the business." The fact is, I am beginning to push at the wheels. This forenoon I had him and John aiding me in some experiments in the old mill. No new idea but an application of old. The experiment thus far has been quite satisfactory and we expect something good from it. Jack, seeing how I am beginning to move myself and him, feels that he has company in his labors. I find that the older members of the firm have not touched a detail of the business for months and hardly kept run of what was being done. I anticipate much good from my interference.

I will not say I am working hard for such is not the case, but I try to keep moving. I am trying to have done about the house and place many things that Father puts off and does not notice. Cleaning my horse, putting the stable in order, and a thousand and one things occupy time. It is much like housekeeping which occupies the time of wives and mothers who do not board.

No news—robbers not caught. John and his family had a scare last evening by three men who wanted to put up with him for the night. Nellie was frightened almost into hysterics. Her sister was there. As her husband is a newspaper man the affair may get into the newspapers. There was nothing of it except the men kept out of the light (they called in the evening) and would not tell who they were.

I have not told Mother about the crab apple jelly as she may ask why—and who is to eat it. I shall keep my foot out of the trap as long as possible. Love, ADELBERT

LOWELL, *September* 16, 1876

DEAR DEL: Dr. Parker called yesterday afternoon, and says that Butler is better. I shall still use the powder. He asked permission to bring a friend of his to call, or rather he asked if I had any "objection to his bringing a friend of his, a French physician from Paris." I answered I should be most happy, and the time is fixed for Sunday evening. I shall get up some excuse to be absent, and leave them to the tender mercies of Hattie.

The books at Fort A. may be in the same condition of those at Northfield. I judge from Sam's letter which I enclosed to you that he had not much money to buy stock—not so much as usual.

But patience, Dearie, and it will all come right. And perhaps is a good lesson in the beginning as it shows how necessary it is to investigate everything occasionally.

Paul is engaged this evening over the books of his clerk who is away for a vacation. Not that he thinks them wrong, but as a precaution to see if everything is up right and in proper order.

You must not allow yourself to feel that you have such a very heavy burden on your shoulders, Del. You will never gain flesh if you do, and it is not necessary to carry out *all* your improvements in one month, or six. The mills have now been running for many years on the present plan, but I can understand better why your Father always felt so poor. I wish I could be with you, with a cheering word now and then. Paul will look for your moisture gauge.

Did I tell you that Father had offered to sell the Pacific Mills at Lawrence 30,000 tons of white ash coal at $4.80 a ton. The present price is $6.00 or $6.50. I believe Pentucket Navigation Co. is starting business.

Love Del, from the babies and your wife. Do your people think that I do not love you because I am not with you? If so, how little they are able to judge.

Good night, BLANCHE

NORTHFIELD, *September* 16, 1876

DEAR BLANCHE: I fed my horse and was seated at breakfast before seven o'clock. After breakfast I saddled up and took a ride. At eight I was at the old mill making some experiments with Jack and there I stayed till twelve. I was late to dinner—finding it nearly cold. It is now one o'clock and I am chatting with you.

I think the information gained by our experiments will be of real value. I doubt if our firm has ever indulged much either in theory or experiments. It has all been practice. However, I have done nothing yet that can be boasted of and I may abandon everything but practice. Our business looks very favorable, in N.Y., but we are getting no wheat. The crop is poor and short and exactly what to expect we do not know. Of course a scarcity of wheat will enhance the price. To me the whole business is full of interest. I am glad as the days pass to see different things developing and of course am absorbing all I can. How long it will take me to become thoroughly impregnated is a question. Our flour does much better out of New England than in it. There they seem to cut closer and look after the nickels much sharper than in the state of N.Y. and those west and south of here. We get better prices at the latter places while freight is not so high.

I have received Webster's letters and shall write him soon in reply. Of course, we have not undertaken to manufacture low shipping grades—but shall if the figures work out right. I have given you an undue allowance of flour business—it will do you for a long time.

Our robbers have escaped and it has been due to the cowardice of those who have been pursuing them. The bank offer $3000.00 for their apprehension. We will save so much by their escape.

I miss you and the babies very much. So far as my beloved ones are concerned, this way of living is a wasting of days. My occupation causes more contentment than idleness ever has. In looking eastward I see no city I can care to go to for in none have I anything to do. Phila., New York, Boston attract not at all. Lowell only pulls at my heart strings and that because the better part of my life is there— Caresses for you all from ADELBERT

WEST POINT, N.Y., *September* 17, 1876

DEAR BLANCHE: Both your letters came all right, and the money too, for both of which I am much obliged. I think Paul might have stopped here, either going or coming, but I suppose it never entered his head to do so.

I have come to the conclusion that the "Mary Jane" and "Annie Maria" must be a bad failure, for I can get no news as to her sailing qualities, or in fact about her at all.

I must tell you something that happened yesterday. Gen. Michie introduced me to a young lady about ten minutes before parade, and I immediately did my best to make myself agreeable. Just after I left, Gen. Michie asked her if she knew who that was. She said "No, I did not catch his name, but he was very pleasant and agreeable, and I should like to know who he is." Gen. Michie said, "That is Gen. Butler's son." "What!" said she. "Gen. Butler's son! Why I am from *Louisiana*, and hate Gen. Butler awfully. But still he was very pleasant and

I should like to meet him again before I leave." But she is going tomorrow, and I shall not have time to see her again, unfortunately. She will go home now very likely with a much better liking for the Butler family than she had before. So you see what a good thing it is to be well and pleasantly represented out of the House as well as in it.

I wish you would tell Father I want fifteen dollars to get a drop light, as it is necessary on account of my eyes in studying at night. Please send me one dozen handkerchiefs, one dozen prs. cuffs, size 10½, six towels, and six pillow cases.

Love to all from *Your affectionate brother*, BEN

LOWELL, *September* 19, 1876

DEAR DEL: I have just come up from the cellar, where Paul and I have been working on the statue for an hour or two this evening. We have a gas arrangement with four burners, which gives us a fine light and will be of great advantage.

I sent you a letter this morning, also two from Prentiss, which seem to me very encouraging. If you set the old mill at work again you may retrieve your *falling* fortunes.

Jack's delight at your interest and energy in the business is easily understood. It is very discouraging to push with all one's might and see others listless and indifferent. It seems to me a few months of your direction will be worth more than a whole year of ordinary supervision. How do you like Kentucky. Is she as poor a horse as you thought at first?

Do not be too hard in your judgment of Fannie, Del. She is very young yet, and feels that the world is made for her. She will not know her duty by intuition, but will have to learn by experience and example. Has she good examples? Do you not think that she gives as much attention to her grandmother as a boy of her age would to your Father under the same circumstances? "Woman's rights," you will say. No, Sweetheart, only you must not think her a woman in knowledge and consideration, although she is one in size.

My pretty babies are all well. The greatest trial is owing to the teasing and fighting of the two elder. When I reflect that it is likely to continue for ten years at least my spirits give way, to revive again when one or the other insinuatingly sidles up with something pleasant in look, or word, or action.

Butler is a very good boy. He is growing better daily, and more companionable. It makes me feel very old when I think what a man he is growing. I should not be surprised to find a grey hair or so. Florence was up this morning. She is very well and happy. I asked Paul about your Father's gun. He says Diamond has not heard from it, but will write to inquire. I can seem to see you in our old room, and wish I were with you to tell you that I love you and wish I could remove all your annoyances with a kiss. We have passed many happy days together, Love, and now are making up the average.

Good night, BLANCHE

NORTHFIELD, *September* 18, 1876

DEAR BLANCHE: I devoted nearly all day yesterday to my papers and letters. When I went to dinner at two o'clock Mother told me that John had been in and wore an expression of weariness and unhappiness. So after dinner, Father and I went up—he in his carriage, I on horseback—to enliven him. Mother and he had talked his case over and decided that his troubles came from the discontented disposition of his wife. We concluded we had never seen her happy. We took John over his farm, looked at his stock, walked through the bushes to the river to see if any wild ducks were feeding and finally returned to his house. Strange to relate I never saw Nellie more agreeable or eager to please than then. Alice gave us some music—we talked of the robbers—John brought out his pistol and I told them of your adventure. Father brought the two older girls down for some grapes while I lingered to chat with John and view his orchard and trees. I think our effort was successful and I felt that I had done something. My efforts to please one devoted to my wife and babies, to expand the heart a little and take in others yields satisfaction both in the effort and the result.

This day has been a little irritating, partly on account of coming bad weather and partly because the papers in the mill are all mixed up and the work to untangle them seems interminable. The mill is doing excellent work now. The margin on our flour is quite satisfactory.

Your letter relating your mishaps and troubles was received this morning. The events were good illustrations of what can happen sometimes till finally they become so numerous as to pass the amusing point. Had I been with you I might have relieved you a little.

Good day, dear one. I am going to the mill to see what has been done and if lost papers have been found. Love,

ADELBERT

NORTHFIELD, *September* 19, 1876

DEAR BLANCHE: I am going to make a proposition which I know will startle you. I have been drifting towards it for some days by reason of the condition of our books, papers and business. What I may think a month hence when I shall leave to go East to visit the Centennial with you I cannot now say; but my present conviction is that I ought and must pass next winter here directing and overseeing. Your father will be in Washington, not as an M.C. but attending to his business as he did last year. Ben will be at West Point. Thus your family reduces itself to one, Paul. Hattie is to be provided for.

Can not your Aunt Nina take Hattie to Washington and keep house for your father—or might not Mrs. Hildreth and Nina, her daughter, go to W— with Hattie. Or what would be simpler, Paul and Hattie could go over to your Aunt Hildreth. If both you and your father be away from Lowell, I presume you would not care to keep up your train of servants by getting an Aunt there to keep house for Paul and Hattie. Perhaps you would prefer to keep your own house in Lowell, and perhaps I may not feel compelled to spend the whole winter here. Now, duty points to such a disposition of the coming months.

John, poor fellow, is not well, and even when well he is not a good manager and financier as the conduct of his farms clearly shows. Some connected thought and purpose is needed and I do not see that we can have it unless it come through me. I began to examine our bank account today but had not proceeded far before I found a number of errors—enough to destroy my confidence in the accuracy of our bookkeeper. We have a grand set of books, ledger after ledger, journal after journal, but they tell nothing. When I get through my present task, I shall know something about bookkeeping and if I make smooth our business lives, I shall be entitled to a leave of absence to go East next spring.

How the Boston papers pitch into your father! I wish he could beat Rice for Gov. and if Hayes should be beaten, I would not care much. I was sacrificed last fall that Mr. Hayes might be made Gov. of Ohio—I can care but little if he should be beaten now.

You can see I am ugly—but not to those I love.

ADELBERT

LOWELL, *September* 20, 1876

DEAR DEL: This will be a pleasant letter to you, for I am going to talk about our little ones. This morning the weather being still rainy, I ordered the carriage to take Butler and Edith to school. Of course, they looked very nice, and were in fine spirits at the thought of going. At nine we were at the house on Willow Street—and were met at the door by Gen'l. or Col. Fish, who lost his wife last spring. He had just brought over his little girl from the other side of the city.

A pleasant, gentle-faced young woman, about thirty or thirty-five, greeted us next, and showed the children where to hang their hats and coats. The rooms, (parlors with an arch where folding doors had been) were very bright, clean, and attractive, even on this dull day. A small conservatory was at one end, with some flowers in it, although not full by any means. I offered to let her have more when the beds were stripped for winter.

The school is small as yet—the term began Monday—but she expects her full number, twelve. There are four besides ours. Butler took his place with the others, but Edith was too shy, and sat by my side while I watched the method of procedure. Each child has a little wooden arm chair, and sits behind a low wooden table, the top of which is evenly checked off with black lines. First the teacher (Miss Flanders) said a little prayer in which the children joined. Then at the words "one," "two," they rose from their seats—put them under the table—and stood each behind his chair. One led off, the others following, into the middle of the front room. Miss Flanders took a basket in which were six colored worsted balls, and asked the oldest girl the order of colors. Then there was a little game, in which the balls were taken out of the basket by the leader in the proper order, and passed from one to the other through the circle, while all sang a song about it. If the wrong color was taken out by the leader, the first child observing the mistake returned it. Each child was leader in turn. Butler was not, of course, as he had not learned about the thing. The other children were at school last spring.

Butler led back to the seats—and the teacher took a little box of stick-like matches, gave one to each child and told them to put it on the line from the upper to the lower side—then another to put in the line from right to left. Quite a number of little exercises to teach them direction, etc. etc. Then told them to make anything they liked with their four little sticks. One child made what she called a roof, another the letter "H."

The teacher told her the letter did not stand straight. She looked at Butler and asked him what he had made. "A derrick" [1] he announced and took her so by surprise she hardly knew what to say to him. In fact, I think she could not remember how a derrick looks. She laughed and passed on to the next—the little Fish child. "What is that?" "A onument" or "noffing" she lisped. "An ornament?" "No, a onument." "Oh! a monument." Which showed where the little child's thought had been directed most lately. By this time Butler had made an anchor, which the teacher praised, as she could not the derrick.

I stayed with them an hour and a half and promised to call for them at twelve. Edith had so far lost her shyness that she was content to have me come away. I said to one little girl, "You have a long distance to come." "I do not care, if I can only come." Our babies were very much pleased, and the system seems to me excellent. Much was done of which I have not written you, giving them knowledge, method, self-reliance, politeness. I trust you will enjoy a morning with me when you return, inspecting this company of little ones.

Everytime I pass the wreath of everlastings I am reminded of our ride from Bay View. The last day we had by ourselves. It is a pleasant memory, and will ever be a sunny time to remember.

Good night, Sweetheart, BLANCHE

NORTHFIELD, *September* 20, 1876

DEAR BLANCHE: We have been having a long rainy spell of weather. It seemed to culminate last night in a northeast storm.

These days of wet weather work disadvantageously to millers inasmuch as the farms have been prevented by the wet from threshing and now there is no wheat coming to market. Two weeks time have been lost this way and we are nearly out of wheat. We will be compelled to stop the mill for a few days to fix the flume which has rotted till we can no longer trust it.

While I am talking about the mill I will ask you to ask Paul to send me the addresses of brush makers, such as he may find in the Boston or New York directories. Should we be able to get some brushes made for a reasonable sum we can save two or three hundred dollars by fitting them up ourselves.

Yesterday I suggested to John T. that he had better go to Milwaukee and see R.R. people about the transportation of

[1] Derricks abounded in the granite quarries at Bay View.

wheat over their road. We expect we will be compelled to buy away from home this season. He will start this afternoon to be gone four or five days. We expect to have our accounts in a comprehensible condition by that time. The trip is not unpleasant to him I can see. I really think it will do him good.

For some unexplained cause Nellie cannot keep her servants. She has but one and as dissatisfaction soon follows, the family is left help-less. Nellie and the girls are doing the cooking. From a few things that have been said I am convinced that Nellie blames me, in her heart, for keeping her on the farm and preventing their living in St. Paul on the interest of the money they would have received had they sold the mill a year ago, as they wanted to. They could not have lived however on what they would have received.

Father has started out for pigeons. He wanted me to go but I could not. Later I will take a trip with my shot gun. I send you love—also the same to the babies.

ADELBERT

LOWELL, *September* 21, 1876

DEAR DEL: Our line storm still continues, and I am trying to take advantage of the dull weather, and do not spend an idle moment. My trials are many—for Martha is away and Virgie is as efficient a cook as she was table girl. She fell asleep this morning shelling beans, while Harriet was trying to help her by washing the dishes, and I was making a pie for dinner. Patience is a great virtue.

You speak of missing papers, Del. Are they anything that I can have here? Perhaps it will surprise you to hear that Paul went over the books of his clerk and made every multiplication, marking those which were correct and putting the corrected answer by those which were not. It was tiresome, but he found eight or ten mistakes, some important, so that it was quite worth while to take the trouble. Your business has probably lacked such supervision.

Poor John! He is unfortunate in not having a comforter at home. Your efforts to cheer him may be of service to you, but I doubt their availing to do him much good. If you have not already found it so, I fear you will. Nellie will oppose any and every new thing you may undertake, and her cue will be to make John think that he is not treated with sufficient consideration.

Don't you make the mistake of believing that you can make

any atonement which will be satisfactory. I do not think human nature will allow it.

Are you going to advertise the house at Bay St. Louis? I have written one to bring the matter under your consideration. Here it is: "Winter residence in the South. For sale or rent. At Bay St. Louis. Within two hours and a half of New Orleans. The sea-side residence of Governor Ames of Mississippi. It is a new and pleasant house with grounds and out buildings, and is within a few rods of the water. Bay St. Louis is an old French town. Orange culture and fishing are the principle employment of the people. The climate is considered equal to that of Florida. Rent for six months ending May 1st $300. Price $6,000. For further particulars inquire of Paul Butler, Lowell Cartridge Co., Lowell, Mass."

I have made you smile, Love. But I am enough in earnest to desire you to write the advertisement rightly and let me have it inserted in the Boston papers. Anyone reading it and seeing that it is your house will say "Well he had some property in the state, if he was a carpet bagger."

I send you, Sweetheart, cheering wishes, and love. The babies are doing finely. Butler and Edith are delighted with school.

Good night, Dearie. BLANCHE

NORTHFIELD, *September* 21, 1876

DEAR BLANCHE: John left last evening, to be gone nearly a week. Going, he told me his household was nervous about robbers and asked me to give them my countenance. I forgot all about his request till last evening at eight o'clock when, on my way upstairs, I saw Mattie's shawl and a basket of grapes in the front hall, which the girls had left there, having forgotten them. Instead of going to my room to read and write, I borrowed a pair of rubber boots and taking shawl and grapes started off through the mud and darkness to John's. There was a light in their sitting room and I could hear voices as I approached the door. When I knocked I heard at once exclamations of surprise at least, and quick movements of feet on the floor—and soon all was quiet. I expected they would be afraid, and I began to call to Nellie. I soon heard Mattie's voice and called to her. After some time the door was unlocked and opened a few inches. I was asked "Who's there?" I replied "I." Everyone knew my voice and there followed exclamations of pleasure and relief. We chatted till half past nine, when I went to bed, as did the whole household.

I have been at our books today, but as yet have not reached any conclusions.

I would like to see Sarah, Edith, Butler and you. Love,

ADELBERT

NORTHFIELD, *September 22*, 1876

DEAR BLANCHE: Yesterday we had despatches from the seat of war notifying us of the capture of four of the six escaping bank robbers. One was killed, three wounded. This town has been very nervous about robbers, and the news of yesterday seemed to relieve every man, woman, and child in town from personal danger. In the evening at about nine o'clock, when I went up to Nellie's on guard duty, I saw a great bonfire in Mill Square, and saw the flash and heard the report of guns, pistols and Anvil Artillery. Everybody talks and laughs with everybody else, and all is happiness. Quite a number of people have received letters from St. Paul threatening to burn the town etc. The writer in St. P. is supposed to be an accomplice of the robbers, as they were in the woods at the time the letters were posted. These letters increased the nervousness. Now, every frightened person feels relieved. But so far as I am concerned, it all seems rather tame. At the time of the attempted robbery there was $15,000.00 in the bank. The bank has given Heywood's widow $5,000.00, one third of what was saved. It offered in the aggregate of $3,000.00 for the capture of the robbers. For the four already captured, $500.00 apiece, it will have to pay $2,000.00. Thus $7,000.00 of the $15,000.00 they have already given. The capture of the other two will make $8,000.00, which will be more than one half of what was in the bank. As our firm owns one fifth of the stock, we will lose by the attempted robbery $16,000.00. My individual share of this is $400.00. This would buy the much-coveted stem-winding watch—and—well, I have forgotten what the other thing is I stand so much in need of.

When I reached Nellie's, I found she was having a party. There is a young lady visiting the girls. Dr. Goodhue and a Rev. Mr. Burnie, a young divine—the first a Canadian, the second a Scotchman—were the lions. Eleven o'clock found the guests gone and me with a lamp in my hand going to bed. I left the ladies to talk over the events of the evening. I was awake this morning when the morning sun shot horizontally across my bed, and getting up, dressing, putting on my rubber boots I waded through the mud to get home at a quarter to seven, to find I was late to breakfast. When John's family began to move, I know not.

Love, Dear One. ADELBERT

LOWELL, *September* 23, 1876

DEAR DEL: I write you a little letter, just to say that all are well and thinking of you.

I did not get up until after two o'clock today, as I had been with Florence until past six. She had a hard sickness, but feels repaid by the birth of a daughter. A pretty baby, weighing eight pounds. Poor girl! her suffering was hard to witness, knowing how little it could be relieved. I am glad she is safely through that trial.

In your letter which came last night you speak of spending the winter in Northfield. You know, Sweetheart, I will do whatever we conclude will be for the best, but I am sorry that there seems to be occasion for our spending the winter there. You will remember that I have always been ready to go with you, but in one respect my mind has changed. I am not prepared to make my *home* in Northfield, and I don't want you to allow your thoughts to drive in that direction. Staying some months, however, is another thing and I am content if it is necessary. I love you, Dearie, and will do my part to make you happy and successful. Matters here can be disposed of in one fashion or another.

The carriage is ready. I must say good-bye.

BLANCHE

NORTHFIELD, *September* 23, 1876

DEAR BLANCHE: I was in hopes I would not have to go up to Nellie's last night, but my hopes were blasted. I had told myself I would not go, but about half past five she was down at the mill, waiting for the half past *six* train for a newspaper to get the last word about the robbers, and insisted on my going up. I was just thinking of starting at nine o'clock when the servant girl came in and said she had just seen two men at the front and that they walked away towards the grapery as she approached the house. At once Father and I put on our boots, armed ourselves, he with his double barrel shot gun to shoot grape stealers, and I with my self-cocking pistol to do heavy work. You must understand the robber scare has not yet passed away. We scattered when we got out of doors. Father went by the front end of the house and I by the back, and extending our line so as to outflank the enemy, we approached the grape vines. We concluded upon examination that the servant girl's imagination had changed a shadow or two, and two bushes, into two men. I put away my pistol and went up to Nellie's, but I did not tell what we had been doing during the fifteen minutes previous. They are timorous enough now.

Father has made arrangements to go on a hunting trip somewhere in the western part of the state. He is also going to unite business with pleasure. He will look for lands. I may go with him, if I can. I do really believe such an excursion would be good for my avoirdupois.

Love, for my dear wife and babies. ADELBERT

WEST POINT, N.Y., *September* 24, 1876

DEAR FATHER: I congratulate you on your success in the Seventh District, although I almost wish that you were not going back to Congress, for it will take up so much of your time after I get home. However, I suppose you enjoy it, so it is all right.

I have been thinking lately a good deal as to what I shall do after I graduate, and can come to no conclusion on the subject. If you remember, there was some talk of my going to the Law School at Harvard after I came home again, and I have been thinking pretty seriously on the subject for some time. The great trouble is that I am certain I could not make anywhere near as good a lawyer as you are, and that makes me very doubtful.

I have written to Paul by the same mail, asking him about the examinations necessary to be passed, in order to enter, and am now going to wait for his reply. He will show you the letter, without doubt.

Do you think it would be a good plan to go in the Army a year or two? It seems to me that the time so spent would not be advantageously used, and would, to speak plainly, be wasted. Blanche will probably have some good ideas on the subject, as will Gen. Ames and the rest.

Write soon. Love to all, and a great deal to yourself.

BEN

WEST POINT, N.Y., *September* 24, 1876

DEAR BLANCHE: Your letter came all right and was very welcome, as also did one from Hattie, which I will answer as soon as I can get time. I have written a letter to Father and also to Paul by this mail, both of which will most likely come to you for your opinion.

I think the grapery will be a great addition to the appearance of the place as well as a very good thing in itself, but I think the character of the ground will have to be greatly changed in order that grapes may grow well. Are you going to have grapes in the greenhouse, as well? I suppose Uncle Parker thinks a great deal of Camp, or rather Park, Parker, and bears himself accordingly. Where on earth did he get that idea into his head?

Are you going to stay in Lowell this winter, and what are your plans? I suppose Hattie is very busy all the time doing nothing, as is my amiable brother. Gen. Ames is the same tease, without doubt.

Things are going on at the Point just the same as ever. Gen. Michie and Mrs. Michie send their regards. The time goes by quite rapidly and rather pleasantly, all things taken into consideration. The mess-hall has been greatly improved lately, and is now quite good.

Gen. Wetzel (I think the name is so spelled) was up here two or three days ago, and wished me to tell Father that he had called on me while here, and seemed very anxious about it.

Love to all. Write soon as you can.

Your affectionate brother, BEN

LOWELL, *September*, 1876

DEAR DEL: I did not write you yesterday, for Saturday's letter was too late for the mail.

Paul and I investigated the encyclopedia and his textbook in regard to hygrometers, and we found that nothing satisfactory has yet been made. There are several kinds, but all require frequent and minute trials to make experiments satisfactory. Even then entire dependence cannot be put upon them. Paul suggests that careful weighing would give you the moisture in the flour—if that is what you desire. By weighing a quart of very dry flour and then an equal amount of damp, you could get a kind of scale by which you could judge of the condition of your flour.

I noticed in that English paper *The Miller*, which I forwarded you, that there was an article upon the use of alum in flour—that it prevented the decomposition of gluten or something of that sort, and thus produced a much whiter bread. Do you think it would have such an effect upon flour as to render it white enough for starch? You remember how dark the soap and flour turned with which we were experimenting. I think I must make a trial of it. I can see a smile on your dear face, and am happy in the thought that even though so far apart I have the power to make you change countenance and for an instant drive dull care away.

I am inclined to reason this way, Love. As the business has not been closely attended to at any time by the older members of the firm—there should be a vast improvement if the younger devotes *any* attention to it, and a month at a time will accomplish wonders.

I am hopeful, and want you to be so. You are inclined to take matters too seriously.

I send you a kiss for every wrinkle of thought there has been on your brow since we parted.

Your loving wife, Blanche

Lowell, *September* 24, 1876

Dear Del: This morning I went to church. Aunt Nina was here to dinner and this afternoon we went over to Dracut as usual. Butler was on the box. I observed that he lifted his hat to someone, and found that Ethel Hastings and her governess were out for a walk. You can judge that the young man is quick to comprehend a situation and act. I am proud of my boy.

In your last letter you write that the books "are getting into a comprehensible condition." Does that mean that we are not to spend the winter in Northfield? I am already trying to adapt myself to this new order of things, and yet I am sorry to start away again—upsetting my plans and projects. But if it will be necessary for you to stay, I must also—come what may.

You say you think Nellie blames you for putting a stop to her living at St. Paul. Tell her that if John still wishes to sell Paul is ready to buy his part. How do you think you and John are going to pull together? If he shares her feeling in the least, I fear it will not be a satisfactory partnership, especially as you will eventually take the directorship of the business. I judge from your letters that you have already begun to do so, which may account for John's poor spirits and consequent poor health. He cannot be well if he is troubled in mind. Of course, he knows as you and I know, that no outsider will buy his portion of the property, and he may feel that he is tied hand

and foot. Perhaps he would feel relieved to know that he can escape if he desires. Although *I* should not advise Paul to buy until he sees how the business prospers under its new head.

Your Father's gun has been sent, and ought to be in Northfield tomorrow. Does he treat you in the way he does John? You know he is somewhat dictatorial at times.

By the way—now we are on business—how would it do to have it understood at Fort Atkinson that the mill is for sale? Some of the people at Decorah, for instance, may wish to buy. I offer this as a suggestion. Paul will look up the brush manufacturers, as you desire.

I am just enjoying the beginning of a cold, the result of some indiscretion doubtless. I can hardly take your prescription—hunting in a fur coat the first of September. I will go on in the usual way and let it wear off. Our babies are well, though this cold damp weather makes me a little anxious.

We send you love, and shall expect you *home* in about three weeks.

Good night. BLANCHE

LOWELL, *September 25*, 1876

DEAR DEL: Your letter saying that your accounts were getting into a comprehensible condition filled me with hope. Your next, saying that you had not yet come to a conclusion about them, shall I say "plunged me into despair"?

I have been reading a French novel to improve my knowledge of that language, and my thoughts naturally take that exaggerated form. I am not in despair but am planning for the winter in Northfield, although your description of mud and rubber boots is not over-inviting.

I no longer send you papers, for the reason that it is hard to get them unless we are down town at just such a time. We expect Father home tonight, and with him will come the usual supply.

I am as busy as I can be, for owing to Martha's absence for eight or ten days in Washington, our household has been in a chaotic condition, and my patience has had more than its ordinary trials. While you are annoyed by some things I am by others, and we ought to have a strong feeling of companionship, although so far apart.

Our babies are well, and will be delighted to go on the cars anywhere.

Love, BLANCHE

NORTHFIELD, *September 26, 1876*

DEAR BLANCHE: I have been very busy today. The greater part of my labor consisting of an effort to give a certain turn to our business. The flume of the mill is rotten and weak. John had intended to repair it as soon as the old stock of wheat was ground out, which will be today or tomorrow. We are doing better now than we have at any time during the year. My idea is to delay repairing the flume, as we can, and put forth every effort to get wheat so we can make flour during this favorable state of the market. My ideas prevailed. Yesterday John saw a man from Castle Rock who had wheat to sell, but he would not buy. Learning this I got him started off in a buggy for Castle Rock and hope he will make the purchase. Then I shall get him to go down the R.R. to do the same thing. He likes to travel and we will give him an opportunity to do so. I do not know that we will be able to get wheat for a few days; but we should *try*. I more than suspect that purposes like John's to shut down at this time have done harm to our business and it is against such that my presence is needed.

Father and I met with an accident yesterday. We were backing away from a store to go to dinner, having one hundred pounds of sugar in the carriage. An ox team with wheat was passing. Father, thinking it had passed, renewed his backing, and the first thing we knew the ox team struck us and broke the hind axle short off, and the rear end of my side of the carriage sank to the ground. That's all. The horses were not frightened, they never are. We got out and walked to dinner.

We are making thirty gallons of wine from our grapes. Father has sold some grapes and given away large quantities with liberal hand.

If you have any of the deeds or mortgage of my Mississippi property, let me know. Send them to me, or a copy of the description.

Love to you, ADELBERT

LOWELL, *September 27, 1876*

DEAR DEL: In about three weeks I shall expect you home. A great deal can be accomplished in that time. Still I shall be ready to go back with you in November, and if our *united efforts* cannot put that business in running condition in four months—why—we will sell out. I enclose slip with all we can learn about the brush makers.

Edith and Butler have gone to school. Sarah is a little ailing this morning—and is now sleeping. Edith would not go yesterday. She had a tantrum in school, and told the teacher she would not come again. I let her have her way, and this morning she was eager to go. Her troubles were forgotten. Butler says he is going to make something pretty for me in school today. He enjoys it very much. More, I fear, than he will the public schools we are going to send him to. Still, he is learning something every day—and is growing accustomed gradually to the discipline and quietude which will be necessary. He is a very good boy.

I find it very difficult to get time to work upon my statue. There are so many things just now which require attention and the weather is so lovely that I dislike to spend the whole day indoors, especially when I think of the cold days coming. Indeed, even if I were not inclined to go out there are so many errands to do—that I should be obliged to go. I have telegraphed for new servants. I should wait before getting new ones until we had been to the Centennial, as I could go on to Washington and select them. But this going to Northfield rather prevents that as I desire to get a cook broken in for Paul, who will doubtless keep the house open—and warm only the library, dining room, cntry and my room and dressing rooms on account of the water. He will prefer to remain here, and as Father is back and forth more or less it will be better. Hattie will go to Aunt Lauretta's or Katie Tucke's. From all this, Sweetheart, do not judge that I am anxious to go—but if you *must* be there I *must*, and that's the end of it.

Remember me to your Mother, and do not allow her to make any change in her arrangements. After all, I think she is to be the most annoyed.

Love, Dearie, from the babies and BLANCHE

NORTHFIELD, *September* 27, 1876

DEAR BLANCHE: Father and his boy of all work went to Faribault this morning. He was inclined to have me drive him over to the depot and keep the horses down at the mill till he came back at one; but I told him it would do him good to walk over—that he never felt so well as when hunting, at which times he would walk miles. So he walked, but said, "Bring the horses over at one when I come back." I agreed. At twelve I left the mill for the house. On my way I bought some beef steak for dinner. I at once went to harness the horses. The harnesses were snatched off in a hurry this morning and were so mixed up with the fly netting that it took me a long while to harness up. At the depot I had to wait some time, and as the *boy* got permission to stay in Faribault till the evening train, I had to unhitch, feed and water the horses. The time lost by me to save Father the walk of five squares was just one hour. He brought a partridge dog—and an invitation to go with a party after ducks and geese. We will tramp on such a trip.

I have already begun a correspondence with a real estate house in Chicago about my property. I think the chances are more favorable for a western than an eastern buyer. However, if you think it advisable, you can advertise, only I would modify your advertisement by an omission of my name. Observe, I do not think the chances for sale are good, with you, and the notice would be converted into a personal item. No harm in that. No. I am inclined to say as little to the public about my Mississippi affairs as possible till the debate on Lamar's claim to his seat in the U.S. Senate shall have terminated. I think I will advertise, impersonally, in Chicago, Milwaukee, St. Louis and St. Paul.

I was glad to receive your letter describing the first day's schooling for Butler and Edith. Your whole story showed Butler off in rather a favorable light. I was much pleased.

Afterwards, however, I recalled the fact that you are his mother, and might possibly have given a coloring to the facts. I forgive you for it. Love, ADELBERT

LOWELL, *September* 28, 1876

DEAR DEL: It is noon, just after dinner, the first moment I have had to sit down and write you. At breakfast this morning Paul told me that two gentlemen—Messrs. Wallace and Hunniford, brass merchants from New York, would lunch with us. Owing to my disorganized household this lunch entailed a hard morning's work. Everything was complete, and I had gone upstairs to dress, when Paul came home with the information that they were not coming. I was content, for it gave me a free afternoon and I had many things to do.

Father returned last night. I told him of your proposition about Northfield. He did not take to it very kindly, and thought the journey very long for the babies. As usual lately, he brought some candy for the children. Butler was delighted to see him. Edith, however, refused to kiss him until he produced the candy from his pocket—then she was ready. This morning Edith went into his dressing room and asked for more candy. "Are you not the little girl who would not kiss me?" "I gave you two kisses yesterday." "Do you like candy?" "Yes." "So do I," said Father, and Edith's face fell—but it brightened again when he told her he would get some for her when he went downstairs. She then asked him to buy her a little wagon. Butler overhearing this told her she had one. "No, that is my little carriage." "Well, I shall give it to Sarah if you have another." You can judge from all this that the children are a good deal of company for Father.

After thinking the matter over last evening, just before going to bed, he said, "What are you going to do with Hattie if you go West?" "She will have to go to Aunt L. or Katie's." "How much would she like to go on to Washington and take charge of the house with Charlotte?" "Very much, I think, more especially as she would feel that she was making herself useful." Now that the matter is almost arranged so that it can be done, I trust you will be able to say it need not be.

Are you still as thin, Del, as when you went away? If so, you must take sweet oil in hard cider three times a day. However, I shall have you under direction again soon, either here or there.

Love, Sweetheart. There is a never-failing supply.

BLANCHE

LOWELL, *September* 29, 1876

DEAR DEL: I made a great mistake again about your Father's rifle in this way. Paul went to Boston this morning and left the box containing the rifle standing in the dining room. I supposed from what he had said that it was all ready to go, and that he had not time to attend to it. So in order to save a day, and allow your Father to go goose shooting as soon as possible, I took the box to the expressman and had it sent. This evening Col. Diamond came up to inquire about it, and seemed quite shocked that it was gone, as he was to have examined it and made some especial cartridges. He said he could write to the Arms Company and get the dimensions. Perhaps I have not done so much harm *after* all. This comes of interesting myself in other people's affairs.

Your letter about your smash-up and difference of business opinion with John came today. Have you all the material for the flume on hand, so as to have no delay when you do wish to renew it?

There is to be a grand torchlight procession a week from Monday and Father has made all kinds of plans, requiring no end of labor, and then mildly says that we will repeat it when he is elected, if he is. I am quite determined to do nothing but direct. I have so many irons in the fire now I am distracted. Sarah is not very well today. Butler and Edith went in to see Florence's baby and Edith insisted that it was her Mamma's baby.

Love, Dearie. BLANCHE

LOWELL, *October* 1, 1876

DEAR DEL: I did not write you last evening, for it was Saturday night and no mail today. Most of my time was spent in the cellar, working in clay. I do not feel sure I accomplished much, however—it is rather discouraging, especially the thought that I must leave what is done to dry up this winter. Still, better that than the mill, and thus I console myself.

This morning I did not go to church. "A bad member" you will say. Yes, rather negligent. I improved the time by writing a letter to Ben and laying my plans for a trip to Boston tomorrow. I have a great many errands and shall not be able to accomplish all.

Aunt Nina was here for dinner and we took our usual Sunday drive. Ned Tucke asked me when we were going to the Centennial. That he is going on the 16th with Katie, and should be glad of our company. I told him I would write you, and advised him to go to some town on the railroad five or ten miles from Philadelphia. He was very much pleased with the suggestion, and will make inquiries among some Boston friends who stopped in one of those pretty towns on the Harrisburg Railroad near Philadelphia.

Mrs. Farrington stopped at the Globe and was not only sick, but entirely uncared for in every way,—3000 guests, with accommodation for 1500 will not permit of much attention or luxury.

Does it make you feel tired Del, to think of going through that old show with me? Say "yes" and I won't believe you. Say "no" and I'll never forgive you. I meant to have written it just the other way, but my wits are wool gathering.

I shall look for you now, in a fortnight, but shall not be ready to go back with you under a month or six weeks, unless it is very imperative. I do not want to leave until after the election.

We shall be very happy to have you home again. It seems as if you had been away three or four months. You must not learn to consider yourself an *old* bachelor so that the cares and demands of your large family will prove burdensome to you.

I am pleased on this account that you have been obliged to keep guard over John's family. I suppose none of them would care to go down into a cellar like ours at twelve o'clock at night to wet the cloths on an old statue. I hear you say "Why did you not go at a reasonable hour"? Because, Dearie, I forgot it, as I forget everything except that I love and miss you.

BLANCHE

LOWELL, *October 2*, 1876

DEAR DEL: Yesterday was mostly spent in Boston. I took Butler down to have him measured for a suit of clothes. The poor little man grew rather tired of shopping and yet he was a very good boy. The day was rather tiresome, but the two letters I found from you on my return were cheering and invigorating.

A man by the name of Boynton from Lawrence spent the night, and left on the twenty minutes past seven train. I did not get up to do the honors. Hattie did, however. She had agreed to last night. Now, with such a lazy wife what do you think you will be able to do in Northfield? There you have breakfast before light. Well, there is one consolation, no one sits up until twelve o'clock.

Your description of your duties as stable boy are very amusing. Are you falling into the duties and annoyances which you always have felt were rather burdensome to John? Don't believe that you can escape by such a flimsy excuse as being afraid of the horses.

I don't feel so sure, Del, that long tiresome tramps through the woods and fields, with poor living, as you would have on a hunting expedition, would be good for you. Do not overexert yourself.

I have hunted all over the places where my papers are kept, but cannot find any referring to the Natchez property. Those must be in Northfield. I send you Tontine and Chandler's deed to the Bay St. Louis. The Wilkinson deed I still have—thinking it not quite safe to trust both in the same mail. One is sufficient for descriptive purposes, is it not?

I think I will have Paul advertise the Bay St. Louis in Boston, omitting your name, as you desire. As you no doubt see from my letter I am not feeling very well this morning and will go for a walk in the sun to brighten up my faculties, not my love, which is always the same for you. BLANCHE

LOWELL, *October* 3, 1876

DEAR DEL: I wrote your last night's letter this morning. So you need not be surprised at the date of this epistle. This day has passed so swiftly that I have hardly had time to get rested for my trip to Boston, still less to prepare for another tomorrow.

I shall never begin another painting or attempt to sculp until I have a housekeeper. Don't be alarmed, Sweetheart. I am not going to propose one, only I will put my *enormous* talents under a bushel or dig a hole and hide them in the ground. It is not that I overwork myself. Not at all. But I have so many things upon my mind that I cannot rid myself of an eager, restless yearning after I don't know what, unless it may be to bring all my ambitious undertakings to a successful end. Beyond this, however, is another feeling, the most disheartening of all—i.e. that I have quite possibly overrated my ability and that all my labor will only end in proving me a conceited fool. Yet I shall not give up, but will strive and try until I am forced to say I have done my best and can no more. There is no doubt about the design, and the position and carriage of my figure is excellent, but alas—I can say no more, but will work. Two or three hours—if I can get so much spare time, will accomplish wonders.

I have nothing new to tell you, Dearie. Butler is rather priding himself upon being a good boy, and is making something pretty at school for me, he says. Edith is happy to go every day. Butler was boasting that he had more of his work done than the others, having twenty sticks in his card, while the others had only six. "I haven't so many," said Edith with a twinkle in her eye. "How many have you?" "Two," and the twinkle extended to the mouth and formed a broad grin. I fear our daughter has neglected her tasks and is rather proud of having done so.

Heigh-ho! I am off to bed. It is after ten, and I must be up in season, for Boston. Good night, BLANCHE

LOWELL, *October* 5, 1876

DEAR DEL: I did not write you last evening. We were visited by a number of torch lighters, although this did not interfere with my writing. But, Dearie, I shall own it. I was so tired by my trip to Boston that after tea I went upstairs, intending to stay but a few moments. The little cot bed in the nursery looked so tempting I threw myself down upon it, face downward and in two minutes was fast asleep and did not wake until half past nine, when the torch lighters made their appearance. Father made a little speech. They went from around by Nesmith Street to Wyman to Major Noyes' who is the commander, for a collation of apples, cheese, crackers, and cider. So that we kept the house lighted up until the departure about half past eleven.

You will see by the papers that Judge Hoar has accepted the nomination on a bolting ticket. He has no hopes of being elected, but thinks he can take enough votes from Father to give the victory to Tarbox. It is as mean a position as ever a man took, as he works not to advance his own interests (that is a proper ambition for any one) but to defeat another. This will make the fight closer, and more exciting. I do not feel entirely satisfied as to the likelihood of success. Father is sanguine, however, as he always is. Hoar did not have thirty men at the Convention at Young's Hotel, and they were not sent by anybody, only went on their own account. The whole thing is very cheap.

How soon are you coming home, Sweetheart? It is now the 5th, and time for you to be thinking of it. How shall we ever get around in the Centennial? The crowd grows greater daily and it was very unpleasant some time ago. Perhaps you will suggest the advisability of staying at home.—No, I thank you—I must go; in spite of everything.

Love and kisses—for my truant. BLANCHE

NORTHFIELD, *October* 5, 1876

DEAR BLANCHE: We see by telegraphic dispatches to the western papers that we received an award on spring wheat flour. This means the "straight" flour and not our "fancy." There are some four persons who receive awards on the same grade as our fancy—they are known as flours made by "patent process." The haste in which we made and shipped ours should have defeated us. Of course we are gratified to get the first award on the "straight." I think we may be able to turn it to as good an account as if we had won on the other quality.

Father's gun came yesterday. After consultation it is decided to return it. The gun itself is well enough—we doubt as to the telescope—but the two together are worthless to Father or anyone else for practical purposes. The trouble is this—the telescope is attached to the gun about as the ramrod of a muzzle loader is. It has a lateral motion which nothing can prevent, and above all there is no graduated scale to indicate any angle between the gun and telescope. In fact, we cannot tell what the point blank elevation is. It is impossible to use it. Should a series of experiments be entered upon and the range for a certain elevation known, there are no means of marking it so as to give an initial point. And a fingering of the screw would destroy everything and a new series of experiments would become necessary. I shall advise Father not to pay for it, unless it be to save Col. Diamond the cost of it. He would gladly take it, if the telescope can be arranged. Of course, his fall rifle shooting is at an end. Today there is a violent rain storm. There was for a few moments a puff of snow. It is quite cold and disagreeable.

Love, ADELBERT

NORTHFIELD, *October* 6, 1876

DEAR BLANCHE: Yesterday I wrote you about Father's rifle, and intended to add that he will not need the cartridges he was expecting from the U.S. Cartridge Company—certainly not until the gun has traveled to the East and back again—a problematical trip. I am sorry Paul and Col. Diamond should have been put to so much trouble. We will try not to have it repeated.

It is very winterish here. During the past few days we have had frost and a skim of ice. Yesterday it rained and blew violently—and under such treatment the leaves on the black walnut trees and the grape vines, which were green the day before, have to the last one fallen to the ground. Other trees and shrubbery have not been so susceptible to the chills of winter. Their turn will come in good time, however.

My days of late have not been so busy. To shorten them somewhat I suggested we should not have breakfast till seven. Acting on my suggestion the delay was made, but we changed back at once on my second suggestion for I did not care to lie in bed awake so late, as we invariably separate at nine o'clock, everybody going to bed but myself—I go to my room, however.

This weather has made Father a little rheumatic. John was never better than now. He so states frequently. Today he has gone a-gunning with a St. Paul friend. The people here desire to send him to the legislature. I do not think he cares to go. He has not spoken to me on the subject, but some one says he has refused to accept a nomination. I am inclined to think he should go if the feeling for him is general.

I see by the Boston papers you sent us that both the Bunting and the Cartridge mills received awards at the Centennial exhibition.

I see by telegraphic dispatch that Judge Hoar has come out as an independent candidate for Congress. The enmity against your Father is far greater than I thought. I hope it will not defeat him.

Love, ADELBERT

NORTHFIELD, *October* 7, 1876

DEAR BLANCHE: Nothing of interest has transpired with us today. The air is cool and bracing, and everyone is only too glad to cuddle up to the fire. We have been especially busy discussing some of the results of the experiments I began three weeks ago, and which I have been steadily at work at ever since.

John's positive tone and still more positive assertions gave way before the facts made known clearly and distinctly for the first time by these same experiments. We have begun to make slight changes in parts of the machinery, but our millwrights are such slow workmen that but little progress is made. Two or three months must elapse before we can put ourselves in a condition to run on satisfactorily.

I am writing in the office, and have just had a discussion with John in which a speech I have often made was repeated—it was as follows— "Why not collect the bill? If the man is to be offended because he is asked to pay for his flour, then take advantage of the opportunity to tell him he need not call again if he cannot pay his honest debts. We are not doing business for the honor of it—at least I am not." And so I spur them up for a moment, to know they will fall back again the next to the old way of letting things run on to be finally lost. It is a little tiresome, but as there is a dollar behind it, and as my business is to get that same dollar, I am quite content.

I had a letter from Noonan—by the way I think you sent it to me—saying he had leased our house at Natchez. Love,

ADELBERT

General Ames returned to Lowell in the middle of October.

WEST POINT, N.Y., *December* 6, 1876

DEAR BLANCHE: I did not write on Sunday as I wrote a day or two before and since then I have been too busy.

In one month we have our semi-annual examination, and we

are now going over the different subjects for the last time, and as the lessons are long, it takes most of the time to learn them. Let us hope I won't be found!! I have not seen Prof. Michie for some time, as his house is in quarantine on account of the measles and we are ordered not to go there.

We had quite a snow storm here four or five days ago, but the snow soon went off, luckily, as it would otherwise spoil our skating which is about the only amusement we have now. Our life here is so uneventful that I have absolutely nothing to write about, for nothing seems to happen.

I am glad you are all going to be home Christmas. It will be so much pleasanter for Father to have you all there. Did Paul get a chance to sell the "Annie Maria?" He said in his last (and I may say only letter) that he was going down to Haggett's Pond and try to sell her to the man who lets boats.

How did the turkey shoot on Thanksgiving turn out? Did Gen. Ames again carry off the palm of victory and several turkeys, chickens, ducks, etc?

It is a race between the watch and myself to see which of us shall win, whether it will be nine-thirty before I finish this page and I am afraid that I shall lose unless thoughts come to me faster than they have done heretofore.

Write soon and tell me lots of news. Good-bye to you all.

Your affectionate brother, BEN

WEST POINT, N.Y., *December* 18, 1876

DEAR BLANCHE: Your letter came all right, and also a short note from Father, and I am much obliged for the contents of both. You need not expect me Christmas, as the high and mighty Superintendent has made up his mind not to grant any leaves, so on Christmas I shall have to stay here through no fault of mine, and chew the cud of my bitter reflections and *pray* silently for the good of his soul. However, I will have as good a time as I can, and wait for "New Years" to make my calls on the people of the Post, omitting the "Super," not that it will make any difference to him, but because I do not know him.

Went to Gen. Michie's yesterday to tea. Had a nice time. He thinks I ought to go to Harvard for four years after I graduate, then two years to a German university, and then four years studying my profession, at the end of which time I shall be thirty-two, and then hang up my "shingle." I thanked him very much for his advice, but declined to follow it for various reasons.

You most likely know before this that Percy's leg was broken at riding about a week ago. He will be laid up in bed, poor fellow, for about a month, and it will put an end to his riding for this year. I hope it will not make him timid hereafter on horseback, for in that case he will never be a good rider.

Wishing you all a Merry Christmas and Happy New Year, I close. Love to all. *Your affectionate brother,* BEN

Conditions in Northfield Mills required General Ames' supervision in the winter of 1877. General and Mrs. Ames, Butler, Edith and Sarah occupied rooms in the house of Captain Jesse Ames.

Reminiscences of Winter in Northfield, Minnesota 1877

The journey from Boston to Chicago was wearying, as the children, Butler, Edith and Sarah required close attention. It was thought best not to take a nurse with us to Northfield, but to hire one there who would not prove homesick.

The Palmer House, in Chicago, where we spent the night, was sickening after our long car ride, on account of the nauseating odor of sewer gas, stale tobacco smoke, and lack of ventilation. On entering our suite of rooms I hastened to put the stopper on the bath tub and fill it half full of water, to cut off the smell of sewer gas. All to no purpose, of course, as the overflow pipe remained open.

A second day's journey took us to Northfield, where Captain and Mrs. Ames gave us a loving and cordial welcome. Mrs. Ames was always loving, considerate and gentle, although the addition to her quiet and orderly establishment of Del's three children must have been a heavy burden. Our family domain was the second story—consisting of three large rooms and a small one.

The first days were given to meeting the family connections and to unpacking our household goods, from Bay St. Louis, Mississippi, that had been sent to Northfield, when we left Mississippi after General Ames' resignation as Governor. All the linen and simple adornment of the Bay St. Louis home were arranged for use, and an effort made to make our rooms homelike. A pleasant week passed in the new environment, with walks to the mills to see and admire the new works and improvements, and returning the neighborly calls, and trying to get in touch and interest with new companions.

But by the tenth day diptheria, caught, no doubt, at the Palmer House in that fetid atmosphere, developed first in Edith, then a few days later in Sarah, and then Butler. The disease ran its course. The house had to be quarantined, and a doctor in daily attendance for three or more weeks. The little girls improved, and were able to be about. Not so Butler. His disease was over, but he steadily grew more feeble and in desperation we took him to St. Paul to the best doctor there, primarily about his eyes, which were becoming crossed. The doctor after hearing about his illness took the boy on his knee, suddenly touched his spine at the back of his neck. The poor child, with a yell, jumped from his knee, and had to be comforted.

"The poison of the diptheria has settled on his spine, and his case requires most careful treatment to insure recovery. I will write directions to your local physician. Do not fail to follow his advice. His eyes will be right when the poison is out of his system. His case admits of no temporizing."

We left St. Paul filled with apprehension and grief. Months of constant attention to the treatment ordered, of poultice and electrical applications—exposure to sunshine in the open air, no matter how cold the weather, in spite of the protests of Captain and Mrs. Ames, who were horrified to see a sick child taken out to sit in the sunshine with the thermometer near zero. Unable to stand, Butler sat in his little sleigh, warmly wrapped up, for two or three hours each day. The clear, dry air of the climate permitted it, and I, warmly dressed, made snow men, and talked and sang to him to help pass the time away. He had all my attention. Edith and Sarah were left to the kindly attention of their grandmother, and withdrew from the contest in the course of six weeks or more, and the boy gradually regained the use of his muscles and could walk.

All this has been written to indicate how most of the winter was spent. General Ames, at the mill, struggled with its problems, and at last returning spring brought hope and beauty.

Captain Ames was very fond of Robert Burns' poems, and in the evening we gathered near the fire while we sometimes read and talked, or talked over the events of the day. Our neighbors usually called in the morning. John would come for fifteen or twenty minutes, tell us the news, and, having said his say, go to the mill. I do not think he cared much to listen to the discussions of others. He did not seem to have the time.

Everything drops into insignificance in face of sickness and death, and the question of whether a thing is agreeable has no place in a struggle of life or death.

General Ames was in Chicago on business during the first part of March, 1877. Mrs. Ames was in Northfield.

NORTHFIELD, *March 2*, 1877

DEAR DEL: Your telegram came this afternoon. It is needless to say that I was disappointed, for I had been hoping that some lucky chance might bring you home on the afternoon train. If I had known you were to be away so long, you should have had a letter every day. I enclose two which may be of use to you.

John returned this afternoon and seems to be hopeful that he can effect a sale. He saw Mr. Glass who seemed very much pleased with the idea and who said he had just bought seven hundred acres of land for $10,000 and could give $12,000 in addition, making $22,000 and wished to know how much more he asked and at what rate of interest. John told him he would want $13,000 more at eight per cent and would give him plenty of time. Glass said he would talk it over with his family and directed John to another—Gorman, who thought he should like the property if his son in California were at home.

Then John went to Spillville. The man who has the mill there has four sons. They all spoke up at once, and were urgent to buy—the old man rather hung back. They agreed to meet John yesterday, but did not put in an appearance. John thinks there was a family dispute on foot. Perhaps all this does not sound very encouraging but it shows at least that there is an inclination to buy, and it is quite likely you can dispose of the mill[1] to good advantage. Of course, people have to think over such an outlay, and cannot decide in a minute.

Meigs has sent the specifications for your patent.

I have not been down to the mill, but day before yesterday they tried your brush machine. It feeds and throws out the wheat— The only difficulty as far as I could learn from your Father was that it was set so near together, the brushes I mean, that the wheat was warm. Your Father added "they

[1] Fort Atkinson Mill, Iowa.

are mighty secret about it." By which I judge he was not entirely confided in.

Fanny slept with me last night but I was more lonely than without her. She needs a whole bed to herself.

I have said good-bye to the twenties, Sweetheart, and begin to realize my years. This afternoon I took a long walk out by the cemetery and then returned and walked out to the college boarding house and back. I heard the birds sing, enjoyed the fresh breeze, and passed a man in a buffalo coat—who had a very perfect face. The days seem long without you, Sweetheart,—come home. BLANCHE

Palmer House, CHICAGO, *March 2*, 1877

DEAR BLANCHE: I do not forget that this is your birthday—I shall not forget it till the shadows fall.

This morning early I got up and took a bath—packed and brought my satchel to the cloak room by the office to be ready to start this evening. I had run through everything and found nothing in it—and to get away tonight refused to look further. But Baldwin asked me to test another offer and upon inquiry I found it to be desirable—and so found it necessary to stay till tomorrow or next week. I may go to Hastings Saturday night and get conveyed across country Sunday.

To make the trade the party offering it must telegraph East for permission. The trade is too good to be realized. I really do not expect it to become an accomplished fact.

It is this—a block of two (2) wholesale stores, each forty-five and one-half feet (45½′) front which are offered at sixty thousand dollars ($60,000.00) each making one hundred and twenty thousand ($120,000.00) dollars. My mill is put at sixty thousand dollars ($60,000.00). The other sixty thousand dollars ($60,000.00) is a mortgage.

The real estate agent to whom I was taken by the Palmer and on whom I rely says he can sell at once one of the two stores for fifty thousand dollars ($50,000.00) and that he will have no difficulty in selling the other at the same price in a brief time. If so and I believe it I would get in the trade forty thousand dollars ($40,000.00) less commissions. But, I do not believe the trade can be accomplished yet—I stay to see.

I have done nothing with the Southern property. Noonan evidently seeks to exchange encumbered property for my Natchez house and then sell it for cash. I suspect him. So, I will have to write down to N. and see about it myself.

So hard have I been working I have not had time to do any errands—not even to get my hair cut.

Love, Dear One, ADELBERT

Palmer House, CHICAGO, *March* 3, 1877

DEAR BLANCHE: As confidently expected my good bargain failed. I have nothing to look to now for the mill. It is possible I may exchange my southern property. Please send me separate deeds of my Natchez and Bay St. Louis places. You need not sign them as by the Code of Mississippi it is not necessary you should. Also send in another package—I will say by express—the original deeds of Bay St. Louis and Natchez.

I miss you much and were I not trying to believe I may do something here would feel that this separation was time wasted.

Never did woman have a more loving lover. ADELBERT

Palmer House, CHICAGO, *March* 5, 1877

DEAR BLANCHE: Today I exchanged my houses at Natchez and Bay St. Louis for property here.

I telegraphed you to have the deeds made out separately—to sign them in blank without going before a notary public or before witnesses and to forward with them the "abstract" and insurance policy of the Bay St. Louis place. I had written you previously not to sign as it was not necessary but it was thought it would be better to have your signature to be certified to here—as suggested by the agent through whom the exchange has been made. If the papers you send come all right I can get thro' the next twenty-four hours after their arrival.

With my two houses I give two thousand ($2,000.00) dollars. I get in exchange a block of six two-story frame houses at the corner of Ashland avenue and Hubbard street. See map. This property is unencumbered. They are situated about two miles west of the mouth of the river. They are second or third class houses—not in the best of repair—not in a desirable quarter of the city—and occupied by working men. They, all, now rent at about one hundred ($100) dollars a month. A few repairs would make them rent at an additional twenty-five ($25) dollars a month each it is said.

I have made careful inquiry and find the land which is one hundred and four (104) feet square on a corner is worth at the lowest estimate eighty (80) dollars pr. foot, making eight thousand three hundred and twenty ($8320) dollars. An experienced builder informs me these houses can not be put up for one thousand ($1000) dollars each—making for land and houses fourteen thousand, three hundred and twenty ($14320) dollars. This builder told me he would make great efforts to raise ten thousand ($10,000) dollars if he could buy the houses at that figure. A mortgage of ten thousand ($10,000) dollars has been on this block till recently.

Such is my information, which I believe. I have seen the houses but was not particularly pleased with them or the surroundings—nor do I suppose I would be with any houses or neighborhood in a city occupied by hard fisted sons of toil. Yet, after all my objections—and with the knowledge that they are not stone fronts on the chief boulevard of the city—the best evidence I can get shows them to be worth ten thousand ($10,000) dollars cash in these times. I also telegraphed you to tell John to send me a letter of introduction to our flour agents here that I may be able to raise the two thousand dollars to complete the bargain. I do not suppose anything will interpose to defeat the bargain.

I send you love, ADELBERT

NORTHFIELD, *March* 5, 1877

DEAR FATHER: Your letter came just in time to change the face of the prism which governs the lights in my horizon and what had been blue became rose colored. After one has been sick it takes some time for the mind as well as the body to recover its usual healthy tone, and I had been fretting about you and Paul, and feeling the loss of Mother's tender sympathy very much.

You must not think of us as suffering from cold weather. Day after day there is a cloudless sky. A half inch of snow fell the other night, but the warm spring sun melts it on all the southern and western slopes.

We propose a riding excursion the first of May to the Hills of St. Croix. They are said to be very beautiful—to visit these and try a little trout fishing will be the inducements. You did not tell me if you had bought the Cushing water power and lands in the town of St. Croix. The people there are anxious that it should be sold and improved.

We are very much amused at the uneasiness of the newspapers as to "what General Butler intends to do." From his long continued silences they think some mischief must be afoot.

Edith has a great deal to say of her "grandfather in Lowell who has no hair in the middle." She thinks she "likes him the best." Butler is growing quite fat. He has gained three pounds and it is all deposited upon his cheeks.

General Ames' affairs look well. We read the foreign war news with quite as much interest as the home telegrams—so heartless is selfishness.

There seems to be so few of us and life is so short that I do not like to have the months fly by while we are so far apart—but—as it must be so, I will try to bridge the distance with love and a kiss. BLANCHE

NORTHFIELD, *March 5*, 1877

DEAR DEL: I expected you home this afternoon—instead of that I received a letter and an old telegram asking for papers which show you are to be gone another week. John and I have fulfilled your directions as far as we are able—we cannot find and I do not think you ever had an abstract of the Natchez or Bay St. Louis property. We sent all the deeds and papers relating to the properties.

I wish you were going to sell the Natchez house—but you know best what you had better do—only look out for a good title—that there is only *one* mortgage on the property and that the taxes are not in arrears, and above all don't take anybody's say so for anything. *Look up the papers*, as you have made *me* do. I don't think much of business which takes you away from your family so much.

I take a little walk every day—sometimes with Butler, sometimes alone. Today I went down to the mill. John was at Faribault, and although Frank and Felix had just completed the rubbing machine and were going to experiment with it, I did not like to stay knowing that they would think me a meddlesome interfering woman. I cannot tell you therefore the result of their labors. If I had thought you were not coming home I should have had the latest news for you.

Oh! I will enclose also the specifications which Meigs has sent in. Tom can save time by signing and forwarding from Chicago. Also a letter about the De Graft property at Mankalo.

Jack's patent was not granted and the strangest thing of all is that the rubber arrangement for supporting mill stones was patented years ago and has expired, so that the patent is now public property, and that man who was so anxious to sell his patent to you has no patent—although he may not know it.

He probably has a patent on *his peculiar arrangement* but the principle belongs to the world.

I have written in haste as John is waiting. Love from

BLANCHE

Palmer House, CHICAGO, *March* 7, 1877

DEAR BLANCHE: The papers came today. You made rather an amusing mistake. I asked you to sign the two deeds *not before a notary*. One is so signed, not only for you but for me—the other is as requested. We are made residents of Minn. We are legally residents of Mississippi and so the papers must show. I think I can scratch out the residence; and make the other mistake answer our wishes. I am not sure that this trade will be accomplished as I do not know if the papers they wish to pass will be satisfactory to my lawyer. I am only anxious for the trade to become a fact—and consequently doubt. I shall try to get away tomorrow evening.

Today Hayes announces his cabinet. What a cabinet for the Republican party to accept! We were right in doubting him. He pretends political virtue in selecting bolting Republicans—*he* who comes in as he does—and I doubt not he will try to ignore the states in the South by which he attained his place—leaving his supporters to the tender mercies of the KuKlux murderers. Well, it makes no difference to us. In fact I rather enjoy the thing. We shall see lively times yet in the Republican party.

I have given up all hope of obtaining a trade for my mill and so repeat that John had better see Glass and make the sale taking security on his farm and the mill. He might telegraph Sam to see if anything can be done. Love,

ADELBERT

NORTHFIELD, *April* 3, 1877

DEAR FATHER: I resent your idea that I resorted to circumlocution to make a request of you—I thought you would recognize the lady at first glance. Was my description so inaccurate that you did not know her? Did she not state at once and most explicitly what she wanted—and is she not always making like demands without the least hesitation? Here she comes with another.

If you have not already rented the house at Bay View, please do not do so. Butler is very much out of health. The diphtheria he had has left a blood poison in his system, which has affected his nerves so that they do not act with the muscles, thus his limbs are very weak and will not do his bidding, and for a time his eyes and neck were feeble. He can hold up his head now and his eyes have recovered their strength but he cannot go up and down stairs without holding on to the balusters and crawling, and if he is on his knees he cannot get up without the aid of the wall or a chair. The doctors tell me that under the most favorable circumstances I must not expect him to get well in less than three months. They give him nerve tonics, and electricity, and wish him to be kept in the open air constantly. Therefore, it will be better for him to spend the summer at the seashore. Do not confound this disease with softening of the bones, Father. It is nothing like that.

Did Hattie tell you, that like you, he has one long and one short-sighted eye? Poor little man! It has been sad to see him so changed, but the improvement in his neck and eyes has given me great encouragement.

Love from your affectionate BLANCHE

During the summer, from June 14th to September, 1877, General Ames' family was at Bay View, Massachusetts. They spent that winter in Lowell.

LOWELL, *September 28, 1877*

DEAR DEL: Your letter from New York came last night, also one from your Father to you in which he seems strongly impressed with the idea that you had better be attending to your business.

Mrs. Fellow's daughter, Mrs. Hill, gave a little party Wednesday to the children. There were about twenty-five present. I made a lovely little dress for Sarah who was pronounced the belle of Mrs. Fellow's. She came home delighted with a bag of candy, a bouquet, and a gold ring which she found in her piece of cake. Edith looked very pretty in her muslin and lace dress—Butler was in fine style. In fact you would have been proud of your family.

Nothing is talked of but the races. Dr. Cilley and wife, friends of Father's, are expected to drive up from Boston with a fast horse which Paul has named Sleepy David. If Dr. Cilley is not a great boaster his horse ought to out trot all the rest. Paul expects to drive the horse.

Goodwin has not returned and everything is working at cross purposes—except the weather. The sky is dark, the wind east, and all the indications are towards rain and two or three days of rain, which will postpone the races and give a chance to clean the house.

Father signed the note and I gave it to Carney—and also had my will finished up.

It is lonesome without you, Sweetheart, and I am glad, very glad, that you are to be gone but a month. BLANCHE

LOWELL, *September* 30, 1877

DEAR DEL: I did not write you yesterday, for I did not have one moment's time. Your telegram came in the morning while we were at breakfast, and I went down to see Carney about half past ten. He agreed to go to Bridgeport tomorrow and on Tuesday I am to see him and write or telegraph the result of his investigations. Your telegram did not give the name of your hotel in Chicago, but I take it for granted that it is as usual, the Palmer House, and sent you a telegram directed there yesterday.

Instead of the predicted storm the weather was beautiful for the race. Father, Dr. and Mrs. Cilley came up from Boston at one, also General Kinsman. As I have not heard from Fannie I conclude Miss McKeen would not allow her to leave.

We had a hurried lunch and then drove to the race track—the races were exciting. Paul beat easily with Kenzie Boy and won great praise for the coolness and skill of his driving. He was received with laughter and clapping of hands as he slowed up his horse and looked back for the others, a rod or two before passing under the wire. Sleepy David came up from Boston on the freight train arriving at half past two. Tom was so much disturbed that he refused to take part in the race if Paul entered. As Paul had already won one race he could not well insist. Tom gave as his reason that he would not run his Fannie and have her beaten. But alas! for Tom. He would not let Paul into the race, Randolph had withdrawn his "Bob Tail" so that Charles Palmer and a hired horse was his only opponent. Palmer beat him the first heat. Florence was so excited that she left the grand stand, and took a seat in her carriage. She watched the second heat until she saw it was hopeless as Tom's horse was behind and breaking so that Tom could not bring her down. Poor Florence could not bear the sight any longer and covered her face with her hands and refused to see the end. She calls the horse hers and was deeply interested.

The last race called "Free to All" Paul was allowed to enter for the second heat—but as Paul looked small Dr. Cilley's horseman was fearful he would not be muscular enough to manage the animal, a tall, finely formed, easy stepping creature, so he strapped him up in every direction and so closely that he really could not go.

Paul drove around, but the other horses were ahead of him and as they had already had a heat (Hasting's horse beating both times) they would not try it again and let Paul in for a second heat. Dr. Cilley's man was very sorry that he had not given the horse more his way, but it would have made no difference in regard to the prizes. So Tom was beaten a second time. He drove a horse belonging to a man in Andover. Altogether Tom appeared very badly and his poor driving lost him the race. He came up last evening and made a kind of apology to Paul for his action, saying that Palmer had told him that "Sleepy David" had just come up from Mystic Park and had a record of 2.30 and of course he could not let Fannie race against such a horse. He also made up with Willis Farrington for his fault finding in regard to the decision of the judges. He had threatened to write to the newspapers and quarreled with Willis a good deal, seeming to hold him responsible for the decisions of the other two judges. He was so mean about the race I am glad he was beaten, but feel sorry for Florence.

Sarah is my bedfellow now. If I put her in Anne's room she wakes up, and comes back to me. All are well and miss the head of *our house* and *home* very much. More than you miss us, Sweetheart, for you are the traveller and have new things to occupy you. Love, BLANCHE

LOWELL, *October* 1, 1877

DEAR DEL: The house is pleasant and quiet. Father, Kinsman, and Hattie have gone to Boston. The children have just returned from school. Sarah is three years old today. She ought to have a party—but will have to take three spankings instead.

Yesterday afternoon we went over to Dracut. Florence and Tom were there. I did not say a word to Florence about the races for I knew she was feeling badly. After she had gone, however, Nina began an attack upon the united assembly saying that she did not see why the whole family should be down on Tom. All disavowed any such intention. I explained to her that the only reason Paul and Prentiss were so anxious to beat was because they thought that Tom had had an advantage over them as his horse had been kept on the track and had been in training longer—that Paul had felt a little hurt and annoyed that Tom would not allow "Sleepy David" to take part in the race, but as Tom had come up to the house and explained that he had been deceived in regard to "Sleepy David"—it was all right and there certainly was no unkind feeling that I knew of. I succeeded in allaying the storm and Nina drove over to Florence's to tell her about it.

Palmer it seems had filled Tom's head full of false notions about "Sleepy David" and the idea that Paul was going to jockey him out of the race by entering an old racer. Tom believed every word Palmer said, and all the time *Palmer* was playing the jockey trick, for the horse he entered was an old racer, that had had its name changed three or four times, and had a record. At Dracut yesterday Tom said "Palmer was no gentleman and a d——n liar." Tom sees that considerable feeling has been stirred up by the race—Tom had better trust his connections rather than outsiders another time.

All are well, as usual. I feel comparatively limber today and mean to take advantage of it to do some shopping this afternoon.

Love from your wife BLANCHE

NORTHFIELD, MINN., *October* 4, 1877

DEAR BLANCHE: I was much entertained by your account of the race. On Florence's account I regret Tom's defeat which as you know I have been wishing all the time. I am sorry she lets her soul go out to such a degree on a trotting horse. How much she has to learn to know better! I can imagine the wife of the old Roman gladiator, witnessing his struggle, would turn away her head to avoid seeing her vanquished husband receive his final blow; but how Florence would permit herself to act so towards her horse is beyond my comprehension.

I went to find my three-year-old today. By the way, I have named her, not Kentucky Second, after her mother, but Minnesota after her place of birth! I shall call her Minni for short. She is very handsome and moves with much grace. Judging from her motion I believe she will make a fine stepper. I was much pleased with her.

I am much absorbed in my gun just now. I spend nearly all the time in the work shop attached to the old mill where I am having a model made. It required some attention and thought to tell a workman just how to make a gun when one has never made one. This I am doing—and in the effort find a thousand and one things to let my brain work on. As machine is entirely novel so are all its separate parts.

I believe I have neglected to say anything about the mill business. The profit we make now is very satisfactory. But owing to the large quantities of flour on its way to the markets we expect lower prices. Then again our water is short. Father is trying to get rain but none of importance has fallen yet.

I wish you would send those pistols in my trunk to me by John when he visits you. Father wants them. Do not fail to give them to John when you see him.

Mother sends her love to you and the babies. Ask the children for me if they are good and dutiful—kiss them and take a world of love from ADELBERT

NORTHFIELD, MINN., *October* 5, 1877

DEAR BLANCHE: I am in our dining room which is lighted, as of old, with kerosene and heated by the most pleasant of wood fires. This room is just cleaned up after being treated with a coat of new paper. The body of the paper is much as the old but around the lower portion of the room is a darker paper, scientific name of which is Dado. I see the suggestion came from you. The room looks very well, indeed.

My day has been a little variable. I am working on some device to revolve the magazine of my gun; and while certain I shall "get it" by and by, I am now laboring with partial success. The apparatus for moving the cartridge forward which was on your mantle piece had five pieces in it. I do the same work with *two* pieces now. I am working to rotate the magazine with one more which will make three in all. Still hopeful you see.

My machine for cleaning wheat came today. It was too large to get into the door so we had to take it to pieces. Now, it is in the room for experiments and we will go to work tomorrow on it with a right good will. When I think of the things I have to do it seems as if two months hence would find me here. I am not going to let Felix waste my time as he did last winter. There are plenty here who want labor and I am not so secret in my work as I was last spring when we were experimenting. I shall put two or three men at work if necessary and rush forward.

By the way, that reminds me that I intended when East to have a good time here, going gunning, visiting Raymond in Dakota Territory, etc. That evidently was fancy. The fact is I am working not on milling but new machines harder than ever. It may be cheering to you to know I have nothing new on.

I end as ever in telling you again of the great fact of my life—my infinite love for my beautiful wife. ADELBERT

LOWELL, *October* 6, 1877

DEAR DEL: I have just returned from a visit to Carney—he has seen Father and has tried to make some headway in regard to Mother's estate. With what success remains to be seen. I told him the Chicago man was ready to give you a mortgage on the property you have there equal to the encumbrance upon the Bridgeport property. He said something that showed he did not quite understand the arrangement, and I did not take the trouble to clear it to his comprehension, for I thought that you could, and had better, see this B. property yourself.

I had a letter from you last night and am sorry that you have no supporters on your wheat cleaning process. It is very discouraging to attempt anything with all the world against you. I believe you can make it work most satisfactorily. The crowd out there are only a set of weather-cocks veering with every breeze which blows. You made flour last Spring and had bread made of it which all agreed was very white and satisfactory considering that the wheat had been so unevenly dried. You remember it was nearly as white as the Fancy. Don't let them make you blue, but work out the problem calmly and slowly—so as to do yourself and your process justice. Is not yours the fate of all innovators and improvers?

Butler is saving chestnuts for you. The children all want to know when you are coming home. They are certainly very fond of their Father. If I were not inclined in that direction myself—I might be a little jealous. As it is, we all run a race to see which one can spoil you first.

I am well, and in better spirits than I have been—rheumatics do not improve the temper, and where one cannot move oneself it is natural to feel that it is difficult to move others.

Love, BLANCHE

LOWELL, *October* 7, 1877

DEAR DEL: In spite of your contemptuous remarks in regard to the dates upon my letters, I shall continue to do as I have done—guess at them when I can—omit when I feel *sure* that I shall not be right, and write them with a feeling of relief when I have lately seen a newspaper or when there is anyone at hand to tell me. Of course, you will have no objection, as in any event you will know the month and year, inasmuch as I shall not be likely to make a mistake about that.

This morning I had a number of hooks put in the closet of the children's room—sewed straps in all their garments, and propose to teach them orderly habits, if possible. It is most distracting when they return from school to see a coat on one chair, a hat or so on the floor, and in fact every place available or unavailable littered with raiment of one or the other of our crowd.

This afternoon I took them to the dancing school. Butler and Edith protested stoutly that they would not dance with Sarah. Edith, however, was better natured than she promised to be, and took her little sister by the hand and showed her how to go.

While they were dancing, I went over to Mrs. Atwood's and to Mrs. Cady's to see about Fannie's dress for the party—returning I found the children all dancing the lancers except Sarah and a little boy who is too shy to take part. Sarah was sitting across the hall from me, all alone, apparently well contented and watching the dancing. Soon there was a great deal of laughing among the scholars in her vicinity. Mrs. Darracutt went to see the cause and there was Sarah going to sleep, her head nodding first one side and then the other. Mrs. Darracutt brought her to me, but she would not stay long. When the children began to practice the polka, she wanted to go and take her place with the others. She has not the slightest doubt as to her capacity to do everything in the most approved manner—in which respect she does not resemble *her mother* although I can hear you say that she does.

Love, from your snubbed and downtrodden

BLANCHE

LOWELL, *October* 15, 1877

DEAR DEL: It is Monday evening, and I am writing to you in our room. Paul, Ben, and Willis Farrington are in the library. Our babies are breathing regularly and quietly in the heavy slumber which comes in the first of the night.

Prentiss has just brought me two letters from you, and I feel as if we had been having an unsatisfactory little chat. "Hearing or reading may be believing" according to the old saw, but it is not *seeing*, and I much prefer those chats where I can see you and you can see me.

You ask about the time Paul made in the race, 2.59. But

he held the horse in all the way and almost walked on the home stretch. Tom's Fannie made 2.49¼. Paul has been trying to get up a race (and the day has been set twice but owing to the bad weather postponed) between Stott's new horse, Tom's "Fannie" and "Kenzie Boy." They were all on the track Saturday speeding the horses. Tom saw "Kenzie Boy" go and now he refuses to race. Paul drove him today in 2.45 and thinks in a week he can make it 2.40.

In the Cartridge case, the result as I understand it, is this—Father has purchased the patents which cover the disputed points between the Lowell and the Metallic Cartridge Co. It seems the Metallic Co. were not the inventors and did not own the patents. This was found out rather accidentally, and now Father says he is going to turn the tables and make the Metallic Co. hum.

I am a little more provoked than amused about the Prairie Creek mortgages—for the reason that Mr. Carney sold in order to forward the money when they drew on him from Northfield, eight hundred dollars worth of government bonds more than they drew on him for—so that in addition to the other two thousand four hundred makes thirty-two hundred which has been lying idle for six months—and you want a stem-winding watch, and I want a desk like Paul's for your papers and a *fancy brass fender*.

Well! Well! Such is life! What do you advise me to do with the twelve hundred I have here? I have had five or six hundred in interest since last March and what I have not spent added to the eight hundred makes the above sum. Should you not be fearful of putting too much in one place?

Now for another air-castle which I am going to knock over. Tom Nesmith went to see Rollin White last summer to see about buying his place. The house is in good repair, with gas but no city water—there is water pumped up from the river below in the house. Mr. White did not wish to sell and would not name a price but gave Tom to understand that twenty-five thousand would not buy it. This drove Tom off as he did not wish to give as much for the White house as the one he now has would cost him. I hear that the place is, however, mortgaged for more than its value, and I am going to see if we can buy up the mortgages. All hope is not gone yet you see. I shall call on Carney again tomorrow and propound this new proposition.

Several persons have spoken to me of Fannie—they think her very pretty. She wore a hat of mine to the concert—which was very becoming to her. Now she has one of her own—a light grey felt with soft feathers the same shade. When she tried it on she looked like a picture.

Capt. Meigs has your papers you left for him. I think I have attended to everything you have spoken about.

I send you love, Sweetheart, and trust you are keeping up your spirits, so that your cheeks are not growing hollow. If you do not plump your face in some way, you will have a son who will be always a mass of bones, hollow-eyed, thin cheeked and weary-looking—so take care.

Good-night. BLANCHE

Merchants Hotel, ST. PAUL, *October 23,* 1877

DEAR BLANCHE: The past week has been most perfect weather. Although within one hundred and fifty miles of the border of British America late in October the weather was so temperate an overcoat was not necessary.

The soil in the Red river section is very rich and the country looks much as it did about Northfield the first time you were there, qualified to this extent—there instead of being a rolling prairie it is perfectly flat; and as it is but sparsely settled, the houses are few and small and fences are unknown. Raymond is charmed with the country and intends to locate there. The climate, the soil, the probable future of Fargo have about concluded him to make it his territorial home. He intends to go into banking. He wants me to join him and possibly go into farming on a grand scale. I do not object to either of his plans for I believe he can make money at either but at present I have no funds for such a purpose.

Yesterday they gave us a special car to go out twenty miles west to the Dalrymple farms. Mr. D. does not live on his farm —has no family on it but hires one hundred or more men to do the work. This last season he raised on one farm 57,000 bushels of wheat and nets fifty cents pr. bushel on it. Such farming seems very attractive especially as no personal attention is needed during the six months of winter. It requires capital to do even that. I much doubt if I shall ever get so far as to undertake anything of the kind with Capt. R. I am glad to say he is a success in the territory and has a host of friends. He has got so far as to say it may be possible that his new found friends may want him to run as their candidate for delegate for Congress. Thus you see he is making progress. His wife is and has been for sometime visiting the Warners in Conn. I think she is to go to Washington soon.

If you want to put some of your money up there in R.'s bank say so and I will not let our agent in Minneapolis lend it.

Last evening I found Gen'l. O. O. Howard at our supper table at Fargo. He had shipped his command down river on a steamboat and he and staff took the cars at Bismarck and came east by rail. I was glad to see him as we are old friends. The abuse the papers have heaped upon him has been like all their abuse of individuals, unjust, wicked. No man could have done more than he. He could not overtake the Indians as they were mounted while the larger part of his force were afoot. But he has been following them since the 20th of June last—four months, and during that time he and his command marched seventeen hundred (1700) miles! He whipped the Indians at first and consequently they would never stop to fight him but kept marching on seeking allies and making for the border line. Genl. H. did not expect to overtake them but kept driving them in the snares the troops on this side of the Rocky Mountains should set for them. Gibbon failed, Sturgis failed and Miles nearly failed, sheer good luck enabled him to retrieve his first error.

The papers say nothing of Genl. H's presence at Joseph's surrender—even though he telegraphed the fact. Yet he was there for the day and a half preceeding Chief Joseph's surrender. In fact Joseph offered him his gun but Howard only magnanimously motioned him to give it to Miles. The duration of his march—the distance traveled, the hardships endured has never been equaled in any of our Indian wars and yet the newspapers of the day have been carping and sneering at him all these long months when in fact he is entitled to the very highest credit. So envious of him have his military confreres on this slope of the Rocky Mountains been that they have suppressed his dispatches and the chief one to do that is my old comrade Genl. Terry. At least so Genl. H. surmises. Since Genl. T. treated me in the same way once and got his Brigadier Generalship by it, I can readily believe he has had a hand in causing Genl. H. a part of his sorrows.

I shall go down to N. tomorrow morning at six. I left there a week ago tomorrow. So for a whole week I have not had one word from you. I am anxious to get the bundle of letters I know awaits me. It is now about a month since I left you. I can not well tell when I shall start East. I think now the last part of Nov. which will make my absence two months.

I send a world of love to my wife and babies.

Adelbert

LOWELL, *October* 20, 1877

DEAR DEL: This is a rainy dull day and our ride to Andover is, of course, given up. Kinsman has gone to the mill with Paul. Butler and Edith have donned their rubber boots and have gone out. Sarah has eaten so many grapes she is complaining "my stomach aches."

When I have finished writing you I shall sit down by the window to look over and mend a formidable pile of winter stockings.

Last evening Paul, Kinsman and I went to a mesmeric performance given by a Prof. Cadwell. It was very amusing. Among other things he had five or six boys called onto the stage, mesmerized them and then made them think they were being challenged by some imaginary boys in the air,—the different expressions and modes of fighting, for he held up his hand and they all hit and lunged at it as if it were a live boy—remarkable. His subjects were all weak looking boys and women. Dr. Parker took part in the entertainment to the extent of sticking a needle into various parts of a boy's hand which the Prof. had rendered insensible. Then the Prof. told the boy that Dr. Parker had gone off of the stage although he was right beside of him—and the boy began to look for him as he was directed to do by the Prof. Dr. Parker in the meantime trying all he could to attract his attention, sticking his needle into the back of the boy's neck so as to draw blood but without making the slightest impression. After the performance the Prof. tried for a moment to mesmerize Mrs. Ludlum but he was unsuccessful, as I think he must always be with any but the most passive, weak natures. I wish you had gone with me. I enjoy so much more when you are seeing or hearing too, and then you ought always to have the same experiences that I do.

Before starting for the show I saw all the children snug in their beds and heard their prayers. Butler was slow and inclined for play, so I said, perhaps pettishly, "What makes you so slow, Butler—you children are a great deal of trouble. It takes so long to get you all to bed one after the other." Butler answered: "If we are so much trouble why did you get married and have us?" These were his exact words. I shall have to be careful what I say hereafter.

Love, BLANCHE

LOWELL, *October*, 1877

DEAR DEL: I think of you tonight as at Fargo and being in a place of which I know nothing—it seems as if you had gone a thousand miles farther off. The two letters which I have had from you to-day do not serve to bridge the distance. I am truly glad your stay is not to be a long one.

If you think best, I shall have two thousand or so here soon and am willing to risk that amount. The money in Northfield, I should like better in mortgages as I had made up my mind to have $12,500 invested, that was, and prefer to carry out that intention, for the simple and foolish reason that having grown accustomed to thinking of such an amount it is easier to remember.

I feel as if I had a good deal of business on hand. Nothing very important however.

Oh! Nina is to give a large party at Urban Hall the 10th of Nov. What do you think about Fannie going? I have no doubt she would enjoy it very much. Ask your Mother.

I told Butler when he was very cross with me that he had better take Hattie or somebody for a Mother. "I don't want any Mamma, only a Papa that's all."

So they can do very well without me if they have you, and as I want you too, you are in great requisition. BLANCHE

NORTHFIELD, MINN., *October* 25, 1877

DEAR BLANCHE: I believe it is a month ago today since I saw you last. Then I thought my face would be turned eastward by this time but now though the month has passed I can not say when I can start—some three weeks or more yet.

My wheat machine was ready for me when I returned yesterday but as we have to get up steam and as everybody was busy I have put off the trial till tomorrow. My gun goes slowly. I have been delayed by the difficulty I find in inventing just what I want to move the cartridges with. I think I have it now. It is the cast piece necessary to complete the gun.

You say I want a stem winding watch and you want to buy me a desk like Paul's for my papers. Do not buy me a desk. At least if you do let me buy you a piece of silk for a dress. I have my *notion* of what I want for a desk and exactly what it is "no fellow can find out." Then again, I do not want a desk till I can get a house to put it in. As for the watch, altho' mine runs and stops in obedience to its own fitful laws,

I do not want one till I get out of debt—so you see we may never be to the expense of a desk and a watch.

I send to you and the babies, many kisses and a world of love,

ADELBERT

LOWELL, *October* 28, 1877

DEAR DEL: I have had two nice letters from you today and one dated Oct. 17, which was too old to be nice. I suspect that somebody I know forgot to mail it before starting for Fargo.

Edith is to go with Butler to the dancing school. Did I write you that on my return from Boston, Butler met me with a formal saying "I don't want Edith to go to the dancing school any more." "Why," I asked, "was she not a good girl?" "No! she would not dance but 'cept with me and I wanted to dance with Julia Fisk. Edith won't dance with the boys who ask her, and the teacher makes me dance with her. She ain't going no more." Edith seemed a little chagrined that I should hear such a report about her and said she would "dance with the boys next time." Butler was very polite to Julia Fisk, but Edith he pulled about by the arm, instead of crooking his elbow and extending his hand graciously as he did to the fair Julia. You must come home and look after your family.

I received the deeds and insurance policies you sent me. I will go in with Mr. Raymond, or rather I want you to go in for me to the amount of twenty five hundred. I shall regard it as a speculation, and make up my mind that I am willing and able to lose that amount for the sake of the chances. Raymond and the rest of the world must think that you do it. It is all the same anyway, for that which makes me richer or poorer does the same for you and vice versa. A kiss from

BLANCHE

NORTHFIELD, MINN., *October* 29, 1877

DEAR BLANCHE: I met Mrs. Wheaton on the street today. I raised my hat and would have passed by but she stopped and I of necessity did likewise. She asked about you and the babies. Then she said "She will spend the winter in Lowell." I said "Yes." She then added, "She (meaning you) is expecting an increase in her family!" I said "Yes, after awhile." The interview then closed. Some women are curious.

Your new scheme of buying a hillside—"Indian Orchard"—does not strike me very favorably. I will not now speak of location for I have not examined it but I will analyze your figures. You say land on the hill above which would be considered more valuable sold for twelve cents (12 cts) a foot. Let us suppose you give ten cents (10 cts) a foot. One acre will cost four thousand three hundred and fifty six dollars ($4,356.00)— Twenty acres (you speak of having fifteen or twenty acres) will cost just eighty seven thousand one hundred and twenty dollars ($87,120.00). Can anybody you are acquainted with put that sum of money in land for a residence? Better hold to the possibility of getting the R. White house or turn your search in another direction.

I am doing nothing just now on my various machines because Felix and his assistant are working on a change or improvement in the new mill. It is probable that I will find the end of November near with my improvement incomplete.

My pen has been moving very unevenly. Father has his papers out and I have to go to his relief to aid him in arranging notes, mortgages and so forth. My ladder will have to wait my return to L. Then I will try to perfect it.

Kiss the babies for me. Some night when you are putting them to bed and hearing them say their prayers and they delay you and you get cross imagine you are hearing them on my account and you will feel better; as I would hold it a great pleasure to hear their sweet voices and see their dear faces. They grow old too fast for me. Caresses for my beautiful wife.

ADELBERT

NORTHFIELD, MINN., *October* 31, 1877

DEAR BLANCHE: You see by the heading of this letter that it is the last day of the month—my birthday. In a recent letter you said I should have a present today but, alas! I did not even receive your usual daily letter. If the time has not passed when I was to be the recipient of a present, a birthday present, I will guess what it is to be as you direct. Of course it is not your love for you gave that to me over seven years ago—unless you made a mistake at that time. It is not a watch or a house, the only two things I aspire to outside of my own home, for you said it was not to be a watch and I am morally certain you have not bought a house and lot. Well, let me see—is it a jacknife? A comb? Or a painted bootjack? Have I failed? If so I give it up. Perhaps I will not receive any.

I had a letter from John T. dated Boston, the 26th inst. It appears he is doctoring there and evidently having a very good time. He writes that he is going to call on you. You doubtless have seen him ere this and from him learned what he wrote me; that he did not expect to return here till about the middle of November. Should he delay till then I will not be back in Lowell till about the first of December.

I have attended to the furs in Minneapolis. I will have the bearskin mounted there and the two robes, one of bear skins, the other of wolf skins, made there also.

Ask Paul if he has any news through Hunt or anybody else about the war in Europe and the possibility of further complications.

I miss you very much. Love from ADELBERT

LOWELL, *November* 1, 1877

DEAR DEL: Last night the fairies, witches, and warlocks made merry and celebrated the birthday of the one I love best. No doubt laid plans for his success and contentment for the coming year, and perhaps one little imp put in a petition that he might be allowed to grow fat.

I send my love, kisses and caresses for a birthday gift altho he does not entirely deserve them, on account of considerable impertinence in his letter of Oct. 26. Of course, my "ailings" and troubles will return with you. How could there be any question in your mind on such a point? You may as well be prepared for groans for I feel it in my bones that there will be plenty of them. As for morals I detest them, and exactly why my finding a moral should make you more deserving of kindness and attention, I am at a loss to know. It is not likely that you will pretend that you have not had your desserts during our seven years of married life.

Ah well, Dearie, I love you, and if it affords you any gratification to try to tease and find fault with your wife—why I shall be the last one to balk your inclination.

YesterdayI did not write you. Paul went off to meet Hunt in Boston and go somewhere shooting. Aunt Nina, and Lottie, Butler and I went down at half past nine. Butler had one tooth filled, but he cried and felt so nervous about it, it was very hard work. Today, however, he says he should like to go down again, that of course he cried the first time. He went upstairs to play with the little Moffat children while I sat for an hour and a half under Dr. Moffat's pincers, scrapers, wheels, etc. At last that was ended. I paid my bill (fifty-five dollars) and went upstairs to call on Mrs. Moffat and thank her for her invitation to lunch. Then Butler and I took the horse car to Tremont St. to join the others and to shop.

John and Nellie came up last night and left at noon today.

They are going to Washington after making a visit of four or five days in New York. I feel that your return is being put off and put off. Butler said, "Uncle John, I want you to go to Northfield so that my Papa can come home." Good night.

BLANCHE

NORTHFIELD, MINN., *November* 3, 1877

DEAR BLANCHE: I received two letters from you today. One was dated "Sunday, Oct. 27." Sunday was not the 27th, and the 27th was not Sunday. You have been very discreet before when you only put "Oct." at the head of your letters and left it to me to guess at their date by the post mark, but in this instance your recklessness has been the cause of your undoing. Don't trifle with dates. You are not equal to them. They "floor" you every time. Till we meet again put at the head of your letters simply "Nov."—unless per chance I remain absent till after Thanksgiving when you must change the "Nov." to "Dec." By following implicitly these directions somebody I know of will not have the opportunity to make such pointless observations as the above.

Surely you are making our children very old when our son has such ideas as your letter shows. Already he has been taught to prefer dancing with the other girl and refusing even to let his own sister go to the dance. He is growing old too fast as I said in a recent letter.

Capt. Raymond is now in Washington. I will write to him before he begins his banking business and agree to take the $2,500.00 you think you can afford to put in such an enterprise. You, yourself, admit it to be something of a speculation—thus you show yourself something of a gambler. Money is money. Do not take many chances. It may be best for you to take the slow and sure ways of the east under the guidance of Mr. Carney and not try the fleet and problematical ways of the West. I believe however that there would be little if any danger of losing your money in R's hands. Banking pays in this country—there is little to be lost in it and this country is so very prosperous that a heavy interest can be paid.

I have done nothing in particular except to move about and observe all that is going on. We are doing very well now and I am in hopes we will have a good season for our business. I see that this business needs more of A. A. and less of J. T. A.

I send as I ever must when absent great love to my Beautiful wife.

ADELBERT

LOWELL, *November 2*, 1877

DEAR DEL: This has been a stormy day—I had a number of errands to do but gave them up on account of the rain. I can always find plenty to do, if not something useful I turn to my poor attempt at art. In this way the day flew by very quickly and when twilight put an end to my labors I found I had been standing nearly all day. Results not satisfactory. I mean the results of my labors.

Ben went to New York at five. Paul returned at six. This morning, they, Willis, Hunt and Paul were wrecked on a gravel bank in Boston Harbor among the islands. The man who owned the boat and undertook to sail it was quite ashamed of himself. They all got out on the bank and tried to get the sail boat off but could not succeed. So all got into the row boat and pulled three miles to land. Fortunately they had the wind with them and could keep the boat strictly before it or the waves would have swamped them.

We expect Father home Monday. I do not suppose it will be for a long stay. Hattie writes that she is full of care. Some one to lunch every day and the prospect that Father is going to keep up the practice. She says she is glad to feel that she is of use—but thinks the time is not far distant when she will be more contented with two rooms and less care. She feels the burden more just now because she has been so free all summer.

I heard Sarah last night singing to herself in her sleep. "I am glad to go, but teacher dear, we'll all be back tomorrow." She sang quite loudly and it sounded strangely enough in the stillness of night. She will hardly be ready to give up her place to you—as it is such a satisfaction for her to wake up and pat my cheek until she goes to sleep again. I have bribed Edith to wear the sponges on her thumbs every night for a week by the promise of a locket. Love from BLANCHE

LOWELL, *November 4*, 1877

DEAR DEL: Father came home on the six o'clock milk train. I have been with him all the evening. He seems in good health and spirits. He is going to try two or three cases this week. As for politics there is nothing new—no fight will be made on Hayes until after the elections in New England and New York, for the reason that it is best it should be understood that Hayes' policy killed the Republican Party in the states, and not any fight or fault finding in Washington.

I agree with you, that my figures were very bad in the

Indian Orchard, but that was owing to my having put trust and confidence in the calculations of a West Pointer and a Heidleburg student instead of using my own poor understanding. However, the calculation is of little importance as the Locks and Canal Co. refuse to sell a foot of land at any price but are ready to lease for any term of years at a nominal rental. They are content to get taxes paid and take a very small per cent looking forward to a future great increase in value of the land.

I have not given up pursuit of the Rollin White place but you know that it is my theory that one ought not to make up the mind to one thing only and think that nothing else will do.

Now, Del, about my getting cross, I shall keep your remarks in mind, and shall not fail to make up a face when I hear, as I shall hear, your voice change, and see the deep lines come between your eyes. I know I am irritable, but I *do* try to be decent, although I must acknowledge that many times my efforts are unavailing.

Sarah cried so grievously with the great tears running down her cheeks, because she could not go to dancing school, that I told her she should go over to Mrs. Pearson's with me, and we would buy some dates. Sarah and I were a little behind hand in getting ready. Butler and Edith were dressed first. Mathew was waiting at the front door and these two enterprising young people took it into their heads to get into the carriage, tell Mathew that he was not to wait for me, and drove off. So that when Sarah and I went down we found ourselves left behind and had to wait until Mathew returned. We then went to Aunt Lottie's and made quite a call, returning called at the dancing school for the children. Edith seemed to be enjoying herself very much. Sarah wished to go and sit beside her on the bench which runs around the hall. I allowed her to do so, although when the children got up to dance she was left all alone. That did not disconcert her in the least, and she quietly watched them dancing grand right and left, the basket, and the Lady Washington's reel. But when the teacher formed them in line for the march, she could restrain herself no longer, and you can image my surprise to see her speak to Mrs. Darracutt, who then led her to Edith and Butler who were standing in line. When the music began she marched off with them. Of course she did not keep step and in her little bonnet and coat she looked so earnest and seemed so convinced that she was doing exactly the right thing, it was comical enough and everyone laughed when she came around into sight.

Many ladies go to take their children or bring them away so that there is usually quite an audience. Edith was in great glee over her own performance. She said she was not afraid and had danced with the other boys. "I danced with that boy who has his hair cut. I like him. I like to dance with him. I like to sit by him forever, and go and live with him and sleep with him and then you could buy another girl and call her Edith." "But what would you do for a Mother?" "You could be my Mother and have another Edith too." It seems to me our oldest daughter is peculiar to say the least of it. Surely it is not common for four year olds to talk as she does.

I have written you a long letter and close it with kisses.

BLANCHE

NORTHFIELD, MINN., *November* 5, 1877

DEAR BLANCHE: This part of the world has lost all trace of John and Nellie and I am grateful to you for your information about him. Father keeps saying "John should come home," but I say so far as the business is concerned there is not need of it—and so I have written him. This is the first time Nellie has been east since their marriage trip and I am not to be the one to force them home at such a time when really there is no need of it. I hear that Nellie has written some friend here glowing accounts of Bay View. It is well. While impressing her friends by descriptions of her own "nice" times she exaggerates for or against just as may suit her purpose. So far as I can learn she can not praise your surroundings enough. I wish you would tell me if John has improved any in health or healthful appearance during his doctoring down in Boston. Their stay east will be almost as long as was mine from June to September.

Love for you, Dear One, and for our babies.

ADELBERT

LOWELL, *November* 5, 1877

DEAR DEL: Butler read your letter and said "that is a nice letter Papa sent me." He was greatly pleased to be remembered. He went to the mill this afternoon with Paul and they drove over to Mr. Wellman's. There is a magpie there which went after Butler at once, and frightened him so that he cried. The little boys in the neighborhood tease the bird, and naturally it does not like children. Your boy will have to learn to control his fears.

Dr. Parker called this evening and wished me to say to you that he will wait your return before doing anything further about the patent—that the paper requires your (yours and his) joint signature—that the paper is satisfactory to him except in that part relating to the selling, etc. He remained to dinner, which is just over, much to my relief, as the room was very warm and my garments are too close for comfort.

I have no birthday present for you, Sweetheart, which is well as it is very evident from your letter that there is nothing within my power to give you which would be satisfactory. Exactly why you should speak as if there were any likelihood of my purchasing a piece of land without your advice and approval—I don't exactly see. The fact is—and my Love ought to know it—that the greatest pleasure I have is in starting some project and talking it over, but to go off and all alone attempt some wonderful performance would not be in keeping with *my conception* of my character.

The children wake about six in the morning and keep up such a movement and make so much noise that sleep is impossible. This is my poor excuse for a feeble letter. My eyelids are actually closing even while I write. Love, Dearie.

BLANCHE

LOWELL, *November* 6, 1877

DEAR DEL: This has been a quiet and uneventful day for me. It is by far the coldest of the season. The children came to me for their fur coats and muffs and even when well wrapped up did not care to remain out long at a time. All my moments are occupied—when there is nothing better I always have plenty of clothes and stockings requiring mending.

Father, Paul and Boynton are in the library talking navigation. The latter, as usual, talking as if he had been wound up and warranted to go just such a time.

Paul went to Boston today and brought home a box of candy. Thinking it might be too late for the children to eat of it, he told me he had some, by spelling out the words without pronouncing them. Butler heard and his curiosity was evidently excited, but he was not to be out done by any such performance as that. So he called out "P-i-g, pig, Uncle Paul, p-i-g." It was rather funny as he happened to say it, for it hit the nail on the head, inasmuch as Paul had candy and was not prepared to share. Of course, Butler could have no sympathy with its being too late to eat candy.

Nina's party has caused considerable comment, for the gossips have decided that it is given for the purpose of announcing her engagement, some say to Palmer, others to McDaniels.

I send you love. We shall all rejoice to have you at home once more. BLANCHE

NORTHFIELD, MINN., *November* 9, 1877

DEAR BLANCHE: Yesterday we had a telegram from John T. who was in New York. Should he go to Washington from there we can not well guess when he will return. I expect to get away from here about the 20th inst. Of course I can not now say I will leave in eleven days but such is my expectation.

In yours of the 5th inst. you say you "have no birthday present for me"! Well, that *is* cool. In a former letter you said "you *shall* have a birthday present." No matter. I do not care so much about the present as I do about being deceived and trifled with—and the sad thought of having a wife who can find it in her heart to treat me in such a way.

Uncle Dave has been up this evening and he and Father have devoted the greater part of the time on repeating stories of the wonderful feats of their Grandfather Perry in the Revolutionary War. They are the same old stories I have heard from my infancy up. Yet, I see they are told with the same interest and same details— There are no additions—no accretions as the years go by—which to my mind is evidence that the stories are true—or at least they are repeated as they heard them from the very identical Grandfather Perry himself.

You take me to task for supposing you would buy a place without consulting me. My reply is—you have some money uninvested which seems to be a great annoyance to you and which you voluntarily propose to put in speculation at Fargo D.T. with Capt. Raymond. The decision seems to have been a great relief(!) to you. Observing how eager you were to put the money out was I not more than justified in imagining that you would buy Indian Orchard or Wellman's or some other similar place—and as 'time is money' you might not be able to communicate with me? So much for nonsense.

I saw the new moon to the front and right this evening! That settles the luck question for this month. I send love to you, Beloved, and to the babies. ADELBERT

LOWELL, *November* 10, 1877

I made no mistake about your birthday, Mr. Ames. It was the day I was in Boston, when it rained so, and when one of your attendant sprites or gnomes ordered a hack for me. None but an imp could have known that I was to be in Hollander's and I am thoroughly convinced that it was one of your uncanny guardians who was at the bottom of it. You can sit out there in Northfield, and because you think I am fast growing old and homely, call me your "beautiful wife" and make fun of my hair. But for all your jokes, some people like red hair and would not object to a lock of it.

You know you never did think your wife attractive *looking* in her palmiest day, and it is not likely that you have discovered any improvement at this late day, although your letters would fain make it appear that you appreciate her in a high degree. "Well" I hear you say, "What is all this apropos of?" "Nothing, only I know what I know."

John seemed to be in very good health when here. In better flesh and spirits. Not so very restless as I have often seen him. Nellie did not display any anxiety about him here. She said "The doctors recommended freedom from care and a long sea voyage" but that she should feel that the time she was separated from him would be just so much lost out of her life, and that she could not make up her mind to let him go. Such sentiments do not give the impression that a person is much disturbed about the health of the nearest and dearest.

You ask also about your horses. They are in Washington. But I keep one horse in use pretty constantly, either for myself or the children, and for the present at least we will pay Mathew.

(*Close of letter missing.*)

NORTHFIELD, MINN., *November* 15, 1877

DEAR BLANCHE: How you pitch into me for writing to you that you are beautiful. My mild mannered remarks to that effect are met by derisive jeers and scoffs. Well, it will teach us never to venture on such ground again. The conservative policy of husbands in keeping their own counsel, especially relative to the personal appearance of their wives, has doubtless been the result of experience from generation to generation since time began—at least since Adam's day if not since his progenitor the monkey—or the still more remote head of our family the clam. Excuse my past offenses and I will ne'er do the like again. Henceforth I cease to make innovations on the old, old style of bearing to the wife.

This day has been uneventful like its fellows. Fortunately for me the mail brought me your letter of your *on* day—of course your *off* days produce no letters for the mail to bring.

I have been at work on my gun. I am approaching its end but delays are great. My whole day's work was spoiled by turning the vise the wrong way which crushed the piece I was working on. My work dwindles as I proceed with it and I have not had the zest of the past. I suppose it will return by and by as the excellence becomes more manifest—but if it fails to become manifest—why, then I shall have lost nothing for I had nothing to lose.

I send you love and kisses—for you and the babies.

ADELBERT

NORTHFIELD, MINN., *November* 18, 1877

DEAR BLANCHE: This is Sunday evening. It is but about an hour since we had our supper of pop corn and milk—with a dash of sugar to give the mixture a flavor. It is rather a delicate dish. Some indefinite time in the future when we have a house of our own and can gather our children before our own hearth we will have pop corn and milk for supper. Then, perhaps, our babies, men and women grown, will, after such a feast, seat themselves to write to their wives and sweethearts.

I had a letter yesterday from Raymond who is now at Yankton D.T. He writes in high feather. He has been confirmed as Marshall by the Senate and feels secure. He has just returned from Washington. He says Hal. Green, one of the banker's sons, has been appointed P.U. of Jackson. This puts Fisher out and disappoints McKee who was eager for the place. In fact the place was almost a necessity as his funds have dwindled to a shadow. What pleases him most is that he did it and his enemies know it and give him credit for it. He is an energetic fellow and will I think make money eventually but—your money will be more satisfactorily placed in Minneapolis than with him at present.

If I dine with you on the 29th inst. I must start this week, otherwise I will not have time to go to Ft. A., to Davenport or some other larger city in Iowa (where I want to go to dispose if I can of my mill) and to Chicago. I will now abandon the idea of visiting New York City on my way to Lowell. I have much to say and do with John and can accomplish everything if he comes by the 20th inst. If not I think it doubtful if I succeed in making the rounds in time. At any rate I will be with you in four or five days after this reaches you. I send you kisses.

ADELBERT

WASHINGTON, D.C., *February* 23, 1878

ADELBERT AMES: Not Dear General, not Dear Ames, not even Ames—if you think of doing such a thing to me as this, I hope Blanche will never give you a chance.

Think of it, you ungrateful fellow, keeping me four days without the knowledge that I had another grandchild.[1] What do you think the telegraph was meant for? If it had been the first one I might pardon you, for such an event might turn an addle pate, but the *fourth!*

I have no patience with you. Blanche, poor child, had other things to think of, so I do not blame her a bit. But you! Do you suppose there was nobody anxious and waiting for news? And then, which was so happily interesting but might have been distressing to yourself?

I will wager a cigar you telegraphed to Minnesota. I am a good mind to say that I will not name the girl. But why should I punish the innocent, you would, if I do not look out, give her some horrid name or other that she will be ashamed of as well as her surname which, I have no doubt, she will be in haste to change.

Give my love and congratulations to Blanche. Tell her I shall be home a week from Monday. You had better be away then and let me get a little mollified by seeing the baby before I see you. Tell the children that Grandfather is coming and we will have a frolic together. Yours, FATHER

LOWELL, *March* 14, 1878

DEAR DEL: I received your letter from Springfield, and was glad to have word so soon from you as it seems less lonesome.

As for the treasurership, although the salary would have been acceptable, you will I have no doubt feel more free to go and come without it and I am not sorry that "this bubble has exploded."

All are well here. This morning Mrs. Faunce, the baby and I went out to ride, did some shopping and made a call on Florence. Sarah and Edith have not any measle spots on the skin yet and seem bright and lively today although yesterday both were a little under the weather.

I enclose a letter from Fannie and one from John. I will answer Fannie's today. John has one burden off of his hands, that is a marriageable daughter. How excited Nellie must be.

[1] Daughter, Blanche, born February 18th, 1878.

The little girl to take care of the baby came yesterday. I like her so far very much and the children are delighted with her, as she can read them stories, and plays games with them. Edith was troubled to know where she was going to eat. She evidently did not think the kitchen the place for her. I expect a new cook today. So much for the changes in our household since you left us.

The baby is being trained to sleep in the crib. This last item may be of some interest to you.

Love for my Sweetheart. BLANCHE

WASHINGTON, D.C., *March* 15, 1878

DEAR BLANCHE: I arrived here yesterday morning. Breakfasted with your Father, Charlotte and Hattie. Mrs. Butler left the day before on a visit to a sister in Illinois.

After breakfast and a chat, I turned my face towards the patent office. I saw Hill and Ellsworth and bore a letter from your father to Mr. Stockbridge, the gun examiner of the patent office.

Away down in my heart I had counted on my wheat machine as you know. Mr. Hill, while not knowing specially about such machines thought the idea of revolving arms in wheat, an old one. He was to find out during the day. I am going to learn the results of his search after finishing this letter.

From the patent office I went to find Kinsman, which I succeeded in doing. Together we came up here to lunch, visit the capitol and he dined with us. In the evening Mr. Stockbridge came up here to see my gun. His opinion is that my whole gun is novel except possibly the arm which sweeps the cartridge in place. That the feature distinction and value is the method of handling the cartridge whatever be the mechanism behind it. He was unqualified in his praise—but the impression left on my mind was that his affability exceeded the future showings of the records. At least my gun fascinated him, your father and Kinsman.

What is true of the gun is also true of the magazine which elicited exclamations of approval from Mr. Stockbridge, but the records alone must decide. I have given you my own state of mind with all the facts up to this morning—and ups or downs, you shall have in detail as this may chance.

I will not attempt to give you household gossip in this letter. Kinsman told me that Charlotte asked him not to tell me about the troubles they have had here. Of course, Kinsman had done so and will continue to give me the spicy items which I will issue to you in due time.

The house is in excellent condition and very beautiful. I have complimented Hattie on her housekeeping. She looks very well. Love to you and the babies, ADELBERT

LOWELL, *March* 15, 1878

DEAR DEL: Another day and we find ourselves well and without the measles. Last night the little girls were very restless and Edith was quite feverish, complaining of a sore throat —this morning however she seems as bright and chipper as usual.

It is not by any means a quiet household—the changes in the kitchen and the presence of Mrs. Faunce keep things at concert pitch. The ground is all covered with snow which fell last night—but the warm bright sun will soon melt it all away.

I expect to hear better accounts of your patents of the Chicopee business. However if they all come to naught do not be despondent, remember that John writes "Glass is on the tenterhooks again" and do not fail to derive hope and consolation from his anxiety.

Your long stay at home with me, so quietly, has spoiled me a little. I miss you more than ever; so do the children. They want you home again. Love and kisses. BLANCHE

WASHINGTON, D.C., *March* 17, 1878

DEAR BLANCHE: Yesterday I went to the patent office to look over patents on fire ladders and then went to see Kinsman at whose table I wrote yesterday's letter. About twelve we went to call on Mrs. Spofford who is occupying our old room at the corner of 15th and I streets. Every thing seemed natural there except they had no bed in the room, making it their sitting room. The house has been extended by an addition on the vacant top—and in the new part they have their sleeping room. It was in that house I first met you, Dearie. It was there I learned to love you. It was there my old life ended and a new one began. In that self same room Edith was born. So well do I remember the incidents. That house—how bright those days. What happy memories it calls up. That past we shall know not again.

From the Spofford's we came up here for lunch but as your Father had two or three people with him at the table we went over to the capitol for something to eat. It is his custom to lunch a number of persons each day. Of course I do not crowd anybody. While lunching, Chase came in. I spent the rest of the day with him. I saw Bruce and Hill there. Of course I got all the news which I will not attempt to give you in this letter.

Returning at nine I found Fay had dined here. He is enjoying "Hamlet." As I was going up to bed I found Hattie dressing for a reception at Rollins'—a Senator from N. H.—a wedding reception. Charlotte was going also—her second evening party this season. I was glad to get to bed. The late hours here—midnight and after had proved too much for me as the rattle of the streets to which I am not accustomed awakes me early dawn.

Yesterday I spoke about Ben to your Father. I asked what Ben was to do. He said "Study law I suppose." I said "With you?" He said, "With me or with anyone else as he may prefer."

Charlotte seems happy though Hattie is eternally sitting down on her. They both are all devotion to your Father and he actually flourishes under it. Hattie's ideas are so peculiar I must give you some. She hates to have Charlotte recognized as a relative[1] of your Father. I think it was at Speaker Randoll's that she said in reply to someone's statement that Charlotte was a relation of Gen. B. that "she is only a half relation." She repeated the conversation at the table here but could see no point in the laughter which followed—nor in Charlotte's quiet innocently intended statement that "half relation is better than none at all."

Hattie says "She never could bear a closed carriage in hot weather and that if she is to stay here this summer she will have an open one." My opinion is she will have an open one if she persists.

Need I add to this letter that I love you and miss you?

ADELBERT

LOWELL, *March* 18, 1878

DEAR DEL: Col. Diamond brought up your first letter from Washington yesterday morning after I had gone out to ride. The sky looked rainy and I took the morning instead of the afternoon for my ride to Dracut.

Edith is in bed with the measles. Yesterday (Sunday) they

[1] Charlotte Stevens was a daughter of Elizabeth Butler Stevens, a half sister of General Butler.

were at the height, and today are fading away a little, and she can open her eyes better. The light was painful and they were a good deal swollen. She will be all well in a few days. Sarah seems to be in perfect condition. She will not probably have the disease unless she takes it from Edith. We are inclined to think the baby has them but such is her natural complexion that an eruption is no indication of disease. A little increased restlessness and disordered stomach are the only things to judge from.

Saturday afternoon Butler did not obey. In the morning I had forbidden him to go near the pond with Georgie Shattuck and he attended to my order. But after dinner Bertha S., a young girl of twelve or fourteen, came over with her brother and Butler thinking her "grown up" concluded it would be safe to play around the pond. As a natural result Georgie ran against him and he went feet first into the water. Bertha pulled him out by the jacket, and he came up to the house crying and crestfallen. His clothes were quickly changed and he was rubbed with alcohol, and apparently has not caught cold. I was a little fearful on account of his recent recovery. Mrs. Faunce will stay until your return. So much for home news.

My hopes have brightened considerably since I have learned Mr. Stockbridge's opinion of *our* gun. I am happy that it meets with approbation even if it should not bring us a million —cents.

Love, Dearie. BLANCHE

LOWELL, *March* 19, 1878

DEAR DEL: You evidently have considerable to enliven you in Washington. Meeting your old friends, listening to Hattie's foolishness and Kinsman's gossip, to say nothing of the excitement in regard to your patents.

I am glad that your recollections of our life in W. are so pleasant. It is true those days can never come back, but I for one have had very many happy days since then and hope for many more. *My* present is not so sad that I have any repinings for the past. Yet—I love you for remembering those hours so pleasantly and send you a kiss for thanks.

Poor Hattie—she is welcome to the open carriage, as far as I am concerned, or anything else. Now is her glorious summer —"The winter of her discontent" is to come later and I fear she will find it very bleak and dreary.

Edith is better. Able to be about today, though her face is very much spotted. Blanche is better, more natural, but she looks measley.

Butler went down to school yesterday. Owing to the weather there was no session of the public schools and he returned, to try again this morning. He has just come in from school and reports that he wants a new book as he is in the second class. I asked if the little girl who did so well was in his class. He answered, "No, she is behind. The teacher told me I should go into the second class when I finished my book and I have finished it and know it pretty well too." I have had him read and spell since you left and no doubt he is right.

I went out to see Lynch this morning and talk to him about the flowers and spring work, about grapes along the stone wall and sowing the pasture with oats.

The baby, dressmaking and house-cleaning occupy all my time. When are you coming home, Sweetheart—I am delighted that you will have to stay in Lowell for the model of your gun to be made.

Love, BLANCHE

WASHINGTON, D.C., *March* 20, 1878

DEAR BLANCHE: Yesterday was a very quiet day with me. I wrote yesterday's letter at Kinsman's room, mailed it on our way to French's studio.[1] He seemed to appreciate the changes you made in the photograph admitting it changed the head and character altogether. He is to make the changes in the clay and then photograph it as before and again submit the photographs to you.

From French's we started to walk around the White House square. On our way we met Chase and Redpath. At the hotel we had lunch. Then K. and I walked back here to Capitol hill.

This morning we have just had breakfast and I write this before setting out on my travels. At this point a son of the murdered Judge Chisholm of Mississippi came in to get me to aid him to a place. The other day he went with his mother to see President Hayes for a place. The young man gave this as the conversation between them.

Mrs. C.— "You know about my husband, Judge Chisholm, who was murdered in Miss. I will spare you a recital of the

[1] Daniel Chester French, the sculptor, who made a medallion portrait of Mrs. Benjamin F. Butler.

facts. We cannot live there and my son here wishes a place under the government." Mr. Hayes, (kind of laughing) "What are your politics, young man?" Young Chisholm, "Republican, of course, I supposed you knew that." Mr. Hayes, (kind of laughing) "Well, you know that they say I only give appointments to Democrats in the South." Young C.— "In that case, as I am a Republican, I stand no chance." Mr. Hayes.— "I do not say it is true, but I have no doubt you can get a place."

Thus ended the interview and Mrs. C. and her son left the White House indignant and outraged. Of course Hayes has not aided him nor will he, nor has it been his purpose to. The feeling of contempt for Hayes is universal here. It is deep and bitter. Even those holding office under him despise him. Even Shaughnessy, a soldier of fortune, curses him, though he has just been appointed Marshall of Utah.

Hayes thinks he is followed by the people in Mass. He will talk by the hour of the new party whenever he can cite some local election in the South where the Democratic party, having no opponent, has divided on local issues. Above all those near him find him weak, vacillating, egotistical, important. He thinks he alone has invented the patent to exalt himself and degrade all the other politicians in the country. G. Washington, Jackson, Lincoln & Co. pale before his splendor in his own estimation. So talk those or some of those who are holding office near him. This will do for politics.

Love, ADELBERT

LOWELL, *March* 21, 1878

DEAR DEL: I enclose you two letters from Sam containing two offers for your Fort A. Mill. If you are sure there will be war in Europe I would not sell for less than twenty-five thousand. One good year's work would be a very nice thing.

Our family is doing finely. Edith's skin is recovering its natural condition, and the baby is less fretty. Butler goes regularly to school, and Sarah is as well as usual. I have hopes although our youngest is not particularly attractive at present that in time she will do herself and us credit.

I have nothing new to write you about. As you well know, life is very quiet here. The same routine from day to day. One change I notice which will please you perhaps. I find myself singing and humming about the house a thing which I have done but seldom for more than a year.

I send you kisses, Sweetheart. BLANCHE

WASHINGTON, D.C., *March* 27, 1878

DEAR BLANCHE: I have been to the Patent Office this morning to learn what progress had been made with the examination of my papers. I saw the Examiner and learned that every part claimed by me as novel is novel and that I can get a patent on every one of my detailed parts; but also that he doubted if the claims would all be allowed in the broad and far reaching way in which they are put. Of course this is his present opinion. He has not completed his investigations. So far as the principals go, he is willing to allow all I claim. So at this moment I feel quite certain of securing a satisfactory patent on my gun. At the patent office I talked with the experts about guns. I found that my gun does too much. It is too capable; and judging by their remarks, men and nations are not educated up to the point that my gun takes them. It fires too fast! The present gun with its magazine seems to be sufficient!

That is, every one has been anxious to get rapidity of fire—now they have got it exactly right! Of course I must contend that with a gun of double rapidity of fire half the number of men will be sufficient. But I won't succeed at first.

Tomorrow at one I will go to the patent office to get the final decision. I hope I will be able to get away on the nine p.m. train. I am tired of staying here and anxious to get away from here and get home.

Kiss the babies for me and take a world of love for yourself.

ADELBERT

LOWELL, *April* 5, 1878

DEAR FATHER: I have been expecting you home, but learn through Col. Diamond that you are not to be here until about the 16th.

We are in the midst of spring cleaning and renovating and hope to be all finished before you come on. The library entry and dining room are in entire confusion for I am having the ceiling painted where the plastering fell and where it has been screwed up: the wood work in the library regrained and in the dining room repairs where the paint had chipped off so badly. The family being so small at present it seemed the most favorable opportunity to have things turned upside down.

You spoke last fall of a new entry and stair carpet. The fur rugs cover the bare places pretty well, but if you think it best to have a new one this spring, I will not have the old carpet put down. The new carpet is not necessary—but it did seem needful to have the painting attended to, as the work has been put off from season to season since the spring before Mother died and the rooms have looked shabby and neglected. If you decide to have a carpet I should like to have you select it when you come on either in New York or Boston.

Spring here comes on very slowly. We have not the warm days and green grass and flowers which Genl. Ames speaks of having enjoyed in Washington.

We are expecting Paul daily owing to what he wrote you. He could not have sailed as soon as he expected or he would have arrived before this. He was to have been home for the annual meeting of the Vesper boat club which was held night before last. He agreed before he went away to give the officers of the club a supper if he failed to return at the time specified. Of course he will have to give the supper. Young Horatio Kimbal (Hattie knows about him) undertook at the meeting to get up a party to vote Paul out of the Presidency of the club. Paul's friends came to the rescue, and every vote but one was for Paul's re-election. That one vote was probably Kimbal's.

Politically things look rather gloomy. The local papers seem to think that you vote for all acts and measures to which your constituents are most opposed.

Love for Hattie and Charlotte and a kiss for my Father from his affectionate daughter, BLANCHE

CHICAGO, *April 21*, 1878

DEAR BLANCHE: I arrived here yesterday morning and was all ready to start last evening for Minn. in fact was buying my R.R. ticket when I learned that as it was Saturday I could reach Northfield as quick by leaving tonight as last night.

I saw Mr. Winchester Hall, my agent, and learned that he has leased all my houses to a new and paying set of tenants at ten dollars ($10) each. He has been putting some repairs on it and is using the rental to pay for them. When all gets running evenly they will get five hundred (500.00) per year in such dull times as these. My agent says they will easily double it in good times. Today I went to see them and found them in good order and rather attractive.

Rhodes is here. He now has work to do. He does not accept the place offered him in Washington. Howe is doing well I should say judging by appearances. I have bought a small French dictionary and a work of V. Hugo. I am surprised to see how many words there are I do not know. I unhesitatingly condemn the way we have fallen into—that of reading without a dictionary. My dictionary is profitable and shall always be at hand.

Since I began to write Mr. Whipple and two other persons have called on me. So the connected letter turns into fragments.

I send you much love. ADELBERT

LOWELL, *Sunday, April* 21, 1878

DEAR DEL: Your letter from Springfield reached me yesterday afternoon. I was surprised to learn of your change of programme. But if your presence is not needed in Washington it would seem to be the best thing to get through with your Western business.

Father left Lowell yesterday morning and I am monarch of this establishment. This morning I was awake quite early and thought, now if Del were here we could have a comfortable little chat.

I have been over at Aunt Lottie's daily since you left, trying to help her about her house. Our progress as you can imagine is slow. House cleaning, painting and dressmaking will occupy my time the coming week. Fannie will be up on Tuesday. I bought some tickets and rewards of merit the other day and our crowd are striving to earn them by good conduct. Poor Sarah has up-hill work, but we are more lenient with her than Edith and Butler. After they have a certain number of cards I am to buy them a new book.

This morning Martha had some colored Easter eggs for them. It was a surprise and the questions at breakfast as to the how and the why were numberless.

Margaret has given her notice for next Saturday. She says the work is too hard for her. I am glad she is going as no doubt we can do better. You see I have only trifles to write you about, but as our wise cousin Hattie says "life is made up of trifles."

One thing however I can tell you which is no trifle as it makes up the sum and substance of my life—I love you and miss you, and shall feel that time is wasted until you return.

BLANCHE

LOWELL, *April* 22, 1878

DEAR DEL: It is half past ten o'clock and all have gone to bed. I am ready at last but will write a few words to you and feel that I have done as I would be done by.

This has been a rainy day and we have improved it by putting the dining room to rights, clearing and repapering all the closets and shelves.

This morning Sarah swallowed a one cent piece. I wrote a note to Dr. Kimball stating the fact and asking if it would do her any harm. He said "Not at all. I need not have the least anxiety." The baby has been riding about the house the greater part of the day in Edith's doll carriage. Butler, Edith and Sarah all taking turns. She seemed to enjoy it immensely. You will remember that there is a squeak about it which may be fascinating to a baby's nerves but excruciating to ours.

Butler and Edith left their school books out in Butler's house last night. They had to be dried this morning.

Ben writes that he has sent in his resignation.

Fannie came up at half past four. She has her hair fixed in the beau catcher style, otherwise she is looking well. As plump and rosy as need be. She heard of herself at Nina's party through her Newton friends, a Mr. Brown of Chelsea who was at the party, said she was "the prettiest girl there and the best dressed—in simple white." He spoke of her as being a sister of Genl. Ames.

So much of the news of the day. I will add to it that I have a headache which makes me cross and have the additional affliction of a very sore mouth. While I write you I have a large lump of alum to keep me in countenance. "Always growling." Love,

BLANCHE

LOWELL, *April 26, 1878*

DEAR DEL: Everything out of doors is looking beautifully now. Nothing can be more charming than the fresh green grass and leaves and the soft rain which has been falling over them all day. When it is so pleasant you ought to be here. But we will not complain.

Last Sunday at the farm when all were assembled, Florence brought in Hilda. She looked so pale and delicate that Katie went home and told her grandmother that she knew she could not live and cried and took on about it for a long time. Poor Katie, her heart is still sore. While we are all well we have no right to grumble or complain about such a trifle as the separation of a month's duration.

I bought a carriage for our youngest and intend to keep her in the open air a great deal of the time. She knows my voice and stops crying the moment she hears it, in expectation of favors coming at once; if delayed for a moment she cries out as if injured beyond endurance.

I have begun the "Boy Hunters" for Butler. He is doing very well with his review lesson. Edith has the privilege of sleeping with me tonight. She is a good little lassie and earns her rewards daily.

I foolishly expected a letter from you today and was a little disappointed. Love, BLANCHE

LOWELL, *April* 30, 1878

DEAR DEL: I have had no letter from you today, but tomorrow will bring me one without doubt. The rain still continues so that I have not been out of the house today, but have mended all the stockings and superintended the cleaning of paint in the upper entry.

Butler is at the head of his class this week and seems quite ambitious not to lose his place. He is not always a good boy however, for yesterday he did not want to go in the afternoon. I said "Oh, yes, my son, you must go regularly whenever school keeps." "Well, I will go then, and I will go all of the time Wednesday and Saturday afternoons and all. I will climb over the fence if the gate is not open, and get in the window." All this was said with so much spite and with such contracted brows that my unfortunate sense of the ludicrous overcame my discretion and I laughed, but was checked by the remark, "Shut up, you old fool." "Butler if you ever say that again I shall punish you severely." "Shut up, you old fool." Thereupon I took hold of the young man and laid him over my knee. He was now thoroughly frightened and begged me to let him go promising to be a good boy. I could not whip him for he clung to me in such a beseeching way, and climbed into my lap sobbing so heavily. I talked to him kindly and gently and finally learned that Willie Mahoney at school had kicked Miss Emerson and called her an old fool. Of course I delivered a lecture upon the impropriety of following such an example.

Edith is a good little girl. She does not seem to suck her thumb much now but bites her nails until they bleed. The latter habit is however preferable to the old one as she is not so likely to spoil the shape of her mouth.

You have been away just a fortnight but it seems like six months. Love and good night. BLANCHE

LOWELL, *May* 2, 1878

DEAR DEL: Your letter enclosing the photographs, which are excellent, came today. I showed them to Edith and Sarah.

They recognized them at once. I did not think that Sarah would remember so clearly.

If you had not made some remarks upon my weakness and foolishness in regard to Mr. McD. expressions of admiration, I would tell you something, as it is I won't. Had anyone but you spoken to me in the way you did upon that occasion, there would have been a *row*—but I took into consideration the fact that *you* were talking and of course could make allowances.

This has not been a very happy day. Quite a number of small things have disturbed my serenity, but I need not inflict my small annoyances upon you, by way of rendering myself entertaining. I have grumbled and growled to you a good deal lately. Fortunately however you were absorbed in your gun and my remarks did not make much impression.

I have not heard a word from Paul except what I wrote you in regard to his presence in St. Petersburg on the 11th of April. I will remember what you say about telegraphing you. Good night, Dearie. I will close my letter with a conundrum—why is this letter unlike a bee? Answer—Because there is no sting in the tail of it. Love. BLANCHE

NORTHFIELD, MINN., *May* 3, 1878

DEAR BLANCHE: This state has been subject to a decided shock and everyone is speculating and wondering about it. Last evening at about seven the largest mill in the state and country, known as the Washburn Mills, at Minneapolis exploded, caught fire and set on fire neighboring buildings. Some half dozen mills were burned, making an aggregate of eighty seven (87) runs of stone. There were one hundred and ninety seven (197) runs of stone in Minneapolis but the eighty seven destroyed were of the principle ones to manufacturing for the Eastern markets. Some fourteen (14) persons were killed. Our cousin Jim Wyman, was again burned out—this being the third time.

The cause of the explosion is yet undecided. Some say there was nitroglycerin on the cars by the mill. Others say that it was caused by the impalpable powder or fine dust from the flour which has always been regarded as explosive. The evidence is in favor of the last theory. You may remember there was a mysterious explosion in New York last Christmas time in a candy shop. The causes were probably similar.

John has gone up to see the ruins. From there he will go down to the southwest corner of the state where he and Father have bought some two thousand five hundred acres of land.

I do not think the business of the mill requires my presence much longer. John's disposition to expand—to borrow money to buy wheat while he leaves large sums in the hands of our commission merchants, I have to repress. Our wheat is three cents off and the tendency is downward. I have faith in the war but find it hard to get the people here up to the sticking point.

I am sorry to think of you all alone in that large house especially in such a violent thunderstorm. I will be at home before the next such shower.

Love, ADELBERT

LOWELL, *May* 3, 1878

DEAR DEL: The papers bring me news of the terrible explosion at Minneapolis. For mercy sake, have the Northfield mill well insured and keep out of it. Why, a cartridge mill is nothing compared to it. I was a little sorry to hear that you have been buying so much wheat. Even if you are sure there is to be a war, I doubt the advisability of bringing your business into the speculation. It seems to me better to take as much money as you feel you can afford to lose and buy margins, rather than to play poker with your daily bread. This time last year you did the same thing and there was a war and in spite of that you lost money.

Of course, Sweetheart, my preaching amounts to nothing. I only desire to put myself on record, but for that desire I would not write about the matter at all, for what is done can not or will not be undone and I hate above all things to keep harping on a subject or to hear others.

Butler wishes me to tell you that "he and Edith have been good boys today, and that he has a pretty picture for having kept at the head of the class a week."

It is now quite late and I will say good night, Dearie. If nothing keeps you in Northfield but the wheat experiments, come home. It will take six months to make all the experiments you will want to make and then you will be disappointed. The old patents go *de mal en pis* and I am down upon them. Still if you are bound to stay and try the thing through, keep up your spirits and keep to work. The moment you feel doubts and misgivings, drop the whole thing and come home.

I miss you and want to make you homesick.

BLANCHE

LOWELL, *May* 6, 1878

DEAR DEL: I have been favored with two letters from you today, and consequently feel that you are not so very far away, but am frightened at your remark that you "don't know whether you will be able to get home again at the end of a month, but you will *try*." I should think so, and succeed, too. Why! You were allowed to go upon the understanding that you were to be away *one* month, and here you are calmly proposing to try to get back in two. But there is one thing to be said in favor of your proposition—and that is—it is better to stay and get through, rather than to feel the moment you get East that you ought to be West.

Paul did not come tonight as he said he would. I expect him in the morning. I had a nice supper ready and in addition was dressed up for the occasion, but the trouble was all in vain.

Yesterday at the farm Prentiss and Aunt Lottie's boys began to play, but as usual ended in earnest much to the disgust of all parties present, actors as well as lookers-on. Butler was in the play too, but he came out all right. Poor Aunt Lottie. She is doing all she can to ruin her boys. Fisher calls her names and she does not prevent him. She blacks their boots for them, and never requires the least service of them in return. Compared with those boys, Butler is an angel.

If there is one in our family who deserves reprimanding and punishing it is myself. I do not keep as even tempered and gentle voiced as I ought. Perhaps I expect too much of my babies, but I do want them to be lovable, nice children. Butler has, as I desire, the little boys up here to play with him. He came in to ask me for four eggs tonight. One for himself and each of his companions. They built a fire, at the end of the green house and cooked the eggs in Edith's milk pan. Butler has a tent which is a great attraction to the boys and he thinks he is camping out. He wishes to sleep out there, but is a little afraid and has coaxed Edith into promising that she will go out there and sleep with him. So he has been teasing me to give my consent to such an arrangement. I answer "No, you must wait until your Father returns and if he gives his consent I have no objection." I want to have the place so attractive that all his playmates will prefer to come here, instead of asking him to visit them.

Edith seems to enjoy her school, but Butler says she whispers to Charlie Mahoney and does not study her lessons. I have not been hearing them lately—for Butler was reviewing and it does not seem very necessary for Edith to be urged forward. She still is so young. She has a year and a half in which to reach Butler's position in the school, and I take him for the standard for I think him well enough advanced for a boy of his age.

Miss Sarah, familiarly known as Sallie Waters and Mother B. is much the same as usual only more so. We had a little understanding day before yesterday in the form of a spanking and she has been more obedient since.

I have written you, Sweetheart, a good many pages about our little family. The only one I have neglected to mention is the baby, who will be grown up, if you stay away a month longer. I shall not feel that anything is perfect until you return. Love,

BLANCHE

NORTHFIELD, MINN., *May* 8, 1878

DEAR BLANCHE: I rejoice to learn that Paul has returned.[1] I shall now feel easier about the dangers of fire and burglars, then again I am glad to have him back on general principles.

We have not been buying wheat because we wanted it but because the elevator had broken down temporarily and as we fix the price—as we do not want the Minneapolis people to come here to buy and as the townspeople are making a disturbance or trying to, we felt obliged to accommodate the farmers by buying.

Paul was to be at home day before yesterday, Monday—and if he had any war news you would have telegraphed. So I conclude he brings no definite news which at this time seems like peace news. I shall so regard your silence.

I am getting to the end of my experiments with my wheat cleaner. To be made a perfect machine, it requires a fan to draw off the dust and bran. It would take some time to do this—more than I care to give it now. I think Jack is interested in the machine and it can be perfected in my absence; in fact I have one important improvement to make which I can do better elsewhere.

So, while I cannot run away today, and my folks would call it running away, if I go now, I feel that I shall be ready any time so far as my own work is concerned. The condition of the business and the bearing on it of a war in Europe render it necessary for me to stay here for awhile.

Kiss the babies for me—for yourself, my love,

ADELBERT

[1] Paul had been in Russia about ammunition business.

LOWELL, *May* 9, 1878

DEAR DEL: Paul has brought quite a number of little trinkets, as mementos of his travels. He says the Russians are peculiar in this respect that you have to explain every little thing just as you would to children and that they ask the most absurd questions. For instance, the Grand Duke Constantine asked him if he had "ever sailed in his father's yacht the 'America'?" Paul looked at him to see if he were joking and seeing that he was not, answered that "he spent considerable time sailing in her every summer." Of course we must come to the conclusion that in that country, sons do not always enjoy the luxury and style of living in which the parents indulge. The more barbarous people are, the less they think of and the more they ill-treat their children.

This sage remark brings me to another point—which is, that of all the gentlemen connected with the family, you are the only one to whom Aunt Lottie would intrust her sons or their interest. She feels sure that with you they would always have consideration and kindness. That is her opinion, but I could have told her that if you treated them at all it would be with kindness, but that if they annoyed you, you would not have anything to do with them but would be as unapproachable and distant as the stars and they would be left to their own devices, that you would never tease or annoy like Prentiss or Tucke but that your standard would be a high one and you would have little patience if they failed to attain it. How is it, Sweetheart? Do you think I am unjust? It is not so, I know, with your own family, but then, we are all yours and you love us and I do not think you would be likely to love the Pearson boys. I do not exactly know why I have written all this. It would seem as if my mind was inclined to speculating upon improbable contingencies.

Do not, Sweetheart, picture to yourself perfect comfort and happiness in store for you when you get back. I can not bear to have you disappointed about anything, and you must remember that your rest will be disturbed and your waking thoughts set wandering by our little ones. I know how prone we are to think only of the pleasant things when we are away and I am fearful least you may be disgusted. I think of this now because our little one increases the turmoil which sometimes troubled you when there were but three absorbers of love, thoughts, and time.

Do not delay returning because Paul is here and you think I need no other protector. You can work better on your gun

here than there. Love, Dearie. I have a feeling that you will not be gone much longer. It may be because I want you here so much.
BLANCHE

LOWELL, *May* 11, 1878

DEAR DEL: A letter came for me last night written Sunday. It was a long time getting here but was very welcome when it did finally make its appearance. In it you speak of John's desiring that you should sell the mill. Of course, Dearie, I need not say do not listen to such advice, for of course you would not dream of such a thing. If John seems too restless and discontented, buy him out. It will to be sure prolong your indebtedness somewhat, but if you were willing, I have no doubt both Paul and Ben will be very ready to buy in with you and in that way you would only be obliged to raise seven thousand a piece.

Your Father, I know, would say "Oh! You can't run the mill unless you will come and live here." But then he is one of the kind who always see how not to do it. My opinion is that the mill will do quite as well under your direction even if you are in Lowell, for when you feel that you are the only one looking after it you will make it your business and attend more closely to it, and to all the details. So you can tell John that he can find purchasers for his portion if he desires to sell, for if you do not feel that you can put any more money into it, I am certain you can get some stock-holders here.

I read your letter to Butler and think it made a good impression. He desires me to say that he has been a very good boy lately. Edith wishes you to know that the teacher says she is a "very good reader," and I am astonished at the progress she has made. Butler commences arithmetic next week and is having some white shirts made to button on the back with studs like his Father's. So you see every week brings its little changes, and we, as well as the children, are growing older.

Are you going to bring on your horse! You do not speak of him this time. Has anything happened to the animal. Is the colt old enough to be used yet?

I am really ashamed of this letter and would not send such a miserable thing in every respect to any one but you. Not that I do not love you, and care more for your good opinion than for that of the whole world, but because I think you know that sometimes I do much better, and that what you care for is not the finely written, well rounded sentences, but the assurance that we are well, thinking of you and missing you.

BLANCHE

LOWELL, *May* 12, 1878

DEAR DEL: I can answer your conundrum with the greatest ease "Why is this letter like an elephant?" Answer, because its TALE is so short. Ha! Ha! Ha!

This is a miserable, cold, gloomy day. The flowers look frozen and the children who have been playing are speckled and blue. Butler and Edith were in the house a few moments ago, but have just gone out again. Sarah was following them with something clasped to her breast, hiding it with her hands. I stopped her to investigate; it was a cigarette. "Sarah, what are you going to do with this?" "I am going to take it out of doors and go puff, puff. I likes to go puff, puff." "Have Edith and Butler cigarettes, too?" "Yes." I hesitated a moment whether it would be best to let them alone and allow them to reap the punishment of their wrong doing—(for they knew they were in mischief or they would not have been sneaking away) or to use authority and make them bring the cigarettes back.

"Sarah if you smoke this it will make you very sick and you will throw up. Your Uncle Paul when he was a little boy tried to smoke and it made him awfully sick. You had better give it to me and go and tell Edith and Butler how sick they will be if they try to smoke." "I don't want to throw up, I will tell Edie and Butler" and she departed. They have not come in yet, so that I can not tell whether or not they have heeded my warning.

The news seems more warlike lately. I hope you understand what I tried to make clear to you, that is that war may be declared any time, but that the Russians want to make all the preparations that England will give them time for, until they are entirely ready, so that all may be quiet for a month or so, perhaps three months.

Now Paul's idea is that the new crop coming in will cause wheat to fall below the margin. You remember last year it went down in the nineties somewhere. Of course the whole thing is uncertain but Paul's idea is to keep close watch and when it reaches the price at which you bought, *sell, unless* the market is steadily advancing.

I sent you a paper containing an interview with Capt. Hunt.

Well, Father of course saw it and he has written a flaming letter to Paul asking him for mercy sake to make Hunt keep his mouth shut, and that if war should be declared he has said enough already to warrant putting him in prison, etc. etc.

The funny thing is that Capt. Semetachkin has been interviewed and talked more than Hunt. I suppose that all who are at all intimate with these Russians will be suspected and watched, and will thus be hampered in all their undertakings.

Father is expecting great things and no doubt feels correspondingly cross when he thinks he may be disappointed owing to the folly of some one.

I am happy to hear that you are eating more slowly and consequently less greedily. Ever since we have been married, you know how much I have had to endure on account of "that gravity—and absence of haste" which you say becomes me so well. All kinds of slurring remarks have been heaped upon me because I could not eat in the same length of time the same quantity that you could. Although something of a traveler I have not had the railroad training that you have. However if you now see the error of your ways, I will say nothing more, except that I wish you were to dine with us today—upon pea soup—broiled shad—stewed chicken and dumplings, and rhubarb pie. Love, BLANCHE

NORTHFIELD, MINN., *May* 12, 1878

DEAR BLANCHE: Rather an amusing incident occurred today. It appears that Kentucky's last colt is the finest one on John's farm. Today for the first time he claimed it as his own. I said, "Yours?" Whereupon Johnny (boys of his age have long ears and loose tongues) said "Well, we have been keeping your horses so long we ought to have the colt!" Later in the day I gave John both the colt and the mare—the mother. So my stock is reduced to a four-year-old and a two-year-old.

Evidently the possession of the colt had become a family matter and even Johnny knew upon what argument the conclusion was reached. It was no great sacrifice on my part as the mare had no particular value; and while I agree that the colt is all claimed for it, its color is bay with a stripe of white down its face and, being so marked, becomes only what all colts are—indifferent. If the family make more points about my expense to them the remaining two horses will be given to them for I set no great value on them.

Yesterday I received yours notifying me of Paul's return. I am glad he is back. It is gratifying to know that business is to benefit even by a war. I hope he will make his fortune out of it. It will surely help us here though as you say we will not make ours on wheat margins.

You cannot write me anything so interesting as the events, great and little, of your daily life. Love, ADELBERT

LOWELL, *May* 14, 1878

DEAR DEL: A welcome letter came from you this morning. It found me busy as a bee as usual. The days are all too short for the work I wish to crowd into them. Yet if you were here a looker-on I have no doubt you would think that it all amounted to nothing.

Therefore I often feel that my time is wasted. What does it all amount to, this weighing of meat, keeping accounts, arranging and cutting out curtains, standing by to see that the walls are properly washed, scolding all dinner time trying to correct bad manners, riding out to do a number of errands and having the baby along to make music, and rest the thoughts and ears, return to nurse the baby and at the same time stand in the parlor to direct about placing the furniture. Take supper with the same pleasing accompaniment as at dinner. Take the baby while the nurse has her tea. Scold Butler in order to get him to wash before going to bed. Hear the prayers all around, kiss them good night, fix the bed clothes and ventilate the room. Pay the servants the wages they ask for. Go down stairs to see that all is well, find parlor window open, can't close it, fly to get Mathew before he goes off. Stand by again to make him use some discretion rather than break the sash by main strength, upstairs to glance at the paper and see that Mrs. Hildreth is a member of the Art Association which is being started here.

This brings me up to the present time when I am writing you, and feeling cross that you are not here, and that I am what I am and that the world is what it is—and pretty soon after I have finished grumbling I shall take a bath and go to bed to sleep as much of the sleep of the righteous as circumstances, Sarah and the baby will permit. All of which is very ungrammatical but you will understand it for all that and also know that I have not written half of the little things which make up the acts performed in one of a series of days.

Butler has changed his stockings every day for a week because of holes in the knees. You will say that they are strapped up too tight—but he says he "can shinny up any tree that he can clasp." He would not wait for Edith when going to school this afternoon. He wanted to run and catch up with Georgie. She had the stomach ache and would not, so he left her and she came back home crying, to be comforted with the promise of a bag of gum drops; and the assurance that Butler was a bad boy.

Butler came in from school with a small blue egg as a peace offering. I said to him that I was sorry to hear he had treated his sister so. "She didn't get anything by it anyway and I shall run off and leave her again." "I don't know what you mean by getting anything by it. She spent the afternoon at home and had a bag of gum drops." After a little reflection he said, "I won't run away from her anymore and the next afternoon I shall stay at home."

I hope you will stop at Fort A. on your return. Can you not have Sam sell out to the Grangers? If the neighbors do not want Glass to buy the mill perhaps it is from a dog-in-the-manger feeling. They can get up a Company, buy you out and then hire Sam and the others to run it for them. At least it will do no harm to propose it to Sam and let him try to start it. I remember John tried something of the kind, but John's efforts are too spasmodic and would not be likely to accomplish much.

Now I will say good night. However much I may growl and find fault with things in *general*, there is one thing in *particular* about which you need have no doubts, i.e., I love you and miss you. BLANCHE

LOWELL, *May* 17, 1878

DEAR DEL: From the tone of your letters received today and in fact from all you have written since you have been away, I fear you have not found your visit West as agreeable this time as formerly. I am anxious to get you home and see if you have been growing thinner, and if the lines between your brows have been deepening. As for your being like John because you follow your wife's lead, I can not make up my mind that you do, and I am sure I don't wish you to, unless you think she is going in the right direction.

Paul returned yesterday morning. He is going to Chicopee Sunday night to meet some of the Russians, I believe there are to be orders for the Lowell gun.

Night before last while attending to Butler, who was sleeping with me, I heard an unusual noise like a muffled blow upon wood. I listened and tried to convince myself that it was a window shaken by the wind, but could not be satisfied and finally it occurred to me that although the cellar door which comes up into the house is locked, the road is always open and that it was quite possible that some of the many tramps who are around might have stolen in there and might be busy trying to get into the wine closet. If so, and they should succeed, in what a dangerous position we should be placed. I could rest no longer, but got up, took the revolver and went to Martha's room, woke her up, knowing her to be the most sensible, and together we explored the rooms downstairs and discovered nothing. We did not have a light, the moon being nearly full and very brilliant. Finally while standing over the entry register, listening for a repetition of the sounds, we heard them up stairs, and I have no doubt it was the swallows or bats in the chimney. Being convinced that there was nothing more to fear, we went to bed and to sleep.

Exactly what I should have done if we had found anyone I don't know, but I do know that they would have stood in great danger of getting shot. Now Paul is at home I shall not feel called upon to know the meaning of every sound or movement.

Paul and Willis telegraphed Kellogg to sell if wheat dropped below 1.09. This evening or afternoon before Kellogg could have received their instructions, wheat fell very rapidly. I did not write you yesterday, but I thought of you many, many times, and sent you love as I do tonight. I am so sleepy I can hardly keep my eyes open. BLANCHE

LOWELL, *May* 19, 1878

DEAR DEL: Our family is under the weather and I do not know what the trouble is unless it is the premonitory symptoms of the whooping cough. I sent for Dr. Kimball yesterday and he came, but could not say that there was any trouble, in fact I don't believe he thought I had displayed great judgment in sending for him. The children were all out of doors. I had to have them brought in to see him and his casual examination showed him only a cold. I told him of the feverish nights and languid days and Butler's complaints of feeling cold. He ordered quinine for Butler and sweet spirits of nitric for the fever. I did not get much satisfaction from his visit, for I am convinced he knows nothing about them. The only thing for me to do is to see that they don't catch cold and wait for the trouble to develop or for them to get well. Butler has felt the worst. For three nights he had a high fever and croupy cough without the loud breathing and now he is very languid, lying on the floor or sofa nearly all of the time, without any appetite and coughing heavily. Edith is in the same condition, but was feverish only two nights. She complains of feeling sick to her stomach and dizzy. Sarah had the fever two nights but seems to have more energy and appetite than the others.

All have just the same cough. I have first one and then another in bed with me all the week, changing them to and from my bed as they called out and seemed to be more uncomfortable or unhappy one than another. The baby also has had a little fever and has now the cough. So you see we again have a houseful of ailing ones and I shall be very glad to have you at home for entirely selfish reasons if no others.

Mr. Carney came up yesterday morning with a letter from Kellogg dated the 15th of May, saying that the wheat had been delivered and that he was now holding it, paying insurance and borrowing the money at ten percent a month, etc., etc. Carney asked if it was my wheat. I said "Yes," and explained that I had telegraphed you about it, and asked him to telegraph Kellogg and ask if he had not received instructions from you in regard to the wheat. He promised to do so and I have heard no more from him but shall call to see him Monday morning. I am sorry that he knows what I did with the thousand dollars—that is—that he knows what kind of a speculation I engaged in, and that you have been attending to it for me. He no doubt will think it was owing to your wishes that I undertook it, and I do not care to have him or his friends making comments of that kind. So if it is possible I wish you would give me a thousand dollars or as much of it as is necessary to return the money into his hands, and I will turn over to you as fast as it comes, the interest on the Western mortgages and bank stock. Five hundred will be due the 1st of June. I know it is somewhat hard on you for I should use the five hundred towards our living expenses and thus you would have so much more towards being out of debt. But we will economize and can do so as the family will soon be returning and we shall bear but a portion of the expense.

I have not written you a very agreeable letter, but you will excuse it because you know that I must have you share the pleasures and also the ills. Love, Dearie. BLANCHE

LOWELL, *May 27*, 1878

DEAR DEL: Our three eldest are able to go out and the baby is nearly well. She has been sicker than the others and I have felt more anxious as she is so young and helpless. Now all anxiety is over and she has only a little cough. The doctor does not know exactly what the trouble has been. If he could have heard the whooping he would have said it was the whooping cough, but as that sound was lacking he did not know what to say. My opinion is, that it was as near the whooping cough as they are likely to get. I have not been out for more than a week, not wishing to leave the baby. I shall go tomorrow or next day.

Your check for the $1,000 came safely. I really feel ashamed to take it, although judgment says it will be better under the circumstances. I don't see why Kellogg need to have made such a mistake.

Paul is here most of the time. He has an order for a million cartridges for Russia and one for twenty (I believe) of the Lowell guns. He is to see Semetachkin in a day or two and expects to get much more. That is, he will be the agent for contracting with others.

Capt. Hunt was up the other day. He is very enthusiastic and says that if it had not been for you Paul would not have gone to Russia and that he wishes to make a close ring of it including only himself, Paul, you and Father. Paul is cooler. He does not depend upon anything until he has it, so that he does not seem to feel so sure about all things as Capt. Hunt. As for the war, Hunt says that the visit of Shinveloff and the pretended concessions made by the Czar is only carrying out the programme that was decided upon, and confided to him before he left Russia. That it is only a pretext to gain time, and that the Czar is bent upon war. Still he says that war or no war, they have done well in going to Russia as there are a great many chances for them. Underneath it all he is a little uneasy and from what I can learn the Russians are great deceivers; in other words, liars. Therefore they can *not* say "go on make your speculation, war is sure to be declared before fall."

Do you feel as lonely when your letters fail to arrive as I do?

Love, BLANCHE

NORTHFIELD, MINN., *May* 28, 1878

DEAR BLANCHE: The expert from Minneapolis came down this morning and I went over the books with him. Tomorrow it is our intention to interview Dudley.

I am on the ragged edge of uncertainty. I know I want to sell my Ft. A. property, but I do not know positively of the advantages of buying the Milwaukee property. But even

Father finds less to oppose in this scheme than he usually does. He will not go into it as a partner and it is well—yet, he will readily lend us money to do so. You can well understand that a debt due him is not like any other debt. At any rate I do not propose to go into debt at all in this new venture if a venture it proves to be.

I do not hold back or offer obstacles. I propose, honestly, ignorance of the advantages of milling in Milwaukee and I put the burden on John where it belongs. He and his do not catch me again either for or against anything they want. He shall have the responsibility. If he fails he will be able to thank himself. If he succeeds I will gladly, in consideration thereof, give him full and ample credit. At the same time, I believe the property to be worth more than we have offered for it. Yet, after all, so little we may not buy. The contingencies are too numerous.

I think I have heretofore told you I love you and miss you very much. These weeks have dragged themselves out to a horrible length. The joy of again beholding you is changing a somber sky into sunshine. To anticipate for a few days my coming, I send all I have—love to my Beautiful.

ADELBERT

NORTHFIELD, MINN., *May* 29, 1878

DEAR BLANCHE: I believe all my business here is closed up as far as I know about it. So I am on my way home which I have missed so much and so long.

I saw by today's telegrams that two masked men made an attempt on Ben's life near El Paso. The driver of his ambulance and his escort were seriously wounded but he escaped unharmed, and the two would be assassins had escaped. I have no doubt they (and they are described as Americans) were avenging the South for some act of your Father. Ben has been there long enough. He had better live in civilized New England and abandon a country where savages are still fighting the battles of the rebellion.

I expect this will be my last letter. The next word will be probably by telegraph, or my own greeting at the door. This may be on Tuesday—at least by Wednesday—unless our business at Ft. A. and M. delay.

Expect to see me a little thinner than when you bade me adieu seven weeks ago. Yet while my avoirdupois is less, my love has augmented. I do not know that you will complain of its hugeness for you have always been burdened with much and may have accustomed yourself to it. ADELBERT

General Ames was making arrangements to go into the commission business in New York and sell Northfield flour—and hunting for a suitable house for his family.

NEW YORK, N.Y., *July* 16, 1878

DEAR BLANCHE: When in Boston yesterday, I saw a telegram from your Father wherein he said he would not be in B. till the first of August. This item of news I send you as it may be of advantage to you in your household arrangements.

I saw Hunt yesterday. I told him I thought of going into business here. He was very anxious that I should not; but that I should go to Russia with him by and by!

I have seen Moulton but not Folsom today. The former is earnest in his desire that I should go into business with the latter. He says if I do go in we "should do only commission business." He thinks "Mr. F. is inclined to do only a strict commission business." Should this be the case, the uncertain ties of the business would be greatly reduced. Nothing has been done as yet. We meet Mr. F. tomorrow.

I saw Carleton and he will inquire about Mr. F.

Yesterday at a meeting of butter and cheese men, Mr. F. was chosen chairman of the meeting. Mr. Moulton wishes to be remembered to you.

The papers say your Father has gone to Atlantic City. Hattie evidently is having a bout at the watering places.

Love for you. Kisses for our babies. ADELBERT

NEW YORK, N.Y., *August* 13, 1878

DEAR BLANCHE: I find in my pocket Judge Ames' letter containing a check for your Minneapolis bank interest. I return it.

We have been doing business for one day. I am simply a looker on. Of course I can judge nothing of the business in so short a time. My opinion is that I will like the business if it pays, as I would any other.

I went up to the 5th Ave. last evening to see your Father, or rather to get the paper he was to make out. He was busy with callers. I shall try tonight, hoping progress. He had spoken to Potter about our coming here and received from him a letter to an agent in real estate. I went to the man's office today but found little satisfactory. I can get anything in the house line by paying for it—but that is the rub.

Last week our friend Maj. Lockwood put an advertisement in the papers and yesterday gave me a long list of replies. I shall investigate as fast as possible.

I am now stopping at the Metropolitan Hotel but it is so crowded I shall leave today unless I get a better room. I send you love. ADELBERT

NEW YORK, N.Y., *August* 14, 1878

DEAR BLANCHE: I have been house hunting this forenoon. I have a house on 56th St. between 5th & 6th Avenues offered to me. That is just three blocks from the park. As I approached the house I saw it was a 25 ft. front. Once inside I began to take observations. The carpet was covered with newspapers. The arrangements of the rooms were excellent. I begin to doubt if the Washington house is built in the best way for economy of space and other advantages. There was a cedar closet large enough for trunks and clothing. There was a jewelry safe up stairs and a silver safe in the dining room. There were bronze and marble ornaments and oil paintings—not to speak of lace hanging and such. I know you would be pleased with the house in every particular. Do you want the house? Rent—$5,000.00.

The next house was at the corner of Madison Ave. and 63rd St. I announced to the lady of the house, an elderly lady, my name and cause of visit. She said, "Ames, Ames, your face is familiar. Did I see you in Europe?" I said I do not know, I was there a number of years ago. She said, "Did you know a family from St. Louis, a Mr.—Mr.—." I helped her on by saying "Chapman." Then we both smiled. The lost was found. We had met a few times and her memory of faces did the rest. She told me she was real estate poor, etc. Her house was good enough but she asked $3,000.00.

This sheet is being stained with Park Ave. Hotel ink. The house was formerly Stewart's Home for old ladies. I have just had dinner and like everything here. The house is elegant and quiet. I could not sleep at the Metropolitan because of the street noises.

Tell Paul to try this hotel next time. It is at the lower end of the tunnel, the upper end of which is at the R. R. depot. I expect to get a fair night's rest tonight. I have not had one since I left you. Love from ADELBERT

NEW YORK, N.Y., *August* 19, 1878

DEAR BLANCHE: I have just had my dinner at the Park Ave. Hotel and came over here to the 5th. Ave. to see your Father. It has occurred to me that you had better come on with Paul and Hattie if they come on about the middle of the week and return with me Friday evening—provided I telegraph you to come; and that I will do if I conclude I have reached my end of the search. I have just had one word with your Father. He says he has found a house for us up by the park. He was to talk with me about it but he is so busy I will not see him tonight.

One of your Father's friends has told me since I began this letter that there is a house on 58th St., which is one street from the park, and near 5th Ave., but recently completed, never occupied, which cost about $80,000.00, and which the owner is anxious to dispose of. That is, it must go for its $30,000.00 mortgage if he cannot make a sale; and that he thinks an advance of $5,000.00 above the mortgage will buy it. Perhaps we will or could buy it and pay interest on mortgage instead of rent. I will see the house tomorrow if I can meet the person spoken of by your Father's friend.

Kisses for the babies and love for yourself. ADELBERT

LOWELL, *August* 22, 1878

DEAR DEL: I received your telegram this morning and have sent your deeds to Sam.

Ben came home last night but returns to Newport this morning. He seems to be enjoying himself.

I went to Boston yesterday to try a dress. Your letters came just before I started and I read them on the cars. If the house you speak of suits you, it may be well to buy. How long does the mortgage run? I am ready to do any or everything you may propose; you see, could anyone have a more agreeable wife?

The baby seems to be troubled with something very like Butler's hay fever. I trust she is not to be afflicted as he has been with the nuisance.

Paul is waiting for my letter. So I will say good bye with love. BLANCHE

NEW YORK, N.Y., *August* 22, 1878

DEAR BLANCHE: I went to see the house on 58th St. that I spoke to you about yesterday. That particular one is not the one forced to a sale by mortgage, though it is for sale and the price is $55,000.00. Further down the same street towards 6th Ave. a similar house 25 x 60 or 20 x 75 new is sold by same builder for I understood, $45,000.00. Anyhow, such a house for $30,000.00 would be cheap but after consideration, I am fully convinced that we had better get out of debt before we attempt such a burden. I think we had better hire and live as best we may till we have more available funds on hand. Next year we are to resume specie payments and I have no doubt times will be worse than now. Then we may be able to buy. I have nothing new. Love, ADELBERT

NEW YORK, N.Y., *September* 3, 1878

DEAR BLANCHE: I will not be in Lowell till Saturday morning and if you will be ready we will start on Monday afternoon.

The cook recommended to me wants $20.00 per month and looked blank when I suggested she would be expected to do the washing. I answered an advertisement of a cook today. Tomorrow I will probably be a little better informed.

Our house is about the width of the Waddel house. It has no windows on the side except the bay windows.

I went to the two places where were advertised auctions of furniture etc., and found them as I expected, auction rooms. Furniture is replaced by other as soon as sold. Both places looked very much alike in style of furniture, fixtures, etc. The furniture sold went cheap enough. In neither place did they have dinner or tea sets.

Unless we have good success in seeking a cook, Liza would be well enough to begin with. In fact, she has her virtues as a cook and servant.

Business is going on as usual.

Love, ADELBERT

NEW YORK, N.Y., *September* 4, 1878

DEAR BLANCHE: This morning I went to a genuine house emptying auction and found nothing worth having. I also called at Sypher's where I saw nothing we wanted except a dozen ornamented cups and saucers for which they asked $10.00. Down in this vicinity I visited an American crockery store. Plain cups and saucers for the kitchen were two dollars ($2.00) a dozen—plates at $1.50 pr. doz. I next went to an importers, and found his quite attractively ornamented crockery offered as follows—dinner set of 140 pieces (see enclosure) price $60.00. This was not the best nor the poorest yet it was very good. A tea set of 51 pieces at from $10 to $78. The tea sets do not include teapots and sugar bowls. It strikes me crockery is not a very expensive article of house furniture.

As I examine the list enclosed on paper I see "12 teas extra" and "12 A. D. Coffees." I suppose they mean cups and saucers. If so, the dinner set will probably do for tea.

If you have any orders for me you had better telegraph unless your letter can reach me before Friday when I shall leave for Lowell.

Love, ADELBERT

General and Mrs. Ames moved their household to their new home at 76 East 61st Street, New York City, N.Y.

LOWELL, *October 12, 1878*

DEAR BLANCHE: Gen. Ames' two letters came together yesterday. Willis, Capt. Reed, Ben and I were on the "ill fated train," as the newspapers have it. We were in the car next to the English coach, and our car was the one "literally obliterated," N.P. again.

Willis and I sat in front of Capt. R. and Ben, Ben and I being on the side next the windows on the left of the car over the wheels. There were about eighty in the car, and I don't believe there were more than six besides our party who got out of the ruins without help. Capt. R., Ben, and I crawled out an opening between the edge of the roof of the car and a pile of rubbish eight or nine ft. high. I think two others went out the same way ahead of us. Willis went through a window on the other side. How any of us ever got out alive, or at least not crushed to pieces, is a mystery.

I crawled onto the roof of the car and laid down. Ben and Capt. R. went to look for Willis, whom we never expected to see again, and met him coming over the roof of the next car. Willis, who in the excitement thought he was not hurt much, went off to look for a team while Capt. R. and Ben helped me off the car. Willis was lucky enough to capture a wagon which took us and a man with his face all cut and shoulder broken to a hotel at Atlantic. After getting Ben and myself beds, Willis went to Neponset for Capt. Hunt and a doctor and Capt. R. to his family in Chelsea. Very soon Willis returned with Hunt and a doctor (Mr. West), quite a pleasant old man retired from his profession. The first thing was to look at my ankle which was bruised and the skin knocked off on both sides. When the doctor saw my big ankle bones, he asked if I had ever had anything the matter with my ankle before. I told him no, that my other ankle bones were the same. "Ah," he said, "I see scrofulous tendency." The examination of injuries stopped until I had given him my opinion about that. *Injuries.* (Ben, Willis and I have been estimating how much we can get from the O.C.R.R. per square inch for skin of which we were unlawfully deprived.)

Capt. R. went home thinking himself not much hurt, aside from his thumb being out of joint, but as soon as the excitement was over, he found he had been very badly bruised and was obliged to go to bed and stay there. Willis was bruised and his left leg skinned. His ideas of damages considerably increased when he stiffened up next day. Ben got a crack over the nose, another in the back, both elbows knocked, also left hip and knee and both legs below the knee and left foot, nothing serious. He went to Huntington Hall to hear Durant last night and I was going to Boston this morning if it had not rained.

For myself, I have three scabs on my nose and a bump on the forehead. A rap on the left shoulder and the left arm from shoulder to half way below the elbow, bruised so that I could not lift it for two days. A punch in the ribs on both sides and a good solid thump in the breadbasket, which was the principal reason why I curled up on the roof of the car after getting out of the wreck. Right shin bruised and left thigh, also left ankle as I said above. I have dwelt more on my own injuries probably because I know more about them.

There was to have been a horse trot this afternoon but I think the rain will cause a postponement. If I can get it put off until after the middle of next week I shall drive Black Diamond, Randolph's horse, so you see I am not very much hurt.

Willis when he got home found himself the happy father of a son born the night of the accident, but before his wife had heard of it. PAUL BUTLER

WASHINGTON, D.C., *March* 10, 1879

Mrs. Blanche Butler Ames,
76 East 61st Street, New York City

MY DEAR BLANCHE: I want you to buy me and send on at once some proper material to upholster my rose-wood furniture. You remember it as the maroon satin. It is not very valuable, and I do not want a very valuable material, but something that will match the rose-wood. Also the proper gimp. It is plain, you know, and I can get a man to put it on here.

I am busy trying to let my house—perhaps I may say houses, for I doubt whether Senator Jones will renew his lease.

The weather is very pleasant here. Before we finally break up, can't you and Ames come on? I shall have to stay here a week. I have been confined to the house with a very bad cold for three days. I seem to have got rid of my cold, but its accompaniment, which has been a very severe pain in the back of my head, sticks to me, and is not pleasant. I have been out today in the pleasant weather, and think I am better for it. I hope to get over it at once.

I send you, enclosed, Hattie's measurement.

Yours truly, BENJ. F. BUTLER

LOWELL, *July* 15, 1879

DEAR DEL: You did not say whether you should write or not, but as I want to hear from you I suppose I shall have to give you a letter now and then to get one in return.

There was a party last night at Miss Burke's. My dress was on the bed and I was nearly ready to go when my heart failed me and I decided that there would be no enjoyment and less comfort such a warm night, under the gas light in a crowded parlor talking to Ludlum and Lawson, Coffin, and others. Hattie, Miss Wadell and Paul represented the household.

Edith asked me to let her go to Haggets Pond with Butler, and when I refused she replied "Butler always has the best things and the nicest time." I thought she was right, so I looked in the closet among my belongings, and found a couple of pieces of flannel of which I made a bathing suit for Edith and some drawers for Butler. This morning West has taken the whole crew, in the park phaeton to the Pond. Martha and the baby have gone too—so that Martha can dress the little girls and the baby have a ride. Sarah's bathing suit is not yet made, so she will wear her white drawers and waist.

The baby this morning had two cups full of oat meal and milk—from which I have hopes she will ere long be a decently plump baby.

Have you bought Mattie's present yet? If you had been here I should have gone to Burke's party.

With love, and many sweet kisses, BLANCHE

129 Broad St., New York, *July 21*, 1879

Dear Blanche: The travel on the boat not being so great as usual I obtained a good stateroom and arrived well and safe, with a good night's sleep.

Charles had caught in all 16 mice and 1 rat—caught in laundry by a cat they invited in for the purpose. He says the bed bugs have disappeared since he painted the floor and mop boards with benzine or kerosene. He now enters a campaign against cock-roaches in the kitchen.

I was to send the sketch of the urn to Brooklyn, but on drawing a line to show my meaning I decided not to do so, for I think he cannot possibly err in such a matter. See how the line runs. But if you think best, return it, and I will do so.

It is very cool here, and I shut the window to keep the draft off.

It would be well for us to go to Bay View this week. I will try to leave so as to be in Lowell Friday.

Love, Adelbert

208 W. 59th St., New York,[1] *July 22*, 1879

Dear Blanche: I write you to say I have nothing to say. To say that this house seems empty would be to say that everything is empty without you. To say that it is not *home* to me is to say that where you are, there is my home. To say the above, when I am with you two or three days a week, is to say something which sounds unmanly. To know I am so weak, and to say I know it should make me blush—at least—should make me say I blush. To say all this in the briefest way, I have but to say—I love you.

I was much interested in "Mr. Smith—A part of his Life." I finished it last night at twelve.

What a clear distinction the writer makes, between "sorrows, sufferings and losses" on the one hand and "disappointments" on the other. I think much of our unhappiness is due to *disappointments* rather than to things more real.

Everything with me is very quiet—absolutely nothing new. Love to you and the babies. Adelbert

129 Broad St., New York, *July 29*, 1879

Dear Blanche: I arrived all right this morning. We were delayed by a fog this morning. I found the house all right. Business is progressing slowly. There are no very high prices but—fair. No great demand, but enough to take all our flour by the end of the season.

[1] General and Mrs. Ames had changed their residence to this address.

My bonanza mine has gone for good and I do not expect to look on the like again. But seriously, nothing is so unsettling as expected bonanzas which yield only bountiful crops of disappointments.

I am curious to know what became of the pic-nic and the sour faces it engendered. In fact, I had a pair of sour faces to remember. Hattie's, about which I care little—but the second—Butler's, concerns me not a little. I never treated my father that way. Pray, what is my error in treatment of the lad? I am in hopes a few years will teach him better.

Love, ADELBERT

208 W. 59th St., NEW YORK CITY, *August* 4, 1879

DEAR BLANCHE: I finished "Theo" before reaching Fall River. I do not think much of her. She is not natural. The lunatic asylum would be a fit home for her. Then again, her belledom did not come naturally out of the situation. It is but the ill directed fancies of a fanciful person. Yet, the story was fairly well told.

About two o'clock Saturday a person called on you, failing to find you at home, he left his card which I enclose. As Saturday was a very hot day, the young man evidently wanted to see you. Sunday was a hot day also. And this day began with an intention of making it hot for everybody, but a sea breeze blew in over the city of Brooklyn, and the temperature was very pleasant. This evening we had a shower, which makes it unnecessary to open wide my windows.

Charles has oiled the front doors. He has not caught another mouse—he regrets that Othello's occupation's gone—five cents a head. I have told the cook that she must wash, etc. the bed spreads—repeating your instructions as near as I was capable of doing.

It was rather amusing that Hattie and I should provoke you into riding down to the depot with me. I was sorry for you. Don't do it again. Tell Hattie that I do not know whether yellow becomes her or not. I based all I said on her wearing that yellow veil about a year ago. If she attempts to act on my talk you had better advise her on the facts as *you* find them.

Love and kisses. I hope your health is improving as it ought under my skillful treatment. ADELBERT

LOWELL, *August* 5, 1879

DEAR DEL: When I left you at the depot we drove home. Mrs. Webster and her friend were still there, but soon left for

Mrs. Reade's. Hattie and I took a long drive in Dracut, and made a call on Aunt Nina, who is a little better than she has been.

The evening we passed at home without callers or incident.

Yesterday I spent an hour or so with Butler over his lessons. Then painted till four in the afternoon.

I had a little shopping to do which had been deferred until this week for lack of funds—such as the purchase of tooth brushes, shoes for the baby, etc. I had Paul's shirts to take to Mrs. Atwood's, and made a call on Aunt Maria. She had nothing new to tell me, so I have no gossip for you.

I shall probably go to the mill today about the magnifying glass for Butler.

I miss you, Sweetheart, and if I do not tell you every hour how dear you are to me—it is because you are as necessary to my happiness as the air I breathe is to existence. I take the air without saying at every respiration how delightful! how satisfying! and in the same way I accept your love, and give you mine—without exclaiming life is perfect with you, without you it is nothing. BLANCHE

129 Broad St., NEW YORK, *August* 6, 1879

DEAR BLANCHE: As business is dull—as I have little to do, and as I want to be with my loved ones, I will leave here Thursday evening. I will not reach Lowell till about midday. If you get this letter in time you may send Mathews for me at about twelve or one—perhaps for both trains due in L. at those hours. I stop in Boston on a matter of business.

Warner is here. I have asked him to stop with me tonight. I meet him at the Astor House, and take him along with me.

I went to see my ear doctor this morning. I spoke about Butler's eyes. The doctor desired that I bring him in.

I understand the public schools begin the first Monday in Sept. which will be the 1st day of that month.

Love, ADELBERT

129 Broad St., NEW YORK, *August* 11, 1879

DEAR BLANCHE: I found a letter from Father notifying me that he is not coming east this summer, and advising me to start west the same day I get this letter. That I cannot very well do. But I have written John I will start a week hence. So next Monday I will take my departure for the northwest.

In thinking over Butler's case, I have concluded he *must*

keep certain hours—above all meal hours. When he fails we must say little or nothing, but request him to keep the house, or a particular room, for a certain number of hours. As he told you he did not want to go to the circus, I would not let him go. Furthermore, I would keep him at home (in the house) that day if he will be likely to go there without permission. He should be made to feel some sort of penalty or punishment for his sins. He has an idea—at least a practice—of fighting every effort to restrain his whims and fancies. It is best to begin the issue on our side so there can be no doubt in his mind that some kind of punishment will attend his viciousness. Our best weapon will be apparent indifference, and he is to be pitted against time to see which can the longer hold out. We to be simple timekeepers.

Love, ADELBERT

LOWELL, *August* 12, 1879

DEAR DEL: I have just received your letter of Monday. In regard to Butler it seems much easier to restrain him in New York than here. For instance, Capt. Meigs took him off somewhere before breakfast, so that when he should have come in he was nowhere to be found. Of course I shall forbid him to go on anybody's invitation without permission. Yesterday the boys made a number of sweet fern cigars and Butler smoked three or four of them. He thinks they tasted good—but he had no desire for his supper—the milk toast was "too soft" for him. He was in a great deal of trouble at tea time. Turner had hit him in the eye with a stick and he had the tooth ache. But he made such a baby of himself, and was so very disagreeable that I was quite out of sorts with him. I had to compel him to clean his teeth, which stopped the pain, and finally I read him a long story. Before he went to sleep he told me all the events of the day and agreed that he would not smoke any more cigars as they spoiled his appetite. Children all have spells of behaving badly and I am in hopes that Butler will be a good boy again in a few months. In the meantime I will follow your suggestions and help him along in the right direction as fast as possible.

Mr. Carney has had a windfall of six thousand dollars, which he has divided between Paul, Ben, and myself. I have paid Aunt Lottie and Hattie at last, and feel that one duty has been attended to. I made Mr. Carney rather a long call—as Hattie went away to do some errands while I was at the Bank and did not return for half or three quarters of an hour. Mr. Carney and I told each other all the stories we knew.

I send you love. BLANCHE

208 West 59th St., NEW YORK, *August* 18, 1879

DEAR BLANCHE: This has been a busy day with me. Rushing through the rain I reached the elevated R.R. and came home for breakfast.

I called up Annie and discussed preserves. She seemed to know well the science of sugar and acids. When I spoke of plums, she said they were more acid than peaches, and would require more sugar. So I told her to "go ahead,"—two crates of peaches and two crates of plums. Charles will paint the roof—iron bars—oil all the wood—work in the house and wax floors on 4th story, as well as the dining room floor.

I found the flour market dull. I drew a number of checks for freight which I signed—and left my salesman to do the rest. I do not expect any money will have to be paid out except for freight, and as the checks for it are made out in the name of the freight company no stealing can be done there. If any other money be used he will have to borrow. The money he collects he can only deposit. So I feel fairly safe.

At half past nine I met Mr. Folsom and signed his release, and took due bills for 3150 dollars. My action is subject to Gen'l. Barlow's review and approval. I left the papers at his office. He is out of town just now.

This afternoon I bought a very handsome clock for $38.00. It will be sent to Northfield insured against breakage, C.O.D.

It is a very desirable article—of more practical use than nine tenths of wedding presents, and much more ornamental. It has two colored marble and bronze ornaments—that is, feet and attachments on the sides.

My dinner and packing have delayed me till it is now half past seven. I go from depot at 8:30. So I must hasten. Love from ADELBERT

Office of Jesse Ames' Sons, Merchant Millers
NORTHFIELD, MINN., *August* 22, 1879

DEAR BLANCHE: This is Butler's birthday. I suppose you are having a party for him. He is eight (8) years old. Before we realize it he will be ready to make a world for himself, separate and distinct from ours. I see by the paper that your

Father reached home yesterday. So while you were chatting with the whole of your own family, I was with mine.

I arrived yesterday morning. Father is a little under the weather—nothing serious. Everybody else is well. John looks well. He has his hair cropped short and sports English side whiskers. I need not say he has a distingué air.

Nellis is fatter than ever. Mattie looks much the same. Fanny looks very well. She will return to Andover in about two weeks. Alice, I have not seen. John says she is very smart. Johnny looks more like Mattie than ever. As for Mother, I need not say she is in excellent health.

Charlotte has another baby—a boy. I need not say they are very proud of him. Before it was four weeks old she brought it into town, caring for it and her girl at the same time.

Everybody else is much as when we were here. No changes have taken place except the trees seem much larger and hide the houses.

Of the mill, I need but tell you that the changes will cost from forty to forty-five thousand dollars. You were shocked, as was I, when I heard of the vast expenditures here. But everyone is hopeful not to say sanguine. They say a change had to be made. Father will help us with some $15,000.00 and so we will get along in a way.

Love, ADELBERT

LOWELL, *August* 24, 1879

DEAR DEL: I have just come from church—changed my dress to get cooled off and am ready for a little chat with you.

Friday Butler had a picnic at Tyngs Pond—Uncle Parker, Aunt Maria, Sadie, Aunt Lottie, Fisher and Gardiner, Gemi Meigs and her three brothers—Percy Parker and his friend, Prentiss Webster, Martha and our children including the baby and myself. We reached the pond about half past two and found the grounds occupied by a town picnic from Pelham. We captured a couple of boats, however, for the children. Butler, while playing in an old paddle boat on the shore disturbed a hornets nest and was stung on his little finger. He can row very well for such a small boy and went nearly across the pond by himself and rowed up and down the shore. His poor little hands were all blistered and when he crawled into bed at night he said he "ached all over, head, arms, stomach and legs."

For all that the children had a delightful time, as all made it a business to wait and tend upon them. We were at home by eight, and Butler found a large box containing an angel cake which his Grandfather had sent up by express for the picnic—but which did not reach Lowell until after we had gone. Butler decided he could have a collation next day. But yesterday he did not feel like play. His hand was as large as three, and he was so tired he preferred to stay at home curled up on armchairs or on the sofa. He is now enjoying the cake with his sisters and the Meigs children under the horse chestnuts.

There was a game of poker here last night. The meeting was called for business relative to the braiding machine. So much for our projects and performances here. I am anxious to learn what you are doing.

Love for you, Dearie. BLANCHE

LOWELL, *September* 3, 1879

DEAR DEL: I know you will say to yourself "Why did she not write yesterday?" I was making preserves yesterday—and the thermometer was up in the nineties. I was obliged to stand over the kettle to take out the pears as they cooked, some getting done before others. Martha helped me, and strange to say we were both sick. I was sick while doing them and the rest of the day. While she was ill after they were all done, and just before she went to bed. I think the heat sent the blood to the head in such a way as to make us faint and dizzy.

The children are in the house more this week. The Meigs boys are at school and there is not that desire to run there has been. I have given Butler the warm bath you proposed. He says that he can breathe a little easier.

I should like to have Charles stain the floor of the basement billiard room and give it a good waxing before we go back. Burnt umber, boiled oil, and turpentine are what he should use.

There is not much chance that the "long name from Maine" will be ready for a sail Saturday. They have been slow about getting her up from Gloucester. So I shall expect you home Saturday morning.

I send you love and kisses, Dearie—don't forget to take the quinine. In addition to my desire to have your throat well for your own comfort, I also have a selfish motive. I shall want you to read to me this winter.

Good-bye, BLANCHE

LOWELL, *October* 21, 1879

DEAR DEL: I was glad to get word from you before you left New York, and pleased that you did not forget Mattie's present.

Our yachting party came home yesterday. They were in Portland harbor during the storm. They passed an anxious night, however, all hands on deck fearing that a big iron clad, anchored in front of them, might get loose from her moorings and drive upon them. Father was not on board, but was passing the night at a friend's near Portland. They seem to have had a very pleasant time. From Portland they had a race with the "Taralinta." She did not mean to race with the America —but tried to steal out of the harbor about midnight. But she was watched, and when her mainsail went up there was a suspicious rattling on the America and they left the harbor together. They soon lost sight of each other in the darkness, and at break of day the "Taralinta" was seen hull down in the distance, with her racing sails all set as they had evidently been during the night.

No doubt there was great excitement on the "America" then, for all sail was crowded on, and they gave chase with such success that passing Thatcher's Light the Taralinta was left two miles behind.

Saturday Father and the boys are to sail around to Bay View and are to have a race with a Marblehead fishing boat. The owner, a Mr. Appleton, who is wealthy, has said he could beat the America and they are going to let him try. I fear there is going to be betting on the race, for Mr. Ludlum has offered to stake a hundred dollars on the result.

208 West 59th St., New York, *May 24*, 1880

Dear Del: This is the second day since your departure, and all goes well. I was provoked to find that I had allowed you to go without your shawl, fur gloves, or Ben's ulster. What else may have been forgotten you will find as you have need of the articles, but I am confident you are not more than half equipped.

You did not have a chance to kiss Blanche good bye. She has asked each morning "Where is Father? Gone to the office?" Butler seems to miss you most. I have been obliged to do double duty in the way of entertaining him. Two or three times he has broken down into tears, and of course I am comforter. He expects to be examined without fail tomorrow. If so, we shall leave for Lowell the last of the week. I had a letter today from Capt. Hunt, in which he politely offers his services during your absence and Ben's, and offers to escort us to Lowell.—That I must not hesitate to ask him as he has "a free pass over the Fall River line."

Sunday I did not go out, but painted some, and read *Mrs. Beauchamp Brown*, which is an amusing, though not a first class, novel. Dennis will get me the papers this evening, so that I can keep along with the events of the day, while my chronicler is away.

Butler sits in your chair at the table, and helps to fish balls, cold meat. etc. This morning he sharply told Edith to "stop sticking her nose in the maple syrup jug." I reminded him that you did not speak in that way.—The servants laughed, he looked red and confused. I think he will be more careful another time.

I have nothing to tell you, Del, except these trifles, and that I miss you very, very much. I dreamed last night that we were together trying to find another house, as we were obliged to give up this one. All the places we looked at seemed half buried in water.

Love, till tomorrow, when you will hear from me again,

BLANCHE

LOWELL, *June* 25, 1880

DEAR DEL: I write you hoping that this will reach Northfield before you leave. I had quite made up my mind that you would give up the idea of stopping at Northfield, as you had said nothing of it in your letters. I had tried to think that you would be so homesick you could not, although reflection might tell you it was best to do so. We have had a very quiet time these six weeks since you left. All have been well and nothing out of the ordinary course of events has happened.

According to directions, the children have been to Sunday school. Butler rides Phil with West on Ben's saddle horse. Blanche has been out to tea with Hilda Nesmith a number of times—but as Florence goes to Bay View today she will have to stop gadding. Sarah, as usual, goes down town every time the team goes. Edith more rarely. She prefers to play with the Ludlum children.

As for me, I ride out almost daily and call to see some of the family, but I find them full of business of one kind or another, and not to be depended upon for companionship. I therefore amuse myself as best I can with reading and daubing, and the days slip by as all uneventful days do, leaving but little impression, except that time is passing.

Your letters have come frequently, often two at a time, and have been the excitement and events of life. The last one, dated the 16th, in which you speak of going to Northfield and express yourself as content with the "Terrible" came last evening. I am happy that the mine is satisfactory to you. I was fearful of a disappointment, and its effect upon your happiness and *flesh*.

Fannie has been up two or three times. She is going home next week, probably with some of her school friends.

Gen'l. Kinsman spent Sunday with me. It was the most tiresome day of the week, chiefly because he smokes so much and the smell of it is very disagreeable just now. He has sold some more "Terrible" stock.

I will not try to give you the small news, and gossip of these last weeks. You will be content to know that we all love you and look forward with delight to your return. BLANCHE

Office of Jesse Ames' Sons, NORTHFIELD, MINN.
June 28, 1880

DEAR BLANCHE: I left St. Louis Friday evening and reached Northfield Sunday morning. I found everyone well except Mother who is fast getting better of a slight sickness. My St. L. trouble was but temporary and I am as well as ever. Father has been waiting my coming with the intention of going East with me. He will go if Mother continues to improve. I shall not, however, invite him to Lowell.

J. T. has grown a full beard and is jolly. He is, as you know, mayor, running Cole for congress, refusing to run for the legislature, etc. and running the mill. The more diversified his duties the better he seems. Really, Jack is the miller and is alone responsible for the flour made. The ground is graded for a railroad track to the mill. In a week or two the track will be down. I am convinced that it will prove very profitable. An arrangement was made today by which the elevator at this point will fall into our hands. This will be very advantageous.

The wheat crop is very promising, never more so, and if results equal indications this section will be very rich in wheat. We hope for a good crop as it will help us along on the way we wish to go. This is a good mill—an excellent mill as it ought to be. The original cost is increased by the changes necessary. I hope—this at least I can say.

I shall start for the East so as to reach New York Saturday morning and to leave there Saturday night for Lowell.

I send you love. Your ADELBERT

General and Mrs. Ames' fifth child, a son, was born August 19th, 1880 and was named Adelbert Ames after his father.

LOWELL, *December* 11, 1880

MY DEAR BLANCHE: Thanks for your very thoughtful invitation. I am lonely, but the needs of my pressing business engagements will keep me here.

I shall be in New York on Tuesday, but without the hope of seeing you, but may on my return from Washington.

Paul heard from on Tuesday last. All well. FATHER

At Home at LOWELL, *January* 28, 1881

DEAR BLANCHE: I am asking Hattie to write a letter to you, as I do not see very well to write at night, and if I did I am too lazy. I owe you an apology for not coming up to see you on my last visit to New York, because—a poor thing to say—I had not time, but yet it is unhappily true.

I want you to do me a favor. You know I am going off yachting and I am getting a little luxurious. I want you to get me at some of the auction or kindred shops in New York, a small set of china. I don't care about platters, teapots, and sugar bowls, or a soup tureen. I have got a small one I shall use. I may have somebody to dine with me on the yacht while I am gone who would think I ought to have such things. I don't want an expensive set, or a large one, as it is likely to be broken up, so you will be glad to learn that you are like John Gilpin and I like his wife "for he was right glad to find that though on pleasure she was bent she had a frugal mind."

I would not trouble you, though you will do it better than anyone else. Kinsman, who does such things for me, is in Washington.—Send it packed to Boston, directed to me, 12 Pemberton Square, for "Yacht America," so it need not be opened.

If you don't get it before, I will pay you out of the first dividend I get out of the Little Chief. You know whom to ask when that will come. It may take the whole stock.

Hattie sends love. FATHER

NASSAU, NEW PROVIDENCE ISLAND, *March* 13, 1881

Mrs. BLANCHE BUTLER AMES, *New York City*

MY DEAR BLANCHE: I write you at our first port of landing, you being the only person in the United States who I suppose cares very much whether I have got here right or wrong. I premise in the first place that we are all well. Ben and Paul have been a little under the weather from the mal de mer, but they are all right now and eating enough to breed a famine.

I suppose you would like to have a little history of our cruise. I will give it to you from narration from Boston until we left Fortress Monroe and thence by actual observation. The "America" started Tuesday, February 22nd at three o'clock p.m. and went to Gloucester. On Wednesday at one p.m. made sail and proceeded with a southwest wind, when it began to blow, and she returned to Gloucester at 5 a.m., there being a strong gale from the northwest. (The days here mentioned are from noon to noon.) On Thursday the 24th she sailed from Gloucester and made Chatham Light, which by the by, is one side of Cape Cod.

It then came on to blow from the northeast, snowing hard, and she came to anchor. On the 25th, at 3:45 p.m. she went into Hyannis Harbor, it having commenced to snow again, and the wind coming out of the northwest, very cold. At six in the morning of the 26th she made sail at G; and struck on the west end of L'Homme Dieu Shoals, there being much vapor on the water; but she only touched. The steam tug "Hunter" came by and was signaled for assistance, and she came toward the yacht, and after a long negotiation agreed to pull her off, which was done.

The Captain of the "Hunter" then demanded four hundred dollars for his services. Capt. Reid offered him $100. He was not engaged more than an hour in the business. Thereupon, soon after, the U.S. Revenue Cutter "Dexter" came out from Vineyard sound, and came within the distance of a mile, and fired a gun, which the yacht took for a salute and kept on.

The "Dexter" then fired a shot across the "America's" bows and she then laid to. An officer came on board and overhauled our papers, and said the Captain of the steam tug "Hunter" told them that the "America" was a rather suspicious looking craft with fourteen working men on board of all nations. The Lieutenant satisfied himself who we were and where we were bound, and then went on board the Cutter to report. After his report, the Commander of the Cutter, Captain Irish, demanded of Captain Reid a written order on the owners of the "America" for one hundred dollars for services rendered by the steamer "Hunter," which he gave.

I need not say to you that this proceeding of Capt. Irish of the Revenue Cutter was an outrage not to be tolerated by civilized nations, and had I been on board he would have received gun for gun until somebody was satisfied. But I will settle with him when I return through his superiors.

Such an act by a foreign vessel would have been causus belli. He knew, or ought to have known if he hadn't been most of the time drunk in his cabin, that the "America" sailed, bound south, who her owners were, and what was her honest errand; and he had no more business firing guns at her than we had firing guns at him, as I should have done if I had been there. But the Captain probably took the wisest course, as I should have taken the most effective one if I had been there.

On the 27th the boys proceeded as far as Montague Light House, when the day ended with a calm and thick fog, which continued until 4 p.m. of the 28th, when a light easterly wind sprung up bringing with it thunder and lightning and heavy rain, and the day ended with wind shifting to the southwest; with heavy and frequent snow squalls.

In this week the yacht has only got as far as Highland Light. On Tuesday, March 1st, the day came in with strong gales from the west southwest, and heavy snow squalls. Barnagat Light about twelve miles off, wind and sea increasing. Went back under Barnagat for smooth weather and the day ended with strong gales and heavy wind squalls. Wednesday, March 2nd, came in with strong gales from the W.S.W. and snow squalls. At noon Obsecomb Light bore west about twelve miles, strong wind and high sea.

At 1:30 a.m. saw a steamer heading for us; had to jibe the main sail in order to clear the steamer, and in so doing the main sheet parted and carried away the main boom, the steamer paying no attention, but went on. We repaired the boom as well as possible and kept on the course with double reefed foresail and bare stay-sail. At 8 a.m. bent on main sail, and at noon weather moderating, it became more pleasant.

Got down as far as Hog Island. (If you don't follow this course on the map and it may be interesting for you and the General to do so, I would say that Hog Island is off the Peninsula of Eastern Virginia).

March 3rd came in with fresh breeze and fine weather. At 3 p.m. Cape Charles was seven miles distant. At 7 p.m. anchors at Fort Monroe.

From this point I may proceed without the aid of the log-book. I came to Fortress Monroe by steamer on Saturday night, the 27th of Feb'y. Remained on the look-out for the yacht, not having heard of her until Ben reported to me at the Soldier's Home at 8 o'clock on the night of the 3rd. In the morning I telegraphed to the Secretary of the Navy for leave to have a new boom made at the Navy Yard. Received permission, and got the Fort tug boat through the kindness of General Getty, to tow the "America" to Norfolk. I came back to the Soldier's Home this afternoon. At 4 o'clock on the next day the boom was ready, and at half-past five they made sail for the Fort but in going out of the harbor they got aground abreast the light house.

Stayed there three hours and then the tide took them off, and they came to anchor at the Fort at eight o'clock. I came aboard of her in the morning of the 6th. On Sunday morning at 6, rather 5 o'clock, passed the light at the Fort with a strong breeze from the northwest, which we run before running southeast. The breeze freshened until 4 p.m. when we furled the main top sail and double-reefed the main sail.

There stayed through the day a strong breeze with increasing sea. During the day we ran by the log 243 miles. The same breeze and some sea and cloudy weather continued through the eighth. At 4 p.m. we were enabled to set the jib. We ran through this day 163 miles. The day ended with a calm and high sea, the vessel laboring very heavily.

Wednesday, the ninth, came with some light winds. At 7 p.m. some wind sprung up, and at 11 p.m. increased to a gale, double reefs in main-sail and fore-sail, and a bonnet out of stay-sail. At one a.m. furled the main sail and stay-sail and laid to under foresail. At 8 a.m. wind going to W.S.W. with heavy squall, jibbed the fore-sail and in so doing tore it from the after leech.

Thursday came in with a brisk breeze from the west with high sea, making the vessel labor very hard and shipping water on deck. At midnight more moderate. From midnight to morning watch was employed setting up rigging which had been very much slackened by the laboring of the vessel. The day ended with fair and pleasant weather.

On Friday, the 11th, day came in with a smart breeze and clear pleasant weather and continued until 9 p.m. and the day ended with calm pleasant weather in which we rolled again, during which we made no progress until about 7 p.m., when a light breeze came up and we made quite a run about before it, although the sea was very heavy, and at 5 o'clock a.m. we saw the outer mast lighthouse on the key at the westerly end of

Abaco Island, the outer island of the Bahamas. This showed us that we were about 25 miles out of our course. The fine weather continued.

The sea moderating, we had to beat up to the southernmost and eastern end of Abaco Island, and then we turned the light and before midnight we saw the light at Nassau. We ran down the light and then waited, watching for a pilot and this morning about seven o'clock we took a pilot and came to Nassau Harbor where we now are, and I am now writing you, for the mail goes out tomorrow at noon.

Running over this log you will see that we have had hardly a pleasant day's sailing. There has either been a very high sea with wind, or a calm with very high sea, or a gale, such as made some of the landsmen on board a little afraid for the outcome. I was as frightened as they were but I did not show it. All agree that there never was so much bad weather in the same space of time; but then the last speech is always the most eloquent ever delivered, and the last cold snap the coldest ever known, and the last storm at sea the worst ever known, so that you can take all this with as many grains of allowance as you like.

But here we are now in the land of the oranges, coconuts, pineapples, Negro washwomen, Port Captains, and forms, all of which we have been through successfully, so far, except the fruits which, being Sunday we can't get in this Godly place, and we are now fitting up the boat.

We shall leave here tomorrow night or Tuesday morning for Havana and hope for kindlier breezes.

I have heard no news—not even who the Cabinet are—and care about as much as I know. When we got here we find that we are the first in. Indeed we passed everybody that we saw, little and big; but that is no news. I still think the "America," properly fitted, is the safest vessel in which to cross the Atlantic. I forgot to mention, however, that when she was pitching in the sea before she got to Fortress Monroe, she sprung her bow sprit. This was not observed until it was pretty fairly displayed by our pitching in the calms. We have fixed it nicely and it is stronger than before and I suppose we will get on.

After you have read this letter I wish you would send it to French, as he may like to know what has happened, and will care about the boat if he don't care about the freight. It is written for both of you. You care about the freight and not much about the boat.

Give my love to Ames and tell him I think he would have

enjoyed it to have been with us. We had some splendid sailing, some grand moonlight views of a storm at sea, and enough wind at some times to be more than interesting; for in the morning when we tore the fore-sail out of the leech, I think the wind was blowing about sixty miles an hour—some say seventy-five.

I will advise you again at Havana and I hope both the tone and substance of this letter will calm all your fears.

Yours, FATHER

HAVANA, CUBA, *March* 19, 1881

MY DEAR BLANCHE: My last, from Nassau, I suppose reached you in due course of mail, containing the beginning of our voyage.

We left Nassau Tuesday morning and in forty hours were off Moro Castle, having sailed 400 miles. We had fair winds, but most of the time a pretty rough sea. Tell Ames that when I speak of 400 miles I mean in a straight line by the chart, but we sailed nearer 500 miles, taking great care to keep off the shore, and had to breast a three mile current in the Gulf Stream. That the Yacht averaged over ten miles by the log, and that for four hours she averaged thirteen.

Of course we could not come into the harbor until after sunrise, when we came to anchor at the man-of-war anchorage.

Mr. Hastings had a letter of introduction to Mr. Froncke of one of the heaviest sugar houses here, who has shown us great attention. The Consul General has been very kind and attentive also.

I have been around the city which you must remember is 350 years old; but it is nasty to a degree. No drainage or preparation for drainage (by that I mean drainage under ground), for that is impossible, the city having been built on the wrong side of the harbor, on low lands, while on the other side there are nice elevations of ground upon which the city could have been beautifully built, and beautifully drained, and they are occupied by very heavy, expensive and useless fortifications from the Moro Castle up. One monitor with fifteen inch guns would knock Moro Castle down in three days. But there is no need of that as you can land almost anywhere on the back part of the city and occupy the heights around it, and the city is at your mercy. I mention this because perhaps I may want to come here some day. There are 20,000 troops here, mostly volunteers. I believe that with 10,000 of ours we could clean them all out. At least I should have no objection to trying.

The harbor is a very fine one, with a very good narrow entrance and plenty of water, eleven fathoms where we are now lying.

I have looked into the yellow fever question. There is no more reason why there should be yellow fever in Havana than there is for having it in Lowell—perhaps much less. The City does not live half a mile from the sea, and a mile and a half, or two miles at the farthest is the length of the harbor. At the upper end of the harbor cutting a mile and a half through the low land would make a canal from the harbor to the ocean so that water would sweep through twice a day by the tide to say nothing of the wind. The tide rises here only about a foot which need hardly be taken into account as against the wind. But at the upper end of the harbor is where this cut should be made, and the lazy, idle, good-for-nothing soldiers should be made to make it without expense to the Government except for shovels.

A small brook runs into the harbor. On that brook are situated the slaughter-houses for a city, including foreigners in port, of 300,000 inhabitants. All the offal and blood is thrown into that brook and runs into the harbor; and the blood sometimes is seen for half a mile down covering the whole surface of the harbor. Of course that generates the waste from an animal substance, which is the father, mother, and grand-father of the yellow fever. There is none here now; but on the deck of the yacht, although there was a fine wind blowing in the day, I smelt last night very decidedly this slaughter-house smell, being a mile below them. One peculiarity of the wind is that there is none at night, and the harbor is like glass. At that time the whole city is a stench. They call the yellow fever here a visitation of God. It is a visitation of nastiness. Six months of energetic administration here would entirely free Havana from the scourge. I would contract to do it pay contingent upon success; but I should want full military power.

I visited the Captain General yesterday. He is a very good looking man of about fifty, very well preserved, of very considerable intelligence; but as we had to communicate through Mr. Hall, the Consul General, as interpreter, there was not a chance for a great deal of conversation. I invited him to come aboard the yacht and he said he would do so if possible, and he found the harbor very smooth but that his stomach turned, even on going across the harbor on a boat.

Ben, Paul and Hastings went to the French Opera, and express themselves favorably. They have two fine opera houses here, seating, one of them as many and the other not quite as many persons as the Academy of Music of New York. One remarkable thing was that there were not more than fifty women present, and that nobody goes in full dress, and everybody goes behind the scenes who pleases. I did not go, my bump of music not being very largely developed.

Capt. Reid and Major went to see the Passion Play last night, or at least one third of it, as it takes three days to get through it, and they have only seen the first day, and have not come to the resurrection yet.

There is one great peculiarity about the people here. They always take one third less than they ask in trade. Let me give you an instance: My ash-tray went on the floor during the gale and broke. I saw a nice little silver tray that suited me, and I asked the price. $5.00 I was told. I didn't much think of buying it, but wanted to try the people, and I said, I will give you $4.00 and the tray was mine. I saw an ornament for a lady's hair which rather pleased me, and I asked the price. $95.00 was put upon a paper and handed me. This was one of the first jewelry establishments, let me say. Wishing to try them, I wrote on a paper, $75.00. The clerk went and consulted with the head of the store, and came back and shook his head. In the meantime, the rest of the party, who had been lingering behind, came up and I went to go out, but he called me back to take it. I didn't want it much, and being a little deaf I didn't hear him and went away.

Currency is two for one in gold, and American gold is two percent above Spanish gold and greenbacks two percent above American gold in any quantity.

I lunched on shore yesterday and we had a very decent lunch with some Spanish wine. I shall not leave here under three or four days. Tomorrow, being Sunday, I am to ride out some eight or ten miles to visit a sugar plantation which is in full blast. They asked two days in which to get ready to see us. In the afternoon we came back to a horse race at four o'clock. How is that for puritan New Englanders?

Ben, who hears me dictating this letter, suggests that we may end up the evening with a bull fight or a cock fight, for both of which he is very anxious. The latter is my suggestion.

I am yet uncertain whether I shall go to Mexico, Galveston or New Orleans. I am waiting advices by telegraph, of which I am a little chary as it costs fifty cents a word, as I want to save all the money I can for cigars, which are very good here.

On Monday night we propose to light up the yacht and give the people some guns and fireworks. But for that we have to get permission from the law for nobody is allowed to fire a gun in the Port or have a light in the harbor after eight o'clock, which regulation however, we, as an American man-of-war pay no attention to. But it is a very queer regulation that the ships all have to lie without anchor lights.

So no more, *Your loving* FATHER

FERNANDINA, FLA., *March* 30, 1881

MY DEAR BLANCHE: We spent a pleasant week at Havana, doing it pretty thoroughly. Were kindly and courteously received.

Grant failing to go to Mexico and others failing me, I concluded to go to this place. We left Saturday morning, that is, before 1 o'clock, and had a nice day and night, sailing till Sunday morning. It came on to blow in the Gulf Stream which runs north, and we had a head northwest wind which blew a very short rough sea being against the stream, and we had a hard battle for 24 hours, when in tacking to make our course, ran out of the stream. The sea all at once calmed down and at night all was pleasant and the wind lulled and about ten o'clock came to the sou'east fair and we made a delightful run for Jacksonville where we arrived off the bar at sunrise.

The pilot came on board and told us there were only ten and a half feet of water on the bar, too little for us as we draw 12½ feet, so we came on here, getting here about 10 o'clock, a.m.

Here the pilot told us we should wait till ½ past five p.m. for high tide before we could get over the bar. We waited. Started to come in, when up came a most violent thunder squall with very high wind. We were just on the bar as it struck us. Too late to go back so we went under reefed mainsail, foresail, and staysail (jib).

The schooner laid clear over her rail under water, yet we must hold our course as we had to vent up five miles in a nasty crooked river at very short work. Ames will tell you what that means.

Gallantly the little craft behaved, one foresail tore out of the reef; we needed it but we came on in an hour and a half, having sailed twelve miles and tacked more than that number of times.

It is now blowing a very heavy Norther in the harbor. Two vessels have dragged ashore, but our ground tackle is sufficient. We are riding at one anchor. Everybody else has two out.

All well. Ben has laid abed a day (yesterday) with a chill

but got up to see the town. Both boys and Major gave in Sunday when we were thrashing about.

We, that is Hastings and self—his family are at Jacksonville to be reached hence by rail—are exploring St. Johns River, 3 & 400 miles. FATHER

PALATKA, FLA., *April* 1, 1881

MY DEAR BLANCHE: If you will put your eye on the Map of Florida and your finger on the port of Fernandina where I last wrote you, and then go south to Jacksonville where the yacht could not get in for want of water as you will remember about, which place is about thirty-five miles south of where we have left *the* boat, and then follow the St. John's River still south 75 miles, you will see whence this note comes.

It set in for a week's westerly blow, so we took the cars at Fernandina and went to Jacksonville. The road is about 70 miles long and we reached that place yesterday at 3:30 p.m. Stayed at the Windsor, and came here by boat at the rate of 15 miles per hour.

This is another watering place in Florida, and has a very good hotel. Our party is just in a cottage adjoining the hotel. Where we are is in the midst of orange groves, the live oak, magnolia, strawberries and sand. All are well. Ben has a ravenous appetite. Has just finished an enormous supper, his third meal today, and threatens an eleven o'clock supper to-night (I write at 7:30 p.m.) and he seems earnest about it too.

We have chartered a small steamer and our party, Mr. and Miss Yulle, Proctor Knott and wife, and West with a box of rum, plates and blankets start at nine a.m. on a voyage of exploration of the Oklawaha River, about 136 miles still farther south up to Silver Springs. These are gushing outpourings of water from under rocks into a lake some 300 yards in diameter, so clear that a penny can be seen at the bottom—30 ft. We are to go through Cypress Swamps, crooked channels and small lakes and the heart of the orange country. What after, you say. The boys after alligators and other like birds, and I to give countenance to the Expedition.

I have said all I can say of love to you and yours, when I say FATHER

FERNANDINA BAR, *April* 8, 1881

MY DEAR BLANCHE: We are off for Fortress Monroe. Fine breeze. Clear weather. The pilot is just leaving us. I supposed we should not start till 4 o'clock. We must, however, be off at 2 p.m. So the curtness of this note.

All well. Cargo, sundry empty wine bottles, some full ones, sundry empty cigar boxes, *some* full ones, one alligator skin 8 ft. long and sundry skins of birds.

Hastings got a telegram from Fortress Monroe, saying his wife is sick there. He has started to join her there by rail. That the reason; fact is, a little scared by waves and winds. Too much for a landsman.

We have been up the Oklawaha River and the St. Marys, but Ben will tell you about that. You may look for news of us three or four days after you get this. But "white man am uncertain" and so are the winds. We may be off for the North Pole, for aught I know.

Love to you and yours. FATHER

BOSTON, MASS., *June* 28, 1881

Mrs. BLANCHE BUTLER AMES, *208 West 59th St., New York City*

MY DEAR BLANCHE: I have learned from experience that in the march of an Army water transportation is the most economical and quite as swift. The boys are engaged in a Fourth of July regatta which chains them at home on Friday, Saturday, and Sunday and Monday.

Now, if I understand it, you are to be on the Fall River boat at Boston next Saturday morning. I can have the yacht, which will have nothing else to do, at India wharf, which is only a short distance from the Old Colony Depot, a very complete and commodious means of embarkation. I will have the yacht there and Capt. Reid there to take you along, perhaps will go myself and spend a day in making the acquaintance of my grandchildren. It is an inside route with the exception of four or five miles, so that I think, with you, you need have no trouble from sea sickness.

I will direct the Steward to have an extra supply of provisions on board, so that enough provisions can be spared to supply you for a day or two till you get your arrangements made with the "butcher, baker and candlestick maker." I think it will be a health-giving excursion. I know it will please Gen'l Ames, and the children will be better than with a further ride in stuffy cars with at least two changes and waiting, so that you will not get to Bay View until probably about eleven o'clock.

If you like this arrangement write me so that I can know

Friday morning, and make the necessary preparations. I will probably spend part of Sunday, and possibly Monday, with you.

Yours, FATHER

HALIFAX, N.S., *August* 13, 1881

DEAR BLANCHE: We arrived here last evening after a run of forty-eight hours, with a fair wind, with a bright sun, during the days and a bright moon by night. It was a pleasant run. Butler was sea-sick a little but it seemed to inconvenience him but little. He said to me just before a meal, "I hope I will throw up soon so I can have some dinner." He has eaten as usual and is very contented and happy.

It is raining this Saturday forenoon. The awning is up and we have not yet been ashore. Breakfast is just over. Your Father is sitting on the opposite side of the table smoking and watching Paul and Butler scuffling in the corner. I was amused yesterday in witnessing a similar scuffle between your Father and Butler. The former had a cloth skull cap and a short blouse on and of the two seemed the most boyish—a big, fat, jolly boy.

Speaking of going to Maine this fall, I stated that a question with us was—what to do with the children. Paul suggested they go to Lowell and be taken care of by Hattie and Fannie, if the latter was not to go to Minnesota. Your Father said take them to Lowell, that is the place for them. So you see how they meet our difficulty. If you are disposed to go to Maine this invitation may help you along.

I eat a good deal and drink at the regulation times which gives me a full supply of liquids. Our amusement is novel reading and thus far two settings which leave us where we began.

Kiss the children for me and tell Edith and Sarah and Blanche that they must be good little girls. Love from,

ADELBERT

HAWKESBURY, N.S., *August* 16, 1881

DEAR BLANCHE: I have just sent you a telegram and expecting we would stay here some time I put off writing till I went aboard again, but the parties who are going with us to see or sell the oil wells are here and we will go at once as soon as a small job of blacksmithing is done.

To show you where and when we are going I must hastily make a map of eastern Nova Scotia. You see the Gut of Canso connects the Atlantic with Gulf of St. Lawrence and is but about twelve miles long. Cape Breton is the eastern part of N.S. Bras d'Or Lake is a large part of it. The canal has been cut to connect it with the southern part of the island. We go then inside of the islands, I have indicated—a run of not more than twenty-five miles. Thence I am ignorant of our course. The men who join us here to go with us to the mines seem to be of the regular mining shack type.

We have been having good weather and fine sailing. Butler is in good appetite and happy. The weather is very cold and we only get warm after going to bed. That is, the temperature is about 54° & 56°—and a strong wind helps to chill. We do as we always do on the yacht, read, sleep, drink and eat and on still nights, sit about the table.

I write in haste as the iron job is about finished.

I send much love and kisses for the babies and yourself.

ADELBERT

WHYCOCOMAH, C.B., *August* 20, 1881

DEAR BLANCHE: We arrived here yesterday. I telegraphed you last evening. I do not suppose you know our locality so I will try to tell you.

Bras d'Or has a number of arms. St. Petus is at canal. The yacht followed the dotted line. When the yacht was at point A, Paul, Butler and I left in the dingy(?) and rowed to a divide a quarter of a mile wide, had our boat hauled over and were soon on the north arm of the lake.

We camped out on the shore for the night. It was very foggy and wet and as our only covering was a small sail, our feet were out where they got covered with mist. Butler complained of being cold so I put my thick woolen socks on his feet over which I put my shoes and then gave him my coat to put on. I do not think he suffered any from cold but the unusual surroundings prevented his sleeping much. The next morning we were up early, rowed out to a fishing boat and bought some codfish and herrings just taken out of the water, went back to the shore and had breakfast. We rowed along to near this point when we had dinner. About two o'clock the yacht came along.

Today we ride up to the oil regions which are about fourteen miles away. Trout are reported as plentiful and we are going prepared to fish. As I understand we start on our return next Tuesday. I shall be heartily glad to get out of this craft.

Here I was interrupted and called to go ashore—we have

had an early breakfast—I am now at the P.O. and have just time to tell you I love you and to send love to our babies.

ADELBERT

During the summer of 1881 General Ames' family were at Bay View, Massachusetts. Ben Butler, who had been a member of the family, studying law at Columbia College, New York, became ill at Bay View and was unable, greatly to his father's disappointment, to accompany him on the yachting cruise to Newfoundland.

Ben grew rapidly worse after the "America" sailed. Mrs. Ames telegraphed for "immediate return." But the flag on the Bay View flag staff was at half mast as the yacht entered the harbor at Bay View. Bennie died that morning, September 1, 1881. The Bay View house was closed. Ben's funeral was at the Lowell house.

NEW YORK, N.Y., *September* 13, 1881

DEAR BLANCHE: Enclosed is a check for $100.00. If you should need more please send to Wyman for check for the amount needed. Please send me at Northfield Glass' mortgage so I can satisfy it.

The house is in good condition. The carpets are especially bright, but a layer of dust is over everything else. Of course, I shall do nothing with furnace or fireplace till we all get home. Dennis and Kitty came all right. The latter will leave today for Norfolk. Dennis reports the breaking of two large jars of blackberry preserves. The keys to the trunks are with you as you may remember. The table ware of the kitchen does for me today. I do not know whether you want the trunks opened or not.

My business at the office is going on smoothly. Some late communications sent to L. contain an epitome of the present condition of it. I shall leave tonight by the N.Y.C. & Lake Shore and will stop one day in Chicago to see Mr. Hall's son as he will leave there before my return.

Home seemed quiet and attractive and I shall be glad when my travels shall be at an end and we are settled again. With love and more love,

ADELBERT

LOWELL, MASS., *September* 14, 1881

DEAR DEL: I was up quite late last night for after I had finished my long letter to you, I undertook to write to Mr. Blair[1] to give him an account, as he desired, of Ben's illness.

[1] Ben's friend and classmate at West Point.

I was undressed and ready for bed and probably caught a little cold for this morning my eyes were nearly closed, result of tears and late hours.

Butler was very good this morning again about his lesson, and I finished with him in good season. Blanche, Fannie and I went in the carriage to see Mr. Carney and over to Aunt Nina's. Mr. Carney ventured to speak of Ben's estate and proposed that you should be appointed administrator of the boat-house property, the rest of the property takes care of itself under the will (Mother's will I mean).

Fannie and I drove over to the burying grounds and spent some time there arranging flowers. Then we reached home at tea-time, and all passed the evening quietly at home. Your letter came bringing kind words, cheering a little, but not like your presence, nevertheless most welcome. The babies are all in fine condition.

Love, BLANCHE

LOWELL, MASS., *September* 15, 1881

DEAR DEL: Another day has gone, in very much the same routine as yesterday. I made a call upon Florence this morning to ask her intentions in regard to the road on the farther side of the burying ground. She says that she means to give a road, sometime but not now as her Mother is quite superstitious. I spoke of my desire to have the present road put in better order and she called my attention to the future of the land near us. If the bridge is built, the old county road which comes into the road which passes the old homestead near the stone house will be continued straight thro' to the river. Florence spoke of the likelihood of buildings backing upon the burying ground road and seemed to think that we might prefer to give up our private road to form a part of a public road, in which case all the houses would face towards us. I decided that for one I should prefer to keep the road, and let the future take care of itself. That trees and a wall could hide the back of houses if necessary. Altogether, I was rather amused.

Father returned tonight, and is trying to get Paul to go to California. I think he will decide to go.

I shall cut this letter short as I have no news for you and you have been having lengthy epistles.

Love and "good night." Adelbert junior is calling.

BLANCHE

NORTHFIELD, MINN., *September* 17, 1881

DEAR BLANCHE: I arrived last evening having spent Thursday in Chicago. When in that city, I gave my houses in charge of a Mr. Cummings who was highly recommended and who came from Lowell.

I found our folks all well. This is especially the case with Father and Mother.

Our business seems not to have flourished as I had hoped. A statement has not been prepared and I cannot now give you any details, but I feel as poor as ever. At this present time our business is good. The margin on flour is better than for a long time. The expenses here have been much greater than they will be for some time in the future and I hope for good profits and independence.

I have spent the day mostly with Father, Mother and John. When not at home we have been riding to Dundas and about this city getting or trying to get dogs and men to go with us on our trip.

Charley Nichols parents, sister and two brothers are here. They are staying with John. Mattie's baby, now a year and a half old is the joy of its parents, grand parents, uncles and aunts. When you see ten grown and nearly grown persons rejoicing over one little human who can say a few words only but who can walk and laugh, you experience a real pleasure. It is a jolly little child and the chances are, of course, that it will be spoilt. The interest John shows in common with the Nichols in something not particularly interesting to me, attracted my attention. Brotherhood, while holding fast on one hand yields on another to ties and affections which become the absorbing ones of life—very naturally. I am glad to say the whole crowd seemed happy and contented.

Mother sends her love. With kisses. Your husband,

ADELBERT

LOWELL, MASS., *September* 18, 1881

DEAR DEL: I suspect that as usual, I have been making mistakes in regard to the date. At any rate this is Sunday afternoon and I did not write you yesterday. I spent most of the day with Aunt Lottie. I went over to do some sewing on the machine and took dinner with her.

She was quite troubled that she did not have more elaborate entertainment for her unbidden guest. But I did such justice to the viands, that she was satisfied.

Governor Sprague came in the morning about his case and will remain until tomorrow. Thus, you see the house is very full. Every bed is occupied. I cannot say the days are very happy ones, but the time passes quickly as I am occupied. This perhaps is all one ought to expect.

I hope that you are content and do not feel worried or troubled with your affairs. I am sorry to have these lovely fall days pass away without being with you. Still we must not regret everything.

I send you kisses, Dearie, and shall be so glad to be home with you again. Edith, who is with me, sends her love. Your wife,

BLANCHE

NORTHFIELD, MINN., *September* 19, 1881

DEAR BLANCHE: I was glad to receive a couple of letters from you today and learn that you and our babies are well.

Our chief business today has been in getting ready to leave tomorrow on a gunning tour. Results—a large trunk packed with clothing, ammunition and other innumerable traps. Of course, I do not expect much success as the fun of getting ready has consumed the whole amount allotted to one trip.

You may remember I gave my horse, Kentucky, and all of her colts but one to John for—well—for—for—their services to him and their keeping. The one I kept was one John did not want. I saw a fine looking young horse on the street Saturday and was told by John that it was a horse of remarkable promise and that it was one of Kentucky's colts. It was the one he did not want a year ago, and which I took as my share. I claimed her of course but alas! John had no recollection of anything that impaired his exclusive ownership.

Nellie today spoke of the horse. I said "Is it not one of Kentucky's colts?" Answer, "No-o-o." What funny people one's relatives are. But to do John justice I should say he offered to give her to me if I would take her and use her. So from this day out I stop raising horses on somebody else's farm.

Usually, I have lost flesh when west here. Now I swelter in grapes, join my parents in lager beer at meals and am holding my own I hope. Mother's health has not been better for years.

John has a full beard. It improves him. He thinks I could raise a similar one. Were my absence from you to be longer, I might have tried it just to show you what I can do, you know. I should hate to go home and not be recognized so this struggle is put behind me for the present.

Give kisses to our babies for your husband.

ADELBERT

LOWELL, MASS., *September* 20, 1881

DEAR DEL: I did not write you yesterday but finished a long letter to Mr. Blair about Ben. I have delayed writing it because I could not avoid crying while writing, and it has such a disagreeable effect on the eyes. I might just as well have done it at first however, as time did not cure the tendency to tears. Yesterday we went over to the grave yard. Poor Ben! The turf is already taking root on his grave, and we all go on the same as if he were still with us. It is hard to realize that we are to hear his happy laugh and see his sunny handsome face no more.

Dr. Spaulding has been again to see Edith, but says that he can not find anything the matter with her, that she probably needs tonics. Iron and quinine. Always the same. Dr. Cilley is coming to Lowell to see Aunt Lauretta, and I will consult him about Edith. She complains daily about her head, and I can see no good reason for it, therefore, am anxious.

I have just read your letter from Renville and am delighted to see that you are in such good spirits and apparently enjoying yourself. I have come to the conclusion that the scenes and pleasant experiences which linger longest in memory and are the pleasantest to dwell upon, are those which are connected with outdoor sports and excursions. I remember the few we took this summer more clearly than anything else in the way of pleasure.

We shall welcome you home with great delight, and trust that you will not have to leave us again for a long time. The boy is a great nuisance at night. I send you love.

BLANCHE

RENVILLE, MINN., *September* 22, 1881

DEAR BLANCHE: This little prairie village is wrapped in slumber (poetical) at this late hour of half past ten. Leastwise, the only sound of wakefulness in this hotel is an occasional snore—(Irish bull). And it is one of those thin skinned western hotels where everything is heard but one's thoughts.

We were in the fields from early morning till sundown today and killed thirteen prairie chickens and ten ducks. The sport was not of the best and was all concentrated at two points. One where we took the ducks when they flew from one small pond to another; the other when we got in a flock of chickens and brought down eight of them. As two of us sometimes shot at the same bird we had double sport of course. Our lunch of prairie chicken, bread and butter and lager beer was a delectable repast. Three or four miles from the station, the land is unoccupied and we have the wild prairie to the horizon. The weather is delightful and we are having a good time.

Yesterday's paper brought the news of Garfield's death. How sad! It was such a needless death in its origin. Alas! for his poor wife and mother. The light is taken out of their lives. How little joy his great office gave them. Office is a monster and men who can only love it and live for it are not entitled to another love than office gives. How suggestive is the nation's grief for Garfield inasmuch as it displays in the same act scowls and threats for Arthur.

I send you, Dear One, love and a tender good night for our little ones. ADELBERT

LOWELL, MASS., *September* 24, 1881

DEAR DEL: A nice long letter came from you yesterday. I have been trying to picture you to myself out hunting with your Father but with indifferent success.

By this time you must have returned and are no doubt settling business prior to taking your departure. Your experience with your horse is amusing, and our relatives certainly are peculiar. I should not be surprised to hear that you have no interest in the mill, that the yearly proceeds do not more than cover your indebtedness, and that you have fully your share of the profit, if not more than you are fairly entitled to, in the form of commissions. It has gone so far already that your requests, commands, and prayers are not worthy of consideration except when made in person.

It seems to me that in some way you will have to turn over a new leaf or step back as you have in the horse matter, and be content to have a gift offered to you once in a while. Do not think that I speak bitterly, I only tell you my thoughts of what is likely to occur.

Hilda Nesmith had a birthday party yesterday which our children attended. "The boy," Adelbert, covered himself with honors. He had a child's high chair and sat at the tea table with the rest of the little folks. He evidently has an idea of propriety for he usually has no hesitation about putting both hands in the plate. But in this occasion he would not even take a piece of sponge cake in his fingers but pushed Martha's hand toward his plate and gave her to understand that she must feed him with a spoon. So she cut up his cake and fed him, to his satisfaction.

Blanche wants to know when her father is coming home, and

her mother has curiosity on the same subject. We shall be so happy to have you back again. I cannot tell why it is, perhaps I am jealous, but I am better content to have you anywhere rather than in Northfield. I never feel that you are happy there or that things will go to please you. That while you are ready to meet them, all with a full heart, and open hand, you do not receive quite the same in return, and that consequently you are always laboring at a disadvantage. No doubt I am morbid, but I have had the same feeling for the last eight years, and time does not lessen it. I suspect that we are very critical and jealous for those we love, and inclined to resent very quickly any real, or imaginary thing. Love and kisses from your babies and wife. BLANCHE

LOWELL, MASS., *September* 23, 1881

DEAR DEL: I cannot give any of Fannie's plans, for like you, I do not know them. Nellie wrote that you are going to bring John east with you. Fannie will probably return with him. You speak of John's interest with the Nicholses. Of course it must be very great and will grow stronger year by year. I hope you will be able to impress upon them the necessity of keeping you more constantly and accurately informed as to the condition of your affairs. Disappointments month by month are not so hard to bear as a big one at the end of the year.

Adelbert Jr. is in fine condition since we came from Bay View. He is strong and jolly and ready for a frolic anytime. Every morning he comes crawling into my room while I am dressing, like a great buzz fly and climbing up to the dressing table pulls everything onto the floor.

I am feeling very well and except one day after I had walked down town, have not had a back ache since the trip to Boston. I send love. BLANCHE

LOWELL, MASS., *September* 27, 1881

DEAR DEL: I shall soon stop writing you as when this reaches Northfield, it will be about time for you to turn your face homeward. Our household does not seem so large as it has been owing to Father's absence.

He had Gen. Pryor and two stenographic writers here yesterday. Major is sick and the two came to fill his place. The Sprague case occupies attention.

Fannie is going to Boston today to see her Aunt Hattie who is to be at the Revere House. She had a letter yesterday from her father, enclosing a check for a hundred dollars. He said that you insisted that he should come east, and spoke as if he might.

Paul tells me that Carney owes me about two thousand dollars; back rents etc. I am very glad to hear it, for I have been failing to get all I thought I was entitled to. However, Carney has not the money to pay, but Paul said he should speak to Father about it.

I think I shall write to Dennis to begin to put the house in order. He will not have much more than time to go all over the house. The prospect of getting home again is very pleasant. I can but think how little real interest we take in the lives of others. It seems that I take more for my relatives than they do for me.

Possibly I am mistaken. Oh, I forgot to tell you that Father said to me, he should have two photographs of Ben enlarged, and would have Bracket paint one, and if I would paint another, he would give me Brackets and take mine. I shall try to do it—although I do not feel equal to the task. My work always turns out unsatisfactory to myself, perhaps to my friends, but they are too kind to say so.

I send you love and count the days until you return, when you will have to take "the boy" in hand for he has his own way in everything, and needs your fatherly correction.

Good-bye for a day. BLANCHE

NORTHFIELD, MINN., *September* 28, 1881

DEAR BLANCHE: Yesterday morning early Father came to my room at the hotel in Appleton and informed me he was not well enough to take the trip to the lakes as arranged. He said he would wait at the hotel a few days for me to go and have some good sport. Of course I could not leave him so sick to go on a pleasure excursion. In less than an hour we were on the train homeward bound.

I find everything here much as I left it. The accounts then unsettled are yet unsettled. But they all relate to wheat buying along the railroad and the joint account with Archibald. Charley has made his monthly statement—regularly but John would not forward them as they were not satisfactory. I have decided to remain till everything is straightened out. Wheat is going up daily. It is now, very high, almost too high for much profit on flour.

I was rejoiced to find a good lot of letters awaiting me from you. I am especially pleased to know your back ache has taken its departure, for good and all, I hope. As I read your letters I find, at least I think I find, that our own home is preferable to any other. That it is mine you have long known. We and our tribe of Arabs can have and ought to have but one Mecca.

I cannot tell now exactly when I shall be able to get away. As this will not reach you till Oct. 1st. any letter from you would find me gone written after you receive this. I send kisses to our babies and love to you from ADELBERT

NORTHFIELD, MINN., *October 2*, 1881

DEAR BLANCHE: Yesterday morning Father and I had an early breakfast and left for Minneapolis at half past seven. We saw Judge Ames. The Case loan is by no means sure. The security of the mortgage is gone. Foreclosing on the mortgage to secure the interest worked a forfeit of the whole as the purchase was made by a judgement creditor. The Judge says he hoped to find other property by which he can make good your principal. I instructed him to sell your 1st. Nat'l Bank Stock. I did so as the bank, though perfectly safe and good, seems to have a president who is regarded generally as too sharp.

I saw our cousin Jim Wyman. He is prospering well and is growing up with the country in such a manner that he now is rated as one of the coming men.

I think you had better devote any spare funds you may be able to seize upon to the payment of the money borrowed to pay for the N. Y. house. In fact I think we had better pay a little, even, on our debts, if we possibly can. The first of August statement shows us to be about $6,000.00 ahead. The mistake last February was due in part to confusion in the wheat accounts with Archibald. Now I believe everything is right. Sept. 1st. 1880 we were in debt about $40,000.00. So in eleven months we got ahead some $46,000.00. The past two months we have made probably including the rise in wheat ten thousand dollars or more. Thus you see while we have done fairly, I can not think of touching the capital on which we do our business for a long time.

I shall leave soon so as to reach N.Y. City Saturday and Lowell Sunday; and will be ready to return to N.Y. any moment thereafter. In a week I hope to be at home. Love from ADELBERT

General Ames' family are in their house in New York for the winter.

WASHINGTON, D.C., *December 22*, 1881

MY DEAR BLANCHE: I ought to write you by my own hand, but as I have not time I do the next best.

I owe you a thousand apologies for not coming up on Sunday; but I came by boat and did not get in until later, and it would have made me too late for my appointments, of which I had a number. I am going to invite myself to breakfast with you on Saturday morning as early as eight o'clock, because I must be at the Fifth Avenue by half past nine. I have also invited myself to dine with you, and perhaps spend a portion of the day, Christmas day, the last being somewhat dependent upon my business calls which will be numerous in New York. I have also taken the liberty to invite Charlotte to go over with me and spend Saturday and Sunday. She wants to see Paul and the children. She has been hard at work here.

Now, one thing further: I have neither time nor taste to select Christmas presents for the babies, and I enclose herewith twenty dollars to buy them. You know what Santa Claus is going to give them, and Santa Claus may have the credit of what he does give them, but somebody else nearly as old as he, wants the credit of giving them what he does give them, and he wants you to fix it so that his present won't duplicate Santa Claus'. So you must go out and buy what you please for them, and they can have two days of delight as well as one. As I am to be there Saturday morning and, as I am no fabled monster, have my presents ready for distributing on Saturday morning and let them enjoy them on that day, and take a new lease of enjoyment on the next day, Christmas morning, of Santa Claus. If you are going to have a Christmas tree Saturday night, why then you can do it the other way.

Yours, FATHER

Mrs. Ames had made inquiries of her father in regard to building a summer residence on Sandy Hook, N.J. in place of using the house at Bay View which had been the scene of such great grief. Also General Ames could be more with his family if it was nearer New York City, now his place of business.

WASHINGTON, D.C., *March* 18, 1882

MY DEAR BLANCHE: I have yours this morning, and of course you had not mine of yesterday when you wrote it.

The land of Sandy Hook was ceded by the State of New Jersey to the United States for military purposes, so long as occupied for those purposes. There have been many attempts in Congress and elsewhere to get a foothold on Sandy Hook to build a hotel, which have been resisted. The land is in the joint occupancy of the Engineer Department and the Ordnance. It so happens that I am specially strong with both of these Departments; but herein lies the difficulty: By law, no executive officer, not even the President, can lease or convey a piece of Government land. And I suppose while the plain letter of the law would permit me to locate a piece of "Sioux half breed" scrip upon the land, which is locatable upon the surveys and unsurveyed lands of the United States, I suppose the land Department would rule against me if I should attempt that "land-grab." I have seen both the Chief of Ordnance and the Chief of Engineers, and they want to aid me. But all I can get would be a simple license that you might occupy to move off when you are told to. Practically that license would last a series of years, unless the Government has some use for the land.

Now, I sent you the chart so that you might find out where you want to go and tell me about it, so that I may know what to apply for *carte blanche*, but to get Blanche's *carte*.

I should have no hesitation in building a shanty on the land if I could get permission. You will note, however, what I said in my last to you about mosquitoes and trees. I would advise, in selecting a location, to get, not far, but a little out of the way where you won't be likely to have it necessary for you to be disturbed, or a plea of such necessity. I would advise a location where the wind sweeps clear across, and I would not advise asking for too much, because you can occupy all the land around you really.

But, keep in mind what I said about mosquitoes. Above all, take care you do not mention it to anybody that you are going there or are to go there because then there will be other applications and they will have to be rejected and possibly yours revoked, but not much danger of that last. Of course you would have to put up what would be very temporary this year to be finished when you get time. General Renham is the Engineer in charge in New York, and as he is an old crony of mine, I sha'n't have any difficulty with him.

Now, I want to scold a little:—I don't think it creditable in my daughter to write about making roads on a sandy beach by carting on loam. If she had said marl or clay, I would have agreed to it; but beach pebbles will make the best road, clay being wanting, which with the sand would make the best. For walks, I should say a thin, and therefore cheap, concrete, the pebbles being on hand, would be the better.

Now you will understand the situation exactly; and if you will tell me within how many feet or rods of the railroad terminus you want the land, and about how much, I will do the best I can for you, as I have always tried and always mean to try to do; especially because I may want to come there myself if the mosquitoes are controllable. *Your* FATHER

208 West 59th St., NEW YORK, *March* 18, 1882

DEAR FATHER: I hasten to answer your letter. Tom gave me very wrong impressions in regard to Sandy Hook land. It certainly would not be advisable to put a house upon land of which we could not have a definite lease, and it would also be most unpleasant to be the object of, or in the way of, flying projectiles. There would be no incentive for improving or finishing a place which the whim of an officer might compel us to leave with short notice. All things considered I do not think you need to take further trouble in the matter, and I am sorry to have annoyed you with it. The fierce mosquitoes we shall no doubt be obliged to put up with anywhere in this climate, but it is not needful to face cannon balls or run the risk of summary ejectment.

Paul came this morning. Florence and Tom are here. Mr. Dunn took dinner with us last night. He seems a pleasant youth, but if I mistake not, he will have to toe the mark. Hattie seems very undecided when she will be married, or where she will take up her habitation. The thought of leaving the "flesh pots" is not agreeable to her. If Mr. Dunn gives her too much time to consider, he may repent. Paul seemed to expect you would be here today. When you do come, if possible stay with us. I know it is not so convenient for you in some ways, and a little far away for your business callers, but I am selfish in the matter, and urge, in spite of your objections. With love,

Your affectionate daughter BLANCHE

General Ames' family passed the year at the New York home, with an occasional outing to Naversink Highlands. Jessie Ames born November 2nd, 1882.

State House, BOSTON, *June* 29, '83

DEAR BLANCHE: I believe I know when Paul will come home. He sails July 3, Farrington is too unwell to come with him.

Mrs. F. goes out to meet her husband. I suppose you have got the papers I sent you, all about the Harvard bother.[1] It was only a little game of skill between self and brother Hoar. It is all described in the old nursery rhyme,

> "He digged a pit
> He digged it deep,
> He digged it for his brother,
> But he fell in
> And was drowned therein
> And died instead of 'tother."

I hope you liked the speech. It was a poor one, not by any means up to concert pitch, but had a real good speech carefully prepared because I supposed I should have a row and then you know one must be prepared and say on the *spur of the moment* the worst possible things in matter and manner the most cool and faultless. But I was so kindly received by President and Fellows and the Just Graduated Alumni that I had to throw all the preparation away and grope about for the speech I did deliver which was honor bright *extempore.* Alas! there was a good speech, that other one lost to the world. Something too much of this.

Love to all the babies including the General from

FATHER

HIGHLANDS, MONMOUTH CO., NEW JERSEY, *July* 6, 1883

DEAR FATHER: We have passed a very quiet Fourth of July and have entered upon a heated term.

I hear that the "America" has been fitted up, and hope that you enjoyed a cool, pleasant sail on Independence Day. Can you not take a cruise in this direction, and see and be seen by a large portion of your family? I am delighted that Paul is to be home so soon, and shall keep the spy glass pointed to the horizon next Thursday and Friday with the thought that each steamship may contain the wanderer.

You speak lightly of your Harvard speech. All here thought it very fine. You seemed so far above the Harvard crowd, and they powerless to affect you, even to anger. A good speech may have been lost to the world, but a good one was given to it, and that is some consolation.

I should like, if it will not inconvenience you, to have some

[1] General Butler was elected Governor of Massachusetts in 1882. As was customary he, as Governor, was invited to attend the Harvard commencement exercises by President Eliot in spite of bitter opposition by a number of its Board of Overseers.

arrangement made by which my portion of the Coast Survey rents can come direct to me without passing through Mr. Carney's hands. I have been subjected to much annoyance, as I have written Mr. Carney twice for money, and am informed that he will let me know when he has any remittances for me, and when I ask how much is due he writes that it is hard he should be called upon to account for what he does not receive.

So my only alternatives are, to ask you to arrange the matter differently, or beg of a comparative stranger with the above results, or wait my uncertain period and have the money doled out to me with a discount of two per cent for the kindness. About a thousand dollars is now due.

Captain and Mrs. Ames are here for a week or so. He is seventy-five and she is seventy—yet they seem fifteen or twenty years younger.

The country and fresh air are doing the children good. They look much better than when we came down. The older ones join me with love for Grandfather.

With best love and a kiss. *Affectionately*, BLANCHE

208 W. 59th Street, November 20, 1883

DEAR DEL: I had a letter from you yesterday written in Chicago, which was evidence that while you claimed to be well you were not. There was no life or buoyancy in it. I hope you are now rested from the jolting of the cars, and feel better. Everything at the office is reported as all right.

Butler has written Johnnie a letter in regard to a printing press and type, etc. which he wishes to trade his bicycle for. John wished him to go and see a boy and inspect the articles of proposed exchange. This he has done and made his report. When I compare our expenditures for Butler with those made for John, I feel we are very economical or else someone is very lavish—Butler's press did not cost a hundred dollars, and we have not felt that we could afford a bicycle for him. I do not wonder that Fanny thinks me close and stingy. If I keep on in this strain you will think I am sick which is not the case. This week I am quite happy for the headache which troubled me last week has gone, and my spirits have risen a number of degrees.

I am very lazy and am doing nothing in particular. I have engaged a new girl as cook and hope she will prove satisfactory.

The babies send love and kisses as does also BLANCHE

208 W. 59th Street, NEW YORK, *November* 21, 1883

DEAR DEL: This is the last letter I am to write you, according to instructions. So far the only word I have had from you was the Chicago letter. I hope the latter part of your absence will be more productive. If not, I think it will be advisable for you to stay away longer.

Adelbert is at my side very busy writing a letter to you. Yesterday, he went to the dentist with Sarah, Blanche and Martha. While waiting in the parlor a lady came in whose face was very much painted. This attracted the young man's attention—so he went up to her, and with fingers opening and shutting as they do when he wants to touch something, said "What is that you got on your face?"

She smiled and answered "Nothing, little boy, run to your nurse" and put up the paper she was reading to cover her face. Martha told Adelbert he should not ask such questions. Ladies put grease on their faces to keep off the chap. "No! that is no grease, Martha," said the boy.

I have been quite an owl since you have been away. It is frequently eleven or twelve before I go to sleep. The fact that I am the main reliance of the household no doubt has much to do with wakefulness.

I have two new novels, which are fairly interesting and help to pass the time. Then as you know the children do not get off to bed until half past eight or nine. I miss you very much Del, far more than you do me, as I am the one left behind and you are with your people and new scenes. I dreamt last night that you had written me you thought you could not get back before Christmas. Was not that a nightmare? With a kiss,

BLANCHE

NORTHFIELD, MINN., *November* 23, 1883

DEAR BLANCHE: I have not been a very good correspondent this trip. I shall see you in a few days and hope not to have occasion to open a correspondence with you again for a year. The days pass very quickly here and I am about packing again.

I was up to John T.'s last evening. I found the house well lighted. Every room on the first floor fitted as sitting rooms and Johnny's printing room upstairs in full blaze. I have not seen much of Fanny. I do not think her grandmother has either. Naturally, her grandparents show that they expect to be called up to gratify all her wishes in the money line—and they will respond favorably.

Our mill business looks very, or I will say, *more* favorable. The price of wheat has been put down to a shipping price, as it has not been for a number of years. Then again, the Mississippi River is so low that the mills at Minneapolis cannot give full time this winter unless there be rain and it is so late in the season that rain is highly improbable. Thus you see the outlook is pleasing.

You can expect me Thursday morning—till then, love from

ADELBERT

LOWELL, *August* 16, 1884

MY DEAR BLANCHE: To whom should I send an advance sheet of my address if not to you. I hope you will like it. I have done the best I can and all I can. It has cost me weary hours; I used not to be weary but I suppose as the Republican Journals say, I am losing my grip, but I trust you will think the old dog has not lost all his teeth, so he cannot bite at all. At least he can growl.

All well. Paul away canoeing. I send much love to all the brood, the mother has what is left.

FATHER

Sweet's Hotel, GRAND RAPIDS, MICH., *September* 2, 1884

DEAR BLANCHE: We have had rather a tiresome journey thus far: due probably to the fact we are not used to the roar and racket of railroading. When I say we, I mean Butler and I. Your Father flourishes like a green bay tree through it all. This State, apparently, is enthusiastic for him. I believe he counts on this as the certain state to give him some electoral votes. He is very enthusiastically received. Curiosity to see the man has something to do with it. Col. Plympton, late Chairman of the Mass. Central Democratic Committee, is with him, a reporter of Boston Globe and West. I am glad to tell you that I like Plympton and believe him honest and faithful. He is also capable. Your Father will go through Iowa and Kansas after leaving Minnesota, getting East about the middle of the month.

I feel that I am progressing West slowly. We will be in Northfield on Saturday next. Butler's hay fever is about the same. He is having a good time with thought mainly on hunting or gunning. I feel the benefits of this change. I wish you were not so closely tied down.

I send you, love for self and babies.

Your DEL

General Butler was on an electioneering trip through the West. General Ames and Butler went with him as far as Minnesota. Mrs. Ames and children were at The Highlands, New Jersey, where the family had a summer residence.

Sweet's Hotel, GRAND RAPIDS, MICH., *September* 2, 1884

DEAR MOTHER: I am now sitting down at a table in the room seventy-nine in Sweet's Hotel, Grand Rapids, Mich.

Last night at Detroit, I was nearly crushed to death by the crowd who went to hear Grandfather speak. There was over 15,000 people there, Grandfather said, in the beginning, but a great many went away because they could not hear him. We came here last night from Detroit. Grandfather will make a speech here this afternoon and one at Muskegon this evening which is forty miles away.

My cold is about the same as when I left you and my home. I saw Niagara Falls and thought them very wonderful. Grandfather feels very well and so does Father and myself.

Your loving son, BUTLER AMES

Palmer House, CHICAGO, *September* 4, 1884

DEAR BLANCHE: We came here last evening after an all day ride through clouds of smoke and dust. Muskegon where we spent the night before last is on the Michigan side of Lake Michigan, a little north of Milwaukee. We traveled by day, like the sun, to be seen. Your Father's meeting last evening was crowded and he feels sanguine—not of being President but of laying a good foundation for a future party, if not for a few electoral votes at this time. Vermont gave him no votes and I reason thereon that the People's Party will need some nursing yet.

Butler's hay fever is troubling him considerably. He has been a very good boy. Last evening while his grandfather was talking we went to Barnum's circus. It is a great show as Mr. B. says. We will reach Minneapolis tomorrow morning. Will stop one hour in Milwaukee for a speech.

Love to you and the children. *Your* DEL

HIGHLANDS, NEW JERSEY, *September* 6, 1884

DEAR DEL: This is Tuesday evening and I am in Edith's room, in undress trying unsuccessfully to keep cool. The warm weather still continues, and everything looks parched except in the shade. This is Florence De Barry's birthday and all but Jessie attended a little party this afternoon. Adelbert seemed to think himself quite a man and behaved like one.

Jessie celebrated in her own account by stepping into the cess-pool by the piazza. It was full and she was wet to the waist. Towards night, she fell down the piazza steps and bit her tongue. She made a pretty picture at the kitchen door with a biscuit in her hands, off of which five chickens as close as they could stand were feeding. Dennis and a bundle of laths have converted the cow-yard into a chicken yard. I hope you will approve, but I know you decided against it, as being too large for so few chickens. While you are away, Sweetheart, I am taking my own way, but in spite of that I am not having a very happy time for it is lonely, and everything loses its charm unless some one I love enjoys it with me.

I send a kiss to Butler and many thanks for his letters, which shows that he remembers those that he has left behind. Kindest regards to your Father, Mother, and best wishes to Fanny. For you, Dearie, a kiss. BLANCHE

HIGHLANDS, MONMOUTH CO., NEW JERSEY, *September* 7, 1884

DEAR DEL: For a whole week, that is over since you left us, we have been having the most trying weather of the season. Day after day the sky has been cloudless and the land breeze (when there was any) intensely hot. The mosquitoes have taken possession. Poor Jessie's little legs are speckled all over. Edith, Jumbo[1] and I went in bathing before breakfast this morning, and as we passed through the grass the mosquitoes rose before us in little clouds, and alighted as the sand flies used to over the bathing dresses and on Jumbo's head.

Mattie was sent away yesterday. Mr. Barrett is trying to get a girl for me in New York. If he is not successful, I may have to go up myself. There are plenty of girls but they prefer the city in the winter.

I forgot to tell you in my last letter that Mr. Clancey called Sunday and took lunch with us. He was very sorry not to find you. I amused him as well as I could. We took a walk to the lighthouse and the keeper showed us the light. It was very wonderful,—much larger and different from any other light I have seen.

I miss you and Butler very much. The girls think I ought to play games with them every evening because I am so lonely. Adelbert is my bedfellow, and Jessie crawls in every morning

[1] Adelbert Ames Jr. sometimes called Jimmy or Jummy.

early. Yet with all this company I am not content, and shall be glad when your visit is a thing of the past. Good night, a kiss for you and Butler. BLANCHE

Office of Jesse Ames' Sons, Merchant Millers
NORTHFIELD, MINN., *October* 9, 1885

DEAR BLANCHE: I arrived on time yesterday afternoon. I was not expected so soon. As I came over the bridge, I saw John and Jack standing in the middle of the square watching a boy riding a mustang pony. The sight was a most natural one especially so far as it pertained to John and Jack. I was a little surprised to find Father in his buggy also a witness. Everyone here seems in excellent health. John has a mustache and side whiskers. It improves his looks. Fanny is here with her baby. I believe they do not claim that the baby is very pretty. Alice is looking better than I ever saw her. It is due to the fact she is fairly fleshy. She walks about but not as far as the village. Nerves—is her bane.

Father is at the door of the office calling me to get in and ride with him. I shall do so as he is persistent, and what I am saying here seems of so little account. Before closing I will say one thing of much account and that is—I love you.

DEL

NORTHFIELD, MINN., *October* 11, 1885

DEAR BLANCHE: Here Sunday morning we had the usual baked beans for breakfast. John came down and I went up to his house and stayed till late this afternoon. Mr. Archibald and Mr. Loyhed called and later Fanny. Mattie is still in Minneapolis. She has a "young English lady" as governess for her children,—one to teach them and "make them mind" as I am seriously informed. This English lady is well versed in German and Johnny, who is studying German in College, takes lessons of her. I have not seen Lizzie yet. Uncle David went up north to see his children before I arrived. I believe Fanny will go to Minneapolis on a visit this week. Our folks here have good times moving about and visiting each other as you can well imagine.

This is a land of plenty. I never saw such profusion. John has thirty cows and sends his milk to St. Paul. His yards are full of pigs (over a hundred) hens, ducks and turkeys. Calves and horses also abound. His barns are full to overflowing with hay and vegetables. He is thrashing out bushels of clover seed worth six dollars a bushel. Father has a wind-mill with tanks in and outside of the barn from which iron pipes conduct the water to all parts of his square. Mother struggles in her need to sell eggs, butter and grapes. This season she has sold (when Father was gunning) some fifty dollars worth of the last. The other day, when the girl was cleaning the rooms, Mother undertook to do the churning. The cream was too cold and Mother, Father and I labored for a half an hour or more unsuccessfully. Then John took me off and Father and Mother had another half hour's work before they got their eight pounds of butter.

Father and Mother send their love to you, all.

I send love and kisses to you and the children. DEL

HIGHLANDS, NEW JERSEY, *October* 13, 1885

DEAR DEL: Your letter on your arrival at Northfield came yesterday. It did not seem as if you were in a happy state of mind, rather inclined to be cynical. I conclude that you were suffering from your long journey and irregular meals.

We are having the heaviest storm I have known here. The wind blew so during the night, that our bed quivered as it does when anyone is walking across the floor. Martha complained of her bed and could not sleep. She got up and lighted a lamp. The children do not go to school this morning. The wind drives the heavy rain so fiercely that they would get very wet.

We shall have but few winter apples. They are all on the ground and being bruised will not keep. I shall have Henry make inquiries about the cider mill and see if we cannot get a barrel of cider which will also give us some vinegar. Some of them can be made into apple butter. We do not keep up our youthful vigor in the matter of letter writing, Del. How do you account for it? In my own case, I know that it is not because I care less but it may be that I feel my affection is so strong that I have grown careless and think that all I might say would be known without the saying. I love you.

BLANCHE

HIGHLANDS, MONMOUTH CO., NEW JERSEY, *October* 15, 1885

DEAR DEL: Your second letter from Northfield made me feel tired. Everyone seems so care free, and bent upon getting enjoyment out of life. How can Mattie stand the expense of a governess? How can Fanny leave her husband and visit about? But there is no use in asking "how." It is evident that we do not take the world easily, or else our relations are very fortunate.

I am glad that you are finding your visit home pleasant, and hope you will have good luck on your shooting trip. Nellie and Alice would not care to be at the Highlands this winter and I am sure I should not care to have them here. Quite the contrary.

I keep very busy, and so kill time. Henry is picking up apples, and if there are enough to make it pay, I shall send them to Middleton and get cider. A gallon and a half is given for a bushel of apples. The toll for grinding comes out of the bushel.

Sarah has written you a letter today. With love and kisses for our absent one.

BLANCHE

HIGHLANDS, *October* 17, 1885

DEAR DEL: I am glad to find you a better correspondent than you have sometimes been. I enjoy your long letters very much. Your remarks about the "lady" governess amuse me, and at the same time my envy and wonder are excited. I fail to understand how such a luxury can be afforded by a Clerk of the firm while the Principal feels and is too poor to indulge in a similar one. No doubt the anomaly is capable of an explanation, but in no event can it be a satisfactory one. But enough of this, let me write about my own affairs.

Henry started this morning with our horse and a wagon borrowed from Weaver, and a heavy load. So heavy that I was rather reluctant to have the horse burdened with it. Mr. Barrett who came down last night seemed to think there would be no trouble and after many injunctions to walk all the way, and to leave part of the load if it proved too much, I let him go. The cider mill is at Middletown. The load consisted of a large brandy barrel and twenty odd bushels of apples. These will give us thirty gallons of cider.

The children have just returned from the woods bringing nine quarts of chestnuts. They are going again this afternoon.

Mr. Barrett[1] says that flour is selling well, the market being much improved. Mr. Colman paid the seventy-five dollars last week, but has not done so this week. Mr. B. will go and see him about it, and also about the roof which he says leaks.

This is my little budget for today and I close with love from self, and children, for our absent one.

BLANCHE

[1] Mr. Barrett, Clerk in commission business of General Ames in New York.

Financial Troubles

Owing to losses due to wheat speculation and the financial management at the Northfield Mills, Western creditors decided to liquidate the property.

John T. Ames was appointed receiver and represented the creditors. Suit was brought against Adelbert Ames and Benj. F. Butler in order to obtain possession of the realty owned by them individually and not assets of the Company. This litigation continued for some years, and was decided in favor of the defendants, Ames and Butler.

The commission business of General Ames, for sale of flour in New York, ended when suit was brought. The 59th Street house was leased, and the family moved to Lowell for the summer and fall.

PUEBLO, COLO., *April* 23, 1886

MY DEAR SON: I received your letter yesterday from Northfield. I felt very bad at the way that you look at it, that is my letter. I did not think I was writing so hard, you did not take it as I meant. I would not stir such views for anything. I was in hopes you could manage to keep the mill for the business. It is dreadful to me to have our little family have such feelings toward each other. I think if you will call to mind our past lives, you must see things in a different light, than when you wrote me. Your Father has been a good father and husband. Done all for his family he was able. We know when things went against him he is apt to get nervous and borrow trouble.

How dreadful this is. You must try to forgive the wrong in your Mother's letter and have sympathy with your family. My little family are very dear to me. Can't there be a reconciliation?

We shall leave here next Wednesday for home. You must write us. I hope this will not sever the ties of our family. I think we can be very happy with very little money if they take the right view of life.

Your Father joins me with much love to Blanche and the children. I hope we shall see each other soon.

From your affectionate Mother, MOTHER AMES

1886

DEAR PARENTS: I cannot tell you how I grieve that your days should be clouded as they are now. The past cannot be recalled and it is our duty to face the future and try to get some sunlight out of it.

The whole trouble has its foundation in money, or the want of it, and I wish to talk with you about it. I am clear in my own mind that litigation will end only in deeper financial ruin. It is proverbial that the law, the courts and lawyers consume the whole substance of the litigants. You know the case against the Grange mill where everything was within sixteen miles of the courthouse dragged along some three years or more. What may you not expect in this case, where Gen'l. Butler will fight not only for his money, but his good name, so needlessly and wickedly assailed.

The duration of the litigation will be, I have no doubt nearer ten years than five. As the persons interested live in different states, the case will be transferred to the United States Courts, and will be appealed if need be, till it is before the Supreme Court. That court is four years behind in its work, and as it will take a year to get the case there, five years will be the shortest possible time to a decision.

Now for the sake of argument, I will assume what I do not believe, that the case is decided against Gen. Butler. The liabilities of Jesse Ames Sons are about $130,000. The assets will not reach over $70,000 as no good will goes with anything. That will leave $60,000 to be paid out of the realty. To it must be added the expense of five years litigation. The interest on $60,000 for five years at 8 percent is $24,000, making a total of $84,000. The cost of litigation for that time will be probably $16,000, making a grand total of $100,000. The mill, at the end of five years, tied up as it must be, will not bring that sum. Certain dower rights will make the property wholly unmarketable and may give five or ten years more litigation. If the courts should finally sustain the view that the real estate is partnership assets, the dower interests in it will render it unmarketable.

I believe Gen. Butler will win, as he should. You know, Father, that the money you received for half of the mill came from Lowell. You know that you received $25,000 direct from him—that check, endorsed by you is in his hands. John knew it. So I say if ever a claim was a just one this is.

You must not forget that the law delays are endless. No end of money will be spent on one side at least to get justice and the result will be that John and I will be old men when this business shall be at an end. We may not want money then.—We will not have it then.—We could not hold it if we had.

If John has made the allegations reported in the papers, I do not want to be compelled to answer them. It can at best be but a mutual besmirching of each other, and whatever we say will have no effect on the point at issue, which is the suit against Gen'l. Butler. The checks, etc, will be absolute proof for Gen'l. Butler and acquit him of the charge of attempted fraud. This acquittal must be the condemnation of those who made the charges against him. I am greatly surprised that the lawyers should be able to get John to second their efforts to slander, when no good could come of it. I have in John's handwriting, documents which show he never believed that our mill realty was vested in a partnership—but just the reverse. The lawyers have put him in a false position in this. I can show he knew of my indebtedness to Gen. Butler and that he suppressed the knowledge (probably) when he borrowed the money. Thus you see my answer must show him guilty of obtaining money under false pretenses. Then again, one of John's letters would convict him of giving excessive valuation to our property for the purpose of deceiving the men of whom he wanted to borrow.

He never had exclusive right to handle our money. I had as much right as he—or you when you were in the mill. Did you give John the exclusive right? Did either of you have an exclusive *legal* right to handle the money? My answer will be direct and cover every point made, in a way which, with documents on hand will wholly satisfy my friends.

But as I have said, I am sorry to be compelled to meet John in such a fight, for my success will be his overthrow.

I send you an accurate account which shows my indebtedness to be $25,500. My book accounts show some $2,000 to collect, giving a remainder of $23,000. John knew this. Why should he say I owed on flour $30,000. I consider it the wisest course for John to shake off the lawyers who have misled him and save himself from condemnation by the courts, and the exposure of my answers.

You must understand that the only legal question at issue is the suit against Gen'l. Butler attachment. To prove him, John and me to be angels or devils can have no effect on the case. So I beseech you to aid me in stopping this kind of work. Let John retract his allegations and swear to only what is necessary in a formal suit. Unless he does, the mill and all its belongings are irrevocably lost to us—and not all your wealth can make up the deficiency.

Marshall, my salesman, disappeared last Tuesday. I have no doubt he has stolen thousands. Blanche joins me in love.

Your affectionate son ADELBERT

Jesse Ames' Sons, Merchant Millers
NORTHFIELD, MINN., *July* 9, 1886

Gen. ADELBERT AMES.

DEAR BROTHER: Our troubles have assumed a new shape since Blanche sued for her note. I think the result will be to throw the firm into Bankruptcy, and with the law suits, waste, and delay, to scatter the whole as well as to disgrace all of us connected with it. As I have written you before, in consequence of the suit of Gen. Butler, the creditors demanded Bankruptcy or a receiver. I thought a receiver best. Our affairs are now in such shape that I can pay fifty or sixty percent this month.

I wish this could be fixed up some way, and for one will give all I have to bring it about. Save—disgrace, and leave me in shape to try again.

If you will settle with the creditors I will give you my part of the mills. Eighty acres of my farm worth $5,000, my part of the outside property we own together. This is all I have except the balance of the farm. I shall secure Father what I owe him on 80 acres, and the 80 acres where the house is I keep for the present as a homestead, as I cannot turn my sick wife and daughter into the street. My bank stock and cash have gone into the mill pool. Beside the above I have $150.00 cash, 24 cows, four horses and some farm tools. The most of that will go with bankruptcy.

This affair I fear will kill Mother. She mourns about it all the time. Father takes it more stoically, but is anxious to have it settled. He says if you will cause it to be settled and will come here and live, he will give you the corner house, worth $4,000 and if you do not want to come here and live, he will give you that much in cash.

I think the creditors will make a discount of 10 or 15 percent to get their money, or even more. (I do not make this statement with authority). Enclosed with this find the statement for May. It will not differ much from that now, except the depreciation of wheat and flour. One was sent you before. It will be much better for you and for all concerned if this can be brought about.

Trusting you will look this over carefully, I am

Your brother, JOHN T. AMES

NORTHFIELD, MINN., *August* 8, 1886

ADELBERT AMES.

MY DEAR SON: Your poor heart broken Mother wishes me to write you. What shall I say? Your conduct has been so mysterious for two or three years that I cannot account for it any other way than you are insane, as Mother soon will be, if she lives a little longer. Oh, what a good Mother you had. Always ready to wait on you and all the rest of us by night or day and never complained. It is enough to break the heart of any one but a fiend, to see her moan and weep her sleepless nights and distressed days away on your account.

As to business, I shall not say much now. What your intention is now, I do not know, but it seems to be to ruin John T. Ames and John Handy, but I may be mistaken in this. There is one fact in this case when it is investigated and that is Gen. Butler cannot get one thing out of these Northfield mills until the debts are paid. If Gen. Butler had taken a mortgage on the mills as he should have done if he intended to hold the mills for his pay, you could not borrow money, if Gen. Butler had held the mortgage. If you and John had left the money in the mill that I lent you and gave you and not drawn any out, you would all have saved about one hundred thousand dollars, that you have paid for interest and had plenty of money to run the mill and paid Gen. Butler long ago and be a hundred times better off than you are now.

I think I never gave you advice but what was correct or very near so, although you seldom followed it. Once more, I will give you my advice. You can take it for what it is worth. I advise you either to give up the mill to the creditors, or take it with the assets and try to pay the debts. I think there's one thing you may be pretty sure of, that is, if this suit goes into court, you will be shown up in a light that you have but little idea of. It will be a bad legacy to leave for such a family as you have and your friends.

On the receipt of this, please write me and I will inform you on anything that I can find out to your advantage.

Your Affectionate Father, JESSE AMES

Testimony in Trial of Case, John T. Ames & John Handy versus Adelbert Ames & Benj. F. Butler

(April, 1887) Not in chronological order

Q. What was the principal subject of discussion between you to which your attention was called by Mr. Upham and John T. Ames?

Answer by GENERAL AMES. The principal discussion was the deficiency in my accounts. That is, my indebtedness to the mill. At that time I held that my indebtedness to the mill was not more than some $20,000. At that time I was not aware of the thefts of my salesman, and the purport or the purpose evidently of the visitation of Mr. John T. Ames and Mr. Upham was first to get me to pay up my deficiency.

We discussed that substantially for two days. I agreed at first to make good so much of that deficiency as I could, not with my own funds, for I had none, but I agreed that my wife who had a note for $5000 money lent the firm mill, and on which the interest probably amounted to another $1000—and an equity on a block of tenement houses in Chicago, which would probably amount to another $5000, should be given to the mill in part liquidation of my indebtedness.

As I say, I agreed at first that this should be done; but it became apparent in that interview, or those interviews, that that was only a part of the purposes of their expedition; they not only wanted me to do that, but they also wanted me in case the business continued, to furnish more means for carrying on the business; either for Mr. John T. Ames to do it,—that is, to carry on the business, or to carry it on myself.

As I say, I was under the impression at first that their only purpose was to collect that deficiency, but I gradually and slowly and painfully awoke to the fact that they had a farther object in view, which was, after the collection of all they could get out of me, to return to Minnesota, and unless the condition of the business affairs should be improved, to put the mill into liquidation.

The question of my indebtedness to the mill was not one where it was considered that any one would suffer loss by such indebtedness. It was agreed in that interview that the realty was worth $100,000, of which I was the sole and exclusive owner of three-quarters, and that my three-quarters of the mill at that price would not only cover my indebtedness to the mill but also my indebtedness to General Butler.

I was advised by them, not at first, but as developments went on, and it also became apparent to me that their purpose was to put us in the melting pot, as Mr. Upham said in that courteous and gentlemanly way of his; and there was no possible escape from that action unless business should improve.

I told them of my indebtedness to General Butler, it was known in the family, and was a matter of constant talk, and was as familiar as any part of my business, or our business, and I invited Mr. Upham and Mr. John T. Ames to go with me to Lowell to see Gen. Butler and have a consultation with him, inasmuch as I had decided eventually that I could not comply with their wishes, and inasmuch as the melting pot process was to be entered upon. Mr. Upham said that he couldn't go, and Mr. John T. Ames declined to go. Mr. Upham said it would be necessary for him to be in St. Paul early Monday morning, and it was agreed; I agreed with him that I would see General Butler, and if he would pay my indebtedness on the mill, or a considerable part of it, and furnish some $20,000 or $30,000 in addition to run the mill,—provided he did that that the creditors here would forbear for a time. If he was to do that I was to telegraph to Mr. Upham early Monday morning "Yes" if in the affirmative, and if not, in the negative.

I left New York Saturday night and reached Lowell Sunday morning. Sunday afternoon about 4 o'clock I left with Gen. Butler after a consultation with him upon this subject with regard to the matter, and he expressed regret that Mr. Upham and Mr. John T. Ames had not come on and consulted with him.

I told him that unless as a business speculation he saw his way to furnish the money, in all that would be some $40,000 or $50,000 and go on with the business, that the whole affair would be in the melting pot, explaining to him in that interview the interview I had had with Mr. Upham and John T. Ames.

He decided that he had no means on hand conveniently to do that, and that if he did have he did not think it would be a desirable business undertaking. And in his characteristic way he suggested that the melting pot business should go on, or begin.

Monday morning in New York I telegraphed Mr. Upham, I think it was either to Mr. Upham or to the First National Bank of St. Paul, Minnesota, the single word "non." Coming on from Fall River that night of Sunday, in continuation of the interview I had had with him on Sunday at Lowell, Massachusetts; I notified the General, or it was agreed that the melting should be done, and that the end of our business career had come, and the creditors should do their best to protect themselves; and that he would probably take immediate steps, inasmuch as his claim was entirely ignored, and the hasty telegram that I sent indicated immediate action on their part and required an immediate action on his part.

I never for a moment thought, nor could I think that there would be any difficulty in raising the other $9,000 or $10,000, to save the credit of the mill, and continue the business. Even my own father would not hesitate to endorse my paper to secure it to them. In fact at that time I regarded myself as well to do, and had considerable property and some capital. And because of my happy state of mind, and a certain amount of certainty of my financial welfare, it took me, as I said, two or three days to fully realize that these gentlemen had come on to get out of me all they could in hard cash, and then pounce down upon the business and take it out of my hands, and own it forever. I say the proceeding was one that I appreciated but slowly, and from being disposed and willing to give this property of my wife's, I came to the conclusion that the whole thing had better be allowed to go on.

General Ames' family were in Lowell preparing for living at the Highlands, New Jersey, as a permanent home. He is on his way to Wisconsin to look up data for General Butler on his St. Croix lands.

CHICAGO, *September 22*, 1886

DEAR BLANCHE: After leaving you Monday, I went to the depot and there struggled for an hour to get a through ticket to St. Croix Falls but it is such an out-of-the-way place that I had to be content with a ticket to this city. This morning I was up early and on the streets.

I get but little satisfaction out of Cummings. He thinks it difficult to sell the houses at any price and gives no assurance that the loan can be adapted so as to let us sell one or more of the houses separately. The loan will run out next July and then we will be more at liberty to act than now. I have seen Baldwin. He thinks he can sell the houses at our figures, $10,000.00. I have given him permission to do so. He feels very sanguine of success. He has been up in Polk Co. three times and knows all about our land. He has no exalted opinion of their value.

I shall start today in an hour for the Northwest.

With love and kisses for you and the children from your husband, ADELBERT

ST. CROIX FALLS, WIS., *September* 23, 1886

DEAR BLANCHE: I am here at last. It was only by persistent struggling with the railroad people I forced my way. The whole trouble was due to the fact that this is not a railroad town.

I have just had a long talk with Col. Baker. He received me in a very friendly way and apparently was glad, he said he was, that some one had come to look into affairs here, action which he had advised (so he said) on two different occasions. He holds that hardwood so remote from a market cannot be handled successfully at present prices. It is my business to settle that question. He springs a novel point. It is, that hard wood lumber from this northern belt of Wisconsin is not so good as that from southern Michigan, Ohio and the other states of that latitude. And he claims it is proven by the fact (if it is a fact) that hardwood manufacturers of St. Paul, Minneapolis and even Stillwater get their hardwoods from the states above named.

Tayler's Falls (village) is strung along the river's brink for a mile or more on the west side and St. Croix Falls (village) about the same distance on this the east bank and together they present a sorry appearance. Great Expectations have been their bane. Instead of being flourishing manufacturing places they seem dead and alive in spots, the dead spots being the most numerous. There is no water power here utilized. The only dam ever built here has long since passed away and only slight traces of its foundation remain. Millions of feet of pine logs are lodged on the banks for a distance of miles and a spring freshet is awaited to get them to market. It is expected that one or two railroads will be built to this place soon, one going east and one north, but I am sorry to say neither will go very near our lands. At least such is the word I have got today.

I send love to you and our children.

Your husband, ADELBERT

LOWELL, *September* 26, 1886

DEAR DEL: I am not at church this morning with the children as you thought it best for me to be, but very well employed just at present, I am sure. Little Blanche is better. She is out walking with the others this morning. It is as warm as summer, and as the doctor thought she looked delicate he advised she should have all the outdoor air she could get.

I asked Father about the necessity of selling the Highland house. He did not seem to think it would be needful. Yesterday morning I told him at breakfast that I hoped he would make a satisfactory bargain with Mr. Staples. He said I don't know when I shall see him again. Then he looked up with a laugh and added, "Oh! I know why you are so disinterested. You want to get Ames back." I didn't catch on at first. "I should be glad to have him back, but that has nothing to do with my kind wishes in your behalf." So it would seem that he has not come to any conclusion with Staples. He wishes you to tell him the nature of the land, whether it is uneven, swampy, cut up with streams, or ditches. In fact what he desires to get at is, what will be the difficulties to be overcome in building a road to be run with a traction engine. I should judge he still has an idea of making you a lumberman.

I wrote a letter to Fanny which reminded me that you did not say you were going to let your Father and Mother know you were going to be in St. Paul. I hope you did send word to them, and that they came to see you.

We miss you, Sweetheart, and if you should become a lumberman, I am a lumberwoman. There is one thing you must remember in season and out and that is don't worry. Do what is before you day by day with no thought of tomorrow.

Blanche

St. Croix Falls, Wis., *September* 26, 1886

Dear Blanche: Today I went to Maj. Baker's to dinner and afterwards we rode out four miles south and one and a half miles east of the St. Croix Falls. By the road the land is about six miles from town. This 40 acres is worthless. It is nearly all trap rock. There is a gorge through the ledge by which the railroad must reach this point. There may be ten acres of level cultivatable land at the bottom with the trap bluff of, say, one hundred feet high on one side, and a less precipitous ledge on the other. The state valuation of this land is I believe $26.00 on which 7 per cent int. is paid. The tax is, I am informed, about $1.50. Through this trap rock are seams of quartz bearing silver and copper. Last spring certain persons sunk a shaft on one of these veins about half a mile from this land. They have been bonding all the land they can in that vicinity for mining purposes. From what I can learn the specimens of ore found are very rich but there is no certainty about the veins and such as found being of but slight dimensions. The railroad say they will build to this place next summer. It may be well to hold the land another year to see the results as they may effect this land. Then if deemed best, we can sell the good acres and drop the ledges.

I have decided not to write formally to your Father as it is impossible at this time to make any conclusions. I can set down the information I get in the way of a memorandum and submit it to him through you. I think it better to carry him along as I advance instead of keeping silent to the last moment and then coming forward with my demonstration. By giving him what I get when I get it, he will have the early opportunity of submitting his ideas and suggestions to me.

All or such parts of my letters to you as you may think instructive I expect you to read to your Father. The preceding part of this referring to my land inspection today necessarily is for his ear. In fact I know our children, if not your Father, will be glad to read my letters, unless perchance they be too long and prosy for such young folk, for you, well, I will have no mercy.

Love and kisses for all. ADELBERT

ST. CROIX FALLS, WIS., *September 27*, 1886

DEAR BLANCHE: I did not start out today as I expected because Maj. Baker's business makes it inconvenient for him to go. I have been somewhat diligent in blocking out the work before me and in seeking information.

I was glad to learn that you and the babies were well and happy. I hope Butler will soon get up in his Latin and look upon it as a pleasant task, to some extent, at least. It is cause of rejoicing that no malaria shows itself in the ills of Blanche and Jessie.

There is one thing in your letter of the 24th inst. I do not quite understand. I do not know that it is of sufficient importance to speak of but I give way to my curiosity. You say "Jessie slept on one side of me last night. Adelbert on the other and Blanche, who was very restless with her throat on the other."

Of course, I know there are lots of sides, right and left may be two but in this particular case which was the third side?

Love and kisses to you all. ADELBERT

LOWELL, *October* 3, 1886

DEAR DEL: We went this afternoon to see the Mikado. By we I mean Butler, Edith, Sarah, Blanche and myself. The performance was not very good, but the children enjoyed it.

Father said this morning that he should buy a covered wagon, so that the children might have something in which to go to school in stormy weather. I think West has put him up to this. I shall interfere as I think the coupe is quite sufficient.

In your last letter you are inclined to question the number of sides which I should lay claim to. In fact, I am many sided and shall insist upon, a right side, a left side, an inside, an outside, a back side, a front side, a wrong side, and a right side. The truth is Blanche was in the cot, on one side, Adelbert *in the bed* on one side and Jessie on the other. Now if I say something about *this side* I believe I have covered them all.

I have borrowed from Joe Meigs a translation of Caesar which will lighten my labors in Latin very much. I shall not give it to Butler, but by reading the lesson I shall know when he has translated correctly. Blanche has been reading to me, so as to keep up with her class. I am trying not to neglect any of my duties. Love and kisses, Del, from all the babies and your wife.
BLANCHE

LOWELL, *October* 5, 1886

DEAR DEL: How is it with you, Dearie? Are you living on nothing and worrying your soul out? I am afraid you are. I wish I could see you, and know just what you are doing. Have you provided yourself with sufficient warm clothing? It seems to me it is about time you were drawing on Father for money to defray expenses.

By the way, he had a chat this morning with Mr. Bennet, a great builder of this city, who told him that he could get lumber board by rail from Chicago at about eight dollars a thousand or seventy-six dollars a car, and that ordinary oak lumber here was worth fifty-five dollars a thousand which would leave a margin of forty-seven for cutting, sawing, getting to Chicago and profit. Father has just given this to me and I pass it on to you. He said to me the other day "the General does not seem hopeful over his enterprise." I answered, "He is not in the frame of mind to be hopeful over anything just now, and moreover, Mr. Barret's exaggerations would tend to make him put everything on a dead level." Keep up your spirits, Sweetheart, we shall pull through all right. Good night, Del.
BLANCHE

St. Croix Falls, Wis., *October* 13, 1886

Dear Blanche: I have reported and reported on the lands till I have reported myself out of any possible employment, that is, I have legislated myself out of office. Then, again, I have reported on this water power when no report was asked and apparently when a report from me was not wished. Though I make no money here I hope my reports will keep your Father from losing any.

I am now waiting instructions. The first echo I get from Lowell is not exactly what I expected. You write your Father said I, evidently, was not very enthusiastic. It was my intention to obliterate myself wholely from the reports and I thought I had done so up to the time you refer to, at least. I did intend to transmit only what I saw and heard, not what I thought. I did not think it a time or a place for enthusiasm. At first I had temporary gushes of it but the despair of this community (the true reason for which I have never been able to learn) made me cautious about expressing it. However, I did not come to enthuse but to gather facts. I now have convictions which I shall hold till some one can knock the reasons therefor from under them. If your Father has any doubt on any point, any question to settle if he will let me know I will address myself to it and report in full.

You ask about my drawing money from your Father. The fact is the bills in New York and the Highlands left me with less than a hundred dollars. So I used one hundred belonging to him. The other day I drew one hundred of the money you deposited in the Appleton Bank to my credit. So far as I know, my work here is substantially done. If so, I will not need the whole of the two hundred received. What difference there may be I pay back.

By the way, your Father wishes me to pursue Baker. This is a side issue of no moment. While we cannot afford to pay him a salary and do not want him he has been lied about most outrageously. His character and acts are false issues interjected into this business by that Mr. Barrett who in my opinion is more than what Paul called him.

Love and kisses for you and the children. Adelbert

Lowell, *October* 18, 1886

Dear Del: I have written you a letter which I have a great mind not to send, and it contains the expression of hopes which I fear will not be realized, but if it goes with this you will not be laboring under false impressions long.

Father did not write you today as he thought he should, but told me this evening he would do so tomorrow, and that he thought you had better hold on, and see what came of the Staples combination. He had no objection to "Baker's doing the work if he wished to" but he did not propose to pay him any more salary. This means of course that Baker is to be relieved. I should judge if the lands are not sold, and nothing is done about the lumber, he will not have any agent there permanently.

He also said "I shall ask Ames if he would like to run the affair, in case Staples buys." To this I said, "I do not think it would be advisable for him to do so, unless you have such a large financial interest in it as to make it necessary. It is something of a wilderness to bring up a family, and the only schooling they could have would be by means of a governess or tutor." "Why it is a larger place than Northfield." "I think you are mistaken. Do you know the number of inhabitants?" "No! I do not, but the moment Staples begins there will be an influx of a hundred or so." "Yes the numbers will increase but not the quality." "Well, if the Meigs railroad goes on, I shall want Ames here, and I don't see anything to prevent it now, but then if it does succeed, we shall never any of us, lack for money." "Do you expect to invest largely in the Staples Lumbering Co.?" "He will expect me to take an interest in it, and it will be better to sell the land at five dollars an acre and invest a fifth of the proceeds in the enterprise, than to sell at four, or not to sell at all." "Oh! by the way, I had a letter from Benton, and he writes that I did well to agree to a division of the money received from sale of assets at Northfield inasmuch as the $50,000 was in the Minneapolis Bank our worst enemy to remain there without interest until the trial of the case in December."

He went on to say that Paul had made $13,000 net in the Cartridge Mill in the last six months, and another six months at that rate would about reimburse them for the thirty thousand dollars they had expended. I give you the conversations about as they were as nearly as I can. In this way you can judge better of the feelings and impulses which dictate decisions and actions. You will hear from Father directly, in a day or so. I think he was glad to hear about the Falls property, and agrees with everthing you have written. When I read him about the property having been "hawked all over the country" he said "that is so."

The other day when we were talking of Northfield, he said,

"If this case were all settled up and I had the mill fully in my possession I would not advise Ames to go there and try to run it. There is no chance for revival there at present."

I had hoped, Sweetheart, that we were to see you in a week or two, but now it looks like Christmas, and it is a great disappointment. Still there may yet be some other decision, and I will not grumble too much. With love and kisses,

BLANCHE

CHICAGO, *October* 25, 1886

DEAR BLANCHE: The "Situation" just at this time, is slightly ridiculous. You will surely agree with me when I state the case and you will smile.

You say you fear I cannot get "home" for some time because your Father thinks I had better "hold on" out here till the Rice option shall end next February. But my Beloved, I cannot "hold on" out here. There is nothing to "hold on" to as I have said in a former letter. The Rice option ends Feb. 2, 1887—100 days from today. In the meantime Staples says we must be silent—silent. So there is absolutely nothing I can do. Board here is $3.00 a day, board at Stillwater is $2.00 a day, board at St. Croix Falls is $1.50 a day. Suppose we take the Stillwater hotel figures $2.00 pr. day—100 days—— $200. When the 2nd of Feb. arrives it will be mid-winter in Wisconsin. Absolutely nothing can be done there. The dam cannot be touched till the water subsides after log driving season, say in July 1887. The canal cannot be begun till the frost is out of the ground, say late in April. In the meantime I am "holding on." It can't be done. Suppose I did the impossible and "held on" till then? The object being to spend your Father's money in the Staples Enterprise. No, sir: that I would not consent to do unless I had the most explicit understanding with your Father.

And here comes a comical phase of this whole business. I have reported and reported, sent protest after protest, given in detail my convictions and facts on which they are based and no response comes which indicates that my labors have had the slightest weight. The same plans seem to be in mind. Well, as I have said I cannot stultify myself by "holding on" and spending, wasting money without arguing in person against it. The "holding on" programme means, if it means anything, waiting till the river opens, the log drives end, the waters subside, the frost out of the earth before any blow can be struck.

After that the work will continue till the next winter a year hence.

You see clearly six months must pass before I can do a stroke of work. Board at $2 pr. day (I will not now consider the cheap boarding-house) say, six (6) months will amount to most $365¼. Even if your Father thought it cheaper to board me in Wisconsin than in Lowell he might, well, in fact this thought has not entered his head. He, in his pressure of business, has not thought of my work at all and he finds it's easier to say "hold on" than to tackle the subject, or even to write a letter. Life is too short for us to live apart. A necessity may separate us for a brief period but we are not so poor or dependent as to carry out this "holding on" programme. The ridiculousness of this whole business is that it can draw forth such a letter as this. I am not met by any counter facts, or arguments, only "hold on."

I shall go "home" in a few days and if need be show the necessity of either selling or giving this business, or rather Wisconsin property, away.

We can do better when we "hold on" together. Don't you think so? Even at the Highlands. Love and kisses.

ADELBERT

NORTHFIELD, MINN., *January 2*, 1887

DEAR BLANCHE: I received a box from Lowell on Christmas day, and many thanks to you. I wish each and all many happy new years. I enclose twenty dollars for presents for the children. We are having very cold weather. The thermometer has been below zero most of the time for a month. We are as well as usual except bad colds.

Your father joins me with love to all. We will always be glad to hear from you. *From your Mother*, MARTHA AMES

Room 605, 62 Nassan St., NEW YORK, N.Y., *February 2*, 1887

DEAR BLANCHE: I enclose a letter which I wish you would forward to Lockwood. I also enclose a letter for Butler. I think it would be well after he has read it to talk with him. Of course, you had better read it over before giving it to him. He must not fall behind his class. And I do not think it would be wise for you to push him along by teaching him as you have formerly. It may be well to give the children a room up stairs where they can have quiet and get away from the bustle and confusion of the parlor, in fact the whole lower part of the house. Sarah does not study. Perhaps it would be well to have hours when they must be at their lessons and also certain hours when they should be kept away from toboggan slides, ice ponds etc.

You will say I am giving you a heavy, unthankful task. Yet, I suppose it is not more than parents ought to assume. I surely will not shirk in this matter. I know I am over indulgent but this is very serious business.

I send you kisses for yourself and the children.

ADELBERT

LOWELL, MASS., *February 2*, 1887

DEAR DEL: All the children but Butler are safely in bed, and all the lessons studied and recited. Butler is sitting by me in our room talking over his studies. It seems Mr. Coburn thinks it is doubtful if Butler will be able to take four studies, but is willing he should try. Butler scoffs at the idea that he cannot, yet I think he will find it rather hard to buckle down to continued study.

This has been a lonesome day without you, Sweetheart. You left us with so little time in which to think that you were going that I hardly realized last night we were not to see you again for a week or ten days.

I was busy all the morning, reading over our old letters, and have found some which may be of use to you. I have marked with a pencil the part which relates to the mill affairs, so that you can tell at a glance what to read. I will send a package by mail in the morning. Do not neglect to read them all.

I enclose in this letter, one from O. D. Barrett to Col. Benton I think. Does Mr. Barrett mean to say that there can be no subsequent suits against you as one of the partners on account of the mill debts? I came across this letter today while putting some papers away, and have been puzzling my brains over it. I shall be sincerely thankful when this law business is over. This suit has been a kind of bugbear lest out of it should grow some annoyance for you.

I send you love.

BLANCHE

WASHINGTON, D.C., *February 3*, 1887

DEAR BLANCHE: I arrived here last evening. I sent you a telegram to forward to me by express my account books. They, here, do not know exactly what Benton wants and so we agreed I should be ready for everything.

I think your Father will sell the houses to the Govt. The

item has been agreed to in the Senate. His argument is this:— The Govt. is paying for one house $6,000.00 pr. year which is 3 pr. ct. (the Govt's rate of borrowing money) on $200,000.00. Now, he lets all go for $75,000.00 more or $275,000.00 total. So if the Gov't. buys it will get rental on all by paying interest on the $75,000.00 extra. As the buildings are necessary to the Gov't. there seems no answer to his argument. He told me this morning that the middle house cost $37,000.00 exclusive of land.

I think you ought to have $100,000.00 for your houses under the circumstances.

Charlotte sends love. She says Hattie is in the country, will not be here this winter, that she, Dunn and the children are well. I perpetrated my sixteen year old joke of threatening Charlotte with getting her removed.

I send love. Del

Lowell, Mass., *February* 4, 1887

Dear Del: This morning about six o'clock the telephone rang, and Martha answered. The call was for you, and when it was learned that you were absent, it was requested that word should be sent to Capt. Meigs that a disastrous fire had taken place at the Meigs Elevated Road and the car had been destroyed. I enclose a newspaper slip giving an account of the fire.

Sarah rode out today for the first time. She is improving steadily though slowly, and in a couple of weeks will I hope be able to return to school. In the meantime we will pay a little attention to studies at home. Butler read your letters, and is, I judge, from his course of action, fully determined to do better.

I intend to take advantage of Paul's painting lessons and follow him along, painting the studies he has. I shall thus learn something of the technique at least, altho' of what benefit it be I am sure I cannot tell you.

I have had no return from the registered letter I sent your Mother some little time ago. I ought to have the return notice by this time. Do see your Father and brother this time, Del. Put yourself, if possible, in their places and think how much we would wish our children to pass over and forgive. Indeed your Mother has done nothing for which she should be made to suffer and to know you are so near and do not go to see her, will I am sure cause her pain.

Your Father has not done anything very bad, and his manner of writing is I am sure caused more by the Ames uncompromising manner of statement than from the least unfatherly feeling toward you.

This is good advise and if followed will lead to the increased happiness and content of three people.

The children send love and the older ones think that I must be, as I am, lonely without you. BLANCHE

MINNEAPOLIS, MINN., *February* 5, 1887

DEAR BLANCHE: I arrived here this morning, days too soon to be of use. I shall possibly get away the last of next week.

Father has sent for me and I shall go to Northfield and pass Sunday.

I had a few hours in Chicago and saw Brown & McKeever and also Hamilton the real estate agent who inspected the Cottage Grove Avenue property for your Father. Brown & McKeeber will not in my judgement do better than $45,000.00. Hamilton told me that in his opinion the rents would continue to hold as good as now. I feel it my duty to recommend the exchange. I know the facts as your Father cannot know them as he has not the time to learn them. An equally good chance is not likely to occur again very soon. He now has to pay out some $3,500,00. I think he can certainly count on rentals to same amount $3,500.00 making a difference yearly of some $7,000.00. A few years of this arrangement will put him far ahead of any position he could possibly hold with those lands on his hands. Please read this to your Father and I am done on the Wisconsin land business.

As to the question of dower, that question is the very gist of the controversy. The other side claim I never held an interest separately but as a partner. In this State there is no dower. The wife inherits on death of her husband one third etc. if she has not signed right away. I say for want of something better that a wife here has no right, but comes in at last as an heir.

Give love to our children and keep much for yourself.

DEL

NORTHFIELD, MINN., *February* 9, 1887

DEAR BLANCHE: I replied to your letter a few days ago but think it best to write you again on this important subject. Adelbert came to see us for which we were very glad. I feel better since seeing him, and now my great wish is that this dreadful business be settled up.

Neither Adelbert or John understand each other. They are

both my darling children and it seems to me I cannot stand this awful suit dragging through years. There is a talk of a settlement which Adelbert will tell you about. It seems to me it would be better for all concerned. If it goes on there will be nothing left but misery.

Now Blanche, I ask you to do all you can to bring this about. I think you never will be sorry. It will make Adelbert a free man. I think the world and all this business will look differently to him, and it surely will lift a cloud from my old age.

I hope this will find you and the children well. Mr. Ames joins me with love and good wishes to you all.

Yours affectionately, MOTHER AMES

LOWELL, MASS., *February* 19, 1887

DEAR DEL: I did not write you last night as my head ached and I felt out of sorts generally. In the afternoon I went to see Miss Webster, Butler's teacher, to thank her for the kindness and attention shown him, and also to tell her my reasons for having him continue Greek.

She was very pleasant, and felt pleased I think at my call. Speaking of Butler she said it seemed to her that he felt badly over his report for the six months, and that she had observed a desire on his part to do better since the new half year.

She had thought that perhaps it would be well for him to give up Caesar, going on with the Latin lessons and reader in the first year class. But she found he understood his Caesar well if she pinned him down to the translation word by word, while he was inclined otherwise to give a very free rendering.

From the whole conversation I judged that he would keep along with all of the studies. I told her my idea was that "Butler would never be a close student, but that he had a great deal of general information." Her reply was "that observation had led her to believe that boys who were more generally well informed never became close students."

I give you this for what it is worth. There is one thing quite certain. The tiger cannot change the spots on her cub, even if she claws him all over, and I do not think we can make any great change in our young cub.

This is a most beautiful day, and all the children are out except Sarah who is very reluctant about it. Perhaps she does not feel strong enough to play much and of course tires of standing, I shall insist upon her going for a while at least. We all miss you and hope you will not have to stay as long as you thought. Love from BLANCHE

LOWELL, MASS., *April* 4, 1887

DEAR DEL: This is a most beautiful spring morning, and if you had been here we should have started today for the Highlands in gay spirits, with this breath of spring giving the feeling of youth to our thoughts and muscles. I feel that I have grown old, very rapidly in the last three or four months. My face shows it too, and I doubt if it is a temporary spell of ill looks.

Yesterday, I called for Florence and we rode over to Aunt Nina's. Tom came in to say a word while I was waiting for F. He is not looking well, but spoke of taking a little stroll in the fresh air. Florence advised he should go to bed, and take a nap.

If I had been in her place, we, that is you and I, would have taken a stroll together, and somebody would have gone to Aunt Nina's alone.

While I was out this morning, Florence came up to see if Blanche could go to Boston with Hilda, who was going to try on a coat and would have to come back on the train alone if Blanche did not go, as F. was to stay in Boston for the theatre. As I was absent Martha got Blanche ready, and then Florence drove all over town to find me, finally meeting me on Merrimac Street. I did not say "No" although I did not more than half like the project. Florence was to see the children on the train in Boston, I suppose it cannot fail to be all right.

We miss you, and count the days as very long while you are away. BLANCHE

LOWELL, MASS., *April* 5, 1887

DEAR DEL: Here is another day, which finds me in the midst of house cleaning. The carpet is up in our room, and all the furniture moved out, except bed, bureau, and desk. I am writing at the latter, while Mrs. Connors is on the top of the step ladder washing the walls. No wonder then that I can think of little else.

Blanche came home last night in great spirits. She had a beautiful time. Florence put the children in Mrs. Pillsbury's care coming home, so they had no difficulty in getting off at the right station. Adelbert and Jessie are quite anxious to know when they are going to take a trip to Boston. I do not give them any encouragement.

Yesterday afternoon for want of something better to do, I called for Aunt Lottie and took her for a drive. She had but little new to say. Fisher is to leave school at the end of the term, and go into a law office. He will be twenty-one this fall. She is a little dissatisfied and would like to do something different. Life is too monotonous. Alas! we are never content.

Butler and Edith have so much spare time this vacation, they don't know exactly what to do with themselves. Sarah, and Bessie Farrington have, you know, been working for a prize which they induced Paul to offer. The effort was to see which could get the largest number of words out of a-d-v-e-r-t-i-s-e-m-e-n-t. Sarah was the champion. She had one hundred and fifty to Bessie's one hundred and twenty. Paul brought a five pound box of candy home today. Sarah tried to tempt me with some but I am too wary and dread headaches and dizzy spells too much to be enticed. She took part of the prize over to Bessie.

Poor little Jessie fell into the pond yesterday and was wet up to her waist. Arthur Pollard did better than that, and went in all over. Such is the record of the simple events, which have taken place in the last twenty-four hours. You know now what we have all been doing. I wish I knew what you are thinking and seeing. I picture you to myself as being at Northfield and hope it is not so unpleasant for you, going back and forth to Minneapolis as you feared it would be. You have nothing to reproach yourself with in the matter and are simply doing your duty.

I love you, and would be glad if you could be spared all annoyances but this cannot be. If we could share them together it would be some comfort but this may not be at present. Give my love to your Father and Mother if it will not be disagreeable to them. Of course I am in disgrace with them as my name was Butler. With kisses, BLANCHE

ST. PAUL, MINN., *April* 7, 1887

DEAR BLANCHE: I did not write you yesterday as I was busy every hour. Breakfast at seven—took the cars at eight at Northfield—listened to Father most of the day—cars again at half past four and bed at ten, an unusual hour for Father and Mother. It is now just before ten when the hearing meets —I having just at this moment arrived.

Yesterday Father testified and in a manner perfectly satisfactory to us. His direct examination showed wholely for the partnership idea but on cross examination he swore that the realty of the mill was held as private, personal, individual property (not his exact words) "just as any other private property." This last line is his exact utterance. Of course, he said on cross examination that we partners could give and take mortgages just as on private property. Also, that "I told Adelbert he should have given that mortgage to Genl. Butler," etc. The other side showed some concern as well they might. They made a feeble attempt to shake his testimony by asking if he knew what a legal partnership was and if the general creditors should not be paid etc. But nothing was made out of him. Col. Benton has just come in and in our conversation said, "By George, I would not be surprised if we win the case." We have the bank president in on the stand and he is showing how he came to loan the money.

Yesterday Col. Benton told me it was likely that the creditors would make an offer of compromise—on some such basis as this—they to receive $10,000.00 from Father and $15,000.00 from me, making $25,000.00 in all. This to be in full for all claims and the mill and the debtors all released and discharged. By such an arrangement the mill will come back to us and your Father's claim perfected by a mortgage etc. Understand this offer has not been made but it has been suggested it *may* be. I think yesterday's testimony will incline them to some kind of compromise.

I expect to leave for Chicago Saturday or Sunday. Love,

ADELBERT

ST. PAUL, MINN., *April* 8, 1887

DEAR BLANCHE: Your loving letters have been received. I appreciate them. I have had time only to send you the scratchiest kind of scrawls. All the same I love you. How much out of place the above sentence is—as the beginning of a letter.

Today all the Northfield testimony is completed. I may take the stand tomorrow and hope to conclude. If I do I will go to Chicago at once. We have no new points in the case nor have I heard much of a compromise since, except this—that the other side may accede to your Father's offer.

Much love to you and the children, ADELBERT

LOWELL, MASS., *April* 10, 1887

DEAR DEL: This is Easter and the most beautiful day of the season. Paul and Butler went up the river canoeing this afternoon. The trip was up the Merrimac through the canal into Stony Brook. Butler and Nichols were in the same canoe, and as they were going under a bridge a cross current struck them just the other side of it, swept the canoe from under them and as they did not balance quickly enough, over they went up stream.

Butler struck out for shore, which was only a few feet distant, and caught a branch, which broke, letting him fall in again. Then he grasped a small tree, drew himself up, and looked about to see what had become of Nichols and the boat.

Paul says the expression of his face was very comical. Nichols was standing further down stream, holding onto the boat, and calling to the fellows coming up to catch the coats, hats, cushions, etc. which were floating down stream. Strange to say, they did not find the water cold, altho' it must have been melted ice and snow. The day was very warm and of course they were sweating from the exertion of paddling under a hot sun.

I called for Florence, and took her over to Aunt Nina's. The family were all there, but had no new thing to talk about. Ned Tucke is longing for a six months vacation in which he shall have nothing to do.

Tomorrow I shall be expecting a telegram announcing the time of your return. We send you love, BLANCHE

BOSTON, MASS., *August* 15, 1887

Mrs. BLANCHE BUTLER AMES
The Highlands, Monmouth Co. N.J.

MY DEAR BLANCHE: I am glad to hear that you are all well at home and I wish I could have come there. I got all ready to go a while since when I was in New York, but was summoned to Boston by telegram. To tell you the truth when you were here and the children, sometimes they were a little annoyance by the noise made by their playful laughter, never otherwise; but I did not know how much comfort they were to me until they were gone. The house appeared very lonely when I came home and that has been growing ever since because Paul has been away a good deal, and now he is away for a fortnight and I am all alone.

I have been yachting very considerably, and I have been racing; that is, I have been sailing along when others race. I have not been allowed to go into the races because I belong to the Boston and not to the Eastern or New York Clubs. There has been some of the most outrageous performances on the part of the time keepers of the Yacht Club, but still this fact exists that the "America" has outsailed every keel schooner of both Clubs on the three occasions, from Newport to Vineyear Haven, from Vineyard Haven to Marblehead, and on the race at Marblehead where everything was exactly fair so far as wind and waves were concerned, without any time allowance. We have outsailed every centre board schooner yacht save the "Sachem" and the "Iroquois," which are mere racing machines, without allowance except in the case of the "Palmer." The "America" does better than she ever did before. Her loss of a race in the Eastern Club early in the season was because of a local squall which changed the wind and left us to the leeward, which was not the fault of the boat.

I approve very much of sending Butler to Exeter. When he goes I will give him a note to my friend and relative, Professor Cilley of Exeter, whose sister lives with me and Charlotte at Washington, who is warmly attached to me, and ask him to keep his eye on Butler and see that he has a fair chance.

Give my regards to the General, and best love to all the children, and keep the love which I have for yourself which is not a gift. *Your father*, BENJ. F. BUTLER

BOSTON, *January 25*, 1888

MY DEAR BLANCHE: I have from Paul your note to me of the 11th, and one to me of the 21st delivered last night. I then learned for the first time that the Jan'y rent had not been received. I sent it as soon as I got it. He says it crossed yours on the road.

I am utterly at a loss to know what you refer to as the Riverside House. You do not mean the Chicago property? If so I would not sell it to you unless I meant to ruin you.

I believed that my sale to Government would be closed as soon as Congress quit, as it would have been if the Sec'y of Treasury had not forgot as he allowed me to send in the appraisement, which Congress directed him to do. We made and returned the appraisment $2600 more than I asked, to wit $275,000. The Committee want the property very much.

I leave for Washington tonight, and as soon as I can arrange matters I will pay what I owe you. If pushed I will send you something that you may get along for a few days.

FATHER

No. 6 Ashburton Place, BOSTON, *January* 29, 1888

Mrs. BLANCHE BUTLER AMES,
The Winona, 8th Ave., New York City.

MY DEAR BLANCHE: I enclose for your and General Ames's inspection, examination, consideration and answer to me, a report of Colonel Benton and a proposition which is made. I do not know that it is hardly of any use for me to say a word about it, for I do not understand it, and you will understand it and get exactly what it means.

I wish you and the General would reduce the whole matter to exact figures. Perhaps you might want also to see at what price your father and brother would buy out your three-quarters of the whole thing, giving a mortgage on the whole of it at a fair rate of interest, say six percent, and if the security is good, of course the longer to run the better. If it is necessary I will try in the course of a week to get on and stay a night with you and confer with you upon this question.

Yours, Father, otherwise called, BENJ. F. BUTLER

WASHINGTON, D.C., *January* 29, 1888

MY DEAR BLANCHE: I want to see you and the General very much, together with Mr. Barrett at my office, say at ten and a half Wednesday. Shall not detain you long. I want the General to look up and bring with him every paper that has any relation to, or will throw any light upon the giving of a deed of the Minnesota property to Paul followed by a deed from Paul to you. I never heard anything about these deeds till recently I learned of their existence from the record of the case. These deeds may have a very important bearing in the case. The case has gone over till June when we hope to have it heard by Judge Miller.

I shall have some papers with me for you to execute about the Highland house.

Ever and Truly Yours, BENJ. F. BUTLER

No. 6 Ashburton Place, BOSTON, *February* 4, 1888

Mrs. BLANCHE BUTLER AMES,
The Winona, 8th Ave., New York City.

MY DEAR BLANCHE: I have your note. I shall wait before I do anything or say anything to Benton until I hear from you except to write him as you will see by the enclosed.

Yours, FATHER

Enclosure.

February 4, 1888

Col. R. C. BENTON, *Minneapolis, Minn.*

MY DEAR MR. BENTON: I have read the proposition you sent me, but I confess I do not see or understand exactly what it means. The proposition is substantially that Mrs. Ames or I shall pay fifteen thousand dollars to the creditors and then that she should release her dividend as creditor, on five thousand dollars and the interest, and then I am to have for my mortgage of $42,000.00 a joint tenancy of three-quarters interest in a mill in Minnesota, my other joint tenant being hostile to me, having started out in this controversy with accusing me, and publishing the accusation, of some fraud upon them and the people in Minnesota perfectly conscious that I never intended any fraud upon anybody.

I could not go into business in carrying on a mill or advising anybody else to do so with Mr. John T. Ames, so that what I should get would be substantially useless to me, and would only make me a payer of taxes in Minnesota and an insurer of property that I do not want.

For Captain Jesse Ames I have nothing but the kindest of feelings and the highest respect, but I see nothing that is to come to General Adelbert Ames or myself from this negotiation which would result in an association, if anything, with his brother in a business which the past has shown they are utterly unable to carry on in company in the best state of feelings.

Now, let whoever is at the bottom of this, and it seems to me as if the Captain and John were probably starting the negotiation, make a proposition to me of just how much they will give me for a full release and assignment of my claim and settlement of the suit and assignment of my judgment.

If they want time on it after paying me fifteen thousand dollars, they may have the rest on a mortgage on the mill property for a term of five years at six percent interest. I would consider such a proposition, and its acceptance would depend upon the amount offered. I do not mean to have Blanche robbed in order to get payment of a mortgage debt, although I may lose a good deal more.

I am, *Very truly yours*, BENJ. F. BUTLER

No. 6 Ashburton Place, BOSTON, *May* 21, 1889

Mrs. BLANCHE BUTLER AMES, *The Highlands, N.J.*

MY DEAR BLANCHE: I think you have the best portrait of anybody that I know of me in my later years. There is some talk of having a portrait painted of me, and I don't know but it is best to have yours enlarged if you will loan it to me.

This portrait that is wanted is for the State House at Concord, New Hampshire, and I would a little rather take one younger looking because I am losing by age some of those beauties which made my daughter the belle of Washington. You see I have a little pride left in that direction, and I know you will do what you can to gratify it.

Yours, BENJ. F. BUTLER

No. 6 Ashburton Place, BOSTON, *June* 4, 1889

Mrs. BLANCHE BUTLER AMES, *Highlands, Monmouth Co. N.J.*

MY DEAR BLANCHE: I have got the portrait, and given it to Mr. Cobb, the painter of the Club portrait. He wants it to get expression and not color. I am a little too old just now to have a portrait painted, and I thought a younger expression would be got from this than anything he could get now.

I think I will satisfy you on the Porter controversy as well as everybody else, and do a little of God's eternal justice.

We are all well here, and I hope you are at your home.

I write you simply confidentially this: Would you and General Ames like to go to any Consulate in Europe where the fees would be $2500.00 to $3000.00 a year, a pleasant place where you can educate the girls in the languages? If so, see the places any one of which would be acceptable to you, and I will try and see if I can get it done. I think the Republican party owes something to General Ames, which, if presented to Harrison, will get a place. I have examined all the places in the line of his old profession which the General would have, and I find them all shut off by carefully drawn laws that they can be only made from promotion, so that I can see no hope in that direction. I will try and send you in a few days a State Department Register. *Yours*, BENJ. F. BUTLER

NORTHFIELD, MINN., *July* 18, 1889

ADELBERT AMES.

MY DEAR SON: Yours of the 8th is at hand. What little money we send you is freely given and we wish it could be more, it may sometime. What I have earned your mother saved it at a penny at a time. Your mother has been a faithful slave, always ready and willing through cold or heat, wet or dry, night or day, to wait upon her family always cheerfully, never complaining. Your mother and I have but few more short steps to the foot of the hill. In that short space I am determined that she shall not be left destitute to be left to the tender mercies of children, grandchildren or great grandchildren or any other children, if I can help it. I know how my poor mother failed after David Cane went away. Thousands of other mothers face the same or worse.

You can come from Boston to St. Paul and back for $40. As to land it is hard to sell land. I have sold one hundred acres for nine dollars an acre. I have sold some before. I don't get more than enough down to pay the taxes, we get it on interest. I think I have a power of attorney from you to sell.

As to mills on the Cannon River, all but the Dundas mill (and they have rich owners) have failed from once to three times or been failed at the time for the last thirteen years.

They used to tax our mills here from seventy-five to one hundred dollars, this year they have put them down to sixteen thousand. They formerly taxed us more than two hundred pr. ct. on our property, more than any other people in town. I don't know what Gen. Butler will do. If I owned the whole property I should not attempt to run the new mill. I should lay out a few hundred dollars on the old mill and have it properly managed. It will considerable more than maintain one family. This is the forth or fifth year the chinch bugs have taken the wheat. If we had wheat here there is little or nothing to make on the Cannon River, Minneapolis keeps the wheat so high.

Your property here I shall look after as well as I can and you shall have it sometime. Use the little money we sent as you think best, and when you need more let us know and you shall have a part of what we have. I don't know what you are doing. If you can leave home I should like to have you come out here about the middle of August. We can have some fine hunting. Chickens are very plenty and health is as good as usual. Please write us often. Love to all. There are many mistakes, but I can't write over again. Mother send much love. *Your affectionate father*, JESSE AMES

NORTHFIELD, MINN., *September 24*, 1889

DEAR BLANCHE: The days pass peaceably and quietly. All the relatives drop in from time to time except John and Nellie who are in Minneapolis. Father never did wholely approve of Nellie but less so now than ever since she refused to take Fanny in and forces her upon Mother who is really too old to trot up and down stairs to care for Fanny and the innumerable things incident to Fanny's many friends, servants, etc. and newcomer. They, Mother and Father, fondly love Fanny and will find, as they expect, full compensation for all their trouble in Fanny's presence.

When I say "relatives drop in" I refer to Uncle Dave's and Frank's families. They are the only ones here now. I showed Frank my pencil sharpener. He was evidently surprised to see the work done with such neatness and dispatch. He said it was the best thing of the kind he ever saw. I believe he meant it. I told him that I might write him if the thing had anything in it, or enough for a reliable assistant.

Last evening we were talking of the children and their music. I expressed my surprise at their musical capacity, a thing I may have done before. Both Father and Mother pitched into me. Mother said, "Both your Father and I can sing and my mother" (my grandmother) "used to sing in the church choir." Whereupon Father and Mother struck up "Lillie Dale" and gave five stanzas much to the satisfaction of us all.

Mother turned to me and said, "Do you remember how I often kept you at home in the evenings when you were a boy? You would want to go out to the stores or lime kilns with the other boys. I did not want you to. At last you would say, "If you will sing to me I will stay." And I would sing to you the whole evening."

If you will read between the lines you will see that I was a very weak boy even in those days. Love and kisses for yourself and all. ADELBERT

BOSTON, MASS., *September* 30, 1889

General A. AMES, *Highlands, Monmouth Co., N.J.*

MY DEAR AMES: I have a deed in due form of the Minnesota property, which Mr. Benton has returned to me after having it recorded.

I understand you have just been out there, and you may know what is the condition of things. Please inform me, and also am I to have any part of the rent of the mill, and if so, what part, and when, and to whom am I to look for it. Please give me any other information which you think I ought to have. *Yours truly*, BENJ. F. BUTLER

BOSTON, MASS., *October* 11, 1889

Captain JESSE AMES, *Northfield, Minn.*

MY DEAR CAPTAIN AMES: I suppose I am now and have been for some months the owner of three-quarters of the mills at Northfield.

They are, I understand, rented, but of course the lease, being rented under the Receiver, must end sooner or later. Please tell me who I shall look to for the rent of my three-quarters of them. I don't know who else to apply to, except to send to my lawyer about it, and I don't want to do that between yourself and myself, for you can tell me exactly about it. Will you also tell me how much anybody will give for my two-thirds of the mill?

Trusting that your health is good, I am,

Very truly yours, BENJ. F. BUTLER

NORTHFIELD, MINN., *October* 22, 1889

ADELBERT AMES.

MY DEAR SON: Yours of the 12th came duly to hand. I had a letter from Gen. Butler. John has collected money enough to pay all the bills. There was $450.00 due the tenth of August and will be $1000.00 due the tenth of January. These two sums will be due to the present owner or the last sum will. I wrote to Gen. Butler that the new mill wanted painting. He can do as he likes about it.

John says there is several hundred dollars due of old debt that he can collect. I will send it to you, your part of it. The court gave the right to run the light. John is trying to get discharged from the receiver and I hope he will soon.

Your Mother joins me in love to you and all your family.

Your affectionate father, JESSE AMES

WASHINGTON, D.C., *December* 6, 1889

MY DEAR BLANCHE: I regret as much as you do the necessity of selling the Coast Survey Building with the other. I will try and see if I can't avoid it, but I doubt; the Government will take the whole building at some time, and as I have fixed the price at $277,000.00 and that price will give them the Coast

Survey and nearly three times as much more, and as that price has been fixed by appraisement, you see the difficulties.

I have a very high appreciation of your abilities as a business woman, but in regard to the house in Boston, you seem to think you couldn't hire the $15,000.00 to be paid down on the house, because you would have to hire the money to do it with.

The house is now rented and pays eight percent and would be paying that on your $15,000.00 that you hired while you would be getting eight. However, I do not know that it can be done, having been away here ten or fifteen days. I will talk it over, when I see you at "our old home" after Christmas, with all the children you choose to bring, especially those older ones for whom we will have a frolic provided. FATHER

NORTHFIELD, MINN., *December* 9, 1889

ADELBERT AMES.

MY DEAR SON: Your letter is at hand. The offer from the creditors is a generous offer. They ask cash and will take nothing else. Cannot Paul help you in this? Blanche would get half of her debt. If Gen. Butler wins the case in the end, she may get more, not otherwise. In my opinion there is no more chance for him to win the case than there is that the sun won't rise tomorrow morning. If you can raise this money there is a good chance to make money on it and what is more it will make you a free man.

Please answer as soon as you receive this and oblige,

Your affectionate father, JESSE AMES

HIGHLANDS, N.J., *December* 30, 1889

DEAR BLANCHE: Yours of Saturday at hand. I am glad to hear of your safe and agreeable journey. It was a high wind you ran before and I was afraid it would kick up sea enough to make you and Edith want the earth.

Everything is peaceful here, yet we have a certain kind of excitement. Day before yesterday Jessie was reading her book but stopped long enough to look up and say, "How exciting this story is, when the mouse got into the draw!" As for me, a like experience was realized when one of the rabbits jumped at me as I was passing his quarters. The wire netting prevented a collision.

I overheard Blanche saying, "When will Mother come home?" I do the best I can for the little orphans left in my charge. I trot them out in the afternoon, across the bridge if pleasant or into the woods when windy. Yesterday we were at the light house and were asked up by the keeper to see the lighting up. This afternoon to avoid the cold northwester, we have planned to go, by land, to Kernachan's, thence to Peterson's and possibly further on to the "widdy woman's"—Mrs. Treat.

Today brought the first letter since you left. I enclose one from Mother. It shows they are happier than a year ago when they did not have the heart to write.

How wonderful is money! No wonder it is worshipped. It makes a young woman of your Aunt Maria! And the want of it an old one of the younger sister Aunt Lottie!

Your letter was read to the children and at dinner our boy wanted to know what you meant when you spoke of missing a warm-blooded bedfellow, quoting Mrs. Treat. I do not know that my scientific knowledge was equal to the occasion. There was, however, a full discussion. And when he named our servants for illustration I had to go back to the foundation and most positively assert that all humans were about the same temperature, 110°F.

The babies join me in love and kisses to you, Edith and Sarah.

DEL

HIGHLANDS, N.J., *January 2*, 1890

DEAR BLANCHE: This is a very remarkable day. The thermometer stood at 68° in the storm entry at breakfast time and now, mid-day, it stands at 72° with the sun hidden most of the time by the soft clouds flying by from the south.

The effect on us is to send us all out of doors. We, all hands, have just been occupying the iron bench. Jessie on one side, the boy on the other and Blanche on my knees, but when the two younger began to play bo-peep between my face and Blanche's back we got tired and here I am for a rest and recreation. This day is also a remarkable one for another thing, our first born begins his first annual examination.

I will meet you at the station at 1:13. I can duplicate the bouquet I gathered for you on our lawn. The dandelions are many and the garlic tall. The lawn is still green but the cold snap of the first of the week took some of its glory from it.

All the babies send love and kisses, as do I.

DEL

WASHINGTON, *January* 31, 1890

MY DEAR BLANCHE: I leave for home tonight—there Sunday. I have had very hard labor. The sale of the house looks promising. The Committee are in favor.

I have got Strong indicted on three indictments, two for forgery and one for theft. His pal on two also.

Charlotte is anxious you should come with me when I return, which will be the last of February of which time I will try and give you some notice. I need not write I wish you to come.

I send check I have dunned the Coast Survey for.

FATHER

February 15, 1890

MY DEAR BLANCHE: Pardon pencil. I cannot use pen. I had an operation on my left eye at 4 o'clock yesterday. It is said to be a success. A half inch of the lid was cut out, and the lower part sewed up to it, so that my eye is "wide open tight." After the swelling has gone down, the face will be somewhat changed, but not enough so that I shall lose my eye-dentity.

FATHER

No. 6 Ashburton Place, BOSTON, *February* 25, 1890

Mrs. BLANCHE BUTLER AMES,
Highlands, Monmouth Co., N. J.

MY DEAR BLANCHE: How could you suppose that I had my eye operated upon to improve my looks? I really did think you knew me better than that. Good gracious. I have gone through life pleased that I was the homeliest man on earth. I have always felt like Mirabeau, "Let me get a chance to shake my boar's head at them." He was not quite as homely as I am.

What I did do was to have an operation performed so as to let light into my eye, so as to enable me to use it. I had great faith in my doctor, and it has been fully verified. He has performed the operation, and I can now see with that eye so as to have the focus adjusted with the other eye, which is failing. It was a little painful, and has been a little troublesome. I don't think it improves my looks, but I know it has improved my sight, and the strength of my eye.

I wrote to you first, as soon as the thing was done, because I thought you might see it in the newspapers and be worried. I do not make jokes with you when there is really anything important.

Yours, BENJ. F. BUTLER

LOWELL, *June* 5, 1890

MY DEAR BLANCHE: So we are jealous are we? Ha! ha! Mark how plain a tale shall but you own.

Paul went up to Camp in his canoe. I went up to see him. Took two ladies with me, one of whom some foolish penny a line mistook for you, and you need not have been ashamed of the mistake when you are not seen together, as she was *Mrs. Prentis Webster* and the other *Florence*, both Tom and Prentis having their business on Decoration Day elsewhere. Now do you not blush at paying any attention to a Newspaper report about your Father?

Paul will be with you on Sunday, having gone off on a canoe race near your house Saturday and Sunday. He won two races. Two cups, and for a wonder one was real silver, so that our house will not be wholly filled up with plated ware.

I am very pleased to send you good report of Butler. He stands about right. Nobody at the head of his class at West Point ever did come to anything save as map makers.

Now to explain my telegram. The proprietor of Poland Springs married his wife in Germany, and is to have a reception at his house, one of the most beautiful establishments I ever saw, about 25 miles from Portland. I am invited as his special friend, and as I am, to come and stay as long as I like, with as large a party of friends as will bring, *and he means it.* I shall go down in the "America" from Boston, if weather is good. A special train will go from Boston Saturday morning to take those who do not wish to go by water. It will be a great treat to see the very fine mountain scenery. If Ames can come, tell him to come. Reed is not Sailing Master now. Don't say no, but come!

Tell Edith that the founder of Wellesley College stood up with her Grandfather, best man at my marriage. Bring Sarah. I want to see her bright eyes once more before she gets over her desire to have a ride down a snow hill belly-bumps, ho!

I enclose the *menu* of today's dinner, which I had to eat all alone.

FATHER

June 6, 1890

MY DEAR BLANCHE: You make a mistake. Edith can finish her examination on Friday 13th. You can all get on board the "Pilgrim" or "Puritan" at 5 o'clock p.m. as well as your own boat, and get to Boston at 8 a.m. and take our special train at 10 and we will all go with you if it rains. I will see you have tickets from New York, and you will not need any after you get to Boston. Paul will be with you when you get this, and will stay a day and come with you.

You can all stay here till Edith takes the examination at Wellesley. Do come, all that can. FATHER

LOWELL, *June* 19, 1890

DEAR DEL: We are to leave here tomorrow afternoon and will go to New York by the Fall River boat—and hope to take the Sea Bird at nine o'clock Saturday morning and reach you and the babies by eleven.

Father is going on to Washington. We are to join him at Ware Junction, as it is easier to go direct from Lowell than by way of Boston.

Hilda, Bessie and Etta are expecting to go with us, so we are likely to have a houseful of young folk for a while. The girls would gladly remain here a while longer, but as Father has asked us to go with him, I thought it best not to delay. He suggested that I should go down and see the family for an hour or so Saturday, then join him at half past three and go on to Washington. I have gracefully retreated from this proposition, however, and go home to stay. The weather is delightful, and the visit has been enjoyable for us all.

I wrote Butler day before yesterday, but fear that he will miss his regular letters.

I have not seen any girls superior to ours, and am proud of my family. I have seen a few husbands, and rejoice that they are not mine, from which it may be inferred that I am well content with my own. With a kiss for babies and yourself,

BLANCHE

December 6, 1890

MY DEAR BLANCHE: I believe I sent you some time since some typewritten sheets of the first Chapter of the Book.[1] If I did not I have lost that Chapter. Will you kindly look the matter up and send me the sheets by registered letter. I hope you have come across them.

Will you not come *home* at Christmas, or as soon as you can? Bring the *whole* family, and specially the General.

Affectionately, FATHER

WEST POINT, N.Y., *December* 28, 1890

DEAR BLANCHE: With sentiments of high esteem for you and yours, I proceed to relate events since I last saw you. "Poor Johnathan" was a treat to the babies. Of course, they

[1] Butler's Book, published in 1892.

could not say much about it as they had nothing to compare it to but they sat upright till the end, eleven o'clock. As we got up I took a look at my watch and decided that you had pulled out of the station.

Yesterday morning we came up the river and saw Butler on our way to the hotel. He was a sight to behold. He had a big black territory under his right eye and a bloody scar from said eye back almost to his ear. He thought the wound would leave a scar but I do not. He, on Xmas day, was playing hockey and was butted on the left side of his head by a fellow cadet. That only dazed him for awhile. Upon recovery he made a dive and brought up against the visor of the cap of his neighbor. Said visor being of stiff leather cut him and the blow blackened his eye. He quit the game. He seems in very good spirits.

The last week he made about 1.5 above proficiency. That makes up all deficiencies, he thinks. Till examination recitations will not count in standing. He spent last evening here. The dissipation of the night before was too much for the babies and they keeled over on the sofas and went to sleep. This morning Jessie did not know how or where she went to bed.

Though it is cold and windy this morning the children and I went to chapel. Then I went to see Prof. Michie. He was busy. His eldest son was to leave immediately after dinner and so I did not trespass long. Of course he did not know much of our boy but said the Math. Prof. passed every boy he could. Prof. M. is, apparently, somewhat concerned about his own boy, who is doing very well in Philosophy but poorly in Chemistry. He told me to ask Butler to come and see him before the examination.

Tomorrow I will take the babies with me to Newark and reach the Highlands at about six.

Butler got his things safely into barracks and no doubt, has had already a partial feast thereon. On the parlor table I have three oranges and a large bunch of raisins. I have done my best to get your boy's stomach out of order.

Adelbert and Jessie are at my side and say they wish their love sent to you and the girls. With them, I join.

Adelbert

Highlands, N.J., *December* 30, 1890

Dear Blanche: We came home last evening, quite content to resume our quiet country life, with no regrets for the rush and frivolities of the city.

The games and books sent by Paul have come, also presents from their grandparents in Seattle. Butler and Adelbert have gold scarf pins and the girls four gold necklaces. The latter are gold beads varying only in size of beads and length. They are costly presents. There is a package for you from, I think, Charlotte or Hattie.

Martha met us at the gate with a lantern. Next to her delight, or before it, was the cat's joy at our return. She even climbed up on me when I was standing at the table unpacking the boxes, a thing she had never done before. The squirrel is very lively and was glad to be fed by me. I gave him a number of nuts. The first one he took in his mouth and held it there while I passed the others into him. He is a wise fellow. He knows a bird in the hand is worth two in the bush, or one nut in his mouth is held while the others are rolling about on the floor of his cage. But the rascal began to scold as I put in more nuts as if I were a bad boy intent on robbing him and no doubt would have tried his teeth on me at that stage of the proceedings if he had been foolish enough to let go of nut number one. Our river is full of ice. It is solid, though not very thick out to the channel, there the procession moves as stately as dancers in the minuet.

The babies join me in love to you all. ADELBERT

Hamilton House, Harlem, N.Y. CITY, *January* 10, 1891

DEAR BLANCHE: As it is but little past nine a.m. I have just returned to the hotel after escorting Edith and Sarah to Madison Ave. On the way, I bought a box of strawberries and four oranges—to be eaten at intervals this forenoon and at lunch with their chicken sandwiches.

Yesterday Edith thinks she made few, if any, mistakes except, perhaps, in some of the grammar questions. Her stomach is not the strongest but she is in the best of spirits and does not fret over the examinations[1] as she did last year. Sarah marches up to the rack like an old soldier, showing concern only by the slightest color in her cheeks.

None of us slept more than the law allows last night. The elevated railroad, street cars, carts, wagons, and humans seemed to make a regular pandemonium. We will do better, in this particular, as time passes.

I now start out to find you a servant and possibly a carpet for the hall. We, all, send love to all. ADELBERT

[1] Entrance examinations for Columbia College.

Law Offices of Benj. F. Butler, Washburn and Webster
BOSTON, *February* 7, 1891

Mrs. BLANCHE BUTLER AMES,
Highlands, Monmouth Co., N. J.

MY DEAR BLANCHE: The State wants a painting of me to put up among the Governors of Massachusetts. What do you say to my sending your painting of me to them?

Won't you also remember that you promised to send me all the photographs you have of scenes or places that I served in during the war? You know I told you I wanted them to have illustrations made from them for the book. The publisher is asking me for a photograph of Ship Island, which I sent to you sometime since. *Yours*, BENJ. F. BUTLER

NEW YORK, *April* 13, 1891

DEAR BLANCHE: I leave on the 5 p.m. train via West Shore. Will reach Chicago at 9 p.m. tomorrow, and if I make connections will reach Seattle at midnight next Saturday.

This is a warm day and I do not miss my old ulster. I send love and kisses to you all. DEL

HIGHLANDS, N.Y., *April* 19, 1891

DEAR DEL: We have all been talking of you and have decided that you are fast asleep in Seattle, as this is eight o'clock Sunday morning. We are all up early as the weather is delightful. The children started in good season and have been looking out of the window at the birds, flowers and sparkling waters. It seemed best to have them dressed, so we—the editorial "we"—led the way. My first thought being of you, my first act is to write you.

Blanche thinks her eyes much better. There is however no very marked improvement visible. Her desire is to have them well by the time you return. Yesterday afternoon all the girls with their mother went into the flower beds and planted seeds. Adelbert went fishing. We had three flounder and two cunners for tea.

I did not put my name on the check sent to Paul to finish paying for the Coast Survey. He returned it to me for endorsement and asked if we wished to loan any more money to the mill. I wrote him that it did not seem best to do so, without some security, that if he were not the treasurer, I should not dream of lending any, and that it was a question how far he could protect my interest when other larger might be at stake. Also that my position was quite different from that of the banks. The moment there was any question, they would have no compunction about withdrawing their loans. While in my case the more prudence might counsel a recall, the more family consideration would compel non-action. I ended by asking for his advice.

Your note from Minneapolis was most welcome. Jessie has brought in a flower which she wishes to have sent you. All join in love. With a kiss, Dearie, BLANCHE

General Ames visited his parents for about two months in Seattle, Washington, where he looked into possible business opportunities. Returning to the Highlands, he and Mrs. Ames interested themselves in building a house on their back lot.

HIGHLANDS, N.J., *November* 4, 1891

DEAR BLANCHE: The unexpected has happened this time. Your visit of a day may extend to three weeks! I hope not, however. Edith[1] will probably regain strength at once and in one week I will drive you both over from the station. It is well you went. We can spare you under the circumstances. Edith must not think she is very sick. Hers is the condition of innumerable others who have been subjected to bad air or water. Fine water and air will restore her. I suggest that only boiled water be used by her and yourself. Blanche will get your things together and we will express them to you.

As I look up through the trees I can catch a glimpse of the roof of the house and see it is nearly shingled. The roof on the other side has the gutter fixed but no shingles have been put on. A part of the gang is putting in the window frames and preparing for shingling the second story. I have not seen Mr. Parmeter today. He is absent. When he comes he will give me his estimate on the attic. What colors have you decided on for the house. Mr. P. spoke about a color for the gable ends as he will paint now (where shingled) as the scaffolding is up. The wall at the back of the house is up except at the kitchen corner. Today they finished grading at the southwest corner of the house and Worth is wheeling out the dirt between the house and wall. I have them at work at the north end of the house grading.

I regret your absence as I counted on you to direct the finish-

[1] Edith, a student at Bryn Mawr College, was stricken with a high fever. Mrs. Ames hurried to Bryn Mawr.

ing touches to the grading, path, etc. Shall I go on or suspend everything till you return?

All join me in much love. Give Edith a kiss for me and tell her to chirp up. Things could easily be worse. DEL

HIGHLANDS, N.J., *November* 6, 1891

DEAR BLANCHE: It is well that Edith has malaria rather than typhoid fever. I hardly expected to hear she was quite so sick. I have no doubt she will soon pull through and be able to come home with you before Thanksgiving. Of course we miss you.

I am helping the children along as well as I can. Blanche has to depend on herself in her Latin. I find her quite capable of learning her French—showing no little capacity. The little boy has finished his geography and taken up French. This is just before dinner and I have been over Blanche's algebra with her—preceded by recitations by the younger ones in reading, spelling, grammar and French. Right here, I recall that I have not heard Jessie's geography. On inquiry, I find that Blanche heard her and that she had a good lesson. I give Blanche her French in the evening. They are all doing well and are happy as children ought to be. I think Blanche misses you most, though she does not say much. When your letters come they group themselves around me for the news.

There is one reason why you should congratulate yourself in being away from home just at this time. Martha has poisoned the rats—so she told me yesterday. I have not heard them for the past day or two but though silent they are loud. Yesterday, James cleaned out the cistern. I had him roll up some wire netting and put it in the pipe which brought the water and also in the waste pipe. Now, if all the rats are dead and never come back no more, and the netting remains in the pipes, we will not find any dead rats in our cistern, I hope.

The roof of the house will be closed in today. I have been putting the mineral wool about the floor. I shall try to close up everything about the kitchen not only to keep the rats and mice away but also smaller pests like cockroaches.

We all send you love and shall be most happy to see you home again with Edith—kisses for both. DEL

BRYN MAWR, *November* 7, 1891

DEAR DEL, AND DEAR CHILDREN.—I address my letter to you all for I have not time to write to each one. A general letter will be as satisfactory when you know that I am thinking of you all, all of the time.

We had a letter from home today and I judge that mine saying that the doctor had decided Edith's disease was typhoid, had not reached you. I asked him yesterday about the milk which comes from Haverford farm. He said he knew that it was good and that the cattle had only pure water. He then wished to know where Edith had been previous to coming to the college. I told him at the Highlands and at White Hall, the other side of the railroad, for a week, the last of September. "All of that part of the town is damp and malarious but I do not know of typhoid there. Stop a moment, yes, I do! My partner had a case at White Hall. There is where Miss Ames got it, no doubt. Please do not quote me as saying so, however, for it will not help our case any and I do not wish to injure the man's business."

Edith today is doing splendidly as shown by the fact that the temperature was two tenths lower than at the same hour yesterday, and would indicate that we have reached a period when the fever is abating. Edith had only liquid nourishment, beef broth and milk.

The nurse will attend to Edith during the night and sleep from eleven a.m. to five or six p.m., during which time I am nurse par excellence, and assist during the other waking hours from seven in the morning until nine in the evening. The doctor has insisted upon a division of duty, saying that if both were on hand all of the time we should soon be good for nothing.

My trunk came today, everything seems to be all right. I thank my dear ones and Blanche especially for the nice letter which came in it. Adelbert and Jessie must write frequently. I have not had a chance to send a line to Butler. My letters are all written on my knee with many interruptions.

I enclose Miss Baldwin's[1] bill. It seems Sarah had already audited it and it is correct. Sarah does not look very well, she is thin and sallow. I have told her to sleep in the little hall bed room with the window open a little, top and bottom. In the larger room there is a stove and I think a constant fire. I have been in the room twice and have found it much too warm to sit in. Sarah went with me to the apothecary's and bought a thermometer, this afternoon. She has promised to regulate the heat by it.

[1] Sarah was a student at Miss Baldwin's School at Bryn Mawr preparing for Bryn Mawr College.

I asked Edith what she wished me to say from her. "Say that I must be at home Thanksgiving."

With love and kisses for you all. MOTHER

BRYN MAWR, *November* 14, 1891

DEAR DEL: Edith still goes on improving, but in spite of that, I have some rather disappointing words for you.

Dr. Gerhard told me yesterday that he was going for two weeks vacation today and asked if I should be willing to have his partner attend Edith in his absence, that he was a good physician and had had many years experience in the Philadelphia hospital with typhoid cases.

Of course I could only say that any one he recommended would be satisfactory to me. "But," I added, "if you are to be away two weeks we shall be gone before you return."

"Oh! Mrs. Ames, don't think of it. You must not run the risks. That is just what makes this fever such a villainous disease. The least indiscretion is so apt to bring on a relapse and then the work has all to be gone over again with the patient in a weakened condition. Six weeks from the commencement will be fully as soon as it will be at all prudent to take her home. I know how anxious you must be to get away, but she must gain strength enough to move about the rooms and get up and down stairs before undertaking to do more. I must certainly find you here when I return."

I answered, "I do not wish to do anything rash, and must abide by your advice for the present."

I hope, Dearie, to shorten the six weeks some, but you see there is no chance for going before Thanksgiving. Sarah will have to go home alone. You can meet her, can you not, and send her word about the trains? I shall probably go into Philadelphia with her and I should think the best route would be to make the change at Elizabethport.

I am very homesick, but Edith's disappointment is such I must not show it. She said "You will have to go home and leave me, they need you there" and the tears rolled down her cheeks. I assured her I should do nothing of the kind but would stand by and we should go together. This seemed to comfort her somewhat, but it was a "Mauvaise quart d'heure."

Thanksgiving itself does not amount to much. It is the extra ten days that count. Ah, well! I will not look forward but get through each day as best we may. Let the weeks take care of themselves. The house will be painted and quite finished before I get back. This however causes no regret. I am glad that you have had it to occupy your thoughts somewhat.

With love and kisses for my babies and you, BLANCHE

BRYN MAWR, *November* 18, 1891

DEAR DEL: Edith and I have been rejoicing over your probable decision to come to Bryn Mawr for Thanksgiving. I think Sarah will not feel much disappointment, because on the 18th of December she will go home for the Christmas holidays, which would be in three weeks from the time of your visit. I shall see her this afternoon and talk it over with her.

This morning's paper has an announcement of Father's illness caused by an abscess in the ear. I do not know whether to put any credence in it or not, but naturally feel anxious.

Edith still does well. I can not say that she is gaining strength for pulse and temperature both show great weakness. Still the fever does not return and in a few days she will be able to eat and can gain rapidly.

How glad I shall be to see you and my babies.

BLANCHE

BRYN MAWR, *November* 23, 1891

DEAR DEL: Edith is eating like a Trojan. The nurse looks on aghast but as she finds that it agrees with Edith, no opposition. When the temperature became normal or below, I gave Edith each day beginning with a piece the size of my thumb nail, graham bread. In the course of three days she had a whole slice, so that by the time the week was out her stomach was all ready for any reasonable amount of food. The doctor knew nothing of this, or the nurse either. The doctor said Saturday that all there was left for him to do was to get Edith on solid diet. He did not know that she was already there. He thought she might have one egg with a very little dry bread broken in it for breakfast and a small quantity of milk toast for tea. She did have however two eggs, a slice and a half of bread, a cup of broth and cracker, a sweet bread and two slices of bread, and crackers, jelly and tea for supper. This morning she is as lively as a cricket and will, I hope, get up this afternoon for a while.

Just think! Day after tomorrow I shall see you all and feel that my exile is drawing to a close. Love and kisses for my dear ones. BLANCHE

General Butler died in Washington, D.C. on January 11th, 1893 in his home on Capitol Hill. A monument erected to his memory by his loving children, Blanche and Paul, in the Hildreth Family Cemetery at Lowell, has on it the following inscription.

BENJAMIN FRANKLIN
BUTLER
JURIST SOLDIER STATESMAN
PATRIOT
HIS TALENTS WERE DEVOTED TO
THE SERVICE OF HIS COUNTRY
AND THE ADVANCEMENT OF HIS
FELLOW MEN

BORN NOVEMBER 5 1818
DEERFIELD NEW HAMPSHIRE
MARRIED MAY 16 1844
SARAH DAUGHTER OF ISRAEL HILDRETH
LOWELL MASSACHUSETTS
DIED JANUARY 11 1893
WASHINGTON DISTRICT OF COLUMBIA

THE TRUE TOUCHSTONE OF CIVIL LIBERTY
IS NOT THAT ALL MEN ARE EQUAL
BUT THAT EVERY MAN HAS THE RIGHT TO BE
THE EQUAL OF EVERY OTHER MAN IF HE CAN

Immediately upon news of General Butler's death, General and Mrs. Ames with their family joined Paul at Lowell, January 12, 1893.

HIGHLANDS, N.J., *March* 8, 1893

DEAR BLANCHE: I am at the old desk again. I have been over the premises with Broady. Everything seems all right. He was giving the finishing touches to passageway from the laundry to the wood-shed. Everything else to be painted is finished, and looks well. The house on the back lot is in excellent condition. I came by the beach to avoid the mud. I saw hens under the bay window and the cat popped its head out from under the piazza. As I came along the shore I met Mr. Peterson. I brought him along, explained how I wanted our very much delapidated dock rebuilt and gave him the job.

I telegraphed to Edith that I hoped to see her tomorrow

afternoon or evening. I shall write to Butler after I finish this, that I will be at West Point Friday or Saturday. I return to the city this afternoon.

Our house here, which we know is so cozy and homelike, is dreary and sad today. I do not know how others may feel but as for me the presence of those I love and who love me is absolutely indispensable. If this be treason make the most of it. Love and kisses for all. ADELBERT

CHICAGO, ILL., *March* 25, 1893

DEAR BLANCHE: I am in hopes I will be able to get $100,-000.00 for the block. I have no doubt I could get $90,000.00 at once, but the building is worth more. I shall not take any other property in part payment.

Two or three different persons will look it over tomorrow, Sunday, and will be ready to talk business Monday. By the way, it seems to me that I have somewhere at sometime said this same thing under the same circumstances.

I hope you will not have to mortgage the home place, even though the money raised is used to pay other debts. Perhaps by so doing you may save some interest—may thereby be led to economical ways, in a way, and have your pride in, say real estate, sat down on, all to some beneficial end. Who knows? Yet, notwithstanding such possible blessings, I am urging the sale of this piece of property thinking it might save the home place from the loss of pride incident to a mortgage.

The two days I was in Northfield I talked incessantly, at least such is my remembrance of the time, and at last my throat was so sore I had to stop talking. It was due mainly to the fact that I talked loud, to be distinctly heard by Father, who is a little deaf as you know.

I am glad to know our babies are happy. What a blessed thing it is to have a margin. Edith must appreciate it. Motto for this life—"Keep a good, wide margin." By the way, Chicago's motto is "Keep a hustling—keep a hustling." Well, I suppose that results in a margin, gives a Worlds Fair, and all else worth having in this Fair World.

I shall remain here till something takes definite form relative to the sale on hand. I may of course fail. Then I shall go to N. again.

I send much love to you and Edith, and Sarah, and Blanche, and Adelbert, and Jessie. ADELBERT

LOWELL, MASS., *April 5*, 1893

DEAR DEL: I can see from your letters that you have the sale of the Chicago property very deeply at heart. I do not care "to preach" as you call it, but let us try to be happy. Paul will be able probably to get a loan on the Wamesit Co. of a hundred thousand additional, and then we need not feel so driven about the Chicago block, although this year would seem to be the time to sell.

Edith went back to college last night. I saw her safely on board the sleeper, in her own section, with buffet in the same car, and trunk checked. Her fellow travelers were several ladies and children and quiet-looking gentlemen. There would seem to be no trouble about her having a comfortable trip. She hated to leave us and will not be ready to go back next year.

Jimmy is having a fine time this vacation. He has been riding with a number of the boys, on a pony, while Sammie takes our brown mustang. Paul smiles many times over the boy's old sayings and ways. He looks over and reads every day the Scientific American.

Paul asked him this morning what he found that he liked—"Oh, everything that is interesting, electrical, machinery and different articles." He made his appearance at the table with a small volume of the poems of Lord Bateman which he read while supping his coffee. This was permissible as Paul and I had the papers. Blanche is just recovering from a very heavy cold and sore throat.

We expect to see you the last of this week or the first of next. You are quite right to insist that your Mother should have skilled attention. I of course have great faith in Doctor Stone, although it by no means follows that because he did well in one case, that he can in another.

Give my love to your Father and Mother and tell them that I wish they could see all your children together, that I am sure they would feel proud of them.

With love for you, BLANCHE

LOWELL, MASS., *August 12*, 1893

DEAR DEL: As you are away[1] I am writing with your own particular gold pen, and I am not a bit afraid to say so because by the time you get back you will have forgotten all about it probably, if not you will be too glad to see me to scold.

Jessie and I passed a very quiet night. She is enjoying the

[1] General Ames, Edith, Sarah and Blanche have gone to the Chicago Fair.

situation greatly. Half a dozen times last evening she asked if it was a bad thought to feel glad that the girls are away. She evidently feels that she is in entire possession of her mother, with no one to dispute her rights.

Tell Butler, that it troubles me when I think of the wine in camp, and that I hope there will be none in Chicago. In case of exposure; and these things come to light sooner or later, it would be a comparatively small matter to have smuggled eatables, but a great scandal to bring in wine, no matter what the kind. The risk is too great for the satisfaction to be had out of it. Let him have patience for nine months more and run no risk of breaking down on the home-stretch. Give him my love and a kiss. I hope he will enjoy every moment of his time at Chicago, and have no drawbacks in the shape of hay-fever.

As for my lovely girls, they must realize that they are favored mortals and make the best of everything. Turn all annoyances into jokes and prove themselves good travelers and pleasant companions to you and to each other. A bright cheerful helping word from each to the other will make all the difference in the world in the pleasure of the trip.

If Blanche's boil troubles her, let her consider it as a kind of head-light to brighten up her travels. Edith must consult her watch very frequently and be sure that she has said forty words in every half hour. Sarah is only going to smile a "rare sweet smile" at all the jokes, and you, my Sweetheart, are not to fret about "our girls." They are perfection and cannot be improved except in our foolish imaginations. With love for each one,

BLANCHE AND MOTHER

WEST POINT, N.Y., *August* 17, 1893

DEAR BLANCHE: It is now seven o'clock in the morning. We have had breakfast. The trunks are all packed and down. In half an hour the corps will march down to the train, which will leave in an hour or two. So you see, we are off.

Last evening ten girls (eight girls and two chaperons) of which I was not one, and ten cadets had a little party at Fort Knox. Watermelon was the food supplied except four pounds of candy by our girls. The boys sang. Unable to get high enough Sarah came to their aid and so had to sing the song alone. She did very well. The girls are fully satisfied with themselves. They are no longer embarrassed in any presence. So far from having the cadet fever they are ready to move on. They were constantly in motion. They dance very well, well enough, and were a shade better looking than anybody else's girls there that *I* saw. They have been the best of girls. You should have been here. I was wholly content with them and think that to be the case with Butler. The girls are perfectly at home. Edith says she knows her old dread has wholly gone.

I send you and Jessie much love. ADELBERT

LOWELL, MASS., *August* 19, 1893

MY DEAR DEL: There is not much mail to send you this morning, only a letter from Miss Oliver that tells its own story. This question of teacher troubles me a little for these reasons.

In the first place, it is among the possible things as I have said before that we may not care to be here this winter. Men are even now begging for work with tears in their eyes, according to the Lowell papers, and unless the mills are to start up again, and of this there seems to be no present prospect, Lowell is not going to be an agreeable residence to say the least. This is one of the uncertainties.

In the second place, has Blanche definitely settled that Bryn Mawr is the best college for her? She has a good voice and some skill in music. All things being equal, is it not possible that she might find Smith College satisfactory, where she will be able to go on with her music? If so would it not be just as well for her to go to Andover or to Rogers Hall where there are girls preparing for Smith, and learn what it is to recite in class and hold her own with other girls? I know she dislikes the thought of going to Rogers Hall and having the crowd know just how much and how little she knows, but there is just the point, she has never measured herself with other girls and is a little uncertain of the result. Perhaps it will be well to talk the matter over with her a little.

We heard yesterday that Mrs. Nesmith's house has been broken into, but do not know the particulars. Of course, this made me think of this establishment and last night I gathered up all the small articles of value and put them in my room and the dressing room. I also told Lizzie that in case I should ring the bell in the dressing room I wanted her to wake up Toy[1] and come to my aid. However, they have both decided that it would be very dangerous for them to appear and they are going to run out of doors. Lizzie asked me this morning "please not to put any dependence" on her. I assured her I would not and that I felt quite able to take care of Jessie and

[1] The Chinese cook.

myself, but if I rang the bell I wanted her and Toy to call up some of the neighbors. It is needless to say that the bell will not be rung.

I am much pleased at your report of our girls. This experience will be worth a great deal to them.

I send love to them, to Butler and to you. BLANCHE

CHICAGO, ILL., *August* 23, 1893

DEAR BLANCHE: You must excuse us all if we prove indifferent correspondents. Yesterday morning we got up at seven and went to bed at eleven. There was no intermediate rest.

I had a telegram from Father just now. He says "come to Northfield and bring the girls—see letter." I expect we will go. No doubt he and Mother are very desirous of seeing their grandchildren. This change will delay our home coming.

This is almost seven and we await Butler's coming to dinner. His hay fever is not troubling him any to speak of. The girls stand the hard work of sight seeing wonderfully well. Sarah is as tough as the other two. They are very good girls of mine. They are absorbing much knowledge and seem to enjoy it.

I send you and Jessie much love. DEL

LOWELL, *August* 23, 1893

MY DEAR *Old* SWEETHEART: What a very funny letter is yours of Aug. 20. I laughed and laughed again as I read it. I seemed to see consternation on your dear faces as you summed up the items. It is evident you are having a "high old time."

I am glad of it. You will not be likely to visit another World's Fair with so many of your loved ones around you, to whom you can give all that they desire in the way of pleasure and gratification of their fancies. I rejoice that you can afford to do it. You will have to draw on the bank again soon; there is no doubt about that.

Blanche's letter pleases me very much—and her efforts to hold her own against the crowd. She must not try to look at more than one thing at a time, or her head will trouble her and spoil all of her enjoyment. Do not let her go too long without eating, a biscuit or a sandwich or fruit will keep the stomach in tone. When the brain is working, as any brain must, that is absorbing so many new impressions, it needs to be well sustained.

Edith signs herself "Your worldly daughter." I am not troubled with fear of any undue amount of worldliness on her part. I know my girls, and there is no question but that they are the best in the world. My bonnie boy Butler is in his glory, I am sure; with such an admiring multitude to look at his manoeuvres, how can he help it. How proud you must be, Del, to feel that you are the father of so much youth and beauty.

If your Father joins you in Chicago, perhaps you will not go to Northfield? With love and kisses for all my dear ones,

BLANCHE

CHICAGO, ILL., *August* 25, 1893

DEAR BLANCHE: It is now half-past seven. Have just had dinner. In a quarter of an hour we are going to a ball in the "Women's Building" given to the cadets. It is a ball where invitations are issued and will not probably be over crowded. At least it will not be a mob of sight seers.

Sunday afternoon we will leave here for Northfield.

We have had a great deal of sight seeing and will leave feeling we have done our whole duty. It has been a good school for the children. They have enjoyed it. It has aged them some as all experience ages folks even when the experience is a pleasant one.

I am glad you enjoyed my letter. I could write you a similar one every day but I will spare your feelings. It is not good to laugh too much.

I send you and Jessie love. DEL

LOWELL, MASS., *August* 26, 1893

MY DEAR TRAVELERS: I am happy this morning because of your letters. I had been quite out of patience with you all. It is evident that you are a mutual admiration society, for Edith writes that "Father is an angel without wings, takes us everywhere, and does everything imaginable for us." To offset this Del writes "They are very good girls of *mine*." Now inasmuch as you all belong to me I feel very proud.

Paul came this morning without Adelbert as that young man thought he would prefer to wait and start this morning and take the steamer through the Grand Rapids. Paul says that he has been a first rate boy, has caught lots of fish, been in swimming every day and sometimes twice a day, but only for a few minutes at a time. He can paddle a canoe and had been fishing in one.

I suppose that it will be somewhat troublesome to raise the money required for payment of notes by the Cartridge Mill. The papers talk of an improved feeling, but Paul does not seem to feel very cheery. Of course, Carney owes us plenty of money, but we don't know if he will pay it now. Paul has said nothing to suggest it, but would it not be well, Del, to inquire of Baldwin if it would be possible to raise money on a second mortgage on the Chicago building? Perhaps money is not so tight there as here.

One good result of this trip is that you are learning all about your girls, traveling etc. are as we all know the best test of disposition. You talk of a trip to Northfield. I should like to know when the crowd is to come home. You girls must take care not to make your visit to Northfield a burden to your grandmother. Take care of your own rooms. Help about the cooking and setting the table and dishes. She is not strong enough to do much. Love and kisses for you all.

MOTHER

LOWELL, MASS., *February* 20, 1894

DEAR DEL: I was blessed yesterday for when Edith and I came home from Boston there were two letters waiting for us, one from you and one from Butler.

Yours seemed a little stiff and formal as if you were somewhat displeased with me and while determined to do your duty, you did it without heart. Perhaps, however, you were displeased with yourself. I do not wish to be fault finding, but while I rejoiced to get your letter, telling me you had reached Northfield safely, I missed something that should have been in that letter. What was it?

We went to Boston to do some shopping for Edith and to get a birthday present for Blanche.

Edith in the evening went with Sadie Meigs to the Opera House to hear Modgeska. Adelbert and I devoted ourselves to Latin. He is a good boy and tries to do his duty. He and Jessie are going to a little party given by Grace Hylan Thursday night. Jessie is to read a piece in the large hall in the Moody School to the assembled scholars in honor of George Washington's birthday. Blanche has asked Gannor to put the express wagon on runners and she intends to have straw in the bottom and rugs and have a straw-ride tomorrow with fifteen or sixteen of the boys and girls.

Now, I think you know about what your family are doing, but what you don't know is, that it is lonely without you. When you are here I feel that there is a strong anchor to windward, and everything is snug. Really are you any happier in Northfield than you are at home?

Give my love to Fannie and your parents. A kiss for you from,
BLANCHE

LOWELL, MASS., *February 22*, 1894

DEAR DEL: Your second letter that came today is just a duck, and I did not read between the lines any of the feeling that I attributed to your first.

We heard from Sarah today, she said that all was going well with her at college. She is very happy. Blanche is in fine spirits, and I try to have her so and have her go out every day. All we can do is to keep her in good condition and let time work a cure for her back.

I rode out this afternoon and called first upon Florence to see if she would ride with me. She was not at home. Then I went to Sadie Webster's and found her ironing but she was ready for a turn out of doors. We did not take a long drive because I had promised Edith to be back by five o'clock to see if she were all right for the Cumnock dinner party. Then the children, Adelbert and Jessie, came in dressed for a card party at the Hylans. They left at seven. Now Blanche and I are alone in the house and I am doing what I should be doing, if you were where you ought to be, talking to you.

Good night, with love,
BLANCHE

NORTHFIELD, MINN., *March 2*, 1894

DEAR BLANCHE: This is your birthday. I think of you and pray that you may have many of them and that all may be as happy as this. What birthday it is I will not say, but let them come to you, the more the merrier.

We have just had dinner. Father and Mother are in the room with me. They are well and I think very happy.

Yesterday I was at Faribault to see a lawyer about sueing this city for damages to Father's square, by the road, between us and the school house. I called on Fanny. She aroused my sympathy. Her children, unused to their surroundings kept close to her and made life a burden. She is to hire a furnished house here, if she can get one. Her husband will travel for a St. Louis hardware manufacturer.

Father's business is still incompleted. I do not know when I shall start east but expect to sometime next week.

I send you and the children much love.
ADELBERT

NORTHFIELD, MINN., *September* 18, 1894

DEAR BLANCHE: As we came into the station I saw Father waiting for me in his carriage. He is in good health and spirits. Mother is looking better than for a year or two. She does not suffer so much from the pain and can sleep better. The cause of her suffering has not been removed but time has so modified it that life is more endurable. She does not complain, in fact, she treats her trouble more lightly than any one about her. She has traveled up to my room to see that everything was in order. And this morning she made arrangements to go down town with Father shopping. I suggested that she go in the low carriage but she would not agree saying she had no trouble in getting into the buggy Father uses. The only thing left for me to say is—nothing.

John has sold his farm and will move into town. What he will do I cannot say. He is the nominee of the Populist party for State senator. He has no chance of being elected. I do not talk politics with him.

I am in good health and send love and kisses to you all.

ADELBERT

NORTHFIELD, MINN., *September* 28, 1894

DEAR BLANCHE: There is nothing new here. John has moved and is settling but I have not called there yet. I shall do so when I learn they are ready for visitors.

Day before yesterday Mother rode down town to do some shopping. She goes with Father in the buggy. They have a wonderful vitality and I more than half suspect that they are as young as some other people we read of. Father's hair is thick and only iron gray. Mother's is about as thick as ever and gray on the back of her head though thin and almost white in front. They send love to you and the children. I send you all love.

ADELBERT

LOWELL, MASS., *December* 6, 1894

MY DEAR DEL: We are as when you left us night before last. I understand that you beguiled the tedium of your trip to Boston by talking to a very charming lady. You see I have an eye to your movements.

Edith had a little ill turn yesterday but is up this morning, and seated opposite to me at the library table, busy with her ivory type.

Florence and Sadie Webster came home with me from the Fortnightly Club and took dinner. They expressed themselves as highly pleased with Edith's picture. Sadie said, "It is wonderful." "I told you it was," replied Florence. "Yes I know you did but I thought you meant for a first picture, not at all like this."

Butler has just brought the telegraph announcement of your Father's death.[1] We all wish to be with you, Dearie, to help lighten your affliction. Butler proposes that we go on to Northfield, he and I, but I do not know what to do, that is, what you would want us to do.

I have telegraphed you, care of Baldwin, asking if I can join you in Northfield. I might be of some assistance to you or to your Mother for whom I feel the deepest sympathy. There can be no position in life so lonely as hers is now.

Do you think, Sweetheart, that it is possible she might be happier with us than in Northfield. The distraction of thought, consequent upon new scenes and new faces might be advantageous. If you think so persuade her to return. We will spare no pains to make her as happy and comfortable as possible. Alas, that it is in our power to do so little! How glad you must be that you were with your parents this fall and that all your relations with them were full of mutual love and trust.

The children all send their love and sympathy to you.

Your loving wife, BLANCHE

LOWELL, MASS., *333 Andover St., December* 7, 1894

DEAR FATHER: You are in trouble now; a trouble that can happen to us but once in a lifetime. As you know, when all is smooth and unruffled, we are undemonstrative in our affection and love for one another; but when trial and sorrows come then we stand by one another and offer what consolation we can, great or small, in the expression of our love.

So you know our hearts go out to you and your mother as the half formed tear on Mother's eye lashes will attest. She can appreciate better, perhaps, than we children, the grief, sorrow and bitterness that must come with crushing force upon the death of so good and dear a parent.

If death be a sleep it is one that knows no sorrows and ours is the lot so hard to bear when our loved ones leave us forever.

So remember, dear Father, though "God's will be done,"

[1] Captain Jesse Ames died in Northfield, Minnesota, December 6th, 1894. He was born February 4th, 1808, in North Haven, Maine.

there are others, still on earth that love you and ask your love in return. Do not mourn or brood too deeply, though your cup of bitterness be full to over-flowing. Though his body be dead, his soul lives on; as a reward for a life so well lived and won, while we will help you drain that "brimming cup" and time will soften the strangeness of God's call.

Mother was about to join you when your telegram came. I suggested that you would like to have me come on, so that you won't feel lonely; but they seem to think I had better not.

Uncle Paul has just brought word that the gas engine is completed and was shipped today. My lessons are getting on quite satisfactorily. Edith is making great work in a miniature of Sarah on the ivory you bought for her. Adelbert has decided to join the Y.M.C.A. for the sake of the gymnasium. He says, "I am not feeling so well since football stopped and I need more exercise."

With love to you and Grandmother, I am,

Your son, BUTLER

NORTHFIELD, MINN., *December* 10, 1894

DEAR BLANCHE: Father was buried yesterday. Poor Mother. Fanny will come here with her children for the winter at least and for an indefinite time thereafter if need be. Her husband suggested she should come and she wants to come. I think her children, who are much loved by Mother, will be a comfort to Mother.

Mother would like a cap. I told her you would send her one. It can come in the box of Christmas presents. I would like the children to put in the box some present to be given by Mother to Fanny's children. Her boy is about eight, one girl about three and one about five. I hear that Mattie's girls are making doll's clothing for them. So a couple of dolls would be acceptable.

I have no wish that our girls should wear mourning. I do not think it goes for much. I leave it for you to decide. Public sentiment, or a respect for it should influence somewhat. Still it may be that the relationship and comparatively slight association would have weight in forming a decision.

I have to thank Butler for a kind, loving letter, and you too, as for that matter, though that can always be said of all of the letters from home. I expect to be with you Christmas.

Mother thanks you for your kind invitation for her to go to Lowell, but it hardly seems practicable.

With love and kisses for you all. ADELBERT

LOWELL, MASS., *March* 16, 1895

DEAR DEL: I send you all that there is of interest in the mail line. Butler has come home. He dined last night with Professor Lanza, two other Professors and one of the Tech fellows. Edith has gone for a walk with Mr. Stevens. She said she would choose the by-ways so that they might not cause comment. This she is anxious to avoid on his account. Blanche is at the theatre with Louise Martin and Mr. Kennard and a chaperone. Adelbert is at the shop, where he almost lives. He ought to learn something in a mechanical line. Time enough is given to it. Possibly he and the boys have skipped out to view the parade in honor of St. Patrick.

It is possible also that there will be some street rows as the A.P.A.s have threatened to sell an orange colored newspaper. This reminds me that I saw a man driving a cart this morning who had adorned his horse's head with green flags but had forgotten that the tail of his cart was filled with oranges.

With love, BLANCHE

NORTHFIELD, MINN., *July* 28, 1895

DEAR BLANCHE: I arrived here yesterday. I was much pleased to find Mother better than she has been for a number of years. She is not stouter, in fact, thinner than I have ever known her, but that I consider an advantage.

That you may judge of her condition I need but tell you that on one occasion recently she walked to Uncle Dave's to make a call, and on another to Charlotte's. Today we drove out over rough enough roads for an hour and a half.

Of course, her old troubles are present with her but in less objectionable form. She seems more cheerful than at any time since Father's death. She has farmed the place till it looks better and is better than I have ever seen it. She has a good man who obeys orders and gives perfect satisfaction. One thing strikes me, when Father was alive he ran everything, Mother rarely interfering. When he died Mother dreaded to take up the burden of managing but really she is an excellent manager.

Miss Hills is here and is a great comfort to Mother. She has got Mother in the way of going out driving almost every day. The outdoor air and moderate exercise seems to have acted as a tonic. Of course, as the months go by Mother does not grieve so much, at least she does not show her grief as at first, fortunately time deadens. She has not much to look forward to.

Her chief work seems to be to get things in order before she goes. While she wrote little of Father's monument, she liked it much as all here do and she is planning to have it up before cold weather.

John is looking better than he has for years. He really looks younger than I expected to see him or thought he was.

I am well. I stuffed in Chicago—am inclined to eat less now having had my spree.

Butler's week of soldiering is ended. I hope you will tie the boy down to his books. He will be sorry next Sept. if he should fail to prepare himself.

Love and kisses to you all. ADELBERT

BAY VIEW, *August* 3, 1895

DEAR DEL: Your second very welcome letter came yesterday. You can imagine that while I have the children for companions there are yet many times when I wonder what I am down here for, or in fact why I should be here or anywhere else. This question will come up more often no doubt during the next week.

Blanche is to have a little house party consisting of Abbott and Laurin Martin; Louise, Betty Bennet, Joe Francis, and Will Fox. The two last are more particularly Sarah's friends. They have been asked to stay from Saturday to Tuesday, then Sarah goes to Lowell to prepare for her next visit to Miss Howard in Burlington. She will probably go up with Paul, who will be on his way to the canoe meet. Adelbert took his weekly trip to Lowell this morning and is to remain over night in order to consult the bee-man and see some of the boys. He and Blanche went in the sail boat to Coffin's beach yesterday and brought home eleven sand peep. Blanche shot three. Sarah feels better than when you were here and is correspondingly more lively and happier.

Night before last we had a fire and the papers reported frost on Mt. Washington. There is no summer. With love

BLANCHE

BAY VIEW, *August* 5, 1895

DEAR DEL: Your third letter telling us that you are to go to New Mexico, came Saturday. That means you will not get back much if any before the first of September, and this summer, at Bay View, in which I had thought you were to find some pleasure as "head of your own household" and in watching the ocean and vessels, has turned out a complete failure.

So it is with all "the best laid plans of mice and men." I will not make any more but just drift along on the current of those made by others.

You say if we or I have anything to suggest about Fort Union to do so before the 10th. There is nothing further I can suggest, unless it may be to state again that I shall be perfectly satisfied with whatever you decide upon.

Will it not be very warm traveling so far South? Had I not better send your new summer suit to Chicago in order that it may be in readiness for your return?

The house is quite full with Blanche's and Sarah's friends. I watch the young folk come and go and to a certain extent it is amusing enough but my companion and the only one with whom I have perfect content is not here.

All send love to you, Del, and kindliest remembrances to yours. BLANCHE

FT. UNION, NEW MEXICO, *August* 16, 1895

DEAR BLANCHE: I reached this place late last Monday. I found Dr. Bailey here. I have agreed with him to lease Ft. Union for twenty-five or fifty years for one fourth of the net profits. He was a pupil of Dr. Kock of Berlin and proposes to run the Sanitarium here under Kock's direction or guidance. Bailey proposes to go to Europe and get endorsements from Kock and other leading physicians who have made consumption a specialty.

Also to get the endorsements of leading American physicians etc. Dr. Bailey is to put some $10,000.00 in improvements at once. If he does he will thereby preserve the buildings, and later improve and extend the facilities for patients.

The term of years of the lease is not definitely fixed. The real point at issue with me is to get some reliable person who can make a success here, or the one who presents himself who apparently can succeed, to take the Fort in charge and try. Better a long lease than none at all. No lease means the destruction and decay of Ft. U.

A successful Sanitarium may be possible. Even a failure requires some $10,000.00 repairs which will preserve the buildings for many years. Upon failure the Fort comes back to us. Then we can try again, somebody else.

I have signed no paper. Any modification or annulment of an "arrangement" not yet made are your right. Dr. Bailey is enthusiastic in the highest degree and sees fame and wealth in this enterprise. You can drive almost any bargain with him. Of course all papers are to be signed by you. You are the master of the situation.

The past three days I have been riding over the Grant, viewing the new fence and getting an idea of the country.

Baldwin came in this morning from Santa Fe. He has had a siege with Catron. The outcome is that Catron agrees to a division so far as he and we are concerned on the 36 parallel of latitude, we to take that south and he take that north of said line. The agreement is before me drawn by Catron. It is no easy matter to decide. I shall start out this afternoon to inspect. I will try to ride over and see all of the Grant so I can come to some intelligent conclusion. Of course Catron is the same person we have known him to be. It is for us to decide if such a division is the least of evils.

I have seen nearly all of the Grant north and south on this Ft. U. line. The north west quarter is mountainous. I will look over the south west quarter and that east of the railroad. I think I can ride over what I have not seen in three or four days, possibly in three days. Of the various purposes of our trip these two, converting Ft. Union into a sanitarium and a settlement with Catron are the only ones we have touched. Nothing, as you see, is settled. I am not over sanguine.

I send love and kisses to you all. ADELBERT

FT. UNION, N.M., *August* 19, 1895

DEAR BLANCHE: I enclose a sketch of the Mora Grant showing by the double line the character of the grant and the relative areas of grazing and timber lands. You must understand that all the land capable of cultivation has been taken and much of the best grazing lands near water have also been taken. I do not consider the timber lands of any present value. Only Mexicans whose labor goes for little can afford to get out timber and that too when they do not have to pay stumpage.

The whole point in the transaction with Catron is we are likely to get as much of what we want, which is grazing lands by a division with him on the 36 parallel, we taking south of it and he north, as if we held on as we are and got some kind of a division in the future. I am clearly of the opinion that if we can now get rid of Catron, we would do a wise thing and in all probability do better than we can possibly some future day.

Of the south east corner of the Grant it can be said that it is poorly watered. But I am told that it is good at all times except the dry season.

Catron's motive for this division is, so I am told and believe, that he hopes and expects to sell a copper mine in the north west corner for a large sum. I hope he may. We cannot look for anything in that direction even if we never divide. By a division we come into possession of our own and may get an income. We may not get our full share by this or any future settlement, but every year diminishes our chances. Love to all,
ADELBERT

CHICAGO, ILL., *August 27*, 1895

DEAR BLANCHE: I do not know that my visit to the Craig Ranch amounted to much. I doubt if it did. It was a hard trip to make, as it was made. I rode over the ranch and back to town, Pueblo, making about sixty miles. I was tired. In a world of cattle there no meat can be had. I propose to straighten myself out again here.

I have just received a letter from Mother who asks me to come to Northfield again on account of business. I shall get there the last of this week. I do not expect to stay more than two or three days.

Doctor Bailey has done some work in the way of a Sanitarium at Ft. Union, but the needed money is not forthcoming. At least he does not indicate how he is to raise it. Schemes, I intend to try another.

Upon my return here from Northfield, I shall look into (as far as I can) the Virginia land business and the better to do it shall go to Grundy, Buchanan County, Va. It is no use to say what I shall attempt. The grand total result will be that I will have the consciousness of having done the best I could. That is supposed to be the highest reward—but it is not always the most satisfactory—especially when success is lacking.

I send you all love and kisses.
ADELBERT

CHICAGO, ILL., *September 2*, 1895

DEAR BLANCHE: I have just come in from Northfield. I find quite a number of schemes on hand which will take time to run through. A new party has been talking to me about the purchase of lands in Virginia. He seems eager to buy. I do not well see how I can neglect to go to Va. and look up the property. This man is the agent of the Union Pacific R.R. and is seeking lands for the people imported by that R.R. He wants some agricultural lands—20,000 acres. Perhaps we can sell him what he wants. I know the Va. lands are spoken of as mineral lands and that the squatters have the best, it may be, of all the agricultural lands. I had better indulge in a little meagre hope of a sale till I go, see and try to harmonize the conflicting interests.

So I don't see how I can get east before the children have to go to school. No doubt you have some preparations to make for them which you can do better in Lowell than Bay View. So I think you had better not stay at Bay View till my return.

Dr. Bailey says he has the money to go on with the Fort Union Sanitarium. I must put that agreement in shape. So, while I am not sanguine it is clearly my duty to continue my efforts as progress seems to have been made.

You must give little Blanche my love and many kisses on her departure to college[1] and tell her I shall take advantage of the first opportunity to pay her a visit at her college. I send you, one and all, much love. ADELBERT

The Wedding of Miss Edith Ames and Mr. C. Brooks Stevens took place at the family home, Belvidere Hill, 333 Andover Street, Lowell, on June 17th, 1896.

LOWELL, *November* 8, 1896

DEAR DEL: The day you left us everything seemed in a turmoil. Each member of the family had plans for as many different directions. Today brings them all back except you. Sarah and Butler returned on the ten o'clock train.

The trip to Manchester proved very satisfactory. Mrs. Clarke telephoned at five o'clock for Butler to pass the night at her house, and has extended the invitation for the other dances. Sarah did not hear the rising bell and missed the early train home so that she did not get back until quarter after ten, barely in time to throw her raiment into a dress suit case and rush for the station to meet Mr. Weld and party for the foot ball game. Butler had a match game of golf at the Country Club. He only reached the house in time to put on his dress suit, leave all of his cast-off apparel on the floor, take with him Sarah's dress suit case and catch the 5:40 train. They met at the Vendome and had a pleasant dinner at the Perkins'. Commodore Perkins amused Sarah very much. He is a great talker. Among other things, he said at the dinner that if I had been willing to marry him his life would have been very different. Even if said as a joke, it could not have pleased Mrs. P. He also told Sarah that he had never met you but

[1] Blanche entered Smith College in September, 1895.

once and that was upon an occasion when you were expected from Washington and I asked him if he did not wish to go to the station with me to meet my Sweetheart. He saw you then and you had a dirty face. Sarah said I can not possibly imagine Father with a dirty face. It is strange how poor my memory is for all such reminiscences.

Adelbert came from Andover and reached here ten minutes before it was time to return to the station. However, as he had been wise enough to get his lunch in Andover, ten minutes was time enough.

Brooks went down to the camp with Del and Jessie. Edith came up to pass the night with me. The hunters were not very successful. Six or eight geese were shot just before they got into camp and some ducks. Del killed a marsh-hen and Jessie brought home some snails and caddises. However, they all had a good time.

The first party, of the series, given by the Lowell young ladies comes off a week from tomorrow and Sarah had planned to ask Miss Perkins to come up for the night, and Harry Cilley. Hilda will entertain a Miss Paterson, daughter of Ex-Governor P. and Sarah is to have a dinner for them just before the dance.

Butler had a call from Arthur Coburn who asked him if he was willing to run as council man. Butler said he would have to consider the question before giving a final answer. He has made out some notes for a smoke talk he expects to give this coming week to four or five hundred of the Militia. So you see the family is full of projects.

Brooks got some ducks and a goose at camp and is to entertain his cousin John Lyles Stevens and wife at dinner tonight, Mr. Bert Norcross and George tomorrow. He thoroughly enjoys his new house.

I am feeling very well and so far could have gone with you without any discomfort. I send you love and good morning.

BLANCHE

LOWELL, MASS., *May* 31, 1897

General AMES, DEAR GRANDFATHER:—DEL: Your telegram of congratulation and love to Edith was pleasant to receive as it seemed to put us in touch with you and also emphasized the fact that this milestone to which I have looked forward with dread had at length been safely passed. Edith was very brave and bore her trial with courage and patience. Poor girl, how one hates to see those one loves suffer. The heavy pain lasted about three hours—Dr. Pillsbury desired to give her a little chloroform towards the last but she did not wish to take it while she had strength to struggle—and her pleasant comfortable condition is her reward. The effect of the drug is to nauseate for some time after the birth of the baby.

Your grandson was born three minutes after one o'clock p.m. and weighed eight pounds and three quarters. He is a perfect, fine, strong baby and while it is impossible to tell at this early stage whom he resembles,—I feel safe in predicting that he will be a fine looking chap. Adelbert, Sarah, and Jessie have all been down to inspect the new comer and pronounce him the cutest thing imaginable.

Adelbert has just gone down to Andover. Decoration Day gave him a little longer visit home. He says the English teacher told him that he had done good work and knew his text books thoroughly, having had ninety-five per cent in his recitations, but that owing to his inability to express himself well he could not recommend him for examinations and advised him to be tutored. The English teacher will tutor him and of course that means he will recommend him. I told Adelbert to begin at once as I was confident that you would advise the same.

Sarah's chicken farm is going finely—she has thirty-three hens, one hundred and sixty chickens and at least four hundred eggs in the incubators.

By Thursday if all goes well, I might be able to leave Edith without any cause for murmurs on her part and would like, if you have decided to prolong your stay there, if you so desire, to join you at the Highlands.

Love from *Grandmother* BLANCHE BUTLER AMES

The Battleship Maine was sunk in the harbor of Havana, Cuba, on February 15th, 1898, and on April 19th, war against Spain was declared by the United States.

LOWELL, MASS., *April* 26, 1898

Hon. GEO. S. BOUTWELL, *Boston, Mass.*

MY DEAR GOVERNOR: Will you write to President McKinley recommending me for appointment as a General, and stating Grant's opinion of me as set forth in your letter to Gov. Wolcott? I see a number of generals are to be appointed. I have no doubt as to my capacity to render service equal to the best named.

As we are at war we should act with vigor. We can land on

Cuba and drive the Spanish army into the cities in short order, —of course capturing them. Moro Castle can be starved out or assaulted—preferably starved out. The Cubans, armed with rifles and artillery as an auxiliary, will make our work simple and speedy.

As you know, I commanded the fighting Division which made two landings on the coast of North Carolina in mid-winter and captured Fort Fisher. I can do a similar thing on the Cuban coast and capture every thing in sight.

President McKinley has wisely and humanely made an ample call for every emergency.

We should take Cuba at once and leave the Fleet at liberty to meet the Spanish squadrons on this or the other side of the Atlantic. *Yours truly,* ADELBERT AMES

LOWELL, MASS., *April* 28, 1898

Hon. GEO. S. BOUTWELL, *Boston, Mass.*

MY DEAR GOVERNOR: Many thanks for your generous letter of recommendation. There are certain elements in the problem before us which you and I give different values to. They are cost, time and Spanish valor. Spain is in the last stages of decay. We are in the early stages of vigorous manhood. Napoleon told his Admiral to count two Spanish warships equal to one of the French. England whipped France. We are the only nation which in modern times ever came out ahead of England in naval warfare.

While you may smile at my "rule of three" demonstration it has not little weight with me. The many fast steam yachts bought by the government are more than an offset to Spanish torpedo boats—I hold, of course, there are many contingencies in a battle by land or sea.

Suppose the Spanish fleet comes to these shores, our fleet could delay action or combat till the coal of the enemy's fleet was exhausted and consequently her ships crippled. As Spain has taken her fleet or rather two of the best ships of her fleet from Havana to Cape de Verde Islands, I am convinced she does not mean to fight on this side of the Atlantic. Had that been her purpose she would have kept those ships here and held a rendezvous for the rest of her ships which would have been dispatched in haste. I agree that a collision of hostile fleets must decide but I do not believe it will be soon or near.

Very truly yours, ADELBERT AMES

WASHINGTON, D.C., *Adjt. Gen. Dept., July* 5, 1898

Brig. Gen. A. AMES, *Lowell, Mass.*

Steamer St. Paul sails from Courtlandt St., N.Y., tomorrow afternoon. Secretary of War directs that if practicable you take that vessel and proceed with it to Santiago de Cuba and there report in person to Maj. Gen. Shafter, for assignment to duty with 5th Army Corps.

S. H. CORBIN, *Adjt. Gen.*

LOWELL, MASS., *July* 6, 1898

DEAR DEL: The morning papers report that Gen. Miles is to go on the St. Paul and that the steamer would sail Thursday. I write, hoping this may be true and have also sent by express some articles that were forgotten in the excitement caused by the receipt of your orders.

Sweetheart, I do not dare to stop to think, except momentarily of where you are going and the work that awaits you. Of course we now know that Butler is to sail from Charleston, but hope he may be in your command when you all reach Santiago.

Impress upon Adelbert the efficacy of a bath every morning even if he has only a cupful of water. Surely it is not needful for me to say a word about the water and yet I must urge you not to drink anything but hot or cold coffee and tea. One of the duties of James should be to keep a supply on hand.

A kiss and all the cautions you can think of for Adelbert. Blanche—in great haste—and much more to say— Goodbye, Dearie.

LOWELL, MASS., *July* 9, 1898

DEAR DEL: My thoughts are always with my three absent loved ones, although I try to keep occupied every moment, and direct all speculations towards the happy possibilities.

Butler wrote us a nice cheery letter from Charleston and said he expected to see you soon as the 8th Ohio belonged to his brigade.

I have been praying that Santiago would capitulate before the arrival of the St. Paul, although I know you are very anxious to be in the fray. It is some consolation that Jimmy is with you as I think he will try to look out for your comfort as well as his own. Enclosed is the report of the Harvard "Exams" which shows his task is not yet accomplished. His best plan now, do doubt, will be to enter the Scientific department and get transferred to the Academic later. He will learn more and develop more quickly in one month with you, in your life than he could in six months at Andover.

Next week we shall probably go to Bay View for a few days. Edith, Brooks and the baby are at Newport for a week. The baby looked rather pale, and a change of air was recommended.

The papers told of Adjutant Ames' presence of mind, as shown in hiring a tug to get the last company of the Sixth on board the steamer, the cheers of thousands of spectators on the wharves, and upon the steamer. Butler must have a pull with the reporters.

Your photographs have come and are very good.—A little stern in expression perhaps, but all the more commanding. Personally I prefer the smile, and a soft light in the eye, but that means more to me than to others.

My love for you, and our two boys—for I feel sure Butler is to be with you, BLANCHE

Extracts from the diary of General Ames.

Left New York dock 7.30 p.m., July 6, 1898 bound to Santiago de Cuba. The U.S.S.S St. Paul is in command of Capt. Sigsbee, Capt. of the Maine when destroyed by the Spaniards in Havana.

8th Ohio Volunteers on board, on way to take part in seige of Santiago de Cuba, also Gen. G. V. Henry.

I go in obedience to orders from Secretary of War to report to Gen. Shafter for assignment to duty with troops engaged in seige. Adelbert goes with me; also, my man, James Everett.

Gen. Henry was a classmate of mine at West Point, my junior in Civil War, but now my senior. He is not a very charitable man. I find he is severe on Miles, Shafter, Lawton and Wheeler who are held responsible apparently by the authorities in Washington for the failure at Santiago de Cuba, failure in the sense that many lives were lost without equivalent gains.

Capt. Sigsbee is most interesting in his accounts of the incidents connected with the destruction of the Maine. He does not give his opinion as to who did the deed, though he has them. He says he told our authorities how the torpedo could be placed "right under our eyes and I not know it." As he has no proof he cannot afford to pass sentence on anyone.

My telegraphic orders direct I report to Shafter for assignment to the 5th Corps, which is Shafter's. Adjutant General Corbin is an old chum, friend and backer of Shafter. So I conclude that Corbin sends me to Shafter to help him out. The 5th Corps is composed of regulars except the 2d Mass. and the Rough Riders. A command in the regulars will be most gratifying to me. The Staff Headquarters will be all arranged and my labor in instruction will be light as compared with what would be necessary with volunteers.

July 10th. We passed the east end of Cuba last night at 12. At six this morning we drew in towards the mouth of Santiago Bay. The first vessel we spoke as we came up was the Vesuvius, then the Texas and Brooklyn. The word we got from the ships is that the garrison at Santiago are talking terms of evacuation. Evidently their situation is getting serious. As we will soon go ashore, I will close my diary and send it with first mail. Adelbert is in our cabin with me and will send his letter with this.

Hd. Qrs. 3d Brigade 1st. Div., 5th Army Corps
FORT SAN JUAN *in front of* SANTIAGO DE CUBA, *July* 11, 1898

DEAR BLANCHE: Yesterday, we, Adelbert and I, landed at Siboney (the nearest landing to Santiago) at about 10 o'clock. We went at once to the telephone office to report to Gen. Shafter. After waiting two hours, I failed to get the telegraph off and was informed by the operator that I might wait there all day without getting a reply. The office was run in a stupid, ignorant, irresponsible way. It was typical of the management of the whole business at Siboney.

This little thing has its counterpart on a gigantic scale in the landing of troops. There is nothing to do it with. Then we have no adequate transporation for food and ammunition to the front. The transportation has not been increased since the troops came in June.

I borrowed a horse and rode out here to Gen. Shafter's Hd. Qrs. in company with one of Gen. Henry's aids. I found Gen. Shafter sitting on a camp stool dressed in hickory shirt and a pair of blue trousers with a pair of dirty suspenders. He is ponderous weighing about 330 pounds. One foot was swathed in a dirty white cloth. His immense abdomen hung down, yes, actually hung down between his legs. The opening or placket of his trousers was forced out at the lowest point, looking as if the cloth has been torn by the weight of said abdomen.

When I said he was looking well, he replied cheerfully that such was the case though he was troubled in his foot by the gout and that it was improving rapidly by virtue of certain pills a surgeon had given him. He was not a pleasing object either in figure or face. His dictation was loose. Strange it is that he seems to find no one to speak well of his management while many condemn it.

He took my telegraphic order, saying he thought I came with troops. After an officer looked over the Commanders of Brigades in this Division, he assigned me to the command of this Brigade. It is composed of three regular regiments, the 9th, 13th and 24th, the last is colored. Love and kisses to you all.

ADELBERT

LOWELL, MASS., *July* 11, 1898

MY DEAR DEL: Brooks has returned from Newport, and brought me a letter from Edith, which I enclose. Adelbert's report from Andover—a very good one by the way—I also send you. Blanche will be home tomorrow, and the house will not be quite so lonely.

Our Relief Entertainment will give us more than two thousand dollars—which is a large sum. Now the city is organized for the Aid Association, and we can get more work done than we can supply materials. I called Ward Nine committee Saturday morning at ten, and this morning—two hundred pillow cases, one hundred and fifty sheets, seventy-one pajamas, fourteen bandages, six shirts have been called for. It has been necessary to ask the ladies to stop asking for workers, as I cannot keep them supplied. My heart is not in the work, and I am tired of seeing so many people. Still it is no doubt a distraction, and serves to fill up the time.

The papers have reported the arrival of the St. Paul and the Yale—and I am sure you and Butler will soon meet. I am full of alarm, because it is said the new troops are to be used to close the road of escape for the Spaniards. That seems a more dangerous position than the fortified lines around the city. We cannot feel easy until Santiago's surrender, and then there will be the dread of the fever.

Adelbert must consider that this letter is for him as well as you and Butler. How I wish I could see you all! To each, I send love and kisses.

BLANCHE

Hd. Qrs. 3d Brig. 1st Div. 5th Corp., July 12, 1898

DEAR BLANCHE: Yesterday there was some firing along the lines till one o'clock when a flag of truce was sent out. The reply to our communication came sealed to Div. Hd. Qrs. The white flag still flies.

Shafter is very reticent, so neither Gen. Wheeler nor Gen. Kent, who have tents side by side, know anything of what is going on. I cannot learn that Shafter has any confidant or that he consults with any one. I have not heard a single officer speak kindly of him. What little is said is just the reverse.

Yesterday we learned that Gen. Miles has come. Any change can be but for the better. No general plan, no system, no method seems to have been followed in the advance to this point. As an illustration of the way things are going, I give this item. Transportation is quite inadequate to supply the troops for which state of affairs there is no excuse. Shafter, who is camped by the road two or three miles from our front, has issued an order or given direction that no team pass his Hd. Qrs. going to the front without his *personal* permission. What inextricable confusion should and does result from such generalship!

General Shafter gave me a horse and orderly. Yesterday I sent the orderly to Siboney for Adelbert. He joins me in love and kisses to you all. ADELBERT

FORT SAN JUAN, *July* 13, 1898

DEAR MOTHER: We are on the side hill about fifty feet from the rifle pits. As the hill is very steep, we are perfectly protected; moreover there has been a truce since day before yesterday which will last until tomorrow noon. Even after that I do not believe there will be much more fighting for the infantry, as our lines run from near the sea way around to the bay back of Santiago, where our lines are very near the city and from where the city could be very easily bombarded. But things are so poorly managed that no one can tell what will happen although we all are hoping and believe that Miles who has arrived will do something.

It is a very beautiful country here. From where we are we look across the field where our regulars charged with such wonderful bravery. I have been told of the incidents of the charge which was made up a hill at the top of which was a large

Spanish force, and all the trees on the hill and also on the plain were full of Spanish sharp-shooters.

The field is covered with the finest, long, green, grass and all sorts of palm trees and other fruit trees. While on the bank of the San Juan are a number of bamboo jungles. Beyond these plains is a fine forest of tropical growth. These woods are full of brightly colored birds, and quail sit on the ramparts in front of the soldiers, who are in the trenches. They are so tame they will remain in a little pond 100 feet across while soldiers bathe in it.

Back of us on the top of the hill are our trenches and beyond them some 400 yards are the Spanish lines.

The only trouble with this country are the creatures that run over the ground. I made a great slaughter in the natives here by killing a scorpion and a centipede, while Captain Sample killed a rattle snake. All of this happened in our tent. I have been very comfortable here.

Although the soldiers are rather hard up for food, Father as he is Brigade Commander, because of his position is fed very well. He was delighted because he had got a good staff and regular troops to command. He seems very happy. The only thing that bothers him is the way things are handled here. We are both very well and I am learning an awful lot. Although I am having to rough it a good deal it is good for me and the pleasure I am getting out of the country makes up for it. Give my love to the rest of the family and take a lot for yourself.

Your loving son, ADELBERT

FORT SAN JUAN, *July* 13, 1898

DEAR BLANCHE: I have just received instructions not to fire on the enemy before 1 o'clock on the 14th inst. and not then without instruction. Gens. Miles, Shafter, and Garcia have just come from between the lines where they have been in communication with the Spanish commander. As we understand it here or as I understand it, the enemy are imitating the Spanish government in its negotiations with Cleveland and McKinley. As the yellow fever is here the Spaniards can depend on an efficient ally. Spanish honor can easily demand the annihilation of its soldiers rather than suffer the disgrace of surrender here. All this will be history before you receive this.

My Brigade is on the line of works with the enemy half a mile in front and beyond him the suburbs of Santiago which is in sight a half a mile further away. Almost immediately after I took command of the Brigade at four o'clock Sunday the truce ended and firing began. Since then a truce has been on most of the time. There has been no firing since Adelbert came up. He is much pleased with his situation. He is very helpful. Lacking transportaton I had to leave Everett at Siboney with all my baggage except my small bag. I have no idea when I can get him. Have I told you that my quarters are only a tent cover and that four of us are in it? Adelbert, Capt. Sample, my Asst. Adjt. Gen. and Lieut. Lawton, my commissary of subsistence. Both are West Pointers. Lieut. Keeler is my Quartermaster also a W.P. Our Aide is Lieut. Simpson a W.P. also. The staff was organized at Tampa and I leave it as it was, to their delight. When Holter comes I will make him an Aide.

Phil Reade[1] was in this forenoon. He is in excellent health and enjoys the situation hugely. He is a most capable gallant and efficient officer. Gen. Kent has recommended him for Brevet which he will surely get—where he will be Lieut. Colonel Reade, or simply Colonel Reade. This will please the Reade family. His mother should be proud of him.

At the late battle here the 71st N.Y. disgraced itself. They blocked the roads and the regulars had to walk over or force their way through them. The material of the 71st like all the vols. is super-excellent. Want of discipline and want of good officers gave results above given. How glad I am that my command is well officered and well instructed.

Adelbert joins me in love to you, Sarah, Blanche, Jessie, Edith and the baby. ADELBERT

FORT SAN JUAN, *July* 14, 1898

DEAR BLANCHE: I have just seen Gen. Kent, Division Comd. who told me that if this city does not surrender today the Secretary of War has ordered an assault. So far as known Miles has not superseded Shafter.

We have had rains by day and night and the condition of affairs is getting worse. The roads are so bad that full rations for the men cannot be had. The Artillery, always used in reducing works, is at the rear. No provisions have been also made to have roads that could be used at all times. The heavy rains raise the streams some eight feet and spread over the bottoms. Though transportation is short, teams and wagons have been lost in the swollen waters.

I have had my Regimental commanders under my tent fly

[1] Phil Reade, a cousin of Mrs. Ames and a Major in the regular army.

for consultation so we may have co-operation in case of assault. They are Lieut. Col. Ewers, 9th Inf., Major Markley, 24th Inf. and Major Auman, 13th Inf. They were in the fight here at the first of the month and look with disfavor on the bald purpose of the Sec. of War. No one has confidence in Shafter and think him possible of any folly. My officers and I agree fully as to the general programme to be followed and the details of formation should we be sent forward. It is very gratifying to me to find one and all seem content to have me here.

Just here I heard a cheer by the soldiers. Everybody wanted to know what it was for. Word came that the enemy had surrendered. I was soon on the parapet. Word was sent along the line that Gen. Wheeler had said the Spaniards had surrendered. This information was not satisfactory to me. I went over to the right of my brigade line behind which Wheeler and Kent have their Hd. Qrs. and learned that Shafter had telephoned Wheeler (in fact Wheeler showed me the message) that the prospects for surrender were very favorable. In the group were all the Generals, Wheeler, Kent, Lawton and Woods of the Rough Riders. We chatted for half an hour when Miles and Shafter rode up. I greeted Miles heartily which he returned. I was glad he is here and he no doubt was glad I was glad. Shafter told Lawton that the chances for surrender were not very favorable. Miles said nothing had been decided. So we are very near the point of interruption on the other page. Miles and Shafter are still between the lines discussing the surrender with the Spanish officers.

1 p.m. I have just received an order from Division Hd. Qrs. to take the troops out of the trenches, put them comfortably into camp and establish a strong line of sentinels with instructions not to permit any one to be beyond the lines. This indicates a surrender of the city. It is certainly a suspension of hostilities for a time at least. As the troops go into camp just behind the trenches we can get into them at short notice.

Today I hear Siboney is quarantined and that the troops of which the 6th Mass. is part will land west of the mouth of Santiago harbor. All my traps are at Siboney. So is Everett. Should they be quarantined my plight will be sad indeed.

3 p.m. July 14, 1898. Word has come that surrender of Santiago is a certainty.

Our next objective will be San Juan. You say everything goes by twos, here is Fort San Juan—the next San Juan, Porto Rico. Adelbert joins me in love to you all. ADELBERT

FORT SAN JUAN, *July* 15, 1898

DEAR BLANCHE: After breakfast Adelbert, Capt. Sample, my Asst. Adj. Gen. and I mounted borrowed horses to ride three or four miles to our right where the city and Bay of Santiago can be looked down upon.

On my way I stopped to chat with Gen. Wheeler. He said he had been up till 1:30 this morning negotiating with the Spaniards as to terms of surrender. They claimed their words had not been rightly interpreted or parts had been omitted. They are very particular about the form rather than substance. They do not want to "surrender" but are willing to "capitulate." They want the honors of the form—though in the end they agree to deportation to Spain. Wheeler said their claims did not differ materially from our demands. He also said they surrendered this whole province, Santiago de Cuba, and 32000 men. And he also said he recommended to our commissioners that I be made Governor General of this Province upon surrender; and that the appointment would make it necessary that I be promoted to Major General. He was very kind in other utterances to the effect that I should have been one of the first M.G.s.

I told him I would take the place if offered. Gen. Lawton who has done so well here wants it. I do not consider my chances of appointment any good—I give you all I know about it. I understand Miles has gone to Porto Rico—that this command may go back to the U.S. The army for Havana (if Spain does not go to pieces before) will be under Lee or somebody else and this army may not be used further. This state of things would leave me out altogether. So a Governor General would be very acceptable. Adelbert joins me in love.

ADELBERT

FORT SAN JUAN, *July* 16, 1898

DEAR BLANCHE: Gen. Kent has just called and reports that Spain has agreed to the surrender of this Province and the 23,000 soldiers in it. I am glad. The situation here, due to Shafter's imbecility, has been uncertain.

Just now word came that the Spaniards were vacating the trenches in front of us. Going to the line of our works, only a few steps, I saw the Spaniards assembled in companies with blue drilling uniforms and straw hats, marching out of sight to the rear. It was a pleasant sight.

Today it looks to me as if there could be no more fighting. We can envelop San Juan and Havana with troops with the certain knowledge that they must surrender. Spain is "going to pieces." Everett and our baggage came yesterday. Love,

ADELBERT

FORT SAN JUAN, *July* 17, 1898

DEAR BLANCHE: At 6 o'clock this morning I received an order to send one of my regiments into the city at 9:30 a.m. and have another receive prisoners of war and to appear with my staff to accompany the Commander in Chief with other Generals into Santiago to receive its surrender at midday.

Butler has not landed. So he has been in no danger. We will proceed in a few minutes to Division and Corps Headquarters to proceed into the city.

Ten minutes past one (such says Adelbert is the time). We have just returned from the formal capitulation of the city and eastern part of the Province of Santiago de Cuba and 24,000 prisoners of war—soldiers of Spain.

At 9:45 a.m. all the general officers of this army with their staffs assembled at Corps Hd. Qrs. We immediately proceeded to a point between our lines in front of mine, where we met the Spanish General, Toral, who with his chiefs, mounted, were drawn up in line. We, the general officers were introduced to the Spaniards after we formed a line with our staffs and cavalry escorts drawn up on the left and rear.

Adelbert was with my staff. Shafter talked with the Spanish General through his interpreter. Lifting of hats were indulged in occasionally. Then Shafter presented the Spanish General with the sword and spurs of their leader who was killed in the early days of the Campaign. They are to be sent to the dead general's family. Soon about 100 Spanish soldiers marched into the field to the right of the Spanish officers. They surrendered formally for the whole force which submits to our arms with trumpets sounding on both sides and hats raised by us; the Spanish officers raising their swords high, points up. It was sad to see them. I refer to the officers. The men seemed indifferent and happy. Then the Spanish soldiers marched by us to our rear a short distance when they stocked their arms and were formally held in a line of the 13th U.S. Infantry, a regiment of my brigade. The Spanish officers withdrew to the city. We soon followed them, Shafter leading, then the generals according to rank; and staff according to rank of their chiefs, followed by a cavalry escort, and still further by the 9th infantry, a regiment of my brigade and a cavalry band. Thus we rode into the city through entrenchments, protected by wire, barrels filled with earth etc. to the governor's palace.

Then we, generals, were introduced to the Mayor of the city, the Archbishop and so forth. There I met for the first time Gen. Costello, the Cuban general. We, generals, were given a lunch of exceptionally good coffee, various wines and cake cut or baked in long slim sticks. The Archbishop came to the governor's palace and again all of us were presented. Gen. Costello, the Cuban leader, showed some feeling in a talk I had with him because Shafter had refused to let the Cubans march into the city, and because the old Spanish officials were left in control.

Facing the governor's palace is a public park, fenced, and across the park the cathedral. Ten minutes before 12 we U.S. officers went into the park, and lined up according to rank with Gen. Shafter at the right, staff officers in rear of their chiefs and the 9th U.S. Inf. drawn up back of us occupying the whole square. A troop of Cavalry was in the street between us and the palace facing it. As the clock on the cathedral struck 12, the stars and stripes slowly hoisted on the flag staff on the palace. We officers, uncovered, the band played "The Star Spangled Banner," the Infantry and Cavalry saluted. It was a most impressive scene.

The streets of the square were occupied by our horses and orderlies. Against the cathedral walls were a crowd of citizens. A cheer was given Gen. Shafter. We all congratulated him a second time.

Two unseemly incidents occurred. A N.Y. Journal man got on the palace roof where the flag was to be raised and insisted on taking photographs. My attention was attracted by Gen. Shafter saying "Won't that man go?" "Throw him off." This was said to the officer about to hoist the flag.

After the beautiful ceremony I have described and we had cheered Shafter, I saw, being within five feet of him, a man's fist in his face and Shafter's also extended towards the man's chest. Instantly those nearer than I pushed the man, almost making him lose his balance. The man was then seized and taken away. Shafter's chin was scratched and showed a streak of blood. It was a pitiable exhibition and checked for a moment the joy of the occasion. I do not know the cause but the newspaper man has made himself notoriously obnoxious to this army. Probably Shafter's "throw him off the roof" was followed by some other like words which were resented. Soon after, we mounted and rode out of the city to our camps. Many Spaniards had marched out and have gone into camp between our lines as our prisoners.

We all are very happy, especially as it seems providential. Not one officer here whom I have met accredits Shafter with any thing more than having a very grand army and—luck. His military management has been most deplorable, hence the delights of this army in this happy issue.

Adelbert joins me in love to you all. ADELBERT

FORT SAN JUAN, *July* 19, 1898

DEAR BLANCHE: This morning early Adelbert and four of my staff officers rode into the city. They expected to do some shopping and get a machete or two. They came back hot and tired with only a looking glass for me. Up to date, since I landed a week ago yesterday, my shaving has been done by the side of a cake of soap and a canteen of water, eyes fixed on the distant hills and fingers groping for the rough places. In the Governor's Palace I saw my face yesterday for the first time in a week. To think I should foresee the need of a looking glass for Butler when informed he was going to the war and then neglect to get one for myself when actually on the way to the front! I am informed he has not been to the wars but is yachting in West Indian waters round about in such a noble ship, as the Yale or Harvard!

Adelbert says he never saw such sorry specimens of humanity as the Santiagoians. They are not of such mixed blood as the Cuban soldiers. They are small, emaciated, colorless, feeble. There is nothing in there of value to our country.

What this army will do is hard to guess. Everything is mismanaged. I have not had a letter since I came. The N.Y. paper of the 6th inst. which I bought, gave latest news we have had here by four days. Officers' mail has just begun to have July letters from home, intersected with the middle of June letters. We are in Egyptian darkness. I am not surprised the Spanish believe Spain has won elsewhere. We cannot believe what we don't hear.

Orders have come to move my Brigade on the hills, over to the R.R. on the north side of the city. It will probably be a better place than this which is the one taken on the day of battle and too, is right on the line of trenches.

I now have a mess of eight including Adelbert and myself.

For the first time we have kettles etc. for cooking and a mess kit. We are made.

Adelbert joins me in love for you all. ADELBERT

LOWELL, MASS., *July* 20, 1898

DEAR DEL: The first word from you since you sailed came this morning, and we rejoice in your diary and Adelbert's letter, as they seem to put us once more in touch with you, even though ten days have elapsed since they were written.

The papers this morning state that Gen'l. Henry is to go to Porto Rico, and this suggests to us the possibility that you may also take part in the movement—but it is useless to speculate.

Your name was given in the list of those who were present at the ceremonies of the surrender. The statement is the only news we have had of you until this morning, and the time seems very long.

Even if Adelbert does not get home in time for college this fall I do not know that it will matter much. He is young in years, and young for his years, as are all the family, and his present experience and contact with older men will be of benefit, beyond anything text books could give.

Yesterday your daughters, Sarah and Blanche, had a most fortunate escape. They were in the small—Paul's—buggy, driving the colt, and had stopped in a wooded road beyond Hood's farm to look at a prize hog which weighed a thousand pounds. As the man in charge prodded it up out of the mud, the creature gave a grunt, the colt made an upward spring in fright, broke the whiffle-tree and dashed through the crooked road, rough with mud holes and stumps. Blanche added her strength to Sarah's in the effort to check him, but the breeching and belly-band gave way, and they pulled the carriage up on the horse's haunches, which made him kick and jump from side to side in his fright, and when they let up on the reins the shafts rose and fell on his back and by his head, striking him as they came down. They guided him, however, safely around the numerous curves, and had almost reached the highway, going sometimes on two side wheels, and then on the other two, when the carriage struck a tree.

Sarah pitched out head first and must have kept hold of the reins, for a moment or so, as she landed on a manure pile far ahead of the carriage. Blanche, who had her feet firmly braced against the dash board went over with the buggy. The horse kept on out of sight. Each girl picked herself up, Sarah covered with mud, her muslin waist all torn in tatters, bruises on her abdomen, back and legs, but all slight injuries. Blanche bruised an elbow, and dizzy with the sudden snap given her head when the carriage stopped. The way it must have snapped was shown by the hat, which flew off of her head and was picked up in advance of Sarah, and all the pins were out of her hair. Sarah said "Are you hurt Blanche?," and Blanche said "No, are you hurt?" Then both sat down on the roadside and were amused to see one whole wheel of the buggy spin around while the rest of it was completely wrecked. The rubber tires alone can be used again—there is not enough of the carriage left to be mended.

The men from the piggery came running down the road, expecting to see the girls injured seriously, but were greeted with smiles and the statement "no harm done." Julian Hood, who drove the girls home, called this morning to inquire after their injuries, and among other things remarked that they were the bravest folks he ever saw. Thus, you see, it is not necessary to go fighting Spaniards to find danger. We live in the midst of it, although not in the midst of alarms.

Edith and the boy are still at Jamestown, but will return next week. The baby is having a hard time with his teeth, and they make him fret, but he is very well considering. With love for our dear ones from all, BLANCHE

Hd. Qrs. 3rd Brig. 1st Div. 5th Corps.
Before SANTIAGO DE CUBA, *July* 21, 1898

DEAR BLANCHE: This is the 21st of July. Perhaps you remember the day.

The excitement of the situation here has passed away. Nothing can be done but wait for the coming of the transports to take us and the Spanish prisoners away. It does not seem possible that there can be any serious fighting at San Juan, Porto Rico, or at Havana.

We are to change camp again going back from the city a mile or more, to the foot hills to clean grounds and handy water. Really this Division is quite unfit for further campaigning, Gen. Kent has so reported to Shafter. Many men are sick, many others are ailing, while comparatively few are in first class condition. The one universal complaint is the slow fever, not yellow fever, also cases of bowel complaint. Of course, the climate is the main cause for it but the troops have been deprived of so many necessities and exposed to the sun and rain so needlessly that they have been broken down before their time.

Such universal condemnation of a commander I never heard before, never, probably, was it more justified. Shafter was sick on his cot at the time of the fight, was not under fire, knew nothing of the battle field by personal observation and is entitled to no more credit than a leader who has not led. The fight was July 1. I arrived July 10. The day of my arrival was the first time Shafter was at the front, so says Gen. Kent. I dwell on the situation, because there is nothing else to think of. No letters, no papers, no news of any kind from the outside world, absolutely nothing. Whether Miles has gone to Porto Rico or somebody else to Havana—or any one of ten thousand things has happened, no whisper of it comes to us.

Adelbert suggests that he is a little anxious about his examinations. If we do not get some satisfactory word about them I will send him home the first opportunity. He says his thoughts are entirely changed from what they were two weeks ago. This has been very absorbing work for all. He does not seem to care for the life he sees about him. I mean to say the officers existence has no attractions for him.

I do not see (we are blind-folded here) why we should be kept here more than a week or ten days longer. Adelbert says "Give them my love and say I will probably see them pretty soon."

Love, ADELBERT

Near SANTIAGO, CUBA, *July* 22, 1898

DEAR BLANCHE: Three days ago Adelbert had a turn of looseness of bowels but was doctored up at once. He and I decided that the U.S. would be a good place for him. Upon inquiry yesterday, I learned that a number of ships would leave today. I turned in every direction for passage and authority for him to leave. It seems the special privilege and pleasure of Army Quartermasters and Ship Captains to refuse all favors. So I sent an orderly with a note to Lieut. Gilmore and received the enclosed reply.

July 21

MY DEAR GENERAL AMES. Gen. Shafter has no control over the State of Texas. The other day he asked Miss Barton's permission to put a wounded officer on board and she informed him that no one would be allowed to go on board for fear of yellow fever. However, there are three of our ships leaving for the U.S. tomorrow morning and the General says you may send Adelbert back on any one. They are the Concho, Leona, and Rio Grande. The Concho is the best ship.

Very sincerely, J. C. GILMORE

This morning Adelbert's trunk and bag were put in a huge wagon going to Santiago for rations and he and Lieut. Lawton, my Commissary, mounted on horses, rode down the hill around the spur out of sight.

About noon, Lieut. Lawton came back and reported that Adelbert was on board the Concho, one of the largest and fastest of the steamships of the New York and Havana lines; that she would leave in a few hours for Fortress Monroe with wounded soldiers. With such passengers, they will be very careful not to get infected with the yellow fever. Sometime next Tuesday, the 26th inst. you should hear of his arrival at Fortress Monroe—and see him the next day.

We are doing nothing but wait—wait, I suppose for the coming of the ships for the Spanish prisoners. They seem perfectly happy. Plenty to eat and Spain but a few days away. Our army would be glad if they had plenty to eat and the U.S. a few days away. As the fighting is over and the sickness so general that no military operations are possible at present, the U.S. seems the natural sanitarium.

The 34th Michigan Vols. is under my command. Its officers are friends of Sec. of War Alger. They feel near the throne. Its surgeon says he is from near Gen. Shafter's home. Shafter is a Michigan man. Hence his power with Alger. Now this Surgeon has just asked my permission to go to see Shafter to ask that his sick men may be taken to the ocean shore or put on shipboard and sent north. As I have been preaching this very thing to the Michigan Surgeon and Colonel, I feel gratified and hope good may result. I miss Adelbert. You will see him before you do this. No word of Butler. Love to all.

ADELBERT

Extract from the New York Herald, July 22, 1898

Mrs. Ames goes to Cuba. Will Sail to Her Husband and Sons in the Yacht America.

Boston, Thursday.—Mrs. Ames, wife of General Adelbert Ames, now at the front with his two sons, proposes to charter the yacht America for a summer cruise and will sail to the West

Indies to visit them. This schooner was owned by the late General Benjamin F. Butler, father of Mrs. Ames, and achieved an international reputation in the early fifties, when it defeated the crack yachts of England.

Paul Butler, a son of General Butler, owns the America, which has been out of commission for several years at the Chelsea Drawbridge. She is 85 tons net, 96 feet long, 22 feet 7 inches beam, 9 feet deep, and was built in New York in 1849. She will be able to sail for Cuba in about four weeks. There will be a crew of twelve men. The America will sail direct for some port in the West Indies, and after learning where General Ames and his sons are located will proceed to them at once. It is understood that the America will be fitted out with stores and provisions to remain in West Indian waters until spring.

Near SANTIAGO DE CUBA, *July* 23, 1898

DEAR BLANCHE: Yesterday word came from the Sec. of War that in eight days 8000 Spanish prisoners would be shipped home. I think this will take about all of those who will want to leave the island. There may be two or three thousand more but they probably are volunteers, residents of the island. When these prisoners are on ship-board our army will have no further duty here, that I can conceive of. Yet, Shafter says he will then withdraw the army to the hills! It is in perfect harmony with everything he has done from the beginning.

More than 35 pr. cent of my command is on the sick lists and a few if any of the men are in first class condition. We could not march five miles without disorganizing. A colder climate is needed as our condition is wholly due to this hot and wet one. Why Shafter proposes such a thing I cannot understand on any other basis than that Caesar at the head of any army out of Rome is quite a different individual from Caesar in Rome subject to higher authority.

This is a peculiar sort of waiting. We cannot do anything here and know others will be taken to do things elsewhere—if anything is to be done. I am glad Adelbert is on his way home. To you all I send love. ADELBERT

Before SANTIAGO DE CUBA, *July* 26, 1898

DEAR BLANCHE: Your letter of the 9th inst. was received last evening—the only word I have had from the U.S. I feel very sorry for Adelbert. It no doubt carries a lesson which he must need, though I would gladly have saved him from it.

He is a brave boy and will buckle down to his work and win.

I have not been able, while here, to get in touch with Butler. —I have not been able to even learn his whereabouts. This whole business is a miserable blunder. The primary trouble comes first from the President's course in acting on political lines, and second, from either favoritism of Miles & Co. or their incapacity to select the capable from the incapable. Between the President and Miles is the Secretary of War. How far he is a factor of evil it is hard for me to say. He, certainly, is no Stanton. Our rations are excellent now and my health was never better. Love to all. ADELBERT

LOWELL, MASS., *July* 28, 1898

DEAR DEL: We are happy tonight because we have just heard from you and Del, and know that you are both well.

Now I feel that we can have telegraphic communication at least. Just after hearing from you I was again called to the telephone and received a telegram from Adelbert at Fortress Monroe.

He is in quarantine there, and does not know how long he will have to remain, but says he is well.

Some of the men who came on the Seneca have reached Lowell. They were not detained more than five days. One of them, named McNamara spoke in great praise of Butler, said that he was the life of the regiment, and related two or three anecdotes to illustrate it. These were published in the Lowell and Boston papers under the heading "Praise for Ames." In a speech made by Hoar at Worcester a short time ago, in which he showed that our soldiers were actuated by a sense of duty, without mentioning your name, he spoke of the soldier who had been a Major General in the Civil War and whose distinguished services entitled him to that rank, as having accepted a Brigadier Generalship, saying that want of rank was no bar to duty.

But to come back to my news from Adelbert. Of course I am more than delighted to have him safely home, but the fact that you are left there alone to face the fever is a nightmare.

Nothing has happened since I wrote you last, of any importance. Edith, Sarah, Ames and Brooks came back Tuesday. Yesterday I saw baby Ames for the first time for about three weeks. He is very brown and looks finely, and puts on numerous little airs. Edith has gained six pounds and is very glad to get home. All your home folks are well. Jessie is now in the billiard-room with John Rogers and Jimmy Abbott. They are playing billiards. Sarah is in the front parlor entertaining Fordyce Coburn. Blanche and Paul are in the library, while I occupy your seat at the table in the back parlor.

Austin Van Greson, a lawyer, has written you to ask your price and terms for the place at the Highlands. At first I thought of sending the letter to you, but have decided to write him that the price for the lower cottage, etc. is eighteen thousand. This will do for an answer until your return, will it not?

Now, Dearie, having given you all the items I can think of that might prove of interest, I will whisper in your ear that the days are slow and lonesome. It seems months instead of weeks since you left. This absence is very different from your Western trips. There is no limit set to the time you are to be away, and the uncertainties and dangers, together with the slow postal conditions, are more than sufficient to make one restless and anxious. I try to keep busy all the waking hours, and have many projects and interests to claim attention, but in spite of all efforts, the condition is one of waiting and watching. If you are happy in the thought that you are doing your duty, and have no regrets, I must be content and make no complaints. I send you love. Good night. BLANCHE

Before SANTIAGO, CUBA, *July* 30, 1898

DEAR BLANCHE: Yesterday Gen. Shafter sent a circular letter to this army saying that "It would be sent to Long Island as soon as the fever *lets up*."

As it happens, yesterday, the sick list of this Division was 29% of its number, a greater percentage than at any previous time. Whether the fever will "let up" while we are here in the sun and rain is the question. The fever would be compelled to "let up" should these sick men be at once put on transports for the North. However, the transports for the Spaniards have not come and according to the programme we can not go till they do.

I had a great treat this morning in a copy of the N.Y. Sun of the 23d inst.—news only a week old. There I learned that Butler has been in my vicinity all this time—at Guantanamo. So imbecile has been the means of communication and the ignorance of the whereabouts of anybody else than self that my letter to Butler has been returned to me. The 6th Mass. and the 6th Ill. are the nucleus of Miles' Army of Porto Rico.

As the war is at an end here, and as I was anxious about Butler, I cabled to Asst. Sec. of the Navy, Allen, day before yesterday, to ask him to get me ordered to Miles' command.

I have received no reply. Yesterday, or the day before, after my telegram, word came that Spain seeks peace. Apparently I shall go North with the command and Butler will not get under fire. We ought to relinquish the Philippines reserving a coaling station from Cuba and take Porto Rico as indemnity. This Spain will accede to, I believe. I make this memorandum as a record.

If Shafter has a friend I have not heard of him. His want of tact is shown in his treatment of Gen. Garcia. The evils of his errors will never be forgotten or forgiven by this army.

Well, we growl and growl, yet there is much complacency on all sides. Love,
ADELBERT

LOWELL, MASS., *July* 31, 1898

DEAR DEL: This has been a happy day. I ran over the Sunday papers in which there were very good pictures of you and Butler taken from your latest photographs and entitled "A Massachusetts Father and Son both serving in the War," and then wrote a long letter to Butler. Just before lunch Paul came in and handed me a package of letters saying: "I heard some soldiers' letters had reached town and thought I would go to the Post Office."

You can imagine that I was delighted for it seemed an age since your last letter came. The latest date of those that came today was July 7. Your letters and Adelbert's seem to have cleared away the mists and gloom that have hitherto hung over all my imaginings.

Just before dinner a telegram came from Adelbert. He is in quarantine in New York and will be home in a day or two. This news was all that was needed to complete my content. Since I read that his steamer "The Concho" had been ordered to sea, from Fortress Monroe, to bury the dead and that malignant typhoid had developed on board I have felt much concern, but the telegram stated that he was well, and now this is the most contented household we have had since you left.

Of course the news will have reached you long before this letter can, that Miles' Army made a landing, the 6th took part in a brisk skirmish in which four of its men were wounded. Ponce surrendered upon the appearance of our gun boats and the inhabitants received our troops with acclamations. As the climate of Porto Rico is delightful and no fever is to be dreaded, Butler could not be in a better place.

We are wondering why you sent Adelbert home unless it was from fear of the fever, reason enough certainly but it was a little comforting to think that he was with you and you were with him. Now you have a staff to be sure and Everett, but that is not quite the same thing. His college work, on account of his age, does not seem to me very important, yet it may seem so to you and to him. Adelbert like all our children is young for his age and one more year would cause him to take a better stand among his fellows. However, in a day or two I shall know his mind and through him, yours.

You speak in your letters, Dearie, of the suggestion that you were to be made Governor of the Province of Santiago. I wish it might be, since you desire it, but Porto Rico would be better. There you would find fewer complications and a better climate. When are you going to send for me to join you? I think it is about time unless you are to be ordered away. Of course, you realize that I must be with you sooner or later.

The children join in love and kisses. BLANCHE

August 1, 1898

DEAR DEL: This morning at seven I was called to the telephone to talk to Adelbert in Boston. He said he would be home on the 8:30 train; that the fever he had on the steamer altho' pronounced by the doctor yellow fever, was not, but that for five days he had nothing but water and the fever left him day before yesterday. He reached home at half past eight and altho' I expected to see a change in him I was not prepared for what I found. He is very much wasted and very weak, but the fever has gone and we will soon bring back luster to his eyes and color to his lips.

He has told us some of the incidents of your life and his and but for this unfortunate fever would have had an agreeable experience. He had to hold his own against the doctors on the steamer who insisted upon putting a Major who was very sick with typhoid fever into his stateroom. He fought them saying that Gen. Ames was his father and he insisted upon being treated with some consideration, but the second day they renewed the attack and brought the Major to his door, upon which Del said he would go out if the man was brought in. This he did and found a place through the kindness of the head nurse who caused two of her nurses to occupy one stateroom and give the other to him.

He is very glad to be at home but cannot think over his experience on the steamer without having his eyes fill with tears. This is due to weakness; in a few days everything will look very different. He thinks he caught the fever before starting as he did not feel quite well for several days prior to sailing.

We are happy to know that you have gone to the hills but in spite of that I feel misgivings lest you have malarial fever. Dearie, take the greatest care. For pity's sake run no risks.

BLANCHE

Before SANTIAGO, CUBA, *August* 1, 1898

DEAR BLANCHE: Yesterday at 3 o'clock we, officers of this army, went to the Governor's Palace in Santiago to organize "The Society of the American Army at Santiago de Cuba"—after the methods of the Loyal Legion. A committee of six was appointed to draw up a programme for organization of which I was one. As I was not in the fight which was on the 1st July and only in two days of the bombardment, I felt that I was half intruder, where honors were going. I said as much and asked to be excused. The assembled officers voted to refuse my request—which certainly was very kind of them. Our committee is expected to have its plan of organization ready by next Sunday.

At the meeting Gen. Wheeler said that the campaign was the most severe that any American army had ever endured! A critic might say it was brief—June 24 to July 17th—and also that the hardships complained of were wholly due to want of fore-thought on the part of the Commanding General or incompetency on the part of all the heads of the various departments. This was not said but it was thought by one certainly and many more probably of those who heard the statement.

General Shafter was inclined to adopt a regal style. After we had organized and appointed our committee, it was voted to notify him of what had been done and request his presence. He came and made some remarks, the chief of which was that the magnitude of our victory was not just apparent—that it ended the War in Cuba. I would say I think it has—but that is due more to the victories of our navy than to ours. It is the two combined which produces such desirable results. The General also said that his was the largest military force that ever left the U.S. Here, too, he was in error. Gen. Scott had, of troops he took into Mexico, at the end of the War, 32,000 men. He discharged 4,000 volunteers, which with losses in battles amounted to 37,000 men. Shafter has about 17,000 men! Well, well, why look a gift horse in the mouth.

This afternoon I rode over to call on Gen. Wheeler. My Division Commander and West Point classmate, Gen. Kent has been slighted by Shafter. Spite and favoritism has had full sway here. In the fighting of July 1st, the battle, Shafter was sick on his cot and Wheeler had command of the line. He told me this morning that Gen. Lawton, Shafter's favorite and recipient of chief honors, was held all day by 460 men at El Caney though Gen. Lawton had some 6,000 men. El Caney is a small contracted village on the hill side having a small brick fort on a hill close at hand. Lawton had a battery of artillery. As he was held so long Shafter sent him word to withdraw. This Lawton would not do. He charged the place and captured it with, relative to the enemy, a large loss.

The wise thing to have done was to have enveloped it with a part of his force and advanced with the rest. The area of ground held by the Spaniards was not more than the hill above your house where the reservoir is. Lawton did not get up on the main line of the rest of the command till the next day. Shafter never saw the field of operations till after it was taken. I hear Miles has taken Porto Rico without opposition.

Love and kisses. ADELBERT

LOWELL, MASS., *August* 3, 1898

DEAR DEL: We are sitting in our room, by "we" I mean Del and myself, by "our room" I mean yours and mine. Del is in the large arm chair facing the window, watching the workmen on the avenue who are using the stone from Andover street for macadam.

He is better each day but can not stand long at a time, only a moment or two, on account of weakness.

I do not remember that I wrote you about Del's trip. His head ached so Sunday and Monday morning he could not get up. Dr. Lesser found his pulse was 105 and told him he had yellow fever. Del had heard Dr. Calhoun talk of yellow fever and did not think that his symptoms were right for that disease. Still he felt that he might die, but could not think very clearly of anything on account of the fever. For five days he had only water, nothing to eat, which was fortunate as the only food on board was beans and hard tack. The doctor or nurses gave him camphor and sulphur from time to time, and the steward took care of the stateroom. When he left it, upon the arrival of the sick officer and went into the nurses' stateroom—there was no pillow and the steward finally called the chief steward when Del protested and brought him one of the sailors' pillows and a blanket—later on a nurse found a sheet for him. The pillow and blanket were foul smelling and the water was not only foul smelling but foul tasting. Del says that he did not mind either very much, when his mouth became parched with fever.

I enclose some newspaper slips that will tell you all about the steamer etc. When it reached New York, the port doctor told Adelbert after he had been disinfected by a bath and his clothes had been steamed, that he might leave the ship. Dr. Lesser, who had doctored him on the steamer, said he must go to the hotel and he would call and see him in the morning. It was nine when he left the steamer, eleven when he reached the city, five minutes of twelve when he arrived at Forty-second street station. There he had a swallow of tea and a piece of toast, and a berth on the night train. Poor old man, the tears rolled out of his eyes when he reached home. Sarah, Blanche, and Jessie had wet eyes also, even Paul looked away after the first glance and straightened his lips. The lad was so weak and his face so pathetic. He has lost just twenty-five pounds since he went away.

I am quite content about him. He is gaining and all right but I am fearful lest you have been suffering as you have had the same exposure. You are liable to the same trouble and I can not bear to think of you in Del's condition so far away from us all.

Delbert says that he would not have missed his trip with you and all the experience he has had for anything. So we must have no regrets. He sends love to you and wants to know why Shafter recommended the Concho when two other boats went up without any sick on them. Love, BLANCHE

SANTIAGO, CUBA, *August* 3, 1898

First part of letter omitted.

Since I began this letter I was notified that Gen. Shafter wanted to see his General officers at 10 a.m. At that time all were there but two who are sick and also the chief medical officers. All the Surgeons and some of the Generals talked and Roosevelt and I made speeches. I said if I had authority I would ship my sick on board the transport now in port today—tomorrow and send them home, etc. etc.

I need not say more on this subject here for the spirit of our work has gone North today by the Associated Press dispatches and that, too, by Shafter's consent as he is now realizing the danger before us. He told us he would remove the censorship on any cablegrams to our friends on this subject we would send. So you will know all this and more too tomorrow.

It would seem Butler is in Porto Rico before the enemy. I send you all love. ADELBERT

LOWELL, MASS., *August* 4, 1898

DEAR DEL: Still another morning and Adelbert and I are in our room. He enjoys looking out at the workmen and as he is much improved and inclined to chat, we have had a cosy time.

I enclose a cut from the day's paper containing startling news from the 6th Mass. What can be the trouble with the officers? Is Henry at his old trick of breaking Colonels? What part has Butler to take? Truly there seems to be no end of surprises—they come fast and furious.

We hear that the cavalry and Rough Riders are to be sent north to Montauk Pt. We were in hopes that you might be coming with the regulars but there is no rumor of that at present.

Great indignation has been expressed everywhere over the condition of the Alamo, Concho, and other steamers that have brought back our sick and wounded soldiers. The papers have been full of the subject and a reporter came up yesterday and another this morning to interview Adelbert. He does not wish to talk and it is not well that he should, on your account.

The Surgeon General, Alger, everybody is disclaiming the responsibility for such a condition of affairs. The result is that more care will be taken in the future.

Del has gained two pounds, and sends his love in which Sarah and Jessie join. There is only a kiss to you from

BLANCHE

LOWELL, MASS., *August* 5, 1898

DEAR DEL: Yesterday when we learned that Shafter's army was to come to Montauk Pt. it seemed possible that we might see you in a couple of weeks. This morning a list of those regiments to be sent at once is given, and the thirty-fourth Michigan is last. No mention is made of the regulars, which means I fear that they can not come until the Spaniards are shipped which may be weeks hence.

The round-robin signed by the officers of the 5th Corps made a profound impression. The whole country is moved and the Secretary of War must move in self defense. Enclosed are some clippings which may reach you in a letter before the newspapers are sent. There are also items about the 6th Mass. Your telegram to Allen was published far and wide. Were you not afraid of the Secretary of War? I hardly know what to expect next. Events are following each other fast and furious.

All the family, except Adelbert, Paul and myself, went to Bay View. Miss Wood, Blanche, Sarah and Jessie will stay over Sunday. Edith and the baby will remain until week after next, perhaps longer. The baby does not sleep well and is broken out with a summer rash. Sarah took twenty-five pounds of honey from the bees yesterday. Del watched and directed operations from the windows. He was not strong enough to lift the super, but enjoyed the sight of the product of his bee farm.

I write without filling any of my letters with expressions of concern in regard to your health and contentment, yet the constant current of thought is in that one direction, no matter how many obstructions oppose it. Love from

DELBERT and BLANCHE

Before SANTIAGO, CUBA, *August* 6, 1898

DEAR BLANCHE: By enclosed clipping from the N.Y. Herald, I see you will sail on the yacht "America" about the 22d of this month. If the War Department has any life in it we should be located in some salubrious part of New England by that time.

Butler will be at San Juan, beseiging or possessing it, at that time. Porto Rico is reported as being a healthy locality—wholly unlike this.

It seems our report of Shafter has had good results. He has received orders to take this army to the U.S. at once. His capacity to effect results is not great, so, like everything else he attempts, our going will be slow. I hope all of us will be off by the 20th inst. Today an order came from Shafter to leave all tents standing and for the men to burn their old clothing and bedding that any infectious disease may not be taken along. The simple order to go and any detailed instructions relative to it are very cheering to the men.

Of late I have been hearing some startling facts about Shafter's generalship. After the battles of the 1st of July, he called together his generals and they decided to withdraw. Among the reasons was one—the bad condition of the roads and swollen streams! No resources, no attempt to utilize material on hand to overcome difficulties! The next day, however, it did not rain, the streams subsided at once, this basin in the hills being flushed. So they held on. The Spaniards were demoralized by the loss of El Caney and Fort San Juan which they thought could not be taken. They were cowed by our fighting and soon gave up. Suppose we had withdrawn with Shafter's statement that he had done all he could! Our country would have been humiliated and a thousand other consequences would have followed. Luck, pure and simple (so far as Shafter is concerned) has made a great man of him and the shingles on the house where he lived in Indiana are selling a dollar apiece, so say the papers. Facts are facts.

Love to all. ADELBERT

Headquarters, 1st Division 5th Army Corps
Near SANTIAGO DE CUBA, *August* 7, 1898

Special Orders No. 17, Extract:

1. Brigadier General Adelbert Ames and staff and the 6th and 13th regiments United States Infantry, each regiment accompanied by a medical officer and the detachment of Hospital Corps men now on duty with them will proceed to Santiago this date and embark on board transport for transfer to the United States.

The sick whom the surgeon designates to remain behind will be left in camp under care of a medical officer.

By command of MAJOR GENERAL KENT
A. C. SHARPE, *Asst. Adjutant General*

LOWELL, MASS., *August* 9, 1898

DEAR MRS. AMES: These are the last letters I have had from Del and were written three weeks ago almost. Since then Adelbert has come home. When he left his father was well and happy. Adelbert is improving every day but is still very weak. A week or two more will do wonders for him.

Butler as you will see by the enclosed slips has been made Lieutenant Colonel of the 6th Mass. This will be a great pleasure to his father. Indeed we have every reason to be very proud of your grandson—he is a good man as well as a capable man. Adelbert will follow in his footsteps.

Edith and the baby are at Bay View for a week or two. When Adelbert is strong enough we will spend a short time before going on the yacht to join General Ames who I hope will be ordered to Montauk Point, Long Island. It seems now as if we might soon have peace, but the army will not be disbanded for sometime after peace is proclaimed.

Give my love to Fanny and tell her I heard that Prof. Churchill spoke of her as the most beautiful and capable girl that had ever been in Andover. So you see she is not forgotten. The children send love to you in which I join. BLANCHE

LOWELL, MASS., *August* 10, 1898

DEAR DEL: This noon I saw the account of the "Embarkation of General Ames and staff on the Vigilencier" and have felt happy ever since although Adelbert's fever has held him again today—this is the third day—I did not like to shoulder the responsibility alone any longer and called in Dr. Irish—Pillsbury is away. Of course he ordered quinine, in larger doses, however, than I had given him and a gargle for his sore throat. Tonight his throat is not painful and his temperature is only 102. I think he will sleep better and cool off still more. Probably this fever will last five days just as the first attack did on the steamer and then he will have another ten days or so in which to pick up.

What a shame that you should have been kept so long in that pestiferous hole! Three letters came in today's mail from you, the latest dated July 30th. In them you speak of the universal sickness. How fortunate you were to have escaped up to that time. I hope your good luck has not deserted you and will not.

I have written you all about Butler and his promotion and sent you various newspaper clippings. Let me again congratulate the father of Lieut. Colonel Ames. You bewail the idea that on account of the prospect of peace Butler will see no fighting. You will know by the time this reaches you that he is away to the front and exposed to we know not what dangers. I pray the Spaniards may retreat after their usual fashion in Porto Rico.

The moment you reach Montauk we want you to telegraph for us to join you. If Adelbert is well you will see us in short order unless you are allowed to come home, which would be better by far, but Del says he does not think you could get away from camp or that you would ask for a furlough.

Adelbert who can not write himself wishes me to give you a loving word of welcome from him. I join, Sweetheart, in his greeting. BLANCHE

LOWELL, MASS., *August* 12, 1898

DEAR DEL: As the Vigilencia is due at Montauk Pt. in my mind I locate you this evening opposite to the South of New Jersey. You will have been in camp a day when this reaches you and I hope you will find better arrangements for your comfort than the newspapers promise. If not the transports will be preferable to the land.

Let us know at once how you are and if you will be obliged to stay there. Perhaps the government will follow the Cuban general Garcia's lead and give the troops a leave of thirty days, and you can come home.

Adelbert has been free from the fever today and will not I think be troubled until another two weeks have passed. Night before last I was somewhat unnerved, the fever was so high and he was a little light-headed. When we walked him up and down the hall to wake him up; his slight weak figure brought Bennie back so forcibly it was very painful.

You need have no uneasiness about him however. In spite of this relapse, his eye is brighter and he is stronger than when he came home. You will see him before long looking himself again.

Good words come from all sides for Butler. I enclose cuttings from the morning papers. He has done well.

It would seem that peace is in sight. The papers say it is here. I shall not so consider it until the Spanish Cortez has ratified M. Cambon's agreement in the protocol.

Sarah and Blanche will go to Bay View tomorrow for Sunday. They would not have left me if Adelbert had not been better. I send you love and kisses of welcome. BLANCHE

On board Steamship VIGILENCIA, *100 miles south of*
MONTAUK POINT, L.I., *August* 13, 1898

DEAR BLANCHE: As I shall telegraph you tonight when we get ashore this brief script will go for but little.

We sailed from Santiago last Monday. We have been on board with the 6th & 13th Infantry, regulars. We go, as will the whole army, to camp at Montauk Point and recuperate for a fall campaign against Havana—perhaps. This army is a sick one and we on this ship feel that we have been particularly fortunate in getting away so early. My health now is good. I felt a little wilted by the hot sun the last few days at Santiago but am all right now.

Your letter of the 18th of July was the last word I received—

almost a whole month ago. I do not know whether Adelbert reached home safely—I have had no communication of any kind from Butler. In fact, I do not know whether he has gone to Porto Rico or not though I suppose he has.

We have no yellow or other contagious disease on board this ship. All the men are getting better. The general sickness and the depression that went with it were remarkable. Gen. Shafter can be held and is held mainly responsible for it. I am glad to get out from under him, even for a few days.

Love and kisses to all. ADELBERT

LOWELL, MASS., *August* 14, 1898

DEAR DEL: Adelbert and I have just strolled down to Edith's house and back. He puts his hand and leans his weight on my shoulder and walks slowly. Still it is an improvement that he can go out at all. The fever seems to have gone entirely but he still has night sweats and bad dreams so that I sleep by him. Last night I woke him up as he was talking and moaning. I think I told you he thinks he will go out of the window, the other night he asked me to hold him and not let him go out, altho' we were walking up and down the upper hall at the time. That however, was unusual but he does not care to be alone at night. By the end of the week he will be all ready to greet you in fair condition.

Since his return I have been away from the house, or I should say from him, only once, to attend a meeting of the Volunteer Aid Association. Labor in that direction can be suspended for a while at least. Woolen pajamas will be more acceptable to the men at Montauk, than the thin cotton we have been making.

Every word that comes from Porto Rico is expressive of delight in the island and the reception of the inhabitants. Butler has been very fortunate. If he should be in garrison there this winter, how would you like to go and see him on the "America?" That is in case you are not on duty elsewhere. I suppose we must now expect a disbandment of the troops. For personal reasons you will regret it, although glad for the country's sake that we are to have peace. A trip to the West Indies again might ease the change from war to domesticity.

The summer has been a long series of excitements and uncertainties. One has a vague notion that the sky has been blue and that the flowers have bloomed but all is like a feverish dream, most unsatisfactory.

Everything seems to be going on quietly at the Highlands.

Del sends his love. You do not need to be told what goes to you with all the passing moments from BLANCHE

Camp Wikoff, MONTAUK POINT, L.I., *August* 15, 1898

DEAR BLANCHE: I rejoice beyond expression at Butler's success. I have had an intuition from the beginning that something would happen to the field officers of his regiment. Today when your letters came was the first intimation I have had of his promotion.

The war is over and your non-combatant son seems to be the only sufferer from it. I quite agree with Adelbert that I know something about war. The regulars under me are constantly rejoicing that they have me as Commander. I know that my old status of Civil War times has not been changed as to the Generals of this War. Deference, respect, recognized superiority are all gratifying to a soldier. I am accorded by all what I attained over ⅓ century ago. Phil Reade told me that the generals at Santiago "respected and feared" me—whatever that might mean.

I telegraphed you today that we will be held in camp aloof from everybody for five days. Then we will go into camp when and where we will be ready to see the world. Should yellow fever be developed here complications may arise.

Now that the war is over, I hope you are content with the parts played by your nearest male relations and connections. Possibly, lack of opportunity is the reason why a galaxy of stars on two pairs of broad soldiers will not blind you when "Johnny comes marching home." Well, a live B.G. is better (?) than a dead M.G. Surely a live Lieut. Col. is my choice to a dead Col. or B.G. Love from ADELBERT

Camp Wikoff, MONTAUK POINT, L.I., *Tuesday, August* 16, 1898

DEAR BLANCHE: Funny things are happening here. This is supposed to be a detention camp for yellow fever cases from Cuba, yet, to us here are coming troops from Tampa and elsewhere! With them is brought typhoid fever cases—a more deadly disease than the yellow fever. Then again the troops are coming in numbers too great to be cared for with means at hand. But it is great fun to sit and enjoy the pure air and sunshine and know that Santiago de Cuba is 1385 miles away and that somebody else is doing the fretting.

My Brigade Staff is a perfect organization—active, thoroughly informed, young regulars, mainly West Pointers. Everything goes like clockwork. I have only to give orders and sign papers.

The 6th Regulars Infantry which came on my steamer but which does not belong to my Brigade solicit that they may be under me till their own Brigade arrives. Thus you see we are a happy family.

Butler's status is this—when the volunteers shall be mustered out, which will be in a couple of months or so, his Colonel, Rice, will go back to the regular army and Butler will be made Colonel of the 6th Mass. Militia. As such he will serve five years, the limit fixed by law last winter. At the end of that time, he will be made a Brigadier General of Mass. Militia for five years—and thereafter he will be compelled to carry about with him the ponderous title of "General Ames." I send you all love and kisses.

ADELBERT

LOWELL, MASS., *August* 16, 1898

DEAR DEL: Your answer to my telegram of welcome and question as to what you would do or what we should do reached us in due time. The wording was a little chill, at "liberty to see you" did not sound over cordial but we held a council of war and concluded that the exigencies of the telegram were to blame and we all cheered up. If you had remained in Cuba we should have telegraphed you, when the yacht was ready, for permission to visit you and if possible for you to take the yacht for headquarters, etc.

The week you left the "America" was put in commission and the work has been hastened right along. She has a shortened boomsprit and main boom and is in good condition for service and I hope you may be able to get some good out of her. The last of this week she will be ready to sail for Montauk and the question now is shall we sail from Boston in her or join her at Newport or New London.

Adelbert thinks it will be well to get our "sea legs" on before appearing before you and your smile of derision at our probable lamentable condition. Joking aside, however, it may be that the sea air will be the best tonic for Del, who is no longer troubled with fever but is weakened by the night sweats.

I should feel happier if I were sure you had not suffered from the fever. Del insists you have not, and that you were very careful of diet, etc. Yet I am not satisfied until I know certainly. All is moving well financially, and if all are in good health we ought to be happy when we meet. With love,

BLANCHE

Camp Wikoff, MONTAUK POINT, L.I., *August* 17, 1898

DEAR BLANCHE: New complications are arising. I see by the papers that the Governor of New York is to quarantine this camp! If so, who can tell when we can get out?

The Army Surgeons here seemed panic stricken and are giving more and more stringent orders about entering and leaving camps. Gen. Kent was ordered to Washington but the Surgeon-in-charge forbade and the Sec. of War has recalled his order. At the same time, new troops from Santiago are camped right beside us thereby nullifying all advantages gained by us thus far by our "detention."

Butler's position in his regiment is better than if he had been appointed Colonel. He has much to learn. Col. Rice is a good soldier who will improve the regiment and teach Butler many things he could not well learn otherwise. When the Volunteers are mustered out Rice will go back to the Regular Army and the 6th to the Militia, the crack regiment probably of Massachusetts. Everything else will naturally follow. I cannot believe the volunteers will be held in service long. Col. Rice being a regular may detain the 6th Mass, for a brief time but Governors of States will demand the return of state troops where and when the work can be done by the regulars. We have regulars enough for Cuba and Porto Rico. So you can count on a relatively speedy return of our son.

Permit me to say that this war has ended much as I predicted. That is "Spain went all to pieces" upon receiving a few severe blows from us. Now we must proceed to adjust ourselves to the new order of things. The volunteers were in *for the war*. It is at an end. Home they must come. Though I am with the regulars I am not needed and my face is to the North not South. Love from ADELBERT

LOWELL, MASS., *August* 18, 1898

DEAR DEL: It is such a comfort to be able to get letters from you with only the interval of a day between the sending and receipt.

The morning papers state that your whole camp Wikoff is being put under strict quarantine. Does this mean that you will not be able to come on the yacht or receive visitors? In view of some such trouble, I wrote Assistant Secretary Allen to procure permission for the "America" to anchor in the bay. He answered that he assumed there would be no difficulty adding "Should you experience any, I hope you will call upon me freely for any assistance I can render." Do you think any permit will be required?

As you say nothing about our expected visit in your letters, I infer that for some reason you do not approve of the plan. I do not quite understand what is wrong about it, as it is only following out the action agreed upon last spring, except that instead of cruising up the shores of New England, we turn to the location of those we love and before you left you said you would make your headquarters on the yacht if we joined you. Of course, I have wit enough to know that you might well not be able to keep this promise as it would depend upon where your Brigade might be, but, at the same time, it was a tacit consent to the plan, and we had looked forward with such pleasure to being with you.

How glad I am to find you so well content with your army life and your staff. You do not see as much of the reporters and do not figure in the papers to the same extent as Roosevelt and Wheeler. I am out of sorts with them for if they had remained quietly in camp this question of strict quarantine might not have come up. Love from all the family and a kiss from

BLANCHE

LOWELL, MASS., *August* 19, 1898

DEAR DEL: We are happy to see, that, the removal of the typhoid patients from Montauk has caused the idea of a general quarantine to be given up and we surmise that you will be a free man tomorrow.

The weather has been very unfavorable for work on the yacht; out of the last twenty-one days there have been but two without rain. Captain Canning is discouraged but will probably be ready to sail Tuesday.

A council was held whether it would be better to go to Newport or New London and meet the yacht or to sail from Boston. All favored going from Boston. I hope you will be able to stay on the yacht and entertain your old friends, I mean your ancient friends. No that is not it, I mean the friends of your youth. Well, anyway, your friends.

Florence was here at lunch and I gave her your statement in regard to the non-receipt at Santiago of the supplies furnished by the Womens' Societies. She will read it at the next meeting which will be reported in the papers. It seems to me that if the vessels at Santiago had been filled with supplies the Army would not have had them. The hospital ship, Bay State, has sailed to Santiago and will perhaps be able to do some good, even at this late hour. Our working force in Lowell is scattered, so many just now are out of town and the Mass. Association has not made any particular call for supplies. If it does there will be a lively response.

All send love and hope you will be as glad to see us, as we shall be to be with you. BLANCHE

Camp Wikoff, MONTAUK POINT, L.I., *August* 21, 1898

DEAR BLANCHE: I am now in permanent quarters in camp. Of my three regiments one only is with me. A second one is here in "Detention" camp while the third has not arrived from Santiago. Of course no military (strictly) duty is possible. I detail men to help do the work at the depots, etc.

You no doubt see by the papers that we do not have hospital tents enough for the sick. Nor have we nurses enough. One of my staff officers, Lieut. Lawton, my commissary, is in the hospital sick. His nurse (he has typhoid fever) has a list of fifteen patients to nurse (so I am told) and is almost worked to death.[1] So it has gone, goes and will go to the end, because of the lack of a right kind of a Chief in the War Dept. at Washington. He has no head and consequently cannot select men with heads.

Shafter sent us well men home first—and we regulars. I told him and others at the Council in Santiago that the sick end of his army should be sent first. He naturally sent *all* the well and left none to care for the sick. Of course, they rotted and died. He also should have sent the volunteers before the regulars as the volunteers were not hardened to the life of soldiering as were the regulars nor could they care for themselves so well. I honestly believe that with a humane, wise policy on Shafter's part not one in ten of the deaths by disease would or need have occurred. I feel the losses and sufferings very strongly perhaps because I know all about it.

When do you expect to be here. I need a blanket, pillow, and a tick for hay. Love, ADELBERT

LOWELL, MASS., *August* 21, 1898

DEAR DEL: Reports seem to show that the supplies at Montauk Pt. are as insufficient and as hard to move as they

[1] Because of this shortage, young Blanche offered her services and worked in the hospital until no longer needed.

were at Santiago. What is the trouble? Is it too much red tape and a reluctance to assume responsibility?

Enclosed are some more slips about interesting matters. Adelbert does not feel quite so well as he has, but he has gained ten pounds and if the fever returns, he is in good condition to fight against it.

We are to sail Tuesday night as at present advised and hope to be with you in a few days. Paul will sail around with us to Montauk but returns at once. It is too bad your Brigade is two miles from the Bay but two are better than five or ten and one never has things exactly as one would like.

We have just received your letter of August the 6th from Santiago enclosing the newspaper slip about the yacht. We have been busy all day packing our things for the yacht and hope to start tomorrow. There has been a little delay with, among other things, the naphtha launch. We could not have taken it to Cuba on account of the danger of breakage while on deck in heavy seas, but it may be useful for Montauk Point. As this whole expedition has been planned for the purpose of adding somewhat to your comfort and pleasure, I trust it may not entirely fail in its object. If so, it will be one more added to the list of disappointments and the only thing to be done is to set up the pins again as we do in bowling, and try once more for luck or improvement in methods.

We have just finished breakfast and have planned to go to Boston on the 1.30 p.m. train. This will give time to get our belongings located before we succumb to the waves. The weather is not very propitious as it looks foggy—however, that is to be expected and as we hope to see you soon, we are to reap the reward of our waiting and efforts.

All send love, Sweetheart, and hope to find you well. Adelbert has lost four of the ten pounds gained in the struggle with the fever for the last day or two. The fever did not return but he has felt very tired. BLANCHE

Headquarters, 1st Division 5th Army Corps,
Camp Wikoff, MONTAUK POINT, LONG ISLAND, *August 25,* 1898

General Orders No. 12

In compliance with Special Orders, No. 10, dated Headquarters U.S. Forces, Camp Wikoff, August 25th, 1898, the undersigned hereby assumes command of this Division.

ADELBERT AMES
Brigadier General, U.S.V. Commanding.

Hd. Qrs. 1st Div. 5th Corps, Camp Wikoff,
MONTAUK POINT, L.I., *August* 28, 1898

TO MRS. MARTHA AMES: MY DEAR MOTHER: Blanche, Sarah, little Blanche, Adelbert and Jessie are sitting in my tent, or in front of it under a tent fly. They left Boston in the yacht "America" last Wednesday and arrived here last evening. They expect to stay about here in the yacht for some time. I believe the idea of yachting this year started with Butler, but he went to War. As we all, Butler, Adelbert and I, were in Cuba, Blanche thought of going there to look us up. So it has resulted in coming here.

Adelbert has been very sick with the malarial fever contracted when before Santiago with me. He is better but has not regained his strength. The fever holds on so long that is why so many continue sick.

Butler has done wonderfully well since he joined the 6th Mass. Vols. as Adjutant and Lieut. He is now Lieut. Col. of that regiment. The Colonel and Lieut. Colonel resigned. Butler was recommended for Colonel by his regiment and by three generals over him. Two of these generals, Wilson and Henry, were friends of mine. But Gen. Miles recommended somebody else for Colonel and his recommendation was accepted. However, Butler got the next place—Lieut. Col. All the papers speak well of him in the little fight the regiment had in Porto Rico. If he comes home well, we will feel very fortunate.

I am well. I had a slight touch of fever. The sun was very oppressive and wilted us. Now I am well again, though my temperature is one or two degrees higher at times than it should be. The temperature here is cool, the air pure, and I shall soon be toned up. I lost a number of pounds in weight but have a good appetite.

I command this Division, eight regiments of regulars, one third of the infantry of the regular army. I expect to be mustered out when other volunteers go. I rather like this business. It recalls old war times when I was a youth.

With much love,
ADELBERT

Hd. Qrs. 3d Brig. 1st Div. 5th Corps, Camp Wikoff,
MONTAUK POINT, L.I., *August*, 1898

MY DEAR COLONEL: I regret that I cannot accept your kind invitation to the Reunion of the 20th Maine on the 26th inst.

We are in a "detention" camp on account of yellow fever the existence of which amongst us is somewhat doubted. We were overpowered by a malarial fever at Santiago, Cuba, which rendered us helpless nearly all being more or less sick, none being perfectly well and strong. This pure air is working wonders for us. Alas! for our comrades who are dying for the lack of it, in the camps about Santiago!

The differences of dates of my two commissions as Brigadier General by Lincoln and McKinley is just thirty five years, yet when I reached the trenches on Fort San Juan hill and found myself among soldiers and heard the bullets and shells that period of more than a third of a century was obliterated and I was again a youth.

Our regular army is unsurpassed, in my opinion, by any military organization in the world. The campaign of Santiago de Cuba is an untold tale wondrously interesting.

I thank you for your kind reference to my boy. While I am glad to see him get military rank especially on the recommendation of his own regiment, I am so much the father as to be thankful that he has not been put through the severe trials of us veterans of the 20th Maine.

Please give my kindest regards to Chamberlain, Spear, Brown, Miller, Prince, Tyler whom you mention and to all others not mentioned. Your friend, A. Ames

The Lochiel, Forrest Hunter, Harrisburg, Pa., *October 22*, 1898

Dear Blanche: As it was after dark when the train reached the station at Camp Meade and as it was storming heavily, I decided not to stop there and prowl about the camps to find some one to take us in but came on, eight miles further, to this city, where we spent the night. After the storm passed this forenoon we took the electrics back to camp. Gen. Graham was not in camp. His Adjutant General did not feel authorized to assign me to my command. So at his suggestion we came back to the hotel again to await orders. The agitation in camp is in connection with the Peace Jubilee in Philadelphia on the 26th inst. Whether Gen. Bates goes with my Brigade, or I, must be decided by Gen. Graham.

The Adjutant General said, in the course of our conversation that he, or a Quartermaster had said that, with the money necessary to move the troops south and care for them there, he could make them perfectly comfortable in their camps here. I interpreted what he said as the expression of his opinion that the troops might not move after all. I read the reports of officers sent to Summerville, S.C. to look up a camp ground. I am surprised the place was selected. It is but 70 feet above tide water. Drainage must be very difficult as water stands in pools and marsh. The surface of the ground is but six or eight feet above the level of the water below. On the other hand a heavy growth of pine is on the land. The report says "a careful system of Scavangering" must be adopted. The drinking water must come from an artesian well belonging to a hotel, but a more powerful force pump will be needed.

I am much struck by the unmilitary aspect of affairs here. I am more than half afraid I shall find myself taking things too seriously. I shall try not to. I do not think I can afford to supply enough "military" to spread over 3,000 volunteers in the brief time that will be alloted me. Don't want to try.

I intend to send you, for Butler's guidance, "A Word of Advice from a Father to his Son." Evidently habits are easily formed—and hard to break. But my advice need not annoy as it need not be followed. I send love to you and the children.

DEL

LOWELL, MASS., *October 23, 1898*

DEAR DEL: Adelbert wrote you of our safe arrival home Saturday morning. The children were glad to have us back as they found the house a little lonely. Paul having gone to Philadelphia, Adelbert and Jessie were housekeepers.

Aunt Maria was at Aunt Nina's. She is apparently as well as ever and looks very finely with her grey hair. Harry was out of sorts and spoke most unfeelingly of his mother's ways as an "infernal nuisance." How little patience we have with those who are obstacles in the path of our wishes. The obligations and love of a lifetime are forgotten.

To keep busy and therefore more contented, I began Saturday the work of changing Adelbert's belongings into Jessie's room and re-arranging Butler's sleeping apartment and study. Sarah, of course, went over at once to her farm and thus the interests are taken up again, but as far as I am concerned with no relish. However this is just as well as anything else can be.

I hope that you will not find you have been too prompt in obeying your orders and that you can have your brigade without delay. From Phil's letters we judge that Gen. Oatis will not care to have you appear. The children send love in which I join them with a kiss.

BLANCHE

The Lochiel, Forrest Hunter, HARRISBURG, PA., *October 23, 1898*

DEAR BLANCHE: I have been assigned to my Brigade—the 2d of the 1st Div. as I expected. The poorest regiment in the

Brigade is the 14th Pa. The morning papers say it is to be mustered out. I hope so. I do not look forward to my work with any enthusiasm. There is nothing back of it. Everything is centered in the Peace Jubilee. I understand we will be two days in Philadelphia—at least we go the day before and get back the day after—the guests of the city all the time there.

Phil Reade has gone to Asheville, N.C. on sick leave.

I send love and kisses to you all. In a few minutes we depart again for the *front*. ADELBERT

LOWELL, *October 24*, 1898

DEAR DEL: Your letters of Saturday and Sunday have just come in the morning's mail, and we are pleased to hear that you are to have a part in the Peace Jubilee. You will probably be in the military parade at the time Butler is disembarking at Boston. "The Word of Advice from a Father to his Son" I shall take pleasure in giving to the young man when he arrives in lieu of a personal greeting from you. It will not be as satisfactory to him, but I think he appreciates your aid and what it has done for him.

Your description of Summerville is disheartening. Perhaps it will be decided to leave the troops at Camp Meade at least until the frosts have killed out the malaria even as far south as Georgia and South Carolina.

Edith who has just been here wishes me to send you her love. Adelbert is studying in the library and joins me in two kisses.

BLANCHE

Hd. Qrs. 2d Brigade 1st. Div. 2d Corps,
CAMP MEADE, PA., *October 24*, 1898

DEAR BLANCHE: I see by the papers that the Mississippi sailed from San Juan with the 6th Mass. on Friday last. This is a day later than we expected.

Gen. Bates has returned from Summerville and reports it unfit for a camp. I think we will go somewhere else. The War Dept. would not act on his report but has ordered him to make it to Gen. Graham. Bates will see Graham tomorrow. Possibly I may be ordered south to select a camp. All the cities and villages in the South are asking for troops—of course—for the money in it. They do not want the colored regiment. Gen. Bates is from Alabama—has been in Congress and Governor of his state. He refused to have the colored regiment in his brigade as it would hurt him politically. Yet it is a fact that the State of Alabama raised a Colored Regiment for this war—probably because that was easier than to raise a white one in its place.

Tomorrow or next day, we will go into Philadelphia as a part of the show for the populace on Peace Jubilee Day.

Last night was cold. I slept on a good mattress and was fairly comfortable. I have ordered a complete bed equipment which will be here tomorrow. My saddle has not arrived. If it does not come in the morning I will telegraph you. I have been in the saddle (not mine) nearly all day and am feeling well.

I send you all love and kisses. ADELBERT

Hd. Qrs. 2d Brigade, 1st Div. 2d Corps,
CAMP MEADE, PA., *October 24*, 1898

DEAR BLANCHE: I have found Gen. Bates a very pleasant gentleman. There has been no friction between us. He has been assigned to another brigade. My late coming has caused my name to be left out of the list of generals taking part in the parade. It is of no moment. I have to use a government horse and my outfit will not be very impressive. That is of no moment.

We will leave here at eleven tomorrow morning and will be in the city two nights and one day as I understand it. There is to be the parade, Union League reception, etc.—a grand time all around.

As a result of Gen. Bates' report to Gen. Graham of the situation at Summerville, S.C., Gen. G. decided he would take no further action about preparing that place for occupancy till after he has visited and inspected it himself. A Philadelphia paper of today says Gen. G. expressed the opinion that it would be the 1st of Dec. before we went South. At least it looks as if we were to loiter here for awhile. I am sure I do not care. The War Dept. is too great a puzzle for me. I am not running the war any more. In fact I take but little interest in it.

Give my love to Butler, Edith, Sarah, Blanche, Adelbert and Jessie, also kisses and the same for you. ADELBERT

LOWELL, MASS., *October 26*, 1898

DEAR DEL: We are glad to hear that you are not to go to Summerville as from your report it seemed a poor place for you and your troops. Since the race troubles in North Carolina are causing so much anxiety you would not care to select that state for a camping ground. It would be a strange coincidence if you should find after the lapse of more than thirty years that you were obliged to champion the blacks against the whites as you did after the Civil War.

Today I shall think of you as on your way to Philadelphia to be admired tomorrow by enthusiastic multitudes. Not an unpleasant mind picture. You can well imagine that it will give me great pleasure to hand your letter to Butler. He will feel pleased and proud to receive it. All the home folks are well and send love, with a kiss. BLANCHE

PHILADELPHIA, *October* 27, 1898

DEAR BLANCHE: I have just seen in the evening paper that the 6th Mass. has arrived in Boston. I am anxious to hear that Butler is not seriously ill and that he is in the way of rapid recovery.

I have been on horseback, at the review, from eight this morning till four this afternoon. It has been cold. I put newspapers on my chest and back holding them in place by my coat and belt and was thus greatly benefited. My thin coat of two rows of buttons was of little protection against this cold northwester. One could not wear an overcoat as one was clad mainly in one's glory clothes. The parade was a grand affair. The personal feature of interest to me was that I came so late to the 2d Army Corps, that the programme put Gen. Oatis in my place. The correction was made in but few papers. So much for glory.

Do you remember the Major Davis who was looking over your Father's papers in Lowell a year ago? Well, he is a Brigadier General and commands a Division in this, our 2d corps. He never did anything in the Civil War. I thought he seemed shamed-face when we met. Somebody has said "Kissing goes by favor." Had that somebody lived till now the saying would be "B.G. appointments go by favor"—great 'favor' and little merit.

I find myself in pleasant touch with all my officers—both above and below me. Capt. Cosby, my Asst. Adj't. Gen'l. was in Troop A, New York City. He had a brother at West Point when Butler was there. Capt. C. was a Rough Rider and one of the heroes of Santiago.

Love to Butler, Edith, Sarah, Adelbert, and Jessie—and kisses and love to you. ADELBERT

LOWELL, MASS., *October* 28, 1898

DEAR DEL: Butler as you know is at home, safe and well, and has received an enthusiastic reception in Boston and

Lowell. He is looking quite thin although he has gained in weight until he weighs one hundred and forty eight pounds in his clothes. He says he has not done any duty walking or riding for two months. His duties were civil administration which permitted him to keep quiet. At one time he was so weak that he fell and had to drag himself up by a chair as he did years ago in Northfield. West tells me that he feared at one time he could not bring him back. You see how fortunate we are.

He and Gardiner are very good friends and seem to have a number of money-making schemes together. Butler is very happy to be at home and was pleased to get your letter. As you have seen in the papers, he finished the Lowell parade about half past six, and came right home with Sarah and Del who had been following the troops with the carriage. Blanche came up from the train almost at the same time and we went out to dinner at once. Your letter I had put upon his plate. Edith and Brooks came up and if you had been at home our circle would have been complete. The excitement caused Butler to talk very steadily and he had numerous relics to show and schemes to present. It was late before we got to bed. This morning at twelve he went to Boston.

Gardiner came over to see us. He has changed very much and his flesh is becoming to him, as are also his mustache and goatee. He is now a soldierly fine-looking man. He told Sarah that Butler was the hero of the Porto Rico Campaign. Butler misses you in many ways, among others, because there is no one to give him good advice and help him about his speeches. He will go to see you at Camp Meade if you let him know when to come.

All send love and as always there is a kiss from

BLANCHE

Hd. Qrs. 2d Brigade, 1st Div., 2d Corps,
CAMP MEADE, *October* 29, 1898

DEAR BLANCHE: I have just received your telegram telling me that Butler is "well and joyous." As I shared your anxiety about him when he was sick and thereby reduced said anxiety one half—so now I will share your joy on his safe return and thereby selfishly reduce said joy one half. Possibly you may doubt my effectiveness in either case.

Last night I received an order to go to Summerville, S.C. and establish a camp there. This morning I had a long interview with Gen. Graham. As a result I am left to do as I think best. Whether our going there is a military necessity or a political necessity I cannot say. I shall stop a few hours in Washington at the suggestion of Gen. Young and see, not the Sec. of War as he advised, but Gen. Corbin, the Adjutant General, who is the power behind the throne. Until then I must be quite undecided as to my final action. I will take Mr. Tayman and the Brigade Quartermaster along with me. I may be gone a week or ten days. It is impossible to anticipate the time.

I regret I cannot be in Massachusetts at this time. I would like to see Butler; and I think if I were there I could get Rice to resign and Butler made Colonel. Perhaps the thing might not be accomplished in a day but it should be before the regiment is mustered out. Every one in the regiment who would be promoted by Rice's resignation—and their friends, should unite in forcing this thing along. Col. R. has been amply repaid for what he has done, especially as he had no claim on the Colonelcy in the first instance. Now, he should move on and give others a chance.

Please extend my deepest sympathy to Sadie Webster. Prentiss' death was a shock. I had no idea that his disease was of such a character. Sadie has further cause to bewail her fate. We, all, should be very tender of her.

With love and kisses to you, one and all—regretting I-am-not-with-you-to-complete-the-circle. FATHER

LOWELL, MASS., *October* 30, 1898

DEAR DEL: Tomorrow will be your birthday, Dearie, and I wish you many happy returns of the day. Your telegram in regard to Butler and your trip to Summerville came yesterday and I did not send your letter knowing it could not reach you until your trip South is finished.

We went to Prentiss' funeral yesterday. General Kinsman was up to attend it and when the subject of Summerville came up he said that he had been there several times, that it was a beautiful place but not considered healthy. I am sorry that you are to struggle with the place but if anyone can do it successfully you can.

Butler is talking over some of his many schemes, but I will not tell you of them as he will wish to do so himself when he visits you. Blanche, Jessie, Sarah and I are going to Boston tomorrow for fall hats for the two younger girls. Blanche returns to Smith College Tuesday. She is happy, does not work too hard and feels that she commands the situation. We visited the chicken farm the other day and found that a chicken had hatched in the incubator from an egg that had been there only nine days—Sarah bought the eggs from the farmers in Tewksbury and this particular egg must have been out in the cold sixteen hours at least.

On Thursday Butler is going with some of his cronies down to the Cape, to stay three or four days. He is not entirely well yet and will have to take care of himself.

Butler says give my love to Father. Blanche and Sarah say the same. With love and a kiss from BLANCHE

SUMMERVILLE, S.C., *November 2*, 1898

DEAR BLANCHE: I arrived here early Monday morning—less than 20 hours from Washington. Since then I have been busy examining possible camp sites.

Gen. Corbin told me Sunday in Washington that Sec. Alger had promised to put troops here. That bit of information made my duty very simple. I had only to select the best place for them *here*,—which I have done.

Gen. Oatis did not have the "true instinct" as I did and tried to get this Brigade to Alabama, his own State. He has been abused in this part of this State for his action as he has been credited with too much zeal for his own State.

That I may have a model camp, I shall have all kitchen refuse burned and use dry earth closets to be carted two miles away. I can get artesian well water for my men to drink. Bored wells 50 to 70 feet deep will give good water for all purposes. I shall have to hold my command with a rigid hand to make them live up to orders.

Gen. Corbin also said he believed that by January 1st. all the troops to go to Cuba would be there and that all others would be mustered out. This, as you know, is what I have already said. The complications in Paris may delay such results—but not for long. Spain has no fight in her.

I am surprised at the great change in public sentiment here as compared to what I have known. In this town are two or three union flags on residences. Some of its young men are in the S. C. regiments. One or two natives are at home on furlough wearing our uniform. I am treated with great courtesy and the City of Charleston is grieving, apparently, that I passed through it without being entertained by its officials! They are trying to get me there but "duty" prevents.

There is a very fine hotel here—complete in every particular. My camp is in the adjacent tract of land. It will not, or does not, usually open till Dec. 1st. What it may do is hard to tell. Every one expects to make a harvest out of us. I expect they will. No doubt Sec. Alger intended all sections of the South should be equally *benefited*. However, the outward respect for our flag and uniform is worth millions to our country.

As the season passes and you have completed all your schemes at home, I shall expect you here if my surroundings be at all acceptable. Love to all. ADELBERT

LOWELL, *November 2, 1898*

DEAR DEL: Here are more slips as by these you can learn about Butler's movements. He is somewhat better today and will be himself again shortly without doubt. The warmth of his reception and the enthusiasm of even the grey-headed men who tell him that he is the logical candidate for any office, going as far as President rather overwhelms him. He says it is "so perfectly ridiculous, I have done nothing to deserve it."

Blanche went back to college Monday. Oakes Ames came yesterday to see Butler. We congratulated him upon his engagement but he denied everything except a business engagement. Adelbert works daily at his lessons and foot ball. He is now quite as tall as Butler.

Rice and his friends are working for a generalship. Butler desires to have him boosted along, of course. Woodward talks of resigning. Butler has been careful not to say anything about him or the other officers. The Sixth is to be furloughed for sixty days tomorrow and after the election Butler will feel more free.

How is it, Del, that you are to have a camp in a location that has been pronounced unhealthy? Does the Hotel keeper have influence? I trust that the cold weather will come soon and strong, and that all your requisitions for lumber and medicine will be filled at once.

You see the feeling is that the Spaniards may "balk." Can you imagine Spain as a heady woman standing on the street corner refusing to cross at the proper time? War and unrest seems to be threatening from several directions in Europe and we may be implicated before we know it.

Your poncho will go by express, and it seems as if there might be other things to add to your comfort. How would you like to have West as your servant? He would be very glad to go—and he hated to come back from Porto Rico. Butler suggested that you might be pleased to have him and

I am sure he could make you more comfortable than some strange man.

Edith has just come in. She says '*the* boy' is first rate. She joins with me in love to "Father." BLANCHE

LOWELL, MASS., *November* 4, 1898

DEAR DEL: It seems a long time since we have heard from you, for telegrams although concise leave much that the imagination must supply.

This is a beautiful Indian summer day, as was yesterday. It is quarter of eight and I am waiting for the family to appear. Sarah rode off to the farm half an hour ago as she had an appointment in regard to some ploughing. The outdoor life and exercise is doing her good. She looks in better color and has no time for moods. Adelbert plays football every afternoon. He weighs one hundred and fifty-two pounds. Jessie feels the importance of her sixteen years. Her birthday was the occasion for gifts of three boxes of candy. At dinner we had the regulation cake.

Butler complains that he feels dull and reluctant to go about or talk much. He is avoiding as much as possible speech making and this makes little difference as the campaign is nearly over. I think he needs you to give him points. He received a letter from the Rep. State Committee asking him to request his democratic friends who would probably vote for him in large numbers to also vote for Knox. Butler answered that he would do all that was in his power or that he could to aid. He did not say, however, that he should ask any favors of his personal followers because he did not feel that it would be right or wise to do so. Love and a kiss. BLANCHE

SUMMERVILLE, S.C., *November* 5, 1898

DEAR BLANCHE: I find that the Secretary of War had promised the people of Charleston that a Brigade of troops should be sent here, at the same time he accepted from them the proffer of financial aid in preparing the camp. The agent of the city is one of McKinley's Quartermasters. *As a quartermaster I accepted his aid.* He sent me laborers. When I found the City of Charleston was to pay them I became concerned as I believe Uncle Sam will be called upon to pay eventually. I would have telegraphed the War Dept. about the situation, advising it to pay all bills, but after learning that Secretary Alger had arranged it all, I became discreetly silent.

This change of base is of great financial benefit to these southern localities. It is not exactly war. It has the smell of politics about it. But the people here like it. Again, I say this war with Spain in many and devious ways is obliterating Civil War animosities.

I have selected the very best site for a camp. My orders to do so are preemptory. I shall have dry earth closets—to be carted a mile or two away. The kitchen refuse will be burned or carted away. If I can get good water, I will keep off sickness. Two hundred and eighty of my Brigade have arrived. My wells are to be bored and not one has yet struck water. The doubts of the Highlands are inclined to present themselves. However, I have demanded the whole power of Charleston and this place to aid me. Water from a second water bearing strata can be had at from forty to eighty feet. In a couple of days I will know exactly what to expect.

I see by today's paper that our division and with it my Brigade is to be a part of the garrison of Havana. It, all, seems very strange. Love and kisses to all. ADELBERT

SUMMERVILLE, S.C., *November* 8, 1898

DEAR BLANCHE: Two of the enclosures will indicate to you what I am doing. The letter in pencil, is my reply to Gen. Young's telegram asking if I was ready for my Brigade. I requested the representative of Charleston to ask the Mayor of that city to telegraph the Sec. of War about the lack of water. I suppose he did so last night. I found a good camp ground and have prepared it for troops as ordered. The water question was not left to me. So I refer it right back to the Sec. of War through or by his friend, the Mayor of Charleston who caused this site to be selected. As we are to go to Cuba so soon it is a great waste to establish new camps. From the present outlook, I doubt if my Brigade gets here.

This is election day. In North Carolina they are putting the shot gun into operation. Of course it will succeed.

Love and kisses to all. ADELBERT

SUMMERVILLE, S.C., *November* 9, 1898

DEAR BLANCHE: You see by the order we go to Havana. Yesterday's paper says we encamp on the line of the aquaduct (for pure water) eight miles from that city. A landing for us is being prepared on the coast so we will not have to go through the city. If we must go to Cuba again, we should congratulate ourselves that our location is the best.

Where fighting was a necessity my sense of duty kept me at my post. Where simple "occupation" is the only necessity I suspect I shall run away in case of sickness, leaving the work to vigorous youth.

I do not agree with those who expect to see us away by the end of this month. Here it is the 9th and I am ordered to expend no end of money in preparing camp. I have just telegraphed I will have a supply of water in about forty eight hours and that my Brigade can be accommodated after that time. I have had coffee made of the artesian water—also had rice boiled—to see the effect of the mineral in the water on the coffee and rice. I have decided to accept the water, part mineral or artesian, part well and part cistern. Tanks and piping will be ready at once. I am glad to settle this question or difficulty in a satisfactory way to myself. My hesitation has set by the ears this whole community, including Charleston. Now, what they wanted they get and the troops will not suffer in the least. I have one company from each of my three regiments on the camp ground. It is being cleared and policed. I am positive we will have no scandal like those at Alger, Tampa, etc.

After being here a week we attempted to pay our board bill but were politely informed that it had been paid. This kindness compels me to get under canvas as soon as I can.

However, for the past few days, I have been in doubt about remaining here. Without water, the Brigade would have had to go up country somewhere. I send love and kisses to you all.

ADELBERT

SUMMERVILLE, S.C., *November* 11, 1898

DEAR BLANCHE: I enclose letters and newspaper cuttings which indicate what I am doing. The last of my Brigade will get here about the 17th inst. Thanksgiving comes on the 24th. By that time, I will be settled. I have the honor to invite you and Sarah to visit me as soon after Thanksgiving as may suit your convenience.

Enclosures show times have changed since 1875. Love to all.

ADELBERT

Brigadier General Adelbert Ames was honorably discharged on January 3rd, 1899, and returned home to complete the family circle. Yet once again he did his duty to his Country when he presented the following report.

Recently, when before the War Investigating Commission, I was asked if I had any statement to make which might help them in their labors; I replied in the negative, adding that we were at the end of a successful war, that a statement from me would necessarily take the form of a criticism which might seem ungracious, and that they, the members of the Commission, should be as well informed on all matters under their consideration as I.

Since then, however, on recalling the evident earnestness of their appeal for help, and realizing that their inquiry failed to touch upon my own experiences in the war or the opinion and convictions which have followed reflection, I have decided to offer some suggestions which I hope may prove of value. At the same time I have no doubt that the official records, if thoroughly studied and properly interpreted, would reveal the causes of the delinquencies now under investigation.

Whether any part of the sickness, suffering and death of our soldiers has been due to neglect or incompetency, or both, is a matter of the gravest importance. The government so regards it, as shown by its act in creating this Commission, and so must it be held by every individual who has the honor and welfare of his country at heart.

Little interest would be aroused if punishment for what has been done or left undone in the past were the only object of this investigation. Guidance for our future wars is the higher purpose and the one not to be lost sight of.

It is remarkable and significant that the investigations into the conduct of the navy and army should have objects diametrically opposed to each other. In the navy they have been for the distribution of honors, while those in the army, most familiar to the public, have been for the distribution of dishonors.

The two arms of the service have been evolved under the fostering care of the same liberal government. The man with the gun and the man behind the gun are of the same order of manhood which finds its highest development, even for warfare, among a free people. The officers of every rank are in intelligence, instruction and valor the peers of the best of any service or any time. Why, then, should only one branch of the service be now subjected to the indignity of a humiliating examination?

It is but fair to assume that had our regular army, under its able and experienced chiefs, conducted the war without interference, on the old and familiar lines of previous wars, as did the navy, it would be, as is the navy, above reproach. To assume otherwise would be to admit that the chiefs of the navy are superior to those of the army. No doubt the cause of much of the deviation from the parallel lines of the two services is to be attributed to the enlargement of the army and the manner in which it has been done. Surely, the inherent difficulties of the management of land service cannot be held as greater than, though possibly different from, those of the sea.

With the conviction, throughout the country, that the soldiers of the war have suffered unnecessarily, though the amount of suffering may have been exaggerated, there is a feeling of resentment because of the belief that those really responsible for such suffering have been shielded, when they should have been exposed and punished.

Statements have been made with the evident purpose of making it appear that the enlisted men were responsible for much, if not all, of their own suffering. As they are little more than machines, always under orders, taught thoroughly the virtue of silence, their amount of responsibility cannot be expanded to cover so important a matter as their own health.

Subordinate commissioned officers are similarly restricted, in degree, corresponding to their rank. It is only when the highest officers are reached that the full extent of responsibility can be placed. Neglect, inefficiency, incompetency, if any there be, must rest with them. It is not sufficient that a leader be able to act, himself, only. He must possess the rare faculty of selecting able subordinates, failing in which, he fails in one of the first attributes of greatness.

It is to be regretted that the experience gained in the Civil War, moving troops by water, was not utilized in the expedition to Santiago, Cuba. The trade winds, smooth seas and sunny days of June offered no such difficulties as were encountered, a third of a century ago, by like expeditions, in midwinter, to the stormiest parts of our Atlantic Coast. Success in those instances was due to the studied care, in every detail, by able and resourceful leaders, and the hearty co-operation of the navy. The slow procession of the fleet of transports, the unsystematic method of handling them after they had reached their destination and the lack of facilities for landing, last June, had no counterpart in the Civil War.

The expedition, the 5th Army Corps, 16,887 strong, sailed from Tampa, Fla., 14th June. Of this force was a Division of Cavalry numbering 2,961. As their horses were not taken they had to act as infantry. It does not appear why this body of unhorsed cavalry was taken when tens of thousands of available infantry were resting idle in their camps.

At Siboney, a point ten miles east of Santiago, the disembarkation of the corps was "practically completed" on the evening of the 24th June.[1]

The Spanish soldiers in Cuba were armed with the best of modern guns and ammunition. Three years warfare against the Cuban patriots had inured them to hardships and dangers. Both in officers and men they represented a fighting force equal to the best Spain has had for many years. However, through the incompetency of their generals, they committed the blunder of permitting our army to land without serious opposition, when they were capable of offering the most heroic resistance as they showed later at El Caney.

Early on the morning of 24th June, a brigade of our cavalry, on foot, numbering 950 men, attacked the enemy, two or three thousand strong, at Las Guasimas, two and one half miles from Siboney, on the road to Santiago, and drove him from his position.[2]

Five days after this battle, the 29th June, the Headquarters of the General Commanding the expedition was still on board of his transport, the S. S. Seguranca.[3] On the 1st July he took command on shore.[4] On this same day the battles of El Caney and San Juan Hill were fought, the last of the campaign.

El Caney is a little village, in the foot hills, some four miles northeast of Santiago, protected by block houses and having on a prominent hill near by, a stone fort with trenches cut in the solid rock. It was defended by 460 Spaniards.[5]

This outpost was attacked early on the morning of the 1st July and was captured at 4:30 in the afternoon, only after nearly all of its defenders were killed or wounded. Our loss was about 400.

Fort San Juan is a mile east of Santiago on the road to Siboney. Near noon 1st July it was assailed by the rest of our army, over 7,000 strong,[6] and carried on the first advance. No subsequent forward movement, under fire, was made by us.

El Caney deserves a passing word. From early dawn 460 Spaniards withstood over 5,000 assailants till half-past ten in the forenoon and over 6,000[7] from that time till 4:30 in the afternoon,[8] inflicting a loss nearly equal to their whole number and only yielding when substantially annihilated.

[1] Gen. Shafter's Report, p. 6.
[2] Gen. S. B. M. Young's Report.
[3] The Santiago Campaign, Major Gen. Joseph Wheeler, p. 264.
[4] Wheeler, p. 272.
[5] Wheeler, p. 197.
[6] Wheeler, p. 81.
[7] Wheeler, p. 81.
[8] Gen. J. C. Bates' Report.

The Spaniards played a heroic role that day at El Caney. Spain has few battle fields where her soldiers showed equal valor. It makes at least one bright spot in her sad and humiliating war. Let her raise a monument to General Vara del Rey and his comrades and sing praises in their honor.

So highly did our government appreciate the victory over these 460 Spaniards that it rewarded its officers who were there by distributing among them four or five commissions as Major General, and others of the grade of Brigadier General. Let Spain inscribe on its monument this evidence of the United States' high appreciation of Spanish heroism.

Notwithstanding the conduct of the Spaniards at El Caney, they are not equal to our soldiers, man for man. They were well covered and defended themselves with the rapid firing gun. Block Houses and trenches are not easily taken by infantry alone, when so defended.

Our officers and men were recklessly brave, but the position was one which could only be reduced by the aid of artillery. This arm of the service was sadly deficient, to which cause must be attributed much loss of life and delay in the capture.

It was well, perhaps, that the order of the Commanding General to suspend the attack on El Caney and withdraw was not obeyed, unless it was his intention to use those troops in an advance on the city of Santiago itself, after Fort San Juan was taken. With such a purpose, so small an outpost might well be passed by, and the disobedience of his order was an act of grave importance. Were there any other motive, the act of disobedience might be defended on the ground that the order was given in ignorance of the exact state of affairs existing there at the time. The failure to capture any point attacked at that stage of the campaign would have given the enemy no little encouragement.

The conduct of the troops which carried Fort San Juan was exceptionally brilliant and worthy of the highest praise. Much of their loss was suffered while getting into position for the assault. The ways of reaching the ground over which they were to charge had not been thoroughly examined. On this point the Commanding General reports as follows:—"It naturally resulted that the progress made was slow, and the long range rifles of the enemy's infantry killed and wounded a number of our men while marching along this road and before there was any opportunity to return the fire.

"At this time Generals Kent and Sumner were ordered to push forward with all possible haste and place their troops in position to engage the enemy. General Kent with this end in view, forced the head of his column along side of the cavalry column as far as the narrow trail permitted and thus hurried his arrival at the San Juan and the formation beyond the stream.

"A few hundred yards before reaching the San Juan, the road forks, a fact that was discovered by Lieut. Col. Derby of my staff who had approached well to the front in a war balloon. This information he furnished to the troops, resulting in Sumner moving on the right-hand road, while Kent was enabled to utilize the road to the left."

As the balloon was made a target by the enemy our troops beneath it suffered not a little from the fire.[1]

It was asserted by those who took part in the capture of Fort San Juan that a vigorous advance by our forces would have resulted in the capture of the city of Santiago that day. The only one who had the authority to decide on such action and order it was the Commanding General. He gives in his report his whereabouts that day as follows:—"My own health was impaired by over exertion in the sun and intense heat of the day before, which prevented me from participating as actively in the battle as I desired, but from a high hill near my headquarters (which was 3 miles from El Caney and about 2½ miles from Fort San Juan) I had a general view of the battle field."

"During the afternoon I visited the position of Grimes' Battery on the heights of El Pozo (El Pozo is about 2 miles from Fort San Juan) and saw Kent and Sumner in firm possession of San Juan Hill." The view from Fort San Juan was the one which should have been taken.

On the night of this day of success when all should have been flushed with victory our generals were ordered to appear at headquarters to consider, not an advance, but a retreat! The Commanding General's dispatch July 3d to Washington:—"I am seriously considering withdrawing about five miles and taking up a new position," shows that even then he did not realize the situation. The retreat of five miles would have put us five miles nearer Siboney, our base of supplies, and five miles further away from Santiago, our objective point. The only advantage to be gained would have been the reduction of the distance over which supplies had to be carted or packed. With a passive enemy in front of us, as was the case from the beginning, these five miles of roads and two or three streams ought

[1] Wheeler, p. 43.

not to have been such serious obstacles as to require a change in the conduct of the campaign.

When the character of the climate is considered, we are justified in believing such a withdrawal and the spirit which prompted it would have delayed the capture of Santiago till the return of a less sickly season of the year.

There was no siege of Santiago in a military sense. No attempt was made to advance our lines or engage in other offensive operations. Few pieces of artillery were at the front, and some of these were posted more than a mile in rear of trenches occupied by our troops.

After the suspension of active hostilities and before the surrender, when doubt existed as to the intentions of the enemy, instructions were received that the authorities in Washington had authorized an assault, should a surrender be refused. This was a startling proposition to those who had had some experience of that kind in the Civil War, especially when our own unpreparedness and the rapid firing guns of the enemy were taken into consideration.

The army waited, enduring some privations and hardships, none of a very serious nature, but all of which ought to have been diminished or avoided by resourceful forethought. The men were becoming day by day more easy victims of a hostile climate. A soldier in health neither asks for nor expects sympathy. One of his traits is to endure in silence; but with the sick and wounded it is different. The extra suffering due to insufficient supplies of ambulances, litters, medicines and other hospital necessities would have been cruel had it been intentional.

In General Orders No. 18, Headquarters 5th Army Corps, dated 20th June, two days before disembarking, is the following:—"All troops will carry on the person the blanket roll (with shelter tent and poncho) three days field rations (with coffee ground) canteens filled and 100 rounds of ammunition per man, tentage, baggage, and company cooking utensils, will be left under charge of the Regimental Quartermaster."

The transports sailed away with the tentage, baggage and cooking utensils, which were left on board, in consequence of which the officers and men were deprived, for weeks, of cooking utensils. Many of the officers suffered for the want of change of underclothing. It was only after Santiago had fallen and the wandering transports had returned that these much needed articles were recovered.

Life in the trenches with the dust and mud caused by a hot

sun and drenching rains made cleanliness of person well nigh impossible. Bathing in the streams was unadvisable for reasons other than those shown in the following communication to the Adjutant General, 5th Army Corps, 4th July:—"There are several dead animals lying in the San Juan river above the point where this command obtains its drinking water. The only way to remedy this is to have a wagon sent up to haul them out. We have not the facilities for doing this here." Reply— "Wagon will be sent you tomorrow forenoon to draw the animals out of the way." [1]

As vessels for carrying water were left on the transports, and as canteens and improvised bamboo tubes were the only means at hand for carrying it, bathing and washing at the trenches were difficult.

The day came when the water for drinking purposes should have been boiled; but, lacking proper conveniences, it was not done. As the men had neither time nor patience to sit over their tin cups and cans long enough to thoroughly cook their rations, another cause of sickness obtained.

On the 13th July, at Fort San Juan, a brigade quartermaster forwarded to his division quartermaster the following:—"I have the honor to request that the companies of this Brigade be supplied with camp kettles. The men are now being furnished beans and rice in addition to coffee; they are also ordered to boil drinking water. The tin cup and empty tomato can are all that they have for these purposes, and are quite inadequate." As the request was not complied with, the men continued to live under the same unfavorable conditions as to their food.

On the 17th July the Spanish commander surrendered the city of Santiago, its garrison of 12,000 officers and men and a part of the Province of Santiago, with other troops making a total of 23,000!

This was a most remarkable proceeding under the circumstances. Our lines were substantially where they had been from the first. Our artillery was still at the rear and many days must needs elapse before works for it could be erected and guns put in place.

The Spaniards had ammunition in plenty and great quantities of rice in their storehouses. With a little tenacity and less endurance—not of the heroic kind shown at Saragossa ninety years ago—and the climate with its diseases as an ally, they could have long held out.

[1] Wheeler, p. 301.

How an army with heroes like those at El Caney could supinely yield as did that at Santiago, and surrender at the same time territory and troops out of the city and beyond our reach, is quite incomprehensible from a military standpoint.

Disease due to the climate, intensified by the upturned soil of the trenches, had begun to affect our troops before the surrender, and every one, appreciating the difficulties before us in case of resistance, felt the most devout thankfulness at the sudden and favorable issue.

After the surrender camps were changed. Still, without wagons and barrels for water, the men in some of the camps had to tramp, in the hot sun, more than a mile and a half, to fill their canteens. Wood for fuel and cots was hard to get, the supply of axes being deficient, and difficult to transport to camp without wagons. The sun, the rains and exposure rapidly increased the number of the sick in some of the brigades to 20, 30, 40 per cent. of the whole number, while at the same time only a very small percent were perfectly well. Gloom began to settle over the camp, and in one Division, at least, the order was issued to discontinue the salute at the burial of the dead.

The situation had become alarmingly serious when on the 3d August, instructions were received that the presence of the general officers and chief surgeons was desired at headquarters for consultation on the condition of the army and on what recommendations, if any, should be made to Washington as to its disposition.

After the officers had assembled, the Commanding General stated that he had received a communication from Washington suggesting that the command be sent against the enemy in the vicinity of Holquin, a point some seventy miles inland, that he was quite ready to assume any responsibility in the matter, and that he would like to hear what his officers had to say on the situation.

The condition of the troops was forcibly presented, especially by some of the surgeons and recommendations were freely made by others. There was no dissenting voice. The Commanding General acquiesced, apparently, in all that was said and recommended, which was that the troops be returned to the United States at the earliest day possible.

So important did he deem the support of his officers that he requested them to draw up a paper setting forth the reasons for their advice that he might forward it to his superiors in Washington.

It must be clearly understood that this paper, which obtained some notoriety later, was not initiated by the officers who signed it. It came into existence through the express request,—which is equivalent to an order coming from a superior,—of the Commanding General.

So far as the signers were concerned, they expected and intended that their action would be enveloped in the same secrecy which properly belongs to such a council. They thought this paper would pass from them to their superior, and from him to the authorities in Washington, in the usual way. It was not for them to give publicity to it.

While the paper was being prepared and signed another step was taken for which the signers were nowise responsible. Word was received from the Commanding General that the censorship would be removed from the cable and that private dispatches, in furtherance of the purpose in hand, could now be sent.

Suddenly, under the influence of the moment, not only the paper written and signed at the command, substantially, of the Commanding General, but private dispatches were given to an agent of the public press.

Of course, all must know that the cable was absolutely under the control of the Commanding General and not a word of all this could have passed over the wire without his approval and consent.

When it was understood he desired to use the papers, ready acquiescence was given, as it was believed that the true situation was not known at home. The signers confidently relied on their Commander that the dispatches would be accompanied with all needed explanations. These dispatches were remarkable only by the manner of their publicity.

The paper signed by the officers has been called a "round-robin." A round-robin is a written paper with signatures arranged in a circular form to conceal the order of signing, and make all of the signers equally responsible for it.

This paper was signed strictly in order of rank, and there is no signer who would not, were it possible, proudly assume all the responsibility for it. Their more than complete justification is found in the records of the hospitals at Camp Wikoff, Montauk Point, L.I., the convalescent camp of this self-same army of Santiago.

This much has been said on this subject, not on my own account, but for the other signers. They were innocent of any offense against military etiquette and, above all, the charge of round-robinism.

That one cannot sit in Washington and successfully conduct a campaign in the field was one of the costly lessons taught in the Civil War. There were at least two reasons for not following the suggestions from Washington that the 5th Army Corps should enter upon a campaign in the interior of the island.

The climatic conditions made success impossible for reasons ably set forth by the highest medical authority of the army. In fact, the main invasion of Cuba had been delayed for such reasons.

The Santiago campaign was a side issue. Troops were sent there on the suggestion of the navy because of the presence in the harbor of a Spanish fleet. When that fleet was destroyed and the city taken, the corps should have been sent elsewhere. The city and harbor could have been held by a small garrison and a few warships. Had the war continued, wise military guidance would have sent that corps, composed almost wholly of regulars, to a more important strategic point.

At the council it was recommended that if the corps were sent home, the sick should go first. For some reason not announced, they were not permitted to go till the last. Weak and depressed, feeling that they were being sacrificed, they were compelled to witness the departure of their comrades. Their appeals by looks and words were pitiable beyond description. As all the well were ordered to the transports, none were left to care for the sick. They fell under the charge of new and unknown troops which replaced our corps.

Before the army began its northward movement there were many transports without passengers from Cuba to the United States, which could have brought home many, if not all of the sick, had wise counsels prevailed. Many things might have been done with the sick, even if cases of yellow fever had existed in the camps about Santiago, which would have been preferable to leaving them under canvas, on the hills, in sun and rain, with water and fuel difficult to get, and destitute of the conveniences of well equipped hospitals.

Camp Wikoff taught many lessons. Now, it must be apparent to all that a camp for a sick army corps cannot be prepared in a few weeks, and that the system for an ordinary army hospital is inadequate when thousands of sick must be treated at one time.

When it was found that the troops were not afflicted with

infectious diseases, they should have been sent at once to their own states or former posts. That there was for a time insufficient quantities of medicines will be found in an official report on that subject; that there was unnecessary suffering and distress is set forth in the same official report in words of the surgeon in charge of the hospitals.

The failure of an adequate comprehension of the situation and inefficient organization were the fundamental causes of the outcry against Camp Wikoff. The difficulties were met at last by the dispersion of the troops.

The most needless infliction of suffering which came under my own observation was that attending the shipment by rail of sick soldiers, in box cars, from Montauk Point to New York City, a distance of some 125 miles. The weather was hot, and the road was long and rough and dusty. The sick soldiers were lying on the floors of the cars with a pitiful handful of straw beneath them, and the nurses pleading in vain for blankets to be used as pillows. What a contrast between such an infliction and the possible quiet, cool and restful journey by steamer up Long Island Sound!

An explanation of the refusal to use water transportation by the government seems to be that the landing of the boats at Camp Wikoff would be objectionable. Why it would be so is not stated. The one single track railroad put no restriction on passengers or freight. It took everything, and in freight, even more than was delivered. The contract with the railroad forbade water transportation!

One of the most remarkable military organizations of the war was that of the 1st U.S. Volunteer Cavalry, known as the Rough Riders. With but little instruction and discipline, its conduct in battle as well as elsewhere, was on an equality with that of its associates, the regulars, than which there is no higher standard.

Assembled from all parts of the country, these rough-riders proved themselves worthy successors of our Revolutionary fathers who fought at Lexington, and of Jackson and his heroes at New Orleans. May the volunteer of the future carefully study and imitate their example.

Unfortunately, the glamour of the gallantry and individuality of these men has blinded the public eye to the merits and services of the regulars. It seems to appear, judging from what we see and hear, that there were in the Santiago campaign 14,000 rough-riders and 500 regulars, whereas, the reverse was the case. There were 14,000 regulars and only 500 rough-riders.

In so far as this fact can be realized, it is to be hoped that efforts will be made to do partial justice, at least, to the regulars in the distribution of official rewards, even though the ratio of 28 to 1, their relative numbers, be not maintained.

The regulars have always proved faithful and reliable both in peace and war. At a time like this when they must expatriate themselves in obedience to the call of duty, consideration, rather than neglect, should be extended to them.

It is well that our country should congratulate itself on the sudden and universal recognition of its greatness; but the time has come when it should carefully consider the nature of the military exploits by which its eminence has been attained.

When war with Spain became inevitable, a wave of enthusiastic patriotism swept over the country. Of the many who were ready to go forth to battle, only 250,000 were chosen. No grander spectacle of a free people rising in its might was ever witnessed.

Proud and once mighty Spain, which had ruled in two continents, had now fallen from its high estate. For many years its colonial members had been sloughing off, leaving her at last in a comatose condition. What was left to her of the two Indies, East and West, was connected by the frailest cords. That to the Philippines was severed by a well directed blow of our fleet on the Asiatic Station.

Her last convulsive effort in the West Indies was made when she sent her fleet to Cuba there to find a final resting place at the bottom of the sea. Spain's offensive power was at an end. The destruction of communication with her islands was in itself equivalent to their loss to her and acquisition by us at no distant day, even without further effort on our part.

To complete what the navy had so well begun and to strike a quick, and what proved final blow, an army was sent to Santiago. It was not an army of 250,000 men which had been enrolled, but one of only 17,000.

Three detached engagements in one week, with a loss of less than 2,000 men, was, substantially, all the land fighting done. Over 200,000 men who had enlisted for the war were left in idleness, or, at most to change camps in search of health.

Such was the modest military performance on land, which, with the brilliant deeds of the navy, transformed us from the unassuming and unpretentious military people of yesterday, to what we are today—globe-encircling, with threatening arms envied and hated, or barely endured by the great powers of the earth.

Some other day, in a contest with a great power, this late holiday pic-nic will not be repeated. That we may be prepared, should be the prayer of all, and the mistakes of this war should not be ignored through any false pride.

Deficiencies in ambulances, litters, medicines, hospital conveniences, tentage, clothing, cooking utensils, rations, transportation for fuel, food and water, inadequate facilities for landing, truant transports, misplaced balloon, neglected roads and bridges, misuse of artillery, one and all, are trifles as compared with the fatal consequences which must follow a contest with a powerful enemy if the Commander-in-Chief should keep himself at the rear.

Without a chief ever present, especially on the battle field, there can be no unity of action, no cohesion of the parts, no esprit-de-corps, no real leadership, all of which are absolutely indispensable in great emergencies.

The General commanding the expedition against Santiago had his headquarters on board of his transport on the 29th June, five days after the troops had practically disembarked and also five days after the battle of Las Guasimas.[1]

He did not take command on land till 1st July,[2] the day of the last battles, and even then did not get within two miles of the fighting.[3] He was unable to view the field with his own eyes, and his inexperienced staff could not supply eyes for him.

In ignorance of what was going on at the front, he ordered the withdrawal of the forces attacking El Caney, which order was not obeyed. Being some two miles from Fort San Juan when it was carried, he could not have ordered a pursuit had the situation been wholly favorable to success.

Unable to see and know, he so far failed to comprehend his position as to consider a possible retreat on the night of the day of victory, and two days later, 3d July, telegraphed to Washington that he was "seriously considering withdrawing" to a point five miles to the rear, though such withdrawal would have resulted in delays which, through climatic causes, might have proved fatal.

As he realized all this and more, it is no wonder that, in a moment of agony of soul, he attempted to turn over his com-

[1] Wheeler, p. 264
[2] Wheeler, p. 272
[3] See Gen. Shafter's report already quoted.

mand to another.[1] Julius Caesar would never have been heard of if he had attempted to lead his armies in like manner.

The following is an extract from the evidence of the Commanding General on the Santiago campaign, viz:—

"Gov. Woodbury asked how the staff officers appointed from civil life turned out. Gen. Shafter said: They were men, as a rule, who had no previous military experience, and might not have been of much use in executing a military manoeuvre. But I had three of them on my staff, and for carrying orders, distributing rations to the refugees and a thousand necessary things, they were invaluable.

Beginning with Colonel ——— (a multi-millionaire), who was perhaps the most inexperienced, they were splendid fellows, and did what they had to do. ——— fell in with the work, ate his beans, and did his duty as cheerfully and expeditiously as though he had not a dollar.

Captain ——— (son of a renowned statesman), was an excellent officer, and did fine work in feeding those hungry people at Caney. At times he had to take an axe helve and stand off some of the men who were keeping back the weaker women and children. And he did it effectively."

The Colonel and Inspector General of any army corps should be the best posted officer in it. He should have the most thorough technical knowledge of all the details of military organization, equipment and service.

These words of the Corps Commander are most significant. Praise of this kind for services which a couple of orderlies could have done must be interpreted as a protest against the injury done him and the service by the assignment of such inexperienced officers to his command. For such appointments and assignments there may have been a necessity, but it was not a military necessity.

That a feeling of annoyance, to say the least, should have been permitted to arise between the army and navy is unfortunate. The best results can be attained only when they are in perfect accord. Experience in the Civil War taught that lesson.

Certain army criticisms on the conduct of the navy at Santiago are most unjust. A fleet of warships could only find justification for laying close under fortifications armed with modern guns when acting in conjunction with important land movements, as an assault, and the fleet should be powerful enough to silence the forts by its overwhelming fire. The at-

[1] Gov. Breckenridge's testimony before Commission.

tempt to enter the harbor of Santiago through the narrow and tortuous channel, in single column, at slow speed, would have resulted, no doubt, in the loss of more than one ship. Even had entrance to the harbor been possible, the fleet would have had to take all the chances of war while the army was sitting inactive back on the hills, a mile, more or less, from the city. With the army siege guns not only not in position, but miles to the rear, it was hardly fair to demand that the work should be done by the guns of the navy. The quarry had been trapped, and it was for the army to dispose of it.

The welfare of our country depends upon perfect harmony between the two services. If wanting, it should be cultivated to the extent, at least, of full and ample justice to the navy's intelligence—its valor has never been questioned.

As successful military leaders are only developed by actual warfare, they, and they only, should be recognized and utilized in time of war. Such men we have on the retired list of the army. They ranked in the Civil War next to our great leaders, and were their worthy successors.

The law which removes them from service shortly after they reach the age of sixty may be a wise one for times of peace, but in time of war it cannot be so regarded. If military success, with the saving of honor, life, suffering and expense, is the chief consideration in war, then the ablest leaders should be selected whatever their ages. The same principle should apply to the active list at all times.

This Commission, composed as it is of statesmen and soldiers, actors in our Civil War, associates of its leaders, students of their methods, familiar with all the principles and practices of warfare, moved only by a sense of duty to the whole country, should fearlessly discover and make known any and all delinquencies of this war, that we may be the better prepared for the next.

ADELBERT AMES

Lieut. Col. & Bvt. Maj. Gen. U.S. Army (Regulars)
Brig. Gen. & Bvt. Maj. Gen. U.S. Volunteers, Civil War
Brig. Gen. U.S. Vols. Spanish War.

NORTHFIELD, MINN., *December 2*, 1899

DEAR CHILDREN: Here we are in December with no snow. We are having the most charming fall days, just cold enough at night for heavy hoar-frosts and bright and warm through the days with little or no wind. We are hoping to have the same conditions a little longer until some timbers can be put in the flume of the old mill and some stone work repaired, in readiness for the spring freshets and ice. All around the square, in the middle of which stands your Grandmother's house, there are tall fir trees in which the blue jays find shelter during the winter. The other morning, as soon as your Father and I stepped out of the front door, one of these old gossips set up a cry and flew on before us from tree to tree screeching out his warning half way down to the mill.

Thanksgiving Day your Father picked in the garden a bouquet of green leaves and berries which was a very festive adornment to my dress. The turkey and accompaniments were very nice but you may be sure I thought often of your bonny faces and would have liked to have seen them around the table.

Butler wrote me a nice Thanksgiving letter and we appreciated the attention and loving thought that dictated it. You know I am always making suggestions and I spoke to your Father about a market for flour in Porto Rico through the agency of the Ames, Pearson Tobacco Co. and urged him to write or telegraph Butler to make inquiries when he goes down. Inasmuch as matters at the mill are in a transition stage and there is no flour to be disposed of, such inquiries would seem, to say the least, a little premature and your Father would not do anything in regard to it. But all the same, it will do no harm for Butler to think the subject over and get some statistics.

I heard your Father say to-day after he had read Sarah's description of the studio which Blanche is furnishing that "he thought he knew where he was going to find a room for himself." Sarah has done good work in getting up her bell signal for the electric incubator. I can see that she is paving the way for an electrical plant.

Edith wrote that little Edith was restless during the night. No doubt the young lady is getting more teeth. Edith will have to take naps during the day and then go to bed expecting to be disturbed and it will not be so annoying. This is what is called adaptability and smoothes the rough places in life immensely.

Jessie must have had a pleasant Saturday with Del. Your Grandmother will probably go to Faribault after we leave. She dreads being here alone and wants the company of the children. I want the company of the children too and send them all love and kisses.

MOTHER

Your Mother has left a little space for me to say how glad we are to have letters from you. I was surprised to see the score of Harvard vs. Yale's freshman football team. Del's must be a superior team. However, I am confident he will make his class team another year.

We are unavoidably waiting for the closing up of the mill business under the old contract so that I may begin under a new one. We expect to be on our way East in a couple of weeks. Our visit and this pleasant weather shortens Mother's winter a good deal. I send love to you all. FATHER

COMMENTARY

Mrs. Blanche Butler Ames' appreciation of the importance of impartiality and freedom from prejudice as primary aids to truth in the writing of history became clearly apparent when she and her brother, Paul Butler, caused the production of a Bibliography of all references to their father, General Benjamin F. Butler, in the Boston Public Library in 1910. This Bibliography was, in their opinion, a more fitting memorial than a statue in a public park.

In 1914, Mrs. Ames collected and had typewritten copies made of the papers of General Butler between the years 1858 and 1868 which were in the possession of the family, and from these was published in 1917 "The Private and Official Correspondence of General Benjamin F. Butler" in sets of five volumes. She also gathered together and examined the remaining large quantity of General Butler's correspondence and papers, and in 1930 she sent them, together with the originals of those already printed in 1917, to the Library of Congress. These papers total fifty three thousand. She added to that collection fifty seven folio sheets of photostat positives of selected papers.

In the years before her death on December 27th, 1939, she interested herself in collecting, sorting, and having copied, her personal letters and those of General Ames. These she requested to have published. It has been my proud task to carry out her wishes. They give a noble record of patriotism and devotion.

JESSIE AMES MARSHALL

INDEX

H

I

J

K

L

M